A HISTORY OF
THE OLD ENGLISH
LETTER
FOUNDRIES

Engrav'd for the Universal Mag

A HISTORY OF
THE OLD ENGLISH
LETTER FOUNDRIES

With Notes

Historical and Bibliographical

on the Rise and Progress of English Typography

by

TALBOT BAINES REED

A new edition revised and enlarged by

A. F. JOHNSON

FABER AND FABER LIMITED

24 Russell Square, London

First published in mdccclxxxvii
This new edition first published in mcmlii
by Faber and Faber Limited
24 Russell Square, London W.C. 1

Printed in Great Britain
at the University Press, Oxford
by Charles Batey
Printer to the University

⌈ Contents ⌉

⌜ *List of Illustrations* ⌝

⌈ *Preface* ⌉

TO THE FIRST EDITION

I N this age of progress, when the fine arts are rapidly becoming trades, and the machine is on every side superseding that labour of head and hand which our fathers called Handicraft, we are in danger of losing sight of, or, at least, of undervaluing the genius of those who, with none of our mechanical advantages, established and made famous in our land those arts and handicrafts of which we are now the heritors.

The Art of Letter-founding hesitated long before yielding to the revolutionary impulses of modern progress. While kindred arts—and notably that art which preserves all others—were advancing by leaps and bounds, the founder, as late as half a century ago, was pursuing the even tenor of his ways by paths which had been trodden by De Worde and Day and Moxon. But the inevitable revolution came, and Letter Founding to-day bids fair to break all her old ties and take new departures undreamed of by those heroes of the punch and matrix and mould who made her what we found her.

At such a time, it seems not undutiful to attempt to gather together into a connected form the numerous records of the Old English Letter Founders scattered throughout our literary and typographical history, with a view to preserve the memory of those to whose labours English Printing is indebted for so much of its glory.

The present work represents the labour of several years in what may be considered some of the untrodden by-paths of English typographical history.

The curious *Dissertation on English Typographical Founders and Founderies* by the learned Edward Rowe Mores, published in 1778, is, in fact, the only work in the language purporting to treat of Letter Founding as distinct from the art which it fosters. This quaint and crabbed sketch, full of valuable but half-digested information, was intended to accompany a specimen of the types of John James, whose foundry had gradually absorbed all the minor English foundries, and, after the death of its owner, had become the property of Mores himself. The enthusiasm of the Oxford antiquary infused new life into the dry bones of this decayed collection. Working backwards, he restored in imagination the old foundries of the seventeenth and eighteenth centuries, as they had been before they became absorbed in his own. He tracked back a few famous historical types to their fountain-head, and even bridged over the mysterious gulf which divided the early sixteenth from the early seventeenth centuries of English letter-founding.

Mores's *Dissertation* has necessarily formed the basis of my investigations, and is, indeed, almost wholly incorporated in the present volume. Of the additional and more anecdotal notes on the later founders, preserved by Nichols and Hansard, I have also freely made use; although in every case it has been my endeavour to take nothing on report which it has been possible to verify by reference to original sources. This effort has been rewarded by several interesting discoveries which it is hoped may be found to throw considerable fresh light on the history of our national typography.

The first century of English letter-founding is a period of great obscurity, to master which it is absolutely essential to have unlimited access to all the works of all the printers whose books were the only type-specimens of their day. Such access it has been beyond my power fully to secure, and in this portion of my work I am bound to admit that I can lay claim to little originality of research. I have, however, endeavoured to examine as many of the specimens of these early presses as possible, and to satisfy myself that the observations of others, of which I have availed myself, are such as I can assent to.

In detailing the rise and progress of the various English Letter Foundries, it has been my endeavour to treat the subject, as far as possible, bibliographically—that is, to regard as type-specimens not merely the stated advertisements of the founder, but also the works for which his types were created and in which they were used. The *Catena on Job*, Walton's *Polyglot*, Boyle's *Irish Testament*, Bowyer's *Selden*, thus rank as type-specimens quite as interesting as, and far more valuable than, the ordinary letter-founders' catalogues. Proceeding on this principle, moreover, this History will be found to embody a pretty complete bibliography of works not only relating to, but illustrative of, English Letter Founding.

The introductory chapter on the Types and Type Founding of the First Printers may be considered somewhat foreign to the scope of this History. The importance, however, of a practical acquaintance with the processes and appliances of the Art of Letter Founding as a foundation to any complete study of typographical history —as well as the numerous misconceptions existing on the part even of accepted authorities on the subject—suggested the attempt to examine the various accounts of the Invention of Printing from a letter founder's point of view, in the hope, if not of arriving at any very definite conclusions, at least of clearing the question of a few prevalent fallacies.

The two chapters on Type Bodies and Type Faces, although also to some extent foreign, are considered important by way of introduction to the history of English Letter Founding in which the 'foreign and learned' characters have so conspicuously figured.

T. B. REED

1887

⌈ _Preface_ ⌉

TO THE NEW EDITION

Rᴇᴇᴅ died in 1893 at the early age of forty-one. He had joined his father's firm, the Fann Street Foundry, when he was seventeen, and for some years before his death had been the manager. For his work as a founder we may refer the reader to Chapter 14 of this book, and for his work as a journalist and writer of boys' stories to the introduction by John Sime to the posthumously published story _Kilgoram_, 1895. It is now more than sixty years since _A History of the Old English Letter Foundries_ was published, and in the meantime the book has become a classic of typographical history. It will be generally agreed that the work is worth reprinting and that the main part of it, the story of the English founders, has not been superseded. That story was based on thorough research and, though additions may be made to it, it is still authoritative. The last sixty years have been productive of much research into the history of typography, and as a result some of the introductory chapters of Reed have become out of date. A summary, therefore, of the alterations which have been made in these chapters is called for.

The introductory chapter deals with the method of type manufacture practised by the earliest printers. A chapter which is based on the work of Van der Linde, Ottley, and other nineteenth-century writers, and not on Zedler, Mori, and Hupp, might on first consideration seem to be unworthy of reproduction. But after all, although disputed points have been discussed afresh and new theories advanced, still our knowledge remains much as it was. Few, if any, new facts have come to light and Reed may still be read as a good account of what is known on the subject. The chapter has therefore been reprinted with the addition of a summary of some theories advanced since 1887.

Chapters 1 and 2 treat of Type Faces and Bodies. Some additions have been made to the historical account of the chief families of types and to the earliest uses of the names of the bodies. The section on initials has been omitted; the subject could not be adequately treated in the space available and, moreover, initials are not primarily founders' material. In Chapter 3 the account of sixteenth-century printers and their types has been much altered. Here we have learnt much since Reed's day and it seemed necessary to emphasize the dependence of English printers on continental sources. The next chapter calling for much revision is that on the Oxford Foundry. The researches of Madan and others have added greatly to our knowledge here, and it is hoped that the revised chapter gives a more lucid and accurate account of what Dr. Fell did for the foundry. At the end of this chapter and the following chapters Reed gave lists of the type-specimens published by each foundry. These lists have been omitted, since the subject is more fully treated in Berry and Johnson's *Catalogue of Specimens of Printing Types*. The revision of Chapters 7–21 consists of additions rather than of reconstruction. Some longer additions, relevant, it is hoped, to the subject, are given as appendixes.

Reed took the year 1830 as the limit of his story. The new edition has added a summary of a further sixty years, ending at a period when new inventions were about to transform the methods of type production.

This new edition was first planned by Mr. Stanley Morison, and I am grateful to him for many notes passed on. The reader will soon observe that I have also taken much information from Mr. Morison's published studies on typographical history. His name stands first among those to whom my thanks are due. Others whom I have to thank for useful notes are Mr. L. Hanson, Mr. Ellic Howe, who has placed at my disposal notes on founders extracted by him from the records of the Stationers' Company, the late R. A. Peddie, Mr. Graham Pollard, Mr. J. S. G. Simmons, Mr. Berthold Wolpe, and Mr. Turner Berry, the librarian of the St. Bride Foundation, where Reed's own books are now preserved. I am grateful to Mr. Berry and to the Governors of the Foundation for permission to consult Reed's own books and for allowing reproductions to be made from some of them. Special thanks are due to three foundries: Messrs. Enschedé of Haarlem, the Oxford University Press, and Messrs. Stephenson, Blake & Co. of Sheffield. They have generously enabled us to show illustrations of type cast from original matrices in their possession, as was done by Reed in the first edition. I have to thank the Cambridge University Press, the Monotype Corporation, and the publishers of *Alphabet and Image* for the loan of blocks, the Record Office for permission to reproduce the specimen of Nicholas Nicholls, and Mr. Geoffrey Stevens of Messrs. Stevens, Shanks & Sons, who now possesses the Minute-Book of the Association of Founders. The publishers of *Alphabet and Image* and of the *Penrose Annual* have kindly allowed me to reprint articles which originally appeared in their pages.

A. F. J.

INTRODUCTORY CHAPTER

THE TYPES AND TYPEFOUNDING OF THE FIRST PRINTERS

For four centuries the noise of controversy has raged round the cradle of typography. Volumes have been written, lives have been spent, fortunes have been wasted, communities have been stirred, societies have been organized, a literature has been developed, to find an answer to the famous triple question: 'When, where, and by whom was found out the unspeakably useful art of printing books?' And yet the world to-day is little nearer a finite answer to the question than it was when Ulrich Zell indited his memorable narrative to the *Cologne Chronicle* in 1499. Indeed, the dust of battle has added to, rather than diminished, the mysterious clouds which envelop the problem, and we are tempted to seek refuge in an agnosticism which almost refuses to believe that printing ever had an inventor.

It would be neither suitable nor profitable to encumber an investigation of that part of the history of typography which relates to the types and type-making of the fifteenth century by any attempt to discuss the vexed question of the invention of the art. The man who invented typography was doubtless the man who invented movable types. Where the one is discovered, we have also found the other. But, meanwhile, it is possible to avail ourselves of whatever evidence exists as to the nature of the types he and his successors used, and as to the methods by which those types were produced, and possibly to arrive at some conclusions respecting the earliest practices of the art of typefounding in the land and in the age in which it first saw the light.

No one has done more to clear the way for a free investigation of all questions relating to the origin of printing than Van der Linde, in his able essay, *The Haarlem Legend*,[1] which, while disposing ruthlessly of the fiction of Coster's invention, lays down the important principle, too often neglected by writers on the subject, that the essence of typography consists in the mobility of the types, and that, therefore, it is not a development of the long-practised art of printing from fixed blocks, but an entirely distinct invention.

The principle is so important, and Van der Linde's words are so emphatic, that we make no apology for quoting them:

I cannot repeat often enough that, when we speak of typography and its invention, nothing is meant, or rather nothing must be meant, but printing with *loose* (separate,

---

[1] *The Haarlem Legend of the Invention of Printing by Lourens Janszoon Coster, critically examined.* From the Dutch by J. H. Hessels, with an introduc-tion and classified list of the Costerian Incunabula. London, 1871. 8vo.

moveable) types (be they letters, musical notes, or other figures), which therefore, in distinction from letters cut on wooden or metal plates, may be put together or separated according to inclination. One thing therefore is certain: he who did not invent printing with moveable types, did, as far as typography goes, invent nothing. What material was used first of all in this invention; of what metal the first letters, the patrices (engraved punches) and matrices were made; by whom and when the leaden matrices and brass patrices were replaced by brass matrices and steel patrices; . . . all this belongs to the secondary question of the technical execution of the principal idea: multiplication of books by means of multiplication of letters, multiplication of letters by means of their durability, and repeated use of the same letters, *i.e.* by means of the independence (looseness) of each individual letter (moveableness).—P. 19.

If this principle be adopted—and we can hardly imagine it questioned—it will be obvious that a large class of works which usually occupy a prominent place in inquiries into the origin of printing have but slight bearing on the history of typography. The block books of the fifteenth century had little direct connexion with the art that followed and eclipsed them. In the one respect of marking the early use of printing for the instruction of mankind, the block books and the first works of typography proper claim an equal interest; but, as regards their mechanical production, the one feature they possess in common is a quality shared also by the playing-cards, pictures, seals, stamps, brands, and all the other applications of the principle of impression which had existed in one form or another from time immemorial.

It is reasonable to suppose that the first idea of movable type may have been suggested to the mind of the inventor by a study of the works of a xylographic printer, and an observation of the cumbrous and wearisome method by which his books were produced. The toil involved in first painfully tracing the characters and figures, reversed, on the wood, then of engraving them, and, finally, of printing them with the frotton, would appear—in the case, at any rate, of the small schoolbooks, for the production of which this process was largely resorted to—scarcely less tedious than copying the required number by the deft pen of a scribe. And even if, at a later period, the bookmakers so far facilitated their labours as to write their text in the ordinary manner on prepared paper, or with prepared ink, and so transfer their copy, after the manner of the Chinese, on to the wood, the labour expended in proportion to the result, and the uselessness of the blocks when once their work was done, would doubtless impress an inventive genius with a sense of dissatisfaction and impatience. We can imagine him examining the first page of an *Abecedarium*, on which would be engraved, in three lines, with a clear space between each character, the letters of the alphabet, and speculating, as Cicero had speculated centuries before,[1] on the possibilities presented by the combination in indefinite variety of those twenty-five symbols. Being a practical man as well as a theorist, we may suppose he would attempt to experiment on the little wood block in his

---

[1] 'Hic ego non mirer esse quemquam qui sibi persuadeat . . . mundum effici . . . ex concursione fortuita! Hoc qui existimet fieri potuisse, non intelligo cur non idem putet si innumerabiles unius et viginti formae litterarum, vel aureae, vel qualeslibet, aliquo conjiciantur, posse ex his in terram excussis, annales Ennii, ut deinceps legi possint, effici' (*De Nat. Deor.*, lib. ii, cap. 37). Cicero was not the only ancient writer who entertained the idea of mobile letters. Quintilian suggests the use of ivory letters for teaching children to read while playing: 'Eburneas litterarum formas in ludum offerre' (*Inst. Orat.* i, cap. 1, § 26); and Jerome, writing to Laeta, no. cvii, propounds the same idea: 'Fiant ei (Paulae) litterae vel buxeae vel eburneae, et suis nominibus appellentur. Ludat in eis ut et lusus ipse eruditio fiat.'

hand, and by sawing off first the lines, and then some of the letters in the lines, attempt to arrange his little types into a few short words. A momentous experiment, and fraught with the greatest revolution the world has ever known!

No question has aroused more interest, or excited keener discussion in the history of printing, than that of the use of movable wooden types as a first stage in the passage from xylography to typography. Those who write on the affirmative side of the question profess to see in the earlier typographical works, as well as in the historical statements handed down by the old authorities, the clearest evidence that wooden types were used, and that several of the most famous works of the first printers were executed by their means.

As regards the latter source of their confidence, it is at least remarkable that no single writer of the fifteenth century makes the slightest allusion to the use of wooden types. Indeed, it was not till Bibliander, in 1548,[1] first mentioned and described them, that anything professing to be a record on the subject existed. 'First they cut their letters,' he says, 'on wood blocks the size of an entire page, but because the labour and cost of that way was so great, they devised movable wooden types, perforated and joined one to the other by a thread.'

The legend, once started, found no lack of sponsors, and the typographical histories of the sixteenth century and onward abound with testimonies confirmatory more or less of Bibliander's statement. Of these testimonials, those only are worthy of attention which profess to be based on actual inspection of the alleged perforated wooden types. Daniel Specklin[2] (who died in 1589) asserts that he saw some of these relics at Strasburg. Angelo Roccha,[3] in 1591, vouches for the existence of similar letters (though he does not say whether wood or metal) at Venice. Paulus Pater,[4] in 1710, stated that he had once seen some belonging to Fust at Mainz; J. F. Bodmann, as late as 1781, saw the same types in a worm-eaten condition at Mainz; while G. Fischer,[5] in 1802, stated that these precious relics were used as a sort of token of honour to be bestowed on worthy apprentices on the occasion of their finishing their term.

This testimony proves nothing beyond the fact that at Strasburg, Venice, and Mainz there existed at some time or other certain perforated wooden types which tradition ascribed to the first printers. But on the question whether any book was ever printed with such type, it is wholly inconclusive. It is possible to believe that certain early printers, uninitiated into the mystery of the punch and matrix, may have attempted to cut themselves wooden types which, when they proved untractable under the press, they perforated and strung together in lines; but it is beyond credit that any such rude experiment ever resulted in the production of a work like the *Speculum*.

[1] *De ratione communi omnium linguarum et literarum, Tiguri*, 1548, p. 80.

[2] *Les Collectanées* ed. R. Reuss, 1890, p. 442. 'Ich habe die erste press, auch die buchstaben gesehen, waren von holtz geschnitten, auch gäntze wörter und syllaben, hatten löchle, und fasst man an ein schnur nacheinander mit einer nadel, zoge sie darnach den zeilen in die länge', &c.

[3] *Bibliotheca Vaticana, Romae*, 1591, p. 412. 'Characteres enim a primis illis inventoribus non ita eleganter et expedite, ut a nostris fieri solet, sed filo in litterarum foramen immisso connectebantur, sicut Venetiis id genus typos me vidisse memini.'

[4] *De Germaniae miraculo*, &c., *Lipsiae*, 1710, p. 10. '... ligneos typos, ex buxi frutice, perforatos in medio, ut zonâ colligari unâ jungique commode possint, ex Fausti officina reliquos, Moguntiae aliquando me conspexisse memini.'

[5] *Essai sur les monumens typographiques de Jean Gutenberg, Mayence*, an 10, 1802, p. 39.

It is true that many writers have asserted it was so. Fournier, a practical typographer, insists upon it from the fact that the letters vary among themselves in a manner which would not be the case had they been cast from a matrix in a mould. But, to be consistent, Fournier is compelled (as Bernard points out) to postpone the use of cast type till after the Gutenberg *Bible* and Mainz *Psalter*, both of which works display the same irregularities. And as the latest edition of the *Psalter*, printed in the old types, appeared in 1516, it would be necessary to suppose that movable wood type was in vogue up to that date. No one has yet demonstrated, or attempted seriously to demonstrate, the possibility of printing a book like the *Speculum humanae salvationis* in movable wooden type. All the experiments hitherto made, even by the most ardent supporters of the theory, have been woeful failures. Laborde[1] admits that to cut the 3,000 separate letters required for the *Letters of Indulgence*, engraved by him, would cost 450 francs; and even he, with the aid of modern tools to cut up his wooden cubes, can only show four widely spaced lines. Wetter[2] shows a page printed from perforated and threaded wooden types;[3] but these, though of large size, only prove by their 'naughty caprioles' the absurdity of supposing that the 'unleaded' *Speculum*, a quaternion of which would require 40,000 distinct letters, could have been produced in 1440 by a method which even the modern cutting and modern presswork of 1836 failed to adapt to a single page of large-sized print.

Johannes Enschedé, the famous Haarlem typefounder, though a strong adherent to the Coster legend, was compelled to admit the practical impossibility, in his day at any rate, of producing a single wood type which would stand the test of being mathematically square; nor would it be possible to square it after being cut. 'No engraver', he remarks, 'is able to cut separate letters in wood in such a manner that

[1] *Débuts de l'imprimerie à Strasbourg, Paris,* 1840, p. 72.

[2] *Erfindung der Buchdruckerkunst,* 1836, Album, tab. ii.

[3] The history of these 'fatal, unhistorical wooden types' is worth recording for the warning of the over-credulous typographical antiquary. Wetter, writing his book in 1836, and desirous to illustrate the feasibility of the theory, 'spent', so Van der Linde writes, 'really the amount of ten shillings on having a number of letters made of the wood of a pear-tree, only to please Trithemius, Bergellanus, and Faust of Aschaffenburg. . . . His letters, although tied with string, did not remain in the line, but made naughty caprioles. The supposition—that by these few dancing lines the possibility is demonstrated of printing with 40,000 wooden letters, necessary to the printing of a quaternion, a whole folio book—is dreadfully silly. The demonstrating facsimile demonstrates already the contrary. Wetter's letters not only declined to have themselves regularly printed, but they also retained their pear-tree-wood-like impatience afterwards.' The specimen of these types may be seen in the *Album* of plates accompanying Wetter's work, where they occupy the first place, the matter chosen being the first few verses of the Bible, occupying nineteen lines, and the type being about two-line English in body. Wetter stated in his work that he had deposited the original types in the Town Library of Mainz, where they might be inspected by anyone wishing to do so. From this repository they appear ultimately to have returned to the hands of Wetter's printer. Bernard, passing through Mainz in 1850, asked Wetter for a sight of them, and was conducted to the printing-office for that purpose, when it was discovered that they had been stolen; whereupon Bernard remarks, prophetically, 'Peut-être un jour quelque naïf Allemand, les trouvant parmi les reliques du voleur, nous les donnera pour les caractères de Gutenberg. Voilà comment s'établissent trop souvent les traditions.' This prediction, with the one exception of the nationality of the victim, was literally fulfilled when an English clergyman, some years afterwards, discovered these identical types in the shop of a curiosity-dealer at Mainz, and purchased them as apparently veritable relics of the infancy of printing. After being offered to the authorities at the British Museum and declined, they were presented in 1869 to the Bodleian Library at Oxford, where they remain to this day, treasured in a box and accompanied by a learned memorandum setting forth the circumstances of their discovery, and citing the testimony of Roccha and other writers as to the existence and use of perforated types by the early printers. The lines (which we have inspected) remain threaded and locked in forme exactly as they appear in Wetter's specimen. It is due to the present authorities of the Bodleian to say that they preserve these precious 'relics', without prejudice, as curiosities merely, with no insistence on their historic pretensions.

they retain their quadrature (for that is the main thing of the line in type-casting).'[1] Admitting for a moment that some printer may have succeeded in putting together a page of these wooden types, without the aid of leads, into a chase: how can it be supposed that after their exposure to the warping influences of the sloppy ink and tight pressure during the impression, they could ever have survived to be distributed and recomposed into another forme?[2]

The claims set up on behalf of movable wood types as the means by which the *Speculum* or any other of the earliest books was printed are not only historically unsupported, but the whole weight of practical evidence rejects them.

Dismissing them, therefore, from our consideration, a new theory confronts us, which at first blush seems to supply, if not a more probable, certainly a more possible, stepping-stone between xylography and typography. We refer to what Meerman, the great champion of this theory, calls the 'sculpto-fusi' characters: types, that is, the shanks of which have been cast in a quadrilateral mould, and the 'faces' engraved by hand afterwards.

Meerman and those who agree with him engage a large array of testimony on their side. In the reference of Celtis, in 1502, to Mainz as the city 'quae prima sculpsit solidos aere characteres', they see a clear confirmation of their theory; as also in the frequent recurrence of the same word *sculptus* in the colophons of the early printers. Meerman, indeed, goes so far as to ingeniously explain the famous account of the invention given by Trithemius in 1514,[3] in the light of his theory, to mean that, after the rejection of the first wooden types, 'the inventors found out a method of casting the bodies only (*fundendi formas*) of all the letters of the Latin alphabet from what they called matrices, on which they cut the face of each letter; and from the same kind of matrices a method was in time discovered of casting the complete letters (*aeneos sive stanneos characteres*) of sufficient hardness for the pressure they had to bear, which letters before—that is, when the bodies only were cast—they were obliged to cut.'[4]

After this bold flight of translation, it is not surprising to find that Meerman claims that the *Speculum* was printed in 'sculpto-fusi' types, although in the one page of which he gives a facsimile there are nearly 1,700 separate types, of which 250 alone are *e*'s.

Schoepflin, claiming the same invention for the Strasburg printers, believes that all the earliest books printed there were produced by this means; and both Meerman and Schoepflin agree that engraved metal types were in use for many years

---

[1] Van der Linde, *Haarlem Legend*, London, p. 72.

[2] Skeen, in his *Early Typography*, Colombo, 1872, takes up the challenge thrown down by Van der Linde on the strength of Enschedé's opinion, and shows a specimen of three letters cut in boxwood, pica size, one of which he exhibits again at the close of the book after 1,500 impressions. But the value of Skeen's arguments and experiments is destroyed when he sums up with this absurd dictum: 'Three letters are as good as 3,000 or 30,000 or 300,000 to demonstrate the fact that words are and can be, and that therefore pages and whole books may be (and therefore also that they may have been) printed from such separable wooden types.'—P. 424. But

see below, p. 16.

[3] *Annales Hirsaugienses*, 1690, ii, p. 421: 'Post haec inventis successerunt subtiliora, inveneruntque modum fundendi formas omnium Latini Alphabeti literarum quas ipsi matrices nominabant; ex quibus rursum aeneos sive stanneos characteres fundebant, ad omnem pressuram sufficientes, quos prius manibus sculpebant.' Trithemius's statement, as every student of typographical history is aware, has been made to fit every theory that has been propounded, but it is doubtful whether any other writer has stretched it quite as severely as Meerman in the above rendering of these few Latin lines.

[4] *Origines Typographicae, Gerardo Meerman auctore*, Hagae Com. 1765, Append., p. 47.

after the invention of the punch and matrix, mentioning, among others so printed, the Mainz *Psalter*, the *Catholicon* of 1460, the Eggestein *Bible*, Strasburg, *c.* 1466, and even the *Nideri Praeceptorium*, printed at Strasburg by Georg Husner as late as 1476, as 'literis in aere sculptis'.

Almost the whole historical claim of the engraved metal types, indeed, turns on the recurrence of the term *sculptus* in the colophons of the early printers. Jenson, in 1471, calls himself a 'cutter of books' (*librorum exsculptor*). Sensenschmidt of Nuremberg, in 1475, says that the *Codex Justinianus* is 'cut' (*insculptus*), and that he has 'cut' (*sculpsit*) the work of *Lombardus in Psalterium*, 1478.[1] G. Husner of Strasburg, in 1473, applies the term 'printed with letters cut of metal' (*exsculptis aere litteris*) to the *Speculum Durandi*; and of the *Nideri Praeceptorium*, printed in 1476, he says it is 'printed in letters cut of metal by a very ingenious effort' (*litteris exsculptis artificiali certe conatu ex aere*). As Van der Linde points out, the use of the term in reference to all these books can mean nothing else than a figurative allusion to the first process towards producing the types, namely, the cutting of the punch;[2] just as when Schoeffer, in 1468, makes his *Grammatica Vetus Rhythmica* of Johann Brunner say, 'I am cast at Mainz' (*At Moguntia sum fusus in urbe libellus*), he means nothing more than a figurative allusion to the casting of the types.

The theory of the 'sculpto-fusi' types appears to have sprung up on no firmer foundation than the difficulty of accounting for the marked irregularities in the letters of the earliest-printed books, and the lack of a theory more feasible than that of movable wood type to account for it. The method suggested by Meerman seemed to meet the requirements of the case, and with the aid of the very free translation of Trithemius's story, and the very literal translation of certain colophons, it managed to get a footing on the typographical records.

Skeen seriously applies himself to demonstrate how the shanks could be cast in clay moulds stamped with a number of trough-like matrices representing the various widths of the blanks required, and calculates that at the rate of four a day, 6,000 of these blanks could be engraved on the end by one man in five years, the whole weighing 100 lb. when finished! 'No wonder', Skeen naïvely observes, 'that Fust at last grew impatient.' We must confess that there seems less ground for believing in the use of 'sculpto-fusi' types as the means by which any of the early books were produced than in the perforated wood types. The enormous labour involved in itself renders the idea improbable. As Bernard says, 'How can we suppose that intelligent men like the first printers would not at once find out that they could easily cast the face and body of their types together?'[3] But admitting the possibility of producing type in this manner, and the possible obtuseness which could allow an inventor of printing to spend five years in laboriously engraving 'shanks' enough for a single forme, the lack of any satisfactory evidence that such types were ever

---

[1] The full colophons of these books printed by Sensenschmidt are set out in the *Catalogue of Books printed in the XVth Century in the British Museum*, vol. ii, pp. 406, 409, and of the work by Nider, printed by Husner, in vol. i, p. 84. The colophon of the *Speculum Durandi* is given in the *Gesamtkatalog der Wiegendrucke*, Bd. 7, p. 755.

[2] The constant recurrence in more modern typographical history of the expression 'to cut matrices', meaning of course to cut the punches necessary to form the matrices, bears out the same conclusion.

[3] *De l'origine et débuts de l'imprimerie en Europe*, Paris, 1853, 8vo, i. 38.

used, even experimentally, inclines us to deny them any place in the history of the origin of typography.

Putting aside, therefore, as improbable, and not proved, the two theories of engraved movable types, the question arises, Did typography, like her patron goddess, spring fully armed from the brain of her inventor? in other words, did men pass at a single stride from xylography to the perfect typography of the punch, the matrix, and the mould? or are we still to seek for an intermediate stage in some ruder and more primitive process of production? To this question we cannot offer a better reply than that contained in the following passage from Blades's admirable life of Caxton.[1] 'The examination of many specimens', he observes, 'has led me to conclude that two schools of typography existed together. . . . The ruder consisted of those printers who practised their art in Holland and the Low Countries, . . . and who, by degrees only, adopted the better and more perfect methods of the . . . school founded in Germany by the celebrated trio, Gutenberg, Fust, and Schoeffer.'

It is impossible, we think, to resist the conclusion that all the earlier works of typography were the impression of cast metal types; but that the methods of casting employed were not always those of matured letter-founding seems to us not only probable, but evident, from a study of the works themselves.

Theo. De Vinne, in his able treatise on the invention of printing,[2] speaking with the authority of a practical typographer, insists that the key to that invention is to be found, not in the press nor in the movable types, but in the adjustable type-mould, upon which, he argues, the existence of typography depends. While not prepared to go as far as De Vinne on this point, and still content to regard the invention of movable types as the real key to the invention of typography proper, we find in the mould not only the culminating achievement of the inventor but also the key to the distinction between the two schools of early typography to which we have alluded.

The adjustable mould was undoubtedly the goal of the discovery, and those who reached it at once were the advanced typographers of the Mainz press. Those who groped after it through clumsy and tedious by-ways were the rude artists of the *Donatus* and *Speculum*.

In considering the primitive modes of type-casting it must be frankly admitted that the inquirer stands in a field of pure conjecture. He has only negative evidence to assure him that such primitive modes undoubtedly did exist, and he searches in vain for any direct clue as to the nature and details of those methods.

We shall briefly refer to one or two theories which have been propounded, all with more or less of plausibility.

Casting in sand was an art not unknown to the silversmiths and trinket-makers of the fifteenth century, and several writers have suggested that some of the early printers applied this process to typefounding. Bernard[3] considers that the types of the *Speculum* were sand-cast, and accounts for the varieties observable in the shapes

---

[1] *Life and Typography of William Caxton*, London, 1861–3, 2 vols., 4to, ii, p. xxiv.

[2] *The Invention of Printing*, New York, 1876, 8vo.
[3] *De l'Origine de l'imprimerie*, i. 40.

of various letters by explaining that several models would probably be made of each letter, and that the types when cast would, as is usual after sand-casting, require some touching up or finishing by hand. He shows a specimen of a word cast by himself by this process, which, as far as it goes, is a satisfactory proof of the possibility of casting letters in this way.[1] There are, indeed, many points in this theory which satisfactorily account for peculiarities in the appearance of books printed by the earliest rude Dutch school. Not only are the irregularities of the letters in body and line intelligible, but the specks between the lines, so frequently observable, would be accounted for by the roughness on the 'shoulders' of the sand-cast bodies.[2]

An important difficulty to be overcome in type cast by this or any other primitive method would be the absence of uniformity in what letterfounders term 'height to paper'. Some types would stand higher than others, and the low ones, unless raised, would not only miss the ink, but would not appear at all in the impression. The comparative rarity of faults of this kind in the *Speculum* leads one to suppose that if a process of sand-casting had been adopted, the difficulty of uneven heights had been surmounted either by locking up the forme face downwards, or by perforating the types either at the time of or after casting, and by means of a thread or wire holding them in their places. The uneven length of the lines favours such a supposition, and to the same cause Ottley[3] attributes the numerous misprints of the *Speculum*, to correct which in the type would have involved the unthreading of every line in which an error occurred. And as a still more striking proof that the lines were put into the forme one by one, in a piece, he shows a curious printer's blunder at the end of one page, where the whole of the last reference-line is put in upside down, thus:

Noe vuas bespot slapende ende niet vutende.
Genesis ix capitel.

A 'turn' of this magnitude could hardly have occurred if the letters had been set in the forme type by type.

Another suggested mode is that of casting in clay moulds, by a method very similar to that used in the sand process, and resulting in similar peculiarities and variations in the types. Ottley, who is the chief exponent of this theory, suggests that the types were made by pouring melted lead or other soft metal into moulds of earth or plaster, formed, while the earth or plaster was in a moist state, upon letters cut by hand in wood or metal; in the ordinary manner used from time immemorial in casting statues of bronze and other articles of metal, whether for use or ornament. The mould thus formed could not be of long duration; indeed, it could scarcely avail for a second casting, as it would be scarcely possible to extract the type after casting without breaking the clay, and even if that could be done, the

---

[1] Blades points out that there are no overhanging letters in the specimen. The necessity for such letters would be, we imagine, entirely obviated by the numerous combinations with which the type of the printers of the school abounded. The body is almost always large enough to carry ascending and descending sorts, and in width, a sort which would naturally overhang, is invariably covered by its following letter cast on the same piece.

[2] It is well known that until comparatively recently the large 'proscription letters' of our foundries, from three-line Pica and upwards, were cast in sand. The practice died out at the close of the eighteenth century.

[3] *An Enquiry concerning the Invention of Printing*, London, 1863, 4to, p. 265.

shrinking of the metal in cooling would be apt to warp the mould beyond the possibility of further use.

Ottley thinks that the constant renewal of the moulds could be effected by using old types cast out of them, after being touched up by the graver, as models. And this he considers will account for the varieties observable in the different letters.

In this last conjecture we think Ottley goes out of his way to suggest an unnecessary difficulty. If, as he contends, the *Speculum* was printed two pages at a time, with soft types cast by the clay process and renewed from time to time by castings from fresh moulds formed upon the old letters touched up by the graver, we should witness a gradual deterioration and attenuation in the type as the work progressed, which would leave the face of the letter at the end unrecognizable as that with which it began. It would be more reasonable to suppose that one set of models would be reserved for the periodical renewal of the moulds all through the work, and that the variations in the types would be due, not to the gradual paring of the faces of the models, but to the different skill and exactness with which the successive moulds would be taken.

The chief objection urged against both the clay and sand methods as above described is their tediousness. The time occupied after the first engraving of the models in forming, drying, and clearing the mould, in casting, extracting, touching up, and possibly perforating the types would be little short of the expeditious performance of a practised xylographer. Still there would be a clear gain in the possession of a fount of movable types which, even if the metal in which they were cast were only soft lead or pewter, might yet do duty in more than one forme, under a rough press, roughly handled. On the xylographic block, moreover, only one hand, and that a skilled one, could labour. Of the moulding and casting of these rude types many hands could make light work. Bernard states that the artist who produced for him the few sand-cast types shown in his work assured him that a workman could easily produce a thousand of such letters a day. He also states that, though each letter required squaring after casting, there was no need in any instance to touch up the faces. Bernard's experience may have been a specially fortunate one; still, making allowance for the superior workmanship and expedition of a modern artist, it must be admitted that, in point of time, cost, and utility, a printer who succeeded in furnishing himself with these primitive cast types was as far ahead of the old engraver as the discoverer of the adjustable mould was in his turn ahead of him.[1]

There remains yet another suggestion as to the method in which the types of the rude school were produced. This may be described as a system of what the founders of sixty years ago called 'polytype'. Lambinet, who is responsible for the suggestion, under cover of a new translation of Trithemius's wonderful narrative, explains this to mean nothing less than an early adoption of stereotype. He imagines[2] that the first printers may have discovered a way of moulding a page of some work—an *Abecedarium*—in cooling metal, so as to get a matrix-plate impression of the whole page. Upon this matrix they would pour a liquid metal, and by

[1] In connexion with the suggested primitive modes of casting, the patent of James Thomson in 1831 (see Chap. IV), for casting by a very similar method, is interesting.

[2] *Origine de l'imprimerie*, Paris, 1810, 2 vols., 8vo, i. 97.

the aid of a roller or cylinder, press the fused matter evenly so as to penetrate into all the hollows and corners of the letters. This tablet of tin or lead, being easily lifted and detached from the matrix, would then appear as a surface of metal in which the letters of the alphabet stood out reversed and in relief. These letters could easily be detached and rendered mobile by a knife or other sharp instrument, and the operation could be repeated a hundred times a day. The metal faces so produced would be fixed on wooden shanks, type high; and the fount would then be complete.

Such is Lambinet's hypothesis. Were it not for the fact that it was endorsed by the authority of Firmin Didot, the renowned typefounder and printer of Lambinet's day, we should hardly be disposed to admit its claim to serious attention. The supposition that the Mainz *Psalter*, which these writers point to as a specimen of this mode of execution, is the impression, not of type at all, but of a collection of 'casts' mounted on wood, is too fanciful. Didot, it must be remembered, was the enthusiastic French improver of stereotype, and his enthusiasm appears to have led him to see in his method not only a revolution in the art of printing as it existed in his day, but also a solution of the mystery which had shrouded the early history of that art for upwards of three centuries.

It may be well, before quitting this subject, to take note of a certain phrase which has given rise to a considerable amount of conjecture and controversy in connexion with the early methods of typography. The expression *getté en molle* occurred as early as the year 1446, in a record kept by Jean le Robert of Cambray, who stated that in January of that year he paid 20 sous for a printed *Doctrinale, getté en molle*. Bernard has assumed this expression to refer to the use of types cast from a mould, and cites a large number of instances where, being used in contradistinction to writing by hand, it is taken to signify typography.[1]

Van der Linde,[2] on the other hand, considers the term to mean printed from a wooden form, i.e. a xylographic production, and nothing more, quoting similar instances of the use of the words to support his opinion; and Van Meurs, whose remarks are quoted in full in Hessel's introduction to Van der Linde's *Coster Legend*,[3] declines to apply the phrase to the methods by which the *Doctrinale* was printed at all; but dwelling on the distinction drawn in various documents between *en molle* and *en papier*, concludes that the reference is to the binding of the book, and nothing more; a bound book being 'brought together in a form or binding', while an unbound one is 'in paper'.

It is difficult to reconcile these conflicting interpretations, to which may be added as a fourth that of Skeen, who considers the phrase to refer to the indented appearance of the paper of a book after being printed. In the three last cases the expression is valueless as regards our present inquiry; but if we accept Bernard's interpreta-

---

[1] *De l'origine de l'imprimerie*, i. 99, &c. The following are the citations: *Escriture en molle*, used in the letters of naturalization to the first Paris printers, 1474. *Escrits en moule*, applied to two *Horae* in vellum, bought by the Duke of Orleans, 1496. *Mettre en molle*, applied to the printing of Savonarola's sermons, 1498. *Tant en parchemin que en papier, à la main et en molle*, applied to the books in a library, 1498. *Mettre en molle*, applied to the printing of a book by Marchand, 1499. *En molle et à la main*, applied to printed books and manuscripts in the Duke of Bourbon's library, 1523. *Pièces officielles moulées par ordre de l'Assemblée*, Procès verbaux des Etats Généraux, 1593.

[2] *Coster Legend*, p. 6.

[3] Ibid., p. viii.

tion, which seems at least to have the weight of simplicity and reasonable testimony on its side, then it would be necessary to conclude that type-casting, either by a primitive or a finished process (but having regard to the date and the place, almost certainly the former), was practised in Flanders prior to January 1446. None of the illustrations, however, which Bernard cites points definitely to the use of cast type, but to printing in the abstract, irrespective of method or process. *Moulées par ordre de l'Assemblée* might equally well apply to a set of playing-cards or a broadside proclamation; *mettre en molle* does not necessarily mean anything more than put into 'print'; while the recurring expressions *en molle* and *à la main* point to nothing beyond the general distinction between manuscript and printed matter. In fact, the lack of definiteness in all the quotations given by Bernard weakens his own argument: for if we are to translate the word *moulé* throughout in the narrow sense in which he reads it, we must then believe that in every instance he cites figurative language was employed where conventional would have answered equally well, and that the natural antithesis to the general term 'by hand' must in all cases be assumed to be the particular term 'printed in cast metal types'. For ourselves, we see no justification for taxing the phrase beyond its broad interpretation of 'print'; and in this light it appears possible to reconcile most of the conjectures to which the words have given rise.[1]

Turning now from the conjectured primitive processes of the ruder school of early typography, we come to consider the practice of that more mature school which, as has already been said, appears to have arrived at once at the secret of the punch, matrix, and adjustable mould. We should be loath to assert that they arrived at once at the most perfect mechanism of these appliances; indeed, an examination of the earliest productions of the Mainz press, beautiful as they are, convinces one that the first printers were not finished typefounders. But even if their first punches were wood or copper, their first matrices lead, and their first mould no more than a clumsy adaptation of the composing-stick, they yet had the secret of the art; to perfect it was a mere matter of time.

Experiments have proved conclusively that the face of a wood-cut type may be without injury impressed into lead in a state of semi-fusion, and thus produce *en creux* an inverted image of itself in the matrix. It has also been shown that a lead matrix so formed is capable, after being squared and justified, of being adapted to a mould, and producing a certain number of types in soft lead or pewter before yielding to the heat of the operation.[2] It has also been demonstrated that similar matrices formed in clay or plaster, by the application of the wood or metal models[3] while the substance is moist, are capable of similar use.

---

[1] A further suggestion as to the meaning of this phrase was made by Degering in a review of Dr. Zedler's book, in the *Zentralblatt für Bibliothekswesen*, 1922, pp. 413–14. He quotes evidence to show that the phrase had a metaphorical meaning, 'precipitate', 'worthless'.

[2] A calculation given in the *Magazin encyclopédique* of 1806, i. 299, shows that from such matrices 120 to 150 letters can be cast before they are rendered useless, and from 50 to 60 letters before any marked deterioration is apparent in the fine strokes of the types.

[3] Several writers account for the alleged perforated wooden and metal types reputed to have been used by the first printers, and described by Specklin, Pater, Roccha, and others, by supposing that they were model types used for forming matrices, and threaded together for safety and convenience of storage.

Benjamin Franklin, in a well-known passage of his autobiography, gives the following account of his experiences as a casual letter-founder in 1727:

Our press [he says] was frequently in want of the necessary quantity of letter; and there was no such trade as that of letter-founder in America. I had seen the practice of this art at the house of James, in London; but had at the time paid it very little attention. I, however, contrived to fabricate a mould. I made use of such letters as we had for punches, founded new letters of lead in matrices of clay, and thus supplied in a tolerable manner the wants that were most pressing.[1]

Bernard states that in his day the Chinese characters in the Imperial printing-office in Paris were cast by a somewhat similar process. The original wooden letters were moulded in plaster. Into the plaster mould types of a hard metal were cast, and these hard-metal types served as punches to strike matrices with in a softer metal.[2]

In the Enschedé foundry at Haarlem there exists to this day a set of matrices, said to be nearly four hundred years old, which are described as leaden matrices from punches of copper, 'suivant l'habitude des anciens fondeurs dans les premiers temps après l'invention de l'imprimerie'.[3] By the kindness of Messrs. Enschedé, we are able to show a few letters from types cast in these venerable matrices.

PATER

FIG. 1. Type cast from leaden matrices, *c.* 1550, now in
the Enschedé foundry.

Lead matrices are frequently mentioned as having been in regular use in some of the early foundries of this country. A set of them in four-line Pica was sold at the breaking up of James's foundry in 1782, and in the other old foundries may be found relics of the same practice.

At Lubeck, John Smith informs us in 1755,[4] a printer cast for his own use, 'not only large-sized letters for titles, but also a sufficient quantity of two-lined English, after a peculiar manner, by cutting his punches on wood, and sinking them afterwards into leaden matrices; yet were the letters cast in them deeper than the French generally are'.

When, therefore, the printer of the *Catholicon*, in 1460, says of his book, 'non calami styli aut pennae suffragio, sed mirâ patronarum formarumque concordiâ proportione ac modulo impressus atque confectus est', we have not necessarily to

---

[1] *Works of the late Dr. Benjamin Franklin, consisting of his Life, written by himself*, 2 vols., London, 1793, 8vo, i. 143. It is a singular fact that in a later corrected edition of the same work, edited by John Bigelow, and published in Philadelphia in 1875, the passage above reads as follows: 'I contrived a mould, made use of the letters we had as puncheons, struck the *matrices in lead*, and thus supplied in a pretty tolerable way all deficiencies.' Whichever reading be correct, the illustration is apt, as proving the

possibility of producing type from matrices either of clay or lead in a makeshift mould.

[2] *De l'origine de l'imprimerie*, i. 144.

[3] From this method of forming the matrices (says a note to the Enschedé specimen, 1867) has arisen the name Chalcographia, which Bergellanus among others applies to printing. The earliest use of these capitals traced is at Geneva, 1570, at the press of Jean Crespin.

[4] *Printer's Grammar*, London, 1755, p. 10.

conclude that the types were produced in the modern way from copper matrices struck by steel punches. Indeed, probability seems to point to a gradual progress in the durability of the materials employed. In the first instance, the punches may have been of wood and the matrices soft lead or clay[1]; then the attempt might be made to strike hard lead into soft; that failing, copper punches[2] might be used to form leaden matrices; then, when the necessity for a more durable substance than lead for the letter became urgent, copper would be used for the matrix and brass, and finally steel, for the punch.

Of whatever substance the matrices were made, the first printers appear early to have mastered the art of justifying them, so that when cast in the mould they should not only stand, each letter true in itself, but all true to one another. Nothing amazes one more in examining these earliest printed works than the wonderful regularity of the type in body, height, and line; and if anything could be considered as evidence that those types were produced from matrices in moulds, and not by the rude method of casting from matrices which comprehended body and face in the same moulding, this feature alone is conclusive. We may go farther, and assert that not only must the matrices have been harmoniously justified, but the mould employed, whatever its form, must have had its adjustable parts finished with a near approach to mathematical accuracy, which left little to be accomplished in the way of further improvement.

Respecting this mould we have scarcely more material for conjecture than with regard to the first punches and matrices. The principle of the bipartite mould was, of course, well known already. The importance of absolute squareness in the body and height of the type would demand an appliance of greater precision than the uncertain cube hollowed in sand or clay; the heat of the molten lead would point to the use of a hard metal like iron or steel; and the varying widths of the sunk letters in the matrices would suggest the adoption of some system of slides whereby the mould could be expanded or contracted laterally, without prejudice to the invariable regularity of its body and height. By what crude methods the first typefounder contrived to combine these essential qualities we have no means of judging,[3] but

---

[1] It has been suggested by some that wood could be *struck* into lead or pewter. In 1816 Robert Clayton proposed to cast types in metal out of *wooden* matrices punched in wood with a cross grain, which had been previously slightly charred or baked.

[2] In the *Spécimen* (*Ancienne Typographie*) of the Imprimerie Royale of Paris, 1819, several of the old oriental founts are thus noted: 'les poinçons sont en cuivre.'

[3] In the 2nd edition of Isaiah Thomas's *History of Printing in America*, Albany, 1874, i. 288, an anecdote is given of Peter Miller, the German who printed at Ephrata in the United States in 1749, which we think is suggestive of the possible expedients of the first printers with regard to the mould. During the time that a certain work of Miller was in the press, says Francis Bailey, a former apprentice of Miller's, 'particular sorts of the fonts of type on which it was printed ran short. To overcome this difficulty, one of the workmen constructed a mold that could be moved so as to suit the body of any type not smaller than brevier nor larger than double-pica. The mold consisted of four quadrangular pieces of brass, two of them with mortices to shift to a suitable body, and secured by screws. The best type they could select from the sort wanted was then placed in the mold, and after a slight corrosion of the surface of the letter with aquafortis to prevent soldering or adhesion, a leaden matrix was cast on the face of the type, from which, after a slight stroke of a hammer on the type in the matrix, we cast the letters which were wanted. Types thus cast answer tolerably well. I have often adopted a method somewhat like this to obtain sorts which were short; but instead of four pieces of brass, made use of an even and accurate composing-stick, and one piece of iron or copper having an even surface on the sides; and instead of a leaden matrix, have substituted one of clay, especially for letters with a bold face.' De Vinne describes an old mould preserved among the relics in Bruce's foundry at New York, composed (with the matrix) of four pieces, and adjustable both as to body and thickness. Bernard also mentions a similar mould in use in 1853.

were they ever so crude, to him is due the honour of the culminating achievement of the invention of typography. 'His type mould,' De Vinne remarks, 'was not merely the first; it is the only practical mechanism for making types. For more than four hundred years this mould has been under critical examination, and many attempts have been made to supplant it. . . . But in principle, and in all the more important features, the modern mould may be regarded as the mould of Gutenberg.'

It may be asked, if the matrices were so truly justified, and the mould so accurately adjusted, how comes it that in the first books of these Mainz printers we still discover irregularities among the letters—fewer, indeed, but of the same kind as are to be found in books printed by the artists of the ruder school? To this we reply that these irregularities are for the most part attributable neither to varieties in the original models, nor to defects in the matrix or the mould, but to the worn

Fig. 2. Variations in the face of type
produced by bad casting.

or unworn condition of the type, and to the skill or want of skill of the caster. Anyone versed in the practice of type-casting in hand-moulds is aware that the manual exercise of casting a type is peculiar and difficult. With the same mould and the same matrix, one clever workman may turn out nineteen perfect types out of twenty, while a clumsy caster will scarcely succeed in producing a single perfect type out of the number. Different letters require different contortions to 'coax' the metal into all the interstices of the matrix; and it is quite possible for the same workman to vary so in his work as to be as 'lucky' one day as he is unprofitable the next. In modern times, of course, none but the perfect types ever find their way into the printer's hands, but in the early days when, with a perishable matrix, every type cast was of consequence, the censorship would be less severe, and types would be allowed to pass into use which differed as much from their original model as they did from one another. Let any inexperienced reader attempt to cast twenty black-letter types from one mould and matrix, and let him take a proof of the types so produced in juxtaposition. The result of such an experiment would lead him to cease once and for all to wonder at irregularities observable in the Gutenberg *Bible* or the Mainz *Psalter* or the *Catholicon*.

With regard to the metal in which the earliest types were cast, we have more or less information afforded us in the colophons and statements of the printers themselves, although it must be borne in mind that the figurative language in which these artists were wont to describe their own labours is apt occasionally to lead to confusion as to whether the expressions used refer to the punch, the matrix, or the cast types. We meet almost promiscuously with the terms *aere notas, aeneis formulis, chalcographos, stanneis typis, stanneis formulis, ahenis formis, tabulis ahenis, aere legere, notas de duro orichalco,* &c. We look in vain for *plumbum,* the metal one would most naturally expect to find mentioned. The word *aes,* though strictly meaning bronze, is undoubtedly to be taken in its wider sense, already familiar in the fifteenth century, of metal in the abstract, and to include, at least, the lead, tin, or pewter in which the types were almost certainly cast. The reference to copper and bronze might either apply to the early punches or the later matrices, but in no case is it probable that types were cast in either metal.

Padre Fineschi gives an interesting extract from the cost-book of the Ripoli press, about 1480,[1] by which it appears that steel, brass, copper, tin, lead, and iron wire were all used in the manufacture of types at that period; the first two probably for the mould, the steel also for the punches, the copper for the matrices, the lead and tin for the types, and the iron wire for the mould and possibly for stringing together the perforated type-models.

It is probable that an alloy was early introduced; first by the addition to the lead of tin and iron, and then gradually improved upon till the discovery of antimony at the end of the fifteenth century[2] supplied the ingredient requisite to render the types at once tough and sharp enough for the ordeal of the press. There is little doubt that at some time or other every known metal was tried experimentally in the mixture; but, from the earliest days of letter-casting, lead and tin have always been recognized as the staple ingredients of the alloy, the hard substance being usually either iron, bismuth, or antimony.

Towards the end of the last century the controversies about the invention of printing and the methods of producing types employed by the first printers appeared to have been settled. The position as laid down in Van der Linde's book seemed to have won fairly general approval. Since that time there has been an intensive study of the productions of the earliest presses and the types used, carried out by a group of German scholars with the support of the Gutenberg Gesellschaft at Mainz. The Society has published a series of monographs by Gottfried Zedler, Paul von Schwenke, Heinrich Wallau, Otto Hupp, and others, each one devoted

---

[1] *Notizie storiche sopra la Stamperia di Ripoli, Firenze,* 1781, p. 49. *Prezzi de' generi riguardanti la Getteria (letter foundry).*

					s.	d.	
Acciaio (steel)	.	. liv. 2	8	0 la lib.	(= 9	0	per lb.)
Metallo (type-metal?)	.	„	11	0 „	(= 2	0¾	„)
Ottone (brass)	.	. „	12	0 „	(= 2	3	„)
Rame (copper)	.	. „	6	8 „	(= 1	3	„)
Stagno (tin)	.	. „	8	0 „	(= 1	6	„)
Piombo (lead)	.	. „	2	4 „	(= 0	5¼	„)
Filo di ferro (iron wire)		„	8	0 „	(= 1	6	„)

Prices of 1887.

[2] It would be more correct to say the discovery of the properties of antimony, which were first described by Basil Valentin about the end of the 15th century, in a treatise entitled *Currus triumphalis Antimonii.*

to the study of one of the books, large and small, printed at Mainz and elsewhere. Discussion has continued in almost every number of the *Jahrbuch* issued by the Society since 1926. Dr. Zedler, in addition to numerous books and articles published by the Mainz Society, has also published similar studies on the so-called *Costeriana*. All this thorough and scholarly research has added greatly to our understanding of the first specimens of printing, but as to the controversial questions such as that between the claims of Haarlem and Mainz and the question as to how the earliest movable types were produced, agreement has by no means been reached. Most of the old theories have appeared again and have been discussed with considerable asperity. It may perhaps be said that a count of heads would show that the views put forward by Van der Linde are still held by the majority, but on the other side are some of the most voluminous and persistent controversialists, especially Dr. Gottfried Zedler. We add here a few notes on the more important publications of this modern period in so far as they bear on the question of the methods of type production.

The two first publications are an account of actual experiments in type-casting carried out by experts. J. E. Hodgkin's *Rariora*, vol. ii, 1902, contains two chapters on 'Wooden Types' and on 'The Evolution of the Type Mould'. Hodgkin claims that the scepticism about wooden types may be due to the fact that the experimenters have been cutting *across* the grain of the wood instead of *along* the grain, and as to the durability of wooden types he claims that if cleaned with oil, and not washed with lye as if they were metal types, satisfactory results can be obtained. At least he has cut wooden letters and shows a 3,500th impression from such letters. He further describes a method of casting in a mould of sand, using a wooden model as a core. Such wooden models could be driven into leaden matrices. He has himself cast type in imitation of the 42-line Bible type from leaden matrices struck by wooden models, and even types as small as the Indulgence types. Hodgkin does not put forward a case that any of these methods were in fact practised by the earliest printers, but as an illustration of what could be achieved his experiments are remarkable.

Herr Gustav Mori, in the account of the experiments he has carried out in *Was hat Gutenberg erfunden?* 1921 (an English translation appeared in *Typographia*, vol. ii, no. 2, 1925), goes a step farther than Hodgkin and claims that Gutenberg did in fact proceed on the same course. Mori begins by describing a method of reproducing wood blocks by casting in sand and claims that the 'Shot prints', usually supposed to be metal cuts, were so produced. This process was then applied to the reproduction of type from letters cut from a wood block, and Mori shows type manufactured in this way in his own experiments. The record in the Gutenberg process of 1439 relating to the 'four pieces' shows, he claims, that Gutenberg was at that time casting in sand. The next process was the casting in sand of brass punches, which were struck into lead matrices. Type was cast from such matrices by means of the casting square made of brass or iron, the sides of which were held together by a spring. At a later date the casting square was covered with wood and became the adjustable hand-casting mould more or less as used by founders for four centuries. All these improvements had been made when the 42-line Bible type was produced. Striking leaden matrices was an unsatisfactory method for producing the smaller Indulgence types, and the need for such small types led to the use of the engraved steel punch, and soon afterwards to matrices of copper. This picture of how Gutenberg worked appears to be accepted by Dr. Zedler and parts of it by other scholars. Dr. Ruppel, for instance, in his latest book *Johannes Gutenberg*, 1939, holds that Gutenberg's earliest type, i.e. before that of the astronomical calendar for 1448,[1] was cast from lead matrices, which fact accounts for their *unscharfe Ränder*. Otto Hupp, on the other hand, contests every conclusion of Mori's book (see especially his article *Gutenberg und die Nacherfinder* in the *Gutenberg Jahrbuch*, 1929, pp. 31–101). Hupp has for years been at variance with Dr. Zedler and firmly holds to the view that Gutenberg, as a goldsmith, was familiar with the engraved steel punch, and had from the beginning always worked from such punches.

Dr. Zedler's book *Von Coster zu Gutenberg*, 1921, contains the most detailed study of the eight types used in the *Costeriana*. We are not here concerned with the author's support of the Coster legend nor with his dating of the surviving specimens from these early Dutch presses. As to the method of type production followed, Dr. Zedler gives the results of further experiments in sand-casting, and supposes, as others have already supposed, that the shanks of the types were separately cast and the shanks then welded on to the letters. This process is known as the 'Abklatsch' method. One of the author's chief arguments for concluding that the Dutch typefounder used the technique of sand-casting is based on the existence of cross-strokes connecting the marks of abbreviation to the main letters. These strokes, he says, represent channels through which the molten metal could flow to these detached parts. As to this argument, other experts have denied that metal could possibly flow through such narrow channels. That types *can* be produced by a process of casting in sand has again been demonstrated by Messrs. Enschedé of Haarlem, who in 1927 published *Het middeleeuwsche Gezang Dies ist Laetitiae*, printed in type cast from sand.

A recent book on the invention of printing, Pierce Butler's *The Origin of Printing in Europe*, Chicago, 1940, has started a new theory. In a copy of the *Speculum* in the Huntington Library there has been found an elevated quad, showing a white letter form on a black ground, which seems to indicate a matrix used as a quad. This would mean that the matrix was struck on the end of the prism and not, as usual, on the side, and would require a different casting mould. Mr. Butler has reconstructed such a mould and suggests that this less efficient instrument would account for the irregularities in early type.

Turning now from type-casting appliances to the early types themselves, we are enabled, thanks to one or two recent discoveries, to form a tolerably good idea as to their appearance and peculiarities. We have already stated that, with regard to the traditional perforated wooden types seen by certain old writers, the probability is that, if these were the genuine relics they professed to be, they were model types used for forming moulds upon, or for impressing into matrices of moist clay or

---

[1] But see Carl Wehmer's *Mainzer Probedrucke in der Type des sogenannten Astronomishcen Kalenders für 1448*, 1948, which upsets this date.

C

soft lead. We have also considered it possible, in regard to types cast in the primitive sand or clay moulds of the rude school, that to overcome the difficulties incident to irregular height to paper, uneven bodies, and loose locking-up, the expedient may have been attempted of perforating the types and passing a thread or wire through each line to hold the intractable letters in their place.

This, however, is mere conjecture, and whether such types existed or not, none of them have survived to our day. Their possessors, as they slowly discovered the secret of the punch, matrix, and mould, would show little veneration, we imagine, for these clumsy relics of their ignorance, and value them only as old lead, to be remelted and recast by the newer and better method.

But though no relic of these primitive cast types remains, we are happily not without means for forming a judgement respecting some of the earliest types of the more finished school of printers. In 1878, in the bed of the river Saône, near Lyons,[1] opposite the site of one of the famous fifteenth-century printing-houses of that city, a number of old types were discovered which there seems reason to believe belonged once to one of those presses, and were used by the early printers of Lyons. They came into the hands of A. Claudin of Paris, the distinguished typographical antiquary, who, after careful examination and inquiry, has satisfied himself as to their antiquity and value as genuine relics of the infancy of the art of printing.

The following outline profile-sketches will give a good idea of the various forms and sizes represented in the collection. There is little doubt that they were all cast in a mould. The metal used is lead, slightly alloyed with some harder substance,

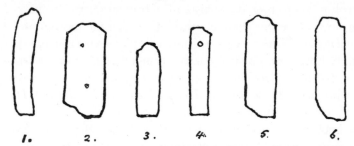

1.   *2.*   *3.*   *4*   *5.*   *6.*

FIG. 3. Profile tracings from M. Claudin's Types. October 1883.

which in the case of a few of the types seems to be iron. The chief point which strikes the observer is the variety in the 'height to paper' of the different founts. Taking the six specimens shown in the illustration, it will be seen that no two of the types correspond in this particular. No. 4 corresponds as nearly as possible to our English standard height. No. 3 is considerably lower than an ordinary space height. No. 2 approaches some of the continental heights still to be met with, while Nos. 1, 5, and 6 are higher than any known standard. It is easy to imagine that an early printer who cast his own types would trouble himself very little as to the heights of his neighbours' and rivals' moulds, so that in a city like Lyons there

---

[1] Printing was practised at Lyons in 1473, only three years later than at Paris. From the year 1476 the art extended rapidly in the city. Panzer mentions some 250 works printed here during the fifteenth century by nearly forty printers. The earlier Lyons printers are supposed to have had their type from Basle, and their city shortly became a depot for the supply of type to the printers of southern France and Spain. Cf. Claudin, *Histoire de l'imprimerie en France*, Paris, 1900–14. Vols. iii and iv deal with Lyons in the fifteenth century.

might have been as many 'heights to paper' as there were printers. It is even possible that a printer using one style and size of letter exclusively for one description of work, and another size and style for another description, might not be particular to assimilate the heights in his own office; and so, foreshadowing the improvidence of some of his modern followers, lay in founts of letter which would not work with any other, but which, as time went on, could hardly be dispensed with. Then, when the days of the itinerant typesellers and the type-markets began, he might still further add to his 'heights' by the purchase of a German fount from one merchant, a Dutch from another, and so on.

The type No. 3, though lower than all the rest, has yet a letter upon its end. But it seems likely that the old printers cut down their worn-out letters for spaces, not by ploughing off the face, but by shortening the type at the foot. So that No. 3 (presuming the bodies to have corresponded) might stand as a space to No. 4, or No. 4 to No. 1. At the same time, the collection includes a good number of plain spaces and quadrats (the latter generally about a square body), which may either have been cast as they now appear or be old letters of which the face and shoulder have been cut off.

The small hole appearing in the side of type No. 4 is a perforation, and the collection contains several types, both letters and spaces, having the same peculiarity. Whether this hole was formed at the time of or after casting; whether the letters so perforated were originally model-types only, or types in actual use; whether the hole was intended for a thread or wire to hold the letters in their places during impression; or whether, for want of a type-case, it was used for stringing the types together for safety when not in use, it is as easy to conjecture as it is impossible to determine. The perforated types which we examined certainly did not appear to be older, and in most cases appeared less old than those not perforated—the outline of type No. 4 itself shows it to be fairer and squarer than any of its companions.

Another peculiarity to be noted is the 'chamfer', or cutting away of one of the corners of the feet of types 2, 5, and 6. This appears to have been intentional, and may have served the same purpose as our nick, to guide the compositor in setting. None of the types has a nick, and types 1 and 3 have no distinguishing mark whatever. The two small indentations in the side of type 2 are air-holes produced in the casting.

With regard to the faces of the types, there are traces in most of the letters of the 'shoulders' of the body having been tapered off by a knife or graver after casting, so as to leave the letter quite clear on the body. In most cases the letter stands in the centre of the body, which is, as a rule, larger than the size the character actually requires. In point of thickness, however, the old printers appear to have been very sparing; and a great many of the letters, though possessing ample room 'body-way', actually overhang the sides, and are what we should style in modern terminology 'kerned' letters. The difficulty, however, which would be experienced by printers to-day with these overhanging sorts was obviated to a large extent in the case of the old printers by the numerous ligatures, contractions, and double letters with which their founts abounded, and which gave almost all the combinations in which an overhanging letter would be likely to clash with its neighbour.

One last peculiarity to be observed is the absence of what is known as the 'break' at the foot of the type. The contrivance in the mould whereby the foot of the type is cast square, and the 'jet', or superfluous metal left by the casting, is attached, not to the whole of the foot, but to a narrow ridge across the centre, from which it is easily detached, was probably unknown to the fifteenth-century typefounders. Their types appear to have come out of the mould with a 'jet' attaching to the entire foot, from which it could only be detached by a saw or cutter. The 'chamfer' already pointed out in types 2, 5, 6, if produced in the mould, may indicate an early attempt to reduce the size of the jet, which, if attaching to the entire square of the foot of a type the size of No. 2, would involve both time and labour in removal.

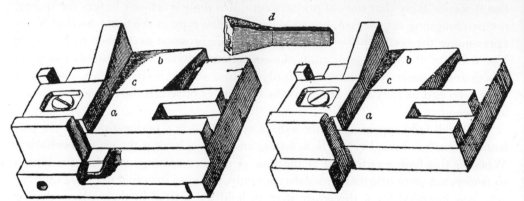

Fig. 4. Sixteenth-century type moulds, from Duverger.
a. The body in which the type is cast. b, c. The 'jet' in which the fluid metal is poured. *d.* The type as cast.

Duverger, in his clever essay on the invention of printing,[1] gives an illustration of the manner in which he imagines the old types would be detached from their jets; and considers that in the three points only of the want of a breaking 'jet', the want of a spring to hold the matrix to the mould, and the absence of a nick, the mould of the first printer differed essentially from that of the printer of his day.

Such are some of the chief points of interest to be observed in these venerable relics of the old typographers. Yet, curious as they are, they prove that the types of the fifteenth century differed in no essential particular from those of the nineteenth. Ruder and rougher, and less durable they might be, but in substance and form, and in the mechanical principles of their manufacture, they claim kinship with the newest types of our most modern foundry.

The old Lyonnese relics are not the only guide we have as to the form and nature of the fifteenth-century types. Madden, in 1875, made a most valuable discovery in a book printed by Conrad Winters de Homborch, at Cologne, in 1479, and entitled *De morali lepra,* by Johann Nider, of the accidental impression of a type, pulled up from its place in the course of printing by the ink-ball, and laid at length upon the face of the forme, thus leaving its exact profile indented upon the page.[2]

A similar discovery, equally valuable and interesting, was made by Henry

[1] *Histoire de l'invention de l'imprimerie par les monuments,* Paris, 1840, fol., p. 12. Duverger gives no authority for the statement that the type-mould was Garamond's.

[2] *Lettres d'un bibliographe,* Paris, 1875, 8vo, Sér. iv, p. 231. Hain,* 11817; Voulliéme, 867.

Bradshaw, of Cambridge, in a copy of a work by Petrus Damascenus entitled *De laudibus Gloriosae Virginis Mariae, sine notâ*, but printed probably about 1475 at Cologne by Nicolaus Goetz.[1] These two impressions are particularly interesting in the light of the old Lyonnese types still in existence. Like them, they are without nick, and tapered off at the face. They are also without the jet-break. The height of both types is above the English standard and more nearly approaches that of No. 2 of the Lyons letters, and Madden points out as remarkable that this height (24 millimetres) is exactly that fixed as the standard 'height to paper' by the *règlement de la librairie* of 1723. The body of the types (assuming the letter to be laid sideways, of which there can be little doubt) is about the modern English, and so corresponds to the body of the text on which it lies.

The chief point of interest, however, is in the small circle appearing in both near the top, which Madden (as regards the type of the *Nider*) thus explains: 'This circle, the contour of which is exactly formed, shows that the letter was pierced laterally by a circular hole. This hole did not penetrate the whole thickness of the letter, and served, like the nick of our days, to enable the compositor to tell by touch which way to set the letter in his stick, so as to be right in the printed page. If the letter had been laid on its other side, the existence of this little circle would have been lost to us for ever.' It would, however, be quite possible for a perforated type, with the end of the hole slightly clogged with ink, to present precisely the same appearance as this, which Madden concludes was only slightly pierced; and were it not for the fact that the pulling-up of the letter from the forme is itself evidence that the line could not have been threaded, we should hesitate to affirm that either of the types shown was not perforated. The sharp edge of the circumference in the type of the *De laudibus*, leaving, as it does, in the original page a clearly embossed circle in the paper, makes it evident that the depression was not the result of a mere flaw in the casting, although it is possible (as we have satisfied ourselves by experiment) for the surface of the side of a roughly cast type to be depressed by air-holes, some of which assume a circular form and may even perforate a thin type. Indeed, at the present day it is next to impossible to cast by hand a type which is not a little sunk on some part of its sides; and this roughness of surface we can imagine to have been far more apparent on the types cast by the earliest printers. We doubt, therefore, whether, in types liable to these accidental depressions of surface, a small artificial hole thus easily simulated would be of any service as a guide to the compositor. A more probable explanation of the appearance seems to be that the head of a small screw or pin, used to fix the side-piece of the mould, projecting slightly on the surface of the piece it fixed, left its mark on the side of the types as they were cast, and thus caused the circular depression observable in the illustrations.[2]

An unusually good specimen of a 'turned-up' early type was found by Gordon Duff in a copy of Richard Arnold's *Chronicle* in the library of Corpus Christi

---

[1] Begins *Incipit Liber de Laudibus ac Festis Gloriose Virginis Matris Marie alias Marionale Dictus per Doctores eximeos editus et compilatus*; at end, *Explicit Petrus Damasceni de laudibus gloriose Virginis Marie*. Hain,* 5918, Voulliéme, 916. The drawn-up type occurs on the top of folio b 4 verso.

[2] Such projections or 'drags' in the mould are not unknown in modern typefounding, where they are purposely inserted so as to leave the newly cast type, on the opening of the mould, always adhering to one particular side.

College, Cambridge.[1] This edition of Arnold is without imprint, but is believed to have been printed at Antwerp about 1503, by A. van Berghen. The book is a curious jumble of civic lore about London. It contains lists of mayors, the charters and liberties of the city, the 'acte for the correction of errours among jugementis in London', weights, measures, laws, oaths, polite correspondence between the 'Sowdan of Babilon and the pope of Rome', and other matters, in the midst of which we find the charming old ballad of the 'Nut-brown Maid'. Our turned type

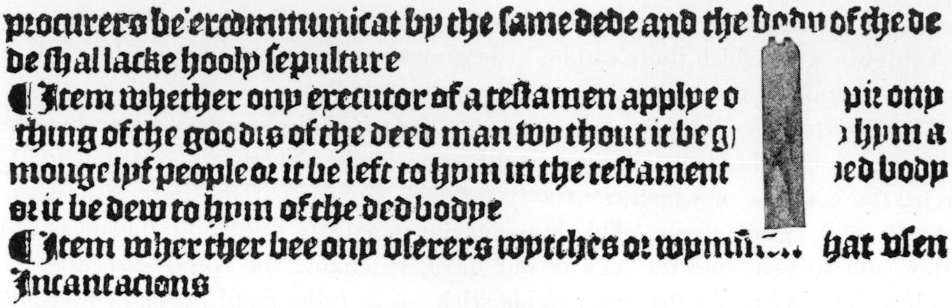
procurers be excommunicat by the same dede and the body of the de
de shall lacke hooly sepulture
¶ Item whether ony executor of a testamen applye o pir ony
thing of the goodis of the deed man wythout it be g hym a
monge lyf people or it be left to hym in the testament ed body
or it be dew to hym of the ded bodye
¶ Item wher ther bee ony userers wytches or wym hat usen
Incantacions

FIG. 5. Turned-up type in Arnold's *Chronicle*, Antwerp, *c.* 1503.

occurs in a passage towards the end reading 'Tharticles founde by the Inquisitours at the visitacion last done in the chirche of saint magnus' at sig. s6 verso. The damaged text should read thus:

applye o[r appro]pir
it be g[yven to] hym
testament [of the d]ed body
(blank line)
or wym[men t]hat

Turning to the truant type, which is possibly an *r* or an *n*, it will be seen that it considerably exceeds in height to paper the ordinary English standard. The body is approximately English. The casting of the type is not very solid, as the marks of depression in the metal are apparent in the side that shows up, one such 'blow' being at the bottom and another and wider one at the top. There is no sign of the perforation common in the earliest types, as in the two turned types described above. But in the present instance there seems to be evidence that type-founding had already reached the stage of 'feet' for the type, although there is no sign of a nick. The manner in which the type, pulled out of its place by the ink-ball and laid flat on the forme, has squashed down the letters round, without bulging out the ends of the lines, indicates that the metal must have been decidedly soft. It will also be noticed that the shoulder of the letter falls away somewhat in the fashion of our type to-day, and not as steeply as the earlier specimens referred to.

In conclusion we give a table of 'turned-up' types noted. The height to paper is given in millimetres, 24 mm. being approximately the standard English height.

[1] This section is taken from an article by Reed in *The Printers' Register* for 6 June 1891.

Date	Title	Place	Printer	Height mm.	Found by	Remarks
c. 1475	Damascenus, P. *Marionale*	Cologne	Nicolaus Goetz	24	Bradshaw; see above	Perforated; sloping shoulders
1479	Nider, J. *De morali lepra*	Cologne	C. Winters de Homborch	25	Madden; see above	,, ,,
1486	*Herbarius*	Augsburg	Schönsperger	22	De Vinne	,, ,,
1487	Clavasius, *Summa Angelica*	Venice	N. de Frankfordia	26¼	J. S. Watson; see *Academy*, 1 Aug. 1885	Not perforated, high shoulders
1503?	Arnold, *Chronicle*	Antwerp	A. van Berghen	25	E. G. Duff; see above	Not perforated, square shoulders, cast feet
1528	*Sarum Breviary*	Paris	J. Kerbriand	..	Bradshaw; copy in University Library, Cambridge	Broken, not perforated, square shoulders

It is worth noting, as indicating that such accidents were not considered serious enough to constitute a 'spoil', that in three of the above instances, at any rate, the rubricator has added his red marks to the damaged text.

Mr. Victor Scholderer, in 'The Shape of Early Type', *Gutenberg Jahrbuch*, 1927, pp. 24–5, has described four further examples of turned types, as well as two of the accidental impression of furniture, found in incunabula in the British Museum. One of his examples, in a *Justinian* printed at Venice by B. de Tortis in 1490, has a height to paper of 27 mm. and has cast feet. None of his examples, all printed in Italy, shows signs of perforation. Mr. Scholderer gives references to other literature illustrating the subject, to Schwenke's *Johann Gutenbergs zweiundvierzigzeilige Bibel*, Ergänzungsband, 1923, p. 39, and to plates 1909 *c* and 1909 *e* in the publications of the Type Facsimile Society.

The quantity of type with which the earliest printers found it necessary to provide themselves turns, of course, upon the question, did the first printers print only one page at a time, or more? On this point we cannot do better than quote the words of Blades.

The scribe [he says] necessarily wrote but one page at a time, and, curiously enough, the early printers here also assimilated their practice. Whether from want of sufficient type to set up the requisite number of pages, or from the limited capability of the presses, there is strong evidence of the early books from Caxton's press having been printed page by page. . . . Instances are found of pages on the same side of the sheet being out of parallel, which could not occur if two pages were printed together. . . . A positive proof of the separate printing of the pages may be seen in a copy of the *Recuyell of the Histories of Troye*, in the Bodleian; for the ninth recto of the third quaternion has never been printed at all, while the second verso (the page which must fall on the same side of the sheet) appears properly printed.[1]

What is true of Caxton's early works is also true of a large number of other fifteenth-century printed books. Hessels refers to a large number of incunabula in which he has found evidence that this mode of printing was the common practice of the early typographers.[2]

Assuming, then, that the first books were generally printed page by page, it will be seen that the stock of type necessary to enable the printer to proceed was

[1] *Life of Caxton*, i. 39. Later on (p. 52) Blades points out, as an argument against the supposed typographical connexion between Caxton and Zell of Cologne, that the latter, from an early period, printed two pages at a time.

[2] *Haarlem Legend*, p. xxiii. See also R. B. McKerrow's *Introduction to Bibliography*, pp. 57–61, and the introduction to the *Catalogue of Books printed in the XVth Century in the British Museum*, vol. i, p. xii.

but small. 2,700 letters would suffice for one page of the 42-line *Bible*; and for the *Rationale Durandi* about 5,000 would be required. It is probable, however, that, as Bernard suggests, the printers would cast enough to enable one forme to be composed while the other was working, so that double these quantities would possibly be provided. Nor must it be forgotten that a 'fount' of type in those days consisted not only of the ordinary letters of the alphabet but of a very large number of double letters, abbreviations, and contractions, which must have seriously complicated the labour of composition as well as reduced the individual number of each type required to fill the typefounder's 'bill'. This feature, doubtless attributable to the attempt on the part of the early printers to imitate manuscript as closely as possible, as well as to the exigencies of justification in composition, which, in the absence of a variety of spaces, required various widths in the letters themselves, was common to both schools of early typography. Bernard states that, in the type of the 42-line *Bible*, each letter required at least three or four varieties; while with regard to Caxton's type 1, which was designed and cast at Bruges, before 1472, Blades points out that the fount contained upwards of 163 sorts, and that there were only five letters of which there were not more than one matrix, either as single letters or in combination. Speaking of the *Speculum*, Skeen counts 1,430 types on one page, of which 22 are *a*, 61 *e*, 91 *i*, 73 *o*, 37 *u*, 22 *d*, 14 *h*, 30 *m*, 50 *n*, 42 *s*, and 41 *t*; besides which there are no less than 90 duplicate and triplicate characters, comprising one variation of *a*, 15 of *c*, 7 of *d*, 3 of *e*, 9 of *f*, 10 of *g*, 3 of *i*, 7 of *l*, 3 of *n*, 2 of *o*, 2 of *p*, 10 of *r*, 9 of *s*, 9 of *t*, varying in the frequency of their occurrence from once to eleven times, leaving but 541 other letters for the rest of the alphabet, including the capitals; and of these last, from 3 to 20 would be the utmost of each required. Altogether, calculating 138 matrices (i.e. two alphabets of 24 letters each, and 90 double and treble letters) to be the least number of matrices required to make a complete fount,[1] the highest number of types of any one particular sort necessary to print a single page would be 91. The average number of the 11 chief letters specified above would be about 44, while if we take into calculation the minor letters of the alphabet and the double letters, this average would be reduced to little more than 10. It will thus be seen that the founts of the earliest printers consisted of a small quantity each of a large variety of sorts. Astle, in his chapter on 'The Origin and Progress of Printing',[2] is, we believe, the only writer who has dwelt upon the difficulty which the first letter-founders would be likely to encounter in the arrangement of their 'bill'. This venerable compilation was, he considers, made in the fifteenth century, probably by the ordinary method of casting-off copy. If so, it must have experienced considerable and frequent change during the time that the ligatures were falling into disuse, and until the printer's alphabet had reduced itself to its present limits.

Of the face of type used by the earliest printers we shall have occasion to speak later on. Respecting the development of letter-founding as an industry, there is

[1] Skeen, *Early Typography*, p. 299, speaks of 300 matrices as constituting a complete fount; he appears accidentally, in calculating for two pages instead of one, to have assumed that a double number of matrices would be requisite for the double quantity of type.

[2] *Origin and Progress of Writing*, London, 1803, 4to, chap. ix.

little that can be gathered in the history of the fifteenth century. At first the art of the inventor was a mystery divulged to none. But the sack of Mainz, in 1462, and the consequent dispersion of Gutenberg's disciples, spread the secret broadcast over Europe.[1] Italy, Switzerland, France, the Netherlands, Spain, England, in turn learned it, and after their fashion improved it. Italy, especially, guided by the master-hands of her early artists, brought it to rapid perfection. The migrations of Gutenberg's types among the early presses of Bamberg, Eltville, and elsewhere have led to the surmise that he may have sold matrices of his letter.[2] In 1468 Schoeffer put forward what may be considered the first advertisement in the annals of typography. 'Every nation', he says, in the colophon to Justinian's *Institutiones*, 1468, 'can now procure its own kind of letters, for he [i.e. Schoeffer himself] excels with every sort of pencil' (i.e. in designing and engraving all kinds of type).[3] For the most part printers were their own founders, and each printer had his own types. But type depots and markets, and the wanderings of the itinerant typographers, as the demands of printing yearly increased, brought the founts of various presses and nations to various centres, and thus gave the first impulse to that gradual divorce between printing and typefounding which in the following century left the latter the distinct industry it still remains.[4]

Such is a brief outline of the chief facts and opinions regarding the processes, appliances, and practices of the earliest typefounders. It may be said that, after all, we know very little about the matter. The facts are very few, and the conjectures, in many instances, so contradictory, that it is impossible to erect a 'system' or draw any but general conclusions. These conclusions we very briefly summarize as follows.

Accepting as a fundamental principle that the essence of typography is in the mobility of the types, we dismiss, as beyond the scope of our inquiry, the xylographic works which preceded typography. Passing in review the alleged stepping-stones between the two arts, we fail to see in the evidence adduced as to the use of movable wooden perforated types anything to justify the conclusion that the earliest printers printed books by their means. Such types may have been cut experimentally, but the practical impossibility of cutting them square enough to be composed in a forme, and of producing a work of the size and character of the *Speculum*, is fatal to their claims. With regard to the 'sculpto-fusi' types—types engraved on cast-metal bodies—the evidence in their favour is of the most unsatisfactory character, and, coupled with the practical difficulties of their production, reduces their claims to a minimum. The marked difference of style and excellence in the

---

[1] Haebler in his *Handbuch der Inkunabelkunde*, pp. 31–2, holds that the importance of the sack of Mainz on the history of printing has been exaggerated. He points out that there were several presses at work before 1462.

[2] The cost-book of the Ripoli press contains several entries pointing to an early trade in type and matrices. In 1477 the directors paid ten florins of gold to one John of Mainz for a set of roman matrices. At another time they paid 110 livres for two founts of roman and one of gothic: and further, purchased of the goldsmith, Banco of Florence, 100 little initials, three large initials, three copper vignettes, and the copper for an entire set of Greek matrices.

[3] Natio quæque suum poterit reperire caragma
Secum nempe stilo præminet omnigeno.

[4] Cf. Dr. Haebler, 'Schriftguss und Schriftenhandel in der Frühdruckzeit', in *Zentralblatt für Bibliothekswesen*, Bd. xli, pp. 81 seq. Dr. Haebler finds no evidence of letter-founders working on their own account in the 15th century. A fount of type could be bought only from another printer. Nevertheless he gives references to many cases where types have changed hands, and, towards the end of the century, of printers supplying a number of other printers with the same types.

typography of certain of the earliest books leads us to accept the theory that two schools of typography existed side by side in the infancy of the art—one a rude school which, not having the secret of the more perfect appliances of the inventors, cast its letters by some primitive method, probably using moulds of sand or clay, in which the entire type had been moulded. Such types may have been perforated and held together in lines by a wire. The suggestion that the earliest types were produced by a system of polytype, and that the face of each letter, sawn off a plate resembling a stereotype-plate, was separately mounted on loose wooden shanks, we dismiss as purely fanciful.

Turning now to the processes adopted by the typographers of the more advanced school, we consider that in the first instance, although grasping the principle of the punch, the matrix, and the adaptable mould, they may have made use of inferior appliances—possibly by forming their matrices in lead from wooden or leaden punches or models—advancing thence by degrees to the use of steel punches, copper matrices, and the bipartite iron mould. We hold that the variations observable in the early works of this school are due mainly to uneven casting and wear and tear of the types. As to the metal in which the type was cast, we find mention made of almost every metal, several of which, however, refer to the punches and matrices, leaving tin, lead, and antimony as the staple ingredients of the type-metal. Of the types themselves, we find these in most essential particulars to be the same as those cast at a later date. We see, however, evidence of perforated, mould-cast type, and, in the absence of a nick, a 'chamfer' at the foot, from which the jet appears to have been sawn or cut, instead of being broken. We remark a great irregularity in the heights of different founts, the average of which height is beyond any modern English standard. The accidental impression of a type in a number of early books proves that about the year 1476 types were made differing only in the two points of the want of a nick and the want of a jet-break from the types of to-day. The quantity of types required by the earliest printers, we consider, would be small, since they appear in most instances to have printed only one page at a time; but the number of different sorts going to make up a fount would be very considerable by reason of the numerous contractions, double letters, and abbreviations used.

Finally, we consider that the art of letter-founding rapidly reached maturity after the general diffusion of printing consequent on the sack of Mainz, and that when the writer of the *Cologne Chronicle*, in the last year of the fifteenth century, spoke of 'the art as now generally used', he spoke of an art which, at the close of the nineteenth century, had been able to improve in no essential principle on the processes first made use of by the great inventors of typography.

$\lceil 1 \rceil$

THE ENGLISH TYPE-BODIES AND FACES

WE have laid before the reader, in the Introductory Chapter, such facts and conjectures as it is possible to gather together respecting the processes and appliances adopted by the first letter-founders, and shall, with a view to render the particular history of the English letter foundries more intelligible, endeavour to present here, in as concise a form as possible, a short historical sketch of the English type-bodies and faces, tracing particularly the rise and development of the roman, italic, and black letters before and subsequent to their introduction into this country; adding, in a following chapter, a similar notice of the types of the principal foreign and learned languages which have figured conspicuously in English typography.

TYPE-BODIES

The origin of type-bodies and the nomenclature which has grown around them is a branch of typographical antiquity which has always been shrouded in more or less obscurity. Imagining, as we do, that the moulds of the first printers were of a primitive construction, and, though conceived on true principles, were adjusted to the various sizes of letter they had to cast more by eye than by rule, it is easy to understand that founts would be cast on no other principle than that of ranging in body and line and height in themselves, irrespective of the body, height, and line of other founts used in the same press. When two or more founts were required to mix in the same work, then the necessity of a uniform standard of height would become apparent. When two or more founts were required to mix in the same line, a uniformity in body, and if possible in alinement, would be found necessary. When initials or marginal notes required to be incorporated with the text, then the advantage of a mathematical proportion between one body and another would suggest itself.

At first, doubtless, the printer would name his sizes of type according to the works for which they were used. His Canon type would be the large character in which he printed the canon of the Mass. His Cicero type would be the letter used in his editions of that classical author. His Saint Augustin, his Primer, his Brevier, his Philosophie, his Pica type, would be the names by which he would describe the sizes of letter he used for printing the works whose names they bore. It may also be assumed with tolerable certainty that in most of these cases, originally, the names described not only the body but the 'face' of their respective founts. At what period this confused and haphazard system of nomenclature resolved itself into the definite printer's terminology it is difficult to determine. The process was probably a gradual one, and was not perfected until typefounding became a distinct and separate trade.

The earliest writers on the form and proportion of letters,—Dürer, Nuremberg, 1525; Tory, Paris, 1529; and Yciar, Saragossa, 1548—though using terms to distinguish the different faces of letter, were apparently unaware of any distinguishing names for the bodies of types. Tory, indeed, mentions Canon and Bourgeoise; but in both cases he refers to the face of the letter; and Yciar's distinction of 'testo y glosa' applies generally to the large and small type used for the text and notes respectively of the same work.[1]

When Claude Garamond, the French typefounder, took to publishing in 1545, he wrote a dedicatory epistle to David Chambellan's *Pia et religiosa meditatio*, in which he refers to the italics he had been cutting. One of these, the smaller, he called a Glossa, a term which no doubt was first used for a type intended for marginal notes. It seems as though this name might have become attached to a particular size among French founders, as did 'Glosilla' in Spanish. The same term was used by Garamond's younger contemporary, Guillaume Le Bé, in some manuscript notes on two different sheets of his specimens preserved in the Bibliothèque Nationale.[2] He uses also the terms Canon, Petit Texte, Gros Texte, Petit Canon, Gros Double Canon, and Moyenne (again this term might have become a regular size, like the German 'Mittel' and Dutch 'Mediaan'). Le Bé's notes refer to types, mostly Hebrew, cut between 1545 and 1591, and the nomenclature seems to be in process of formation. Other references to type sizes are found in Coyecque's *Recueil des actes notariés*, Paris, 1905. 'Petit romain' is mentioned in vol. i, Nos. 3137 and 5505, of 1545 and 1550. A 'Nonpareil' of Robert Granjon's is referred to in No. 5985, dated 1551. In a document of August 1547, reproduced by Baudrier, we read of St. Augustin and Nonpareil to be supplied by Granjon to one Gaspard de Molina. In Coyecque, vol. ii, No. 5237, 1549, the term *lectres de cicero* occurs. Probably the *lettre de Bourgeois, à faire breviaires* in Coyecque, vol. i, No. 15, 1515, and the *petite lettre bourgeoyse* of François Regnault in No. 1907, 1542, mean the face of the type and not the body. When we come to Christophe Plantin of Antwerp we find from the inventories of his types made in 1562 and 1563, and his subsequent dealings with various typefounders, that most of the recognized names of sizes are in use,[3] from Gros Canon down to Nonpareil. The earliest published specimen on which sizes are given is that of the Egenolff Berner foundry, Frankfort, 1592.

In the *Dialogues françois pour les jeunes enfans*, Plantin, 1567,[4] written in French

---

[1] Both *Texto* and *Glosilla* subsequently became the names of Spanish type-bodies, the former being approximately equivalent to our Great Primer, and the latter to our Minion.

[2] See H. Omont, *Spécimens de caractères Hébreux, Grecs, Latins et de musique gravés par Guillaume Le Bé*, 1889.

[3] See Max Rooses, *Le Musée Plantin-Moretus*, 1913.

[4] A portion of this book, with an English translation and notes by Ray Nash, was printed in 1940 by Harvard College Library, under the title *An Account of Calligraphy and Printing in the Sixteenth Century*. Already in 1907 J. W. Enschedé had edited these

and Flemish by Jacques Grevin, in the section on printing there is a passage on the names of types. The author says that some types have received their names from the kind of book for which they were often used, such as Canon, Canon de messel, lettre de Cicero, lettre de S. Augustin; others were named from the country of their origin, as Romain, Italique, lettre françoise (Civilité); others because of their beauty, as Mignonne, and Paragon. Finally, some have got their names elsewhere, as Bourgeois, lettre bâtarde, lettre de somme ou moderne. The writer seems in general to be thinking of the face of the types, but partly also of sizes. For instance, he speaks of Gros romain, romain commune, and petit romain.

In England the earliest reference to type sizes so far recorded is contained in an indenture dated 1 September 1539 of the sale of material by the printer John Wayland to John Mayler. In an article in *The Library*, 4th series, vol. xi, 1931, p. 323, H. Byrom reproduced part of this document, in which are the words: 'tres sortes litterarum videlicet, the englyshe letter the grete prymer the small letter'. At the time in question Wayland had only three types, according to Isaac, all Texts, Great Primer, English, and a smaller size. Thus the English and Great Primer of the document appear to be sizes. The two printers both produced *Primers*, the English Book of Hours, which supports the view that Primer as a size was derived from Primer the service book. The two larger sizes and a Pica are mentioned in their Latin form in another document quoted in the same article by Mr. Byrom (p. 337), an agreement made on 16 November 1539 between Wayland and John Butler. The passage in question mentions Primers *in magna primoriali littera nigri*, others *in le pica littera nigri*, others in *Anglicana littera nigri*.

The next reference is of the year 1553 and is contained in an inventory of the stock of the printing house at the Sun in Fleet Street, formerly Wynkyn de Worde's house. The inventory was drawn up in connexion with an action brought against the printers William and Humphrey Powell. There is mention of 'Canon letters duo boxes of grete Roman . . . one forme of the grete primer letter in a chase one forme of pica bounde vp in pagis duo forme of the longe primer letter in pages . . .'.[1]

We find nothing more until 1588, when in a minute from the Court Book of the Stationers' Company, quoted more fully below (p. 117), there is mention of Pica roman and italic of Robert Waldegrave, printer of the Marprelate tracts, types which were confiscated by the company. In the inventory of the stock of the Cambridge printer Thomas James, who died in 1588, we read of Brevier, Long Primer, Pica, and Great Primer.[2] In a regulation made by the Stationers' Company in 1598, Pica, English, Long Primer, and Brevier are mentioned as well-established bodies at that time (cf. below, p. 119). In Sturtevant's *Metallica*, 1612, p. 89, we read 'Goe but to a Printer, and you shall heare many strange words of his invention and misterie, as . . . the Long Primer, the Pica.' Charles Butler in his *Oratoriae libri duo*, Oxford, 1629, writes: 'Genera literarum varia sunt, quae corporum proceritate distinguuntur: Primier, Pique, English: & supra haec, Great Primier, Double

---

sections in an article entitled 'Vlaamsche Drukkerswoorden en 1567' in the *Tijdschrift voor Boek- en Bibliotheekwezen*. Enschedé commented on the origin and meaning of the words applied to faces and bodies.

[1] See H. R. Plomer, 'An Inventory of Wynkyn De Worde's House', in *The Library*, 1915, p. 228 et seq.

[2] See Gray and Palmer's *Abstracts from the Wills of Printers of Cambridge, 1504–1699*, Bibliographical Society, London, 1915.

Pique, Double English: atque, quod omnium maximum est, Canon: infra vero
Primier brevius, quod ideo Brevier, & cujus respectu, prius illud, long Primier,
vulgò dicitur: atque, quod minimum est, Nonpareil.' That is the full list as given
by Moxon, except for Pearl. Each of the names is set in its own size of type. To
this, two of the early English dictionaries add Minion. T. Blount's *Glossographia*,
1656, has Minion and Pearl, and J. Howell's *A Particular Vocabulary*, 1659, in
section li, 'Other mechanical trades', mentions 'Letters of all sorts, as Pearl, Non-
paril, Minion, Brevier,' &c.

Moxon, our first writer on the subject, in his *Mechanick Exercises*, in 1683,
described ten regular bodies in common use in his day, and added to his list the
number of types of each body that went to a foot, viz.:

Pearl	. 184 to a foot		English	. 66	to a foot
Nonpareil	. 150	,,	Great Primer	. 50	,,
Brevier	. 112	,,	Double Pica	. 38	,,
Long Primer	. 92	,,	2-line English	. 33	,,
Pica	. 75	,,	French Canon	. $17\frac{1}{2}$	,,

We have one body more [he adds] which is sometimes used in England; that is, a Small
Pica: but I account it no great discretion in a master-printer to provide it, because it differs
so little from the Pica, that unless the workmen be carefuller than they sometimes are, it
may be mingled with the Pica, and so the beauty of both founts may be spoiled.

In this sentence we have the first record of the introduction of irregular bodies
into English typography, an innovation destined very speedily to expand, and
within half a century increase the number of English bodies by the seven following
additions:

Minion	. 132 to a foot		2-line Pica	. $37\frac{1}{2}$	to a foot
Bourgeois	. 100	,,	2-line Great Primer	. 25	,,
Small Pica	. 76	,,	2-line Double Pica	. 19	,,
Paragon	. 46	,,			

The origin of these irregular bodies it is easy to explain. Between Moxon's
time and 1720 the country was flooded with Dutch type. The English founders
were beaten out of the field in their own market, and James, in self-defence, had
to furnish his foundry entirely with Dutch moulds and matrices. Thus we had the
typefounding of two nations carried on side by side. An English printer furnished
with a Dutch fount would require additions to it to be cast to the Dutch standard,
which might be smaller or larger than that laid down for English type by Moxon,
and yet so near that even if it lost or gained a few types in the foot, it would still
be called by its English name, which would thenceforth represent two different
bodies. If, on the other hand, a new fount were imported, or cut by an ill-regulated
artist here, which when finished was found to be as much too large for one regular
body as it was too small for another, a body would be found to fit it between the
two, and christened by a new name. In this manner, Minion, Bourgeois, Small
Pica, Paragon, and two-line Pica insinuated themselves into the list of English
bodies, and in this manner arose that ancient anomaly, the various body-standards
of the English foundries. For a founder who was constantly called upon to alter
his mould to accommodate a printer requiring a special body would be likely to

cast a quantity of the letter in excess of what was immediately ordered; and this store, if not sold in due time to the person for whom it was cast, would be disposed of to the first comer who, requiring a new fount, and not particular as to body, provided the additions afterwards to be had were of the same gauge, would take it off the founder's hands. *Facilis descensus Averno!* Having taken the one downward step, the founder would be called upon constantly to repeat it, his moulds would remain set, some to the right, some to the wrong, standard, and every type he cast would make it more impossible for him or his posterity to recover the simple standard from which he had erred.

Such we imagine to have been the origin of the irregular and ununiform bodies. Even in 1755, when Smith published his *Printer's Grammar*, the mischief was beyond recall. In no single instance were the standards given by him identical with those of 1683. Indeed, where each founder had two or three variations of each body in his own foundry it is impossible to speak of a standard at all. Smith points out that, in the case of English and Pica alone, Caslon had four varieties of the former, and the Dutch two; while of the latter, Caslon had three, and James two. Nevertheless, he gives a scale of the bodies commonly in use in his day, which it will be interesting to compare with Moxon's on the one hand, and the standard of the English foundries in 1841 as given by Savage, on the other.

	Moxon, 1683	Smith, 1755	Caslon, 1841	Figgins, 1841	Thorowgood, 1841	Wilson, 1841
Canon	17½	18 and G. P.	18	18	18	18
Two-line Double Pica	—	20¾	20¾	20¾	20½	20¾
Two-line Great Primer	—	25½	25½	25½	26	25½
Two-line English	33	32	32	32	32¼	32
Two-line Pica	—	35¾	36	36	36	36
Double Pica	38	41½	41½	41½	41	41½
Paragon	—	44½	44½	44½	—	44½
Great Primer	50	51 and an r	51	51	52	51
English	66	64	64	64	64½	64
Pica	75	71½	72	72½	72	72
Small Pica	—	83	83	82	82	83
Long Primer	92	89	89	90	92	89
Bourgeois	—	102 and space	102	101½	103	102
Brevier	112	112½	111	107	112	111
Minion	—	128	122	122	122	122
Nonpareil	150	143	144	144	144	144
Pearl	184	178	178	180	184	178
Diamond	—	—	204	205	210	204

This list does not include Trafalgar, Emerald, and Ruby, which, however, were in use before 1841.[1] The first-named has disappeared in England, as also has Paragon. The *Printer's Grammar* of 1787 mentions a body in use at that time named 'Primer', between Great Primer and English.

It is not our purpose to pursue this comparison further or more minutely; nor does it come within the scope of this work to enter into a technical examination of the various schemes which have been carried out abroad, and attempted in this country, to do away with the anomalies in type-bodies and restore a uniform invariable standard. The above table will suffice as a brief historical note of the growth of these anomalies.

[1] See also below, p. 36, for Brilliant.

As early as 1725, in France, an attempt was made to regulate by a public decree, not only the standard height of a type, but the scale of bodies. But the system adopted was clumsy and only added to the confusion it was designed to remove. Fournier, in 1737, invented his typographical points, the first successful attempt at a mathematical systematization of type-bodies, which has since, with the alternative system of Didot, done much in simplifying French typography. England, Germany, and Holland have been more conservative, and therefore less fortunate. Attempts were made by James Fergusson in 1824,[1] by Bower of Sheffield about 1840,[2] by the Patent Typefounding Co. in 1868, and by the Caslon firm in 1886, to arrive at a standard of uniformity; but their schemes were not warmly taken up and failed.

Before proceeding to a brief historical notice of the different English type-bodies we shall trouble the reader with a further table, compiled from specimen-books of the eighteenth century, showing what have been the names of the corresponding bodies in the foundries of other nations—premissing, however, that these names must be taken as representing the approximate, rather than the actual, equivalent in each case:[3]

	English	French	German	Dutch	Italian	Spanish	Points
1.	French Canon	Double Canon	Kleine Missal	Parys Kanon	Reale	..	48
2.	Two-line Double Pica	Gros Canon	Grobe Canon	Groote Kanon	Corale	Canon Grande	44
3.	Two-line Great Primer	Trismegiste	Kleine Canon	Kanon	Canone	Canon	36
4.	Two-line English	Petit Canon	Doppel Mittel	Dubbelde Augustyn	Sopracanoncino	Peticano	28
5.	Two-line Pica	Palestine	Roman	Dubbelde Mediaan	Canoncino	..	24
6.	Double Pica	Gros Parangon	Text or Secunda	Dubbelde Descendiaan (or Ascendonica)	Ascendonica	Misal	22
7.	Paragon	Petit Parangon	Parangon	Parangon	Parangone	Parangona	20
8.	Great Primer	Gros Romain	Tertia	Text	Testo	Texto	18
9. ⎰ (Large English)	Gros Texte	Grobe Mittel	..	Soprasilvio	..	..	
⎱ English	St. Augustin	Kleine Mittel	Augustyn	Silvio	Atanasia	14
10.	Pica	Cicero	Cicero	Mediaan	Lettura	Lectura	12
11.	Small Pica	Philosophie	Brevier	Descendiaan	(Filosofia)	..	11
12.	Long Primer	Petit Romain	Corpus or Garmond	Garmond	Garamone	Entredos	10
13.	Bourgeois	Gaillarde	(Borgis)	Burgeois or Galjart	Garamoncino	..	9
14.	Brevier	Petit Texte	Petit or Jungfer	Brevier	Testino	Breviario	8
15.	Minion	Mignonne	Colonel	Colonel	Mignona	Glosilla	7
16.	Nonpareil	Nonpareille	Nonpareille	Nonparel	Nompariglia	Nompareli	6
17.	Pearl	⎰ Parisienne or Sedan ⎱ Perle	Perl	⎰ Joly ⎱ Peerl	Parmigianina	..	5
18.	Diamond	Diamant	Diamant	⎰ Robijn ⎱ Diamand	..	..	4½

A few notes on the origin of the names of English type-bodies will conclude our observations on this subject.

CANON. The Canon of the Mass was, in the service-books of the Church, printed in a large letter, and it is generally supposed that this size of letter being ordinarily employed in the large missals, the type-body took its name accordingly, a supposition which is strengthened by its German name of Missal. Mores, however (who objects equally to the epithets of Great or French as unnecessary and delusive),

---

[1] Hansard's *Typographia*, London, 1825, 8vo, p. 388.

[2] See below, p. 350.

[3] In several of the German specimens thus examined, not only do the bodies of one founder differ widely from those of others, but the variations of each body in the same foundry are often extraordinary. Faulmann, in his *Geschichte der Buch-*

druckerkunst, Vienna, 1882, 8vo, p. 488, has a table professing to give the actual equivalents of each body to a fraction, but we conceive that, in the absence of a fixed national standard, such an attempt was futile. For the American point system, which was adopted in England in 1898, see Updike, *Printing Types*, vol. i, pp. 33–4. See also below, p. 252.

considers this derivation to be incorrect, and quotes the authority of Tory, who (*Champ fleury*, fol. lxxiv) uses the term Canon to apply to *lettres de forme*, as distinguished from *lettres bastardes*. So that the *lettre qu'on dict Canon* originally meant the design of the face and subsequently came to be confined to the largest size in that category. The theory is ingenious and interesting, but it seems more reasonable to lay greater stress on the actual meaning of a word than on its equivocal interpretation. In other countries two-line Great Primer was commonly called Canon, and our French Canon was called by the Dutch Parys Kanon; by which it would seem that both England and Holland originally received the body from the French. In modern letter-founding the name Canon applies only to the size of the face of a letter which is a three-line Pica cast on a four-line Pica body.

Passing the next four bodies, which with us are merely reduplications,[1] we note that—

DOUBLE PICA, which at present is Double Small Pica, was in Moxon's day what its name denotes, a two-line Pica. When the irregular Small Pica was introduced, Double Pica was the name given to the double of the interloper, the double of the Pica being styled two-line Pica. In Germany, Double Pica was called Text or Secunda—the former name probably denoting the use of this size in the text of Holy Writ, while the latter indicates that the body was one of a series, the Doppel Mittel, corresponding to our two-line English, being probably the Prima.

PARAGON, the double of Long Primer, though a body unnamed in Moxon's day, was a size of really old institution, it having been a favourite body with many of the earliest printers, and particularly affected by Caxton in this country. Its name points to a French origin and it occurs in the inventory of Plantin's types in 1563 and in the *Dialogues françois pour les jeunes enfans*, 1567; and, like most of the other fanciful names, proves that the appellation had reference in the first instance, not to the depth of its shank, but to the supposed beauty of the letter which was cut upon it. In the letters between Thomas Marshall and Dr. Fell, 1671 and 1672, the Paragon Greek is mentioned several times. In the Oxford specimen of 1693 this Greek is called Double Pica, but Paragon in the list of matrices (cf. below, p. 144). The references also show that the name came into this country from Holland. It was a body which did not take deep root in this country, and for the most part disappeared with the first quarter of the last century. It is noteworthy that Paragon and Nonpareil are the only bodies which have preserved their names in all the countries in which they have been adopted.

GREAT PRIMER. For this body Mores claims an indisputable English origin. He considers it possible that it may date back to before the Reformation, and that it was the body on which were printed the large primers of the early Church.[2] This derivation[3] would be more satisfactory were it found that these works, or the

---

[1] Two-line English, Mores points out, was originally a primitive, and not a derivative body, corresponding to the old German Prima.

[2] Henry VIII, in 1545, allowed his subjects to use an English Form of Public Prayer, and ordered one to be printed for their use, entitled *The Primer*. It contained, besides prayers, several psalms, lessons, and anthems. *Primers* had been printed in English from 1535. See 'The Prymer in English' by E. Birchenough in *The Library*, Sept. 1937, p. 177 seq.

[3] We have nowhere met with the suggestion that Primer may be connected with the Latin *premere*, a word familiar in typography, and naturalized with us in the old word 'imprimery'. Great Primer might thus merely mean the large print letter.

D

school primers of a later date, were, as a rule, printed in type of this size.[1] But this is not the case. *Primers*, *Pyes*, and *Breviaries* occur printed in almost all the regular bodies. Great Primer was a favourite body with the old printers, and having been adopted by many of the first Bible printers, was sometimes called Bible Text. The French called it Gros Romain; and the 'Great Romaine letter for the titles', mentioned in Pynson's indenture in 1519 (see below, p. 87), may possibly refer to an already-recognized type-body of this size. In Germany it was called Tertia, being the third of the regular bodies above the Mittel. In Holland, Italy, and Spain it was called Text.

ENGLISH is also a body which undoubtedly belongs to us. Until the end of the eighteenth century the name served not only to denote a body, but the face of the English black-letter; and many of the old founts used in the law books and Acts of Parliament were English both in body and face. As in Germany, where it is called Mittel, English was the middle size of the seven regular bodies in use among us: the Great Primer, Double Pica, and two-line English (the Tertia, Secunda, and Prima of the Germans) being on the ascending side, and Pica, Long Primer, and Brevier on the descending. The French call it St. Augustin,[2] and the Spaniards Atanasia, apparently from its use in printing the works of these Christian Fathers. Although the middle body, its standard has been subject to much variation, particularly in France and Germany, where large and small English are two distinct bodies.

PICA. This important body, now the standard body in English typography, presumably owes its name to its use in printing the ordinal of the services of the early Church, and is coeval with Great Primer. 'The Pie', says Mores, of which this is the Latin name, 'was a table showing the course of the service in the Church in the times of darkness.[3] It was called the Pie because it was written in letters of black and red; as the Friars de *Pica* were so named from their party-coloured raiment, black and white, the plumage of a magpie.' 'The number and hardness of the rules of this Pie' is referred to in the preface to our Prayer-book; and it will be remembered that Caxton's famous advertisement related to 'Pyes of Salisbury use'. But as a larger type-body than Pica was generally used to print these, it is possible the name may refer to nothing more than the piebald or black-and-white appearance of a printed page. Some authorities derive Pica from the Greek $\pi i \nu a \xi$, a writing tablet, and, hence, an index. The name was, in fact, applied to the alphabetical catalogue of the names and things in rolls and records. In France and Germany the body was called Cicero, on account of the frequent editions of Cicero's *Epistles* printed in this size of letter.[4] It was the Mediaan body of the Dutch.

SMALL PICA, as already stated, was an innovation in Moxon's day, and was probably cast in the first instance to accommodate a foreign-cut letter, too small for

---

[1] The religious origin of the names of types is in harmony with the occurrence in typographical phraseology of such words as *chapel*, *devil*, *hell* (the waste type-pot), *friars* and *monks* (white and black blotches caused by uneven inking), &c.

[2] Ulric Hahn's *Augustini De Civitate Dei*, Rome, 1474, is printed in a letter almost exactly this body. Others derive the name from the great edition of

St. Augustine printed by Amerbach at Basle in 1506.

[3] 'Liber presens, directorium sacerdotum, quem *pica* Sarum vulgo vocitat clerus,' &c., is the commencement of a work printed by Pynson in 1497, *S.T.C.* 17724.

[4] Both the *Cicero* of Fust and Schoeffer at Mainz, 1465, and of Hahn at Rome, 1469, were in type of about this size.

Pica and too large for Long Primer. It subsequently came into very general use, one of the first important works in which it appeared being Chambers's *Cyclopaedia*, in 1728. The French called it Philosophie, and appear to have used it as a smaller body on which to cast the Cicero face. The Germans called it Brevier, the Dutch (it being one body below the Mediaan) called it Descendiaan, and the Italians, when they had it, followed the French and called it Filosofia.

LONG PRIMER, Mores suggests, was another of the old English bodies employed in liturgical works. He explains the use of the word Long to mean that Primers in this size of type were printed either in long lines instead of double columns, or that the length of the page was disproportionate to the width, or more probably, that they contained the service at full length *a long*, or without contraction.[1] These *Primers*, however, are rarely to be met with in this body. The French named the body Petit Romain, preserving a similar relationship between it and their Gros Romain, as we did between our Long Primer and Great Primer. The other countries evidently attributed the body to France, and named it after Claude Garamond, the famous French letter-cutter, one of whose Greek founts, cut for the Royal Typography of Paris, was on this body. The Germans, however, also called the body Corpus, on account of their *Corpus Juris* being first printed in this size.

BOURGEOIS. This irregular body betrays its nationality in its name, derived probably from the fact that it was the commercial hand used by the *bourgeois*, although some have derived it from the city of Bourges, the birthplace of Geofroy Tory. Tory in his *Champ fleury* uses it of the face of a letter. After describing the *Lettre de Forme* and *Bâtarde*, he says there are also the *Lettre ronde, bourgeoise* and *Lettre de somme*; he has nothing further to say on these three Gothic hands. We shall return to the *Lettre de somme* below (p. 49). In the *Nouveau Traité de diplomatique*, 1755, ii. 87, the *Lettre bourgeoise* is compared to the contemporary *coulé*, so that it may have been a hand similar to the *Lettre française* or *Civilité*. As a type-body I find it used first in Holland, e.g. by J. Elzevir, 1658, Van Dijk, 1681. The French called the body *Gaillarde*, perhaps after the founder Jean Guaillard who cast types for Plantin in 1568, or possibly the name may be fanciful, like Mignon. It occurs on the specimen sheet of the Egenolff–Luther Foundry, Frankfort, 1592, and in the book of Jean Jannon, Sedan, 1621. The earliest use of Bourgeois in England appears to be on the Caslon specimen sheet of 1749, and John Smith in his *Printer's Grammar* informs us that it was originally used as a large body on which to cast Brevier or Petit.

BREVIER. The smallest of the English regular bodies claims equal antiquity with Great Primer, Pica, and Long Primer. The conjecture that it was commonly used in the *Breviaries* of the early Church is not borne out by an examination of these works, most of which are printed in a considerably larger size.[2] The name, like the French and German 'Petit', may mean that, being the smallest body, it was used for getting the most matter into a brief space. The Germans, when they cut smaller-sized letters, called the Petit 'Jungfer', or the Maiden-letter.

[1] *This Prymer of Salysbury use, is set out a long, wout ony serchyng*, &c., Paris, 1532. 16mo. Many editions were printed in England and abroad.

[2] The German Brevier, corresponding to our Small Pica, is of more frequent occurrence in these works.

MINION, although a body unknown to Moxon, was used in England by 1656, e.g. in T. Blount's *Glossographia*, 1656, and in James Howell's *Lexicon*, 1659, and like the other small fancifully named bodies, appears to have originated in France. Mignonne is mentioned as a body in the *Dialogues françois pour les jeunes enfans*, 1567, and in E. Binet's *Essay des merveilles de nature*, Rouen, 1622, p. 299, and also on the specimen sheet of the Luther Foundry, Frankfort, of the same year. The Dutch and Germans call it Colonel, and the Spaniards Glosilla.

NONPAREIL, an indispensable body, because the half of Pica, was introduced as a peerless curiosity long before Moxon's day, and has preserved its name in all the countries where it has gone. Robert Granjon had cut a Nonpareil for Gryphius and Jean de Tournes of Lyons by 1547.[1] The word occurs also in the deed relating to the close of partnership between Granjon and M. Fezendat of 1551.[2] Mores supposes that, because the Dutch founders of Moxon's day called it 'Englese Nonpareil' in their specimens, the body was first used in this country. The Dutch name, however, evidently refers to the face of the letter, cut in imitation of an English face, or adapted to suit English purchasers. Paulus Pater[3] says that on account of its wonderful smallness and clearness the Dutch Nonpareil was called by many the 'silver letter', and was supposed to have been cast in that metal.

PEARL, though an English body in Moxon's day, appears to have been known both in France and Holland at an earlier date. In the former country it was celebrated as the body on which the famous tiny editions at Sedan were printed by Jean Jannon, *c.* 1620. The Dutch Joly corresponded more nearly to our modern Ruby than to Pearl. But Luce, in 1740, cut the size for France, and provoked Firmin Didot's severe criticism on his performance—'Among the characters, generally bad, which Luce has engraved, . . . is one which cannot be seen.' In T. Blount's *Glossographia*, 1656, under the word 'Characters', Pearl, together with Minion, is given as a size.

DIAMOND was unknown in England until the close of the eighteenth century, when Dr. Fry cut a fount which he claimed to be the smallest ever used, and to get in 'more even than the famous Dutch Diamond'. This Dutch fount was of some antiquity, having been cut by Voskens about 1700. Thomas Marshall's letters to Dr. Fell, 1672, mention a Diamond roman among the matrices of Jacques Vallet. Van Dijk cut a letter on a body below Pearl, called Robijn, a specimen of which appears on the sheet of the widow of Daniel Elzevir in 1681. Henri Didot, however, eclipsed all these minute-bodied founts by a Semi-nonpareil in 1827.[4] The 'Non plus ultra' of the Enschedés of Haarlem, apparently derived from the foundry of Jules Didot, was of about the same size.

It now remains to trace briefly the origin and development of the leading type-faces used in English Typography.

---

[1] See Baudrier, *Bibl. Lyon.*, vol. i, art. 'Molina'.
[2] See Coyecque, *Recueil d'actes notariés*, Paris, 1925, tom. ii, No. 5985.
[3] *De Germaniae Miraculo, Lipsiae*, 1710, 4to, p. 37.
[4] The Brilliant of Messrs. Miller and Richard, shown at the Exhibition of 1851, called 'Ruby' in the Report of the Jurors and in *Whitaker's Almanack* for 1888, was the clearest of all these small sizes. Pickering's small series, printed by C. Corrall from 1822, was in Diamond. Minnikin was another name for a type of about the same size as Brilliant.

ROMAN

To trace the history of the roman character would almost require a résumé of the works of all the greatest printers in each country of Europe. It must suffice to point out very briefly the changes it underwent before and after reaching England.

ITALY. At the time when printing was introduced into Italy the humanistic scholars were practising a revived Carolingian hand for the copying of classical Latin manuscripts, which were being eagerly sought for and collected. Many fine specimens of these fifteenth-century copies have survived. It was inevitable that the German printers, Sweynheim and Pannartz,[1] when they set up their press at Subiaco and found that they were expected to print Latin texts, should cut letters after the model of the calligraphy of the humanists. With the exception of a lost Donatus,

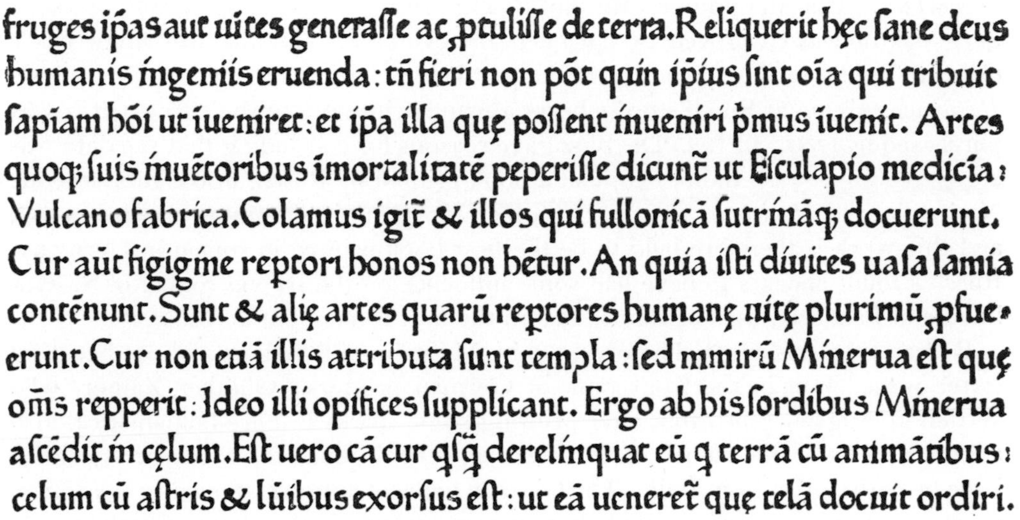
fruges ipas aut uites generasse ac ꝓtulisse de terra. Reliquerit hęc sane deus
humanis ingeniis eruenda: tñ fieri non põt quin ipius sint oĩa qui tribuit
sapiam hõi ut iueniret: et ipa illa quę possent inueniri ꝑmus iuenit. Artes
quoq; suis inuẽtoribus imortalitatẽ peperisse dicunt̃ ut Esculapio medicia:
Vulcano fabrica. Colamus igit̃ & illos qui fullonicã sutrinãq; docuerunt.
Cur aũt figigine reptori honos non hẽtur. An quia isti diuites uasa samia
contẽnunt. Sunt & alię artes quarũ reptores humanę uitę plurimũ ꝓfue-
erunt. Cur non etiã illis attributa sunt templa: sed mirũ Minerua est quę
oĩs repperit: Ideo illi opifices supplicant. Ergo ab his sordibus Minerua
ascẽdit in cęlum. Est uero cã cur qsq̃ derelinquat eũ q terrã cũ animãtibus:
celum cũ astris & lũibus exorsus est: ut eã ueneret̃ quę telã docuit ordiri.

FIG. 6. Earliest roman. Subiaco Press, 1465.

the edition of Cicero's *De Oratore* of 1465 is believed to be the first book produced in the new type, although a Lactantius, finished on 29 October 1465, is the first dated book. Since the engravers of the type faithfully carried out their intention of reproducing the letters of the humanists, letters at a later date to be called roman by the printers, we may be satisfied to call the Subiaco type the first roman. Mr. Morison[2] has discussed this point in a recent article and has objected to the tradition of referring to the semi-Gothic characteristics of the fount. The first Venetian romans of Johannes de Spira, 1469, and Nicolas Jenson, 1470, are nearer to what we know as roman because they have abandoned the calligraphic qualities of the letter of Sweynheim and Pannartz.

Jenson's fount is on a body corresponding to English. The form is round and clear. The capital alphabet consists of twenty-three letters (J, U, and W not being

[1] It seems that the Subiaco Press was not the first to be set up in Italy. Dr. Konrad Haebler in *Die Italienischen Fragmente vom Leiden Christi das älteste Druckwerk Italiens*, Rosenthal, Munich, 1927, described a small Italian book printed in Rotunda, which he considers was produced in northern Italy not long after 1462. The type is connected with that of a calendar for 1462 printed at or near Vienna.

[2] 'Early Humanistic Script and the First Roman Type', *The Library*, June–Sept. 1943, pp. 1–29.

yet in use); the 'lower-case' alphabet is the same, except that the 'u' is substituted for the 'v', and in addition there is a long ∫, and the diphthongs æ and œ. To complete the fount, there are fifteen contractions, six double letters, and three points . : ? making seventy-three punches in all.[1] Jenson's roman letter fell after his death into the hands of a 'firm' of which Andrea Torresani was head. Aldus Manutius subsequently associated himself with Torresani, and, becoming his son-in-law and heir, eventually inherited his punches, matrices, and types. The roman founts of Aldus form a group by themselves, and that this group was the immediate ancestor of the 'Garamond' roman and the standard European roman for over two centuries has been established by Mr. Stanley Morison.[2] He has shown that the new roman of Robert Estienne, 1531, which, if not cut by Garamond, was at any rate the forerunner of the 'Garamond' roman, was closely modelled on the Aldine letters.

GERMANY. That the printer with the 'R' bizarre fount was Adolf Rusch of Strasburg has now been proved by documentary evidence,[3] but that this fount has a claim to be the earliest roman is no longer held. The Basle copy of Durandus's *Rationale* printed at Rusch's press bears a manuscript note to the effect that it was purchased in 1464. In 1925 Dr. Binz gave reasons for concluding that the date was a mistake for 1474. Another copy of a book printed by Rusch, in the Bibliothèque Nationale, the *Hrabanus Maurus*, has a manuscript note containing the date 1467, and this work is therefore held to be the first book printed in roman in Germany. Rusch's fount appears to have had some influence on the second roman of Sweynheim and Pannartz, used at Rome, and on the first romans cut at Venice.[4]

Roman type was adopted before 1473 by Mentelin of Strasburg, whose beautiful letter placed him in the front rank of German printers. Günther Zainer, who settled at Augsburg in 1469, after printing some works in Fere-humanistica, also adopted, in 1472, the roman of the Venetian school, founts of which he is said to have brought direct from Italy. The German name of antiqua, applied to the roman character, has been held to imply a reluctance to admit the claim of Italy to the credit of introducing this style of letter. As, however, the Italians themselves called the letter the 'Lettera antiqua tonda', the imputation against Germany is unfounded.[5] The French, Dutch, and English called it 'roman' from the first.

FRANCE. The French received printing and the roman character at the same time, the first work of the Sorbonne Press in 1470 being in a handsome roman letter about Great Primer in size. The fount, according to Claudin, was modelled on the type of Sweynheim and Pannartz used at Rome. The Paris fount is rudely cast, so that several of their words appear only half-printed in the impression, and have

[1] For a full account and analysis of Jenson's roman and other type the reader is referred to Sardini's *Storia Critica di Nic. Jenson*, Lucca, 1796–8, 3 parts, fol. See also V. Scholderer, 'Printing at Venice to the end of 1481', in *The Library*, Sept. 1924. For a criticism of the fount, hitherto regarded as the perfect roman, see S. Morison, 'Towards an Ideal Type', in *The Fleuron*, No. 2 (1924), pp. 57–75.

[2] 'The Type of the Hypnerotomachia Poliphili' in the *Gutenberg Festschrift*, 1925, pp. 254–8.

[3] Dziatzko, *Sammlung bibliothekswissenschaftlicher Arbeiten*, Heft xvii, 1911.

[4] See V. Scholderer, 'Adolf Rusch and the Earliest Roman Types', in *The Library*, vol. xx, 1939, pp. 43–50.

[5] Sardini (iii. 82) cites an interesting document wherein Zarotus, in forming a typographical partnership with certain citizens of Milan, covenants to provide 'tutte le Lettere Latine, e Greche, antique, e moderne'. Bernard points out that *antique* undoubtedly means roman type, the traditional character of the Italians, while *moderne* applies to the Rotunda. The books of the Italian writing masters consistently use these terms.

been finished by hand. It has been stated erroneously, by several writers, on the authority of Chevillier, that their fount was without capitals. The fount is complete in that respect, and Chevillier's expression, *lettres capitales*, as he himself explains, refers to the initial letters for which blank spaces were left to be filled in by hand. Besides the ordinary capital and 'lower-case' alphabets, the fount abounds in abbreviations. This letter was used in all the works of the Sorbonne Press, but when Gering left the Sorbonne and established himself at the 'Soleil d'Or', in 1473, he made use of a Fere-humanistica. In his later works, however, new and greatly improved founts of the roman appear. Jodocus Badius, who by some is erroneously supposed to have been the first who brought the roman letters from Italy to France, did not establish his famous 'Prelum Ascensianum' in Paris till 1503, when he printed in roman types—not, however, before one or two other French printers had already distinguished themselves in the same direction.

SPAIN. Lambert Palmart, the introducer of printing into Spain, began with roman types in 1474. But the Spaniards, like the French, soon returned to the national gothic.

NETHERLANDS. The roman was introduced into the Netherlands by Johannes de Westfalia, who, it is said, brought it direct from Italy about the year 1472. He settled at Louvain, and after several works in Fere-humanistica, published in 1483 an edition of the *Epistolae Familiares* of Pope Pius II in the Italian letter. His fount is elegant, and rather a lighter face than most of the early roman founts of other countries. This printer appears to have been the only one in the Low Countries who used this type during the fifteenth century; nor was it till Plantin, in 1555, established his famous press at Antwerp that the roman attained to any degree of excellence. It should be mentioned that the Elzevirs did not cut their own punches. The roman types of the Leyden branch which they made famous, and which are known by their name, were most of them acquired from the Egenolff–Luther Foundry at Frankfort.[1] Daniel Elzevir at Amsterdam had some of their letters, together with others of Christoffel van Dijk, the form of whose letter was subsequently adopted by the English printers.

SWITZERLAND early distinguished itself by the roman letter of Amerbach of Basle and still more so by the beautiful founts used by Froben of the same city, who between 1491 and 1527 printed some of the finest books then known in Europe. His roman was very bold and regular. German printers of that generation made use of a peculiar and not unpicturesque form of the roman letter, in which the round sorts were thickened, after the gothic fashion, at their opposite corners instead of at their opposite sides.

---

[1] See C. Enschedé, 'Die Druckerei der Elsevier und ihre Beziehung zu der Lutherschen Schriftgiesserei', in *Die hochdeutschen Schriften . . . von J. Enschede en Zonen*, Haarlem, 1919. In this article Enschedé has thrown much light on the question as to where the Elzevirs obtained their types. He has shown that the attempt to represent Christoffel van Dijk as the engraver of their letters arises from confusing the two firms, the Elzevirs of Leyden and Daniel Elzevir at Amsterdam. Daniel bought Van Dijk's foundry in 1673, and about half the letters shown in the specimen of his widow of 1681 were cut by Van Dijk. But in the specimen of Johan Elzevir issued at Leyden in 1658 there is only one letter by Van Dijk, an italic. Of the rest the majority have been traced by Enschedé in the specimens of the Luther foundry, beginning with the sheet of 1592.

ENGLAND. The roman did not make its appearance in England till 1509, when Richard Pynson printed Petrus Gryphus's *Oratio*, in a handsome letter, of which we show a facsimile. The letter was used on the title-page of the *Sermo Fratris*

Oratio quam erat habiturus Petrus Gryphus:
Sędis Apoſtolicę prothonotarius/ac iterũ nũcius:
Ad Sereniſſimũ Hḗricũ.vij.Anglię Regḗ: Ni para
tã expoſitionḗ immatura Regis mors preueniſſct.
Siqui ſunt fortaſſe Sereniſſime ac Inuictiſſi
me Rex/Siqui inquam fortaſſe ſũt/qui nõ
ex mediocritate mea/ſed ex Maximi San=
ctiſſimicȝ Pontiſicis/a quo venio/ſumma dignita=
te:et ex tuæ Maieſtatis ſingulari eximiacȝ præſtan
tia/hunc meum ad te aduentum metiãtur:expecla
re eos quidem arbitror/me primo hoc cõgreſſu ita

FIG. 7. First roman in England. Pynson, 1509.

Hieronymi (*S.T.C.* 21800), of the same year, and for the Latin text of Alexander Barclay's translation of the *Ship of Fools* (*S.T.C.* 3545), the English text being in black-letter, also 1509. The type was acquired from Paris (cf. below, p. 86). The fount is about Great Primer in body, and though generally neat and bold in appearance, displays considerable irregularity in the casting and, like most of the early roman founts, contains numerous contractions.

The roman made its way gradually in English typography during the first half of the sixteenth century, and in the hands of such artists as Pynson, Berthelet, and Day maintained an average excellence. But it rapidly degenerated, and while other countries were dazzling Europe by the brilliancy of their impressions, the English roman letter went from good to bad, and from bad to worse. No type is more beautiful than a beautiful roman; and with equal truth it may be said no type is more unsightly than an ill-fashioned and ill-worked roman. While Claude Garamond[1] in France was carrying out into noble practice the theories of the form and proportion of letters set out by Geofroy Tory and copying the fine design of the roman which Aldus used for the *De Aetna* of P. Bembo (Venice, 1495) and in a recutting for the *Hypnerotomachia Poliphili* (1499); while Froben at Basle, the Estiennes at Paris, Sebastien Gryphius at Lyons, Froschouer at Zurich, and Christopher Plantin at Antwerp, were moulding and refining their alphabets into models which were to become classical, English printers, manacled body and soul by their patents and monopolies and state persecutions, achieved nothing with the roman

---

[1] Garamond's roman was cut about 1531, see P. Beaujon, 'The Garamond Types', in *The Fleuron*, No. 5. The roman character was an object of considerable royal interest in France during its career. In 1694, on the reorganization of the press at the Louvre under Louis XIV, arbitrary alterations were made in the recognized form of several of the 'lower-case' letters, to distinguish the *Romain du Roi* from all others, and protect it from imitations. Cf. Reed's paper read before the Royal Society of Arts, 18 Apr. 1890.

type that was not retrograde. For a time a struggle appears to have existed between the black-letter and the roman for the mastery of the English press, and at one period the curious spectacle was presented of mixed founts of the two. No English work of the time, printed in English roman type, reproduces within measurable distance the elegant *embonpoint*, the harmony, the symmetry of the types of the famous Dutch printers. The seeker after the beautiful looks almost in vain for anything to satisfy his eye in the English roman-printed works of the seventeenth century. A few exceptions there are; and when the English printers, giving up the attempt to cut roman for themselves, went to Holland to buy it, or when, as in the case of Oxford and Thomas James, the English foundries became furnished with Dutch matrices, our country was able to produce a few books the appearance of which does not call forth a blush.

The first *English Bible* printed in roman type was Bassendyne's edition in Edinburgh, in 1576. We have it on the authority of Watson[1] that, from the earliest days of Scottish typography, a constant trade in type and labour was maintained between Holland and Scotland; and he exhibited in his specimen pages the Dutch romans which at that day were the most approved letters in use in his country.

Utilitarian motives brought about one important departure from the first models of the roman letter in the different countries where it flourished. The early printers were generous in their ideas, and cut their letters with a single eye to artistic beauty. But as printing gradually ceased to be an art, and became a trade, economical considerations suggested a distortion or cramping of these beautiful models, with a view to 'getting more in'. In some cases the variation was made gracefully and inoffensively. The slender or compressed roman letters of the French, Italian, and in some cases the Dutch printers, though not comparable with the round ones, are yet regular and neat; but in other cases, ours among them, there was little of either delicacy or skill in the innovation. From about 1672 the German founders in particular cut many romans of a large 'x' height. They are to be seen in the specimens of Anton Janson of Leipzig, the Baumanns of Nuremberg, Christian Zinck of Wittenberg, and others.[2] The early part of the seventeenth century witnessed the creation abroad of some very small roman faces, foremost among which were those of the beautiful little Sedan editions of Jannon,[3] which gave their name to the body of the microscopic letter in which they were printed. Van Dijk cut a still smaller letter for the Dutch in black-letter and afterwards in roman; and for many years the Dutch Diamond held the palm as the smallest fount in Europe. England followed the general tendency towards the minute, and though it is doubtful whether either Pearl or Diamond were cut by English founders before 1700, an English printer, Field, accomplished in 1653 the feat of printing a 32mo Bible in

[1] *History of the Art of Printing*, Edinburgh, 1713. 8vo.

[2] On these types see S. Morison's 'Leipzig as a Centre of Typefounding' in *Signature*, No. 11, 1939, with a supplement in *Signature*, No. 15, 1940, and A. F. Johnson's 'The "Goût Hollandois"', in *The Library*, Sept. 1939, p. 180, &c.

[3] The *Horace*, printed in 1627, may be mentioned as one of the most interesting of these little typographical curiosities. The type is exactly the modern pearl body. The text is $2\frac{5}{8}$ inches in depth and $1\frac{1}{2}$ inches wide. Cf. the specimen issued by Jannon in 1621, though the smallest size there shown is Petit Text (Brevier). In the facsimile reproduction of this specimen, London, 1928, the editor, Paul Beaujon, shows that Jannon's types were those used by the Imprimerie Royale, started in 1640, and known, on their revival in recent times, as 'caractères de l'Université'.

Pearl.[1] Among English printers in the seventeenth century who did credit to their profession Roycroft is conspicuous, especially for the handsome large romans in which he printed Ogilby's *Virgil*,[2] 1654, and other works. This type—that in which he printed the Royal Dedication to the *Polyglot* of 1657—was the fount used nearly a century before by Day,[3] whose productions few English printers of the seventeenth century could equal, and none, certainly, could excel. Of Moxon's attempt in 1683 to regenerate the roman letter in England we shall have occasion to speak elsewhere. His theories, as put into practice by himself, were eminently unsuccessful; and though the sign-boards of the day may have profited by his rules, it is doubtful if typography did. His enthusiastic praise of the Dutch letter of Van Dijk may have stimulated the trade between England and Holland, but at home his precepts fell flat for lack of an artist to carry them out.

That artist was forthcoming in William Caslon about 1725, and from the time he cut his first fount of Pica, the roman letter in England entered on a career of honour. Caslon went back to the Dutch for his models, and throwing into his labour the genius of an enlightened artistic taste, he reproduced their letters with a precision and uniformity hitherto unknown among us, preserving at the same time that freedom and grace of form which had made them of all others the most beautiful types in Europe. Caslon's roman became the fashion, and English typography was loyal to it for nearly eighty years. Baskerville's exquisite letters were, as he himself acknowledged, inspired by those of Caslon. They were sharper and more delicate in outline, and when finely printed, as they always were, were more attractive to the eye. But what they gained in brilliance they missed in sterling dignity; they dazzled the eye and fatigued it, and the fashion of the national taste was not seriously diverted. Still less was it diverted by the experiments of a *nouvelle typographie* which Luce, Fournier, and others were trying to introduce into France. The Dutch type was now no longer looked at. Wilson, whose letter adorned the works of the Foulis Press, and Jackson, whose exquisite founts helped to make the fame of Bensley, as those of his successor Figgins helped to continue it, all adhered to the Caslon models. And all these artists, with Cottrell, Fry, and others, contributed to a scarcely less important reform in English letter-founding, namely, the production by each founder of his own uniform series of roman sizes— a feature woefully absent in the odd collections of the old founders before 1720. Towards the close of the century the roman underwent a violent revolution. The few founders who had begun about 1760 in avowed imitation of Baskerville had found it in their interest before 1780 to revert to the models of Caslon, and scarcely had they done so when about 1790 the genius of Didot of Paris and Bodoni of Parma took the English press by storm and brought about that complete abandonment of the Caslon models which marked, and in some cases disfigured, the last years of the eighteenth century. The famous presses of Bell, Bensley, and Bulmer introduced the modern roman under the most favourable auspices. The new letter was

---

[1] *The Holy Bible, containing the Old and New Testaments*, London, printed by John Field, 1653. 32mo. The inexperience of English compositors and correctors in dealing with this minute type is illustrated by the fact that Field's Pearl Bibles are crowded with errors, one edition, so it is said, con- taining 6,000 faults.

[2] In one of the Bagford MSS. (Harl. 5915) ap- pear, with the title 'Mr. Ogilby's Letters', the drawings and proofs of an alphabet in capital and lower-case. It is Moxon's Canon roman.

[3] See Fig. 17.

honest, businesslike, and trim, but in its stiff angles, its rigid geometrical precision, long hair-serifs, and sharp contrasts of shade, there is little place for the luxuriant elegance of the old style.[1] In France the new fashion, even with so able an exponent as Didot, had a competitor in the Baskerville type, which, rejected by us, was welcomed by the French literati. Nor was this the only instance in which the fashion went from England to France, for in 1818 the Imprimerie Royale itself, in want of a new *typographie* of the then fashionable roman, came to London for the punches.

The typographical taste of the first quarter of the nineteenth century suffered a distinct vulgarization in the unsightly heavy-faced roman letters, which were not only offered by the founders, but extensively used by the printers; and the date at which we quit this brief survey is not a glorious one. The simple uniformity of faces which characterized the specimens of Caslon and his disciples had been corrupted by new fancies and fashions, demanded by the printer and conceded by the founder—fashions which, as Hansard neatly observed in 1825, 'have left the specimen of a British letter-founder a heterogeneous compound, made up of fat-faces and lean-faces, wide-set and close-set, proportioned and disproportioned, all at once crying "Quousque tandem abutêre patientia nostra?"'

Some of the coarsest of the new fashions were happily short-lived, and about 1840 the beautiful old-face of Caslon was, in response to a demand from outside, revived and has since, in rejuvenated forms, regained both at home and abroad much of its old popularity.

It will not be out of place to add a word, before leaving the roman, in reference to letter-founders' specimens. When printers were their own founders the productions of their presses were naturally also the published specimens of their type. They might, like Schoeffer, in the colophon to the *Justinian* in 1468, call attention to their skill in cutting types or on an advertisement of books for sale print the words *hec est littera psalterij* in the Psalter type; or, like Caxton, print a special advertisement in a special type; or, like Aldus, put forward a specimen of the types of a forthcoming work.[2] But none of these are letter-founders' specimens; nor was it till letter-founding became a distinct trade that such documents became necessary. Apart from specimens issued by printers, such as those of Ratdolt at Augsburg, 1486, Johann Petri at Nuremberg, 1525, Geyssler at Nuremberg, 1561, and Plantin at Antwerp, 1567, perhaps the earliest letter-founder's specimens are those of Guillaume Le Bé. Even these are not published specimens, but printed proofs accompanied by notes in Le Bé's own hand. Le Bé's first proof is described by H. Omont, who published a facsimile in 1887, as *Spécimens de caractères Hébreux gravés à Venise et à Paris par Guillaume Le Bé* (1546–1574) and the second, published in 1889, as *Spécimens de caractères Hébreux, grecs, Latins et de musique gravés à Venise et à Paris par Guillaume Le Bé* (1545–1592). These important documents

---

[1] A French typographer, Claude Motteroz, attempted to combine the excellences of the Elzevir and modern roman with a view to arriving at an ideally legible type. The experiment is curious but disappointing. For though the *typographie* of Motteroz justifies its claim to legibility, the combination of two wholly unsympathetic forms of letter destroys almost completely the beauty of each. The first French printers to revert to old-face models were Louis Perrin at Lyons, 1847, A. de Berny, Paris, 1852 (cf. Updike, fig. 326), and Théophile Beaudoire at Paris, 1857. Cf. M. Audin, *Le Livre*, Lyons, 1924. Motteroz's roman was shown in *The Printing Times* for 15 Apr. 1882.

[2] *Specimen Bibliorum Editionis Hebr. Gr. Lat.* s. sh. fol., N.D.

preserved in the Bibliothèque Nationale give details of printers for whom the types were cut, such as Hebrew for Giustiniani at Venice, Canon roman for Torrentino of Florence, Greek for Zanetti at Venice, and music for Le Roy and Ballard at Paris. Le Bé further mentions two other engravers of Hebrew types, Jean Arnoul le Picard and Michel Du Bois. The next letter-founder's specimen is the sheet of romans and italics printed by the Egenolff–Berner firm at Frankfort in 1592. The importance of this sheet is in the fact that the names of the engravers are given, most of the romans being by Claude Garamond and the italics by Robert Granjon. This sheet has already been referred to in connexion with the Elzevirs' types. The next French specimen, and the first book of specimens published by a French founder, is that of Jean Jannon, 1621.

England was, therefore, well behind other nations when, in 1665, the tiny specimen of Nicholas Nicholls was laid under the Royal notice. It is doubtful whether any founder before Moxon issued a full specimen of his types. He used the sheet as a means of advertising not only his types but his trade as a mathematical instrument maker; and his specimen, taken in connexion with his rules for the formation of letters, is a sorry performance, and not comparable to the Oxford University specimen, which that press published in 1693,[1] exhibiting the gifts of Dr. Fell and Junius.[2] Of the other English founders before 1720 no published type specimen has come down to us, that shown by Watson in his *History of the Art of Printing* being merely a specimen of bought Dutch types, while those of James Orme, B. Motte, and H. Meere are printers' specimens, also for the most part, doubtless, of Dutch letter. Caslon's sheet, in 1734, marked a new departure. It displayed at a glance the entire contents of the new foundry; and by printing the same passage in each size of roman, gave the printer an opportunity of judging how one body compared with another for capacity. Caslon was the first to adopt the since-familiar *Quousque tandem* for his roman specimens. The Latin certainly tends to show off the roman letter to best advantage; but it gives an inadequate idea of its appearance in any other tongue.

> The Latin language [says Dibdin] presents to the eye a great uniformity or evenness of effect. The *m* and *n*, like the solid sirloin upon our table, have a substantial appearance; no garnishing with useless herbs . . . to disguise its real character. Now, in our own tongue, by the side of the *m* or *n*, or at no great distance from it, comes a crooked, long-tailed *g*, or a *th*, or some gawkishly ascending or descending letter of meagre form, which are the very flankings, herbs, or dressings of the aforesaid typographical dish, *m* or *n*. In short, the number of ascending or descending letters in our own language—the *p*'s, *l*'s, *th*'s, and sundry others of perpetual recurrence—render the effect of printing much less uniform and beautiful than in the Latin language. Caslon, therefore, and Messrs. Fry and Co. after him [and he might have added all the other founders of the eighteenth century] should have presented their specimens of printing-types in the *English* language; and then, as no disappointment could have ensued, so no imputation of deception would have attached.[3]

Several founders followed Caslon's example by issuing their specimens on a broadside sheet which could be hung up in a printing-office or inset in a cyclopaedia.

---

[1] Cf. *A specimen of the several sorts of letter given to the University by Dr. John Fell, Oxford, 1693*.
[2] See Berry and Johnson, *Catalogue of Specimens of Printing Types*, Oxford, 1935.
[3] *Bibliographical Decameron*, ii. 381–2.

Baskerville appears to have issued only specimens of this kind; but Caslon, Cottrell, Wilson, and Fry, who all began with sheets, found it necessary to adopt the book form. These books were generally executed by a well-known printer, and are examples not only of good types, but of fine printing. Bodoni's splendid specimens roused the emulation of our founders, and the small octavo volumes of the eighteenth century gave place at the commencement of the nineteenth to quarto, often elaborately, sometimes sumptuously got up. Alexander Wilson, in 1772, was the first to break through the traditional *Quousque tandem,* by adding a passage in the same-sized letter in English. But it has not been till comparatively recent years that the venerable Ciceronian denunciation has finally disappeared from English letter-founders' specimens.

ITALIC

The ITALIC letter, which is now an accessory of the roman, claims an origin wholly independent of that character. The earliest italic was cut by Francesco Griffo[1] da Bologna for Aldus Manutius of Venice on the model of the Chancery hand which had been adopted by the Papal Chancery for the engrossing of briefs about the year 1450. The Italians also called the script *corsivo* from the fact that it was rapidly formed, and the Germans have continued to call it *cursiv* down to the present day. Aldus intended to use it for printing his projected small editions of the classics, which would have been bulky volumes if printed either in the roman or gothic character. The fount is a 'lower-case' only, the capitals, as in the Chancery scripts themselves, being upright, i.e. roman. It contains a large number of tied letters, to imitate handwriting, but is quite free from contractions.[2] It was first used in the *Virgil* of 1501, and rapidly became famous throughout Europe. It was counterfeited almost immediately in Lyons and elsewhere. The Giunta Press at Florence produced editions scarcely distinguishable from those of Venice. The new letter was introduced into Germany by Sebaldus Striblitza at Erfurt in 1510 and into Paris by Guillaume Le Rouge about the same year. In 1513 Thielman Kerver printed a Book of Hours in an Aldine italic, and at a rather later date several Paris printers seem to have acquired Froben's version, which the Basle printer used in many books from 1519.[3] Griffo himself cut at least two other italics, one for Soncino at Fano in 1503 and a smaller one in which he himself printed some sextodecimos at Bologna from 1516.

In spite of the popularity of the Aldine italic, a second family of Chancery types

---

[1] That Francesco da Bologna was not the painter Francesco Francia, as maintained by Sir A. Panizzi in *Chi era Francesco da Bologna?* 1858, was established by Adamo Rossi. See his article in *Atti della r. dep. di storia patria per le provincie di Romagna,* 1883, p. 412. See also G. Manzoni's *Studii di bibliografia analitica,* Bologna, 1881–2. Another old-established error about the origin of italic is that it was copied from Petrarch's handwriting. This is due to a misreading of a statement in the Aldine *Petrarch* of 1502 that the *text* was based on the manuscript in Petrarch's hand. This manuscript was then in the possession of Cardinal Bembo and is now in the Vatican Library.

[2] Chevillier, *Origine de l'imprimerie de Paris,* Paris, 1694, 4to, p. 110, gives a curious instance of the tendency of the old printers to contract their words. The example is taken from the *Logica* of William of Ockham, Higman and Hopyl, Paris, 1488, Hain* 11948, on sig. q1 verso, a work in which there scarcely occurs a single word not abbreviated. 'Sic̃ hic ẽ fal. s̃m qd ad simpl̷r a ẽ p̣ducibile a Deo g̃ a ẽ & sil̷r hic a ñ ẽ g̃ a ñ ẽ p̣ducibile a Deo', which means: 'Sicut hic est fallacia secundum quid ad simpliciter; A est producibile a Deo; ergo A est. Et similiter hic. A non est; ergo A non est producibile a Deo.'

[3] Froben is often said to have had italic by 1513. This mistake is probably due to a confusion with his Greek, which he used from 1513.

proved in the long run to be of greater importance in the history of typography. This family is based on the Italian cursive hand known as 'Cancellarescha formata' which was employed for many humanistic, domestic, and diplomatic purposes, and as a type was first designed by the calligrapher and printer Lodovico Vicentino degl' Arrighi at Rome in 1523. We have seen that the Venetian italic was based on one version of this hand. A less rounded and more pointed hand was practised in Rome. Unlike the Aldine italic this formal Chancery was not intended for the printing of long texts in a book of a handy size, but was rather for the production of shorter pieces of fashionable 'modern' prose or verse deemed worthy of fine typography.

Arrighi's italics are divided into two groups; the one group has 'swash' capitals and calligraphic ascenders, and to this group belong the founts of Francesco Calvo at Milan and the first italic of Colines at Paris (used from 1528); to the second group, a severe letter, belong the italics of Antonio Blado at Rome and Colines's larger fount. Robert Granjon's italics are derived from this second group, and it was from Granjon that most of the italics cut in France after 1550 are descended. Under his hands the letter had acquired a decided slope and had finally adopted capitals inclined at the angle of the lower-case.

The italic was at first intended and used for the entire text of a classical work. Subsequently, as it became more general, it was used to distinguish portions of a book not properly belonging to the work, such as introductions, prefaces, indexes, and notes; the text itself being in roman. Later, it was used in the text for quotations; and finally served the double part of emphasizing certain words in some works, and in others, chiefly the translations of the Bible, of marking words not rightly forming a part of the text.

PATER NOSTER qui es in cœlis, ſancti-
ficetur nomen tuum. Veniat regnum tuum: fiat
voluntas tua, ſicut in cœlo, ita etiam in terra.
Panem noſtrum quotidianum da nobis hodie.

FIG. 8. Italic cut by C. van Dijk. From matrices in the
Enschedé Foundry.

In England it was first used by De Worde, in Lucian's *Complures Dialogi*, in 1528. The italics of Berthelet, of William Rastell, Reyner Wolfe, and John Day are described below. Vautrollier, also, in his *New Testaments*, made use of a beautiful small italic, which, however, was probably of French cut. Like the roman, the italic suffered debasement during the century which followed Day, and the Dutch models were generally preferred by English printers. These were carried down to a minute size, the 'Robijn Italic' of Christoffel van Dijk being in its day the smallest in Europe.

It is not easy to fix the period at which the roman and italic became united and interdependent. In France italic was still an independent letter in the seventeenth century. Many of Racine's plays were printed entirely in that letter. Few English works occur printed wholly in italic. In many of the early foundries, and till a later date, one face of italic served for two or more romans of the same body. We find the same italic side by side with a broad-faced roman in one book and a lean-faced in another. Frequently the same face is made to serve not only for its correct body but for the bodies next above or below it, so that we may find an italic of the Brevier face cast respectively on Brevier, Bourgeois, and Minion bodies. These irregularities were the more noticeable from the constant admixture in seventeenth- and eighteenth-century books of roman and italic in the same lines, the latter being commonly used for all proper names as well as for emphatic words. The chief variations in form have been in the capital letters and the long-tailed letters of the lower-case. The tendency to flourish these gradually diminished on the cessation of the Dutch influence and led the way to the formal, tidy italics of Caslon and the founders of the eighteenth century, some of whom, however, consoled themselves for their loss of liberty in regard to most of their letters, by more or less extravagance in the tail of the *Q* which commenced the *Quousque tandem* of their specimens. As in the case of the roman, Caslon cut a uniform series of italics, having due relation, in the case of each body, to the size and proportions of the corresponding roman. The extensive, and sometimes indiscriminate, use of italic gradually corrected itself during the eighteenth century; and on the abandonment, both in roman and italic, of the long *∫* and its combinations,[1] English books were left less disfigured than they used to be.

BLACK-LETTER

The so-called 'gothic' letter employed by the inventors of printing for the *Bible*, *Psalter*, and other sacred works was an imitation of the formal hand of the German

Our Father, which art in heaven; Hallowed be thy Name. Thy kingdom come. Thy will be done in earth, as it is in heaven. Give us this day

FIG. 9. Textura, *c.* 1480. From matrices in the Enschedé Foundry.

scribes, chiefly monastic, who supplied the clergy of the day with their liturgical books. This letter was called by the Germans TEXTUR, MISSALSCHRIFT, or MÖNCHSCHRIFT, and by the French LETTRE DE FORME, as distinguished from the rounder and less regular manuscript-hand of the Germans of the fifteenth century, which was adopted by Schoeffer in the *Rationale* of Duranti, in the *Catholicon*, and other works, and which has been given the name GOTICO-ANTIQUA or FERE-HUMANISTICA. The pointed Gothic TEXT, or LETTRE DE FORME, a name[2] generally supposed to have reference to the precision in the figure of the old ecclesiastical character (although

---

[1] This reform, which was an incident in the general typographical revolution at the close of the eighteenth century, is usually credited to John Bell, who discarded the long *∫* in his *Shakespeare*, 1785 Long before Bell's time, however, in 1749, Ames had done the same thing in his *Typographical Antiquities*, and was noted as an eccentric in consequence.

Hansard notes the retention of the long *∫* in books printed at the Oxford University Press as late as 1824.
[2] The suggestion that *Lettres de Forme* may have meant merely letters commonly used in print (adopting the early printers' use of the word *forma* as type) appears to be somewhat far-fetched.

some authorities have considered it to be a corrupt, rather than a standard form of handwriting), preserved its character with but little variation in all the countries to which it travelled. It is scarcely necessary to detail its first appearance at the various great centres of European typography. In England it appears first in Caxton's type No. 3,[1] and figures largely in nearly all the presses of our early printers. De Worde was, in all probability, the first to import French matrices into this country, and to produce the letter which henceforth took the name of 'English', as being the national character of our early typography. De Worde's English, or as it was subsequently styled, black-letter, was for two centuries and a half looked upon as the model for all his successors in the art; indeed, to this day, a black-letter is held to be excellent, as it resembles most closely the character used by our earliest printers. The black being employed in England to a late date, not only for Bibles, but for law books and royal proclamations and Acts of Parliament, has never wholly fallen into disuse among us. The most beautiful typography of which we as a nation can boast during the sixteenth and seventeenth centuries is to be found in the black-letter impressions of our printers. The Old English was classed with the roman and italic by Moxon as one of the three orders of printing-letter; and in this particular our obligations to the Dutch are much less apparent than in any other branch of the printing art. Indeed, the English black assumed characteristics of its own which distinguished it from the LETTRE FLAMAND of the

Our Father/ which art in heaven; Hallowed
be thy Name. Thy kingdom come. Thy will
be done in earth, as it is in heaven. Give us
this day our daily bread. And forgive us our

FIG. 10. Lettre Flamand, cut by Fleischman, 1743, from matrices in the Enschedé Foundry.

Dutch at one end of the scale, and the FRAKTUR of the Germans at the other. It has occasionally suffered compression in form, and very occasionally expansion; but till 1800 its form was not seriously tampered with. Caslon was praised for his faithful reproduction of the genuine Old English; other founders, like Baskerville, did not even attempt the letter. The old blacks were looked upon as the most useful and interesting portion of James's foundry at its sale;[2] and the Roxburghe Club, those black-letter heroes of the early years of the nineteenth century, dismissed all the new-fangled founts of modern founders in favour of the most venerable relics of the early English typographers. Of these new-fangled blacks it will suffice to recall Dibdin's outburst of righteous indignation: 'Why does he [i.e. Whittingham], and many other hardly less distinguished printers, adopt that frightful, gouty, disproportionate, eye-distracting and taste-revolting form of black-letter, too frequently visible on the frontispieces of his books? It is contrary to all classical precedent, and outrageously repulsive in itself. Let the ghost of Wynkin de Worde haunt him till he abandon it!'[3]

---

[1] See Fig. 14.   [2] See Fig. 42, below.   [3] *Bibliographical Decameron*, ii. 407.

Of the other groups of gothic letters, the Fere-humanistica, the round hand in which many of the earliest and finest incunabula were printed, in this country is found only at the first Oxford Press. It is possible that the French printers called this hand *Lettre de Somme*. Tory uses the term, but does not explain or illustrate it. If it was derived from early editions of the *Summa* of St. Thomas Aquinas, e.g. that of Mainz, 1467,[1] then it probably was the letter which we call Fere-humanistica, but on the other hand the *Lettre de Somme* shown by Fournier in his *Manuel* is a Rotunda. In the *Dialogues françois pour les jeunes enfans*, Plantin, 1567, one face is called 'Lettre de Somme ou moderne', and the *Lettera moderna* was the usual term for Rotunda. The Rotunda is the round form of gothic which had developed in Italy and which by 1500 had become the commonest European type. In England we shall meet a few examples, with Lettou, Machlyn, De Worde, Pynson, and Berthelet, but the letter was entirely superseded before the middle of the sixteenth century by the traditional English BLACK-LETTER or TEXT.

BÂTARDE AND SECRETARY[2]

The BURGUNDIAN, or GROS-BÂTARDE, was the manuscript-hand employed by the English and Burgundian scribes in the fifteenth century for works in the vernacular. It was, therefore, only natural that Caxton, like his typographical tutor, Colard Mansion of Bruges, should adopt this character for his earliest works, in preference to the less familiar Rotunda, or roman letter. The French possessed a similar character, which was used for works in the French language, beginning with *Les Grandes Cronicques de France*, printed by Pasquier Bonhomme in 1477. In some cases the resemblance between the French and English types is remarkable. The Rouen printers, who executed some of the great law books for the London printers early in the sixteenth century, used a particularly neat small-sized letter of this character. Like the Rotunda, the Bâtarde, after figuring in several of the early London and provincial presses, yielded to the English black-letter, and after about 1544 did not reappear in English typography. It developed, however, several curious variations, the chief of which were what Rowe Mores describes as the SET-COURT, the BASE SECRETARY, and the RUNNING SECRETARY. Of the first-named, James's foundry in 1778 possessed two founts, come down from Grover's,[3] but as the old deformed Norman law hand which they represented was abolished by law in 1733, the matrices, which at no time appear to have been much used, became valueless. The name COURT HAND has since been appropriated for one of the modern scripts. Its place was taken in law work by the ENGROSSING hand, which Mores denominates as Base Secretary. Of this character the only fount in England appears to have been that cut by Cottrell about 1760.[4] The RUNNING SECRETARY, described by Mores as the law Cursive of Queen Elizabeth's reign, was based on Elizabethan handwriting. It was similar to the French Cursive, of which Robert Granjon, in 1556, cut the first punches at Lyons. Granjon's letter at first was called

---

[1] The *Secunda Secundae* of St. Thomas was printed by Schoeffer at Mainz in 1467, in the type of the *Rationale*, Proctor's Type 3.

[2] Mores, followed by many later writers, used the word 'Secretary' of all the bâtarde types in England. But as the word does not appear to have been in use as applied to handwriting in the fifteenth century, it seems better to confine it in typography to the script type corresponding to Civilité. See Fig. 47. [4] See Fig. 80.

by its author *lettres françaises,* but subsequently became known as LETTRE DE CIVILITÉ, on account of its use in *La Civilité puerile,* a translation from Erasmus by J. Louveau, printed at Antwerp by J. Bellère in 1559, and in Gilbert de Calviac's *Civile Honesteté,* Paris, 1560. Plantin possessed similar characters in more than one size, which he made use of in dedications and other prefatory matter. Some

Rursus detestatus sum omnem industriam
meam/qua sub sole studiosissime laboravi/
habiturus heredem post me/quem ignoro/
Utrum sapiens an stultus futurus sit/et
dominabitur in laboribus meis/quibus desu-

FIG. 11. Civilité cut by A. Tavernier, *c.* 1570. From matrices in the Enschedé Foundry.

were cut by Granjon and some by A. Tavernier. The popularity of the letter in the Netherlands is illustrated by the fact that the Enschedé firm possesses matrices of five founts dating from the sixteenth century.

Of the Secretary (Mores's Running Secretary) founts used in England the earliest appears first in the colophon of A. Guarna's *Bellum grammaticale,* H. Bynneman, 1576 (*S.T.C.* 12420). It was used on single sheets of various official documents. Hilary Jenkinson[1] in 'English Current Writing', showed a wine licence issued by Sir Walter Rayleigh under his monopoly in this fount. A circular letter relating to the affairs of John Stowe, authorizing him to collect contributions in relief of his poverty, is set in the same letter.[2] It was used also for printing circular letters demanding loans issued by James I, in the second, ninth, and eleventh years of his reign. A later fount of this class is shown in a Privy Council Notice of 19 August 1670, relating to the infringement of the privilege held for law books by Richard Atkyns. James I's circular letter issued in the third year of his reign is also in this second fount. Mr. Jenkinson, in the article referred to, mentions the use of Secretary in recognizances entered into by victuallers and in forms for marriage licences. The earliest of the recognizances preserved were issued in the forty-second year of Elizabeth's reign and were printed in the first fount. Others issued in the sixteenth year of James I's reign are in the second fount. From the seventeenth year they appear to have been printed in italic, with the conditions on the back in roman. The first fount was in Grover's foundry, called Great Primer Secretary. A third fount, somewhat resembling the second but of a much larger face, was used for the text of a remarkably fine music book printed by Edward Griffin in 1641, entitled: *The First Book of Selected Church Musick . . . Collected . . . by John Barnard one of the Minor Cannons of the Cathedrall Church of Saint Paul, London.* 3 parts in folio.

[1] See *Trans. Bibl. Soc.*, vol. xiii, 1916, pp. 273–95.
[2] See Fig. 46.

⸤2⸣

TYPE FACES (*continued*)

THE LEARNED, FOREIGN, AND PECULIAR CHARACTERS

GREEK[1]

GREEK type first occurs in the Cicero, *De Officiis*, printed at Mainz in 1465, at the press of Fust and Schoeffer. The fount used is exceedingly rude and imperfect, some of the letters being ordinary Latin. In the same year Sweynheim and Pannartz at Subiaco used a good Greek letter for some of the quotations occurring in *Lactantius*; but the supply being short, the larger quotations were left blank, to be filled in by hand. The earliest entire Greek text printed is an edition of the *Batrachomyomachia* with an interlinear Latin prose translation on the recto of each page and a metrical Latin version on the verso, assigned by Proctor to the press of Thomas Ferrandus at Brescia, *c.* 1474 (Hain 8783). The type belongs to the group which Proctor called the Greco-Latin and is copied from Nicolas Jenson's Greek, cut in 1471. The only known copy of this badly printed book is in the John Rylands Library at Manchester. Possibly the second Greek text is the Ἐρωτήματα, a Greek grammar by Manuel Chrysoloras, presumed to have been printed at Vicenza, *c.* 1476, by Giovanni da Reno (Hain 5018, Gesamtkat. 6696). This is the first attempt to reproduce in type contemporary Greek calligraphy; the accents and breathings were cast separately. Another Greek grammar, the Ἐπιτομή of Constantine Lascaris (Hain 9920), was completed at Milan on 30 January 1476, by Dionysius Paravisinus for Demetrius Damilas, a Cretan who may have designed the fount, the earliest to be equipped with Greek capitals. From this year onward the printing of Greek texts was continuous, especially at Milan and Florence. At Florence in 1488 the *editio princeps* of *Homer* was printed by Bernardus Nerlius (Hain 8772) in the type of the *Lascaris* of 1476. In the same city Janus Lascaris, in 1494, published the *editio princeps* of the *Greek Anthology* in a type designed by himself, consisting entirely of majuscules and printed by Laurentius de Alopa (Hain* 1145, Gesamtkat. 2048).

But it was Aldus Manutius at Venice who finally set up a tradition in Greek typography which lasted for some three centuries and is in some respects still un-

---

[1] See R. Proctor, *The Printing of Greek in the Fifteenth Century*, 1900, Monograph 8 of the Bibl. Soc., and British Museum, *Greek Printing Types, 1465–1927*, 1927, ed. V. Scholderer.

broken. He began to prepare for his editions of the Greek classics about 1490 and in 1495 issued his first book, the grammar of Lascaris already printed at Milan (Hain* 9924). In the printing of Greek texts he was so successful that his new letters drove out all the earlier experiments towards a Greek typography. Aldus turned away from the book-hands of the earlier calligraphers and modelled his types on contemporary Greek script. He made Greek type cursive like italic, as it still is in essentials to-day, rather than a formal letter like roman type. If his successors finally after many generations rid themselves of Aldine ligatures, they are still under the tradition of the current script of the fifteenth century.

The fame of the Italian Greek presses roused early emulation in France. Among the first printers of Paris, however, the Greek quotations and words introduced in their works were scanty and indifferent. Gering used but a very few letters, and Jodocus Badius, in 1505, excused the poverty of his edition of L. Valla's *Annotationes in Nov. Testamentum* by pleading the paucity of his types. The early works of the first Henri Estienne were similarly defective. In 1507, however, Greek punches were cut and matrices struck by Gilles de Gourmont, and the first wholly Greek work was printed at his press in this year, being a reprint of the Aldine Theocritus, with rules for pronunciation and reading. In the same year he also printed the *Batrachomyomachia*. Greek printing, once started in Paris, made rapid progress. Jodocus Badius, Vidoue, Colines, and Chrestien Wechel all distinguished themselves. But it was not till Robert Estienne, with the title of 'Regius in Græcis Typographus',[1] commenced his career, that Greek printing reached its greatest perfection in France. Claude Garamond,[2] the first typographical artist of his day, was entrusted with the care of engraving punches and preparing matrices for three founts of Greek, about an English, Long Primer, and Double Pica in body, which henceforth became famous throughout Europe as the 'Characteres Regii'.[3] These characters, modelled as to their capitals on the alphabet of Lascaris, and as to their 'lower-case' and abbreviations from the beautiful Greek calligraphy of Angelus Vergetius of Candia, first appeared in the *Eusebius*, printed, in 1544,[4] by Robert Estienne, to whom the use of the types was, by virtue of his office, conceded, and who employed them in the production of some of the most brilliant Greek impressions Europe has ever seen.[5] During the seventeenth century the Royal Greek punches and matrices lay for the most part idle; but in 1691 Anisson, Director of the Imprimerie Royale, rescued them from obscurity and caused new punches to be cut and matrices struck, to supply what were missing, by Grandjean, the famous Parisian founder.

In the Low Countries, as early as 1501, Thierry Martens, at Louvain, had Greek

[1] Robert Estienne was not the first to hold this title, Conrad Néobar, his predecessor, having enjoyed it from 1538 to 1540. In some of his early impressions before 1543 Estienne used occasionally Greek types, apparently the same as those of Badius, acquired from Basle.

[2] The Imprimerie Royale at the Louvre, of which the present Imprimerie Nationale is the direct successor, was not founded till 1640, by Louis XIII. Francis I granted the letters patent in 1538 whereby Néobar and his successors received the title of Royal Printers, but did not create a royal printing establishment.

[3] Renouard states that the last, type 9 (1557), of the Greek founts of the Aldine Press was without doubt designed from Garamond's models.

[4] Gresswell mentions an *Alphabetum Graecum*, published in 1543, as a preliminary specimen. Possibly this is a mistake for 1548.

[5] The history of these famous types may be read in Bernard's *Les Estienne et les types grecs de François Ier*, Paris, 1856. See also R. Proctor, 'The French Royal Greek Types', in *Bibliographical Essays*, 1905, pp. 89–119.

types with which he printed occasional words. He produced an edition of *Æsop* in 1513, and in 1516 a Grammar of Theodore de Gaza's, and a little book of Hours, in Greek. The latter is considered an excellent piece of typography. Greek printing attained to considerable celebrity in the Low Countries. The Greek fount used in Plantin's *Polyglot*, in 1569–72, was cut by the famous French founder and engraver, Robert Granjon.[1]

Spain claims a prominent place in the history of early Greek printing in Europe, as it was at Alcalá in that country that the famous *Complutensian Polyglot* of Cardinal Ximenes was printed in 1514–17,[2] including the entire text of the Bible in Greek. The fount employed in the New Testament is very grand and imposing, and is said to have been cut specially for the work on the models of Greek manuscripts of the eleventh or twelfth century. It is the chief example of a Greek outside the Aldine tradition.

Before the completion of this great work Switzerland had secured the honour of producing the first entire *Greek Testament*, 1516, at the press of Froben of Basle. Froben's Greek is somewhat cramped and stiff. Oporinus, who printed in the same city from 1536, besides using a fount identical with that of Froben, introduced a smaller and much neater letter at the same time. See his edition of Hesiod in Greek and Latin, printed in 1544. Numerous printers produced Greek works in Germany at this period, perhaps the most famous being André Wechel, who began at Paris with types inherited from his father, but in 1573 established himself at Frankfort, where he printed several very fine works in the Royal Greek types acquired from the Estiennes.

The first appearance of Greek type in England is observed in De Worde's edition of R. Whittinton's *Syntaxis*, 1517, *S. T. C.* 25543, where a few words are introduced cut in wood. Cast types were used at Cambridge in a Galenus, *De Temperamentis*, translated by Linacre, and printed by Siberch in 1521. Siberch styles himself the first Greek printer in England; but the quotations in the Galenus are very sparse, and he is not known to have printed any entire book in Greek. In 1524 Pynson also used some Greek words and lines, without accents or breathings, in Linacre's *De emendatâ structurâ Latini sermonis*; but added an apology for the imperfections of the characters, which he said were but lately cast, and in a small quantity. The first printer who possessed Greek types in any quantity was Reginald Wolfe, who held a royal patent as printer in Greek, Latin, and Hebrew, and printed, in 1543, Ὁμιλίαι δύο of Chrysostom, edited by Sir John Cheke, the first Greek Lecturer at Cambridge. The type was of Basle origin. Eight years later, in the first volume of William Turner's *Herbal*, printed at Mierdman's press in London, the Greek words were given in black and quotations in italic. In Edinburgh, in 1563, and as late as 1579, the space for Greek words was left blank in printing, to be filled in by hand. The Oxford University Press, re-established in 1585, was well supplied with Greek types, which were used in the *Chrysostom* of 1586 and the *Herodotus* of 1591. The beautiful Greek fount used in the Eton *Chrysostom*[3] in 1610–12—a work

---

[1] See Max Rooses, *Le Musée Plantin-Moretus*, Antwerp, 1913, p. 159.

[2] Greek printing did not become common in Spain till a later period. A book printed at Oriola in 1603 contains an apology for the want of Greek types.

[3] See Fig. 25, and Proctor, 'The French Royal Greek Types and the Eton Chrysostom'.

which takes rank with the finest Greek impressions in Europe—is supposed to have
been obtained from abroad, probably from Frankfort. Its similarity to the Greek of
the Estiennes is remarkable. Indeed, the 'characteres regii' of France were at that
time, and for long afterwards, the envy and models for all Europe. A Greek press
was established in London in 1636, under peculiar circumstances, which are detailed
in our account of the Oxford Press. There is every reason to suppose that of the
handsome Greek letter provided for this press,[1] not only the types, but the matrices
were acquired abroad. After this, Greek printing became general in London and
Oxford. The various typefounders all provided themselves with a good variety
of sizes, some of which were very small and neat. There was a very fine Brevier
Greek in Grover's foundry in 1700, and a Nonpareil in that of Andrews in 1706;
but for minute Greek printing England could produce nothing to equal the Sedan
Greek Testament, printed by Jannon in 1628.

As was the case with the roman letter, many of our printers at the close of the
seventeenth century preferred the Dutch Greeks, which at that time were good.
Thomas James, in 1710, brought over the matrices of four founts from Amsterdam.
In 1700 Cambridge University, still badly off for Greek, made an offer for the
purchase of a fount of the King's Greek at Paris; but withdrew on the French
Academy insisting as a condition that every work printed should bear the imprint,
'Characteribus Graecis e Typographeo Regio Parisiensi'. The large number of
ligatures and abbreviations in the Greek of that day made the production of a fount
a serious business. The Oxford Augustin Greek comprised no fewer than 354
matrices, and the Great Primer as many as 456, and the Pica 508; Fournier, however, went beyond all these, and showed a fount containing 776 different sorts!
The impracticability of such enormous founts brought about a gradual reduction
of the Greek typographical ligatures—a reform for which the Dutch founders,
under the guidance of Meibomius and Leusden, deserve the chief credit. Fournier,
in 1764, stated that for some years previously, in Holland, Greek printing had been
carried on with the simple letters of the alphabet. Wilson's beautiful Double Pica
Greek,[2] used in the Glasgow *Homer* of 1756, was in its day the finest Greek fount
our country had ever seen. A new departure, however, was initiated by the production, in 1763, of Baskerville's Greek fount[3] for the Oxford *New Testament*. The
letter is neat, but stiff and cramped, and apparently formed on an arbitrary estimate
of conventional taste, and without reference to any accepted model. The fount was
praised and provoked imitation. Baskerville's imitator, William Martin, produced
a letter still less Greek than his model's, and the general tendency was countenanced
by the form of Bodoni's types, which were so much admired in this country at the
close of the century. A reaction, however, had begun before Bodoni's time. The
Glasgow Greek kept its place in Wilson's specimens; and Jackson, encouraged by
the younger Bowyer's remark that the Greek types in common use 'were no more
Greek than they were English', cut a beautiful Pica about 1785 for his rising
foundry. Early in the nineteenth century a new fashion of Greek, for which Richard
Porson of Cambridge was sponsor and furnished the drawings, came into vogue, and
has remained the prevailing form to this day. It may be doubted if the Porsonian

---

[1] See Fig. 26.   [2] See Fig. 73.   [3] See Fig. 76.

letter would be recognized by an ancient Greek scribe as the character of his native land; but at any rate it is neat, elegant, and legible, and dispenses with all useless contractions and ligatures. In taking leave of this subject it would be an omission not to mention the most beautiful little fount in which Pickering printed his *Homer* in 1831. Probably no finer masterpiece of minute Greek printing exists anywhere.

HEBREW

There was no Hebrew type in Germany in the fifteenth century. In the *Tractatus contra perfidos Judaeos*, printed by Conrad Fyner at Esslingen in 1475, Hebrew letters cut on wood appeared, and also in Breydenbach's *Itinerarium* (E. Reuwich, Mainz, 1486) along with other oriental alphabets. Salamon Jarchi's *Commentary on the Pentateuch*, printed at Reggio in Calabria by Abraham ben Garton ben Isaac, is dated 5 February 1475, and the four-volume edition of the *Arba Turim* of Rabbi Jacob ben Ascher, printed at Piove di Sacco, is dated 5 July in the same year. It is thought that work on the second must have started earlier than on the volume printed at Reggio. The most distinguished of the early Jewish printers was a family of German Jews surnamed Soncino from the town where they first printed. Joshua Solomon Soncino printed his first book in 1483, and in 1488 produced the first Hebrew Bible. His son Gershom Soncino printed many fine Hebrew books in various towns in northern Italy and later, in the sixteenth century, at Constantinople.[1] In all about one hundred Hebrew incunabula are known, the great majority produced in Italy. Three Spanish towns had Jewish presses, the first, Guadalajara in 1483, and three Portuguese towns, the first, Faro, in 1487. There is also known one work printed in the fifteenth century at Constantinople, an edition of the *Turim* by David and Samuel Nachmias in 1493.

In the sixteenth century many Italian presses had Hebrew types, including that of Aldus. Perhaps the most distinguished printer of Hebrew was Daniel Bomberg of Amsterdam, who established his press at Venice in 1516, and second only to Bomberg was Antonio Giustiniani, also at Venice, for whom the French founder Guillaume Le Bé cut founts from 1545. The press at Constantinople after a break resumed printing in 1505, and a press was established at Salonika in 1515 by Judah Gedaliah, a refugee from Lisbon.

The first Hebrew types in Germany were cut at the instigation of the famous Renaissance scholar Johann Reuchlin. He found a printer in Thomas Anshelm of Pforzheim, who cut three Hebrew types. The first, a cursive letter without points, is found in Reuchlin's *Teutsch Missive*, Pforzheim, 1505, the second, the normal design, in his *De Rudimentis Hebraicis*, 1506, in the *Grammaticae institutiones* of J. Henricmannus, 1508, and in other books printed by Anshelm at Tübingen. At Tübingen also Anshelm used a third, smaller Hebrew from 1512. A Jewish press was established at Prague in 1513 by Gershom Cohen ben Salomo, who printed several prayer books. At Augsburg Erhard Öglin had two founts of Hebrew, used from 1514. In 1534, at Basle, the first Hebrew Old Testament printed by a Gentile was produced at the press of H. Bebel, and in 1536 the younger

---

[1] See G. Manzoni's *Annali tipografici dei Soncino*, Bologna, 1883–6.

Froben printed another edition, with the running titles in a Rabbinical or cursive letter. In 1587 Elias Hutter published at Hamburg, at the press of J. Lucius, a Hebrew Bible in large type, in which the inflexional letters are left in outline, while the root letters are solid. There were several reissues of this typographical curiosity.

In France an *Alphabetum Hebraicum et Graecum* was printed by Gilles de Gourmont about 1507; and in 1508 that able typographer, whose distinction as the first cutter of Greek type in France we have already noticed, produced, under the conduct of his patron, Tissard, a Hebrew *Grammar*, together with the *Oratio Dominica* and other passages in the sacred language. The types made use of were ill formed and imperfect. Although thus early initiated, Hebrew printing made little or no progress for some years. Jodocus Badius showed a few lines in 1511; and in 1516 Gourmont printed an *Alphabetum Hebraicum et Graecum*. In 1519 Agostino Giustiniani, a native of Genoa, who had already distinguished himself by superintending the production of Porrus's *Polyglot Psalter* at that city in 1516, being invited to Paris by the King, caused new punches and matrices of the Hebrew to be made by Gourmont. The work took a year and a half to complete, when, in 1520, was published the *Liber viarum linguae sanctae* of the Rabbi Moses Kimhi, the first wholly printed Hebrew work produced in Paris. From this time Hebrew printing made steady progress in France. Most of the printers possessed types, the Wechels and the Estiennes being the most distinguished in their use of them.

In Spain the printers of the *Complutensian Polyglot* made use of a fine Hebrew fount in 1514–17.

In the Low Countries Hebrew words, probably cut in wood, occur in the *Epistola apologetica Pauli de Middleburgo*, printed at Louvain by Joannes von Westfalia in 1488 (Hain 11150). The first dated Hebrew work of Thierry Martens of Louvain was a *Grammar*, in 1528. Martens's earliest founts were a large Hebrew with vowel points, and a small, without.[1] The splendid type cut by Le Bé for Plantin's *Polyglot*, printed at Antwerp in 1569–72, placed the Netherlands in the front rank of Hebrew typography. Amsterdam, during the seventeenth century, excelled all other cities in its Hebrew printing. The Portuguese Jews established two presses in 1627, the first under Daniel de Fonseca and the other under Manasseh ben Israel. The Hebrew and other oriental types of Thomas Erpenius were bought by Isaac Elzevir of Leyden in 1625 and used in that city by his successors Abraham and Bonaventura Elzevir.[2] The Hebrew *Bibles* of Jansson in 1639, Athias in 1667, and Van der Hooght in 1705 are justly regarded as masterpieces of Hebrew typography.[3]

The first specimen of Hebrew printing in England occurs in Wakefield's *Oratio de laudibus & utilitate trium linguarum*, printed by De Worde in 1528,[4] where a few words appear, rudely cut on wood. In the same work the author complained that

---

[1] See Gand, *Recherches . . . sur la vie et les éditions de Thierry Martens*, Alost, 1845. 8vo. Gand wrongly attributes Reuchlin's *De Rudimentis* to Martens.

[2] The specimen book of Johannes Elzevir, 1658, shows six sizes of Hebrew, one Rabbinic, a Syriac, an Arabic, an Ethiopic, and a Samaritan.

[3] On Hebrew typography see *The Jewish En-*cyclopaedia, art. 'Incunabula and Typography', and the *Encyclopaedia Judaica*, art. 'Druckwesen', and the references there given. See also A. Marx, 'Some Notes on the Use of Hebrew Type in Non-Hebrew Books', in *Bibliographical Essays, a tribute to W. Eames*, 1924, p. 380 seq.

[4] Isaac dates this book 1528, not 1524, as in *S.T.C.*

he was compelled to omit a third part because the printer had no Hebrew types. Hebrew words cut in wood are also used in Humphrey's *J. Juelli vita*, printed by John Day in 1573, and in the preface of a work of Dr. Peter Baro, *In Jonam prophetam praelectiones*, printed at the same press in 1579, occur several verses of Hebrew. As late as 1603 Dibdin points out that in a poem, published at Oxford, composed by Dr. William Thorne, Regius Professor of Hebrew at that University, a phrase in Hebrew is added, with the remark, 'Interserenda hoc in loco . . . sed enim Typographo deerant characteres' (Madan 229). However, Hebrew is found at Oxford in 1596 among poems in memory of Sir Henry Unton (Madan 159), while a translation from *St. John Chrysostom*, of John Willoughbie, printed by Barnes in 1602, shows two distinct founts in use. The first English book in which any quantity of Hebrew type was made use of was Dr. J. D. Rhys's *Cambrobrytannicae Cymraecaeve linguae institutiones*, printed by Thomas Orwin in 1592. Minsheu's *Ductor in Linguas*, printed by W. Stansby in 1617, shows Hebrew which serves not only for its own language but also for the Syriac. In 1621 John Bill used a newer and better letter for printing Dr. John Davies's *Antiquae linguae Britannicae . . . rudimenta*. Thomas Buck at Cambridge used Hebrew type in 1632 in Joseph Mede's *Clavis Apocalyptica*. The Hebrew fount made use of in Walton's *Polyglot* in 1657 was probably the first important fount cut and cast in this country; and, as we shall have occasion to notice, was found fault with by the critics of that great undertaking. Oxford bought Hebrew types in Leyden in 1637. In their first specimen book of 1693 three founts are shown, and both in Oxford and in London several Hebrew works were printed at the close of the seventeenth century, although none of striking importance. It is significant of the superior reputation of the Oxford Hebrew that the Hebrew and Chaldaean versions in the *Oratio Dominica* of 1700 were among the versions printed for the London publisher of that work in the University types. Thomas James, although he visited Amsterdam in 1710, at that time the centre of the best Hebrew printing in Europe, failed to secure any matrices; and most of those which subsequently were added to his foundry appear to have been cut by English founders. Among them were four founts of Rabbinical Hebrew,[1] for which character there existed no matrices in England in Walton's time, as he was compelled to cut the alphabet shown in his Prolegomena in wood. Mores counted as many as twenty-three different founts in James's foundry in his day, eight of which were with points, the remainder without. For those without points it was early the practice to cast points on a minute body, to be worked in a separate line below the letter. Caslon cut several good founts of Hebrew (one of which was of the open or outline description first introduced by Hutter), and during the eighteenth century the character became a necessary part of the stock of every founder. It would be difficult, however, to point to any striking achievement in Hebrew typography earlier than Bagster's *Polyglot* in 1817–21, in which the Hebrew text is printed in a very small and beautiful type cut by Vincent Figgins, which in its day had the reputation of being the smallest Hebrew with points in England, and of equalling in size and exceeding in beauty even the elegant letter of Jansson of Amsterdam, two centuries before.

[1] See Fig. 41.

ARABIC

The first book printed in Arabic types is said to be the *Kitab Selat el Scoua'i*, printed at Fano by G. de Gregoriis in 1514. In 1516 Porrus's *Polyglot Psalter*, containing the Arabic version, was printed at Genoa. About 1518 Paganini de Paganini printed at Venice an edition of the *Koran* in Arabic. No copy of this edition is now known to have survived, but the existence of copies in the sixteenth century is well authenticated.[1] An order for the destruction of the edition was issued by the Pope. Thus three Italian printers had employed Arabic type many years before the printers of any other European country.

In 1505 an Arabic Vocabulary, Pedro de Alcala's *Arte para saber la lingua arauiga*, was printed at Granada by J. Varela in Rotunda with the Arabic points placed over the letters. In 1539 Guillaume Postel's *Grammatica*, printed by Pierre Gromors at Paris, made use of an Arabic type, but the fount was apparently not used again, and as late as 1596 in a book printed in Paris, Thomas de Vio's *Paradigmata de quatuor linguis Orientalibus*, the Arabic words were set in Hebrew.[2] The first Arabic fount cast in Germany appeared in an edition of the *Epistola Pauli ad Galatos* in Arabic and Latin by Ruthger Spey, printed by J. Mylius at Heidelberg in 1583. The *Alphabeticum Arabicum* of Jacobus Christmannus, Neustadt an der Hardt, 1582, has woodcut letters. In 1585 at Rome Domenico Basa printed an Arabic work, *Salamese ben Cand Ghadi*, which bears on the title-page the name of the French type-cutter Robert Granjon. The printer Basa sold the type to the newly established Stamperia Orientale Medicea, for whom Granjon cut various other oriental types. Among these was a smaller Arabic, finished on 6 September 1586, used in the Gospels in Arabic, 1590, 1591, in an *Alphabeticum Arabicum*, 1592, and in an Avicenna, 1593. These types were afterwards removed to Florence, and an account of their subsequent history was given by G. E. Saltini in 'Della Stamperia Orientale Medicea' in the *Giornale storico degli Archivi Toscani*, 1860, vol. iv, p. 267 seq. The Vatican Press also had a fount of Arabic by 1591, a specimen of which is given by Angelo Roccha in his *Bibliotheca Apostolica Vaticana*. For this press also Granjon cut many founts.

At Leyden Franciscus Raphelengius, himself the compiler of an Arabic Dictionary, was celebrated for his Arabic letter, and in 1595 issued a *Specimen characterum Arabicorum*. Thomas Erpenius appears to have acquired his Arabic from Raphelengius. When sending his edition of *Arabian Proverbs* to Casaubon, in a letter of March 1614, he says the book was printed 'Typis Raphelengianis'. In 1626 an attempt was made to secure the oriental matrices of Erpenius for Cambridge, but the Elzevirs forestalled the move. Savary de Brèves had Arabic types cut in Constantinople and finished by Le Bé in Paris, and with these types he printed an Arabic version of the Psalter in Rome in 1614. De Brèves died in 1627 and his oriental types were purchased by Vitré in 1632 for the Imprimerie Royale. According to Vitré the English also were negotiating for these types. The Congregatio de Propaganda Fide showed specimens of Arabic in 1636. Another Arabic scholar,

---

[1] See Fumagalli's *Lexicon typographicum Italiae*, and his Figs. 41, 74, and 148. See also G. B. de Rossi's *De Corano Arabico*, Parma, 1805.

[2] J. de Guignes's *Essai historique sur la typographie orientale et grecque de l'Imprimerie Royale*, Paris, 1787.

Peter Kirsten of Breslau, who had already published at Breslau in 1608 his *Tria specimina characterum Arabicorum*, was living in Uppsala from 1636 to 1640 and had his Arabic works printed there. The types were afterwards acquired by the University.[1]

In England there was no printing in Arabic until about the middle of the seventeenth century. In Wakefield's *Oratio de laudibus trium linguarum*, De Worde, 1528, a few rude Arabic letters are introduced, cut in wood, and in Minsheu's *Ductor in Linguas*, 1617, the Arabic words are printed in italic. William Bedwell, who is called in the *D.N.B.* the father of Arabic studies in England, visited Leyden in 1612 and had his edition of *St. John's Epistles* in Latin and Arabic printed there. From a letter of John Greaves[2] we learn that Bedwell bought Raphelengius's press, but found defects in the types. According to the *Epistolae selectiores* of Georg Richter, 1662, p. 485, Bedwell, who died in 1632, left his Arabic type to Cambridge University in order that his Arabic lexicon might be printed there. The work was not printed and it is not known what became of the type. Laud's gift of Oriental MSS. to the University of Oxford in 1635, and the appointment of an Arabic lecturer, was the first real incentive to the cultivation of the language by English scholars. In 1637 the Oxford Press bought their first oriental types, including Arabic, from the foundry of Corston van Hoogenacker in Leyden, as related below (p. 133). The Arabic words in Thomas Greaves's *De Linguae Arabicae utilitate*, Oxford, 1639, were written in by hand, and in John Greaves's *Elementa linguae Persicae*, James Flesher, London, 1649, the author explains that the printing of the work had been delayed for five years for lack of type. The type used by Flesher had appeared already in 1648 in an anonymous tract entitled *De Siglis Arabum et Persarum astronomis*. At Oxford John Bainbridge's *Astronomy*, 1648 (Madan 2003), contains Arabic type, and also Pocock's edition of Abul Faraj's *Specimen historiae Arabum*, 1650 (Madan 2034). Pocock's *Carmen Tograi*, H. Hall, Oxford, 1661 (Madan 2576), is stated to be printed 'Typis Arabicis Academicis', perhaps the type bought in 1637, different both from Flesher's type and from the English Arabic shown in the Oxford specimen book of 1693. The Oxford fount, the type used in the London *Polyglot*, and the Arabic cut by William Caslon (see below, p. 231) shared among them most of the Arabic printing in England for about a century. Mores, however, mentions three other Arabics cut by English founders among the lost matrices of the James Foundry.

SYRIAC

Syriac type was first used in the *Introductio in Chaldaicam linguam, Syriacam atque Armenicam*, by Teseo Ambrogio, printed at Pavia by J. M. Simonetta in 1539.[3] The Syriac letters in Guillaume Postel's *Linguarum duodecim alphabetum*, P. Vidoue, Paris, 1538, were probably woodcut, but are so rude in execution as to be scarcely legible. In 1555, however, Postel's designs were used for the punches, cut by Kaspar Kraft of Ellwangen, for the famous Syriac Peshito *New Testament*,

---

[1] Klemming and Nordin, *Svensk Boktryckeri-Historia*, 1883, p. 182.
[2] *Domestic State Papers*, 1637–8, p. 245.

[3] See Fumagalli's *Lexicon typographicum Italiae*, pp. 292–3.

printed by Michael Cymbermannus at Vienna, the first portion of the Scriptures printed in that language. In 1569–72 Plantin at Antwerp included the Syriac *New Testament*, set in type cut by Robert Granjon, in his *Polyglot* Bible, and reissued it in separate form in 1574. Leonhard Thurneysser, alchemist and printer at Berlin, had Syriac type about 1580, along with a number of other oriental alphabets. These are shown in the tables in his *Magna Alchymia*, 1583. Besides Hebrew, Arabic, and Syriac they include alphabets of Armenian, Ethiopic, Georgian, and other languages. The designs are unusual and seem to have had no use outside Thurneysser's own press.[1] The Vatican Press had a good fount in 1584, which appears in the *Orationes Ecclesiae Maronitarum* and in Roccha's *Bibliotheca Apostolica Vaticana*, 1591. The *Nomenclator Syriacus* by J. B. Ferrarius, Rome, 1622, was printed with the Syriac type of Savary de Brèves. In 1636 the Congregatio de Propaganda Fide issued a specimen of the Estranghelo and Syriac alphabets, and in the same year A. Kircher's *Prodromus Coptus*, from the same press, contained passages in both these characters and in Heraclean. A Syriac *Testament* was printed at Cöthen in Upper Saxony in 1621, and at Hamburg Aegidius Gutbier's edition in 1663, and several later editions. In France, after the disappearance of Postel's types, there was no printing in Syriac for nearly a century. Henri Estienne in 1569 printed his Syriac *New Testament* at Geneva in Hebrew type, and in Cardinal Thomas de Vio's *Paradigmata de quatuor linguis Orientalibus*, Paris, 1596, the Syriac character was cut on wood, and longer passages set in Hebrew. Syriac matrices were among the oriental types brought by Savary de Brèves to Paris in 1614; these were used by Vitré for a *Psalter* in Syriac and Latin, 1625, and subsequently in Le Jay's *Polyglot*.

In England Syriac in the earlier books was usually set in Hebrew. James Usher, Archbishop of Armagh, was one of the first English scholars to acquire Syriac and Samaritan manuscripts and he made more than one attempt to obtain abroad types for the printing of his manuscripts, though without success. He employed Thomas Davies, chaplain of the English merchants in Aleppo, to seek out the texts in which he was interested. In a letter of 29 August 1624 to Usher Davies reports that he has sent off a copy of the Samaritan Pentateuch—a text of which Usher acquired several copies. In a letter of July 1625 there is reference to a manuscript of the Old Testament in Syriac and in a letter of 13 March 1626 we hear of the dispatch of this manuscript.[2] On the death of Thomas Erpenius of Leyden Usher made an attempt to procure his library and oriental types, including Arabic, Syriac, Ethiopic, and Samaritan, for the University of Cambridge, as we learn from a letter to Dr. Samuel Ward, Master of Sidney Sussex College, dated 16 June 1626. In a further letter of 23 June Usher has to report that he has been forestalled by the Elzevirs.[3] (These orientals are shown in Johannes Elzevir's specimen book of 1658.) Again in 1637 Usher was trying to buy Syriac type. Writing to Louis de Dieu in Leyden on 7 July 1637[4] he says that the bearer is instructed to buy Syriac or Hebrew with the object of printing the Syriac Old Testament. J. Battière, writing to Usher from

[1] See E. Crous, *Die Schriftgiessereien in Berlin*, 1928, pp. 15–17.

[2] Usher's letters form vols. xv and xvi in the edition of his *Works*, edited by C. R. Elrington, Dublin, 1847–64 (the letters were edited by J. H. Todd). The letters from Davies are Nos. 71, 90, and 388.

[3] Letters 109 and 110.   [4] Letter 210.

Paris on 29 August 1637,[1] refers to efforts to buy Syriac in Paris or from Geneva. This attempt also appears to have failed. But in the same year the Oxford Press succeeded in acquiring a fount of Syriac from the foundry of Corston van Hoogenacker in Leyden, as recorded below (p. 133). But it was not till the prospectus and preliminary specimen of Walton's *Polyglot* were issued in 1652 that we find Syriac type in use in this country. The *Polyglot* contains the entire Bible in Syriac. In 1661 the Oxford Syriac appears in Pocock's *Carmen Tograi* (Madan 2576), and differs from the fount subsequently presented by Dr. Fell, which was used in the *Oratio Dominica* of 1700, and other oriental publications of the University. The Syriac in J. Viccars, *Decapla in Psalmos*, London, 1655, fol., differs from the type of the *Polyglot* and the Oxford fount of 1661. The *Polyglot* fount[2] found its way to Caslon's foundry, who added two new founts of his own cutting. In 1778 Mores noted six founts altogether in the country. A fresh interest was taken in Syriac printing by the exertions of Dr. Claudius Buchanan, who, in 1815, had the *Gospels and Acts* printed in types cut and cast under his supervision by Vincent Figgins. After his death his work fell into the hands of Dr. Lee to complete, who, objecting to the omission of the vowel points, printed the entire *New Testament* in 1816. In 1825 Dr. Fry produced the beautiful English Syriac for Bagster's *Polyglot*, and in 1829 Richard Watts cast the fount of Estranghelo for the edition of the *Bible* published that year, which at the time was the only Syriac Bible in Nestorian characters printed in this country.

ARMENIAN

The earliest Armenian type appears to have been cut at Rome in 1563 at the instigation of an Armenian, Abgar, and is said to have been the work of a German. Armenian Psalters were printed at Rome in 1565 and at Venice 1587, followed by many other editions. In 1591 Angelo Roccha showed a specimen of Armenian in his *Bibliotheca Apostolica Vaticana*, printed at the Vatican Press, and the Congregatio de Propaganda Fide published their specimen in 1636. According to C. F. Neumann's *Versuch einer Geschichte der armenischen Literatur*, Leipzig, 1836, there was an Armenian press at Lemberg in 1616. In 1621 Francesco Rivola printed at Milan his *Dictionarium Armeno-Latinum* with Armenian type, and in 1633 had another edition printed at Paris by Antoine Vitré. But the most important centre of Armenian printing in the seventeenth century was Amsterdam. An Armenian ecclesiastic, Uscan or Osgan, who had been living in Rome with the intention of having Bibles printed for his countrymen, in 1660 went on to Amsterdam and was successful in establishing an Armenian press at which the *Bible* was printed in 1666, and a *New Testament* in 1668. According to W. P. van Stockum, who reproduces the title-page of the Bible of 1666,[3] the type was cut by Christoffel van Dijk.[4] In 1669 the press was moved to Marseilles, but apparently towards the end of the century again returned to Amsterdam.

In England the first Armenian types were those acquired by Oxford after 1695

[1] Letter 211.
[2] See Fig. 34.
[3] Pl. 72 in his *La Librairie, l'imprimerie et la presse en Hollande*, La Haye, 1910.

[4] See also J. Berg, 'De voormalige Armenische drukkerijen te Amsterdam' in *Bibliotheekleven*, ix, 1924, pp. 29–33. Van Dijk had signed a contract to cut the punches on 27 Nov. 1658.

(see below, p. 142). In the Prolegomena of Walton's *Polyglot* the alphabet there given had been cut in wood. In 1736 Caslon cut a neat Armenian[1] for Whiston's edition of Moses Chorenensis's *Historia Armenica*, and these two were the only founts in England before 1820.

ETHIOPIC

The earliest type of this language appeared in Potken's *Psalterium Aethiopicum*, printed at Rome by M. Silber in 1513. The work was reprinted at Cologne by J. Soter in 1518, in Potken's polyglot *Psalter*. In 1548 the *New Testament* was printed at Rome by V. and L. Dorici for some Abyssinian priests. The press of the Congregatio de Propaganda Fide issued a specimen of its fount in 1631, and again in A. Kircher's *Prodromus Coptus* in 1636. Thomas Erpenius at Leyden had an Ethiopic fount, which in 1625 was acquired by Isaac Elzevir. James Usher attempted to procure the fount for this country, but his attempt failing, punches were cut, and matrices prepared by the London founders for the London *Polyglot*, which showed the Psalms, Canticles, and New Testament in the Ethiopic version. Various portions of Scripture were printed at Leyden and Frankfort about the same time, of which the most important work was the *Psalter*, &c., of J. Ludolf, printed at the latter place in 1701, in a letter bolder and larger than either the Vatican or London fount, which was cut by the Luther Foundry at Frankfort at Ludolf's cost.[2] The Oxford Press possessed a fount of Ethiopic[3] 'bought of Dr. Bernard' which appears, with the other Oxford orientals, in the *Oratio Dominica* of 1700 and 1713—the Amharic being in the same character. Chamberlayne's *Oratio Dominica*, printed at Amsterdam in 1715, shows these versions in copperplate. Mores mentions a second English fount in his list of the matrices of the 'Anonymous' foundry, besides the fount cut by Caslon[4] for his foundry. There were thus four founts in England in 1778. The Polyglot fount[5] and that of the anonymous founder came into the possession of James, and at the sale of his matrices in 1782, were acquired by Dr. Fry. The reprint of Ludolf's *Psalter* by the Bible Society in 1815 was in the latter type. But the Ethiopic *Gospels* printed by the same society in 1826 were in a fount of type cast from the matrices presented by Ludolf to the Frankfort Library in 1700. No new fount of Ethiopic in England had been added to the four already named when Hansard wrote in 1825.

COPTIC

Of this character the press of the Congregatio de Propaganda Fide possessed a fount, of which a specimen was issued in 1636, in which year also Kircher's *Prodromus Coptus* appeared at the same press. No fount, however, appeared in England till about 1672—the alphabets shown in the Introduction and Prolegomena to the London *Polyglot* in 1655 and 1657 being cut on wood. About 1672 Dr. Fell purchased Coptic matrices[6] for Oxford, and it was from these that the types were cast for David Wilkins's edition of the *New Testament*, printed in 1716. In 1731 the same scholar published an edition of the *Pentateuch*, this time at the press of Bowyer, in types specially cut by William Caslon.[7] A Coptic fount is shown by

---

[1] See Fig. 60.
[2] See K. F. Bauer, *Hiob Ludolf*, 1937; his type is reproduced.
[3] See Fig. 31.
[4] See Fig. 63.
[5] See Fig. 33.
[6] See below, pp. 141, 142.
[7] See Fig. 58.

the Voskens of Amsterdam in their specimen of exotic types, *c.* 1700; and, besides the fount at Rome, there was one (or more) at Paris. A specimen is shown in Fournier; and in 1808, in Quatremère's *Recherches critiques et historiques sur la langue et la littérature d'Égypte*, printed by J. J. Marcel, considerable portions of Scripture in Coptic were included. In England the Oxford and Caslon founts were the only two in 1778, when Mores wrote, nor had the number been increased when Hansard compiled his list of foreign founts in 1825.

SAMARITAN

Samaritan type followed closely on the purchase of the celebrated manuscript of the Samaritan Pentateuch by the traveller Pietro della Valle at Damascus in 1616, which was deposited in the Oratory in Paris in 1623. The type was first used in 1631 in J. Morin's *Exercitationes ecclesiasticae in utrumque Samaritanorum Pentateuchum* and appeared again in 1636 in the *Linguarum Orientalium . . . Alphabeta*, printed by Vitré, along with the other oriental types subsequently used in the Paris *Polyglot*, completed in 1645. We have seen that James Usher had acquired a Samaritan Pentateuch by 1624, but had been too late to purchase the Samaritan type of Thomas Erpenius in 1626. Mores[1] refers to a Samaritan type of the Congregatio de Propaganda Fide. The fount used in the London *Polyglot* of 1657 (Fig. 33) appears to have been produced in England, cut perhaps under the supervision of James Usher, who between 1620 and 1630 was active in procuring Samaritan manuscripts for this country. The Samaritan letters in J. J. Scaliger's *De emendatione temporum*, Geneva, 1629, are very rough, while in J. Leusden's *Schola Syriaca*, Utrecht, 1672, the Samaritan type is very like that shown in J. Elzevir's specimen book of 1658. There is a Samaritan shown on the specimen of exotics of J. A. Schmidt, Frankfort, 1674, and another was cut by Anton Janson at Leipzig in the same year, perhaps the fount used by C. Cellarius in his *Horae Samaritanae*, Cizae, 1682. Another type was in the Voskens' foundry, shown on their specimen of *c.* 1700. The Oxford Foundry acquired a Samaritan before 1693, the type used in the *Oratio Dominica* of 1700. Although shown first in the 1695 book, the punches and matrices are mentioned in the inventory of 1693. The Polyglot Samaritan passed into Grover's hands, thence to James, at whose sale it was bought by Dr. Fry. A fount belonging to Robert Andrews also came to James's foundry. It is called by Mores 'Leusdenian', presumably the type used by Leusden in 1672. It is illustrated in the James's Sale Catalogue. James's foundry also had a set of punches in Long Primer, but these appear never to have been struck. In Hansard's list of learned founts in 1825, the only other Samaritan in this country besides those from the James's foundry and the Oxford fount was the one cut for William Caslon by Dummers.

SLAVONIC AND RUSSIAN

Early Slavonic types were of two kinds, Cyrillic, used by the Greek Orthodox Church, and Glagolitic or Hieronymian for the Roman Catholic use, though found also in Orthodox books. Cyrillic first appears in a dated book at Cracow in 1491,

---

[1] *Dissertation*, p. 13.

where Sweipolt Fiol printed the *Octoëchus* and a *Psalter*, followed by several service books. A monk, Makarije, cut Cyrillic and in the monastery at Cetinje printed at least four books, *c.* 1495. The same man, or probably the same man, printed a *Liturgiarion* at Târgoviște in Wallachia in 1508, an *Octoëchus* in 1510, and the *Liturgical Gospels* in 1512. Andreas Torresanus of Venice had Glagolitic type and printed a *Breviary* in 1493 (GKW. 5171), and in that city in the sixteenth and seventeenth centuries many books in Cyrillic were printed for the Greek Church. There was Cyrillic type at Vienna in 1529 and in many cities of eastern and south-eastern Europe. The type is found also in Sweden, where a Dutch founder, Peter van Selow (1618–49), cast the type for the King, Gustav Adolphus, and in 1628 printed a Russian *Catechism* at Stockholm, also an undated *Alphabetum Rutenorum* and a Finnish *Catechism* in 1644.[1]

In Russia the first dated book appeared in 1564, the *Apostol* (Acts and Epistles of the Apostles) and was followed by an *Horologion* in 1565. The printer was Ivan Thedorov, who probably brought the press and types from Poland. There was great prejudice against the new art and Thedorov's press was burnt out in a riot. Thedorov escaped to Poland and after working at Lemberg in 1581 printed the Russian *Bible* at Ostrog. New presses were set up at Moscow and printing there was fairly continuous. There was a press at Kiev, then in Poland, from 1616.

There are, however, six unsigned liturgical books which are probably of earlier date than Thedorov's and from a different press. They have recently been connected with the name of Marucha Neped'ev.[2]

There was no modern Slavonic or Russian before 1700, and the new letter owed its inception to Peter the Great. During Peter's residence in Holland at the end of the seventeenth century he was on intimate terms with a family of merchants, the Thessings. He induced one of the brothers, Jan Thessing, to start printing Russian books in Amsterdam. Several books appeared in 1700 and 1701 with Thessing's imprint. There seems to be a tradition that the types were cut by the Voskens firm, but the 'Mediaen Russis' shown on the specimen sheet of Johannes Rolu appears to be one of the types used. At any rate, Thessing's type is Cyrillic, not modern Russian, although the books were non-religious. Thessing died in 1701 and his employees set out to move the press to Russia in 1708, but they were captured by the Swedes, then at war with Russia, at Danzig, and the types were used by the captors for propaganda purposes. Thessing's assistant for the production of Russian texts was a Pole, E. F. Kopievich, who soon parted from his master and began to print Russian books on his own account, also at Amsterdam and also in Cyrillic. Kopievich was printing there down to 1705. Afterwards he migrated to Russia, but without his types. A list of all these Amsterdam books in Russian will be found in P. Pekarsky's *Наука и литература въ Россій при Петрѣ Великомъ*, St. Petersburg, 1862, 2 tom. This work includes a catalogue of all Russian books from 1698 to 1725, those in Cyrillic being clearly marked off from those in modern Russian.

---

[1] See S. Dahl's *Bibliotekshandbok*, 1924, pp. 246–7, in the chapter on Swedish printing by Dr. Isaac Collijn, with a reproduction.

[2] See A. A. Sidorov, *История оформления книги*, 1946, p. 42.

In 1707 a new press was established in Moscow by three printers who had brought with them punches and matrices for three types from Amsterdam. These types were modern Russian, the first of their kind. The three men were Hendrik Seelbach (?), a compositor, Voskuyl, a pressman, and Anton van der Mey, type-caster. Who cut the punches is not recorded, but the printers called them Amsterdam letters. The types were cast in Moscow by Mikhail Efremov, the head of the new press, and the first book finished was a *Геометрия*, in 1708. In 1710 there appeared a list of fifteen books produced in the new letter. The intention of the Czar Peter, who had complete control of all printing in Russia, was to produce books of practical value, especially works on navigation, ship-building, and the like, hence the new letters were called 'graždansky', that is, secular. In 1711 some of these types were taken to St. Petersburg, and the first press in that city was set up under M. P. Abramov, who produced his first book, the *Книга Марсова*, in 1713. Lithographic facsimiles of the earliest 'graždansky' letters were issued in 1877 by the 'Общество Любителей Древней Писменности', entitled *Азбука*.[1]

The only Slavonic fount in England was that purchased in 1695 from J. A. Schmidt at Amsterdam. The *Oratio Dominica* of 1700 gives a specimen of this fount, but renders the Glagolitic version in copperplate. Chamberlayne's *Oratio Dominica* at Amsterdam in 1715 does the same, as also for the Cyrillic type. Gessner in his *Buchdruckerkunst*, Leipzig, 1740, shows Cyrillic and Glagolitic printed from type, but his Russian is engraved. The press of the Congregatio de Propaganda Fide showed founts both of Cyrillic and Glagolitic in 1739 and 1753, and founts occur in nearly all the Polyglot specimens of the chief European foundries.

Breitkopf of Leipzig had matrices of Russian prior to 1787; Fournier, at Paris, in 1766, showed a specimen of a fount in his foundry; Marcel, in his *Oratio Dominica*, 1805, showed another; and Bodoni of Parma, in his *Manuale Tipografico*, 1818, had no less than twenty-one sizes.

In England Mores notes that in 1778 there was no Russian type in the country, but that Cottrell was at that time engaged in preparing a fount. It does not appear that this project was carried out, and the earliest Russian we had was cut by Dr. Fry from alphabets in the *Vocabularia*, collected and published for the Empress of Russia in 1786–9. This fount appeared in his *Pantographia* in 1799. About 1820 Thorowgood procured matrices in two sizes from Breitkopf, and these three founts were the only ones enumerated by Hansard in 1825.

ETRUSCAN

A fount of this character is shown in the Oxford broadside, *c.* 1750, and was cut by William Caslon[3] about 1746 for John Swinton of Oxford. Fournier, in 1766, showed an alphabet engraved in metal or wood. In 1771 the Congregatio de

---

[1] See also A. G. Shitsgal, *Графическая основа русского гражданского шрифта*, Moscow, 1947; R. A. Peddie's *Printing, a Short History*, 1927, the chapter by L. C. Wharton on eastern Europe, pp. 245–305; and Wharton's 'Miscellaneous Notes on Slavonic Bibliography', in *The Library World*, May–July 1915. For reproductions of Russian types see Bulgakov's *Иллюстрированная история Книгопечатанія*, St. Petersburg, 1889.

[2] But cf. below, p. 143.   [3] See Fig. 62.

Propaganda Fide published a specimen of their fount, and Bodoni of Parma, in 1806, exhibited a third in his *Oratio Dominica*. The character is one rarely used, and prior to 1820 it is doubtful whether there were more than the four founts above mentioned in existence.

RUNIC

Types of this character were first used at Stockholm in J. T. Bureus's *Runa A.B.C. Boken*, A. Gutterwitz, 1611. They are said to have been cut at the expense of King Gustav Adolphus, but no doubt Bureus, one of the earliest scholars who wrote on runes, was responsible for the design. A second edition was printed at Uppsala by Gutterwitz's successor, E. Matzson, in 1624, and the type afterwards became the property of the University of Uppsala. Another scholar at Copenhagen, Ole Worm, also designed a Runic type, to be seen in his *Runer, seu Danica Literatura antiquissima*, M. Martzan, Copenhagen, 1636, with a second edition in 1651. These books are entered in C. G. Warmholtz's *Biblioteca historica Sueo-Gothica*, 1815, Nos. 8960, 8961, and 8962. The Voskens firm at Amsterdam showed Runic in their specimen of exotic founts issued about the end of the century. The Pica Runic which Junius presented to Oxford in 1677 he had himself used at Dordrecht, along with his Gothic, in his *Gothicum Glossarium*, 1665, printed 'typis & sumptibus Junianis'. This fount appears in the *Oratio Dominica* of 1700, and in Hickes's *Thesaurus*, 1703–5. Mores mentions a second fount, incomplete, in James's foundry, which, however, was lost; so that the Oxford fount remained the only one in the country. Fournier and Fry show the alphabet engraved.

GOTHIC

Matrices of this language were presented to the Oxford Press by Francis Junius in 1677. The type had been used in an edition of the *Gospels* in Gothic and Anglo-Saxon printed at Dordrecht in 1665 and in Junius's *Gothicum Glossarium* of the same year, printed 'typis & sumptibus Junianis'. The Gothic text of the Gospels was based on the famous 'Codex Argenteus' of Ulfilas. The Stockholm edition of 1671 of the *Gospels* printed the Gothic text in roman. There appear to have been other matrices in Holland, as the Gothic in Chamberlayne's *Oratio Dominica*, Amsterdam, 1715, differs from the Oxford fount, which was used in the *Oratio Dominica*, London, 1700, and also in Hickes's *Thesaurus*, 1703–5. Mores speaks of another fount in the James's foundry, acquired from the 'Anonymous' foundry, but since lost. The *Gospels* in Gothic were again printed at Oxford in 1750 in the type presented by Junius. In 1820 the only other fount in England was Caslon's, shown on his specimen sheet of 1734. Breitkopf of Leipzig had a fount, used in F. A. Knittel's edition of the *Epistola ad Romanos* in Gothic and Latin, 1762. On the specimen sheet of A. G. Mappa, Delft, 1785, a Gothic is shown under the name 'Moesogothique'. Mappa's types came from the Voskens and ultimately, after he had gone to the United States, went to Binny and Ronaldson of Philadelphia.

SAXON

The first type for this language was cut by John Day about 1566, under the direction of Archbishop Parker, and appeared in Ælfric's *A Testimonie of Antiquitie* in 1567, and in the *Ælfredi Res Gestae* of Asser Menevensis, published in 1574. Parker, in his preface to the latter work, makes mention of Day as the first who had cut Saxon characters. This interesting fount[1] is rather less than a Great Primer in body, and in general appearance is handsomer than many of its successors. Day used the type and a smaller size in several other works. William Stansby (1597–1639, used Day's type, for example, in John Selden's *Eadmer*, 1623, and *Mare Clausum*, 1635. It was used again by James Flesher in 1647 in Selden's *History of Tithes*. Saxon type was used by Stansby in 1617, in Minsheu's *Ductor in Linguas*; and Haviland, who printed the second edition of that work in 1626, had in 1623 already made use of the character in Lisle's edition of Ælfric's *Homily*. Another fount was used by Badger in 1640 for Spelman's *Saxon Psalter*, so that, as Mores points out, at that date there were already four founts in the country. Hodgkinson, one of the Star Chamber printers, used Haviland's Pica Saxon in Dugdale's *Monasticon*, 1655; and two founts, a Great Primer and a Pica, were in use at Cambridge by Roger Daniel in 1643 and 1644, for example, in Whelock's edition of *Bede*. In 1654 Francis Junius had a fount of Saxon 'cut, matriculated, and cast', at Amsterdam, which, after printing Cædmon's *Paraphrasis poetica Genesios* in 1655, and some other works in that town, he brought over to England, and in 1677 presented to the University of Oxford. As early as 1659 the University had possessed a Saxon fount cast by Nicholas Nicholls (see p. 165). Junius's fount was used in Hickes's *Institutiones gramaticae Anglo-Saxonicae*, 1689, and in his *Thesaurus*, 1703–5, but was not employed by the printer of the *Oratio Dominica* of 1700, where a different fount appears—the same, apparently, which in 1709 Bowyer used to print Miss Elstob's *Homily on the Birthday of St. Gregory*. The Amsterdam printers of the *Oratio Dominica* of 1715 used a handsome fount of their own. The great interest taken in the study of the Northern languages at this period in England produced many Saxon works, and some of our scholars devoted themselves to the study of the most beautiful of the old manuscripts, with a view to the improvement of the character in print. But the failure of the typefounder Robert Andrews to do justice to Humphrey Wanley's drawings, in cutting the punches for Bowyer's new fount in 1715,[2] apparently discouraged further endeavours. Miss Elstob's *Anglo-Saxon Grammar* was printed in that year in the new type, the matrices of which were subsequently presented to Oxford, where they still remain.[3]

The Voskens of Amsterdam had Anglo-Saxon matrices towards the end of the seventeenth century, shown in their specimen of exotic types, but, except in England and Holland, the character was not used. Caslon and most of his successors cut Saxon founts. Mores noted eleven different founts existing in England in 1778. This number was afterwards increased by numerous new founts cut by Fry, Figgins, and Wilson; and Hansard enumerated twenty-three in 1825.

[1] See Fig. 16.
[2] See Fig. 43.
[3] See E. N. Adams's *Old English Scholarship*, *1566–1800*, Yale Studies in English, No. 55, 1917. There is an appendix, with reproductions, pp. 157–81, on Anglo-Saxon types.

The Anglo-Norman Saxon character in which the *Domesday Book* was written was twice imitated in type during the eighteenth century, once by Cottrell, whose attempt was not wholly successful, and again by Joseph Jackson, under the supervision of Abraham Farley, in 1783. Jackson's types were used in the facsimile printed by Nichols in that year.

IRISH

An account of the first Irish fount and of Joseph Moxon's Irish is given below under Moxon. The Irish Franciscans abroad were better supplied with Irish type than our countrymen. At Antwerp, in 1611, O'Hussey's *Catechism* was printed in an Irish fount, which subsequently reappeared in 1616 at Louvain, and was afterwards used to print a number of works published by the Irish College in that place. In 1641 a second and larger Irish fount appeared at Louvain in the *Riaghuil Treas Uird S. Froinsias*, and again in Colgan's *Acta Sanctorum Hiberniae*, 1645. This second fount was used till 1662, but the Franciscans continued to print with their first fount until 1728. In 1676 the press of the Congregatio de Propaganda Fide at Rome published O'Molloy's *Lucerna Fidelium* in a handsome and bold character, Great Primer in body, which was used again in the following year in O'Molloy's *Grammar*, and in 1707 for the *Catechism* of O'Hussey. Previous to this, however, Irish printing had revived in England, and Moxon, in 1680, had cut the curious fount of Small Pica Irish, used in Boyle's *New Testament*, printed by Robert Everingham in 1681, followed by Bedell's *Old Testament* in 1685, and in several further publications from the same press. Until the year 1800 this fount was the only Irish in this country. Abroad, a new fount appeared at Paris in 1732, where it was used in McCurtin's *Dictionary*, and in 1742 in Donlevey's *Catechism*, printed by Jacques Guérin. The matrices for this fount appear to have been held, if not prepared, by Fournier, as in the *Manuel Typographique* (ii. 196), 1766, a specimen of it appears among the foreign founts of his foundry. The fate of this fount is a matter of uncertainty. After 1742 a general cessation of Irish typography at home and abroad took place, and the few Irish works which appeared between that date and 1800 were for the most part in roman type (like John O'Brien's *Dictionary*, Paris, 1768), or with the Irish characters in copperplate (like Vallancey's *Grammar*). The chief exception is Charlotte Brooke's *Reliques of Irish Poetry*, George Bonham, Dublin, 1789, printed in a new fount, apparently privately cut. In 1804, however, a revival took place, beginning in Paris, where Marcel, being at that time in possession of several of the founts belonging to the press of the Congregatio de Propaganda Fide, which Napoleon had impounded for the use of the press of the Republic, printed his *Alphabet Irlandais* in the Irish fount of the *Lucerna Fidelium* together with a larger fount which came from Rome, but had apparently not been used before, and issued a short sketch of the character and language, illustrated with readings in these types. In his beautiful *Oratio Dominica*, printed in 1805 in the presence of Napoleon, the same types are used. Strikes of these founts were retained in Paris, and the letter reappeared in specimens issued in 1819 and 1840. The matrices probably remain part of the stock of the Imprimerie Nationale to this day. The revival in our kingdom was more rapid. Moxon's fount, which had passed through the hands of

Robert Andrews, came in 1733 into the foundry of Thomas James, at the sale of which, in 1782, the punches and matrices were purchased in a somewhat defective condition by Dr. Fry. A specimen was shown in Dr. Fry's specimen of 1794, and in his *Pantographia*, 1799, after which the fount occasionally reappeared until 1820, when it was last seen in O'Reilly's *Chronological Account of Irish Writers*, printed in Dublin in that year. Neilson's *Grammar*, printed at Dublin in 1808, appeared in the type of Charlotte Brooke's *Reliques*.

In the first twenty-five years of the nineteenth century two new Irish types were cut in Dublin and three further designs by the London founders. The Dublin printer John Barlow had a Long Primer type cut in 1808, which was in use until 1821. James Christie, who was a printer and typefounder in Dublin from 1809 to 1855, in 1815 printed *The Proverbs of Solomon* in Irish in a new fount cut and cast by himself; the type appears occasionally down to 1844. The first of the London founders to cut an Irish type since Moxon was Richard Watts. Several sizes of this design were used for fifty years in the publications of the British and Foreign Bible Society. An even more popular design was that of Dr. Edmund Fry which first appeared in 1819, 'cut . . . from original Irish manuscripts made under the care and direction of Mr. Thaddeus Connellan', as stated in the first books. The third design was that of Vincent Figgins cut for the second volume of Charles O'Conor's *Rerum Hibernicarum Scriptores*, 1825, after the copperplate examples of Irish in Vallancey's *Grammar of the Irish Language*, Dublin, 1773. James Hardiman's *Irish Minstrelsy*, 1831, is the only other book in which the type was used, but the matrices are still in the possession of Messrs. Stevens, Shanks & Sons. It is impossible to enumerate all the new founts cut subsequently in the nineteenth century, but mention may be made of the fine design used by the Irish Archaeological Society from 1841.[1]

INDIAN LANGUAGES

The first of the Indian languages to be translated into type was Tamil and was due to the efforts of Jesuit missionaries. In De Backer's *Bibliothèque de la Compagnie de Jésus*, in the account of the work of Antoine de Proença, whose *Vocabulario Tamulico* was printed at Ambalacata on the Malabar coast in 1679, it is stated that a Spaniard, Joannes Gonzalvez, cut some Indian types in 1577, and that in 1578 the Jesuit Joannes Faria printed his *Flos Sanctorum* in Tamil type. An account of the assistance given to the Danish Protestant missionaries at Tranquebar by the S.P.C.K. is given below in a note on p. 231.[2] This Mission printed the *Gospels* in Tamil in 1714, in the translation of Bartholomaeus Ziegenbalg. The type was sent out from Halle in Germany, and using this type Ziegenbalg printed a *Tamil Grammar* at Halle in 1716. The Tranquebar press found the type too large and succeeded in producing a more suitable size by their own efforts, and in this they printed the rest of the New Testament. The Congregatio de Propaganda Fide

[1] See Dr. E. W. Lynam's 'The Irish Character in Print', in *The Library*, 1924, pp. 286–325, an article which includes many reproductions. See also R. I. Best's *Bibliography of Irish Philology*, 2 vols., 1913, 42; E. R. M. Dix and S. U. Casaide's *List of Books printed in Irish*, 1905, and the Bradshaw Collection of Irish Books. Many reproductions of Irish types will be found in Colm Ó Lochlainn, 'Irish Script and Type in the Modern World', *Gutenberg Jahrbuch*, 1932, p. 9 seq.

[2] See also an article by V. Rosenkilde in *The Library*, Dec. 1949.

showed a Malabaric alphabet in 1772, and the first cut by an English founder was that of Dr. Edmund Fry.

The second Indian language cut as type was also from the south, Sinhalese. The Dutch missionaries at Colombo printed a book of *Prayers* in Sinhalese in 1737, followed by the *New Testament* in 1739. The founts of this press appear to have been the only ones used in the eighteenth century. They also had a Tamil type. As to an English-cut Sinhalese I can find nothing earlier than the specimen shown in 1859 by W. M. Watts (cf. below, p. 357).

The earliest Sanskrit was the Alphabetum Brammanicum of the Congregatio de Propaganda Fide, 1771. Next came the founts of Joseph Jackson and of Dr. Charles Wilkins, accounts of which are given below on p. 313 and the note on p. 314.

The Baptist Mission at Serampore, under the leadership of William Carey, was very active in cutting types and printing books in various Indian languages in the early part of the nineteenth century. Their first punch-cutter had been trained by Dr. Charles Wilkins. The Mission issued frequent reports on the progress of their translations and editions of parts of the Bible, and also *Specimens of Editions of the Sacred Scriptures in the Eastern Languages translated by the Brethren of the Serampore Mission*, Serampore, 1818. One of the specimens, the Cingalese, is signed: 'Dodd sculp.' Second only to the Serampore Mission was the College of Fort William in Bengal. Claudius Buchanan published a book on their translations and oriental types in 1805. All these types were the work of the missionaries or of native craftsmen trained by them, with little or no technical help from England. The total represents a remarkable achievement in the history of type-cutting. Of the English founders, besides Jackson already mentioned, Edmund Fry showed two sizes of Guzarattee in 1824, whilst Vincent Figgins had cut a fount of Telegu for the East India Company about 1802. According to Hansard the Caslon firm had a Sanskrit by 1825. The firm of Stephen Austin of Hertford, a firm whose history goes back to the eighteenth century (founded 1768) and which had connexions with the East India Company, had a large collection of founts of the Indian languages. They were awarded a medal at the Exhibition of 1862, and about 1880 issued a specimen book. The East India Company's College was opened in 1806 at Hertford Castle and moved to Haileybury in 1809. I cannot find any of the Austin oriental types earlier than the Sanskrit used in the *Hitopadesa*, 1847, nor who cut their types.

CHINESE AND OTHER FAR EASTERN TYPES

Since the Chinese written language is formed by thousands of ideographs, a fount of types consists of an unwieldy number of sorts, and as a result few Western founders have attempted the task of cutting such founts. The earliest European writers on the language had wood blocks made for the characters. The first appears to have been Andreas Müller of Greiffenhagen, who in 1685 presented his fount of 3,000 characters to the library of the Elector of Brandenburg. The Royal Library at Paris possessed a large number of Chinese books and many thousands of Chinese characters were cut on wood under the superintendence of the orientalist Étienne Fourmont. They appeared in two works by Fourmont, his *Meditationes Sinicae*,

1737, and *Linguae Sinarum Mandarinicae grammatica duplex*, 1742. Chinese letters had already been shown, but on a much less ambitious scale, at St. Petersburg in 1735 in T. S. Bayer's *De horis Sinicis*.[1] As to Chinese cast types, first in the field appears to have been Breitkopf of Leipzig, who in 1789 issued his *Exemplum typographiae Sinicis figuris characterum e typis mobilibus compositum*. But this was just an experiment with some twenty characters. The next fount was that of the Congregatio de Propaganda Fide, which appears in the *Oratio Dominica*, Paris, 1805; sixty-seven characters are shown. In these cases it seems unlikely that sufficient numbers of types were cast to make possible the printing of books. The earliest translations of the Bible or parts of the Bible were printed from woodcut blocks, and at a later date such translations were reproduced lithographically. But the missionaries of Serampore had produced a Chinese version of Genesis printed from movable types by 1819, and the whole Bible by 1822. The type is shown among their specimens of 1818. Marcelin Legrand of Paris had cast a large fount by 1844, and exhibited in Paris 4,600 punches and as many matrices. Books printed from the types were shown at the Great Exhibition of 1851. A. Beyerhaus of Berlin also exhibited a complete Chinese fount.

The first English founder to attempt Chinese was Vincent Figgins the younger, in 1826, but probably only a few letters were cut. The specimen appears on a slip dated 1843 and inserted in the Figgins specimen book, *c.* 1850. W. M. Watts showed Chinese and other Far Eastern languages on the sheet of his exotic types issued about 1850. His note says that portions of the New Testament were printed in 1845 for the British and Foreign Bible Society in the Chinese type. The firm of Stephen Austin of Hertford also display the type in their specimen book of *c.* 1880.

MUSIC[2]

The reproduction of music in the fifteenth century was effected in a variety of ways, from leaving blank spaces to be filled in by hand to wood or metal blocks. Where type was used for the notes, the staves might be added by hand, drawn with a rastrum, a kind of five-pronged pen, or printed from rules. In the case where both notes and staves were printed, it was always a two-impression process. These various methods did not succeed one another in time. There were two styles of notes; the roman style showed square notes, printed from quads or inverted types, and the gothic style 'horse-shoe nail' notes or lozenge-shaped notes. The two earliest pieces of music printing are found in 1473. In Charlier de Gerson's *Collectorium supra Magnificat*, Conrad Fyner, Esslingen, 1473, the notes are of the roman style and the staves have not been added.[3] The second specimen is a *Graduale*, printed at Augsburg without date, but believed to be of 1473. The notes are in the gothic style and the staves are separately printed. A page from this book is repro-

---

[1] See De Guignes's *Essai historique sur la typographie orientale*.

[2] See H. Riemann, *Notenschrift und Notendruck*, Leipzig, 1896, and the article 'Notendruck' in Riemann's *Musik-Lexikon*, 1922.

[3] There is a reproduction in Miss Kathi Meyer's 'The Printing of Music 1473–1934' in *The Dolphin*, 1935, an article which gives a good summary of the subject, with a number of reproductions. Miss Meyer also contributed to *The Library*, Dec. 1939, an article on 'The Liturgical Music Incunabula in the British Museum', with a catalogue of the German and Italian incunabula in which music is found.

duced in the *Guide to the King's Library*, British Museum, 1939 edition. Square notes in the roman style may be seen in the *Missale Romanum*, Ulrich Han, Rome, 1476, and this was the style followed in the earliest specimen of music printing in England, in Higden's *Polychronicon*, Wynkyn de Worde, 1495. 'Horse-shoe nail' notes were used in a *Missal* printed at Wurzburg by Georg Reyser in 1481.

The printing of measured or figured music was a much more difficult task than reproducing plainchant. The first successful printer of such music was Ottaviano Petrucci of Venice and Fossombrone. His process was a two- or three-impression one and success was obtained by the excellence of the register. Petrucci received a privilege from the city of Venice in 1498, but his first book appeared in 1501, *Harmonice musice Odhecaton A*.[1] The printer returned to his native Fossombrone in 1511 and was then associated with Francesco Griffo da Bologna, the type-cutter who worked for Aldus. It is suggested by Fumagalli in his *Lexicon typographicum Italiae*, 1905, that Griffo may have cut Petrucci's music. His process was soon copied in Germany, first by Erhard Öglin, Augsburg, 1507. One of the best of early English music books, *The Book of Twenty Songs*, 1530 (*S.T.C.* 22924), is in the same style (Steele's type No. 2) with a resemblance to Öglin's type. The English book was formerly attributed to Wynkyn de Worde; this is now known to be a mistake, but who the printer of this excellent piece of work was is still a mystery. There is also in the British Museum a fragment of a ballad with music of the same style and bearing the device of John Rastell, which may have been printed some years earlier. The type is Steele's No. 1 and was used also by Rastell's successor Gough.

The next advance in music printing was made by Pierre Haultin at Paris about 1527, who contrived to print with a single impression by casting each note on the staves and then fitting them together. The process was used by Pierre Attaignant, the first King's printer of music in France; his notes were lozenge-shaped (cf. a reproduction in Updike, fig. 137). Round notes appeared at Avignon in 1532 and were cut also by Robert Granjon. In the *Spécimens de caractères Hébreux . . . et de musique gravés par Guillaume Le Bé*, edited by H. Omont, 1889, three sizes of music are shown, two of them cut for Le Roy and Ballard, the Paris firm which kept the privilege for music printing for several generations. Plantin had music type from Granjon and also from Henri Du Tour of Ghent. In England most of the music books after 1530 for a century or more followed the Haultin process. Reproductions may be seen in R. Steele's *The Earliest English Music Printing*, Bibliographical Society, London, 1903. Steele gives a list of thirteen types in the sixteenth century, three of them at least imported, one of Day's (1560) from Geneva, one used by Vautrollier (1575) from Johann Petreius of Nuremberg, and one of Short's (1597) from Louvain. Steele's book includes also a catalogue of English music books. As in Paris, the printing of music in England was controlled by privileges; Day held the privilege for metrical psalters, and Thomas Trallis and William Byrd for other music. Vautrollier printed for Trallis and Byrd from 1575 and afterwards for

---

[1] A list of his music books is given in Bruce Pattison's 'Notes on Early Music Printing', in *The Library*, March 1939, pp. 389–421.

Thomas East. After the expiration of their patent another was granted in 1598 to Thomas Morley. Tied notes, by which the heads of sets of quavers could be joined, were introduced by the Ballards in Paris in 1644, and in England by John Heptinstall about 1688, with improvements by William Pearson.

In the meanwhile the process of engraving had been applied to the reproduction of music and was to prove the most successful method down to the lithographic processes of the nineteenth century. Music was first engraved by Simon Verovio at Rome in 1586, and in England first appeared in Gibbons's *Fantasia for Viols*, variously dated 1606 and 1609. The plates in *Parthenia*, 1611, were engraved by William Hole. Later in the century Thomas Cross, 1683 (?) to 1720, maintained almost a monopoly for the publishing of engraved music.[1]

Oxford University possessed music matrices, some apparently purchased by Dr. Fell about 1672, and others cut by Walpergen. The punches and matrices of the latter are still preserved,[2] and are very curious, many of the matrices being without sides in the copper, and justified so that the mould shall supply the side, and the lines thus be cast so as to join continuously in the composition. Grover's foundry also had a Great Primer music, and Andrews had matrices of several sizes of the square-headed or plainchant character. Caslon possessed a set of round-headed matrices in two sizes, which came to him from Mitchell's foundry. In 1754 Breitkopf of Leipzig succeeded in casting a music-type, in which the notes were composed of several pieces, which were 'built up' by the compositor. Fleischman cut an improved music on the same principle for the Enschedés at Haarlem. Rosart of Brussels, and Fournier of Paris,[3] succeeded in reducing the number of pieces of a fount to 300 and 100, respectively. Henry Fougt, a German, in England in 1767, invented sectional types, which divided so as to admit the staff lines, working more or less on the lines of Breitkopf. About 1770 his plant was bought and the business continued by R. Falkener.[4] The principal improvements after Fougt's time aimed at overcoming the hiatus caused by the joining of the lines. Attempts were made to cast the notes separately from the lines, or to adopt a logographic system of casting several notes in one piece. After the beginning of the nineteenth century the production of music-type was left in the hands of specialists, amongst whom Hugh Hughes, as late as 1841, had the reputation of possessing the best founts in the trade. Of the plainchant and psalm music, both Dr. Fry and Hughes had matrices in several sizes.

BLIND

Printing for the blind was first introduced in 1784, by Valentin Haüy, the founder of the Asylum for Blind Children in Paris. He made use of a large script character, from which impressions were taken on a prepared paper, the impressions so deeply sunk as to leave their marks in strong relief, and legible to the touch. Haüy's pupils not only read in this way, but executed their own typography, and in 1786

---

[1] See also H. Riemann, *Musiklexikon*, 11th ed. 1929. There is also an English edition; W. Gamble, *Music Engraving and Printing*, 1923; O. Kinkeldey, *Music and Music Printing in Incunabula*, Papers of the Bibliographical Society of America, 1932.

[2] See Fig. 50.

[3] Cf. Fournier's *Manuel*, and on the relations of Breitkopf and Fournier see L. Volkmann in the *Gutenberg Jahrbuch*, 1928.

[4] See Kidson's *British Music Publishers*.

printed an *Essai* giving an account of their institution and labours, as a specimen of their press.[1]

The first School for the Blind in England was opened in Liverpool in 1791, but printing in raised characters was not successfully accomplished till 1827, when James Gall, of the Edinburgh Asylum, printed the *Gospel of St. John* from angular types. John Alston, the Treasurer of the Glasgow Asylum, introduced the ordinary roman capitals in relief, and this system was subsequently improved upon by the addition of the 'lower-case' letters by Dr. Fry, the typefounder, whose specimen gained the prize of the Edinburgh Society of Arts in 1837.

A considerable number of rival systems have competed in this country for adoption, greatly to the prejudice of the cause of education among the blind. The most important of these we here briefly summarize:

1. LUCAS SYSTEM (T. M. Lucas of Bristol, *c.* 1835). The letters were represented by curves and lines, having no connexion with the form of the characters they denoted. In this type the Scriptures occupied about 36 volumes.

2. FRERE'S SYSTEM (J. H. Frere, *c.* 1838). Wholly phonetic, the sounds being represented by circles, angles, and lines. These symbols were cut in copper wire and soldered upon sheets of tin. From this form a stereotype-plate was taken.

3. MOON'S SYSTEM (W. Moon of Brighton, 1847). Based upon the two preceding, but professed to be alphabetic. Nearly every symbol represents the form of a portion of the Roman letter it denotes. The plates were prepared by Frere's method.

4. CARTON'S SYSTEM (C. L. Carton of Bruges, 1802–63). Also arbitrary, though following somewhat the form of the lower-case alphabet.

5. ALSTON'S SYSTEM (J. Alston of Glasgow, 1836). This great improvement consisted in the rejection of all arbitrary symbols, and the adoption of the plain Roman alphabet of capitals. In addition to the simplicity both to the teacher and the scholar, its adaptability to typography was obvious. Instead of soldering the wire outlines on to tin, the letters were now cut and cast by the ordinary process of typefounding.

6. BRAILLE'S SYSTEM (Louis Braille of Paris, 1834). A series of dots in various combinations, designed as a universal system. This system was introduced in the 'Institution pour les jeunes aveugles' in Paris, in place of the alphabetical system which had prevailed since Haüy's time.

The Braille system is now the one universally used. For a full description see Legros and Grant, *Typographical Printing Surfaces*, pp. 104–7. The Reports of the Juries at the Great Exhibition include a long account of the various systems in use up to that date, together with lists of books printed, pp. 413–23. See also the *Encyclopaedia Britannica*, art. 'Blindness'.

TYPE ORNAMENTS AND PRINTERS' FLOWERS

The woodcut initials and borders with which so many early books are decorated were the work of the woodcutters and not the typefounders. But the 'petit fers', copied from the work of the binders, were cast metal pieces, produced by the same

---

[1] *Essai sur l'éducation des aveugles.* Dédié au Roi. À Paris. Imprimé par les Enfants Aveugles. 1786. 4to. The work is printed in the large script letter of the press, but not in relief. Appended are specimens of circulars, addresses, &c., printed in ordinary type, for the use of the public.

men who cut the types. They could be used for decoration either singly or arranged
in series as a border. In the earliest recorded appearance of such ornaments, in an
Ars moriendi printed at Verona by Giovanni Alvise in 1478, they are arranged within
rules to form a border. The books of several London printers of the early sixteenth
century show 'petit fers', e.g. Wynkyn de Worde, Pynson, and William Faques.
De Worde had four varieties of such pieces, one an arabesque unit and three entre-
lacs, and closely similar ornaments are found at Paris, for example, in the *Quincuplex
Psalterium*, printed by Henri Estienne in 1509. But it was the arabesque on which
sixteenth-century book-decoration was largely based. The subject was dealt with
and well illustrated in Messrs. Meynell and Morison's article on 'Printers' Flowers
and Arabesques' in No. 1 of *The Fleuron*, 1923. This oriental mode of decoration
came into Europe via Venice and 'petit fers' of arabesque design soon spread to all
centres of printing. The more elaborate designs were copied from the pattern or
lace books, such as the work of Francesco Pellegrino, Paris, 1530, and of Peter
Flötner of Nuremberg. The printers of Lyons, and especially Jean de Tournes,
were attached to the arabesque, and the books of Tournes are full of arabesque
fleurons, head-pieces, and borders. Much of this work was woodcut, but it was a
founder who took the next step of breaking these designs up into their component
parts and casting them as type units. This founder was Robert Granjon according
to a rhymed chronicle in Flemish by Marcus van Varnewyck, printed in 1568. It
is in the latter part of the sixteenth century that we find the elaborate arabesque
borders built up from separate cast units, and nowhere were they more popular
than in England. They went out of fashion in the seventeenth century and Moxon
speaks of them as old-fashioned in his day. However, some of the old flowers are
still to be seen on the early Caslon specimen sheets, along with some later designs
of the seventeenth century, such as crowns, roses, harps, and thistles.

The Paris founder P. S. Fournier was responsible for the revival of flowers in
the middle of the eighteenth century, this time in a rococo style. These were
rapidly copied, and the Caslon specimen books of 1764 and 1785 show their imitations and illustrate the manner of building up the units. Edmund Fry's *Specimen
of Flowers* issued from Type St. about 1790 is a most elaborate display of eighteenth-century flowers.[1] By this time William Caslon III had introduced a new kind
of cast ornament, imitating the work of Thomas Bewick and the new school of
wood-engravers. There followed a flood of ornaments in this style, reflecting in
part the social history of the times; thus we get ships, balloons, coaches, and rail-
way carriages.[2]

[1] Reproduced in Berry and Johnson, *Catalogue of Specimens of Printing Types*, pl. 8.
[2] See O. and E. Howe's 'Vignettes in Type-founders' Specimen Books' in *Signature*, No. 11, 1939.

THE PRINTER LETTER-FOUNDERS, FROM CAXTON TO DAY

I N taking a brief survey of that early period of English typography when printers
are assumed to have been their own letter-founders, we shall attempt no more
than to gather together, as concisely as possible, any facts which may throw
light on the first days of English letter-founding, leaving it to the historian of
printing to describe the productions which, as we have already stated, must be
regarded, not only as the works of our earliest printers, but as the specimen-books
of our earliest letter-founders.

Respecting many of our early printers, our information, especially with regard
to their mechanical operations, is extremely meagre. But the researches of William
Blades[1] have thrown a stream of light upon the typography of Caxton and his contemporaries, of which we gladly avail ourselves in recording the following facts
and conjectures as to the letter-founding of the period in which they flourished.
Adopting as a fundamental rule 'that the bibliographer should make such an accurate and methodical study of the *types* used and *habits of printing* observable at
different presses, as to enable him to observe and be guided by these characteristics
in settling the date of a book which bears no date upon the surface', Blades has
succeeded not only in establishing a precise chronology of the productions of the
first English printer but an exhaustive catalogue of his several types.

As we are concerned with Caxton only in his capacity as letter-founder, we must
refer the reader for all details respecting his life and literary industry to Blades's
admirable biography; and for later research to articles by W. J. B. Crotch in *The
Library*, 'Caxton Documents' (vol. viii, 1928, p. 426 seq.) and 'Caxtoniana' (vol.
xi, 1931, p. 102 seq.), and the introduction by the same author to Caxton's *Prologues
and Epilogues*, Early English Text Society, 1928. Documentary evidence has been
discovered from the Register of Aliens at Cologne of Caxton's residence in Cologne
in 1471 and 1472. There is reason to believe that he then learnt something of
printing in the office of the printer of the *De proprietatibus rerum* of Bartholomaeus.[2]
He made his first essay at printing in the year 1474–5 at Bruges; in 1476 he settled

---

[1] *The Life and Typography of William Caxton,
England's first Printer*, 2 vols., London, 1861–3.
4to.

[2] See J. G. Birch in *The Library*, 1923, pp. 50–2,

and Henry Thomas, *Wilh. Caxton uyss Engelannt*,
London, 1938. Blades's account of the relations
between Caxton and Colard Mansion is no longer
accepted.

as printer at Westminster, where he remained an industrious and prolific worker until the year of his death in 1491.

As we have already observed, the history of the introduction of printing into England differs from that of its origin in most other countries in this important particular, that whereas in Germany, Italy, France, and the Low Countries letter-founding is supposed to have preceded printing, in this country it followed it. Caxton had already run through one fount of type before he reached this country, and it appears to be quite certain that his type No. 2, with which he established his press at Westminster, was brought over by him from Bruges. The English origin of his type No. 3 is also open to question. There seems, however, reasonable ground for supposing that type No. 4 was both cut and cast in England; so that Caxton had probably been at work for a year or two in this country as a printer before he became a letter-founder. It must be admitted that any conclusion we may come to as to Caxton's operations as a letter-founder are wholly conjectural. In none of his own works (in several of which he discourses freely on his labour as a translator and a printer) does he make the slightest allusion to the casting of his types, nor does there remain any relic or contemporary record calculated to throw light on so interesting a topic.

That Caxton made use of cast types it is hardly needful here to assert. Even admitting the possibility of a middle stage between xylography and typography, the general identity of his letters, the constant recurrence of certain flaws among his types, and the solidity of his pages, may be taken as sufficient evidence that his types were cast and not separately engraved by hand.

It is scarcely likely that during his residence at Bruges, where, as he himself states in the prologue to the third book of the *Recuyell*, 'I have practysed and lerned at my grete charge and dispense to ordeyne this said book in prynte', he would omit to make himself acquainted with the methods used in the Low Countries for the production and multiplication of types; and it is at least reasonable to suppose that, once established in this country and removed from the source of his former supplies, he would put into practice this branch of his knowledge and produce for himself the remaining founts of which he made use.

As to the particular process he employed, we have, as Blades points out, only negative evidence on which to rely. The frequent unevenness and irregularity of his lines, as well as the variations of the letters themselves, lead to the conclusion that the method employed was a rude one, inferior not only to that now in use but even to that adopted by the advanced German school of typography of his own day. Rude, however, as his method may have been, we are not disposed to allow that Caxton could have produced the types he did without the use of a matrix and an adjustable mould. Despite his rough workmanship, his types are as superior to those of the *Speculum* and *Donatus* as they are inferior to those of the Mainz *Bible* and the *Catholicon*; and we consider it out of the question that works like the *Dictes*, or the *Polychronicon*, or the *Fifteen Oes*, could have been produced from types cast by a clay or sand process, which we have elsewhere described as possibly employed in the most primitive practice of the art.

It is more probable that Caxton, possessing the principle of the punch, matrix, and adjustable mould, but ill furnished with the mechanical appliances for putting that principle into practice, made use of rough and perishable materials in all three branches of the manufacture. Some such rough appliances we have already suggested in our introductory chapter. His punches, as Blades has pointed out, were, in the case of at least two of his founts, touched-up types of a fount previously in use. A matrix formed from such a punch, either in soft lead or plaster, could not be anything but rough and fragile; and such a matrix, when justified and applied to a mould of which the adjustable parts may have lacked mathematical finish and accuracy, could scarcely be expected to produce types of faultless precision.

As we have freely admitted, it is impossible on this subject to go beyond the regions of speculation, but we decidedly incline to the opinion that the irregularities and defects of Caxton's types may be accounted for in the way here suggested, rather than by the assumption that he made use of a method of casting differing wholly in principle from that which was presently to become the universal practice.

We shall now briefly follow Blades's chronological summary of Caxton's six types known to him, with the additional types 7 and 8, with a view to point out such particulars respecting them as may have special bearing on the object of this work.

TYPE 1. This type, as already pointed out, was never used in England, but appears in the works of the Bruges press in the years 1474 and 1475. Caxton appears to have used it in at least two English books, the *Recuyell* and the *Game of Chesse*, the former of which was the first book printed in the English language. The body of the type corresponds to the present Great Primer; and a fount comprised 163 sorts, of which a considerable number were varieties of the same letters, 'there being only five sorts for which there were not more than one matrix, either as single letters or in combination'.

TYPE 2 was the fount with which Caxton printed in 1476 an *Indulgence*, discovered in the Public Record Office.[1] The Indulgence was issued by John Sant, Abbot of the Benedictine Monastery at Preston; the last word of the date, 'sexto', and 'xiii die decembris Westm'' are added in manuscript. The first word of the text [*J*]*ohannes* is printed in type 3. Hitherto the *Dictes or Sayengis of the Philosophres*, finished on 18 November 1477, was the earliest-known dated book printed in England, although there is some reason for supposing that the undated *Jason*, and possibly some of the small quarto poems, printed in the same type, may have preceded it. Before Caxton brought it over to England it had been used at Bruges to print *Les Quatre Derrenieres Choses*. Twenty-one works in all are known to have been printed in type 2, which is on a body equal to two-line Long Primer, or 'Paragon', and consists of 217 sorts. The capital letters are extremely irregular, not only in size but in design, some being of the simplest possible construction, while others have spurs, lines, and flourishes. It was used from 1476 to 1479, when, on its becoming worn out, selected letters were trimmed up with a graver, new matrices formed, and a recasting made. This recasting, known as type 2*, is the same body as type 2, but in all cases the letters are slightly thinner, while in the case of ascend-

---

[1] See an account of this discovery by A. W. Pollard in *The Times*, 7 Feb. 1928.

ing and descending types it is found that the process of trimming has resulted in the amputation of certain portions of the letters. There are also some thirty-seven sorts more in the second fount, consisting largely of double and compound letters, which do not appear in the first. It was used from 1479 to 1481, and nine books are known to have been printed in it, including the second edition of the *Game and Playe of the Chesse*, from which Vincent Figgins[1] in 1855 took the models for his facsimile of the 'Caxton Black'.[2]

TYPE 3. This handsome fount appears to have been used from 1476 to 1483, chiefly for headlines, although one or two small church books, as well as Caxton's *Advertisement*, were printed entirely in it. The body is the same as that of type 2, with which it is sometimes used, to distinguish proper names. The fount consists of 194 sorts, of which the points are remarkable as being smaller than those of type 2. It is the first appearance of the Text or Textura[3] in English typography; although, as Blades has pointed out, this character belongs only to the 'lower-case' letters, the capitals partaking more of the features of Mansion's 'Gros Bâtarde'. The fount possesses a special interest in being the first letter put forward as an English printer's type-specimen. In the *Advertisement* Caxton calls attention to the fact that he is prepared to sell cheap copies of the Pica or Ordinary of the Salisbury service, printed in the same type as the specimen shown, to anyone, spiritual or temporal, who may come to his shop at the Red Pale, Westminster. There is nothing to show whether this fount was brought by Caxton from Bruges or whether it is entitled to the distinction of being the first fount wholly cut and cast in this country. The German cut of the 'lower-case', as well as the slight use which Caxton made of it, would almost suggest that it was not the product of his own genius. On the other hand, the frequent use which De Worde made of the fount after his master's death seems to point to the existence of the matrices as well as the types in this country.

TYPE 4. This letter was in use by Caxton from 1480 to 1484, and there is strong reason for believing that (whatever may have been the case with type 3) it was both cut and cast in this country. That Caxton possessed punches of it appears highly probable from the fact that in the recasting of the fount as type 4* we do not find the face of the old letters to have been trimmed up, as was the case with type 2*. On the contrary, as far as face is concerned, the two founts are identical— a result which could hardly be expected had the matrices for the second fount been produced by any means but a re-striking of the original punches. The fount is smaller in size than type 2, though the design is similar. It consists of 194 sorts, of which seven were not re-struck for 4*. Twelve works were wholly printed in type 4, and two partly in 4 and 4*. The one difference between the first and second

---

[1] Vincent Figgins, apparently misled by the irregularities in form consequent on the touching-up of type No. 2, concluded that the whole of the types in which this book was printed were cut separately by hand.

[2] On Type 2 see Dr. C. F. Bühler's articles in *The Library*, 'The Dicts and Sayings of the Philosophers', in vol. xv, 1935, pp. 316–29, and 'Three Notes on Caxton', vol. xvii, 1937, pp. 155–66. Also Mr. G. Legman's article 'A Word on Caxton's

Dictes', ser. 5, vol. iii, no. 3, Dec. 1948, p. 155 seq. Dr. Bühler sought to prove that Type 2* was cut as early as Type 2, but Mr. Legman's reply seems conclusive, and Blades's account stands.

[3] We use the term *Text* in this chapter, but later we shall use the term *Black*, since that was the name generally used by the English founders. On the nomenclature of Gothic types see Johnson's *Type Designs*, chap. i.

fount is that, whereas type 4 is very close to English body, type 4* is cast on a body equal to two-lines Minion; or more precisely, nineteen lines of type 4* are equivalent to twenty lines of type 4. It appears, therefore, that, either purposely or accidentally, Caxton shifted his mould between the two castings. It is easy to imagine that his supply of moulds might be very limited; and even that it might be limited to but one mould capable of being varied in 'body' as well as in 'thickness', which he would adapt as necessity required to cast any size of letter; so that if, for instance, after casting type 4, he had had occasion to 'break' his mould in order to cast some additional letters in type 3, he might easily fail to readjust it to the precise body of his former fount, particularly if he used a worn or foul type by which to 'set' it. The fact that in Gower's *Confessio Amantis* and the *Knyght of the Toure* both castings are used shows at least that 4* was intended to supplement rather than replace its predecessor. Besides the two partly printed works, sixteen entire works were printed in type 4* between 1483 and 1485. (See Fig. 12.)

TYPE 5. In this fount the Text, first introduced with type 3, reappears in a smaller but very similar form. Eleven books were printed in it between about 1487 and 1491, the majority of which were Latin works of devotion. The body is rather larger than two-line Brevier, and the fount consists of only 153 sorts, there being very few double letters. With this fount is a set of bold Lombardic capitals, cast full on the body and used as initials. These Caxton afterwards cut down for quadrats, shortening them, as was usual at that time, at the foot-end of the type, and so not destroying the face.

TYPE 6. (Fig. 13.) This fount was for the most part produced from matrices formed from trimmed-up letters of types 2 and 2*, supplemented by a few new letters and some from other founts. The body on which it is cast is considerably smaller than type 2, being nearly a Great Primer as against a two-line Long Primer. This reduction in size necessitated the compression of a number of full-faced letters of the original founts, some of which have been forcibly squeezed into the compass and others truncated. The fount comprises only 141 sorts, and has a set of Lombardic capitals. It was used by Caxton between 1489 and the time of his death in 1491, during which period eighteen works were printed in it.

TYPE 7. This is a Text found in two editions of an *Indulgence* of 1489. It was unknown to Blades.

TYPE 8. Also a Text used in 1491 in an *Ars moriendi* and one or two other works. Blades did not admit that this type was used in Caxton's lifetime, but later discoveries have established its claim.[1]

We add a table of Caxton's types taken from Haebler's *Repertorium* together with the reproductions in Duff.

Type 1	M 59	121/2	mm. for 20 lines		Duff, pl. 1	
,, 2	,, 80	132	,,	,,	,,	pls. 2, 3
,, 3	,, 12	136	,,	,,	,,	pl. 4
,, 4	,, 80	95	,,	,,	,,	pls. 5, 6
,, 5	,, 12	113	,,	,,	,,	pl. 7
,, 6	,, 80	119/20	,,	,,	,,	pl. 8
,, 7	,, 12	80/1	,,	,,	,,	pl. 9
,, 8	,, 80	119/20	,,	,,	,,	pl. 10

[1] See Seymour de Ricci, *A Census of Caxtons*, Bibl. Soc. Monograph, No. 15, 1909, fol.

ranne in to the forst / And whanne the wylde beestes sawe
hym come / they were so ferdfull that they alle beganne to flee /
For they wende / that it had be the lyon / And the mayster of
the asse serched and soughte his asse in euery place al aboute
And as he had soughte longe / he thought that he wolde go in
to the forst for to see yf his asse were there / And as soone as
he was entryd in to the forst / he mette with his asse arayed
as before is sayd / But his mayster whiche had soughte hym
longe sawe his erys / Wherfore he knewe hym wel / and anone
toke hym / and sayd in this manere / Ha a mayster asse / arte
thow clothed with the skynne of the lyon / thow makest the be
stes to be aferd / but yf they knewe the / as wel as I do / they
sholde haue no fere of the / But I ensure the / that wel I shalle
bete the therfore / And thenne he toke fro hym the skynne of
the lyon / and sayd to hym Lyon shalt thow be no more / But
an asse shalt thow euer be / And his mayster toke thenne a
staf / and smote hym / soo that euer after he remembryd hym
wel of hit / And therfore he whiche auaunceth hym self of other
mennes goodes is a very foole / For as men sayn comynly /

                                    o   iiij

FIG. 12. Aesop, 1484. Caxton's type 4*.

Whether it be in Batapllces sieges/rescowse/ɇ all other faytes
subtyltees ɇ remedyes for meschieues/Whiche translacyon
Was finysshed the/viij/ day of Juyll the sayd yere ɇ enpryn
ted the/viiij/ day of Juyll next folowyng ɇ ful fynysshyd/ thē
ne syth I haue obeyed his most dredeful commaudement/I hū
bly bysecke his most excellent ɇ bounteuous hyeues to pardo
ne me of this symple ɇ rude translacion Where in be no cury
ous ne gaye termes of rethorpk/but I hope to almighti god
that it shal be entendyble ɇ Vnderstanden to euery man/ɇ al
so that it shal not mocke Varye in setence fro the coppe recey
ued of my said souerayn lord/ And Where as I haue erryd
oz made defaulte I besecke them that fynde sucke to correcte it
ɇ so doyng I shal praye for them/ɇ yf ther be ony thig ther
in to his pleasir/I am glad ɇ thinke my labour Wel enplo
yed for to haue the name to be one of the litel seruantes to the
hiest ɇ most cristen kyng ɇ prince of the World/Whom I by
secke almyghty god to preserue/kepe/ɇ contynue in his noble
ɇ most redoubted enterprises as Wel in Bretayn/ flaudres ɇ
other placis that he may haue Victorie honour/ɇ renōmee to
his perpetual glorye/ For I haue not herd ne rede that ony
prynce hath subdued his subgettis With lasse hurte ɇ ē and
also holpen his neighbours ɇ frendis out of this londe/In
Whyche hye enterprises I bysecke almyghty god that he may
remayne alleWay Vyctoryous/ And dayly encrease fro Ver
tu to Vertue ɇ fro better to better to his laude ɇ honour in this
present lyf/that after thys short ɇ transitorye lyf he may at
teyne to euerlastyng lyf in heuen/ Whiche god gaunte to
hym and to alle his lyege peple AMEN/

Per Caxton

Fig. 13. Christine de Pisa, 1489. Caxton's type 6.

Such is a brief summary of the types of our first printer. It would be interesting, were it possible, to continue in an equally detailed manner an examination of the types of all the early English printers. But the rapid increase of printing which followed Caxton's death would render such a task one of great labour and difficulty. We shall content ourselves with notes on some imported types and with collecting such references to typefounding as may throw general light on the progress of the art during the first century of its existence.

We have elsewhere stated that the first Oxford press began with types brought from abroad. Of the St. Albans printer and his contemporaries, Lettou and Machlin, in the city of London, we know very little. The types of both presses were extremely rude, and might therefore suggest that an attempt was made to produce them by untrained English artists, or, as is equally probable, that the old and worn-out soft lead types of an earlier printer were made use of. The St. Albans printer used three Bâtarde types and one Text, all resembling Caxton's types. Lettou had one Rotunda and one Text very like Caxton's type 3. With Machlin he used also a Bâtarde, whilst Machlin, when printing alone, had two Rotundas, another Bâtarde, and a Text. All these types are well illustrated in E. Gordon Duff's *Fifteenth Century Books*, and are listed in Haebler's *Repertorium*. The other three printers who were at work before 1501, Wynkyn de Worde, Richard Pynson, and Julian Notary, are referred to below in our account of the typography of the sixteenth century.

THE SIXTEENTH CENTURY

In the course of the sixteenth century typefounding became a separate trade in continental countries, and possibly in England also at the very end of the century. Whereas in the early years of the history of printing every printer had his own types, cut by himself or by one of his employees, a hundred years later we find all the printers of one city using much the same types, which they bought, or matrices of which they bought, from a man practising the trade of a typefounder. When, once the methods of type production ceased to be a secret, the uneconomic process of cutting a new set of punches whenever a printer desired a new type was bound to be superseded. The change took place very gradually and had begun many years before 1500. There are many instances in the Incunable period of types changing hands, of the bigger houses supplying the smaller men with founts, and finally of the same type being in the hands of many printers. Konrad Haebler collected the references to the commerce in type in an article which appeared in the *Zentralblatt für Bibliothekswesen*, 1924, 'Schriftguss und Schriftenhandel in der Frühdruckzeit' (a translation was published in the American periodical *Typographia*, vol. iii, July 1926). But Haebler concludes that there is no evidence that typefounders formed as yet a separate profession.

In the first half of the sixteenth century the supply of types seems to have been provided by the larger printing-houses, men like Johann Froben of Basle and the younger Peter Schöffer. One of the first professional type-cutters of whom we have any information was Francesco Griffo of Bologna, who cut many of the types used by the great Venetian printer, Aldus Manutius, and by Soncino at Fano, and later on engaged in printing for himself at Bologna. Claude Garamond (d. 1561) was the first independent typefounder in France, who conducted his business in much the same way as did William Caslon.

The numerous documents preserved in the Plantin Museum at Antwerp relating to the printing-house of Christophe Plantin, summarized by Max Rooses in *Le Musée Plantin-Moretus*, 1913, show that Plantin bought his types from many different founders. There is, however, one difference between Plantin's office and later printing-houses. Plantin had a foundry attached to his press, in which were employed men capable of casting type from matrices bought elsewhere, of replacing defects, extra sorts, and the like. Such foundries must have formed part of most large establishments, since the trade was generally in matrices.

In England we find a similar state of affairs, and also we find that our printers were very largely, perhaps one might say almost entirely, dependent on the continental printers or founders for their supplies. In Colonel Isaac's two volumes on *English and Scottish Printing Types*, *1501–58*, 1930, 1932, we have lists and reproductions of all the types used by our printers within those dates, and an attempt will here be made to trace the source of some of these types. The sizes will be given, as in Colonel Isaac's volumes, in measurements of twenty lines in millimetres, since to use the terms Great Primer, English, Pica, &c., would be an anachronism.

WYNKYN DE WORDE in 1500 moved into London from Westminster and after that date used only two of his fifteenth-century types. He had eight Texts (blacks), one Rotunda or Round Text, two romans, and two italics, and except for two Texts, including the earlier of the two fifteenth-century types, all can be traced to a French or Low Countries source. His *Text 95* (Duff's type 8—Isaac, figs. 3, 6–8), with Haebler's M 32, the usual M with English blacks, was used by Trepperel and Le Noir in Paris from 1497, and is illustrated in Claudin's *Histoire de l'Imprimerie en France*, tom. ii, p. 161. It was used also by other Paris printers and by other London printers, some of whom no doubt had their own matrices, whilst others acquired a fount of the type from one of the larger houses; e.g. John Scolar at Oxford had the type from De Worde. De Worde made certain alterations in the type in the course of time, using, for instance, three different *s*'s and three *w*'s. Such alterations were no doubt made in his own foundry; in the case of *w* English printers would find no such letter in a French fount and were forced to cut their own. Pynson also had the type, but had an entirely different *w* cut (cf. Isaac, figs. 13 and 15). The reproductions in Isaac show that many other printers had a Text of this design and size, in which one can detect occasional small differences. How many were copies made in this country—and it would be easier to copy a heavily inked Text than the finer lines of a roman—it is impossible to estimate.

Text 116 (Isaac, fig. 5), used from 1508 to 1515, is found with Wolfgang Hopyl of Paris from 1506. Hopyl printed a number of service-books for the English market, and it is probably from him that many English printers acquired matrices. This 116 is a Great Primer in size, and the design is shown by Samuel Palmer in his *General History of Printing*, 1732, along with a two-line Great Primer. Palmer says that these types were used by all printers in London and expresses his belief that they were struck from the punches of Wynkyn de Worde. Both sizes were in the Grover Foundry, and Rowe Mores, as we shall see later, shared this belief as to the larger size. If De Worde acquired matrices from Paris, then the Grover foundry punches must have originated from some later copier of the design.

The firſt is the two lin'd *Great Primmer* black,

bp me Winken de Worde

The next is the *Great Primmer* black,

This Work was finiſhed by me, Winken de Worde.

He

FIG. 14. Black Letter, sixteenth century.
From Palmer's *General History of Printing*.

William Caslon jun.'s copy is shown on the Caslon specimen of 1742. The Type Index to Isaac shows that some eight other printers had this 116 Text.

Text 62 (Isaac, fig. 6) is another fifteenth-century type, shown in Claudin, ii. 353, from the press of Antoine Chappiel, Paris. It was used at Rouen by P. Violette in the *Legenda Aurea*, 1507, also by Pynson (Isaac, fig. 16) and Julian Notary (Isaac, fig. 28). It was in Rouen before 1501 and is shown among the plates issued by the Gesellschaft für Typenkunde, pl. 1379. It is often said that English printers of this period acquired types from Rouen, and the connexion with Normandy is well established, for instance in the case of Pynson and the first printer in Scotland, Andrew Myllar; but in many cases types used at Rouen are found at an earlier date in Paris.

Text 220, with M. 68, used from 1532. Found with many Paris printers from about 1512. It was often used in missals for the Canon of the Mass. The design is that of the two-line Great Primer black of the Grover Foundry, the punches of which Rowe Mores said he had found. John Rastell had the design by 1516. A heavy black type of this size would be easy to copy, and it is clear from the reproductions in Isaac that the contemporaries of De Worde had more than one type of this size.

Text 70, with M. 36a, used in 1533 (Isaac, fig. 10a). W. Hopyl of Paris had this type by 1504. It was used by Pynson (Isaac, fig. 17) from 1509, Robert Redman, 1531–40, Richard Kele in 1545, and others.

Rotundas or *Round Texts* were not commonly used in England and did not survive, but De Worde's only Rotunda, dating from the fifteenth century, Duff 9, was a very popular Paris type. This Rotunda 53 (Isaac, fig. 8) is found at Paris with Philippe Pigouchet from 1499, and is shown in Claudin, ii. 55 and on G.F.T. 1781. Thomas Berthelet used the type in 1528, John Day in 1551, and others.

De Worde had two romans, both acquired from Paris. *104 roman* (Isaac, figs. 11 and 12), used from 1523, is found in Paris at several presses, the first being that of

Pierre Vidoue, about 1510. *81 roman* (Isaac, fig. 11), used from 1520, is another common Paris type, found from the early years of the century. It was the only roman in Rouen up to 1520, at the press of M. Morin, and was the principal text type used by Geofroy Tory. In England Pynson had the type by 1519, William Copland was using it as late as 1558, and Thomas Davidson took it to Edinburgh.

De Worde was the first printer in England to use italic, in a Latin translation from Lucian, *Complures Dialogi*, 1528. There were two sizes, 86 and 75 mm. (Isaac, fig. 10*b*). This very poor design was of Antwerp origin and is shown in Nijhoff's *L'Art typographique dans les Pays-Bas*, under J. Grapheus, figs. 4 and 5. John Herford was using the smaller size as late as 1547.

Although characterized as a better printer than scholar, De Worde was the first to introduce letters of some of the learned languages into his books. In 1517, in Whittinton, *De concinitate grammatices*, he used some Greek words, the first in England, cut in wood. Later, in 1528, in Wakefield's *Oratio*,[1] printed in roman characters with marginal notes in italic, he printed some Greek words in movable types, and showed Arabic and Hebrew cut in wood, the first used in this country. The Hebrew is rabbinical, and the author complains that he has been obliged to omit a third part because the printer lacked Hebrew types. As early as 1495, moreover, De Worde, as we have elsewhere noted, in his edition of Higden's *Poly-chronicon*, used the first music types known in England. He died in 1534, after printing about 800 books.

His contemporary, PYNSON, who also acknowledged Caxton as his 'Worshipful Master', appears to have been in regular correspondence with the typographers of Rouen, one of whom printed in his name.[2] His first types were extremely rude; but in this particular he seems to have made rapid progress, and some of his later works are distinguished as fine specimens of typography.

We have already mentioned three Texts and a roman which Pynson used in common with De Worde. His *Text 130* (Isaac, fig. 20) is another Paris type of the fifteenth century, shown in Claudin, ii. 215, from the press of J. Morand, 1497; Pynson used it from 1504, and William Faques had it in the same year. His *Rotunda 64* (Isaac, fig. 18; Duff 3[3]) was another Hopyl type, found from 1490 (cf. Claudin, ii. 68). He was also the first printer in England to use roman, in 1509. This 114 roman (Isaac, figs. 21 and 22) is found at Paris in 1501 with Joannes Antonius Venetus, and afterwards with other Paris printers. The first book in which Pynson used the type was a speech by Petrus Gryphus, of Pisa, Papal Collector in England. Owing to the death of Henry VII, the speech was not delivered, but it may be supposed that it was the influence of this Italian humanist which induced Pynson to import a type unknown in this country. The fount passed to Thomas Berthelet (cf. Isaac, fig. 66).

A document preserved in the Record Office, dated 28 June 1519, contains an

---

[1] *Roberti Wakefeldi . . . oratio de laudibus et utili-tate trium linguarum Arabice, Chaldaicæ et Hebraice atque idiomatibus Hebraicis quæ in utroque testamento inveniuntur. Londini apud Winandum de Vorde* (1528). 4to. The date appears to be 1528, not 1524, as in *S.T.C.*

[2] Pynson was not the first English printer who 'put out' his work to foreign typographers. Caxton, in 1487, employed W. Maynyal of Paris to print a Sarum *Missal* for him; and one book, at least, is known to have been printed for De Worde by a Parisian printer.

[3] *Letters and Papers of the Reign of Henry VIII*, vol. iii, 1867.

interesting mention of Pynson's types. It is an indenture between Wm. Horman, Clerk and Fellow of the King's College at Eton, and Pynson, for printing 800 copies of such *Vulgars* as be contained in the copy delivered to him, 'in suffycient and suyng stuff of papyr, after thre dyverse letters, on for the englysh, an other for the laten, and a thyrde of great romayne letter for the tytyllys of the booke'.[1] But the book was printed in two types only, his two sizes of roman.

In 1524 Pynson possessed a fount of Greek which he used in Linacre's *De emendata structura*. This is of special interest, since the preface contains the first distinct reference to letter-founding which occurs in any English book. The Greek accents and breathings, it appears, were not sufficient for the whole of the quotations in the book, and their paucity is made the subject of the following interesting apology: 'Lectori. S. Pro tuo candore optime lector æquo animo feras, si quæ literæ in exemplis Hellenissimi vel tonis vel spiritibus vel affectionibus careant. Iis enim non satis erat instructus typographus videlicet *recens ab eo fusis characteribus græcis*, nec parata ea copia, quod ad hoc agendum opus est.'[2] The Linacre is printed in the 114 or Great Primer roman, with which the Greek ranges fairly. The letters of the latter character are cast wide, so that each letter stands apart from the next instead of joining close.

A further mention of Pynson's types occurs in a Latin letter of his own, printed at the end of the *Lytylton Tenures* of 1528, in which he thus inveighs against the piracy of his rival and contemporary, Robert Redman:

> Richard Pynson, the Royal printer, salutation to the Reader. Behold, I now give to thee, candid Reader, a Lyttleton corrected (not deceitfully), of the errors which occurred in him; I have been careful that not my printing only should be amended, but also that with a more elegant type it should go forth to the day: that which hath escaped from the hands of Robert Redman, but more truly Rudeman, because he is the rudest out of a thousand men, is not easily understood.[3]

The new fount here referred to was his 64 Rotunda recast and must have been among the latest productions of this printer's industrious labours, as he ceased printing in 1528. He died early in 1530.

After noting another Hopyl type in the *Text 93* of John Rastell (Isaac, fig. 36) shown in Claudin, ii. 161, 1497, we come to a printer, PETER TREVERIS, who seems to have been among the first to import types from the Netherlands. His 94 roman (Isaac, fig. 54a) was used at the press of Simon Corver at Zwolle, 1519–22, and is illustrated in Nijhoff, op. cit., figs. 18 and 22. It was used by James Nicholson in 1537 (Isaac, vol. ii, fig. 136). Treveris's 81 *Lettre Bâtarde* (Isaac, fig. 64) is found at Antwerp in 1525 with Willem Vorstermann.

THOMAS BERTHELET, who succeeded Pynson as King's printer in 1530, introduced two, or possibly three, new romans and an italic from Cologne, where there was an anonymous punch-cutter at work in the twenties, one of whose designs has survived to our generation. Whether he worked as an independent founder or was an

---

[1] *Letters and Papers of the Reign of Henry VIII*, vol. iii, 1867.

[2] i.e. 'Greeting to the Reader: Of thy candour, reader, excuse it if any of the letters in the Greek quotations are lacking either in accents, breathings or proper marks. The printer was not sufficiently furnished with them, since Greek types have been but lately cast by him; nor had he the supply prepared necessary for the completion of this work.'

[3] Cf. E. G. Duff's *The Printers of Westminster and London*, 1906, p. 173.

employee of one of the leading Cologne printers, Quentel or Cervicorn, cannot be discovered. Berthelet's 73 roman (Isaac, fig. 64) is found at Cologne with E. Cervicorn in 1531. The type was later at Basle and Antwerp, and in 1541 was used by M. Vascosan at Paris. Thomas Powell, Berthelet's successor, was using it in

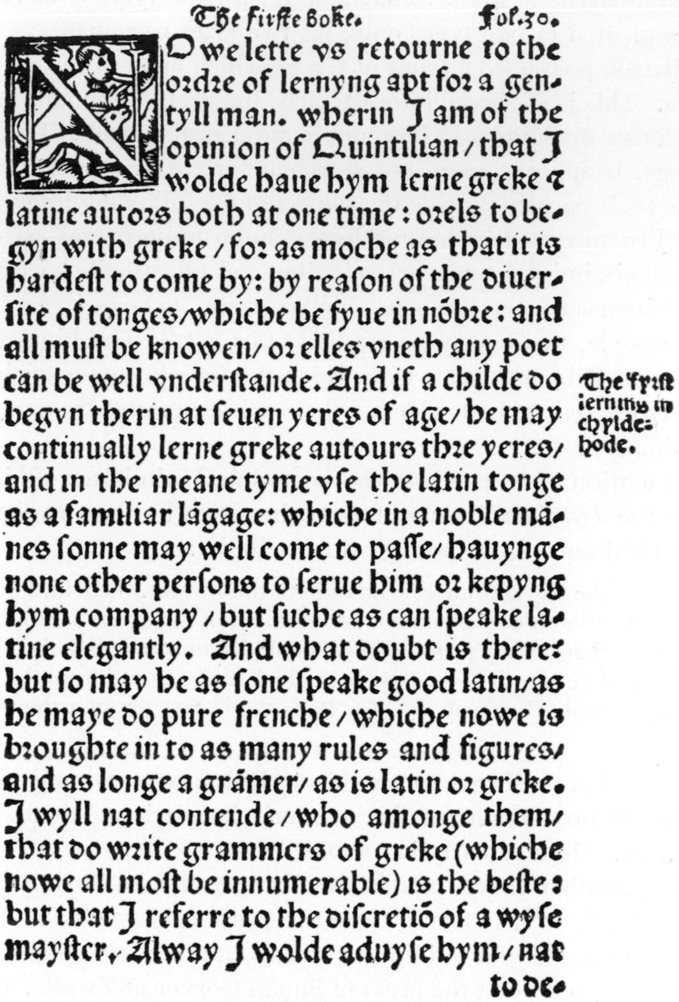

The firſte Boke. fol.30.

Owe lette vs retourne to the ordre of lernyng apt for a gentyll man. wherin J am of the opinion of Quintilian / that J wolde haue hym lerne greke & latine autors both at one time : or els to begyn with greke / for as moche as that it is hardeſt to come by: by reaſon of the diuerſite of tonges / whiche be fyue in nóbre : and all muſt be knowen / or elles vneth any poet can be well vnderſtande. And if a childe do begvn therin at ſeuen yeres of age / he may continually lerne greke autours thre yeres / and in the meane tyme vſe the latin tonge as a familiar lágage: whiche in a noble mánes ſonne may well come to paſſe / hauynge none other perſons to ſerue him or kepyng hym company / but ſuche as can ſpeake latine elegantly. And what doubt is there? but ſo may be as ſone ſpeake good latin / as he maye do pure frenche / whiche nowe is broughte in to as many rules and figures / and as longe a grámer / as is latin or grcke. J wyll nat contende / who amonge them / that do write grammcrs of greke (whiche nowe all moſt be innumerable) is the beſte ? but that J referre to the diſcretió of a wyſe mayſter. Alway J wolde aduyſe hym / nat to de-

The firſt iernmg in chyldehode.

FIG. 15. Berthelet's Rotunda, 1531.[1]

1557. The 109 roman (Isaac, fig. 67) was used at Cologne by J. Soter in 1531, and is found at Antwerp in 1540, but with a different M. The 88 roman (Isaac, vol. ii, fig. 4) is found at Antwerp with J. Steelsius in 1539. This type seems to have some relation to Quentel's roman first found in 1527, a type which has survived, at least in part. The Enschedé foundry at Haarlem have some matrices and have attributed the type to Peter Schöffer (cf. their specimen: *Een romeinsch letter type uit de vijftiende eeuw*, Haarlem, 1926). The other Cologne type of Berthelet's is the 95 italic (Isaac, fig. 65a) which is found with E. Cervicorn in 1525, a remarkable and popular design with tall capitals, still upright, as with all the early italics.

[1] This Rotunda has not been traced, but resembles Cologne models.

It rapidly won popularity, was in Paris by 1530, is found in the Netherlands and in Italy also. The many printers in England who acquired the type may be followed in Isaac. Another interesting italic is the 92 of William Rastell (Isaac, fig. 75), which came from Antwerp; cf. Nijhoff, H. Peetersen, figs. 13 and 15. It resembles an italic of Simon de Colines and belongs to the group of formal italics based on the *cancelleresca formata* of the writing masters, such as Lodovico degli Arrighi da Vicenza. A number of London printers acquired the Antwerp type, including Humphrey Powell who took the type to Dublin. It seems likely that Rastell bought the punches as well as matrices, since after its first appearance at Antwerp in 1530 it seems to have been used in England only.

RICHARD GRAFTON, with EDWARD WHITCHURCH, printed the seven editions of Cranmer's Bible, called the *Great Bible*. The printing of the first edition began in 1537 in Paris at the press of François Regnault. The work was stopped through the interference of the Sorbonne and the types were brought to London; hence two more Paris types are found in Grafton's books, 104 Text (Isaac, vol. ii, figs. 29 and 30), with M. 69, not the usual M. 32, and 68 Text with M. 70 (Isaac, vol. ii, fig. 29).

Between 1540 and 1545 a number of Basle types were introduced, possibly by REYNER WOLFE, a native of Gelderland, who is said to have visited the Frankfort Fair regularly, where matrices as well as books could be purchased. These Basle types, two romans, three italics, and a Greek, are found at the presses of Grafton, his former partner Whitchurch, Reyner Wolfe, and others. First is the Froben italic of about 85 mm., which appears in 1540 with Grafton (Isaac, fig. 39) and Whitchurch. This italic, produced by Johann Froben of Basle in 1519, was sold all over northern Europe. Whether all the founts of this design used in England came from one source or whether some were copies it is impossible to decide, so rare is it to find a good impression. Next is the Basle roman of *c.* 112 mm., a design persisting for many years in Basle books, although in fact it is found in Germany rather earlier than at Basle. John Mayler had this size by 1540 (Isaac, fig. 52), Wolfe in 1542 (Isaac, figs. 67 and 75), Grafton (Isaac, fig. 36 *a*), and Whitchurch (Isaac, fig. 41) in 1545. The second size of the Basle roman is shown under Wolfe, 1543, at Isaac, fig. 74, but Thomas Berthelet had this type by 1537 (Isaac, fig. 3a). Next comes the Basle italic, a sprawling design with an inclined upper case, dating from 1538, another general European type, including Italy. According to the index in Isaac nine London printers had this italic, the earliest being Wolfe in 1543 (Isaac, fig. 70). There was also a smaller size of the same design, which Grafton alone appears to have purchased (Isaac, fig. 33*b*). As to the Greek, used by Wolfe in an edition of St. John Chrysostom, Ὁμιλίαι δύο, 1543, the first entire Greek text printed in England, this fount was used at Basle by the younger Froben and Episcopius from 1531.

Whitchurch had a 78 roman, which was little used in England, but is of interest historically because of its long life and appearance in many centres of printing. It is a German design and is found at the press of Johann Schott of Strasburg and at that of Quentel of Cologne at the end of the fifteenth century (cf. G.F.T., pl. 1545 and 285). It was used in Germany for wellnigh a century, and is found at Antwerp, Lyons, and in Italy. Whitchurch had acquired it by 1545 (Isaac, fig. 43*b*). Hugh Singleton (Isaac, fig. 119*b*) and Robert Stoughton (Isaac, fig. 122) also had it.

The last type to be mentioned of those illustrated in Isaac's two volumes is an italic 79, used by Wayland (Isaac, fig. 23) and Richard Tottell (Isaac, fig. 140). This italic came from Paris and appears there first in 1549. It may be noted that by this date the upper case also is inclined. Of all the types illustrated in Isaac only a small proportion have here been traced to a continental source. Doubtless further research could enlarge the number, but there would still remain a residue cut probably in England, if not by English workmen. Many of these are poor copies of the standard designs, but there are also the 'Lettres bâtardes' used for law books in Norman French, and the curious Rotundas (cf. Fig. 15) of Thomas Berthelet, which have not been traced.

JOHN DAY occupies an important place in the history of early English letter-founding. What is mainly conjecture with regard to most of his predecessors we are able to state on the authority of historical records with regard to him, namely, that he was his own letter-founder; and from his day English letter-founding may be said to have started on a separate career.

He was born in 1522 at Dunwich in Suffolk, was apprenticed to Thomas Reynoldes, and in 1546 was in partnership with William Seres in St. Sepulchre's parish. In 1549 he removed to Aldersgate, where he continued for the rest of his life. The persecutions of Queen Mary's reign led to his arrest for printing heretical books. He escaped and sought refuge abroad.[1] He returned in 1556, in which year he was the first person admitted to the livery of the Stationers' Company, newly incorporated by the charter of Philip and Mary. On the accession of Queen Elizabeth he became an important printer, and was chosen Warden of the Company in 1564 and three subsequent years, and Master in 1580.

Early in the Queen's reign he found a generous patron in Archbishop Parker, under whose auspices he cut some of his founts. One of the earliest of these was the fount of Saxon, which appeared first in Ælfric's Saxon Homily, edited by the Archbishop under the title of *A Testimonie of Antiquitie*, and printed about 1566. It was used again in Lambard's *Archaionomia*, 1568, in the *Saxon Gospels*, printed in 1571, and subsequently in the Archbishop's famous edition of Asser Menevensis' *Ælfredi Res Gestæ* in 1574.[2]

This last-named work contained a preface by Parker, in which Day's performance in cutting the punches is thus particularly alluded to: 'Jam vero cum Dayus typographus primus (et omnium certé quod sciam solus) has formas æri inciderit; facilé quæ Saxonicis literis perscripta sunt, iisdem typis divulgabuntur.'[3]

The Saxon fount, as will be seen by the facsimile, is an English in body, very

---

[1] See C. H. Garrett's *Marian Exiles*, 1938, pp. 142–3.

[2] *Ælfredi Regis Res Gestæ* (without imprint or date), fol. The work was bound up and published with Walsingham's *Historia brevis*, printed by Bynneman, and his *Ypodigma Neustriæ*, printed by Day, both in 1574. The text of the *Ælfredi*, though in Saxon characters, is in the Latin language.

[3] i.e. 'And inasmuch as Day, the printer, is the first (and, indeed, as far as I know, the only one) who has cut these letters in metal; what things have been written in Saxon characters will be easily published in the same type.'

clear and bold. Of the capitals, eight only, including two diphthongs, are distinctively Saxon, the remaining eighteen letters being ordinary roman; while in the lower-case there are twelve Saxon letters as against fifteen of the roman. The accuracy and regularity with which this fount was cut and cast is highly creditable to Day's excellence as a founder.[1] He subsequently cut a smaller size of Saxon on Pica body.

OMINO MEO VENERABILI
PIISSIMOQVE OMNIVM BRI
TANNIÆ INSVLÆ CHRISTIA-
NORVM RECTORI ÆLFRED
ANGLORVM SAXONVM RE.
GI: ASSER OMNIVM SERVO-
RVM DEI VLTIMVS MILLE-
MODAM AD VOTA DESIDE-
RIORVM VTRIVSQVE VITÆ PROSPERI-
TATEM.

I.

10 ANno Dom. incarnationis, 849. natus est Ælfred angulsaxonũ rex in villa regia quæ dicitur Vuanating in illa paga; quæ nominatur Bennocscire, quæ paga taliter vocatur a Bennoc silua vbi buxus habundantissime nascitur; cuius genealogia talis tali serie cótexitur. Ælfred rex filius Æþelpulsi regis qui fuit Ecgberhti; qui fuit Ealhmundi; qui fuit Eafa; qui fuit Eoppa; qui fuit Ingild. Ingild ꝗ Ine *Ælfred*
ille famosus occidentaliũ rex Saxonũ Germani duo fuerũt; qui Ine Ro- *genealogia*
mam pergexit; ꝗ ibi vitam præsentem finiens honorifice cœlestem patriam cum Christo regnaturus abiit; qui fuerunt filii Coenred;

<small>Fig. 16. Day's Anglo-Saxon. From *Ælfredi Res Gestae*, 1574.</small>

The typography of the *Ælfredi Res Gestæ* is superior to that of almost any other work of the period. The Archbishop's preface is printed in a bold, flowing Double Pica italic, and the Latin preface of St. Gregory at the end in a roman of the same body.

Day's Double Pica roman and italic are found, together with other types which were in his press, on an unsigned specimen sheet of types, which is preserved in the Folger Shakespeare Library in Washington.[2] I understand that the sheet was

[1] Astle, in his *History of Writing*, p. 224, remarks: 'Day's Saxon types far excel in neatness and beauty any which have since been made, not excepting the neat types cast for F. Junius at Dort, which were given to the University of Oxford.'

[2] We have to thank the authorities of the Folger Library for information about this sheet and for a photostat.

found in a copy of Humphrey Dyson's *Collection of Proclamations*, published in 1618. The sheet bears no heading, date, or description of any sort. In the margins are some manuscript notes in Flemish relating to the price of the types. It seems to be a proof sheet sent by a founder in the Low Countries probably to a printer in London, and, in view of the history of the types shown, we may perhaps conclude that the founder was François Guyot. There are six types displayed very fully,

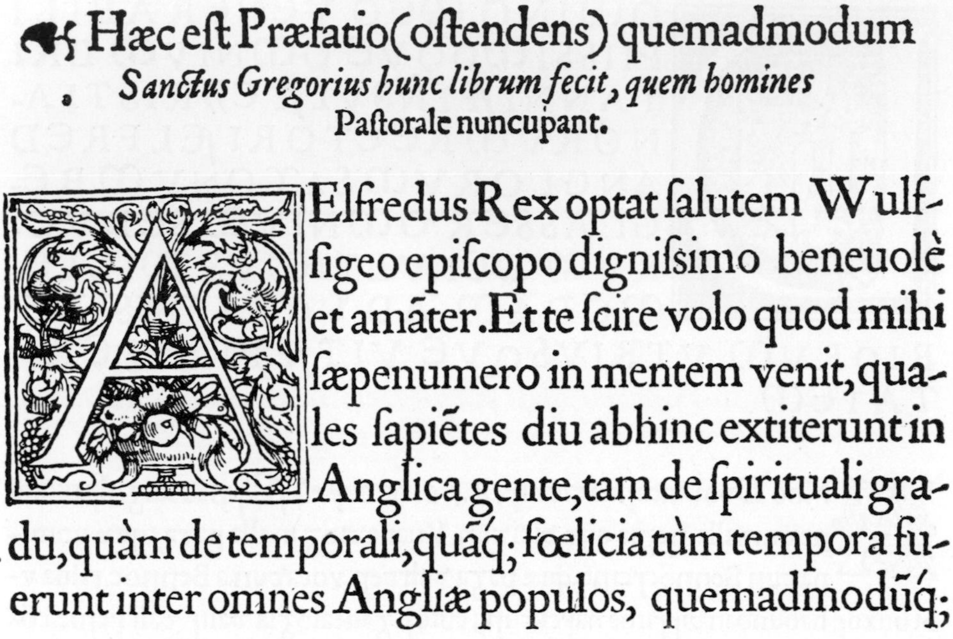

<Haec est Praefatio(ostendens) quemadmodum
Sanctus Gregorius hunc librum fecit, quem homines
Pastorale nuncupant.

Elfredus Rex optat salutem Wulf-
sigeo episcopo dignissimo beneuolè
et amâter. Et te scire volo quod mihi
saepenumero in mentem venit, qua-
les sapiétes diu abhinc extiterunt in
Anglica gente, tam de spirituali gra-
du, quàm de temporali, quáq; foelicia tùm tempora fuerunt inter omnes Angliae populos, quemadmoduq;

FIG. 17. Day's Double Pica roman. From *Ælfredi Res Gestae*, 1574.

that is to say, with full alphabets of all the sizes. First comes a Canon roman, which is found in an edition of the Vulgate printed in Louvain by B. Gravius in 1547. This Vulgate was an important publication, recognized by the Church as the authoritative text down to the publication of the Vatican Vulgate at Rome in 1590, and possibly some of the types on this sheet were cut for its use. The Canon may be seen as a heading in many English Bibles, for example in Richard Jugge's edition of 1572 and the so-called Authorized edition of 1611. Next comes Day's Double Pica roman and italic. The roman is found in the preliminaries of the Louvain Vulgate. Plantin at Antwerp had both roman and italic and they appear in his *Index characterum*, 1567. He was using the italic in 1557, and in 1563 he bought back, after his temporary failure, the Ascendonica (Double Pica), apparently this type, and according to Max Rooses the founder was François Guyot. Day had the roman by 1558 and the italic by 1559. They were used by many other English printers down to about 1700. We shall meet them again in the London *Polyglot Bible* of 1657, in Oxford printed books of the second half of the seventeenth century, in the Grover and the James foundries. A very late appearance of the roman is in a Postscript to *The Postboy* for 26 September 1700, reproduced in Morison's *The*

English Newspaper at p. 64, and its last appearance of all in the James Sale Catalogue, 1782.

The Double Pica roman and italic appear on another specimen sheet of the middle of the seventeenth century which was reproduced in Berry and Johnson, *Catalogue of Specimens of Printing Types*, pl. 19. This sheet, at the Oxford University Press, has no heading or date, but the sizes are added in a hand which is believed to be that of Gerard Langbaine, Keeper of the Archives at Oxford, d. 1658.

Vbi si quis cum codicibus manuscriptis, impressos comparare voluerit, enimuero nihil nos aut detraxisse, aut addidisse inueniet, sed summam vbiq̃ fidem & religionẽ præstitisse. Quapropter si quid emolumenti ex huius historiæ lectione sine alicuius alterius iam per me euulgatæ ad te (humanissime lector) redundauerit lætabimur: et nos instituti ac voluntatis nostræ (quandoquidem id solum concupiuimus) fructus amplissimos consecutos existimabimus.

Vale.

¶.i.

FIG. 18. Day's Double Pica italic. From *Ælfredi Res Gestae*, 1574.

First is a Canon, the same as that on the Folger Library sheet, then a Small Canon or two-line English, and last the Double Pica roman and italic, as Day. The two-line English Day also had by 1558, and several others of his contemporaries. It was a Basle type, or at least it was much used at Basle from about 1554.

The next type shown on the Folger Library sheet is a Great Primer italic, found in Antwerp at the press of J. Richardus in 1547 and of Plantin in 1557. It is perhaps the 'Text italique de Guyot' of the inventory of Plantin's types drawn up in 1563. The type was much used in Germany and in Spain. Day used this italic in William Cunningham's *Cosmographical Glasse*, 1559, and several other London printers acquired it, first Nicholas Hill in 1548 (cf. Isaac, vol. ii, fig. 112) and especially Richard Tottell (Isaac, fig. 143). No Great Primer roman was shown on the Folger Library sheet, but a roman of that size which was often used with the Great Primer italic appeared at Antwerp about 1557, a roman characterized by a broad upper-case M. It is found in the preliminaries of Rembert Dodoens's *Histoire des plantes*, J. Loe, Antwerp, 1557, and Plantin had it in the following year. Day was using it from 1570 (cf. an illustration in Isaac's *English Printers' Types of the Sixteenth Century*, pl. 66), and it is often found in the next century, for instance in the edition of the *Works of Charles I*, James Flesher, 1662. We shall meet it still later on an unpublished specimen of types from the Bagford collection.

The last two types shown on the Folger Library sheet are a Pica roman and italic, of which the roman is found in the preliminaries of the Louvain Vulgate, and the italic in the same year with J. Steelsius at Antwerp. These were both in London, though not used by Day. The roman may be seen in an edition of Calvin's *Sermons*, H. Bynneman, 1574, while the italic was in London from 1553 at the press of H. Sutton and J. Kingston (Isaac, fig. 154). Day had a different italic of this size, also an Antwerp type, in use from 1553. It is the italic of the first books printed by Plantin. An example from a book printed by Day is given in Isaac's *English Printers' Types of the Sixteenth Century*, pl. 73a.

It appears that in 1572 Archbishop Parker was engaged in providing replies to a Popish polemic of Nicholas Sanders, entitled *De visibili monarchia*. Dr. Bartholomew Clerke of Cambridge was selected for the task, and his *Responsio* was entrusted to Day to print. In a letter to Lord Burleigh, dated 13 December 1572, the Archbishop thus refers to the typography of the forthcoming work:[1]

To the better accomplishment of this worke and other that shall followe, I have spoken to Daie the printer to cast a new Italian letter, which he is doinge, and it will cost him xl marks; and loth he and other printers be to printe any Lattin booke, because they will not heare be uttered and for that Bookes printed in Englande be in suspition abroad.

Strype, referring to the transaction, adds a note: 'For our Black English letter was not proper for the printing of a Latin Book; and neither he (Day) nor any one else, as yet had printed any Latin books.'[2] This misleading statement is corrected by Herbert,[3] who points out that many Latin books had been printed, few of which, after 1520, had been in black-letter. Moreover, many English books had long before 1572 been printed in roman or italic, and even such as had generally been printed in black-letter usually had the notes and quotations in roman or italic.

By 'Italian letter' the Archbishop appears to have meant roman, and we may infer that the ultimate name in English of the letter which the Italian and Germans called 'antiqua' was still unsettled. At any rate Clerke's work, entitled *Fidelis servi subdito infideli Responsio*, 1573, was printed in the Great Primer roman which Day had been using from 1570, though he probably recast it afresh for this book. Another reply of the same year by George Acworth, entitled *De visibili Romanarchia*, introduces three other interesting types. The body of the text is set in an English roman, which is a common European type. It appears to have been cut in France in the fifties, and differs from Garamond's roman in the narrowness of the M and R, and in the design of the *g*. Paolo Manuzio of Venice had bought this type from France in 1558 for use in the books of the 'Accademia Veneziana', founded in 1556,[4] and it is found in very general use throughout Europe. In England the type lasted throughout the seventeenth century; it was used, for instance, for the main text of the folio editions of Burton's *Anatomy of Melancholy*. Manuzio had a Cicero roman of similar design, which is also found in the Acworth and with other London printers (cf. Isaac, op. cit., pl. 69). The italic used with this English roman by

[1] *The Correspondence of Matthew Parker*, Parker Society, 1853, p. 411.
[2] *Life of Parker*, vol. ii, pp. 178 and 525–6.
[3] *Typographical Antiquities*, i. 656.
[4] See Renouard, *Annales de l'Imprimerie des Aldes*, 1834, p. 270.

Day is the St. Augustin italic of Robert Granjon as shown on the Egenolff–Berner specimen sheet of 1592, which seems to have been cut about 1566. Finally in the same book we find another Granjon italic, the so-called 'Immortelle', a Long Primer also on the Egenolff sheet (cf. also Isaac, op. cit., pl. 73*b*). In Parker's great work, however, *De antiquitate Britannicæ ecclesiæ*, published the year before (1572), and supposed by some to have been printed by Day at a private press of the

Fig. 19. Portrait of John Day, 1562.

Archbishop's at Lambeth, the entire text, consisting of 524 pages, was in the Granjon English italic. The preface only to this work was in roman; the various titles and sub-titles being in the larger founts of Clerke's *Responsio* and the *Ælfredi Res Gestae*.

In addition to the characters already mentioned, Day had a good Greek letter. Alexander Nowell's *Christianæ pietatis prima institutio*, printed by him in 1578, is in a beautiful type, one of the copies of the French royal Greek types.

Among his further enterprises in letter-cutting may be mentioned the Hebrew words, cut in wood, which he used in Humphrey's *J. Juelli vita*, in 1573, and in Baro's *In Jonam Prophetam prælectiones*, in 1579; and the musical notes which he introduced into his editions of the metrical *Psalter*. These notes are chiefly lozenge-shaped and hollow, differing from those used by Grafton in 1550, in Merbecke's *Booke of Common Praier, noted* (*S. T. C.* 16441), which are mostly square and solid. He also, as he himself stated in a *Psalter* printed in 1572, 'caused a new print of note to be made, with letters to be joined to every note, whereby thou mayest know how to call every note by its right name'. Besides these, he made use of a considerable number of signs, mathematical and other, not before cast in type; while his works abound with handsome woodcut initials, vignettes, and portraits, besides a considerable variety of metal 'flowers'.

In Strype's *Life of Parker*, already quoted, is preserved an interesting account of Day's business, with which we close this short notice:

> And with the Archbishop's engravers, we may joyn his printer Day, who printed his *British Antiquities* and divers other books by his order . . . for whom the Archbishop had a particular kindness. . . . Day was more ingenious and industrious in his art and probably richer too, than the rest, and so became envied by the rest of his fraternity, who hindered, what they could, the sale of his books; and he had in the year 1572, upon his hands, to the value of two or three thousand pounds worth, a great summ in those days. But living under Aldersgate, an obscure corner of the city, he wanted a good vent for them. Whereupon his friends, who were the learned, procured him from the Dean and Chapter of St. Pauls, a lease of a little shop to be set up in St. Pauls Churchyard. Whereupon he got framed a neat handsome shop. It was but little and low, and flat-roofed and leaded like a terrace, railed and posted, fit for men to stand upon in any triumph or show; but could not in anywise hurt or deface the same. This cost him forty or fifty pounds. But . . . his brethren the booksellers envied him and by their interest got the mayor and aldermen to forbid him setting it up, though they had nothing to do there, but by power. Upon this the Archbishop brought his business before the Lord Treasurer, and interceded for him, that he would move the Queen to set her hand to certain letters that he had drawn up in the Queen's name to the city, in effect, that Day might be permitted to go forward with his building. Whereby, he said, his honour would deserve well of Christ's Church, and of the prince and State.—ii. 525–6.

Day died in 1584 at Saffron Walden in Essex, aged 62, and was buried at Bradley Parva. He was twice married and had twenty-two children.

Worman's *Alien Members of the Book-Trade* contains a few references to founders working in England, all relating to the second half of the century. There is one Antonius d'Anvillier, 'fusor typorum', 1562; Hubert D'Anvillier, 'caster of printing-letters', 1553–94; Amell de Groyter, 'letter-maker for printers', 1583 (there was an Aimée de Gruyter who worked for Plantin); Gabriel Guyett, 'letter-maker for printers', 1576–88 (perhaps a member of the family of the Netherlands founder François Guyot); Jerome Haultin, 'letter-caster for printers', 1574–85; a nephew of the founder Pierre Haultin of Paris and La Rochelle (there is a record of a sale of matrices by P. Haultin at La Rochelle to his nephew, dated 5 Feb. 1575[1]); Poll Rotteforde, 'founder of lettres for printers', 1571 (had been then in England for fourteen years); and Charles Tressell, 'a graver of letters for printers' and 'a carver to the printers (? wood-cutter)', 1571–83. Whether any of these men were independent founders or were employed in a particular printing-office is not known, nor whether any of them were engravers of punches.

[1] See G. Musset in the *Bulletin archéologique du Comité des travaux historiques et scientifiques*, Paris, 1889, pp. 202–4.

$\begin{bmatrix}4\end{bmatrix}$

LETTER-FOUNDING AS AN ENGLISH MECHANICAL TRADE 1477–1830

IT will be convenient, now that we have reached a point at which letter-founding enters upon a new stage as a distinct trade, to take a brief survey of its progress as a mechanical industry; availing ourselves of such records and illustrations as may be met with, to trace its development and improved appliances during the period covered by this narrative.

As has already been stated, the reticence of our first printers leaves us almost entirely in the dark as to the particular processes by which they produced their earliest types. Blades leans to the opinion that Caxton, in his first attempts at type-founding, adopted the methods of the rude Flemish or Dutch school, of whose conjectured appliances we have spoken in the introductory chapter. 'The English printers,' he says, 'whose practice seems to have been derived from the Flemish School, were far behind their contemporaries in the art. Their types show that a very rude process of founding was practised; and the use . . . of old types as patterns for new, evinces more of commercial expediency than of artistic ambition.'

At the same time there seems reasonable ground for inferring, from the peculiarities attending the re-casting of Caxton's type 4 as 4*, to which allusion has already been made, that at least as early as 1480 Caxton was possessed of the secret of the punch, and matrix and adjustable mould; while the excellent works of De Worde and his contemporaries demonstrate that, however rudely the art may have begun, England was, in the early years of the sixteenth century, abreast of many of her rivals as to the workmanship of her founts.

The frequent indications to be met with of the transmission of founts from one printer to another, as well as the passing on of worn types from the presses of the metropolis to those of the provinces, are suggestive of the existence (very limited, indeed) of some sort of home trade in type even at that early date. For a considerable time, moreover, after the perfection of the art in England, the trade in foreign types, which dated back as early as the establishment of printing in Westminster and Oxford, continued to flourish. With Normandy, especially, at the beginning of the sixteenth century, a brisk commerce was maintained. Not only were many of the English liturgical and law books printed abroad by Norman artists, but

Norman type found its way in considerable quantities into English presses. A. Claudin, whose researches in the history of the early provincial presses of France entitles him to be considered an authority on the matter, states that Rouen at the

Der Schrifftgiesser.

Ich geuß die Schrifft zu der Druckrey
Gemacht auß Wißmat/ Zin vnd Bley/
Die kan ich auch gerecht justiern/
Die Buchstaben zusammn ordniern
Lateinisch vnd Teutscher Geschrifft
Was auch die Griechisch Sprach antrifft
Mit Versalen/ Puncten vnd Zügn
Daß sie zu der Truckrey sich fügen.

E iij   Der

FIG. 20. From J. Amman's *Beschreibung aller Stände*, 1568.

beginning of the sixteenth century was the great typographical market which furnished type not to England only, but to other cities in France and to Switzerland. 'It evidently had special typographical foundries,' he observes. 'Richard Pynson, a London printer, was a Norman; Will Faques learned typography from J. le Bourgeois, a printer at Rouen. These two printers had types cast expressly for themselves in Normandy.'[1] And with regard to the first printer of Scotland, Claudin

---

[1] R. Dickson, *Introduction of the Art of Printing into Scotland.* Aberdeen, 1885. 8vo, Appendix.

has no doubt that Myllar learned his art in Normandy, and that the types with which his earliest work was printed were those of the Rouen printer, Hostingue. However, it should be added that many of the Rouen printers acquired types from Paris.

It is reasonable to suppose that English printers would endeavour, if possible, to provide themselves, not with types merely, but with matrices of the founts of their selections; and, indeed, we imagine some explanation of the marked superiority of our national typography at the close of the fifteenth century over that of a century later is to be found in the fact that whereas many of the first printers used types wholly cut and cast for them by expert foreign artists, their successors began first to cast for themselves from hired or purchased matrices, and finally to cut their own punches and justify their own matrices. Printing entered on a gloomy stage of its career in England after Day's time, and as State restrictions gradually hemmed it in, crushing by its monopolies healthy competition, and by its jealousy foreign succour, every printer became his own letter-founder, not because he would, but because he must, and the art suffered in consequence.

Of the operations of a sixteenth century letter foundry we are fortunately able to form some idea from the quaint engraving preserved to us by Jost Amman in his *Book of Trades*[1] in 1568. The picture represents the Frankfort founder seated at his small brick furnace, casting type in a mould. This mould differs from the modern hand-moulds in being pyramidical in shape and holding the matrix as a fixture in its interior. One of the moulds on the shelf shows a hole in the side into which the matrix was probably inserted. From the manner in which the caster is grasping the mould it would seem that it was bipartite and needed the two halves holding together during casting. The cast types lying in the bowl have 'breaks' attached to them, which at that date were in all probability cast so as to be easily detached. Behind the caster are some drawers, probably intended to contain matrices, of which one or two lie on the top waiting their turn for use. On the lower of the two shelves above the furnace are some crucibles in which the metals would be mixed before filling up the casting-pan. On the upper shelf, besides three more moulds, are some sieves, suggestive of the use of sand, either for moulding large letters or, as Blades suggests, for running the small ingots of metal into for use in the melting-pot. The small room in which this caster is operating in all probability formed part of a printing-office; and another interesting engraving of a still earlier date, 1545,[2] shows the two departments of the typographer's art going on in adjoining apart-

---

[1] *Eygentliche Beschreibung aller Stände und . . . Handwerker, Frankfurt*, 1568. 4to. *Der Schrifft-giesser.*

[2] The following sentence from T. C. Hansard's *Treatises on Printing and Typefounding*, Edinburgh, 1841, 8vo, p. 223, refers to the same woodcut: 'This evidence [of the process employed by the early letter-founders] is afforded us by the device of Badius Ascensius, an eminent printer of Paris and Lyon, in the beginning of the sixteenth century, and also by that of an English printer, Anthony Scoloker of Ippeswych, who modified and adopted the device of Ascensius, as indeed did many other printers of various countries. This curious design exhibits in one apartment the various processes of printing, the foreground presenting a press in full work, the background on the left the cases and the compositor, and on the right the foundery; the matrix and other appliances bearing a precise resemblance to those at present in use.' Hansard has here confused the matrix with the mould. We have to thank Mr. F. S. Ferguson for the information as to the origin of the cut. See also a reproduction in R. B. McKerrow's *An Introduction to Bibliography*, Oxford, 1927, p. 43. Chap. V of that book contains a detailed description of the mechanism of the early presses. On early representations of the printing press see F. Madan in *The Bodleian Quarterly Record*, iv, pp. 165–7.

ments. In this case, as in the Frankfort cut, the caster is sitting; but his mould, large as it is, appears to be furnished with a spring at the bottom, more like the later hand-moulds. The cut was first used by Jost Lamprecht at Ghent in a book by Cornelius van der Heyden and was later acquired by Scolaker of Ipswich.

FIG. 21. From C. v. d. Heyden, Ghent, 1545. Later the cut was used at Ipswich. Enlarged from 55 × 68 mm.

In the lines accompanying Amman's picture the founder is made to say that he casts types made of 'Bismuth, tin and lead', a statement which, if correct, shows that the Frankfort types of that day must have been cast in terribly soft metal, of about the substance and durability of modern solder. The presence of the crucibles, however, points to the use of some fourth metal, of sufficient hardness to require a violent heat to fuse it. The founder also states that he can correctly justify his letters, which may refer either to the dressing of the types after casting or the more important justification of the matrix to adapt it to the mould.

Another interesting memorial of a sixteenth-century foundry is to be met with in a visit to the once-famous printing-office of Christophe Plantin at Antwerp.[1] The foundry of the great Netherlands 'Archi-typographus', which is still preserved in its pristine condition, was on the upper floor of his house, and consisted of two rooms, one devoted wholly to the casting, the other being a storeroom for types awaiting use at the press. In the casting-room is still to be seen a large brick furnace covered with an earthenware slab. To the right of this is a smaller furnace, surmounted by the metal pot, which even yet contains some of the old type-alloy. On the walls hang tongs, ladles, knives, and moulds. In a box are preserved small parcels of pattern-types for setting the moulds by, among which the visitor is

---

[1] A description of this interesting establishment will be found in Max Rooses's *Le Musée Plantin-Moretus*, 1913, chap. xxiii.

shown three or four types of silver.[1] In another box are a large number of punches and moulds of all sizes. A bench extends along one side of the room, doubtless for the use of the dressers or rubbers.

In the *Dialogues françois pour les jeunes enfans*, Plantin, 1567, already referred to, there is a fairly detailed account of the process of type production, composition, and press-work. There is an even earlier one, though less detailed, in an Italian work first published in 1564, *Dello specchio di scientia* by Leonardo Fioravanti, Venice. The passage was quoted by Don C. Allen in 'Some Contemporary Accounts of Renaissance Printing Methods', *The Library*, vol. xvii, 1937, p. 167 seq., but from the edition of 1567. There was also an edition of 1572, and a French translation by Gabriel Chapuis, Paris, 1584. The same article mentions a similar work by a French author, Louis Le Roy's *De la vicissitude ou varieté de choses en l'univers*, Paris, 1579, and quotes the relevant passage from an English version made by Robert Ashley. The English translation was printed in London in 1594 under the title *Of the Interchangeable Course or Variety of Things*. This passage seems to be the earliest account in the English language of the process of punch-cutting.

In all these points we recognize that even in Plantin's day the general appointments of a letter foundry differed very little from those of the modern foundry before the introduction of machinery. Although we have no description of any English foundry before Moxon's time, we know that the processes in use among us boast a much earlier origin. Moxon described no new method, but the old-established practice which had obtained, if not from the infancy of the art, at least from the commencement of that gradual divorce between printing and letter-founding which led, about 1585, to the establishment of foundries for the public use. We have no reason to suppose that the foundries connected with the presses of Day, Wolfe, and others differed in practice from those of their Frankfort and Antwerp contemporaries, or that when, in 1597, Benjamin Sympson, a letter-founder, gave bond to the Stationers' Company not to cast type for the printers without due notice, he, or the founders who followed him, knew any other methods of producing their type than those already familiar to every printer at home and abroad.

Turning now to Moxon's account of English letter-founding as it was in his day,

---

The legend of the silver types has been a favourite one in the romance of typography. L. Giucciardini states in his *Descrittione di tutti i paesi bassi*, 1587, that Aldus Manutius was generally said to have used them; and Hulsemann describes the Bible printed by Robert Estienne in 1557 as *typis argenteis sanè elegantissimis*. The same extravagance was attributed to Plantin. Possibly the famous productions of these great artists impressed their readers with the notion that their beautiful and luxurious typography was the result of rare and costly material; and, ignoring the fact that silver type would not endure the press, they credited them with the absurdity of casting their letters in that costly material. It is difficult to believe that any practical printer, however magnificent, would make even his matrices of silver when copper would be equally good and more durable. Didot was said, as late as 1820, to have cast his new Script from steel matrices inlaid with silver. The use of the term 'silver' as a figurative mode of describing beautiful typography is not uncommon. Sir Henry Savile's Greek types, says Bagford, 'on account of their beauty were called the Silver types'. Field's Pearl Bible in 1653 has been spoken of as printed in silver types. Smith, in 1755, referred to the fiction, still credited, that 'the Dutch print with silver types'. On the other hand, we have the distinct mention in the inventory of John Baskett's printing-office at Oxford, in 1720, of 'a sett of Silver Initiall Letters', which we can hardly believe to be a purely poetic description, and probably referred to the coating of the face of the letter with a silver wash. It should be stated here that Ratdolt, the Venetian printer, in 1482 was reported to have printed one work in types of gold!

we find no lack of detail as to every branch of the art and every appliance in use by the artist. It is not our purpose here to follow these descriptions farther than as they give a general idea of the practice and method of letter-founding two centuries ago—a practice and method which, as we have said, existed long before his day, and were destined to be in common use for nearly a century and a half after. We shall best indicate the processes and appliances he describes by giving a brief analysis of that portion of his book which is devoted to the mechanics of letter-founding,[1] reserving for a later chapter a general summary of the complete work.

Naturally beginning with punch-cutting, he first describes in detail the various tools made use of by the engraver, viz. the forge, the using file, the flat gauge, the sliding gauges, the face gauges, the italic and other standing gauges, the liner, the flat table, the tach, and other furniture of the bench. Every one of these tools is to be found in the punch-cutter's room of the present day, scarcely changed in form or use from the woodcuts which illustrate Moxon's description.

Turning from the tools to the workman, Moxon next proceeds to describe his choice of steel for the punches; the making and striking of the counter-punches on the polished face of the punch; the 'graving and sculping' of the insides of the letters; together with certain rules in the use of the gravers, small files, &c., employed in this delicate operation.

With regard to the process described as counter-punching, it is necessary to admit that this constituted a refinement of the art of punch-cutting apparently unknown to the first printers. The freedom of their letters, consequent on the imitation of handwriting, which served as their earliest models, makes it evident that they cut by eye rather than by mathematical rule. But as typography gradually made models for itself, the best artists, particularly those who aimed at producing regular roman and italic letters, discovered the utility and expediency of arriving at uniformity in design and contour, by the use of these counter-punches, which stamped on to the steel the impress of the hollow portions of the letters they were about to cut, leaving it to the hand of the engraver to cut round these hollows the form of the required character.

The punches being cut, finished, and hardened, Moxon next deals with the various parts of the type-mould, describing in turn the 'Making' of the mould: The Carriage,[2] (a); the Body, (b); the Male Gauge, (c); the Mouthpiece, (d e); the Register, (f i); the Female Gauge, (g); the Hag, (h); the Bottom Plate, (a); the Wood, (b); the Mouth, (c); the Throat, (d); the Pallat, (e d); the Nick, (f); the Stool, (g); the Spring, (b).

Here again we have described, with scarcely a difference, the mould in which scores of men in the nineteenth century cast types for the trade. The justification of the mould is then described; after which the important operation of striking the steel punch into copper, and forming and justifying the matrix, is treated of, with instructions for 'botching' matrices in the event of a mistake in the latter process. The matrices being thus ready, the founder is instructed how to adjust them to the

---

[1] *Mechanick Exercises, or the Doctrine of Handy-Works applied to the Art of Printing*, vol. ii. London, 1683. 4to.

[2] The index-letters following each part refer to Moxon's illustration of a mould in the *Mechanick Exercises*, a reduced copy of which is placed by the artist of the *Universal Magazine*, 1750, at the foot of his View of the Interior of Caslon's Foundry.

mould in preparation for casting—a solemn process which may be best described in the writer's own language:

Wherefore, placing the under-half of the Mold in his left hand, with the Hook or Hag forward, he clutches the ends of its Wood between the lower part of the Ball of his Thumb and his three hind-Fingers. Then he lays the upper half of the Mold upon the under half, so as the Male-Gages may fall into the Female Gages, and at the same time the Foot of the Matrice place itself upon the Stool. And clasping his left-hand Thumb strong over the upper half of the Mold, he nimbly catches hold of the Bow or Spring with his right-hand Fingers at the top of it, and his Thumb under it, and places the point of it against the middle of the Notch in the backside of the Matrice, pressing it as well forwards towards the Mold, as downwards by the Sholder of the Notch close upon the Stool, while at the same time with his hinder-Fingers as aforesaid, he draws the under half of the Mold towards the Ball of his Thumb, and thrusts by the Ball of his Thumb the upper part towards his Fingers, that both the Registers of the Mold may press against both sides of the Matrice, and his Thumb and Fingers press both Halves of the Mold close together. Then he takes the Handle of the Ladle in his right Hand, and with the Boll of it gives a Stroak two or three outwards upon the Surface of the Melted Mettal to scum or cleer it from the Film or Dust that may swim upon it. Then he takes up the Ladle full of Mettal, and having his Mold as aforesaid in his left hand, he a little twists the left side of his Body from the Furnace, and brings the Geat of his Ladle, (full of Mettal) to the Mouth of the Mold, and twists the upper part of his right-hand towards him to turn the Mettal into it, while at the same moment of Time he Jilts the Mold in his left hand forwards to receive the Mettal with a strong Shake (as it is call'd) not only into the Bodies of the Mold, but while the Mettal is yet hot, running swift and strongly into the very Face of the Matrice to receive its perfect Form there as well as in the Shanck.

This done, the mould is opened and the type released, Moxon adding that a workman will ordinarily cast 4,000 such letters in a day.

Then follow rules to be observed in breaking off, rubbing, kerning, setting-up, and dressing, with descriptions of the dressing-sticks, block-groove, hook, knife, and 'plow'. That these operations, as well as the casting, had undergone no alteration nearly a century after Moxon's day may be judged from the fact that Moxon's descriptions are used verbatim to accompany the view of the interior of Caslon's foundry shown in the *Universal Magazine* of 1750, where all these operations are exhibited in active progress.

With regard to the preparation of the type-metal, Moxon's account is minute and a trifle peculiar. This metal was, according to his account, made of lead hardened with iron.[1] Stub-nails were chosen as the best form of iron to melt, and the mixture was made with the assistance of antimony, of which an equal amount with the iron was added to the lead, in the proportion of 3 lb. of iron to 25 lb. of lead. The great heat required to melt the iron necessitated open furnaces of brick, built out of doors, in a broad, open place, well exposed to the wind, into which the iron and antimony mixture was put in pots surrounded with charcoal. After half an hour's time the metal men were to 'lay their Ears near the Ground and listen to hear a Bubling in the Pots', which is the sign that the iron is melted. They then were to erect another small furnace, 'on that side from whence the Wind blows',

---

[1] Iron does not appear to have continued much longer as a staple ingredient of English type-metal. There was, however, no rule as to the composition of the alloy. The French type-metal at the beginning of the eighteenth century was notoriously bad, and drove many printers to Frankfort for their types, where they used a very hard composition of steel, iron, copper, brass, tin, and lead.

which was to contain the large pot full of lead. The lead being melted, they were to carry it at a great heat, with a 'Labour would make Hercules sweat', to the open furnace, filling up the pots of iron and antimony with the lead, and stirring at the same time. The open furnace was to be then demolished, and the mixed metal left to cool in the pots. And 'now', says Moxon, '(according to Custom), is Half a Pint of Sack mingled with Sallad Oyl provided for each Workman to Drink; intended for an Antidote against the Poysonous Fumes of the Antimony, and to restore the Spirits that so Violent a Fire and Hard Labour may have exhausted'.

Such is a brief account of the practice of typefounding in Moxon's time. Of the trade customs of the day our author also presents us with a curious picture, in his account of the Chapel.

A Founding-House [he says] is also call'd a Chappel: but I suppose the Title was originally assum'd by Founders to make a Competition with Printers. The Customes used in a Founding-House are made as near as may be those of a Printing-House; but because the Matter they Work on and the manner of their Working is different, therefore such different Customes are in Use as are suitable to their Trade, as:

    First, To call Mettle Lead, a Forfeiture.
    Secondly, A Workman to let fall his Mold, a Forfeiture.
    Thirdly, A Workman to leave his Ladle in the Mettle Noon or Night, a Forfeiture.

We are given to understand that in the case of other offences, common to both printing and typefounding, such as swearing, fighting, drunkenness, abusive language, or giving the lie in the chapel, or the equally heinous offence of leaving a candle burning at night, the journeyman founder was liable to be 'solaced' by his fellow workmen, in the same hearty and energetic way which characterized the administration of justice among the printers.

After Moxon's time we meet with numerous accounts of foundries and their appointments. The interesting inventory of the Oxford foundry, appended to the specimen of the press in 1693, gives a good idea of the extent of that establishment. There were apparently two casters, two rubbers, and two or three dressers, and the foundry possessed twenty-eight moulds. The punches were sealed up in an earthen pot, possibly to protect them from rust or injury; or possibly because, having once served their purpose in striking the matrices, they were put aside as of little or no use. The small value put upon punches after striking is constantly apparent about this period. Very few punches came down with the foundries which were absorbed by that of John James; and of those that did, the greater portion were left to take their chance among the waste as worthless. The small value set upon the punches of Walpergen's music, in the inventory of his plant,[1] shows that they were considered the least important of his belongings. Matrices did not wear out in the old days of hand-moulds and soft metal, as they do now under steam machines and 'extra hard'; but the liability to loss or damage, and the importance of protecting and preserving the steel originals of their types, can hardly have been less with the founders of two centuries ago than it is to-day.

The entertaining letters of Thomas James from Holland, in 1710,[2] point to a curious practice in that country which we believe has never obtained in this. We

[1] See pp. 203, 204.   [2] See p. 209.

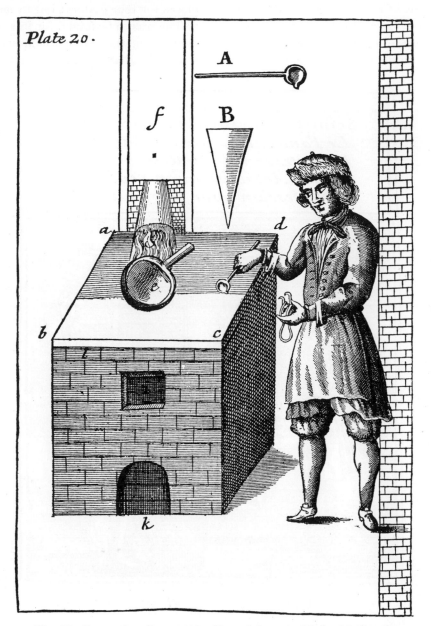

Fig. 22. Letter-founding, 1683. From Moxon's *Mechanick Exercises*.

refer to the habit of lending casters and matrices by one founder to another. In each of the two foundries he visited there were places for four casters; but in one case only one man was at work, and in the other no one was to be found, for this reason. This system of interchange is hardly consistent with the jealousy and suspicion shown by the same Dutch founders towards their English rival in his endeavours

Ecce Typis additn on parvum Fusor honorem
Scilicet ut niteant, splendida Signa facit,
Le Fondeur donne au Caractere
La justesse et la netteté :
Par son Art il fait qu'on revere
L'Impression pour sa beauté. Thib

FIG. 23. From Thiboust's *Typographiae excellentia*, 1718.
Enlarged from 79 × 60 mm.

to procure sets of matrices from their punches. In this endeavour, however, he succeeded, much to his own satisfaction. He also purchased moulds, which, like all the other Dutch moulds he saw, were made of brass. Voskens's foundry, which he visited, appears to have been 'a great business, having five or six men constantly at the furnace, besides boys to rub, and himself and a brother to do the other work'. He also found artists who, like Cupy and Rolu, were punch-cutters only, not attached to any one foundry, but doing work for founders generally. The Voskens at this time did their own casting, but their punches and matrices were supplied them by Rolu, who, as an independent artist, was free to sell duplicate matrices of his letters to James. This division of letter-founding into one or more trades, though common abroad, was never a common practice in England, where jealousy and lack of enterprise conspired to keep each founder's business a mystery known only to himself.[1]

In the course of this book we shall have constant occasion to point out the intimate relations which existed at the beginning of the eighteenth century between English printers and Dutch founders. There was probably more Dutch type in England between 1700 and 1720 than there was English. The Dutch artists appeared for the time to have the secret of the true shape of the roman letter; their punches were more carefully finished, their matrices better justified, and their types of better metal and better dressed, than any of which our country could boast. Nor was it till Caslon developed a native genius that English typography ceased to be more than half Dutch.

Thiboust's quaint Latin poem on the excellence of printing,[2] though throwing little new light on the practice of the art, is worth recording here, not only for the description it gives of letter-founding in France at the time, but for the sake of the curious engraving which accompanies it. The latter represents a round furnace in the centre of a room, surmounted by a metal pot, at which two casters are standing, with ladle and mould in hand. The moulds, of which a number are to be seen in a rack against the wall, are almost cubic in shape, and apparently without the hooks shown in Moxon's illustration. One of the casters is holding his mould low, as in the act of casting. A workman sitting on a stool is setting up in a stick the newly cast type from a box on the floor—possibly breaking them off at the same time. Beyond is a dresser grooving out the break in a stick of types.

Of the portion of the poem devoted to letter-founding[3] we venture to give the following rough translation:

> The founder see, whose molten metal glows
> Above the blazing furnace. From the pot
> His ladle nimbly feeds the curious mould,
> Whence straight the type in perfect fashion falls.
> The willing servant, he, of all the Schools,
> Whether in Latin they would write, or Greek,
> Or in the Hebrew tongue their minds disclose,

[1] Psalmanazar, in referring to Samuel Palmer's projected second part to his *History of Printing*, which should describe all the branches of the trade, says that this project, 'though but then as it were in embryo, met with such early and strenuous opposition from the respective bodies of letter-founders, printers and bookbinders, under an ill-grounded apprehension that the discovery of the mystery of those arts, especially the two first, would render them cheap and contemptible . . . that he was forced to set it aside' (Psalmanazar's *Memoirs*, 1764, pp. 284–5).

[2] *Typographiae Excellentia. Carmen notis Gallicis illustratum à C. L. Thiboust, Fusore-Typographo-Bibliopôlâ*, Paris, 1718. 8vo.

[3] 'LIQUATOR.

'Ecce Liquator adest; en crebris ignibus ardet
Ejus materies; praebet Cochleare, Catillum
Et Formas queis mixto ex aere fideliter omnes
Conflat Litterulas; Hic paret sponte Peritis,
Sive Latina velint conscribere, Graecáve dicta;
Sive suam exoptent Hebraeâ dicere mentem
Linguâ, seu cupiant Germanica verba referre,
Cunctas ille suâ fabricabitur arte figuras.
Cernis quâ fiat cum dexteritate character
Singulus Archetypo, quod format splendida signa,
Cum mollis fuerit solers industria scalpri.
Illum opus est fusi digito resecare metalli
Quod superest, Ferulisque Typos componere lêves,
Ut queat exaequans illos Runcina parare.
Sed solet esse gravis nimiis ardoribus aestus.'

Or in the German. He, for all prepared,
Skilful, for each his character provides.
See with what art the several types are cast,
Each from its parent matrix; see how bright,
Trimmed by the dresser's cunning knife, they lie.
He the redundant metal first breaks off,
Then on the stick in order sets the type,
And with his plane their equal height assures.
Such is the founder's craft, whose arduous round
Of toil 'midst ardent heats is daily found.

In Gessner's *Buchdruckerkunst*, Leipzig, 1740/1, vol. i, p. 130, there are illustrations of various founders' tools, and on the frontispiece of vol. iii a caster is represented with an almost round mould, with long hooks. The interior of another German foundry is shown on the frontispiece to vol. ii of Täubel's *Allgemeines Wörterbuch der Buchdruckerkunst*, Vienna, 1805. In the same volume there is a plate of a mould, &c.

A still more satisfactory view of an eighteenth-century foundry is to be found in the *Universal Magazine* of 1750. This engraving represents the interior of Caslon's foundry, with the processes of casting, breaking-off, rubbing, setting-up, and dressing, all in operation. The casting is specially interesting in the light of Moxon's graphic account of the attitudes and contortions of the caster. Unlike their French brethren, each of Caslon's casters stands partitioned off from his neighbour, with a furnace and pan to himself. One of them is dipping his ladle in the pot for a new cast; the next holds his mould lowered, at the commencement of a 'pour'; the third has evidently completed the upward jerk necessary to force the metal into the matrix; and the fourth, with his mould again lowered, is apparently throwing out the type and preparing for the next casting. (See the Frontispiece.)

A set of three views of the interior of a French foundry, from Diderot's *Encyclopédie*,[1] 1762–72, presents a few interesting points of contrast between foreign and English methods. In the first view the process of punch-cutting is displayed.[2] One man is finishing a punch with his file; another is striking a counter-punch (with perhaps undue energy) into the steel face of a punch; while the third, at a large forge, is hammering a piece of steel in readiness for the engraver. The second view shows metal-making, casting, breaking-off, and rubbing in operation. There are two men at the large furnace, one watching the melting of antimony in a crucible, the other pouring off the mixed metal into ingots. At the small metal pot with three divisions, in the centre of the room, are three casters, one of whom is about to cast, another has finished his 'throw', and the third is loosening his spring so as to open the mould. At the table in the rear sit two girls, one breaking off, the other rubbing. The third view represents a dressing-room, where a girl is setting up the rubbed types on a stick. The dresser is ploughing the 'break' from the foot of a

---

[1] *Recueil de planches*, tom. ii, pl. 1. *Fonderie en caractères de l'Imprimerie.* 4 pp., and 4 pp. of plates. Fol.

[2] Smith (*Printers' Grammar*, p. 8) blames the French founders of his day for the shallow cut of their punches, which being naturally reproduced in the types, was the cause of much bad printing. Some sorts, he said, as late as 1755, only stood in relief to the thickness of an ordinary sheet of paper. He contrasts English punch-cutting favourably with French in this particular. But, on the other hand, see Breitkopf in his *Nachricht von der Stempelschneiderey*, 1777, who, in defending Fournier against Fleischman, says there is no point in these deep-cut punches. If the matrices are struck too deep, the operation of casting will be rendered more difficult.

stick of types, which is placed in the blocks, not lengthways along the bench, but across it. An apprentice sitting at the table completes the dressing, holding one end of the stick tilted while he passes his scraper over the front and back of the row of types. Drawings of all the tools and parts of tools used in typefounding complete the illustration.

Fournier, in 1764, devoted the latter part of vol. i of his *Manuel Typographique*[1] to the appliances and instruments used in type-casting. His work enters in detail into the form and use of every tool used in every department of the trade, from the cutting of the punch to the storage of the finished types, giving careful and accurate engravings of each. Allowing for a few national peculiarities, and certain improvements in casting, there is scarcely anything but the date of the book to distinguish it from a mechanical handbook to typefounding in the middle of the nineteenth century.

The operations of punch-cutting and justifying appear to have been kept a mystery from the earliest days of the trade. To lay minds the one work of the founder was to cast types, but the preliminary operations on which his whole reputation as a founder depended were little understood by any but the founder himself. And even he, as in the case of the first two Caslons, carried on this part of the mystery stealthily, and with closed doors even against his own apprentices. In many cases, especially with the originators of the great foundries, Caslon, Cottrell, and Jackson, it was the master himself who designed and cut his own punches. It was not till the unusual demand for artists at the close of the eighteenth century broke down this exclusiveness that outsiders arose to work for the trade in general. And even these it was the policy and endeavour of each founder to attach to himself, treating him as a gentleman at large, and free from the obligations imposed on his other workmen.

The Rules and Regulations of Thorne's Foundry, printed about the year 1806, give an interesting glimpse into the internal economy of a foundry of that period. After fixing the prices to be paid for work (for casting, rubbing, and kerning were all paid by 'piece'), they provide that the dressers shall have 25s. a week, 'abiding by the old custom of leaving work at four o'clock on Mondays. Each man to dress after four casters.' The fines for 'foot-ale' imposed on new hands are ordered to be deposited with the master, who is to keep an account of the same and divide it equally among the men at Christmas. The foundry hours are from six in the morning to eight in the evening in summer, and from seven to eight in winter, 'beginning when candle-light commences'. The dressers are to work from seven to eight in summer, and eight to eight in winter. Any man losing or damaging a mould, matrix, or tool, to make good the loss on the following Saturday. Any man leaving his lamp or candle alight after hours is to pay 6d., and the master for a similar offence is to fine himself 1s. Rubbers must grind their stones once a fortnight, 'if requested to do so either by the master or foreman'. No work to be taken out of the foundry. Casters and rubbers must take their turn at carrying in metal. Breaking-off and setting-up boys shall earn 10d. a week for each man they set-up after. Many of these customs are traditional, and survived throughout the nineteenth century.

---

[1] *Manuel typographique, utile aux gens de lettres,* Paris, 1764–6, 2 tom. 8vo. Mr. Harry Carter published a translation of vol. 1 of the *Manuel*, with valuable notes, in 1930.

Conservatism, indeed, has been a marked feature in the history of British letter-founding. Between 1637 and 1837 the number of important foundries rarely exceeded the limit prescribed by the Star Chamber decree of the former year. The methods and practice of the art, as we have seen, remained virtually unchanged during the whole period. The traditional customs, the trade *argot*, the relations of men to men, and men to masters, even the tricks and gestures of the caster, suffered nothing by the lapse of two centuries. The relations of the founders among themselves during the period underwent more vicissitudes. At all times jealous of their mystery, they mistrusted in turn the printers and one another. As the new school of Caslon and his apprentices rose up to oust the old Dutch school of James, mutual antagonism was the order of the day. The literary duel between the Caslons and the Frys was perhaps the least injurious outcome of this spirit. This antagonism resolved itself, at the close of the eighteenth century, into a combination of London founders against their rising Scottish competitors. An Association was formed in 1793, which continued for three years. In 1799 it was re-formed, and this time lasted four years; and again in 1809 it was revived and continued till 1820, when it terminated. In the early days of this Association the lady Caslons took a prominent part in its deliberations, which, however, frequently consisted of little more than the imposition of fines for non-attendance. The prices of type during this period, chiefly owing to the fluctuations in the value of metals during the French war, were constantly changing. Pica in 1793 was 1*s*. 1½*d*. a pound, in 1800 1*s*. 4*d*., in 1810 3*s*., and in 1816 (after the price of antimony had gone down from £400 to £200 a ton), 2*s*. The Scottish founders, however, joined presently by the Sheffield houses, continued to underbid the London founders in their own market; and at one time a combination of all the English houses existed in opposition to the unfortunate new foundry of the Frenchman, Pouchée.

Before concluding this outline of the progress of letter-founding as a mechanical trade, it will be interesting to notice the gradual changes in the process of casting which led to the final abandonment of the venerable hand-mould in favour of machinery.

We cannot do better than give a brief summary from the Patent Book[1] of the chief improvements proposed to be made in typefounding prior to 1830, premissing that many of the schemes advanced no farther than the proposal, and that some of the most important improvements which actually did take place were not registered in the Patent Book at all.

1790. WILLIAM NICHOLSON (of New North St., Red Lion Square) proposed to cast type in the usual manner, except that instead of leaving a space in the mould for the stem of the letter only, several letters are cast at once in ordinary moulds, communicating by a common groove at the top. The types are also to be scraped in dressing, so as to render the tail of the letter gradually smaller the more remote it is from the face; thus enabling them to be set imposed upon a cylindrical surface.[2]

1790. ROBERT BARCLAY (the brewer, of Southwark). A method of making punches on

---

[1] *Patents for Inventions.—Abridgments of Specifications relating to Printing*, 1617 to 1857, London, 1859. 8vo.

[2] A fuller account, with a plate, of Nicholson's invention is given in the *Repository of Arts*, vol. v,

pp. 145–70. See also W. Savage's *Dictionary*, where under the article 'Machines' there is an appreciation of Nicholson. He was a chemist and editor of *The Journal of National Philosophy*.

broken steel, the irregular figures in the grain of which will effectually obviate counterfeit. Punches may be formed of steel broken as above, by cutting, drilling, punching, bending parts of the letters, and leaving the grain of the steel to form the lines or strokes; and in this way complex founts of type might be cast, every letter of which would vary in its lines from every other.

1802. PHILIP RUSHER.[1] Improvements in the form of printing types. Each capital letter, with few exceptions, should be comprised in the compass of an oval. Each small letter is to be without tail-piece or descender, and the metal (both in small letters and capitals) is to extend no lower than the body of the letter. The letters above the line have their heads shortened or lowered about one-third.

1806. ANTHONY FRANCIS BERTE. A machine for casting type. The casting is performed by applying the mould to one of several apertures in the side of the metal pot, through which, by the removal of a lock or valve, the metal is made suddenly to flow into the mould with a force proportionate to the height of the surface of the type-metal in the vessel.[2]

1806. ELIHU WHITE.[3] A machine for casting types; consisting of a matrix-box containing a certain number of matrices, which is applied to a complex mould having a similar number of apertures, through which the metal is poured, thus forming several types at one operation.

1807. ANTHONY FRANCIS BERTE. Improvements on his former patent. The metal is forced through the aperture by means of a plug or piston, and the machine is so contrived as to regulate the quantity of metal ejected at each application of the mould.

Another improvement consists of making the body of the mould in four adjustable pieces instead of two, which will admit of changes in the body, as well as the thickness of the types. The moulds are without nicks,[4] and the type, when cast, is expelled by a punch or other tool, without opening the mould.

1809. JOHN PEEK. A machine for the more expeditious casting of types, by which three motions out of the five ordinarily made use of in casting are saved. This consists in the addition of two parts to the ordinary hand-mould, that to the upper part being a plate with a socket in which the matrix is suspended on pivots, and that to the lower part being a bolt which presses the matrix to the mould, where it is kept by a spiral spring round the bolt, and by the withdrawal of which the matrix is tilted, another spiral spring keeping it in that position till the mould recloses. The bolt is worked by a lever.

1812. WILLIAM CASLON. An improved printing type. The face or letter part of the type is made of the usual thickness and in the usual way, 'but the body, which is commonly made about seven-eighths of an inch, I make only three-sixteenths of an inch in thickness; and the front of the said body I make sloping or bevelling upwards from the outer side towards the face, as well as the opposite side or back, by which means the upper part of the body is about one-eighth of an inch narrower than the under part of the same.' These short types are raised to the requisite height to paper by stands of the necessary thickness. 'Or the

---

[1] This misguided reformer lived at Banbury, where, in 1804, he printed an edition of *Rasselas*, 8vo, in his 'improved' types. The result is more curious than beautiful, and the public remained loyal still to the alphabets of Aldus, Elzevir, Caslon, Baskerville, and Bodoni. Nevertheless, Rusher's edition of *Rasselas*, 'printed with patent types in a manner never before attempted', will always claim a place among typographical curiosities.

[2] This is apparently the first suggestion in England of the 'hand-pump', which was subsequently adopted by all the founders, and formed, in combination with the lever-mould, the intermediate stage between hand and machine casting. Berte was a merchant living at St. Dunstan's West. See also the *Repository of Arts*, 2nd ser., vol. xi, pp. 241–5.

[3] White's address is given as Threadneedle St., but he is the American who started a foundry in New York in 1810. See also the *Repository of Arts* 2nd ser., vol. xi, p. 97, with plate.

[4] The origin of type-nicks is doubtful. Some have considered them to have resulted from a modification of the old alleged system of perforation, and to have been intended as a receptacle for the wire or string used to bind the lines together. The types of the first printers were certainly without them, and as late as 1540 French moulds had none. A nick forms part of Moxon's moulds in 1683. In French founding the nick is at the back of the type, while in England it is always on the front. In Fournier's day the Lyonnese types were an exception to the general French rule, and had the nick on the front, as also did the types of Germany, Holland, and Flanders. Some of the old founts procured abroad by English founders were struck in the copper inverted, so that when cast in English moulds they have always had the nick at the back.

body may, without being bevelled, be fixed by nails or otherwise, upon blocks of wood of a proper width and height. Or the stands may be made of the whole width of the body of the type, with only one projecting part, the other being screwed on after the types are put on the stands. The advantage of these types is in economy of weight and space; the former being one-half, and the latter one-third to one-half of the ordinary types.'

1814. Ambroise Firmin Didot. An improvement in the method of making types. In roman text, running hand or any other hand consisting more or less in hair strokes or fine lines, from letter to letter, the projecting extremities of each letter are extended so as to form a join with the next. In the case of inclined letters 'I do, by suitable alteration in my moulds, cast my types and the beards and shanks or tails thereof with the same or nearly the same inclination or slope of surface as aforesaid; and to prevent such types sliding upon each other when set up, a protuberance or projecting part is cast on one face, and a cavity or indentation corresponding to it in the opposite one; or otherwise I do, by angular or curved deviations from, in, or as to the straight direction of the said surfaces, render it impossible that any sliding should take place between the same.'

1816. Robert Clayton (an artist, of Dublin). A new method of preparing metal . . . types. The specification mainly relates to plate-printing, but concludes: 'Thirdly, I obtain what I shall term alto or high-relief, by producing metal castings from wooden moulds or matrices, punched in wood with a cross-grain, which has been previously slightly charred or baked.'[1] The metal is bismuth, tin, and lead in equal parts, or tin (4), bismuth (4), lead (3), and antimony (1).

1822. William Church. Machine for casting the types and arranging them ready to be transferred to the composing machinery. A matrix-bar containing a series of matrices is applied to a mould-bar, with a corresponding number of moulds. At the time of casting the latter is applied to jets leading from the metal chest, which is supplied from a metal fountain connected with the metal pot, and furnished with a valve to prevent the return of the metal. After the casting, the mould-bar, drawn endways, cuts off communication with the metal, and brings the said types beneath a series of punches, which descend and force them out at the same time that the matrix-box is unlocked, and descends clear of the types. . . . The mould-bar is kept cool during the process by a stream of water passing through it. . . . The metal is injected by the descent of a plunger into the metal chest. The type, as cast, is carried direct into a composing machine, where it is set up by means of a mechanism worked by keys, resembling the notes of a piano.[2] There is an illustration of this machine in Legros and Grant, *Typographical Printing Surfaces*, p. 321.

1823. Louis John Pouchée[3] (communicated by Didot of Paris). Machine calculated to cast from 150 to 200 types at each operation, the operation being repeated twice or oftener in a minute. The moulds are composed of steel bars. The first has horizontal grooves at right angles to its length, and forms the body of the letter. The second is a matrix-bar, screwed to the bottom of the first. The third bar forms the fourth side of the type-body. The feet of the type are made by the fourth, a 'break bar', with orifices communicating with each type-mould. Two of these moulds are placed side by side so as to form a trough between them, in which the molten metal is poured, nearly as high as the orifices on the 'break bar'. On pulling a trigger by a string, a plunger at the end of a lever falls into the trough, and injects the metal into the moulds. The lever is slightly raised after the casting, by a treadle, after which the workman raises it by hand until it passes a catch, which retains it until the string is pulled again. The mould is then unclamped, the mould-bars drawn asunder by wrenches, the types are found adhering to the break bar like the teeth of a comb, when they are broken off and dressed in the usual way.

---

[1] Clayton issued a pamphlet printed from plates produced by this process.

[2] It was calculated that 75,000 types could be produced by two men in an hour. Dr. Church was an American, at this time living in Nelson Square, Southwark. See the *London Journal of Arts*, vol. iv,

pp. 199, 200.

[3] See below, pp. 355, 356. Prior to Pouchée's introduction of this system of casting into England, Hansard informs us, the younger Henry Caslon made trial of it, but it was not found practicable.

1823. JOHN HENFREY AND AUGUSTUS APPLEGATH.[1] Certain machinery for casting types. The type is cast in a space between two flanges, set at right angles on a spindle, and pressed to and drawn from one another alternately by a spring and a peculiarly arranged eccentric piece. A piece of steel, called the 'body', adjustable to the thickness of the particular type, is screwed to one of the flanges. The matrix is on a carriage, and is run through holes in the flanges for the casting, and kept in its place by a spring. The metal is injected by the descent of a plunger, which recovers itself by a spring. After the casting the spindle begins to revolve, immediately upon which the matrix is disengaged from the type and withdrawn clear of the flanges. The flanges are then opened, and the cast type pushed from the mould by the action of spring pins. A type is thus cast for each revolution of the spindle. The 'break' is disengaged from the letter by two small pins, one of which protrudes from each jaw after the casting.

1828. THOMAS ASPINWALL (of Bishopsgate Churchyard). An improved method of casting types, by means of a 'Mechanical Type Caster'. The working parts of this machine are mounted on a table suspended so as to move to and from the melting-pot. The mould is in two parts, mounted on two sliding 'carrier pieces' on the table, inclined to each other at a slight angle. The matrix is held during the casting by a spring. On the revolution of the crank shaft (by hand) a sliding rod on the table is made to move towards the melting-pot, and the carrier pieces being acted upon by a cross-bar attached to it by springs, are drawn forward so as to unite the two parts of the mould for the casting. By a further revolution of the crank shaft, a projecting piece on the end of the sliding rod, coming in contact with an adjusting screw on one end of a bent lever, causes it to turn on its centre, and by a friction roller at the other end forces down the plunger of a cylinder communicating with the metal pot, so as to inject the metal into a chamber, whence it ejects a portion previously there through a nozzle into the mould as it is moved forward by the forward motion of the table. The handle of the crank is then turned the reverse way, the table swings back from the metal pot, the plunger rises by a spring, the parts of the mould separate, the matrix is withdrawn from the cast type by a lever (which overcomes the force of the spring by which it is held during the casting), and the type itself loosened from the mould by coming in contact with an inclined plane.[2]

We conclude these extracts with a proposal suggestive more of the primitive experiments of the first printers than of nineteenth century letter-founding.

1831. JAMES THOMSON (of Spencer St., Goswell Rd.). Certain improvements in making or producing printing types. 'My improvements consist in making printing types by casting or forming a cake of metal having letters formed and protruding on one side of it, and in afterwards sawing this cake directly or transversely, so as to divide it into single types.' The casting is effected in two ways. First by forming a mould from types set up, and immersing this within an iron box in a pot of melted type-metal, 'as in making stereotype plates; with this difference, however, that in the present case, the plate must be as thick as the length of the intended type; and further, that in setting up the types for the cast, proper spaces must be made between each letter and between the lines, in order to allow for what will be taken away in the sawing.' The second mode is 'by taking a plate of copper or other suitable metal, and making in it indentations or matrices with a punch having on it the letter for the intended type, taking care to make them in straight rows, direct and transverse. The plate being so indented, is put into an iron box and immersed in a pot of liquid type-metal, and kept there the proper depth and proper time, so as to enable the metal fully to enter into those indentations or matrices, that the letter may be well formed. The cake thus cast or formed, after being taken out and cooled, is sawed as before.'[3]

---

[1] Henfrey was an engineer of Waterloo Rd. and Applegath a printer in Duke St., Stamford St. On this machine, see the *London Journal of Arts*, vol. viii, p. 169, with plate. Applegath is the well-known builder of newspaper printing machines. Cf. the article in Bigmore and Wyman's *Bibliography*

of Printing.
[2] On this patent, see also *London Journal of Arts*, 2nd ser., vol. v, p. 212, with plate.
[3] For further notes on 19th-century inventions see below, pp. 360–4.

I

⌈5⌉

THE STATE CONTROL OF ENGLISH
LETTER-FOUNDING

O UR Statute Books and Public Records do not throw any very important light on the early history of English letter-founding. Although a busy import trade in type appears to have been maintained by the earliest printers, and although as early as the days of De Worde there were English printers who not only cast types for themselves but are supposed to have supplied them to others, we search in vain for any definite reference to letter-founding in the decrees and proclamations which, prior to 1637, had for their object the regulation or repression of printing. It is true that the term printing was at that period wide enough to cover all its tributary arts, from paper-making to book-selling. At the same time, it is noteworthy that, whereas in many of the early decrees paper-making, book-binding, and book-selling are distinctly mentioned, letter-founding is invariably ignored. If any inference is to be drawn from this fact, it is that type was one of the latest of the printer's commodities to go into the public market. A printer's type was his own and no one else's; and if occasionally one great printer was pleased to part with founts of his letter to his brother craftsmen, either by favour or for a consideration, it was not till late in the day—that is, not for about a century after the introduction of printing into England —that English-cast types became marketable ware in the country.

It is not our purpose here to review in detail the various decrees and proclamations which regulated printing in this country,[1] but it will be interesting to notice such of them as appear to have special reference to letter-founding.

The earliest Statute relating to printing was made in 1483, before the art had well taken root in the country, and proclaimed free trade in all printed matter imported from abroad. In 1533 this enactment was repealed, on the ground that 'at this day there be within this realm a great number of cunning and expert in the said science or craft of printing'.[2]

---

[1] The reader is referred to the concise summary given under the title 'Parliamentary Papers', in Bigmore and Wyman's *Bibliography of Printing*, also to the *Abridgments of Specifications relating to Printing, 1617 to 1857*, published by the Commissioners of Patents in 1859, and for more minute particulars to Arber's *Transcript of the Registers of the Stationers' Company*, *The Records of the Court of the Stationers' Company*, edited by W. W. Greg and E. Boswell, Bibliographical Society, London, 1930, and the *Calendars of Domestic State Papers*.

[2] Notwithstanding this flattering announcement, we find that five years later Grafton and Whitchurch, who held the King's Bible patent, received the royal permission to print the revised edition of Matthews's Bible in Paris, 'because at that time there were in France better printers and paper than could be had here in England'. The project, as history records, was cut short by the Sorbonne; but the presses, types, and workmen were with great difficulty brought over from Paris to London, where the Bible was finished in 1539.

More direct control was assumed in 1556, when the charter was granted to the Stationers' Company, constituting that body the 'Master and Keepers, or Wardens and Commonalty, of the Mystery or Art of a Stationer of the City of London'.[1] Under this comprehensive term, there is little doubt, founders of type, had any at that time been practising in London, would be included; and such being the case, it would become necessary for them as well as for paper-makers, printers, binders, booksellers, and others, to become members of the Stationers' Company, and subsequently, in compliance with the enlarged powers conferred on the Company in 1559 and 1586, to give surety to that body for the due observance of the ordinances by virtue of which they held their privileges.

The powers conferred on the Company by its charter related exclusively to the publication of printed matter; and the rights of search granted in the subsequent Acts confirming the charter appear to have been directed rather against the possession of smuggled or illegally printed books than against the possession of the materials necessary to produce them.

In 1582 was tried a celebrated lawsuit known as the Star Chamber case of John Day *versus* Roger Ward and William Holmes, for illegal printing of an *A B C* and *Catechism*.[2] In the course of the inquiry occurs an interesting reference to the practice of printers as their own letter-founders, which we reproduce as being one of the earliest direct notices of letter-founding in the Public Records. Amongst the questions put to the recalcitrant Roger Ward[3] the following three were intended to discover whether the illicit *A B C* was printed by him in his own type, or whether (with a view to remove suspicion from himself) he had printed it in the type of another printer:

QUESTION XIII. Did any person or personns Ayde help or assist you with paper letters (*type*) or other necessaries in this work?

ANSWER. He was not with paper letters (*type*) or other necessaryes in the said worke aidyd holpen or assistyd by any manner of personne or persons but that one Adam a Servant of Master Purfo(o)ttes dyd lend him some letters wherewith he imprinted the said boke.

QUESTION XVIII. Whether were the Letters wherewith you imprinted the sayd *A B C* your owne yea or no? If not whose were they and by what meanse came you by them, And whether with the Consent of the owner or not? And whether have you redelivered them back againe and how long since, And what nomber of Reames did you imprint with the said letter?

ANSWER. That all the letters wherewith he impryntyd the said *A B C* were not his owne for he dyd borrowe of one Adame, a man of one master Purfott all the Inglisshe (i.e. *black*) Letters to the said worke and he borrowyd these letters without the consent of the said master Purfytt and hath the same as yet in this defendants custodye and have not Redelyvered

[1] A brotherhood of Stationers, consisting of 'writers of text letter', 'lymners of bokes', and subsequently admitting printers to its fellowship, had existed since 1403. The term Stationer, at the time of the incorporation, included booksellers, printers, bookbinders, publishers, typefounders, makers of writing-tables, and other trades, amongst which were 'joiners and chandlers'. Cf. Mr. Graham Pollard's article 'The Company of Stationers before 1557', and 'The Early Constitution of the Stationers' Company' in *The Library*, vol. xviii, 1938, pp. 1–38, 235–60, 335–7.

[2] Arber's *Transcripts*, ii. 753–69.

[3] This unruly printer troubled the Company's peace for eleven years and demonstrated, by his persistent defiance of their authority, the insufficiency of their powers to execute the control they nominally possessed. John Wolfe, the City printer, distinguished himself in a similar way. According to McKerrow, *An Introduction to Bibliography*, 1927, p. 142, some of these troubles arose from a serious protest against monopolies granted in certain classes of books.

of the same sithes he borrowyd the same as aforesaid and to his Remembrance he Did imprynt with the sayd letter the nomber of Twentie Reames of paper.

QUESTION XIX. Whether have you cast any new Letter of your owne since the first printinge of the said *A B C*, and what nomber of the same have you printed of that letter (*in that type*)?

ANSWER. He confessyth that he hath sythes the first imprintyng of the said *A B C*, cast a newe letter of his owne and yet he hath not pryntyd any of that letter (*in that type*).

This testimony was generally corroborated by the other printers and persons examined, to many of whom it appeared to be notorious that Roger Ward had printed the book in a letter not his own, and that he had since cast a new fount of type for his own use. The whole inquiry throws a curious light on the methods of business of the printers of the day. Composition then, as Arber points out, was not necessarily done in the master-printer's house where he kept his press. Of course that which was done by himself and his apprentices was done there, but work given out to journeymen (who were generally householders) was probably done in their houses and paid for by piece-work.

A custom which [continues Arber] was facilitated by most of the books then printed being almost always in some one size of type. Therefore there could not be so much control exercised over the literature in respect to the guardianship of the type—however easy it was for printers of that day to identify the printer of a book by its typography—neither do we find any such attempted; but only in respect to the custody of the hand printing press, which was doubtless well secured every night as a dangerous instrument, lest secret nocturnal printing should go on without the owner's consent.[1]

In the same year, 1582, Christopher Barker, the Queen's printer, drew up an able report on the condition of printing as it then existed, in which among other matters he referred to the cost of making type, and its consequent effect on publishers and printers.

In King Edward the Sixt his Dayes [he says] Printers and printing began greatly to increase; but the provision of letter, and many other thinges belonging to printing was so exceeding chargeable, that most of those printers were Dryven throughe necessitie, to compound before[hand] with the booksellers at so low value, as the printers themselves were most tymes small gayners and often loosers. . . . The Bookesellers . . . now (1582). . . keepe no printing howse, neither beare any charge of letter, or other furniture, but onlie paye for the workmanship . . . so that the artificer printer, growing every Daye more and more unable to provide letter[2] and other furniture . . . will in tyme be an occasion of great discredit to the professours of the arte.

The report goes on to mention that at that time (December 1582) 'there are twenty-two printing howses in London, where eight or ten at the most would suffise for all England, yea, and Scotland too'.[3]

In May of the following year there were twenty-three printers with fifty-three presses among them, and during the next two years the number appears to have increased so considerably as to call for that sweeping enactment, the Star Chamber decree of 1586. This famous measure prohibits all presses out of London, except one each at the two Universities, and 'tyll the excessive multytude of Prynters

---

[1] Arber's *Transcripts*, ii. 22.

[2] A commission appointed to inquire into the disputes at that time agitating the Company gave as one of its chief reasons why the monopolies should be sustained, that if anyone were to print any book he chose, this inconvenience would follow, viz., 'want of provisions of good letters', in other words, the quality both of type and printing would degenerate.

[3] Arber's *Transcripts*, i. 114, 144.

havinge presses already sett up be abated', permits no new press whatsoever to be erected.[1] The Stationers' Company have authority to inspect all printing-offices, 'to search take and carry away all presses, letters and other pryntinge instrumentes sett up, used or employed . . . contrary to the intent and meaninge hereof; . . . and thereupon shall cause all suche printing presses, or other printing instruments, to be Defaced, melted, sawed in peeces, broken, or battered . . . and the stuffe of the same so defaced, shall redelyver to the owners thereof againe within three monethes next after the takinge or seizinge thereof as aforesayd'.[2]

The Company were not slow in making use of their enlarged powers, and the refractory Roger Ward appears to have had considerable experience of the rigours of the new decree. In October 1586 the wardens seized on his premises '3 presses and divers other parcells of pryntinge stuffe', and ordered them to be defaced and rendered unserviceable, according to the tenor of the decree. In 1590 they made a further visitation, and discovered that 'he did kepe and conceale a presse and other pryntinge stuff in a Taylor's house near adjoyninge to his owne, and did hide his letters in a hen house near St. Sepulchure's Churche, expressely against the Decrees of the Star Chamber. All the whyche stuff were brought to Stacioners Hall' and duly destroyed. But the dauntless Roger Ward was not thus to be extinguished, and scarcely six months later, at Hammersmith, another press, 'with 5 formes of letters of Divers sortes and 3 cases with other printing stuffe', were impounded and rigorously defaced.

Nor was Ward the only victim. In the Records of the Court of the Stationers' Company for 13 May 1588 we find:

Whereas Mr. Coldock warden, Tho Woodcock, Oliver Wilks and Jo Wolf on the 16 of April last, upon serche of Robert Walgraves house, did seise of his and bringe to the Staccon's hall accordinge to the late decrees of the Starre Chamber and by vertue thereof, A presse with twoo paire of Cases with Certen pica Romane & pica Italian letters with diverse books entituled: The state of the churche of England laid open in a conference betwene Diotrephes a byshop . . . and Paul a p'cher of gods woord ffor that the said Walgrave without aurthority and Contrary to the said decrees had printed the said book it is nowe in full Court holden this day ordered & agreed by force of the said decrees & accordinge to the same. That the said books shal be burnte and the said presse letters and printinge stuffe defaced and made unservicable. [See the Records edited by Greg and Boswell, Bibliographical Society, 1930.]

In a Secret Report presented in September 1589 to Lord Burleigh respecting the authors of the famous Marprelate Tracts, it is stated that the printer of the first three of these, 'all beinge printed in a Dutch letter', was Robert Waldegrave; and 'towchinge the printinge of the two last Lebells in a litle Romaine and Italian letter', the report states—once more showing how in those days a printer was known by his types:

. . . the letter that these be printed in is the same that did printe the *Demonstration of Discipline* aboute Midsommer was twelve moneth (24 June 1588), which was printed by Waldegrave

---

[1] A return of presses and printers, made in the same year to the Master and Wardens of the Company after the publication of the decree, shows that this provision had reduced the number to twenty-five printers, with fifty-three presses. A list of these is given in C. R. Rivington's *Records of the Company*

[2] The provisions of this decree were commended in *The London Printer his Lamentation*, published in 1660, and reprinted in the third volume of the *Harleian Miscellany*. The writer contrasts it favourably with subsequent decrees.

of Stationers, London, 1883, 8vo, p. 28.

neere Kingston upon Thames, as is discovered. When his other letters and presse were defaced about Easter was twelve moneth (7th April 1588) he saved these lettres in a boxe under his Cloke, and brought them to Mistris Cranes howse in London, as is allso confessed; and they are knowen by printers to be Waldegrave's letters; And it is the same letter that was taken with Hodgkys. These two last Libells came abroade in July (1589) last. Now it is confessed by the Carier that John Hodgkys that is taken, did send from a gentlemans howse in Woltonam in Warwikeshier unto Warrington immediatlye after whitsontyde last (18 May 1589), a printinge presse, two boxes of letter, a barrell of nicke (*incke?*), a baskett and a brasse pott, which were delyvered to him at Warrington, etc.[1]

The Stationers' Company, on the whole, had a busy time during the few years following the Star Chamber decree in hunting up and destroying disorderly presses and the 'stuffe' appertaining thereto. The numerous monopolies and patents of which they were the appointed guardians provoked a regular secret organization of unprivileged printers,[2] who pirated right and left, sometimes with impunity, sometimes at the cost of losing their whole plant and stock-in-trade by a raid of the authorities. These raids must have kept the type-casters of the day well occupied, and it is even possible that the 'stuffe' which from time to time fell into the hands of the Company may have included punches, matrices, and moulds, which it would be far less easy to replace than presses, ink, and balls. A printer liable to such visitations would prefer, if possible, to procure his type out of doors rather than maintain the valuable plant requisite to make it himself; and it is probable that the outside demand thus created may have been among the causes which led to the establishment of one or two small foundries, unconnected with any one printing-office in particular, whose business it would be to supply any purchaser with type from its matrices.

The Stationers' Company, who from time to time supplemented the powers conferred upon them by the Star Chamber with regulations of their own on matters such as standing formes, apprentices, and prices, would naturally recognize a source of danger in a new foundry starting under the circumstances described, and were prompt to assert their authority. Accordingly we find the following entry in the Index to the Court Books of the Company under date 1597:

BENJAMIN SYMPSON, letter founder, to enter into a £40 bond not to cast any letters or characters, or to deliver them, without advertising the Master and Wardens in writing, with the names of the parties for whom they are intended.—1597.

Here we have the first historical record of letter-founding as a distinct and recognized trade.[3] Of Benjamin Sympson and his types little is known. He is mentioned

[1] Arber's *Transcripts*, ii. 816. At the time of the raid in April 1588 Waldegrave's house was at the sign of the Crane in Paul's Churchyard, and the book seized, the *Diotrephes*, was by John Udall. The press referred to in the report of September 1589 was at East Moseley and was not discovered. Here was printed the first of the Marprelate Tracts in Waldegrave's 'Dutch letter', i.e. a Lettersnijder type. This type is illustrated in W. Pierce's *An Historical Introduction to the Marprelate Tracts*, 1908, opposite p. 156. The *Demonstration of Discipline*, printed in the 'litle Romaine and Italian letter', was also by John Udall. The italic, probably cut by Jerome Haultin, we shall find again in Walton's *Polyglot*

Bible of 1657. The Pica roman and italic which were seized, and the 'litle Romaine' were all common London types.

[2] A licensed stationer might, with the leave of the Company, employ an unlicensed stationer to reprint a work of his own, on payment of a fine. (Arber, ii. 19.)

[3] In France, as early as 1539, typefounding had been legally recognized as a distinct trade. The edict of 1539 contains the following clause, applying the provisions and penalties of the decree to type-founders: 'Et pour ce que le métier des fondeurs de lettres est connexe à l'art de l'imprimeur, et que les fondeurs ne se disent imprimeurs, ne les imprimeurs

in the Registers (Arber, ii. 224) in 1598 as having an apprentice, George Ward. Nashe in *Have with you to Saffron Walden*, 1596, refers to one 'Beniamin the Founder' (sig. O 1 vº.). His name does not occur in any of the lists of printers of the period, nor does it appear that he was even a member of the Stationers' Company. Whether he was called upon at his own request to qualify as a type-founder, or whether the resolution of the Court was arrived at in consequence of his previous transactions with one or more of the disorderly printers, is equally uncertain.

In 1598 the Stationers' Company made a regulation respecting the price of work, which is also of interest as indicating the bodies of type at that time most commonly in use for book-work. It was as follows:

No new copies without pictures to be printed at more than the following rates: those in pica Roman and Italic and in English (i.e. *black letter*) with Roman and Italic at a penny for two sheets; those in brevier and long primer letters at a penny for one sheet and a half.[1]

A further regulation regarding typefounders shows that in 1622 the trade had more than one recognized representative:

The Founders bound to the Company by bond, not to deliver any fount of new letters, without acquainting the Master and Wardens—1622.

The second English founder of whom there is a record is Richard Adams, who was made free of the Stationers on 22 October 1618.[2] In the Acts of the Privy Council for 9 January 1625 it is stated that Adams is threatened with being pressed into the armed forces as a drummer; the Council instructs that he shall not be pressed for the reason that he is a founder of letters for the King's Printing-house. Also his two servants, Abraham Bradshaw and Thomas Wright, are not to be molested. There is no further information about Adams or Bradshaw, but Wright is the man who in 1637 became one of the four Star Chamber founders. Alexander Fifield also was apprenticed to Adams.

The Act of 1586, despite the rigour with which, at first at any rate, it was enforced, appears to have fallen into contempt, and to have been openly disregarded by the printers of the first quarter of the seventeenth century. According to the account of the 'London Printer', who wrote his *Lamentation* in 1660, printing and printers, about 1637, were grown to such 'monstrous excess and exorbitant dis-

---

ne se disent fondeurs, lesdicts articles et ordonnances auront lieu . . . aux compagnons et apprentifs fondeurs, ainsi qu'en compagnons et apprentifs imprimeurs, lesquels oultre les choses dessus dictes seront tenus d'achever la fonte des lettres par eux commencée et les rendre bonnes et valables.' The whole decree is in curious contrast with the Acts regulating English printing and founding. The French *compagnons* are forbidden to band together for military, festive, or religious purposes, to carry arms, to beat and neglect their apprentices, to leave any work incomplete, to use any printer's marks but their own; and so great is the fatherly solicitude of the Crown for the honour of the press that printers are made amenable to law for typographical errors in their books. (Lacroix, *Histoire de l'Imprimerie*, Paris, pp. 124–8.) In Rebuffi's edition of the *Ordonnances*, Lyons, 1559, this edict appears under the date 12 Aug. 1542, no doubt a reinactment.

[1] In 1635 the journeymen printers presented a petition to the Stationers' Company respecting certain abuses which they desired to have reformed. The report of the referees appointed to inquire into the matter, with their recommendations, is still preserved. Amongst other things is a provision against standing formes; also that no books printed in Nonpareil should exceed 5,000 copies, in Brevier 3,000 (except the privileged books); and further, that compositors should keep their cases clean, and dispose of 'all wooden letters, and two-line letters, and keep their letter whole while work is doing, and after bind it up in good order'. The Company approved of the report and ordered it to be entered on the books. (*Calendar of State Papers, Domestic, 1635*, 1865, p. 484.)

[2] Additional notes relating to apprentices, &c., have been extracted from the Stationers' Registers by Mr. Ellic Howe.

order' as to call for the prompt and serious attention of the Court of Star Chamber, who in that same year, because the former 'Orders and Decrees have been found by experience to be defective in some particulars; and divers abuses have sithence arisen and been practiced by the craft and malice of wicked and evill disposed persons', put forward the famous Star Chamber Decree of 1637.[1]

In this decree, the severity of which, or of its partial renewal by Parliament in 1643, called forth from Milton his noble protest, the *Areopagitica*,[2] letter-founding is formally recognized as a distinct industry, and shares with printing the rigours of the new restrictions. The following is the text of the clauses relating to founders:

XXVII.—*Item*, The Court doth order and declare, that there shall be foure Founders of letters for printing allowed, and no more, and doth hereby nominate, allow, and admit these persons, whose names hereafter follow, to the number of foure, to be letter-Founders for the time being, (viz.) *John Grismand, Thomas Wright, Arthur Nichols, Alexander Fifield*. And further the Court doth Order and Decree, that it shall be lawfull for the Lord Arch-bishop of *Canterbury*, or the Lord Bishop of *London* for the time being, taking unto him or them, six other high Commissioners, to supply the place or places of those who are now allowed Founders of letters by this Court, as they shall fall void by death, censure, or otherwise.

Provided that they exceede not the number of foure, set down by this Court. And if any person or persons, not being an allowed Founder, shall notwithstanding take upon him, or them, to Found, or cast letters for printing, upon complaint and proofe made of such offence, or offences, he, or they so offending, shal suffer such punishment, as this Court, or the high Commission Court respectively, as the severall causes shall require, shall think fit to inflict upon them.

XXVIII.—*Item*, That no Master-Founder whatsoever shall keepe above two Apprentices at one time, neither by Copartnership, binding at the Scriveners, nor any other way whatso-ever, neither shall it be lawfull for any Master-Founder, when any Apprentice, or Appren-tices shall run, or be put away, to take another Apprentice, or other Apprentices in his, or their place or places, unless the name or names of him, or them so gone away, be rased out of the Hall-booke of the Company, whereof the Master-Founder is free, and never admitted again, upon pain of such punishment, as by this Court, or the high Commission respectively, as the severall causes shall require, shall be thought fit to bee imposed.

XXIX.—*Item*, That all Journey-men-Founders be imployed by the Master-Founders of the said trade, and that idle Journey-men be compelled to worke after the same manner, and upon the same penalties, as in case of the Journey-men-Printers is before specified.[3]

XXX.—*Item*, That no Master-Founder of letters, shall imploy any other person or persons in any worke belonging to the casting or founding of letters, than such only as are freemen or apprentices to the trade of founding letters, save only in the pulling off the knots of mettle hanging at the ends of the letters when they are first cast, in which work it shall be lawfull for every Master-Founder, to imploy one boy only that is not, nor hath beene bound to the trade of Founding letters, but not otherwise, upon pain of being for ever disabled to use or exercise that art, and such further punishment, as by this Court, or the

---

[1] *A Decree of Starre-Chamber, concerning Printing. Made the eleventh day of July last past*, 1637. Lon-don, 1637, 4to. The 'London Printer', previously quoted, writing in 1660, styles this decree 'the best and most exquisite form and constitution for the good government and regulation of the press that ever was pronounced, or can reasonably be con-trived to keep it in due order and regular exercise'. It was the lapse of its authority in 1640 which led to the abuses over which he lamented.

[2] This famous tract has been reprinted by

Arber among his *English Reprints*, together with a verbatim copy of the decrees which evoked it. London, 1868, 12mo.

[3] That is, the Master and Wardens are obliged to find employment for all honest journeymen out of work, the master-printers and founders being bound to give work to anyone thus brought to them. Masters requiring additional hands can compel the services of any journeyman out of work, who can only refuse the summons at his peril.

high Commission Court respectively, as the severall causes shall require, be thought fit to be imposed.

XIV.—*Item*, That no Joyner, or Carpenter, or other person, shall make any printing-Presse, no Smith shall forge any Iron-Worke for a printing Presse, and no Founder shall cast any Letters for any person or persons whatsoever, neither shall any person or persons bring, or cause to be brought in from any parts beyond the Seas, any Letters Founded or Cast, nor buy any such Letters for Printing, Unlesse he or they respectively shall first acquaint the said Master and Wardens, or some of them, for whom the same Presse, Iron-works, or Letters, are to be made, forged, or cast, upon paine of such fine and punishment, as this Court, or the high Commission Court respectively, as the severall causes shall require, shall thinke fit.

Respecting the four founders thus nominated, and their types, we shall have occasion to speak in a following chapter. Continuing here our cursory review of the Statutes which affected letter-founding, it is necessary to remind the reader that this tremendous decree, which for severity eclipsed all its predecessors, was short-lived.

On 3 November 1640 the Long Parliament assembled, and with it the Star Chamber disappeared, and its decrees became dead letters. Then for a season there was virtually free trade in printing, and advantage was taken of the new condition of affairs to infringe existing rights on every hand, the King's Patent Printers (if we are to believe the 'London Printer', above quoted) being the chief and most unscrupulous transgressors.

Parliament was not slow to take up the mantle dropped by the late Star Chamber, and in June 1643 attempted to stem 'the very grievous' liberty of the press, reinvesting the Stationers' Company with powers to search and seize all unlicensed presses and books, and to apprehend the 'authors, printers and other persons whatsoever employed in compiling, printing, stitching, binding, publishing and dispersing the said scandalous, unlicensed and unwarrantable papers, books and pamphlets.'

This ordinance, in which once more typefounders are conspicuous by their absence, was strengthened by a further decree in 1647, and two years later the Act of 20 September 1649 virtually reimposed the old Star Chamber regulations, requiring, among other provisions, that printers should enter into a £300 bond not to print seditious or scandalous matter; also that no house or room should be let to a printer, nor implements made, press imported, or letters founded, without notice to the Stationers' Company. The penalties attached to a breach of these orders were severe. This Act was renewed in 1652, but it failed to remedy the abuses it was intended to meet. Private presses sprang up on all hands; the art was degraded and prostituted to all manner of base uses; workmen as well as master printers joined in their complaints against disorders which were working their ruin. The number of printers, restricted since 1586 to twenty, had grown to sixty; the Royal printers themselves were interlopers, two of them not even being practical printers (Barker and Bill).[1]

Such being the condition of affairs it is not surprising that in 1662 the remonstrances raised on all sides should result in an Act of Parliament intended to dispose finally of the abuses complained of.

The Act of 1662 (13 & 14 Charles II, c. 33) reimposes the provisions of the

[1] See *The London Printer*, 1660.

Star Chamber Decree of 1637 with additional rigour.[1] It enacts that no type is to be founded or cast, or brought from abroad, without licence from the Stationers' Company. The number of founders is again limited to four, and all vacancies in the number are to be filled up by the Archbishop of Canterbury or the Bishop of London.[2] Masters of the Stationers' Company, past and present, may have three apprentices, liverymen two, and the commonalty only one. Master founders must see that their journeymen are kept at work; and these journeymen must be all Englishmen and freemen, or sons of freemen. Founders working for the trade who offend are to be disabled from following their craft for three years, and on a second offence to be permanently disqualified, besides suffering punishment by fine or imprisonment, or 'other corporal punishment not extending to life and limb'.

This uncompromising Act was continued from time to time, with temporary lapses, until 1693,[3] when, in the tide of liberty following the Revolution, it disappeared. Despite its stern provisions, we find from a petition entitled *The Case of the Free Workmen Printers*, presented to the House about 1665, praying for its renewal, that the number of printing-houses had already grown to seventy, with 150 apprentices; and in 1683 we have the evidence of Moxon that the number of founders, as well as of printers, was grown 'very many'. It does not, however, appear that at any time during the continuance of the Act, the number of founders ever exceeded four. How far they complied with the regulation requiring them to account to the Company for all type cast we are unable, in the absence of any register of such accounts, to say; but that a register was duly kept is evident from the following important minute of the Court in 1674:

All the Letter-founders to give timely notice to the Master and Wardens, of all such quantities of letter as they shall cast for any person; which notice shall be entered by the Clerk in a register book to be provided for that purpose.—1674.

In 1668, as will be seen in a subsequent chapter, the Company had, in discharge of their authority, nominated Thomas Goring to the Archbishop of Canterbury as 'an honest and sufficient man' to be one of the four founders allowed by the Act, there being then a vacancy in the number. And that the penal clauses were not

---

[1] In a rare tract entitled *An Exact Narrative of the Tryal and Condemnation of John Twyn, for printing and dispersing of a treasonable book, &c.* (London, 1664, 4to), several curious particulars are given as to the operation and enforcement of this Act as regards printers. But although a bookseller and bookbinder were arraigned at the same time, no reference was made to the founder of the types, who was apparently not held responsible for a share in the offence. In the evidence given by L'Estrange, however, as to Dover, one of the prisoners, we have a curious glimpse of the technical duties devolving on the Surveyor of the Imprimery and Printing Presses under this Act. He states, 'I was at his (Dover's) house to compare a *Flower* which I found in the *Panther* (a dangerous Pamphlet), that flower, that is, the very same *border*, I found in his house, the same mixture of Letter, great and small in the same Case; and I took a Copy off the Press.' The sentence passed upon the unfortunate John Twyn gives a vivid idea of the amenities of a printer at that period: 'That you be led back to the place from whence you came, and from thence to be drawn upon an Hurdle

to the place of Execution, and there you shall be hanged by the Neck, and being alive shall be cut down, and your privy Members shall be cut off, your Entrails shall be taken out of your body, and you living, the same to be burnt before your eyes: your head to be cut off, your body to be divided into four quarters, and your head and quarters to be disposed of at the pleasure of the King's Majesty. And the Lord have mercy upon your soul.'

[2] Printers were ordered to enter into a bond of £300 to the Crown not to misconduct themselves, but no bond appears to have been exacted by this Act from letter-founders.

[3] The Act of 1662 was a probationary Act for two years. In 1664 it was continued till the end of the next session, and again until the end of the session following; and in 1666 again until the end of the first session of the next Parliament. In 1685 it was revived for seven years, at the end of which, in 1692, it was continued for one year more, after which it dropped. According to this account, it must have been dormant at any rate between 1679 and 1685.

neglected is equally evident from the resolution of the Court in 1685, withholding Godfrey Head's dividend until he should comply with the Act by giving an account to the Company of what type he was casting.

The latest minute in the Court Books relating to letter-founding was in 1693—the year in which the Act expired—when the following order was made:

Printed papers to be delivered to all Founders, Press Makers and others concerned, requiring obedience to that Clause in the Act for preventing abuses in Printing, whereby all Letter Founders, Press Makers, Joiners, and others are commanded to acquaint the Master or Wardens what Presses or Letters they shall at any time make or cast.—1693.

After 1693, letter-founding came from under all restraint. Laws of copyright and patent still clung to printing,[1] but, except for a proposal made about 1695 by one W. Mascall[2] that every printer, letter-founder, and press-maker should enter with a statement on oath the number of his presses, the weight of his letter, and the extent of his other utensils, we find no reference to letter-founding in the Public Records for upwards of a century.

Notwithstanding this liberty, the number of founders during the eighteenth century appears rarely to have exceeded the figure prescribed by the Star Chamber Decree of 1637, and occasionally to have been less.

One more attempt was made in the closing days of the eighteenth century to control the freedom of the press by law. There is something almost grotesque in the efforts made by legislators in 1799 to refit, on a full-grown and invincible press, the worn-out shackles by which the Stuarts had tried to curtail the growth of its childhood; and the Act of 39 George III, cap. 79,[3] in so far as it deals with printing, will always remain one of the surprises, as well as one of the disgraces, of the Statute-book. Among its worst provisions, the following affect letter-founders and letter-founding:

Sec. 23 ordains that no one, under penalty of £20, shall be allowed to possess or use a printing-press or types for printing, without giving notice thereof to a Clerk of the Peace, and obtaining from him a certificate to that effect.

Sec. 33 provides that any Justice of the Peace may issue a warrant to search any premises, and seize and take away any press or printing-types not duly certificated.

The following sections we give in full:

Sec. 25. That from and after the Expiration of Forty Days after the passing of this Act, every Person carrying on the Business of a Letter Founder or Maker or Seller of Types for Printing or of Printing Presses, shall cause Notice of his or her Intention to carry on such Business to be delivered to the Clerk of the Peace of the . . . Place where such Person shall propose to carry on such Business, or his Deputy in the Form prescribed in the Schedule of this Act annexed.[4] And such Clerk of the Peace or his Deputy shall, and he is hereby

---

[1] In 1724, according to the list presented by Samuel Negus to Lord Townsend, the number of printers in London had increased to seventy-five, and in the provinces to twenty-eight. There were also at that time eighteen newspapers.

[2] *A Proposal for Restraining the great Licentiousness of the Press throughout Great Britain, &c.* No date.

[3] *An Act for the more effectual Suppression of Societies established for Seditious and Treasonable Purposes; and for better preventing Treasonable and Seditious Practices.* [12 July 1799.]

[4] 'VI. FORM *of Notice to the Clerk of the Peace that any person carries on the Business of a Letter Founder, or Maker or Seller of Types for Printing, or of Printing Presses.*—To the Clerk of the Peace for (*as the case may be*) or his Deputy.—I, A. B., of   do hereby declare, That I intend to carry on the Business of a Letter Founder, or Maker or Seller of Types for Printing, *or* of Printing Presses (*as the case may be*), at   and I hereby require this Notice to be entered in pursuance of an Act passed in the 39th Year of the Reign of His Majesty, King *George* the Third.'

authorized and required thereupon to grant a Certificate in the Form also prescribed in the said Schedule,[1] for which such Clerk of the Peace or his Deputy shall receive a Fee of One Shilling and no more, and shall file such Notice and transmit an attested Copy thereof to one of his Majesty's Principal Secretaries of State; and every Person who shall, after the expiration of the said Forty Days, carry on such Business, or make or sell any Type for Printing, or Printing Press, without having given such Notice, and obtained such Certificate, shall forfeit and lose the Sum of Twenty Pounds.

Sec. 26. And be it further enacted, That every Person who shall sell Types for Printing, or Printing Presses as aforesaid, shall keep a Fair Account in Writing of all Persons to whom such Types or Presses shall be sold, and shall produce such Accounts to any Justice of the Peace who shall require the same; And if such Person shall neglect to keep such Account, or shall refuse to produce the same to any such Justice, on demand in Writing to inspect the same, such Person shall forfeit and lose, for such offence, the Sum of Twenty Pounds.

Such was the law with regard to typefounding at the time when the widows of the two Caslons were struggling to revive their then ancient business, when Vincent Figgins was building up his new foundry, and Edmund Fry, Caslon III, and Wilson were busily occupied in cutting their modern romans to suit the new fashion. And such the law remained nominally until the year 1869,[2] just upon four centuries after the introduction of the art into this country. It is probable that, during the first few disturbed years of its existence, the Act may have been enforced, that certificates may have been registered, and accounts dutifully furnished.[3] But its provisions appear very soon to have fallen into contempt, and certainly, as far as we can ascertain, failed to trouble the peace of any British letter-founder.

Such is a cursory review of the various laws which from time to time have taken letter-founding under control. Whether they succeeded in placing any real check on the progress of the art it is difficult to determine. But it is certain that the heaviest restrictive measures have generally been accompanied not only by the most grievous abuses in the spirit of the press, but by distinct degeneration in the quality of the typographical work executed. A privileged printer, sure of his monopoly and safe from competition, would have little or no inducement to execute his work at more cost or pains than was necessary. Old type would do as well as new, and bad type would do as well as good. Free trade and open competition were the great evils to be dreaded, because free trade and open competition would demand the best paper and type and workmanship. The typography of the entire Stuart period is a disgrace to English art. Fine printing was an art unknown; and only a few works like Walton's *Polyglot*, which were produced in an atmosphere untainted by mercenary considerations, stand out to redeem the period from unqualified reproach.

---

[1] 'VII. FORM *of Certificate that the above Notice has been given.*—I, G. H., Clerk (or Deputy Clerk) of the Peace for   do hereby certify that A. B. of   hath delivered to me a Notice in Writing, appearing to be signed by him, and attested by E. F. as a Witness to his signing the same, that he intends to carry on the Business of a Letter Founder, or Maker or Seller of Types for Printing or of Printing Presses, at   and which Notice he has required to be entered in pursuance of an Act of the 39th Year of His Majesty,

King *George* the Third.'

[2] The clauses relating to printers and typefounders were repealed by 32 and 33 Vict., cap. 24: *An Act to Repeal certain enactments relating to Newspapers, Pamphlets, and other Publications, and to Printers, Typefounders, and Reading Rooms.* [12 July 1869.]

[3] 'Now register'd—now ticketed we move,
  Our slightest works the double label prove.'
                                        (McCreery, *The Press*, p. 25.)

On the other hand, the removal of the restrictions was the signal for a revival which may be traced in almost every printed work of the early eighteenth century. In the absence of any great English founder, the best Dutch types came freely into the English market. Books came to be legible, paper became white, ink black, and press-work respectable. Caslon came in on the tide of the revival, as also did Bowyer, Watts, Bettenham, and artists of their rank; and the emancipated press, among them, made up the leeway of a wasted century, and, no longer in the grip of faction, but the free servant of the great and wise of the land, raised for itself monuments which will remain a lasting glory not only to English scholarship and English eloquence, but also to English typography, for which liberty has been, and always will be, the surest road to achievement.

6

THE OXFORD UNIVERSITY FOUNDRY

THE Oxford Foundry may be said to date from the year 1669, when the Sheldonian Theatre was opened. Before that date the early printers at Oxford and the so-styled University printers carried on their business in much the same way as their contemporaries in London or any other city. A full account of the first printers at Oxford in the fifteenth century will be found in F. Madan's *The Early Oxford Press*, 1895, with an additional note in his second volume, *Oxford Books, 1641–1650*. To bring the account into conformity with more recent methods of type description, we give a table of the types used according to Haebler's *Typenrepertorium der Wiegendrucke*. The first press, of whose work three books have survived from the years 1478–9, used only one type, and this is type 1 of Gerhard ten Roem of Cologne, 20 lines measuring 97 mm., with Haebler's M. 5. It is illustrated at pl. 141 of the reproductions of the 'Gesellschaft für Typenkunde'. Of the second press, that of Theodoric Rood (together with Thomas Hunte according to the imprints of two of the books), eleven books are known to have been produced between 1481 and 1486. Apart from the books themselves nothing is known of Rood, who is presumed to have come from the Cologne district but cannot be the Cologne printer Theodoricus Molner, and little of the Englishman Hunte, who was a stationer at Oxford.

This firm made use of six types as follows:

Type 1. M. 70. 100 mm.	Type 4. M. 70. 88 mm.
,, 2. M. 20. *c*. 210 mm.	,, 5. M. 70. 116 mm.
,, 3. M. 70. 88 mm.	,, 6. M. 72. 116 mm.

Type 2 is a Rotunda, resembling type 5 of the Cologne printer J. Koelhoff, type 6 is a Text, and the four body types belong to that early group of fifteenth-century types known as 'fere humanistica' or 'gotico-antiqua'. All closely resemble types used at Cologne, and the press as a whole is a sort of appendix to the history of Cologne printing. Reproductions of the types are given in Duff's *Early English Printing*, 1896, pls. XXVII–XXXI, and Duff's *Fifteenth Century English Books*, pls. XXXVIII–XLII.

The next Oxford printer was John Scolar, who produced a few books in 1517 and 1518, followed by one further production at Abingdon in 1528. One Charles Kyrforth issued one book from Scolar's address in Oxford in 1519, printed also with Scolar's types. These types were two sizes of Text and a 53 Rotunda, which came from Wynkyn de Worde. They are shown in Isaac at fig. 47. This printer, like all his successors at Oxford up to the establishment of the foundry, was typographically dependent on the London press.

There follows a gap in Oxford printing of nearly sixty years, when in 1585 begins the career of Joseph Barnes, the first University printer. It appears that

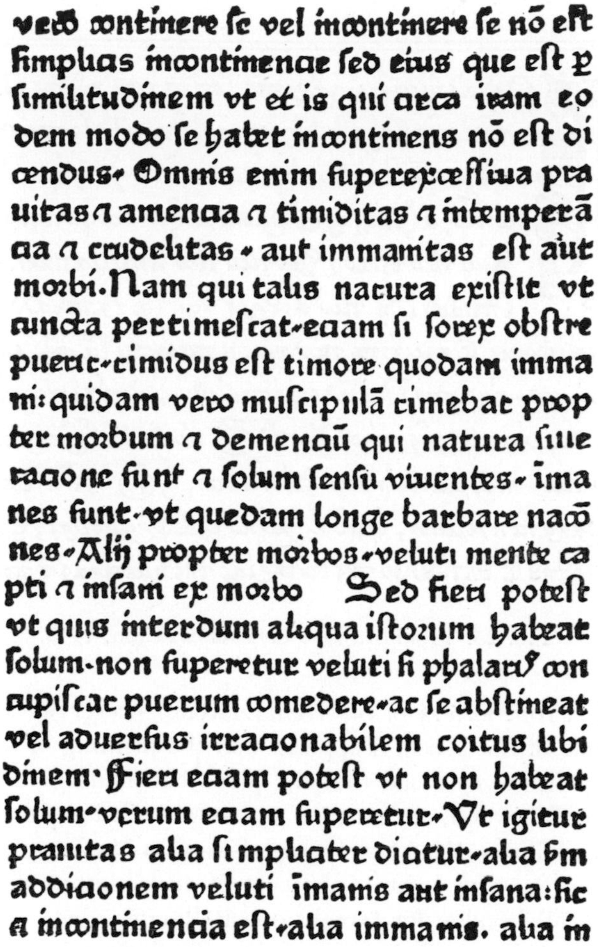

vetõ continere se vel incontinere se nõ eft
fimplicis incontinenciae fed eius que eft p
fimilitudinem vt et is qui arca iram eo
dem modo fe habet incontinens nõ eft di
cendus· Omnis enim fuperexceffiua pra
uitas τ amencia τ timiditas τ intemperã
cia τ crudelitas · aut immanitas eft aut
morbi. Nam qui talis natura exiftit vt
cuncta pertimefcat·eaam fi forex obftre
pueric·cimidus eft timore quodam imma
ni: quidam vero mufcipulã timebat prop
ter morbum τ demenau qui natura fiue
racione funt τ folum fenfu viuentes· ima
nes funt·vt quedam longe barbare naõ
nes·Alij propter morbos·veluti mente ca
pti τ infani ex morbo   Sed fieri poteft
vt quis interdum aliqua iftorum habeat
folum·non fuperetur veluti fi phalaris con
cupifcat puerum comedere·ac fe abftineat
vel aduerfus irracionabilem coitus libi
dinem· Fieri eaam poteft vt non habeat
folum·verum eaam fuperetur·Vt igitur
prauitas alia fimpliciter dicitur·alia fm
addicionem veluti imanis aut infana:fic
τ incontinencia eft·alia immanis. alia in

FIG. 24. From *Aristotelis Ethica*, Oxford, 1479.

when the University assisted Barnes to set up his business with the loan of £100, no one was aware that he had had any predecessor at Oxford; all trace and memory of Rood and Scolar had vanished. Barnes's typography was much like that of his contemporaries in London and was probably derived from there. In particular the Pica Greek, in which he printed an edition of Aristophanes' *Knights* in 1593 and a number of other Greek books, was the same as that used by John Day and other London printers. He was one of the first English printers to use the Plantin roman capitals. They appear on the title-page of his first book, reproduced in Madan, *A Chart of Oxford Printing*, pl. IV.

The reputation of the University for its Greek types was enhanced some years afterwards by the acquisition of the letter in which the magnificent edition of *St. John Chrysostom*[1] had been printed at Eton, nominally by John Norton, but in fact by Melchisedec Bradwood of the Eliot's Court Press in the Old Bailey in 1610–13, at the charge and under the direction of Sir Henry Savile.[2] This work, one of the most splendid examples of Greek printing in this country, is said to have cost its

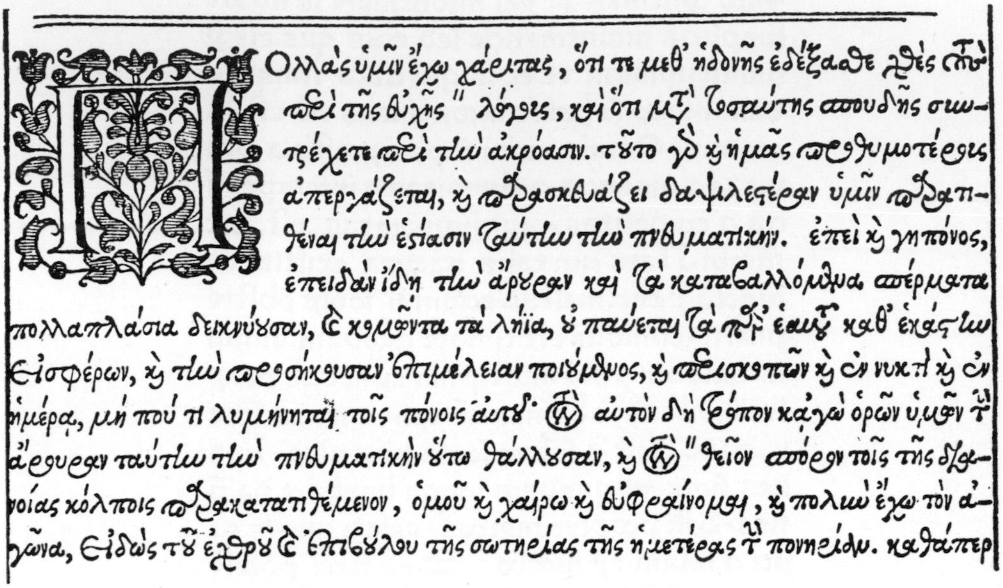

Πολλὰς ὑμῖν ἔχω χάριτας, ὅτι τε μεθ' ἡδονῆς ἐδέξασθε τοὺς τοῦ
περὶ τῆς εὐχῆς λόγους, καὶ ὅτι μετὰ τοσαύτης σπουδῆς συν-
τρέχετε περὶ τὴν ἀκρόασιν. τοῦτο γὰρ καὶ ἡμᾶς προθυμοτέρους
ἀπεργάζεται, καὶ παρασκευάζει δαψιλεστέραν ὑμῖν παραπι-
θέναι τὴν ἑστίασιν ταύτην τὴν πνευματικήν. ἐπεὶ καὶ γηπόνος,
ἐπειδὰν ἴδῃ τὴν ἄρουραν καὶ τὰ καταβαλλόμενα σπέρματα
πολλαπλάσια δεικνῦσαν, καὶ κομῶντα τὰ λήϊα, οὐ παύεται τὰ παρ' ἑαυτοῦ καθ' ἑκάστην
εἰσφέρων, καὶ τὴν προσήκουσαν ἐπιμέλειαν ποιούμενος, καὶ περισκοπῶν καὶ ἐν νυκτὶ καὶ ἐν
ἡμέρᾳ, μή πού τι λυμήνηται τοῖς πόνοις αὐτοῦ· τὸν αὐτὸν δὴ τρόπον κἀγὼ ὁρῶν ὑμῶν τὴν
ἄρουραν ταύτην τὴν πνευματικὴν οὕτω θάλλουσαν, καὶ τὸν θεῖον σπόρον τοῖς τῆς δια-
νοίας κόλποις παρακατατιθέμενον, ὁμοῦ καὶ χαίρω καὶ εὐφραίνομαι, καὶ πολλὴν ἔχω τὸν ἀ-
γῶνα, εἰδὼς τοῦ ἐχθροῦ τὴν ἐπιβουλὴν τῆς σωτηρίας τῆς ἡμετέρας τοῦ πονηροῦ. καθάπερ

FIG. 25. From *St. John Chrysostom*, Eton, 1613.

author £8,000. From letters of Sir Henry Savile, preserved among the manuscripts of the Duke of Buccleuch, it appears that the printing of the work had been contemplated for many years and that the plans had undergone several changes. A letter to Raphe Winwood, at that time ambassador in France, of 7 March 1602, is summarized[3] as follows: 'Had first resolved to print his work in London, Norton having undertaken to bring some of the best [Greek] letters from Paris, but the only workman in all London for Greek, one Bellyfant, died. Refused Frankfort, which Norton then offered, their paper being ill, their correctors perchance unlearned. We were then driven to Paris, whither Norton will go himself, with his associates.' The Bellyfant here mentioned is Edmund Bollifant alias Carpenter, printer, 1584–1602.[4] From a further letter of Savile's to Winwood, of 1 August 1602, we learn that after all the printing was to be done in London and that Norton

[1] *S. Joannis Chrysostomi opera Graece, octo voluminibus. Etonae, in Collegio Regali, Excudebat Joannes Norton, in Graecis, &c., Regius Typographus*, 1610–13. fol.

[2] Sir Henry Savile (who is not to be confounded with his kinsman and namesake, Long Harry Savile, Camden's friend) was formerly Greek tutor to Queen Elizabeth. In 1585 he was made Warden of Merton, and in 1596 became Provost of Eton College, where he died in 1621, aetat. 72. H. R. Plomer in 'The Eliot's Court Printing-House' in *The Library*, 1921, showed that the other types and ornaments used in the *Chrysostom* belonged to Bradwood. Norton was probably never a printer.

[3] *Reports on the Manuscripts of the Duke of Buccleuch*, Historical Manuscripts Commission, 1899, vol. i, p. 33.

[4] R. B. McKerrow's *Dictionary of Printers, 1557–1640*.

was not going to Paris. In the papers of Sir Thomas Edmondes, which are preserved in the Stowe MSS. in the British Museum, there is a letter from Winwood,[1]
written from The Hague on behalf of Savile, to Sir Thomas Edmondes, dated
7 May 1608, in which he asks that Mr. Sanford, Edmondes's chaplain, might go
to Antwerp to treat with Moret the printer about certain Greek characters, 'whereof he [Savile] shall have use for the printing of Chryostom's works, which long he
hath had in hand'. Whether these negotiations with Jean Moretus, Plantin's
son-in-law and successor, came to anything is not known. At any rate the Great
Primer Greek used for the main text of the *Chrysostom* was found by Robert Proctor[2]
to be identical with a type used at Frankfort by the Heirs of André Wechel in a
Demosthenes of 1604. It is not the original fount of the 'Grecs du Roi' which Wechel
himself used, but a close copy. Proctor concluded that Savile's fount was bought
in Frankfort, but it is of course possible that Moretus at Antwerp had strikes of the
same letter, although Plantin himself did not. It is curious that another attempt
was made to buy Greek types in Antwerp in 1634 (see below, p. 132). Norton
had already in 1603 been appointed King's printer in Hebrew, Greek, and Latin.
Scarcely less high an honour had been paid to him in 1594, when we are told Paul
Estienne (son of Henri Estienne II) visiting England, and appreciating his merit,
permitted him to make use of the device of the Estiennes.[3]

At what date these famous Greek types came into the possession of the Oxford
University Press is unknown, but in *Ultima linea Savilii*, Oxford, 1622, a set of
verses issued on Savile's death, we read: 'Officinam Universitatis typographicam
literis graecis innumeris, literarumque matricibus ditavit.' Evelyn,[4] in a letter to
Pepys, dated 12 August 1689, after lamenting the loss of Sir Simon Fanshaw's
medals, says that 'they were after his decease thrown about the house for children
to play at counter with, as were those elegant types of Sir Henry Savill's at Eton,
which that learned knight procured with great cost for his edition of *St. Chrysostom*'.
The types, of which we give a specimen (Fig. 25), were of a Great Primer body,
very elegantly and regularly cut, with the usual numerous ligatures and abbreviations which characterized the Greek typography of that period.

During the early part of the seventeenth century the Oxford Greek types do not
appear to have been extensively used; and in 1629 we find it recorded that Lord
Pembroke, the then Chancellor of the University of Cambridge,[5] applied for and

---

[1] *Catalogue of the Stowe Manuscripts,* 1895–6,
170, f. 37.

[2] R. Proctor, 'The French Royal Greek Types
and the Eton Chrysostom' in *Bibliographical Essays,*
1905.

[3] Dupont, *Histoire de l'Imprimerie,* Paris, 1854,
2 vols., i. 488. The devices are Nos. 348–51 in
McKerrow's *Devices used by English Printers.*

[4] *Diary and Correspondence,* London, 1850–2,
4 vols., iii. 300.

[5] Printing was introduced into Cambridge in
1521, when John Siberch printed Bulloch's *Oratio.*
On the title-page of a book printed at Cologne in
1520, Richard Croke's *Introductiones in rudimenta
Graeca,* he is styled 'Ioannes Laer de Siborch' [i.e.
Siegburg near Cologne]. He styled himself the first
printer in Greek in England, although none of his
works were wholly printed in that language. The

fount used for the quotations in the *Galeni de Temperamentis* was probably procured from abroad. See
G. J. Gray, *The Earlier Cambridge Stationers . . . and
the first Cambridge printer,* Bibl. Soc. Monograph
XIII. Siberch was the third printer in England to
use roman, in which he printed seven other books
in 1521 and 1522 besides the *Bulloch.* A fragment
of a ninth has also been found. On printing at
Cambridge see also S. C. Roberts, *A History of the
Cambridge University Press,* 1921. The residence of
Erasmus at Cambridge lent undoubted impetus to
the art, which progressed actively while the Oxford
Press was idle. The first University printers, three
in number, were appointed in 1534, by virtue of a
charter granted by Henry VIII, in terms considerably more liberal than those first granted to Oxford.
At no period of its career has the Cambridge Press
boasted of a type-foundry. In 1626 Archbishop

K

obtained the loan of one of these founts for the purpose of printing the *Greek Testament*,[1] which was issued in 1632 by Buck, the University printer, and which, says Beloe,[2] 'has ever been admired for the perspicuity of its types as well as for the accuracy of its typography'. The reason urged for this loan was that the Oxford Press made no use of the Greek type itself. This reproach was, however, shortly afterwards removed by the bounty and interest of Archbishop Laud, whose generous encouragement of printing at Oxford must always entitle him to an honourable mention in any record of the history of the art. Laud, at that time Bishop of London, was appointed Chancellor of the University in 1630, and in the same year projected, among other acts of bounty, two important measures for the advancement of printing at that Academy. These were:

To procure a large Charter for Oxford, to confirm their Ancient Privileges, and obtain new for them, as large as those of Cambridge, which they had got since Henry the 8th and Oxford had not.

To set up a Greek press in London and Oxford, for printing the Library-Manuscripts, and to get both Letters and Matrices.[3]

The former of these projects was carried out in 1632, when Charles I granted a charter to Oxford, giving her equal privileges with the sister University, authorizing her to employ three printers, and securing to her a right for a certain term over all books issued. In forwarding this charter to the University Laud mentioned by name two of the printers—King and Motteshead—but urged Convocation as yet to nominate no one as the third, in order, he said, 'that you may get an able man, if it be possible, for the printing of Greek when you shall be ready for it'.[4] This is clearly an allusion to the Bishop's other project, which, however, was only partially fulfilled during his lifetime.

A Greek press was established in London in 1636, under peculiar circumstances, which, though not strictly bearing upon the history of letter-founding at Oxford, we may here refer to as an interesting episode in the history of English printing. Robert Barker and Martin Lucas, the King's printers in London, were arraigned before the High Commission Court for a scandalous error in a *Bible*[5] printed by

---

Usher made an effort to procure from Leyden, for the use of the press, matrices of Syriac, Arabic, Ethiopic, and Samaritan letters, as already related (see above, p. 60). The University made an effort in 1700 to enrich their press by the purchase of a fount of the famous Paris Greek types of Francis I, known as the King's Greek. But as the French Academy insisted, as a condition of the purchase, that all works printed in these characters should bear the imprint 'characteribus Graecis e Typographeo regio Parisiensi', the Cambridge Syndics, unable to accede to the terms, withdrew from the negotiations (Gresswell's *Early Parisian Greek Press*, Oxford, 1833, i. 411; and De Guignes's *Typographie Orientale et Grecque de l'Imprimerie Royale*, Paris, 1787, p. 85). For Van Dijk's types at Cambridge see below, pp. 226–8.

[1] *Novum Testamentum, Cantabrigiae. Apud Tho. Buck*, 1632. 8vo.

[2] *Anecdotes*, i. 119. Elsewhere (v. 111) Beloe asserts that the type thus used was the Greek of Sir Henry Savile. Although the same size, and in many points closely resembling this letter, it differs from

it materially in other respects. This may possibly be accounted for on the supposition that some of the Savile characters having been lost, they had been replaced either by new matrices or by the addition of letters from some other fount. Buck discarded many of the cumbrous abbreviations used in the *Chrysostom*, greatly to the advantage of his text (see *4th Report Historical MSS. Commission*, p. 464). The documents relating to this loan are given in Madan's *Oxford Books*, vol. ii, App. D, pp. 517–20. The matrices were returned in June 1631.

[3] Rushworth's *Collections*, ii. 74.

[4] *Works of Laud*, Oxford, 1847–60, 7 vols., v. 80. For the text of the Charter, dated 12 Nov. 1632, see Madan, vol. i, p. 281, and the confirmation, dated 10 March 1633, p. 283. A further charter is dated 3 March 1636, see Madan, vol. ii, pp. 526–30.

[5] *The Holy Bible, containing the Old Testament and the New, &c. Printed at London by Robert Barker . . . and by the Asssignes of John Bill. Anno 1631*. 8vo. The King's Printing House was at this time in Hunsdon House, Blackfriars, on the site

them in 1631, whereby the seventh commandment was made to read, 'Thou shalt committ adultery.' For this grave offence the impression (which numbered 1,000 copies and was full of typographical errors) was called in, and the printers were ordered to pay a fine of £300.[1] This sum of money Laud received the royal authority to expend in the purchase of Greek types, according to the terms of the following letter addressed to him by the King, dated 13 January 1633:

Most reverend father in God, right trusty and right entirely beloved counsellor, we greet you well. Whereas our servant, Patrick Young, keeper of our library, hath lately with great industry and care published in print an epistle of Clemens Romanus[2] in Greek and Latin, which was never printed before, and has done this to the benefit of the church, and our great honour, the manuscript, by which he printed it, being in our library; and whereas we further understand that the right reverend father in God, Augustin,[3] now Bishop of Peterborough, and our said servant Patrick Young, are resolved for to make ready for the press one or more Greek copies every year, by such manuscripts as are either in our library or in the libraries of our universities of Oxford and Cambridge, or elsewhere, if there were Greek presses, matrices, and mony ready for the work which pains of theirs will tend to the great honour of our self, this church, and nation; we have thought good to give them all possible encouragement herein, and do therefore first require you, that the fine lately imposed by our high commissioners upon Robert Barker and Martin Lucas for base and corrupt printing of the Bible, being the sum of three hundred pounds, be converted to the present buying of such and so many Greek letters and matrices, as shall be by you thought fit for this great and honourable work. And our further will and pleasure is that the said Robert Barker and Martin Lucas, our patentees for printing, which either now are, or shall hereafter succeed them, being great gainers by that patent, which they hold under us, shall at their own proper costs and charges of ink, paper, and workmanship, print, or cause to be printed in Greek, or Greek and Latin, one such volume in a year, be it bigger or less, as the right reverend father aforesaid, or our servant Patrick Young or any other of our learned subjects shall provide and make ready for the press, and shall print such a number of each copy, as yourself, or your successors for the time being, shall think fit; and all this they shall perform, whether the said copy or copies be to be printed in London, Oxford, or Cambridge, which shall be left free to their judgments and desire, whose pains prepare the copy or copies for the press. And last of all, our further will and pleasure is, that the aforesaid patentees do without any delay procure such, and so many matrices and letters, as aforesaid, that no hindrance be put upon the work, and that they be at the charge of printing in the mean time with such letters, as are already in the kingdom. Of all which or any other necessary circumstances for the furtherance of this work, we shall not fail to call for a strict account from you; and therefore do look that you call for as strict a one from them: provided always, that it shall be, and remain in your power to mitigate their fine aforesaid, according as you shall see their diligence and care for the advancing of this work.[4]

This letter Laud forwarded to the printers, who in reply, 'accounted it so great a happiness' to receive the royal commands in the matter, and stated that they

where is now *The Times* Printing House. The house had formerly been the residence of George Carey, 2nd Baron Hunsdon. It was burnt down in the Great Fire of 1666 and the King's Printer moved temporarily to the Savoy. The house was rebuilt by Major John Bill, burnt down again in 1738, at the time when John Basket held the privilege, and again rebuilt. Under Charles Eyre and William Strahan the press was moved to New St., Gough Sq., and the old building was purchased by John Walter in 1784. There is some account of the King's Printers in Bigmore and Wyman, but the view there reproduced is not the King's Printing House, but the Apothecaries' Hall in Water Lane, Blackfriars, a building still surviving. See also Plomer, 'The King's Printers under the Stuarts', in *The Library*, 1901.

[1] Bagford and others erroneously mention the fine as £3,000.

[2] *Clementis ad Corinthios Epistola prior, Oxonii*, 1633. 4to.

[3] Augustine Linsdell.

[4] D. Wilkins, *Concilia*, iv. 485.

were already labouring 'to find out the best fount and matrices, and to purchase the same at what cost soever'.[1] From the introduction of an edition of the Letters of Patrick Young[2] it appears that an attempt was made to buy Greek matrices in Antwerp. A letter is quoted from Balthazar Gerbier in Brussels to Sir Francis Windebank in September 1634, from which we learn that Mr. Naviland (the printer John Haviland) had failed in his mission, as the Antwerp printer (? Moretus) would sell neither type nor matrices, but that he himself intended to prosecute the matter. A week later he reports that he has been to Antwerp and arranged for the purchase of types, but not matrices. That 'Naviland' of the letter was the printer John Haviland is confirmed by a petition to Archbishop Laud, signed by Haviland and dated 6 October 1638, in which Haviland says: 'Whereas your Petitioner about foure years since being imployed in France and other parts beyond the Seas for providing of Greeke Letters, Matrices and such other things for his Ma[tie's] printing office. . . .'[3] The King's Printers had two Greeks, Double Pica and Great Primer; they possessed, as we shall see, matrices of the Double Pica, so that this size, unless Haviland did after all secure matrices, cannot have been bought at Antwerp in 1634.

The King's Printing House in Blackfriars produced three volumes in Greek in the years 1636, 1637, and 1638. The first was an edition of Theophylact's Commentary on St. Paul's Epistles, edited by Augustine Lindsell, Bishop of Hereford. The second was Patrick Young's *Catena in Job*. In these interesting works, from which we here give a facsimile, two Greek founts are used, the larger being a handsome Double Pica,[4] not dissimilar to that in which Estienne's great folio *Greek Testament* was printed in Paris in 1550. The smaller fount, a Great Primer, bears so close a resemblance to the fount used in the Eton *Chrysostom* that it is probable it may have been cast abroad from the same matrices. The Double Pica roman and italic used in the works are the same as those employed by Day in the preface to the *Ælfredi res gestae* in 1574. The English used for the Latin text belongs to the series of romans cut in England about 1635, described on p. 181. The third Greek volume was Gilbert Foliot's, Bishop of London's, *Expositio in Cantica Canticorum*, edited by Patrick Young, 1638. With Laud's downfall the printers escaped from their obligation and no more Greek books appeared.

Although Laud's project for the establishment of a Greek press at Oxford similar to that in London was not fully realized, his efforts on behalf of the University and its press continued unabated. In 1635 he presented his fine collection of oriental manuscripts, and established a Chair of Arabic, which greatly encouraged and promoted the study and printing of works in that and other Eastern languages. This favour he followed up with a gift of oriental types, which is alluded to in a

---

[1] According to documents in the Record Office, the fine was entered 18 Feb. 163¾, 'Fined for errors in printing the Bible, Barker £200, Lucas £100'. It was allowed to stand over from time to time, 'to see whether they would set up their press for the printing of Greek'. On 23 June 1635 it was ordered that all Bibles now in Stationers' Hall which had been erroneously printed should be redelivered to them 'with charge to see all the gross faults amended before they vent the same'. See the *Reports of Cases in the Courts of Star Chamber and High Commission*, edited by S. R. Gardiner, 1886, pp. 296 and 304.

[2] *Patricius Junius, Mitteilungen aus seinem Briefwechsel*, Herausgegeben von Johannes Kemke, Leipzig, 1898.

[3] From a Bodleian MS. (Tanner 67): see H. R. Plomer, 'Some Petitions for Appointments as Master Printers', in *The Library*, 1919, p. 101 seq.

[4] The matrices of this fount, as will be seen hereafter, passed into Grover's foundry, and were sold at the dispersion of James's foundry in 1782.

letter from John Greaves to Dr. Peter Turner, dated 1637.[1] Greaves approves of the bargain formed by the proctor's brother, Samuel Browne, for the purchase at Leyden of some printing types, of probably an Eastern language. The only danger is that some are wanting. Bedwell, when he bought Raphelengius's Arabic press, found some characters defective, which he was never able to get supplied. The writer hopes that, 'now that Archbishop Laud has taken such care for furnishing the University with all sorts of types, and procuring so many choice MSS. of the

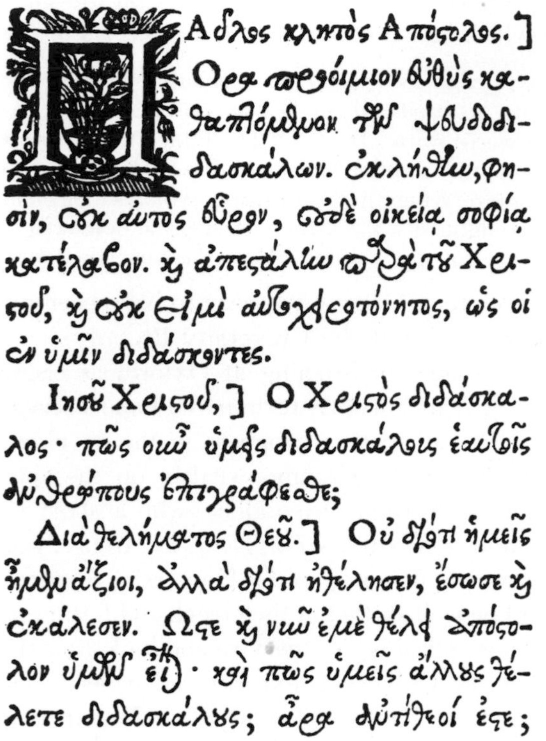
ΠΑῦλος κλητὸς Ἀπόστολος.] Ὅρα προοίμιον εὐθὺς καθαπτόμενον τῶν ψευδοδιδασκάλων. ἐκλήθην, φησίν, οὐκ αὐτὸς εὗρον, οὐδὲ οἰκείᾳ σοφίᾳ κατέλαβον. καὶ ἀπεστάλην παρὰ τοῦ Χριστοῦ, καὶ οὐκ εἰμὶ αὐτοχειροτόνητος, ὡς οἱ ἐν ὑμῖν διδάσκοντες.

Ἰησοῦ Χριστοῦ.] Ὁ Χριστὸς διδάσκαλος· πῶς οὖν ὑμεῖς διδασκάλους ἑαυτοῖς ἀνθρώπους ἐπιγράφεσθε;

Διὰ θελήματος Θεοῦ.] Οὐ διότι ἡμεῖς ἦμεν ἄξιοι, ἀλλὰ διότι ἠθέλησεν, ἔσωσε καὶ ἐκάλεσεν. Ὥστε καὶ νῦν ἐμὲ θέλει ἀπόστολον ὑμῶν εἶναι· καὶ πῶς ὑμεῖς ἄλλους θέλετε διδασκάλους; ἆρα ἀντίθεοί ἐστε;

FIG. 26. From the Theophylact, King's Printers, 1636.

Oriental languages, that some will endeavour to make true use of his noble intentions, and publish some of those incomparable pieces of the East, not inferior to the best of the Greeks or Latins.'[2] An agreement relating to these types is preserved at the Oxford Press. The contract is dated 7 January 1637, new style, and under it Samuel Browne agrees to pay to Renold Henricson, the executor of the late Arnold Corston van Hoogenacker, founder at Leyden, the sum of 2,300 gilders for oriental punches and matrices. These consisted of two sorts of Arabic, seven or eight of Hebrew, 'Siriac, Rabinis, Arabis, Greeke greate and smalle'. Corston van Hoogenacker is first heard of as a founder in 1614.

[1] *State Papers, Domestic,* 1637–8, No. 75; cf. also Madan, vol. iii, p. 456.

[2] Thomas Smith at a later date referred to the same gift: 'Circa id temporis . . . D. Guilielmus Laudus . . . postquam ingentem Codicum omne genus manu exaratorum molem pecuniis largissime effusis, ubi ubi merx ista literaria erat reperienda, conquisivisset, elegantissimos typos, omnium ferè linguarum, quae hodie obtinent, efformari procuravit' (*Vitae quorundam virorum . . . Patricii Junii,* London, 1707, 4to, p. 27).

In a letter addressed 5 May 1637 to the Vice-Chancellor the Archbishop himself refers to these recent acquisitions in the following terms:

You are now upon a very good way towards the setting up of a learned press; and I like your proposal well to keep your matrices and your letters you have gotten, safe, and in the mean time to provide all other necessaries, that so you may be ready for that work.[1]

One of the last recorded services of Laud to the Oxford Press was the recovery, in 1639, of the Savile Greek Types, which had been clandestinely abstracted by William Turner, the University printer. His letter on the subject is characteristic of the fatherly care which he exercised over the interests of the Oxford Press:

I am informed [he says] that under pretence of printing a Greek *Chronologer* . . . Turner, the printer . . . got into his hands all Sir H. Savil's Greek letters amounting to a great number, some of them scarce worn. It was in Dr. Pink's time. I pray speak with the Dr. about it and call Turner to an account before the heads what's become of them. I doubt Turner's poverty and knavery together hath made avoidance of them. Oct. 18, 1639.

Feb. 13th. Turner brought back the Greek letters, and delivered them by weight as he received them: there were not any wanting. He came very unwillingly to it.[2]

This celebrated Greek fount does not appear to have been much used after this, and no trace of it now remains at the University Press.[3]

Unfortunately for the cause of learning at Oxford, as elsewhere, the political troubles of the following years abruptly terminated Laud's services in that direction, and suspended for a time all further progress in the development of the press.[4] A revival took place during the Commonwealth, on the appointment, in 1658, of Dr. Samuel Clarke, the learned Orientalist (who a short time previously had assisted in the correction of Walton's *Polyglot*), as Archi-Typographus. This responsible functionary was 'a person', so the University Statute ordained, 'set over the printers, who shall be well skilled in the Greek and Latin tongues, and in philological studies, . . . whose office is to supervise and look after the business of Printing, and to provide at the University expence, all paper, presses, types, &c., to prescribe the module of the letter, the quality of the paper, and the size of the margins, when any book is printed at the cost of the University, and also to correct the errors of the press'.[5] To this office was, by the same Statute, annexed that of superior law bedel.

After the Restoration, printing at Oxford made still greater advances, chiefly through the instrumentality and munificence of Dr. John Fell. This eminent scholar and theologian was born in the year 1625. He entered as a student of Christ Church at the age of 11, and in 1643 bore arms in the civil wars for the king in the garrison of Oxford. At the Restoration he received ecclesiastical promotion, and from 1666 to 1669 was Vice-Chancellor of the University.[6] In this

[1] *Works of Laud*, v. 168.
[2] Ibid. v. 236.
[3] Latham's *Oxford Bibles and Printing in Oxford*, 1870, p. 46.
[4] The University supplied a press and type to King Charles I during the Civil War. The Court was at Oxford during the first years of the Civil War. See Madan's *Oxford Books* for the official publications printed there.
[5] Lemoine, *Typographical Antiquities*, London.

1797, p. 87. The office of Archi-Typographus had been instituted by Laud in 1636, but no appointment had been made.
[6] He it was on whom Tom Brown wrote his famous epigram:
 'I do not love thee, Doctor Fell,
 The reason why, I cannot tell;
 But this alone I know full well,
 I do not love thee, Doctor Fell.'

capacity, and as one of the Delegates of the Press, he exerted himself strenuously to continue the work begun by Laud for the advancement of learning and encouragement of printing at the University.[1]

We have seen that Oriental types had been purchased in 1637, and under the founders Nicholas Nicholls and Joseph Leigh below we give some account of the dealings between them and the University for further types. These University-owned types were at first kept by Gerard Langbaine, Keeper of the Archives, at his own lodgings in Queen's College. In 1652 the Old Congregation Hall was

FIG. 27. The Sheldonian Theatre. From the original wood block.

assigned to the press for storing the Hebrew, Arabic, Syriac, and Greek types. But a new building was needed for the projected learned press and at the cost of Gilbert Sheldon, Archbishop of Canterbury, the Sheldonian Theatre was built by Christopher Wren and opened in 1669. Even this building was inadequate or unsuitable, and 'Tom Pun's House' was acquired as an annexe, and other premises to the east of the Sheldonian. In fact few of the learned press books were actually printed in the Sheldonian, in spite of the imprints, for when in 1678 the right to print privileged books, that is Bibles in the main, was farmed out to four London booksellers, William Leake, Moses Pitt, Joseph Parker, and Thomas Guy, the rooms in the Sheldonian were handed over to them.[2]

In 1671 there took place an important event in the history of the press when Dr. Fell persuaded the University to lease the privilege of printing to four members

[1] Bagford (Harl. MS. 5901, fo. 89) mentions that Dr. Fell encouraged the fitting up of a paper-mill at Wolvercote by George Edwards, 'who was a cutter in wood of the great letters, and engraved many other things made use of in the printing of books, and had a talent in maps, although done with his left hand'. Of this mill Hearne wrote in 1728, 'Some of the best paper made in England is made at Wolvercote Mill' (*Reliq.* ii. 85, ed. 1869). There are several references to Edwards in Madan's *Oxford Books*.

[2] For the story of this agreement and of other agreements made by the University with the Stationers' Company and the King's Printers concerning the printing of privileged books, see J. Johnson and S. Gibson, *Print and Privilege at Oxford*, 1946.

of the University, Sir Leoline Jenkins, Thomas Yate, John Fell, and Joseph Williamson. The first three were Heads of Houses and already Delegates of the Press. Williamson was an important man in public life and was shortly to become Secretary of State. The new company was to pay £200 a year to the University, the sum which the privileged London printers had formerly paid on the condition that the University should refrain from using their overriding privilege. The Vice-Chancellor's accounts for the year September 1668 to September 1669 show that already the furnishing of a new printing-house was well under way. In the new company Thomas Yate appears to have been the managing director and book-keeper, whilst Fell, after the death of Samuel Clarke in 1669, concerned himself especially with the building up of the type-foundry.

Under the date 1672, in a Draft Statement in Fell's hand, we find this passage: 'Since our undertaking the Affair of Printing we have layd out above fourteen hundred pound, particularly are furnisht with Arabic, Hebrew, Greek, Latin & English matrices, as also letters in the aforesaid languages to the value of five hundred & fifty pounds'.[1] In a report dated 6 January 1679 [1680], written by Fell, and concerned primarily with the everlasting dispute between the Universities and the London printers on the matter of printing Bibles, we read: 'In the year 1672, several persons members of the University . . . took upon themselves the charges of the Press in the said University; and at the expense of above five thousand pounds furnisht from Germany, France and Holland an Imprimery, with all the necessaries thereof'.[2] Further details are supplied by the letters of Robert Scott, London agent of the press, and the Rev. Thomas Marshall, chaplain to the English merchants in Holland and later Rector of Lincoln College, which are given by Horace Hart in the appendix to his *Notes on a Century of Typography*.

Marshall acted as Fell's agent for the purchase of punches and matrices in Holland. The letters reproduced date from April 1670 to February 1672—the correspondence actually began in 1668—and from them we learn a number of interesting facts. From the first letter we hear that Christoffel van Dijk and the elder Voskens had both died in the preceding winter. Then we read of negotiations with Abraham van Dijk for a Greek and four sorts of Latin letters. Finally, after many delays we find that the Latin letters, which prove to be Brevier and Descendiaen roman and italic matrices, have been dispatched to Robert Scott in London. The Greek, at any rate, was ultimately delivered. It is the English Greek shown in the Oxford specimen of 1693 and was identified as by Van Dijk by Charles Enschedé, who found it in a specimen issued by one of the heirs of the foundry, the widow of J. J. Schipper. In Marshall's letter of 26 December 1671 there is reference to the possible purchase of a whole range of Van Dijk's romans and italics, but whether anything was finally delivered does not appear. In January 1672 mention is made of Voskens's Coptic and of Greek matrices of one Katzenberger. In this letter too we first hear of Jacques Vallet, a specimen of whose work was enclosed. From the three following letters we hear that Vallet would be willing to come to Oxford if the press would purchase his matrices. Marshall points out that he was not a

---

[1] Madan's *Oxford Books*, iii. 412.
[2] There is a copy of this printed account in the Bagford Collection (Harl. 5929). Gutch in his *Collect. curiosa*, i. 271, gave the amount as *four thousand*. Cf. also *Dom. State Papers* for Jan. 1680.

punch-cutter. He had in earlier letters complained of the lack of punch-cutters in Holland since the death of the elder Van Dijk and Voskens, and had foretold that the English would have to learn to do these things for themselves, a prophecy which was not to be fulfilled in a satisfactory manner for another half-century. The last letter of February 1672 tells of the death of Abraham van Dijk and of the fire at Blaeu's press in Amsterdam. But no doubt the chief reason for the closing of Marshall's mission was the war between England and France and Holland, which broke out in March of this year. As to Vallet,[1] according to Enschedé his matrices remained in Amsterdam and in December 1673 were added to the stock of Dirk Voskens. Vallet himself it appears, strangely enough, had died in England in that year. But he was not the founder secured by Oxford. That founder was Herman Hermansen, formerly in the Van Dijk foundry; after being detained in Helvoetsluys he reached Oxford on 1 August 1672. However, he proved unsatisfactory and was succeeded by another Dutchman, Peter Walpergen. There is a record of Hermansen being again at work in Amsterdam in 1681. Probably Marshall made considerable purchases during the second part of his mission, since a stock of material reached Oxford in August 1672. It had been expected in the previous year and old type had been sold to make room for the new. Marshall himself was back in Oxford by the end of March, but had left the types behind. The papers of Sir Joseph Williamson, now in the Record Office, include a number of letters relating to the efforts to have the types sent over via Antwerp.[2]

It appears to be established that the foundry, now in the Sheldonian Theatre, was well equipped by 1672, and it is rather strange that some years elapsed before the press began to use these types, at least the larger sizes of roman and italic, that is to say, those which are to-day especially associated with the name of Fell. The first of them that I have found in Oxford printed books is the English roman and italic in I. Vossius's *De Sibyllinis*, 1679. A little of the Double Pica italic is found in the folio Bible of 1682, and the Double Pica roman was used for the main text of the large folio Bible of 1685. The Oxford Press printed two sizes of Bibles in folio, a larger for lectern Bibles, and a smaller for family Bibles. The first appearance noted of the Double Pica roman is the address 'Lectori' of the Cyprian, edited by Fell in 1682. The Cyprian has also the Pica roman and italic, but the main text of the work is still set in Nicholls's roman. The Fell Canon appears first for the Dedication to James II in R. Plot's *Natural History of Staffordshire*, 1686.

The suggestion that the chief body-types of the 'Fell' series were not used for some years after 1672 is borne out by a recently published discovery. In 1940 Mr. Philip Hofer issued a reproduction with notes of a hitherto-unrecorded advertisement sheet of Bibles and Prayer Books printed by the University Press. The sheet is undated but can be assigned to 1685, since Prayer-book alterations due to the accession of James II are announced. Five sizes of type are used, Double Pica to Long Primer, each size being 'a specimen of the letter on which every book is

---

[1] Enschedé's *Fonderies de caractères dans les Pays-Bas*, p. 97, records that in March 1645 Vallet made a contract with a London punch-cutter, John Collet, to engrave punches of a fount of 'petites lettres allemandes'.

[2] *Domestic State Papers*, vol. for Dec. 1671–17 May 1672. The Calendars for the years in which Williamson was Secretary of State index many letters from Fell and his partners dealing with the affairs of the press.

Double Pica Roman.

ABCDEFGHIKLMNOPQR
STVUWXYZ ABCDEFGHIK-

Pater noſter qui es in cœlis, fanctificetur
nomen tuum. Veniat regnum tuum : fiat
voluntas tua, ſicut in cœlo, ita etiam in
terra. Panem noſtrum quotidianum da
nobis hodie. Et remitte nobis debita
noſtra, ſicut & remittimus debitoribus noſtris. Et ne nos inducas in tentationem, ſed libera nos ab illo malo.
AMEN.

Double Pica Italick.

AABCDEFGHIJKLMM
NOPQRSTVUWXYZ ÆÆ

*Pater noſter qui es in cœlis, ſanctificetur
nomen tuum. Veniat regnum tuum : fiat
voluntas tua, ſicut in cœlo, ita etiam in terra.
Panem noſtrum quotidianum da nobis hodie.
Et remitte nobis debita noſtra, ſicut & remittimus debitoribus noſtris. Et ne nos inducas in tentationem, ſed libera nos ab illo
malo. Amen.*

FIG. 28. The Fell Double Pica roman and italic. From the original
matrices.

printed'. The only 'Fell' type is the Double Pica in which a 'Church-Bible in large folio' and a 'Common Prayer Book for the use of Parish-Churches' are advertised. The Bible is the edition of 1685 mentioned above. The other sizes are not those shown in the specimen book of 1693. The Great Primer in which the matter at the foot of the sheet is set is the Oxford version of the Great Primer imported by Moxon.

We will now turn to the type-specimen books and sheet issued by the Oxford Press and give such notes as we can as to the origin of the types shown. For the bibliographical description of the specimens the reader may be referred to Berry and Johnson's *Catalogue of Specimens of Printing Types*. The display begins with two sets of roman capitals and a Canon roman, which are English types and which are all shown on the anonymous sheet No. 1 described below. The first series of capitals is a five-line Pica, and is said to have been cut by George Edwards, the man who with the support of Dr. Fell started the paper-mill at Wolvercote. There is a record of payment to Edwards for a set of initials (Hart, p. 147), undated. However, these capitals were not confined to Oxford, as we see from the anonymous sheet described below (p. 180). The second set of capitals is also on sheet No. 1 together with a lower-case. It goes back, at any rate, to 1639 and on sheet No. 2 is called 'Fatt Cannon'. Next follows Moxon's Canon, also on sheet No. 1, and a number of other English specimen-sheets. After some large Greek capitals (four-line Pica) we come to the Canon (three-line Pica), Double Pica, and Great Primer roman and italic, which are the types which printers of to-day think of as 'Fell'. They may be presumed to be Dutch, but they have not been found on any extant Dutch specimen-sheets. Oxford has the punches as well as matrices of these types, but that does not necessarily mean that they were engraved especially for the press. Hart in fact suggests that Marshall's anxiety to secure punches was due to his ignorance of the fact that matrices were all that was needed.

In November 1930 an exhibition of Oxford books was held in London, and on that occasion posters set in Fell types were exhibited, with historical notes by Mr. Stanley Morison. After referring to the Dutch origin of the larger sizes of roman and italic, he continues:

To the trained eye the *english* roman with small capitals is in a finer, an earlier and a French tradition. It has the capital M with spreading, instead of vertical, supports, while the fount as a whole reaches so high a level in design and cutting that it has only to be placed side by side with the larger bodies to reveal their comparative amateurishness. The english, pica, small pica, long primer, brevier and nonpareil are all cut by a highly experienced hand—hardly that of any Hollander—though it is conceivable that they could have been cut by Christoffel van Dijck, a German and the ablest punch-cutter working in Holland.

Mr. Morison then states that some of these romans and italics are identical with the Garamond romans and Granjon italics shown on the specimen sheets of the Luther Foundry of Frankfort, beginning with the sheet of 1592. As to the English, the capitals certainly seem to be those of Garamond, but there have been some changes in the lower-case; the *g* is a later design, with a curled instead of a straight ear. The Pica, both roman and italic, came from Frankfort, and in the case of the italic Mr. Morison was able to show its complete identity with one of the best of the Granjon italics, the 'Cicero currens', cut originally for Christophe Plantin of Antwerp in 1565. The Oxford Press in 1693 showed it with the wrong upper-case, a larger set; this was no doubt deliberate, for we meet other instances of seventeenth-century founders rejecting the capitals of the sixteenth century as being too small. However, the Oxford Press had the correct upper-case and it was shown by

Engliſh Roman.

A Æ B C D E F G H I J K L M N O P Q R S T V U W X Y Z

A B C D E F C H I K L M N O P Q R S T V U W X Y Z.

Pater noſter qui es in cœlis, ſanctificetur nomen tuum. Veniat regnum tuum : fiat voluntas tua, ſicut in cœlo, ita etiam in terra. Panem noſtrum quotidianum da nobis hodie. Et remitte nobis debita noſtra, ſicut & remittimus debitoribus noſtris. Et ne nos inducas in tentationem, ſed libera nos ab illo malo. Quia tuum eſt regnum, & potentia, & gloria in ſecula, Amen.

FIG. 29. The Fell English roman. From the original matrices.

Pica Italick.

A Æ B C D E F G H I J K L M N O P Q R S T V U W X Y Z

Pater noſter qui es in cœlis, ſanctificetur nomen tuum. Veniat regnum tuum : fiat voluutas tua, ſicut in cœlo, ita etiam in terra. Panem noſtrum quotidianum da nobis hodie. Et remitte nobis debita noſtra, ſicut & remittimus debitoribus noſtris. Et ne nos inducas in tentationem, ſed libera nos ab illo malo. Quia tuum eſt regnum, & potentia, & gloria in ſecula, Amen.

FIG. 30. The Fell Pica italic. From the original matrices.

Hart on p. 26. Plantin called the italic 'Philosophie' and included it in his specimen book of 1567. Besides the specimens already mentioned, Plantin, the Luther Foundry, and Oxford, it is found on at least seven other specimens. Although very popular in Germany and the Netherlands, only one other English printer is known to have used it, namely, Roger Daniel. It will be found in several books printed by Daniel in London in the years 1655 to 1657. The type was used also in Ireland at Cork and Waterford by Peter de Pienne, for example in an edition of the *Eikon Basilike*, Cork, 1649, and John Cook's *Monarchy no Creature of God's Making*, Waterford, 1651.

There is a difficulty as to the smaller sizes of the Fell romans and italics. We have seen that Marshall acquired for Oxford Brevier and Descendiaen roman and italic from Van Dijk. What became of these types, if we suppose that all the smaller sizes of 'Fell' came from Frankfort? Mr. Morison suggests that Van Dijk may have sold matrices which were struck from the Frankfort punches. We know in fact that not all the types shown on the specimen-sheets of his heirs were cut by Van Dijk. But this conflicts with Charles Enschedé's statement that these particular sizes were actually cut by Van Dijk, since the Enschedé firm acquired the punches in the eighteenth century. Unfortunately these have not survived, as the first Enschedés with their admiration for Fleischman set no value on this old-fashioned style. It is difficult to come to a definite opinion with these small sizes of roman without a clear impression from freshly cast type. The italics are more distinctive and there seems to be no doubt that the 'Fell' Brevier is identical with the 'Cursiv Petit Texte de G.' (Granjon) of the Frankfort sheets. These small sizes were much used at the Daniel Press at Oxford from 1877, and it is not surprising that the books of that press remind one of Lyons printing in the sixteenth century.

Of Greek types, besides the capitals to accompany the Canon roman, the 1693 specimen-book shows six sizes, Double Pica, Great Primer, English, Pica, Small Pica, and Long Primer (these last two are the same design cast on different bodies), as well as another Pica among the types presented by Francis Junius. Three of these can be identified. We have already seen that the English size was bought by Marshall from Van Dijk. The Double Pica and Long Primer are the Parangon and Garamond Greeks of Robert Granjon. The scanty display of these Greeks on the Frankfort sheets, including the special Greek specimen-sheet issued in 1670, would hardly enable us to be sure of this identification, but we have another source-book which is much more useful. In 1566 Plantin issued an *Alphabetum Graecum*, in which three sizes of Greek (the Parangon is called 'Characteres maiores' and the Garamond 'Characteres minores'; no name is given to the St. Augustin) are fully displayed, with the whole alphabet and all the ligatures set out. It is not stated that any of the types are Granjon's, but the purchases by Plantin of some Granjon Greeks are known from the documentary extracts given by Max Rooses, and comparison with the Frankfort sheets of the Parangon and Garamond leaves no doubt. The Long Primer Greek was used for the text of the Oxford *New Testament* of 1675. It should be added that neither of these Greeks is in quite the original state. The Oxford Press had an additional set of large capitals for the Double Pica, and a number of other new letters cut for both types, as may be seen from the punches which exist at Oxford, according to Hart.

Of the exotic founts there is some difficulty in discovering what founts there were at Oxford, at what period they were acquired, and from what source. We have already mentioned that as early as 1637 the press had bought Hebrew and other Oriental types and that in 1652 they were in the possession of Hebrew, Arabic, and Syriac types, as well as Greek. Under Nicholas Nicholls we shall note that that founder had supplied Hebrew and Saxon in 1656 and that these types may be those shown on C 4 of the 1693 specimen-book. As to Arabic and Syriac, the founts in this specimen differ from the two founts used in Pocock's *Carmen Tograi*, 1661 (Madan, No. 2576), where, as to the Arabic, the work is said to be printed 'Typis Arabicis Academicis'. As to Coptic, from a prospectus of 1672 (Madan, vol. iii, p. 411) we learn that the publication of the Gospels in Coptic and of a Psalter was intended, and it is known that Thomas Marshall was working on the Coptic Gospels. From the preface of David Wilkins's edition of the *New Testament in*

Coptic and Latin, Oxford, 1716, we learn that Dr. Fell had a fount cut at his own expense after the designs of Maurice Wheeler, Rector of St. Ebbe's in Oxford and compiler of the *Oxford Almanack* for 1673. After Marshall's death in 1685 a Cambridge scholar, Thomas Edwards, was invited to Oxford to carry on the work, but nothing was then printed, although Edwards compiled a Coptic Dictionary, which remains in manuscript in the Bodleian.[1] The Coptic fount was not used for the text of a book before Wilkins's edition of 1716, although it had appeared in the Oxford Specimens and the *Oratio Dominica* of 1700. According to the Latin life of Edward Bernard, Professor of Astronomy at Oxford, which is appended to the edition of the *Epistolae* of Bishop Robert Huntington, London, 1704, edited by Thomas Smith, another fount of Coptic as well as Ethiopic was presented to Oxford through Bernard in 1686 by Nicolas Witsen, Burgomaster of Amsterdam, but there seems to be no trace of these founts. Other exotics acquired somewhat later than the original Fell collection are the Ethiopic 'bought of Dr. Bernard', some

Ethiopic

ወእምድኅሪሁ: ነገሮሙ: አስማቲሁ: ሊያልሃ: ሃብ:
ግሪም: ሱራሂ: ብሃል: ዓቢይ: ዶምናኤል: ብሃል: ኃያል:
......ምርዮኅ: ብሃል: ዓቆቤ: ኵሉ: አእ: ብሃል: ረደሊ:
አፉራኅ: ብሃል: መዶኅኅ: መናቱር: ብሃል: ዖላዊ: ሌል:
ሌል: ብሃል: ከደኔ: ኵሉ: አከ: ብሃል: ተዓጋዜ: አሎሄ:
ብሃል: ፀዮሪ: ኵሉ:......ያዌ: ያዌ: ብሃል: አማኅ: ርቶዕ:

FIG. 31. Ethiopic, purchased 1692. From the original matrices.

supplementary Arabic sorts and Syriac vowels 'bought by Dr. Hyde', i.e. Thomas Hyde, Bodley's Librarian and Professor of Arabic, and the Armenian, acquired after 1695. No Armenian is shown in the early specimens, but in the account of matrices in the second issue of the 1695 book seven Armenian matrices are entered. Possibly these are part of the fount which was shown in 1768. In the *Oratio Dominica*, 1700, the Armenian is engraved, and no use appears to have been made of the type at Oxford.

After the exotics are shown the types presented by Francis Junius in 1677. Junius was a German, born at Heidelberg in 1589. After studying in Holland he came to England in 1621 and became librarian to the Earl of Arundel. He was again living in Holland from 1651 to 1674, but spent the last few years of his life in England. In 1676 by a deed of gift he presented his books in the Northern languages, as well as his punches, to Oxford.

From Madan's notes we learn that Junius's types did not reach the press until April 1679. Some of the founts Junius had to have specially cut, and it seems that it was in such a manner that many of the lesser-known languages first got into type. A scholar interested in the printing of a manuscript in some abstruse language would find no fount available among the foundries and would have to start his task by paying for the cutting of punches. In 1654 Junius writes to John Selden from

[1] See W. D. Macray's *Annals of the Bodleian Library*, 1868, pp. 149, 150, and *D.N.B.* under 'Edwards'.

Amsterdam: 'In the meanwhile have I here Anglo-Saxonic types (I know not whether you call them puncheons) a cutting, and I hope they will be matriculated and cast within the space of seven or eight weeks at the furthest.' The type was used in Junius's edition of the *Pentateuch* in Anglo-Saxon, printed at Amsterdam in 1655,[1] and at Oxford in Edward Thwaites's edition of the *Heptateuchus*, 1698, in Hickes's *Thesaurus*, 1703–5, and other works. Junius's Gothic, as well as the Saxon, was used in the *Quatuor Evangeliorum Versiones perantiquae duo*, Dordrecht, 1665, edited by Junius and Marshall, and in a later edition, Amsterdam, 1684. The Runic, Saxon, and Gothic may be found in Junius's *Gothicum Glossarium*, Dordrecht, 1664, and in Hickes's *Thesaurus*, that compendium of Oxford types. What Junius called 'Icelandic' is nothing but one of the traditional designs of Schwabacher, which goes back to the fifteenth century. A reproduction of the design is given at fig. 63 in Proctor's *German Books in the British Museum, 1501–1520*. The same may be said of the Swedish, also one of the Junius series, although first shown in the specimen of 1706. This may very well have come from the Luther Foundry of Frankfort, who had matrices, now in the possession of the Enschedé of Haarlem. It is their Cicero Schwabacher, No. 1531. The Danish probably is another similar case, but a few letters only of that fount are shown. Last of all Junius's Pica italic is another fount acquired in Holland. It is the Mediaen Cursiif shown on the sheets issued by the Heirs of Van Dijk, although, according to Charles Enschedé, it was not cut by Van Dijk. This italic had already appeared on the specimen-sheet of Joseph Moxon in 1669.

In the second issue of the Oxford specimen, 1695, three new types are shown which require a note. First is the two-line English italic belonging to the pseudo-Janson series, which is commented on below (see p. 181). Next is the Sclavonian, the ancient Cyrillic, Great Primer in size. In March 1695 Dr. Arthur Charlett in a letter to Archbishop Tenison refers to the founts of Slavonic and Armenian 'very elegantly cut, which Mr. Ludolfus is bringing to Oxford from Holland'.[2] This is H. W. Ludolf, whose *Grammatica Russica*, printed at Oxford in 1696, used the Great Primer Sclavonian. The type came from the foundry of J. A. Schmidt of Amsterdam, formerly of Frankfort. We refer below to the fragments of a specimen of Schmidt's types which is in the Bagford collection, and where the Oxford Sclavonian appears as 'Text Ricisch'. Mores states, probably in error, that this type superseded one presented by Dr. Fell. There were two founts of music, the one shown in the appendix to Hart (p. 142), of unknown origin, and the other cut by Peter Walpergen.[3] This second fount was used in the *Yattendon Hymnal*, edited by Robert Bridges, 1895–9, and helped to make that volume one of the handsomest productions of the Oxford Press.

All the material acquired by Fell and his partners was, under the terms of Fell's will, to become the property of the University four years after his death, which took place in 1686. The extent of this noble gift, the importance of which can only be estimated by recalling the low condition of letter-founding in England at the

---

[1] *Caedmonis monachi paraphrasis poetica Genesios . . . edita a Francisco Junio.* C. Cunradi typis & sumptibus editoris, Amsterdam. 1655. 4to.

[2] Lambeth MS. 942 (Gibson, xiv), no. 14. On Ludolf and his grammar see J. S. G. Simmons,

'H. W. Ludolf and the Printing of his *Grammatica Russica* at Oxford in 1696' in *Oxford Slavonic Studies*, vol. i, 1950.

[3] For Walpergen, see below, pp. 202–4.

time, will best appear by the following Inventory, published by the University in 1695:

An Account of the Matrices, Puncheons, etc., given by Bishop Fell to the University of Oxford:—[1]

34 BOXES OF MATRICES

1. Great Primer Roman . . 121	27. Music 70
2. Double Pica Roman . . 123	28. [Pica Roman and Italic, bought
3. Pica Greek . . . 513	by the University, an. 1692.]
4. Augustin Greek . . . 353	Roman, 93; Italic, 78; Small
5. Long Primer Greek . . 354	Caps., not justified, 27; in all . 198
6. Great Primer Greek . . 456	,, Great Primer Italic . . 87
7. Long Primer Italic . . 121	29. Astronomical Signs, Pica . . 25
8. Small Pica Italic . . 142	,, Samaritan, English . . 30
9. Long Primer Roman . . 155	,, Mathematical Marks . . 21
10. Pica Roman . . . 156	,, Cancelled Figures, Pica . . 10
11. Brevier Roman . . . 156	,, Brasses, Long Primer . . 16
12. Great Brass Roman Caps. . . 40	,, Mathematical Marks, Small Pica 10
13. Augustin Roman . . . 142	30. Hebrew, Great and Small . . } 292
14. English Black. . . . 73	31. ,, ,, ,, . . } 254
15. Small Pica Roman . . . 142	,, Armenian 7
16. Coptick 135	32. Arabic, Syriac, and Hebrew . 228
17. Augustin Italic . . . 114	,, Arabic Figures . . . 10
18. Pica Italic 130	33. Sclavonian Great Primer . . 110
19. Nonpareil Italic . . . 121	A paper of Flower Matrices.
20. Nonpareil Roman . . . 134	A paper of Great Primer Roman
21.} Paragon Greek . . . 445	and Italic, cut by Mr. Nichols—
22.}	not good.
23. Syriac 121	New Music Puncheons and
24. Double Pica Italic . . . 87	Matrices, cut by Peter Wal-
25. Great Canon 204	pergen.
26. Brevier Italic 134	

PUNCHEONS SEALED UP IN AN EARTHEN POT

For the Double Pica Roman and Italic, and some for the Double Pica Greek.
For the Great Brass Roman Capitals.
For the Black, English.
For the Coptick.
For the Syriack.

For the Samaritan.
For the Cannon Roman and Italic.
For the Astronomical Signs and Figures.
[For the Pica Roman and Italic.]
[For the Sclavonian also there were 109 punches.]

UTENSILS FOR PRINTING

1 small anvil.
4 hammers.
28 moulds.
1 engine to make brass rules with a plane.
1 wyer sieve.
332 dressing sticks.
2 great vices.
2 hand vices.
21 great files.

1 pair of sheers.
2 iron pots.
4 dressing planes.
3 dressing blocks.
3 plyers.
2 rubbing stones.
1 grinding stone.
26 copper borders.
32 copper letters.

[1] This list, which was appended to the specimen of 1695, second issue, includes several items acquired by the press since Dr. Fell's death. The first specimen, 1693, has a list of twenty-eight boxes only. See Hart, *Notes on a Century of Typography at Oxford*, 1900, and Berry and Johnson, pp. 6 and 7.

7 printing presses, with all things belonging to them.	5 pair of capital cases.
2 rolling presses, with all things necessary to them.	5 pair of fund cases.
132 upper and lower cases.	13 pair of Greek cases.
	50 chases.

In 1675 Dr. Fell was created Bishop of Oxford, and continued his active services to the cause of learning until the time of his death in 1686, having, as Anthony à Wood remarks, 'advanced the learned press, and improved the manufacture of printing in Oxford in such manner as it had been designed before by that public spirited person, Dr. Laud, Archbishop of Canterbury'.[1]

Junius died in 1677 at Windsor, at the great age of nearly ninety. A quaint tribute to his memory exists in a note from Dr. (afterwards Bishop) Nicolson, who, writing to Thwaites in May 1697, says, 'My acquaintance with that worthy personage was very short, and in his last days, when he was near ninety . . . alas! I can remember little more of him than that he was very kind and communicative, very good, and very old.'[2] The custodians of his valuable gift scarcely appear at first to have been impressed with an adequate sense of their responsibility, for we find that the Junian punches and matrices disappeared shortly after their presentation, and remained lost for a considerable period, when they were discovered by chance under the circumstances thus humorously narrated in a letter from Dr. (afterwards Bishop) Tanner, dated All Souls College, 10 August 1697, and addressed to Dr. Charlett:

Mr. Thwaites and John Hall took the courage last week to go to Dr. Hyde about Junius's Matrices and Punchions, which he gave with his books to the University. These, nobody knew where they were, till Mr. Wanley discovered some of them in a hole in Dr. Hyde's Study. But, upon Mr. Hall's asking, Dr. Hyde knew nothing of them; but at last told him he thought he had some old punchions about his Study, but did not know how they come there; and presently produces a small box full, and taking out one, he pores upon it, and at last wisely tells them that these could not be what they look'd after, for they were ethiopic:[3] but Mr. Thwaites desiring a sight of them, found that which he look'd on to be Gothic, and in the box were almost all Junius's Saxon, Gothic and Runic Punchions, which they took away with them, and a whole Oyster barrel full of old Greek letter, which was discovered in another hole.[4]

Apart from the value as specimens of the Oxford foundry, considerable interest attaches to the specimens of 1693 and 1695, as being the first polyglot productions

[1] *Athenae Oxonienses*, London, 1813–20, vol. iv, pp. 193–201. Wood, in speaking of Mill's *Greek Testament*, begun in 1681, says that the first sheets were begun at his Lordship's cost, 'at his Lordship's printing house, *near the Theater*' (*Fasti Oxon.*, 3rd ed. ii. 381). This was probably the hired house concerning the site of which Hearne remarks (*Reliq.* i. 254), 'One part of the wall, being a sort of bastion, is now to be seen, just as we enter into the Theater-yard, at the west corner of the north side of the Schools, viz., where the late printing-house of Bp. Fell stood.' Moxon, in 1683, recognized the Bishop's 'ardent affections to promote Typographie' in England, by dedicating to him the second volume of his *Mechanick Exercises*, the first practical work on printing by an Englishman.

[2] Nichols, *Literary Anecdotes*, iv. 147.

[3] In 1716 Wilkins notes, in the preface to his Coptic *New Testament*, p. xl, that the Ethiopic was in a chaotic condition. Dr. Mawer, writing to the Archbishop of Canterbury in 1759 respecting his proposed Supplement to Walton's *Polyglot*, says that the use of the University types had been offered him (in 1743) for printing a specimen of his work, 'but', he adds, 'an obstruction was here thrown in my way by reason of the Ethiopic types being most of them lost, and incapable of printing half a page' (Todd's *Life of Walton*, London, 1821, i. 332).

[4] Bodleian MS. Ballard 4, f. 30a. I owe this reference to Mr. J. S. G. Simmons. One of the first works printed in the recovered types was King Alfred's Saxon version of Boethius' *De Consolatione Philosophiae*, Oxford, 1698, 8vo. It was edited by Christopher Rawlinson, from a transcript by Francis Junius among the manuscripts at Oxford. Opposite the title is a head of Junius by Burghers, from a sketch by Van Dyck, in the Picture Gallery.

in this country in which a stated portion of the Scripture—the Lord's Prayer—appears in as many as forty-five different forms and nineteen different languages. In this respect, however, it was shortly afterwards eclipsed by a polyglot *Oratio Dominica*, published in London in 1700,[1] exhibiting the Lord's Prayer in upwards of one hundred versions. This may, to some extent, be regarded as a specimen of the University Press, as the two principal sheets of the work were printed at Oxford containing the prayer in the Hebrew, Samaritan, Chaldee, Syriac, Coptic, Ethiopic, Amharic, Arabic, Persic, Turkish, Tartaric, Malayan, Gothic, Runic, Icelandic, and Sclavonic, of the University foundry.[2] These constitute the most interesting part of the collection, as the remaining versions, requiring special characters, are produced chiefly in copperplate.[3] Rowe Mores points with some pride to this specimen as showing how far superior we were at that time to our neighbours abroad in the variety of our metal types.[4]

Specimens of Dr. Fell's and Junius's gifts, and an account of the foundry with its recent acquisitions, were frequently printed in the early part of the eighteenth century. Rowe Mores mentions four between 1695 and 1706. In the latter year the document had grown to twenty-five leaves, and included a Great Primer and a two-line Great Primer, purchased in 1701, and other additions. The inventory mentions twenty-eight moulds as being the number still in use in the foundry, and seven presses in the printing-house. It also distinguishes certain types as being of the Dutch height, a discrepancy to which may be traced that unfortunate anomaly of 'Bible height' and 'Classical height'. 'Bible height' was the height of the types used in the Bible Press provided by the London printers who were lessees of the privilege of printing.

A later specimen, without date, was issued in broadside form, in which the old title gave place to the more simple one of *A Specimen of several Sorts of Letters in the University Printing-House, Oxford.*[5] In this specimen, while including all the recent acquisitions, several of the older and less sightly founts comprised in Dr. Fell's gift are discarded.

In the year 1712 the University Press was removed from the Sheldonian Theatre to occupy its new quarters in the Clarendon Printing-House, erected for its accommodation—a building considered at the time one of the finest printing-houses in the world.[6]

[1] *Oratio Dominica,* πολύγλωττος πολύμορφος, nimirum, plus centum Linguis, Versionibus, aut Characteribus reddita et expressa. Londini, 1700, 4to. 76 pp. The editor was B. M(otte), Typogr. Lond. B. Motte was printing from 1693 to 1738 (see H. R. Plomer, *Dictionary of Printers, 1668–1725*) and issued a specimen of his types.

[2] This circumstance is thus frankly noted in the preface: 'Porrò, ne Characterum alienorum copiâ me jactitare videar, scias velim, schedas duas, Linguas Hebraicam, et cæteras usque ad Slavonicam complexas, in Typographéo instructissimo inclytæ Academiæ Oxoniensis excusas esse, cui faustissima quaeque comprecator quisquis est qui patriam amat, et bonam mentem colit.'

[3] These include the Malabaric, Brahman, Chinese, Georgian, Sclavonic (Hieronymian), Syriac (Estrangelo), and Armenian. The Anglo-Saxon versions are from type, as is also the Irish, which is Moxon's fount cut for Boyle.

[4] A second edition appeared in 1713. In 1715 a similar work was published by Chamberlayne in Amsterdam, entitled *Oratio Dominica in diversas omnium fere gentium linguas versa et propriis cujusque linguæ characteribus expressa. Amstelodami* 1715, 4to, with dissertations by Dr. David Wilkins and others. This production is superior in general appearance to the English book, but the oriental and other foreign characters being almost entirely copperplate, its typographical value is decidedly inferior.

[5] This sheet was reproduced, reduced, by D. C. McMurtrie in 1931.

[6] Writing in 1714, Bagford boasted that 'the Sheldonian Theatre, Plantin's Office at Antwerp, the King's Office in Paris, the King of Spain's Printing-house (Plantin's Office at Leyden—since Elzevir's—is a sorry shed), Janson's in Amsterdam, and that of the Jews in the same city, were not to compare with the Oxford House' (Harl. MS. 5901). The imprint, *E Theatro Sheldoniano,* was continued on Oxford books till 1743.

The encouragement given by Junius to the study of the Northern languages resulted in the production of many important works in that branch of literature at the University Press during the early years of the eighteenth century. Foremost among these was Dr. Hickes's *Thesaurus*,[1] printed in 1703–5, a learned and elaborate work in which the types presented by Junius are many of them displayed to advantage. Rowe Mores, for the honour of his University in general, and his own college in particular, gives a list of the famous 'Saxonists' of Dr. Hickes's time.

FIG. 32. The Clarendon Building. From the original wood block.

Amongst these, not the least eminent was Miss Elizabeth Elstob, who published in 1715 an Anglo-Saxon Grammar printed in types which, as they subsequently found their way into the Oxford Foundry, call for a particular mention here. William Bowyer the elder had printed in 1709 a work entitled *An English-Saxon Homily on the Birth-Day of St. Gregory*, translated by the Rev. William Elstob of Oxford and his sister, a young lady of great industry and learning, whom Mores describes as the 'indefessa comes' of her brother's studies, and a female student of the University.[2] In 1712, in the same types, was issued a specimen of Miss Elstob's Anglo-Saxon Grammar. Before, however, this work could be completed, Bowyer's printing-house in Dogwell Court, Whitefriars, was destroyed by fire, and his types, including the Anglo-Saxon, perished in the flames. This disastrous event was the occasion for a remarkable display of sympathy on the part of Bowyer's many friends, both in and out of the profession, which found expression in several forms,[3] one of

---

[1] *Linguarum Vett. Septentrionalium Thesaurus grammatico-criticus et archaeologicus, Oxon.* 1703–5. fol., 3 vols.

[2] This learned lady, mistress of eight languages besides her own, was the daughter of Ralph Elstob, a Newcastle merchant, and was born in 1683. Besides making the English translation which accompanies her brother's Latin version of the *Homily on St. Gregory's Day*, she transcribed and translated many Saxon works at an early age. 'Miss Elstob', says Rowe Mores, 'was a northern lady of ancient family and a genteel fortune. But she pursued too much the drug called learning, and in that pursuit failed of being careful of an one thing necessary. In her latter years she was tutoress in the family of the Duke of Portland, where we have visited her in her sleeping-room at Bulstrode, surrounded with books and dirtiness, the usual appendages of folk of learning. But if any one desires to see her as she was when she was the favourite of Dr. Hudson and the Oxonians, they may view her pourtraiture in the initial G of the *English-Saxon Homily on the Birthday of St. Gregory*' (*Dissertation*, p. 29). Miss Elstob died in 1756, and was buried at St. Margaret's, Westminster.

[3] It is interesting to note that among the money contributors on this occasion (a list of whom is preserved in Nichols's *Anecdotes of Bowyer*, pp. 496–7), Robert Andrews and Thomas James, the letter-founders, appear as donors of five guineas each, and Thomas Grover of two guineas.

the most practical of which was the offer of Lord Chief Justice Parker (afterwards Earl of Macclesfield) to pay for cutting a new set of Anglo-Saxon types for Miss Elstob's Grammar. The drawings for the new types were made, at Lord Parker's request, by Humphrey Wanley,[1] the eminent Saxonist, and the cutting of the punches entrusted to Robert Andrews the letter-founder, who, however, proved unequal to the task. 'I did what was required', Wanley wrote, 'in the most exact and able manner that I could in all respects. But it signified little; for when the alphabet came into the hands of the workman (who was but a blunderer), he could not imitate the fine and regular stroke of the pen; so that the letters are not only clumsy, but unlike those that I drew. This appears by Mrs. Elstob's *Saxon Grammar*.'[2]

Poor as the letter-founder's performance was, the Grammar duly appeared in the new letter in 1715,[3] and the punches, matrices, and types remained in the possession of Bowyer and his son, being used occasionally in some of their subsequent works, though not in any other of which Miss Elstob was the authoress.[4] In 1753 they were sent by William Bowyer the younger, to Rowe Mores, with the following letter, for presentation to the University of Oxford:

To EDWARD ROWE MORES, Esq., at Low Leyton.   *4th December*, 1753.

Sir,—I make bold to transmit to Oxford, through your hands, the Saxon punches and matrices, which you were pleased to intimate would not be unacceptable to that learned body. It would be a great satisfaction to me, if I could by this means perpetuate the munificence of the noble donor, to whom I am originally indebted for them, the late Lord Chief Justice Parker, afterwards Earl of Macclesfield, who, among the numerous benefactors which my father met with, after his house was burned in 1712–13, was so good as to procure those types to be cut, to enable him to print Mrs. Elstob's *Saxon Grammar*. England had not then the advantage of such an artist in letter cutting as has since arisen,[5] and it is to be lamented, that the execution of these is not equal to the intention of the noble donor, and, I now add, to the place in which they are to be reposited. However, I esteem it a peculiar happiness, that as my father received them from a great patron of learning, his son consigns them to the greatest seminary of it, and that he is, Sir, your most obliged friend, and humble Servant,   W. BOWYER.

The adventures of this epistle and the gift which accompanied it, before reaching their destination, are almost romantic. For some reason which does not appear, Rowe Mores, on receipt of the punches and matrices, instead of transmitting them

---

[1] Humphrey Wanley, son of Nathaniel Wanley, was secretary to the Society for Promoting Christian Knowledge, and afterwards librarian to the Earl of Oxford. He was an adept in the Saxon antiquities and calligraphy, and was an important contributor to Hickes's *Thesaurus*, for which work he compiled the historical and critical catalogue of Saxon and other manuscripts. He died in 1726, aged 54. Much of his correspondence and his diary are preserved among the Harleian MSS. See also D. C. Douglas, *English Scholars*, 1939.

[2] Nichols's *Anecdotes of William Bowyer*, London, 1782, 4to, p. 498.

[3] *The Rudiments of Grammar for the English Saxon Tongue*, London, 1715. 4to. A specimen of the letter is given at fig. 43, p. 189.

[4] 'This type Miss Elstob used in her *Grammar*, and in her *Grammar* only. In her capital undertaking, the publication of the *Saxon Homilies*, begun and left unfinished, whether because the type was thought unsightly to politer eyes, or whether because the University of Oxford had cast a new letter that she might print the work with them, or whether (as she expresses herself in a letter to her uncle, Dr. Elstob), because "women are allowed the privilege of appearing in a richer garb and finer ornaments than men", she used a Saxon of the modern garb. But not one of these reasons is of any weight with an antiquary, who will always prefer the natural face to "richer garb and finer ornaments". And on his side is reason uncontrovertible.' (Rowe Mores, *Dissert.*, p. 29.)

[5] i.e. William Caslon.

to Oxford, took them to Caslon's foundry to be repaired and rendered more fit for use. Caslon having kept them four or five years without touching them, Bowyer removed them from his custody, and in 1758 entrusted them to Thomas Cottrell, from whom in the same year he received them again, carefully 'fitted up' and ready for use, together with 15 lb. of letter cast from the matrices. In this condition the whole was again consigned by Bowyer to Rowe Mores, together with a copy of Miss Elstob's *Grammar*, for transmission to Oxford. On hearing, two years later, that his gift had never reached the University, he made inquiries of Mores, from whom he received a reply that 'the punches and matrices were very safe at his house', awaiting an opportunity to be forwarded to their destination. This opportunity does not appear to have occurred for three years longer, when, in October 1764, the gift was finally deposited at Oxford. Its formal acknowledgement was, however, delayed till August 1778, exactly a quarter of a century after its presentation.[1]

The correspondence touching this transaction, amusing as it is, throws a curious light on Rowe Mores's character for exactitude, and it is doubtful whether the publication of Bowyer's first letter in the *Dissertation*,[2] together with a few flattering compliments, was an adequate atonement for the injury done to that gentleman by the unwarrantable detention of his gift. Nor does the title under which the gift was permitted to appear in the University specimen, suppressing as it does all mention of the real donor's name, and giving the entire honour to the dilatory go-between, reflect any credit on the hero of the transaction. The entry appears thus: 'Characteres Anglo-Saxonici per eruditam fœminam Eliz. Elstob ad fidem codd. mss. delineati; quorum tam instrumentis cusoriis quam matricibus Univ. donari curavit E. R. M. e Collegio Regin., A.M. 1753.

> Cusoria majuscula 42 (desunt Ꝥ et ꝑ)
> Matrices majusculæ 44.
> Cusoria minuscula 37 (desunt e et ᵹ)
> Matrices minusculæ 39.

It does not appear that these types were ever made use of at Oxford in the eighteenth century. The punches and matrices remain in the University Press to this day,[3] and the type was used as a phonetic script, with some extra sorts, by Robert Bridges in his *Tract on the Present State of English Pronunciation*, 1910, 2nd edition 1912.

Between the Broadside sheet following the specimen of 1706, and 1768, no specimen of the Oxford Foundry occurs. There exists, however, in the works issuing from the press during that period ample testimony to its activity. The proposal to print Dr. John Mawer's *Supplement to Walton's Polyglot*, with its types, is evidence of the continued reputation of its 'learned' founts; while such an admirable specimen of typography as Blackstone's *Charter of the Forest*, printed in 1759,[4]

---

[1] Nichols's *Anecdotes of Bowyer*, p. 319; *Literary Anecdotes*, ii. 361, seq.

[2] *Dissertation*, p. 28.

[3] A few of the punches and matrices were shown in the Caxton Exhibition of 1877.

[4] *The Great Charter and Charter of the Forest*, Oxford, at the Clarendon Press, 1759, 4to. This fine work is printed in Caslon's Great Primer roman. The copperplate initials and vignettes are very fine, the former containing views of several of the different colleges and public buildings at Oxford. Further dealings with Caslon are recorded, on 28 March

affords proof that Oxford was not behindhand in that famous revival of printing which received such impetus from the taste and genius of Baskerville. The Delegates of the Press had, indeed, so high an opinion of the talents of this famous artist that they employed him in 1758 to cut a fount of Great Primer Greek type for a *Greek Testament* shortly to be issued.[1] The performance was pronounced unsuccessful, but the Greek types duly appeared, together with numerous other acquisitions, including a Long Primer Syriac purchased from Caslon, in the *Specimen* of 1768–70.[2]

Of this specimen Rowe Mores (who informs us that it was printed at the request of foreigners) falls foul as inaccurate.

The materials from which this account [i.e. his summary of the contents of the Foundry] is drawn [he says] are not so accurate as might have been expected from an Architypographus and the Curators of the Sheldonian. In excuse may be alleged that neither the Architypographus nor the Curators are Letter-founders; certainly that the matter has not been treated with that precision which in so learned a body should seem to be requisite. For one instance among others, which might be produced, take the Double Pica, Brevier and Nonpareil Hebrew, the only Hebrew types the University then had. They are two-line English, English and Long Primer. And this mistake has run through all the editions of the Oxford specimen, and in the last of 1770, the leanest and the worst of all, appears most glaringly. For this Brevier is placed immediately under Caslon's Long Primer, a diversity sufficient one would think to show the blunder without the aid of a magnifier. The Nonpareil as it is called is omitted in this last specimen, and so are many other sets of matrices which have been given to the University, touching which enquiry should be made out of respect (at least) to the memory of the donors.[3]

Another specimen appeared in 1786, in which more of the old founts are discarded in favour of more modern letters, among which are noticeable several roman founts cast on a large body, to obviate the necessity of 'leading'; including an English, cast for John Richardson's *Dictionary*. Almost all the 'learned' founts presented by Fell and Junius are here shown, as well as a considerable number of borders and ornamental initials.

In 1794 a still fuller specimen appeared, which included a Great Primer Greek, cut by Caslon, and several new titling letters. To this specimen is appended a detailed inventory, both of the punches and matrices at that time in the possession of the University, and of the quantity of type of various kinds in stock, with the utensils for printing.

1766 for roman and italics and in 1767 for Arabic, Syriac, Samaritan, and Greek. See Hart, op. cit., and below, p. 242.

[1] *Novum Testamentum, juxta exemplar Millianum. Typis Joannis Baskerville. Oxonii e Typographeo Clarendoniano* 1763. *Sumptibus Academiae*, 4to and 8vo. (See also Chap. 13.) The Baskerville Greek punches, matrices, and types, still preserved at Oxford, are supposed to be the only relics in this country of the famous Birmingham foundry.

[2] Though dated 1768 on the title, this specimen appears not to have been completed for two years, as it bears the date 29 Sept. 1770 on the last page, and includes specimens of purchases made in that year.

[3] *Dissertation*, p. 45. These strictures we cannot but regard as somewhat hypercritical. It was no uncommon thing to cast a small face of letter on a body larger than its own; and in the case of Hebrew and other orientals, where detached points were cast to work over the letter, it was by no means unusual at that time, and till a later period, to designate the latter by the name of the body which it and the point in combination collectively formed. With regard to the gradual lapse of obsolete and superannuated founts from the specimen, Mores's antiquarian zeal appears to have blinded him to the fact that the Oxford Press may have issued their specimens as an advertisement of their present resources, rather than as an historical collection of their typographical curiosities.

The following is a summary of the foreign and 'learned' punches and matrices included in this catalogue:

PUNCHES

Anglo-Saxon	79	Greek, two-line English	10
Arabic	33	Hebrew, with points	20
Armenian	65	Music	220
Black, English	72	Runic	24
Coptic, Pica	116	Samaritan, English	28
Gothic	25	Saxon	21
Greek, Great Primer	114	Slavonian	106
,, ,, (Baskerville's)	148	Syriac, English	90
,, Double Pica	190	Turkish, Persian, Malayan	47

MATRICES

Arabic, Syriac, and Hebrew	228	Greek Long Primer	352
Arabic figures	10	,, two-line English	11
Anglo-Saxon	83	Hebrew, large and small	230
Armenian	77	,, ,,	250
,,	7	Music	228
,,	7	,,	70
Black, English	73	Runic, Dutch, Saxon, Gothic, and	
Coptic	135	Greek	89
,,	27	Samaritan	30
Ethiopic	224	Saxon, Small Pica, Long Primer, Pica	20
Greek, Augustin (or English)	351	Slavonic	110
,, Great Primer	493	Syriac, English	120
,, ,, (Baskerville's)	167	,, vowels	5
,, Double Pica (bad)	239	Turkish, Persian, Malayan	47
,, Paragon (Double Pica)	432	Welch	10

Of the printing utensils, the following items will give an idea of the extent of the press at that date:

CASES (FILLED WITH TYPE)		Frames	30
Common cases	267	Chases	129
Single cases and boxes	44	Letter boards	37
Fount cases	26	Presses	5
Long Greek cases	34	Proof press	1

Of the presses, one is described as 'mahogany, set up in the year 1793', and another as 'on the new constitution which works with a lever, set up in 1793'.

The revival of the Fell types in the nineteenth century is due in the first place to the Rev. C. H. O. Daniel, who started a small private press at Frome in 1845. Afterwards he became Provost of Worcester College, and at Oxford between 1877 and 1919 printed privately a number of books in the Fell types, using also old sixteenth-century flowers.[1] A still more important name in the story of the revival

[1] See *Memorials of C. H. O. Daniel*, Oxford, 1921/2.

is that of Horace Hart, who in the 1890's rescued the punches and matrices from neglect and recast the types. The culmination of his work may be seen in his book *Notes on a Century of Typography.*

The famous gifts of Fell and Junius, in company with Baskerville's Greek, Walpergen's music, and Miss Elstob's Anglo-Saxon, remain to this day the most interesting monuments our country possesses of the art and mystery of its early letter-founders.

7

THE STAR CHAMBER FOUNDERS AND THE LONDON POLYGLOT

PRIOR to 1637, letter-founding is not specifically mentioned as a distinct industry in any of the public documents. We are not on that account, however (as we have endeavoured to point out), to assume either that the restrictive provisions of previous enactments which regulated printing did not apply to letter-founding, or that, as a trade, it had no separate existence before that date. The divorce of letter-founding from printing was in all probability a long and gradual process; and although it would be difficult to fix any precise date to the completion of that process, we may yet infer from the fact that the Decree of 1586 (which includes by name almost every other branch of industry connected with printing) makes no mention of letter-founding, while the Decree of 1637 particularly names it, that between these two dates printers ceased generally to be their own letter-founders.

As we have elsewhere noticed, the Stationers' Company as early as 1597 took cognizance of letter-founding as a distinct trade when it called upon Benjamin Sympson to enter into a bond of £40 not to cast any letters or characters, or to deliver them, without previous notice to the master and wardens. And that there was a certain body of men known in the trade as 'founders' owning the authority of the Stationers' Company in 1622 is evident from the fact that in that year the Court called upon 'the founders' to give bond to the Company not to deliver any fount of new letters without notice. It would be erroneous, therefore, to imagine that the Star Chamber Decree of 1637 in any sense created letter-founding as a distinct trade. Its purpose, as in the case of printing, was to restrict the number of those engaged in it, which had probably grown excessive under the milder régime of the Decree of 1586.

In the curious little tract, to which allusion has already been made, entitled *The London Printer, his Lamentation*,[1] the author, writing in 1660, after highly com-

---

[1] There is a copy in the British Museum. Reprinted in *Harl. Miscell.* London, 1745, 4to, iii. 277. The full title of this curious tract is as follows: *The London Printer, his Lamentation; or the Press oppressed, or overpressed. September 1660. Quarto, containing 8 pages. In this sheet of Paper is contained, first, a short account of Printing in general, as its Usefulness, where and by whom invented; and then a Declaration of its Esteem and Promotion in England by the several Kings and Queens since its first Arrival in this Nation; together with the Methods taken by the Crown for its better Regulation and Government till the year 1640; when, says the Author, this Trade, Art and Mystery was prostituted to every vile Purpose both in Church and State; where he bitterly inveighs against Christopher Barker, John Bill, Thomas Newcomb, John Field and Henry Hills as Interlopers, and, under the King's Patent, were the only instruments of inflaming the People against the King and his Friends, etc.*

mending the Decree of Elizabeth (23 June 1586) limiting the number of printers, says that about 1637, notwithstanding the above decree, 'printing and printers were grown to monstrous excess and exorbitant riot', and that the law was infringed at all points. In this 'monstrous excess and exorbitant riot' it is highly probable that the letter-founders of the day figured. And it seems equally probable that John Grismond, Thomas Wright, Arthur Nicholls (or Nichols)[1] and Alexander Fifield, who were appointed by the Decree of 1637 as the four authorized founders, had already been founding types for several years with or without the sanction of the authorities.

In the Registers of the Stationers' Company the names both of John Grismond and Thomas Wright occur as publishers of a number of works, from which it would appear that both before and after 1637 they may have combined the trade of bookseller and printer with that of letter-founder.[2]

In another curious document, preserved among the Bagford collections, and entitled *The Brotherly Meeting of the Masters and Workmen Printers, began November 5, 1621; the first Sermon being on November 5, 1628, and hath been continued by the Stewards, whose names follow in this Catalogue to this present third of May 1681*,[3] the names of Thomas Wright, Arthur Nichols, and Alexander Fifield all appear as having served their stewardship, although unfortunately the list does not assign dates to the respective terms of service.[4] In the lists of the Stationers' Company, however, we find that the four founders took up their freedom in the following order: John Grisman (*sic*), 2 December 1616 (apprenticed to Edward White, 18 Dec. 1609); Thomas Wright, 7 May 1627 (apprenticed to Richard Adams, 3 May 1620); Arthur Nicholls, 3 December 1632; and Alexander Fifield, 20 July 1635 (apprenticed to Richard Adams, 20 Dec. 1627).[5]

Respecting Wright and Fifield, after their nomination as Star Chamber founders history records little. Wright, as appears from the Poll-Tax Returns, was in 1641 of St. Botolph's Ward, Aldersgate. Fifield's name is found in the imprint of the *Directory of the Assembly of Divines*, 1644. We know of three addresses of Grismond, first at Little North Door, St. Paul's, then in Paul's Alley, and next in Ivy Lane, always at the sign of the Gun. The two first addresses are perhaps the same, since, as may be seen from the view of old St. Paul's in William Dugdale's *The History of St. Paul's Cathedral*, 1658, Paul's Alley was opposite the Little North

---

[1] Mores makes a mistake in calling this founder Arthur Nicholas.

[2] In the British Museum *Catalogue of Early English Books to 1640*, the name of John Grismond appears as publisher of some thirty books. He died in 1638. John II, who was printing till 1664, was probably a nephew. See Plomer's *Dictionary of Printers, 1640–67*.

[3] Harl. MS. 5910, pt. i, p. 148.

[4] Moxon, in his account of the Customs of the Chapel (*Mechanick Exercises*, ii. 363), gives a full description of this yearly feast, which, he says, 'is made by Four Stewards, *viz.*, two Masters and two Journey-men; which Stewards, with the Collection of half a Crown apiece of every Guest, defray the Charges of the whole Feast'. The List of Stewards, above referred to, contains, among others, the names of nearly all the seventeenth-century letter-founders.

Seventy feasts were held between 1621 and 1681, the first few probably being half-yearly. Three or four stewards officiated at each. The names of the founders occurring in the list are as follows, the figures appended to each indicating the number of the feast at which each served his stewardship, with the approximate date:

(24) Thomas Wright (1635)
(26) Arthur Nichols (1637)
(31) Alexander Fifield (1642)
(42) Nicholas Nichols (1653)
(61) James Grover (1672)
(63) Thomas Grover (1674)
(64) Joseph Leigh (Lee?) (1675)
(66) Godfrey Head (1677)
(67) Thomas Goring (1678)
(69) Robert Andrews (1680)

[5] Arber's *Transcripts*, iii. 363–8.

Door. John Grismond, named in a State Paper in 1649 as having on the 19 October of that year entered into a bond of £300, and given two sureties, not to print any seditious work,[1] was John II.

Of Arthur Nicholls there remains a record of a more ample and satisfactory nature, being undoubtedly one of the most valuable and interesting memorials of early English letter-founding which we possess. It appears that Nicholls, at the time of his nomination as Star Chamber founder in 1637, was also a candidate for the vacant place of printer at Oxford, at that time at the disposal of Archbishop Laud, who, as we have seen in the preceding chapter, had been reserving it for a printer well versed in the Greek language. Nicholls, being unsuccessful in this matter, and driven by his straitened circumstances to seek some addition to his slender pittance as letter-founder, thereupon made application to Laud to be admitted as a licensed master-printer in London, that so he might make use of his own type. His letter and the 'Cause of Complaint' annexed are preserved among the State Papers,[2] and are so important that we make no apology for quoting them *in extenso*:

To the Right Reverend Father in God, WILLIAM, LORD ARCHBISHOP OF CANTERBURY, *his Grace, Primate and Metropolitane of all England.*

The humble peticion of Arthur Nicholls. Showeth unto your grace:

That the said peticioner hath spent much tyme and paines in cuttinge and foundinge of letters for divers of the printers in London, and at this tyme hath greate store of letters ready cast lying upon his hands, they refusing to take them from him att any rate.

Besides this his imployment of founding letters is of soe small gaine that alone it will not mainteyne him and his familie but that of necessitie hee must betake himself to some other course whereby to be freed from extreame povertie, and utterly to quitt himself of that, unless your Grace be pleased out of your wonted goodness to comiserate his case.

May it therefore please your Grace, since you have otherwise determined to dispose of the printers place att Oxford, to give him leave, for the better encouragement of that course wherein he hath so long exercised himself, to bee a printer here in London, That soe he may make use of his owne letters for the elegant performance whereof hee doth promise to use his best care and industry And ever to pray for your Grace's honour and happinesse.

The 'Cause of Complaint' gives a lively picture of the tribulations of letter-founders at that time:

The Cause of Complaint of ARTHUR NICHOLLS [endorsed '*Mr. Nicholls his reasons to be made printer.*']

The Complainant being the cutter and founder of Letters for Printers is 3 quarter of a yeares time cutting the Punches and Matrices belonginge to the castinge of one sorte of letters, which are some 200 of a sorte, after which they are 6 weekes a castinge, that done some 2 monthes tyme is required for triall of every sorte, and then the Printers pay him what they themselves list; thus he is necessitated to lay out much money and forebeare a long tyme to little or noe benefitt.

Likewise for the Greeke the Printers came unto him promisinge him the doinge of all

---

[1] *Calendar of State Papers, Domestic,* 1649, pp. 362, 523. Among the entries of admission to Merchant Taylors' School occurs: 'Johannes Grismond, filius unicus Johannis Grismond, Typographi, natus Londini, in paroeciâ de Giles, Cripplegate, Aprilis 1, 1647: an. agens 8. Admissus est Aprilis 3, 1654.'
[2] *Domestic,* 1637–8, vol. ccclxxvi, Nos. 13 and 14.

the common worke, which drewe him to doe 400 Mattrices and Punches for 80 *l.* which weare truly worth 150 *l*:

Further they caused him to spend 5 weekes tyme in cutting the letters for the small Bible, it beinge finished was approved for the best in England, notwithstandinge they put him off aboute it from tyme to tyme for 15 weekes till (as they pretended) Mr. Patricke Yonge came out of the contry.

All which tyme he kept his servants standinge still, in regard whereof he refused to doe it, except he might doe the common worke likewise, when for feare of the displeasure of my lord his Grace, they came to him agayne but told him that if they should lett him have worke enough, he would growe to ritch.

Albeit, of soe small benifitt hath his Art bine, that for 4 yeares worke and practice he hath not taken above 48 *l.*, and had it not bine for other imploymente he might have perrisht.

He seeinge himself soe slightly regarded by them, was the rather annimated to sell off' the proffitablest of his worke thinking to take some other businesse in hand, whereby to free himselfe from want, being not able to subsist by workinge only for 2 or 3.

Notwithstandinge his longe tyme spent in that Art, wherein he hath brought up his sonne to bee soe expert and able that if it please God to call him, the other is able exactly to performe anythinge touchinge the same.

Wherefore he requesteth my lorde Grace not to confine him to these miserable uncertainties, but promiseth if he will bee pleased to grant his peticion, he shall see more done in one yeare than was ever done in England for all kindes of languages which he is assured will bee for the good of the commonwealth in general and his Graces particular content.

Whether Nicholls's application was successful or otherwise is not known. In the disastrous times which immediately followed the four Star Chamber founders are lost sight of. It is scarcely likely, judging from the dismal account given above of the trade in times of peace, that they were able, any of them, to keep a business together in times of civil war. Nor is there any certainty that when, in 1649, the Commonwealth re-enacted the main provisions of the Star Chamber Decree, that the four founders then appointed were the same who had been licensed in 1637. Mores, however, leads us to suppose that they were, and for the purpose of enumerating the oriental and learned matrices which about the year 1657 were in use in the country, treats their four foundries as one. There is, however, no reason for supposing that they worked in partnership, or that their business was in any way connected. But in one great undertaking they were associated; and the *London Polyglot* of 1657 has generally been regarded as the product of the types of some, if not all, of their number.

By these or some of them [observes Mores] we may suppose to have been cut the letter used in *The English Polyglott*: but as we cannot assign to any of them their particular performances we shall till we are better able to ascertain them, call their labours by the name of the Polyglott Foundery, which, as nearly as that work and the *Heptaglott* which accompanies it instructs us, is described at the bottom of the page.[1] But it is not to be doubted, considering the elegance and simplicity of the assortment which we see, that the foundery was as completely furnished with that which we see not, and which, for that reason we cannot mention.[2]

The *London Polyglot* ranks deservedly as one of the most conspicuous landmarks of English typography. Great works had gone before it, and greater followed. But in few of these has the learning of the scholar, the enterprise of the publisher,

---

[1] The list of matrices is given on p. 160.   [2] *Dissertation*, p. 40.

the industry of the editor, the ability of the printer, and the skill of the letter-founder been combined to so extraordinary a degree as in the production of this *magnum opus* of the Commonwealth press. A brief sketch of the typographical history of this famous work may be interesting, and not out of place here.

The *London Polyglot* was the fourth great Bible of the kind which had been given to the world.[1] In 1517[2] the *Complutensian Polyglot* had been printed at Alcalá, at the charges of Cardinal Ximenes, in six volumes, containing the Sacred Text in Hebrew, Latin, Greek, and Chaldean, including an 'Apparatus' consisting of a Hebrew and Chaldee Lexicon, &c. This work will always be famous, if for no other reason, for the grand, bold Greek type in which the Septuagint and New Testament are printed.

In 1572 the *Antwerp Polyglot* of Arias Montanus was completed, in eight magnificent volumes, by Christophe Plantin. It comprises the whole of the Complutensian texts, with the addition of the Syriac, and an Apparatus containing lexicons and grammars of Hebrew, Chaldee, Syriac, and Greek.

In 1645 the *Paris Polyglot*, edited by Le Jay and others, was published in ten sumptuous volumes. It comprises the whole of the texts of the *Antwerp Polyglot*, with the addition of Arabic and Samaritan. Owing to the abrupt completion of this work, no Apparatus of any description was included. This work was seventeen years in the press.

The *London Polyglot*, as we shall observe, added to the languages used in the *Paris Polyglot* the Persian and Ethiopic, with an Appendix containing additional Targums, also a complete 'Apparatus' and Prolegomena, with alphabetical tables of the various languages employed, and others besides.

The following table will show clearly the gradual advances made by the four great *Polyglots* in respect of the versions they comprise:[3]

	Complutum, 1522	*Antwerp, 1572*	*Paris, 1645*	*London, 1657*
1	Old Test., *Heb.*	Old Test., *Heb.*	Old Test., *Heb.*	Old Test., *Heb.*
2	Vulgate, *Lat.*	Vulgate, *Lat.*	Vulgate, *Lat.*	Vulgate, *Lat.*
3	Septuagint, *Gr. Lat.*	Septuagint, *Gr. Lat.*	Septuagint, *Gr. Lat.*	Septuagint, *Gr. Lat.*
4	Pentat., *Chal. Lat.*	Old Test., *Chal. Lat.*	Old Test., *Chal. Lat.*	Old Test., *Chal. Lat.*
5	New Test., *Gr. Lat.*	New Test., *Gr. Lat.*	New Test., *Gr. Lat.*	New Test., *Gr. Lat.*
6	..	New Test., *Syriac, Heb. Lat.*	New Test., *Syriac, Heb. Lat.*	New Test., *Syriac*
7	..	..	Old Test., *Syriac Lat.*	Old Test., *Syriac*
8	..	..	Bible, *Arab. Lat.*	Bible, *Arab.*
9	..	..	Pentat., *Samar. Lat.*	Pentat., *Samar.*
10	..	..	..	Pentat. Gospels, *Per. Lat.*
11	..	..	..	Ps., Cant. New Test., *Eth. Lat.*
12	..	..	..	Add. Targums
13	Apparatus	Apparatus	..	Apparatus, Proleg., &c.

[1] The first project of a Polyglot Bible is due to Aldus Manutius, who, probably between 1498 and 1501, issued a specimen-page containing the first fifteen verses of Genesis, in collateral columns of Hebrew, Greek, and Latin. The typographical execution is admirable. A facsimile is shown in Renouard's *Annales de l'Imprimerie des Aldes*, 2nd and 3rd editions.

[2] The first volume was finished in 1514 and the work completed in 1517, but not published till 1522.

[3] For the bibliography of the *Polyglots* see the *Historical Catalogue* of the British and Foreign Bible Society, London, 1911, vol. i. That work contains much information on Bibles in all languages and on the types of the less well-known languages.

The first announcement of the *London Polyglot* was made in 1652, when Dr. Walton published *A Brief Description of an Edition of the Bible in the Original Hebrew, Samaritan, and Greek, with the most ancient Translations of the Jewish and Christian Churches, viz. the Sept. Greek, Chaldee, Syriac, Ethiopic, Arabic, Persian, etc., and the Latin versions of them all; a new Apparatus, etc.*[1] This Description, which set forth the various improvements in the proposed *Polyglot* on its predecessors, was accompanied by a specimen-sheet[2] containing the first twelve verses of the first chapter of Genesis in the following order: On one side, Hebrew with interlinear Latin translation, Latin (Vulgate), Greek (Septuagint) with Latin, Chaldean paraphrase with Latin, Hebrew-Samaritan, Samaritan. On the other side, Syriac with Latin, Arabic with Latin, Latin translation of the Samaritan, Persian with Latin. The imprint to this highly interesting specimen (a copy of which is said to be in the Library of Sidney Sussex College, Cambridge) was: *Londini, Typis Jacobi Flesher*; from which it appears that James Flesher was the first possessor of some of the types cast by the polyglot founders, and subsequently used by Roycroft in this great work.[3]

Flesher's *Specimen*, which we have unfortunately not been able to discover, met with many critics. Amongst others was Dr. Arnold Boate, the Dutch scholar (who had already found fault with the Hebrew character used in the Paris *Polyglot*, which he described as 'a very scurvy one, and such as will greatly disgrace the work'), was very disparaging to the new undertaking. It was probably in deference to this critic that Dr. Walton added the following manuscript note to the copy of the specimen now at Sidney Sussex College, Cambridge: 'Typos Hebr. et Syr. cum punctis meliores, parabimus.'

The time occupied in securing the co-operation and assistance of the learned men of the day, in getting subscribers,[4] in arranging copy, and finally in providing the necessary types, delayed the commencement of the undertaking till September 1653. Writing to Usher on the 18 July of that year, Dr. Walton thus notes the near completion of the preliminary arrangements: 'I hope we shall shortly begin the work; yet I doubt the *founders* will make us stay a week longer than we expected. . . . We have resolved to have a better paper than that of 11*s*. a ream, viz., of 15*s*. a ream.'[5]

---

[1] These *Proposals* were printed by R. Norton for Timothy Garthwaite at the lesser North Gate of St. Paul's Church, London, 1652.

[2] It is described by the Rev. H. J. Todd in his *Memoirs of the Life and Writings of the Right Rev. Brian Walton, D.D.*, London, 2 vols., 1821. Todd's work contains much valuable information respecting the *Polyglot*.

[3] Among the manuscripts in Sidney Sussex College is a letter written by Abraham Whelock to the Vice-Chancellor of Cambridge, dated 5 Jan. 1652, in which, referring to the specimen, he says: 'When the sheete, here sent, was printed off, I corrected at least 80 errata in it. It as yet serves to show what letters Mr. Flesher, an eminent printer, my friend and printer of my booke, hath' (Todd's *Memoirs*, i. 56). James Flesher, son of Miles Flesher (one of the twelve Star Chamber printers named in the Act of 1637), entered into a bond of £300 to the Stationers' Company in 1649, and held the office of City printer in 1657. His name occurs in the list of

the *Brotherly Meeting of Printers* as Steward at the 42nd Feast. In 1664 he served, together with Roycroft, on the jury at the trial of John Twyn; see above, p. 122.

[4] Walton's *Polyglot* is supposed to be the second book printed by subscription in England. In 1617 Minsheu's *Ductor in linguas* was published by subscription, the names of those who took a copy of the work being printed. Minsheu's venture, however, turned out a failure. In Dr. Walton's case this mode of publication was, owing to the energy of the promoter and the number of his friends, successful. The subscription was £10 per copy, or £50 for six copies. The estimated cost of the first volume was £1,500, and of succeeding volumes £1,200 each. Towards this, £9,000 was subscribed four months before the first volume was put to press.

[5] Usher's *Works*, vol. xvi, letter 304. Dr. Walton received the Protector's permission to import the paper for his work, duty free.

Towards the end of September 1653 the impression of the first volume was begun at the press of Thomas Roycroft, in Bartholomew Close, whose name will always by honourably associated with this famous work. Very little is known of the actual manual labour employed in the production, beyond the fact that two presses only were said to have been kept at work, and that the types were supplied by more than one of the four authorized founders. Chevillier[1] speaks somewhat contemptuously of the typographical execution (*fabrique de l'Imprimerie*) of the London as compared with that of the Paris *Polyglot*. And if, as Le Long points out, 'he means by that term the beauty of the paper and the magnificence of the types, it must be admitted that the Paris edition is superior; but if he means the arrangement of the texts and versions, and the general disposition of the entire work, then it is much inferior; for Walton has mapped out his work so precisely that at a single opening of the book you see the texts and versions all at a glance; thus giving a great facility for comparison, wherein the chief usefulness of compilations of this sort consist'.[2]

Not the least noticeable feature about the work is the fact that from the time of its first going to press to its completion, the printing barely occupied four years. The first volume was completed at the beginning of September 1654. A month later, from the same press was published Dr. Walton's *Introductio ad lectionem linguarum orientalium* for the use of subscribers.[3] In 1655 the second volume of the *Bible* was finished; in 1656 the third, and about the close of 1657 the remaining three.[4] 'And thus,' says Twells,[5] 'in about four years was finished the English Polyglot Bible,[6] the glory of that age, and of the English Church and Nation; a work vastly exceeding all former attempts of the kind, and that came so near perfection as to discourage all future ones.'

Apart altogether from the literary and scholastic value of the Bible, the amount of labour and industry represented in its mere typographical execution is astonishing. Each double page presents, when open, some ten or more versions of the same passage divided into parallel columns of varying width, but so set that each comprehends exactly the same amount of text as the other. The regularity displayed in the general arrangement, in the references and interpolations, in the interlineations, and all the details of the composition and impression, are worthy of the undertaking and a lasting glory to the typography of the seventeenth century.

---

[1] *Origine de l'imprimerie de Paris*, Paris, 1694, 4to, p. 59.

[2] *Discours historique sur les principales éditions des Bibles Polyglottes*, Paris, 1713, 12mo, p. 209.

[3] This useful little tract was reprinted with improvements in the following year, entitled: *Introductio ad lectionem linguarum orientalium, Hebraicae, Chaldaicae, Samaritanae, Syriacae, Arabicae, Persicae, Æthiopicae, Armenae, Coptae . . . in usum tyronum . . . praecipuè eorum qui sumptus ad Biblia Polyglotta (jam sub prelo) imprimenda contulerunt. Londini. Imprimebat Tho. Roycroft*, 1655. Republished at Deventer in 1658. The Armenian and Coptic alphabets were cut in wood, and reappeared in the Prolegomena of the *Polyglot*.

[4] 'The latter part', says Bowyer, 'is much more incorrectly printed than the former, probably owing to the editor's absence from the press, or to his being over-fatigued by the work. The Hebrew text suffered much in several places by the rapidity of the publication.'

[5] Rev. Leonard Twells, author of *Life of Dr. Pocock*, contained in Pocock's *Works*, 1740.

[6] *Biblia Sacra Polyglotta, complectentia Textus Originales, Hebraicum cum Pentateucho Samaritano, Chaldaicum, Graecum; Versionumque antiquarum, Samaritanae Graecae LXX Interpr. Chaldaicae, Syriacae, Arabicae, Æthiopicae, Persicae, Vulg. Lat. Quicquid comparari poterat. Cum Textuum & Versionum Orientalium Translationibus Latinis . . . Omnia eo ordine disposita, ut Textus cum Versionibus uno intuitu conferri possint. Cum Apparatu, etc., etc. . . . Edidit Brianus Waltonus, S.T.D. Londini. Imprimebat Thomas Roycroft*, 1657. 6 vols., fol.

With regard to the types which concern us most the following is the list of the characters employed, as extracted by Rowe Mores:

ORIENTALS.—*Hebrew*: Two-line English, Double Pica, English.
Samaritan (with the English face): English.*
Syriac: Double Pica, Great Primer.*
Arabic: Double Pica, Great Primer.
MERIDIONAL.—*Ethiopic*: English or Pica.*
OCCIDENTALS.—*Greek*: Great Primer and Small Pica.
Roman and Italic: Two-line English, Double Pica [Day's],[1] Great Primer, English, Pica, Long Primer, Brevier, five-line Pica, two-line Great Primer, Small Pica.
SEPTENTRIONAL.—*English* (Black): Pica.

The matrices of two of these founts, the Ethiopic and the Samaritan, have survived to the present day, and in the course of this work we shall have occasion to

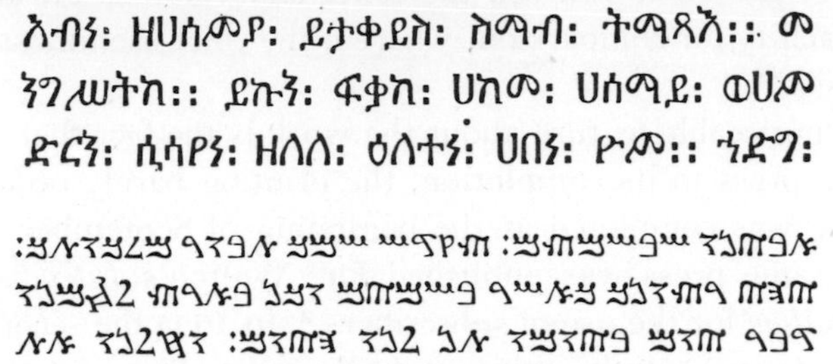

FIG. 33. Ethiopic and Samaritan of the *London Polyglot*. From the original matrices.

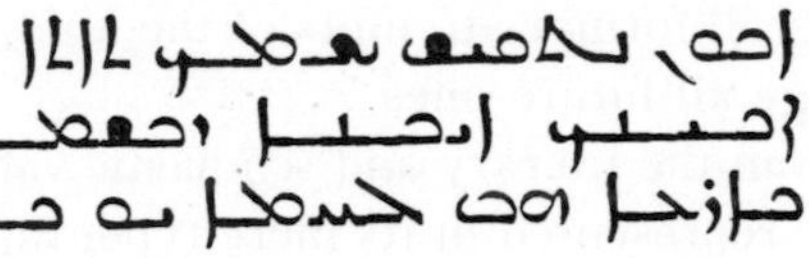

FIG. 34. Syriac of the *London Polyglot*.

trace their descent from the original makers to the present owners.[2] Of the Arabic fount, some of the punches and matrices also exist, but in too incomplete and dilapidated a state to allow of their being used.

Of the orientals, the Hebrew is, perhaps, the least good. The Syriac and Arabic are fine bold characters. The Greek is neat, though somewhat insignificant. The Ethiopic[3] and Samaritan[4] are both good and elegant faces. The italic is particularly neat. As might be expected from founts procured from various foundries in that

* Of the founts marked thus (*) in the present and following summarized lists of the contents of the English foundries, the matrices or punches, and in some cases both matrices and punches, still exist.

[1] See above, pp. 91–93.

[2] In some cases a few of the matrices have undergone renovation in the hands of their successive owners.

[3] 'The Æthiopic of the Congregation', i.e. of the Congregatio de Propaganda Fide at Rome, 'is not to be compared with ours. And Ludolphus, whose abode was at Gotha, sent his Lexicon to be published at London, where it was printed by Mr. Roycroft upon the type of the English *Polyglot*' (Mores,

p. 12). This work of Hiob Ludolff was printed in 1661.

[4] 'The elegant face of the Samaritan is justly attributed by Cellarius to the English, for it was first used in our *Polyglot*. It differs widely from the type used by Scaliger in his *Emend. Temp.*, and by Leusden at the end of his *Scholae Syriacae*, and from another used in an encomiastic of Abr. Ecchelensis upon F. Kircher, which type belonged to the Congregation at Rome; and which was afterwards more neatly cut by Voskens' (Mores, p. 13). However, the Samaritan used in the Paris *Polyglot* preceded the London type.

day, there is a certain absence of uniformity in the bodies on which the different founts are cast. This only makes the more remarkable the accuracy and precision with which the columns are arranged. In most copies the columns are divided by red lines, ruled by hand—in itself an enormous task.

A few notes may be added about the romans and italics used in the *Polyglot*, following Mores's list:

The five-line Pica is found on the title-page.

The two-line Great Primer is the heading type in the series of English-cut romans, an account of which is given below (p. 181).

The two-line English is a sixteenth-century type of Basle origin and is found on the unsigned specimen preserved at Oxford, reproduced in Berry and Johnson, pl. 19.

The Double Pica roman and italic, in which is set the address to Charles II, is the type used by John Day and many other London printers, and which, as already shown (pp. 91–93), was imported from the Low Countries. It is a curious comment on the standards prevailing at the time that the part of this address which was reset after the Restoration was printed in an English-cut Double Pica belonging to the same series as the two-line Great Primer above.

The Great Primer is another sixteenth-century Low Countries design, also among John Day's types and described above on p. 93, and with the italic usually found with it.

The English roman and italic, found in the Appendix in vol. vi, belongs to the same series as the two-line Great Primer and Double Pica mentioned above; we have already met with this size in the *Theophylact*, 1636, and *Catena in Job*, 1637.

The Pica roman, found in the 'Prolegomena', is a condensed design, probably English, and similar to the type used in the *Herodotus* printed by Grover and described on p. 189. The italic found with it is the Cicero Cursiv of Robert Granjon, shown on the Frankfort specimen-sheets and used in England from the time of Elizabeth's reign.

The Long Primer is used for the Vulgate text and other Latin versions and is a widely used sixteenth-century roman.

The italic used for the Latin version of the Samaritan text appears to be identical with that used by Robert Waldegrave in the Marprelate Tracts, probably cut by J. Haultin of La Rochelle.[1]

The Brevier, used for the interlinear version of the Hebrew, is probably another sixteenth-century type.

It will be seen then that few of the roman and italic types used can have been cut by contemporary founders.

Nine languages are used in the *Polyglot*, but no single book is printed in so many. The following is the arrangement of texts according to volumes:

VOL. 1. *Prolegomena.*
      Pentateuch. Hebrew, Greek, Latin, Syriac, Arabic, and Samaritan.
  „ 2. *Joshua to Esther.* Hebrew, Greek, Latin, Syriac, and Arabic.
  „ 3. *Job to Malachi.* Hebrew, Greek, Latin, Syriac, Arabic, and *Psalms* also in Ethiopic.

---

[1] Cf. the reproduction in Isaac's *English Printers' Types of the Sixteenth Century*, pl. 78.

M

Vol. 4. *Apocrypha.* Greek, Latin, Syriac, Arabic (some of the books, however, have not the Arabic. *Tobit* is in a twofold Hebrew.) An appendix to this volume contains two Chaldee Targums and a Persic *Pentateuch.*

„　5. *New Testament, Gospels* in Greek, Latin, Syriac, Arabic, Ethiopic, and Persian; other books, Greek, Latin, Syriac, Arabic, and Ethiopic.

„　6. *Various readings.*

It will thus be seen that the Greek, Latin, Syriac, and Arabic texts run throughout the work. The Chaldean text and Targums are all given in Hebrew type. The Hebrew text is printed throughout masoretically (that is, with points and accents).

In addition to the above fundamental characters used, the Prolegomena show the following alphabets cut in wood, viz.: Rabbinical Hebrew, Syriac duplices, Nestorian and Estrangelan, Armenian, Coptic, Illyrian, both Cyrillian and Hieronymian, Iberian, Gothic, Chinese, and the character of the Codex Alexandrinus. These are, for the most part, rudely cut, and valuable only as curiosities.

From our point of view, the chief glory of the English *Polyglot* is that it is largely the impression of English type. It marks an epoch in the history of our national letter-founding, as, before it appeared, no work of importance had been printed in any of the learned characters except Latin and Greek. The Hebrew, Samaritan, Syriac, Arabic, and Ethiopic were probably cut expressly for the work, under the supervision of its learned editors, and became thus the models or prototypes of the numerous oriental founts which during the eighteenth century figured so largely in the works of English scholarship.

The original preface to the *Polyglot* contained an honourable reference to Cromwell, who had, from the first, encouraged the undertaking and materially assisted it by remitting the tax on the paper imported from abroad for the use of the work. But the Protector's death took place in the year after the publication; and the Restoration, which followed two years later, was made the occasion for a somewhat ignoble act of time-service on the part of Walton, who cancelled the last three leaves of the preface, and added a Dedication to Charles II, in which, among other attacks on the memory of his former patron, he referred to Cromwell as 'Draco ille magnus'.[1] The particular typographical interest of this Royal Dedication is that it is printed in the handsome Double Pica roman and italic used by Day in the *Ælfredi res gestæ* of 1574, and subsequently by Barker and Lucas in Young's *Catena in Job*, in 1637, and in other works. The somewhat worn condition of the types leads Dibdin to condemn the founts as inferior;[2] but in point of elegance and grandeur this venerable letter remained still one of the best of which our national typography could boast.

In recognition of his services, Charles made Walton his chaplain-in-ordinary, and created him subsequently Bishop of Chester. Nor was he the only worker to whom the completion of this great enterprise brought honour. Roycroft, after what

---

[1] In his 'loyal' dedication Walton asserts that from the outset he had intended to dedicate the work to Charles II, and that Cromwell's patronage of the work had been offered only as the price of a public compliment for himself (Todd, i. 82 seq.).

[2] 'The first view of this dedication', he says, 'will prove it to have been printed with different and inferior types, the hasty produce of a courteous after thought' (*Introd. Classics*[4], i. 27). In fact, in the middle of the dedication Day's Double Pica roman gives place to the Double Pica roman of the series of English types described below on p. 181

may be considered a feat of rapid and skilful typography, was permitted to take the title *Orientalium Typographus Regius*.[1]

The value of the English *Polyglot* was vastly enhanced by the addition to it of Dr. Edmund Castell's Heptaglot *Lexicon*,[2] which, after seventeen years of incessant labour, commencing with the first announcement of the *Polyglot*, was printed, at Roycroft's press, in 1669, in two volumes, uniform in size and style with the *Bible*, of which henceforth it formed a necessary complement. Respecting this famous work, there is little to add from a typographical point of view to what has already been noted with regard to the *Polyglot*. The same types are, with few exceptions, used in both. Mores considers, but wrongly, that the Amharic shown in Castell's work is metal and the same as that used in the *Oratio Dominica* of 1713. This letter (which also appeared in the edition of the *Oratio Dominica* in 1700) belonged to Oxford University, who procured it in 1688, being the Ethiopic character with additions. But the few letters shown in the *Heptaglot* are evidently engraved by hand, and not cast.

It is to be regretted that Castell's work, which has been pronounced one of the greatest and most perfect works of the kind ever performed by human industry and learning, and which represented an amount of heroic perseverance in the midst of adverse circumstances scarcely credible, was almost the ruin of its author, both in constitution and fortune. It sold slowly, and at the time of his death upwards of 500 copies were left on hand. The encouragement he received both from royal and episcopal patronage was inadequate to cover the losses which the undertaking had involved, and he died in comparative obscurity in 1685.[3]

Roycroft's office appears to have suffered severely by the Fire of London in 1666, and a large number of copies of Castell's *Lexicon*, then in course of printing, were destroyed. To the same disastrous event may also be attributed the disappearance of some of the founts of the *Polyglot* founders, after the completion of the *Lexicon*. Mores, however, succeeds in tracing the most interesting of these; and the fact that all the matrices did not go down to posterity as a single property is additional proof that they were not all the production of one artist. The Arabic, larger Syriac, and Samaritan passed into the foundry of the Grovers, and the Ethiopic into that of Robert Andrews, who, it seems probable, also inherited the Hebrew and black. The smaller Syriac came into William Caslon's hands.

NICHOLAS NICHOLLS. This founder was son of Arthur Nicholls, the Star Chamber founder, and, as appears by the mention of him in his father's petition to Archbishop Laud, already quoted, was brought up to the art, in which, as early as 1637, he was 'so expert and able as to be able to perform anything touching the same'. During

---

[1] 'Thomas Roycroft died 10 August 1677. In 1675 he was master of the Stationers' Company, and in 1677 he gave to them two silver mugs, weight 27 ozs. 3 dwts. In the rear of the altar at St. Bartholomew's the Great is this epitaph:—"M.S. Hic juxta situs est Thomas Roycroft, armiger, linguis Orientalibus Typographus Regius, placidissimis moribus et antiquâ probitate ac fide memorandus, quorum gratiâ optimi civis famam jure merito adeptus est. Militiæ civicæ Vicetribunus. Nec minus apud exteros notus ob libros elegantissimis suis typis editos, inter quos sanctissimum illud *Bibliorum Polyglottorum*, opus quam maxime eminet. Obiit die 10 Augusti, ann. Reparatæ Sal. MDCLXXVII, postquam LVI ætatis suæ annum implevisset. Parenti optimè merito, Samuel Roycroft, filius unicus, hoc monumentum pie posuit".' Timperley, p. 616.

[2] *Lexicon Heptaglotton, Hebraicum, Chaldaicum, Syriacum, Samaritanum, Æthiopicum, Arabicum*, conjunctim; *et Persicum* separatim, *etc., etc. Authore Edmundo Castello, S.T.D., etc. Londini, Imprimebat Thomas Roycroft, L.L. Orientalium Typographus Regius*, 1669. 2 vols., fol. [3] See *D.N.B.*

the Civil Wars he appears to have suffered in the royal cause, and, like many others, at the Restoration to have looked for substantial reward at the hands of the son of the Royal Martyr.

In 1665 he presented to the King a petition to be appointed His Majesty's Letter Founder. The original document is in the Record Office,[1] and is as follows:

To the KINGE's MOST EXCELLENT MAJESTIE. The humble peticion of Nicholas Nicholls. Most humbly sheweth

That the petitioner in the worst of tymes was a constant and loyall sufferer for the causes of your Majestie and that of your Royall ffather of glorious memory, and thereby reduced to greate extreamities.

Now soe it is, That the peticioner by Industrie hath attained to a considerable skill in the Art of cutting and casting all kinds of Letters and faire Characters (as by the annexed may appeare) And your Majestie beinge the great encourager of good Literature

Your Majestie's peticioner most humbly prays your Grace and ffavour to serve in the place of Letter Founder to your Majesties Presses That soe your Majesties presses may be supplyed with Characters in some measure worthy of your Royall Greatness. And the peticioner makes no question but he shall perform that service (with the blessing of God) to your Majestie's full content and satisfaction.

And the peticioner (as in duty bound) shall alwaies pray for your Majesties long and prosperous Reigne over us.

Attached to the petition, in the centre of a folio sheet, is the tiny polyglot specimen, of which we here present our readers with an enlarged reproduction. English typography possesses few relics more interesting than this quaint little page—the earliest-known typefounder's specimen in the country. The execution, particularly of the roman fount, is very poor, and one wonders, in examining it and comparing it with the recently completed *Polyglot*, at the artist's claim 'to considerable skill in cutting and casting of faire characters'. It is possible, however, that the unusual minuteness of the type may have been held to be a merit compensating for defects in execution. And as none of the founts are known to have been used in any other work of the time, it may be presumed the letters were cut specially for this specimen. The roman and Greek founts are Pearl in body, and the orientals Nonpareil, and display the text 'Vivas o rex in perpetuum' in Latin, Greek, Hebrew (with points), Syriac, Samaritan, Ethiopic, and Arabic. This loyal aspiration, effusively dedicated as 'the prayer of the devoted heart, and the specimen of the Art of the least of the subjects of the greatest of the Kings', is surrounded by a neat flower-border (also Nonpareil in body), and printed somewhat roughly on coarse paper. Despite its defects, it appears to have found favour with the august personage to whom it was offered, as we find, on 29 January 1667, a minute of a 'Warrant for swearing Nicholas Nicholls, Letter Founder to His Majesty'.[2]

The earliest mention of Nicholls in connexion with Oxford is in a statement, preserved at the press, dated 20 January 1649. John Greaves, the orientalist and Professor of Astronomy, had been entrusted with Arabic matrices, which he was to have perfected. This he did, but he allowed Miles Flesher, the London printer, to cast a fount from these matrices. Nicholls reported that many of them were spoilt.

---

[1] *State Papers, Domestic*, 1665, vol. 142, No. 174.　　[2] Ibid., 1667, Ent. Book 23, p. 337.

The Oxford Press has also some papers referring to the casting of a fount of Brevier Hebrew by Nicholls in 1652. There is first an agreement between Gerard Langbaine, Keeper of the Archives, and Nicholls, dated 31 March 1652, under which the founder is entrusted with the University matrices, from which he is to cast a complete fount of 200 pounds weight, and to make good all defects of punches and matrices. Nicholls is to receive the matrices at his house in Aldersgate Street, London, by 1 July. He is to be paid 4s. a pound for the type and 2s. 6d. for each

FIG. 35. Specimen of Nicholls. Enlarged from the original in the Record Office.[1]

new punch. There are also letters from Nicholls to Langbaine about the progress of the work and payment for it. The work was finished in November and the sum paid for the Hebrew came to £52. 10s. 6d. From one letter to Pocock, Professor of Arabic at Oxford, it seems that Nicholls was also casting an Arabic fount. It appears further that at this time Nicholls had a servant named Thomas Grover, possibly a relative of James Grover the founder.[2]

From Madan's *Oxford Books*, vol. iii, p. xxix, we find that in 1656 £23. 7s. 2d. was paid to Nicholls for a fount of Saxon type. In the University Archives there is preserved an undated and unsigned sheet, measuring 17·6 × 28 cm., showing a Hebrew about English size, cast from Dutch matrices belonging to the University, and a Pica Anglo-Saxon. The Hebrew is perhaps the fount cast by Nicholls from

[1] The original measures 8·5 × 4·5 em.
[2] We have to thank Dr. John Johnson, late University Printer, for the information in this paragraph.

matrices acquired in 1637 (see p. 133), and the Saxon a fount cut by Nicholls. This Saxon was used in William Somner's *Dictionarium Saxonico–Latino–Anglicum,* W. Hall, Oxford, 1659 (Madan 2458), and appears on C 4 of the Oxford Specimen Book of 1693, although some of the capitals then shown, e.g. N and R, have been changed. On the same leaf are shown a Brevier Hebrew and an English Arabic, also probably early Oxford, i.e. pre-Fell, types.

In *The First Minute Book of the Delegates of the Oxford University Press*[1] we find that £11 was 'lent' [? advanced] to Nicholls and £15 more 'when he shall have finished the Italick Letter to the Roman, which he has now in hand to the printing of ye Catalogue'. This catalogue of the Bodleian Library appeared in 1674, the main text being set in a roman and italic of the sixteenth century, but in the preliminaries we find the roman and italic cut by Nicholls, which is described below. On 8 April 1669 Nicholls presents an account for £76. 10s. 9d. of which £40 had already been paid. There is a further payment of £60 on 7 February 1670, and of nearly £120 in 1671.

At the end of the Oxford specimen of 1693 there is an 'Account of the Matrices, Puncheons, &c.' and in this list is a 'Paper of Great Primer roman and italick, cut by

Great Primer Roman.

ABCDEFGHIKLMNOPQRSTVUWXYZ J Æ

abcdefghiklmnopqrstvuwxyz j æ œ

.,;:?!'-)] 1234567890 &

And I, even I Artaxerxes the king, do make a
decree to all the treasurers which are beyond the
river, that whatsoever Ezra the priest, the scribe
of the law of the God of heaven, shall require
of you, it be done speedily.

FIG. 36. Nicholls's roman. From the original matrices.

Mr. Nicols, not good'. The type was not shown in the specimen, but was fully shown in the Appendix to Hart, and turns out to be a type which is fairly common in English books of the period. The earliest date noted is on *Proclamations of the Lord Mayor of London* printed by James Flesher in 1666. In view of this date we may conclude that the cutter was Nicholas Nicholls. Another book from Flesher's press in which the type was used for the Dedication is John Pearson's *An Exposition of the Creed,* 1669. One may agree with Oxford's verdict of 'not good', but nevertheless it was much used at Oxford in the years preceding the employment of the Fell types. The first appearance at Oxford noted is for the Prolegomena of William Beveridge's *Pandectæ Canonum Apostolorum,* 1672 (Madan 2916). It is found in

[1] Edited in 1943 by Dr. Strickland Gibson and Dr. John Johnson for the Oxford Bibliographical Society.

the preliminaries of the *Catalogus librorum Bibliothecæ Bodlejanæ*, 1674 (Madan 2999), as already stated, and in Anthony à Wood's *Historia Universitatis Oxoniensis*, also 1674 (Madan 2996). From the size of the type it was naturally not often used for the main text of a book, but it was so used in R. Plot's *Natural History of Oxfordshire*, 1677 (Madan 3130), and again in a parallel volume, Plot's *Natural History of Staffordshire*, 1686. Some of the letters in this Great Primer are somewhat condensed, e.g. the H, M, and R. The R has a curled tail and the U the design of the lower-case, both forms popular, as we shall see, in English romans of the seventeenth century. The latest appearance of the type noted is in a London printed book of 1704. There was also an English size of the same design, presumably cut by Nicholls, found at Oxford in the preface of *Abu Jaafar*, 1671 (Madan 2877), and in Daniel Brevint's *Missale Romanum*, 1672 (Madan 2921).

[8]

JOSEPH MOXON, 1659

JOSEPH MOXON, whose distinction it is to have been the first practical English writer on the mechanics of typography, was born at Wakefield, in Yorkshire, on 8 August 1627, and appears to have been brought up as a mathematical instrument maker, in which profession he showed himself highly proficient. The earliest mention of his name is on a broadside, *Victories obtained . . . both by land and Sea. Printed by James[1] and Joseph Moxon for T. Jenner*, London, 1647. The address of the brothers was the upper end of Houndsditch, near Bishopsgate. In the year 1659, being settled in the metropolis, Joseph added to his stated business that of a typefounder, in which, according to Mores, he continued till 1683.

It is difficult to fix the precise condition of the laws relating to typefounders in the last year of the Commonwealth. The Ordinances of 1647 and 1649, which re-imposed the main provisions of the Star Chamber Decree of 1637, remained nominally in force till the Restoration, so that we are to suppose that Moxon, unless he practised his art surreptitiously or *sub rosa*, was formally installed into a vacancy in the body of authorized founders on execution of the usual bond to the Company of Stationers.

If, as seems probable, he commenced operations with little or no previous experience, and with no plant ready to his hand, the progress of the new foundry must at first have been very slow, particularly as he appears to have devoted much of his time to his other scientific pursuits, to which in 1665 he added that of hydrographer to the king. To this office a considerable salary was attached. He petitioned for this post in January 1662, and the petition was backed by Sir Isaac Newton.[2]

After leaving his brother in Houndsditch, his shop from 1653 to 1664 was in Cornhill, near St. Michael's Church, at the sign of the Atlas. Pepys has two entries in his *Diary* of visits to this shop in October 1663 and in March 1664 and bought a globe there. Moxon remained interested in St. Michael's even after he had left Cornhill. From the publications of the Wren Society (vol. xix, p. 45) it appears that he had a lease of the Quest House built over the church cloisters and burnt

---

[1] James Moxon printed the *Mercurius Pragmaticus* and *Mercurius Scommaticus* in 1651, and the *Mercurius Britannicus* in 1652. He was printing in Edinburgh in 1689. See Plomer's *Dictionary*. James Moxon must have been the senior, as his name on the joint imprints always occurs first. He is presumably identical with the English printer of that name who is found at Delft in 1637 and at Rotterdam in 1638. See *Tijdschrift voor Boek- en Bibliotheekwesen*, 1910, pp. 266 seq. He was a printer in Houndsditch about 1650, and appears in the list of the 'Recognisances to the Council of State' given in the *Calendar of Domestic State Papers* for 1649–50, pp. 522–3. The printers had to give sureties not to print any seditious or unlicensed books. After the Great Fire of 1666 James Moxon had a shop near Charing Cross.

[2] See *State Papers, Domestic*, 1661–2, p. 241.

Joseph Moxon.
Born at Wakefeild August. 8.
Anno 1627

FIG. 37.

down in the Great Fire. Also in 1672, at the time of the rebuilding of the church, he was a churchwarden. His first wife, Susannah, was buried in St. Michael's on 28 June 1659. He appears to have married again, as on 26 June 1664 Hanna, daughter of Joseph Moxon and Hanna his wife, was christened in St. Michael's.[1] From 1665 for the rest of his life, except for an interval due to the Great Fire, Moxon lived at the same sign on Ludgate Hill, near Fleet Bridge, that is, outside the City gate. Rowe Mores states that in 1668 he was in Warwick Lane, but I can find no authority for this, nor any book of that year with which Moxon was connected either as author, publisher, or printer. It seems unlikely that he would have taken a shop in 1668 in Warwick Lane, which was in the area of the Great Fire as much as Ludgate Hill. His book entitled *Mechanick Dyalling*, a book on the sundial, was issued from Ludgate Hill and bears the date 1668. But this is a misprint for 1678, as appears from the advertisements printed on the last quire of the book. This list includes several books printed after 1668, e.g. the first six numbers of *Mechanick Exercises*, which brings us down to June 1678. *Mechanick Dyalling* is entered in the Term Catalogues for 18 February 1679. The second volume of *Mechanick Exercises*, 1683, has the address the 'West Side of Fleet Ditch'.[2] The Fire of London in 1666 caused him to quit Ludgate Hill for another shop of the same sign in Russell Street, Westminster, where he is found from 1669 to 1671 and whence in 1669 was issued his famous specimen of types, the first complete typefounders' specimen known in England.[3]

In a passage in the *Mechanick Exercises*, published several years later, Moxon speaks of the art of letter-cutting as a mystery, 'kept so conceal'd among the Artificers of it, that I cannot learn anyone hath taught it any other, but every one that has used it, Learnt it of his own Genuine Inclination'. If this be the writer's own experience—though his subsequent intimate acquaintance with the minutest details of the art almost disproves it—his specimen must be taken as the production of a self-taught typographer after ten years' intermittent practice. Viewed in this light, the exceedingly poor performance which the sheet presents can to some extent be accounted for. It must also be borne in mind that Moxon's theoretical and mathematical studies of the proportions and form of letters had not yet been begun, or, at least, elaborated; so that in no sense is his specimen to be assumed to be a reduction into practice of those theories.

This specimen, which is entitled *Prooves of the Several Sorts of Letters cast by Joseph Moxon*, is a folio sheet, showing in double column:

Great Canon Romain

Double Pica Romain	Pica Romain
	Pica Italica
Great Primmer Romain	Long Primer Romain
	Long Primer Italica
English Romain	Brevier Romain
English Italica	Brevier Italica

[1] See the *Parish Registers*, edited by J. L. Chester, 1882.

[2] Moxon's addresses as given in Plomer's *Dictionary* are incorrect, partly because of reliance on Rowe Mores and partly because Moxon and his son James are confused. It was James Moxon the younger who was in Warwick Lane down to 1704 and who had also a stall in Westminster Hall. The son James is not known to the *Dictionary*.

[3] Nicholas Nicholls's tiny specimen, printed four years earlier, exhibited only a few lines specially cut, and dedicated privately to the King.

The imprint is *Westminster, printed by Joseph Moxon in Russel Street, at the sign of the Atlas*, 1669.

In all respects it is a sorry performance. Only two founts, the Great Canon and the Pica, have any pretensions to elegance or regularity. The others are so clumsily cut, so badly cast, and so wretchedly printed, as here and there to be almost undecipherable. Moxon's proficiency in the processes of the art does not appear as yet to have attained the pitch of justifying his matrices to any regularity of line, or of casting his types square in body. Some lines of the specimen curve and wave so as to make it a marvel how others kept their places in the forme, and the press-work and ink are so bad that at a first glance the beholder is tempted to mistake the larger letters with their sunken faces for open instead of solid-faced romans. The sheet was apparently put forward not solely as a specimen of types. The matter of each paragraph is an advertisement of Moxon's business as a mathematical instrument maker. In Great Canon Romain he calls attention to the 'Globes Celestial and Terrestrial of all sizes made by Joseph Moxon, Hydrographer to the King's Most Excellent Majesty, 1669'. In Double Pica Romain he announces his Spheres; in Great Primmer 'a Large Map of the World'; in Pica Italica, 'a book called a Tutor to Astronomie and Geographie', and so on. To one or two of the founts, such as the Great Canon, the Pica, and the Brevier, he adds a line of accents or signs.

As to the types themselves, the only successful design cut by Moxon was the Great Canon roman, which we have found already at Oxford and which still survives in the copy cut by William Caslon. There is a fine display of this roman in the preliminaries of vol. i of Moses Pitt's *English Atlas*, printed at Oxford in 1680. It appears on half a dozen English and Scotch specimens. The other types seem to have found little sale. The Double Pica and the English may be seen in Moxon's book *Practical Perspective*, 1670, and the Double Pica in John Evelyn's *Discourse of Medals*, 1697. The Pica italic is found also in the Oxford specimen-books, one of the types presented by Francis Junius in 1677, and appears on the specimen-sheet of the heirs of Christoffel van Dijk, 1681. According to Charles Enschedé it was not cut by Van Dijk, since no punches were acquired by the Enschedé firm. One must suppose that it was a Dutch type and not sold by Moxon to the Van Dijk Foundry in Amsterdam.

It would appear, from the imprint already quoted, that Moxon combined printing with typefounding. His translation of Vignola, 1655, his *Tutor to Astronomie* 1659, and *Practical Perspective*, 1670, are all stated to be printed by Moxon. Also J. Caus's *New and Rare Invention of Water Works*, 1659, and John Newton's *Help to Calculation*, 1657, bear his imprint.

About 1672 he moved back to the sign of the Atlas, in Ludgate Hill. Rowe Mores considers it probable that for some time he resided in Holland, during which time he acquired a certain proficiency in the Dutch language.[1] During the same period it is probable that he may have come across and been struck by specimens

[1] In 1677 he published *Compendium Euclidis curiosi, Geometrical Operations*, London, 4to, translated by himself from Dutch into English. He also engraved maps for editions of the *Bible* in English, printed at Amsterdam.

of the beautifully proportioned letters of Christoffel van Dijk, which he admitted were the inspiration of his *Regulæ Trium Ordinum.*

Of this curious work,[1] which was published in 1676, it will suffice to say here, it is a work intended not so much for the letter-cutter as for the sign-board and inscription painter. Taking the Van Dijk letters as his models, the writer attempts to demonstrate that each letter is a combination of geometrical figures, bearing regular proportions one to another; and by subdivision of the square of each letter into forty-two equal parts, he professes to be able to erect in any other square, similarly subdivided, the same letter in precise proportion and harmony. This theory he illustrates by copperplate figures of the various letters of the roman, italic, and black alphabets, and their subdivisions. The result is not pleasing. The letters are stiff, and in some cases distorted; although this we believe to be the fault not so much of the theory itself as of the rules of proportion for the different parts of each letter predicated in the first instance. The book, as we have observed, is clearly not intended as a guide to punch-cutting. We regard it rather as an interesting attempt to reduce to precise mathematical rules a set of characters which never have and never will yield themselves entirely to such treatment.[2] In the text the letters of his own Great Canon roman are used as illustrations. Of his predecessors Moxon was certainly acquainted with Dürer's work, which he mentions, and may also have known an English translation of Pieter Coecke's version of Sebastiano Serlio's book on architecture. Coecke added an alphabet of roman capitals at the end of Book 4. This alphabet, printed from the same woodcuts, appeared in the English edition, Simon Stafford, 1611.

At the conclusion of the section devoted to 'the ordering of Inscriptions', Moxon says (p. 11), 'But of this and several other Observations of this Nature, I have written more at large in a book I intend to publish on the whole Art of Printing.' From this it is evident that, as early as 1676, his treatises on typography, which formed the second volume of the *Mechanick Exercises* and were published in 1683, were already written.

---

[1] *Regulæ Trium Ordinum Literarum Typographicarum; or the Rules of the Three Orders of Print Letters, viz.: the Roman, Italick, English,—Capitals and Small; showing how they are compounded of Geometrick Figures and mostly made by Rule and Compass. Useful for Writing Masters, Painters, Carvers, Masons and others that are Lovers of Curiosity; by Joseph Moxon, Hydrographer to the King's Most Excellent Majesty. London. Printed for Joseph Moxon on Ludgate Hill at the Sign of Atlas.* 1676. 4to. (Dedicated to Sir Christopher Wren.)

[2] The Renaissance artists, especially the Italian, were keenly interested in the roman lettering found on inscriptions, and several of them designed alphabets modelled on the inscriptional letters and wrote treatises on the method of constructing the letters by geometrical means. Most of those which have survived have been reproduced and studied by writers of this and the preceding century. The earliest to which a date can be given, a manuscript of Felice Feliciano of Verona, 1463, preserved in the Vatican, was edited by R. Schoene in 1872 (in *Ephemeris Epigraphica,* i, pp. 255 seq.), and further discussed by A. Khomentovskaia in *La Bibliofilia,* April 1935, pp. 154 seq., with a reproduction.

Another fifteenth-century Italian manuscript, copied by the German medical scholar Hartmann Schedel, is preserved at Munich and was described by Dehio in 'Zur Geschichte der Buchstabenreform in der Renaissance' (*Repertorium für Kunstwissenschaft,* iv, 1881, p. 269). The earliest printed treatise of the kind was produced at Parma about 1480 by Damianus Moyllus, a treatise which was reproduced by the Pegasus Press in 1927, with an introduction by Stanley Morison. The better-known work by Luca de Pacioli, entitled *De Divina proportione,* Venice, 1509, has also been reproduced by the Grolier Club, New York, 1933, again edited by Stanley Morison. Other Italian books on the subject are Sigismondo Fanti's *Theorica et practica de modo scribendi,* Venice, 1514, F. Torniello's *Opera del modo di fare le littere maiuscole antique,* Venice, 1519, and by G. B. de Verini's *Luminario,* 1527. The work of Albrecht Dürer on the same subject in his *Underweyssung der Messung,* and of Geofroy Tory in his *Champfleury,* 1529, are both well known. Roman capitals are displayed in the books of many of the writing-masters from Ludovico Vicentino onwards.

To this highly interesting work[1]—the first work on the mechanics and practice of printing and letter-founding—we have already alluded in a previous chapter. It is impossible here to give more than a brief summary of its contents. Its publication commenced in 1677 with a series of monthly 'Exercises' devoted to the smith's, joiner's, carpenter's, and turner's trades. These formed the first volume. Moxon himself informs us that their publication was interrupted by the excitement of Oates's plot, 'which took off the minds of his few customers from buying them, as formerly'. It was not till 1683 that the work was resumed. The second volume (which appeared in twenty-four monthly parts), treating wholly of the art of printing, commences with a brief account of the invention of the art (in which the reader is left to decide between the titles of Haarlem and Mainz), and with a claim on behalf of typography equally with architecture to be regarded as a mathematical science.[2]

A scientifick man [says Moxon] was doubtless he who was the first Inventor of Typographie; but I think few have succeeded him in Science, though the number of Founders and Printers be grown very many: Insomuch that for the more easie managing of Typographie, the Operators have found it necessary to devide it into several Trades. . . . The several devisions that are made are—1. The Master Printer. 2. The Letter Cutter. 3. The Letter Caster. 4. The Letter Dresser. 5. The Compositer. 6. The Correcter. 7. The Press Man. 8. The Inck-Maker. Besides several other Trades they take in to their Assistance, as the Smith, the Joyner, etc.

These divisions he proceeds to treat of seriatim and in detail. We have elsewhere quoted freely from this work, with a view to illustrate the condition of letter-founding as a mechanical trade in his time.[3] But we notice here that, in the advice which he gives to the master printer on the choice of letter for his office, he takes the opportunity to reiterate his admiration of the Dutch form of letter, particularly that adopted by Christoffel van Dijk, and his conviction that as the roman letters were originally made to consist of circles, arcs of circles, and straight lines, the cutting of those letters should invariably be according to strict mathematical rule of form and proportion. His advice on the choice of letter is fourfold.

1. 'That the Letter have a true shape.'
2. 'That they be deep cut' (i.e. in the punch).
3. 'That they be deep sunck in the Matrices' (with a good 'beard').
4. 'That his Letter be cast upon good Mettal.'

He then proceeds to indicate the quantities of each body of letter with which the printer should provide himself; and from that proceeds to notice in turn every possible requisite for a well-ordered printing-office, from the 'ball-nails' to the press.

His 'Exercises on Letter Founding' may be best introduced in his own language: 'Having shown you the Master Printers Office,' he says, 'I account it suitable to

---

[1] *Mechanick Exercises, or the Doctrine of Handy-Works. Began Jan. 1, 1677. And intended to be Monthly continued. By Joseph Moxon, Hydrographer to the King's Most Excellent Majesty. London. Printed for Joseph Moxon on Ludgate Hill at the Sign of the Atlas.* 2 vols., 4to.
Vol. I (14 numbers). *The Smiths, the Joyners, the Carpenters, and the Turner's Trades,* 1677–80.

Vol. II (24 numbers). *Applied to the Art of Printing,* 1683–6. (Dedicated to Dr. Fell, Bishop of Oxford.) It was reprinted by T. L. De Vinne in 1896.
[2] Mores says that before Moxon's time letter-cutters worked by eye and hand only, and practised their art by guess-work (*Dissert.*, p. 43).
[3] See Chap. 4.

proper Method to let you know how the Letter Founder Cuts the Punches, how
the Molds are made, the Matrices sunck, and the Letter Cast and Drest. . . . Wherefore the next Exercises shall be (God willing) upon Cutting of Steel Punches.'
The minuteness with which he enters into every detail connected with this mysterious art, and his familiarity with the terminology of the craft, prove that Moxon,
although he professed to have learned it not from any master, but 'of his own
genuine inclination', was an experienced and even enthusiastic punch-cutter. He
devotes considerable attention to the tools and gauges necessary for the work, and
returns once more to the charge on behalf of geometry as the foundation of typography. Anyone acquainted with the modern practice of punch-cutting cannot but
be struck, on reading the directions laid down in the *Mechanick Exercises*, with the
slightness of the change which the manual processes of that art have undergone
during the last two centuries. Indeed, allowing for improvements in tools, and the
greater variety of gauges, we might almost assert that the punch-cutter of Moxon's
day knew scarcely less than the punch-cutter of the nineteenth century, with the
accumulated experience of 200 years, could teach him.

Moxon's observations, as in the *Regulæ Trium Ordinum*, apply only to the
roman, italic, and black-letter, and these he illustrates by a series of plates devised
on the same method as in his former work, showing each letter in a magnified form
on a square subdivided into forty-two parts, with the proportions for the various
parts of each letter minutely laid down. He imagines an objection that it may be
deemed impossible in the case of a small letter to divide the square of the body into
forty-two equal parts. 'But yet,' he says, 'it is possible with curious working,' and
proceeds, evidently to his own satisfaction, to demonstrate the fact in a very curious
way, by suggesting a series of graduations in the rubbing of spaces and points,
whereby a thin[1] space may be enlarged by sixths until a series of forty-second parts
of each body is arrived at. Impracticable as such a system appears, it is consistently
carried out in the enlarged letters which illustrate the *Exercises*. The result is not
more successful than that produced in the *Regulæ Trium Ordinum*; and we venture
to think if any proof were needed that geometry is not, and cannot be, the Alpha
and Omega of typographical beauty, these reductions into practice of Moxon's
ingenious theories will supply it.[2]

Passing from letter-cutting, Moxon next describes with much minuteness the
various parts of the mould and the method of putting them together. Here the
practical instrument maker is on familiar ground, and the directions he gives remained the best authority on the subject, until the venerable hand-mould which he
describes began to give place, a century and a quarter after his time, to the lever-
mould from America.

Next to mould-making, the *Exercises* deal with the important processes of striking and justifying the matrices, operations which, like that of punch-cutting, have
undergone but little change since his day. Then follow descriptions of the furnace,

---

[1] Or rather a hair space, of which seven go to the
body; so that one such space divided by six would
gave a 42nd part!
[2] With this passage may be compared the story
of the 'Romain du roy Louis XIV' cut by Grandjean
and first used in 1702. See Updike's *Printing Types*,

i. 241–4. In a paper read before the Royal Society
of Arts, 18 April 1890, entitled 'Old and New
Fashions in Typography', Reed discussed the French
geometrical scheme and the introduction of flat
serifs in Grandjean's letters.

the alloy of the metal, and the methods of casting and dressing the type, with the implements necessary for these branches of the work; and this portion of the work closes with a few highly interesting plates, amongst which that of the caster at work[1] is the most curious and valuable.

The remainder of the book is devoted to various departments of the letter-press printer's trade, those of the compositor, the corrector, the pressman, and the warehouse keeper. To this is added an appendix, describing the ancient customs of the 'Chapel', and a dictionary of typographical terms.

Such is a brief outline of the contents of this first English book on printing and letter-founding. It is a work which no one interested in English typography can omit to consult. For almost a century it remained the only authority on the subject; subsequently it formed the basis of numerous other treatises, both at home and abroad, and to this day it is quoted and referred to, not only by the antiquary who desires to learn what the art once was, but by the practical printer, who may still on many subjects gather from it much advice and information as to what it should still be.

Reverting now to Mores's description of the contents of Moxon's foundry, we meet with one fount which calls for particular mention here.

The Pica Irish was cut expressly for the purpose of printing the *Irish New Testament*, published in 1681 at the cost of Robert Boyle, son of the Earl of Cork, and is described by Mores as the only fount of purely Irish type he had ever seen in the country. We may, perhaps, be excused a slight digression in this place for the purpose of giving a sketch of the efforts which before Moxon's day had been made to propagate the Irish language by means of typography.

The first fount of Irish type known was presented in 1571 by Queen Elizabeth to John O'Kearney, treasurer of St. Patrick's, with a view to encourage the diffusion of the Scriptures in the Irish character. By whom this character was prepared we are not informed. It is not the genuine Irish, but a hybrid fount, consisting chiefly of roman and italic letters, to which the 'discrepants', or seven distinctively Irish sorts, are added.[2] It is accompanied by a small and equally neat letter for notes, which, however, appears to be Saxon. The earliest specimen of this fount appears in a broadside *Tuar Ferge Foighide*, by Philip O'Huiginn,[3] printed in 1571, and sent over to the Archbishop of Canterbury, apparently as a specimen of the type. This was followed almost immediately by the *Church Catechism* and *Articles*, translated by O'Kearney and Nicholas Walsh, afterwards Bishop of Ossery, and printed in 1571 at the cost of John Ussher (*S.T.C.* 18793).[4]

The object of the royal donor was further realized in 1602, when there appeared from the press of John Francke, William O'Donnell's (or Daniel's) Irish *New*

---

[1] See Fig. 22.

[2] Of the eighteen letters of the alphabet, the b, c, h, l, m, n, o, s, u, are in roman, the *a* and *e* in italic.

[3] A copy of this rare broadside is in the library of Corpus Christi College, Cambridge.

[4] The full title of this rare little tract, consisting of eight leaves only, is translated as follows: *Aibidil Gaoidheilge Caiticiosma, &c.* (*The Irish Alphabet and Catechism, precept or instruction of a Christian, together with certain articles of a Christian faith which* are *proper for everyone to adopt who would be submissive to the ordinance of God and the Queen of this Kingdom. Translated from Latin and English into Irish by John O'Kearney . . . Printed in the town of the Ford of Hurdles, (Dublin), at the cost of Master John Ussher, Alderman, at the head of the Bridge, the 20th of June 1571, with the privilege of the great Queen. 1571.*) 8vo. See a reproduction in E. W. Lynam's 'The Irish Character in Print', *The Library*, 1924, p. 291.

Testament (S.T.C. 2958),[1] the first version of that or any portion of the Holy Scriptures in the native character. In dedicating the translation to James I, Daniel thus refers to the royal origin of the types: 'And notwithstanding that our late dreade Soveraigne Elzabeth . . . provided the Irish characters and other instrumentes for the presse in the hope that God in mercy would raise up some to translate the Newe Testament into their native tongue, yet hath Sathan hitherto prevailed, and still they remain *Lo-ruchama Lo-ammi*, &c.'

The type did further service in 1608, when Daniel's *Common Prayer (S.T.C. 16433)*[2] was printed by Franckton, a well-executed work, with engraved title and beautiful ornamented initials, each page being enclosed in a rule border. After the appearance of this book nearly a quarter of a century elapsed before the type reappeared in Bishop Bedell's *A B C*, or English and Irish *Catechism*, printed by the Stationers' Company at Dublin in 1631 (*S.T.C.* 1785).[3] This *Catechism*, with additional matter, was republished by Godfrey Daniel in 1652, also in Dublin,[4] after which the Irish type of Queen Elizabeth disappeared. There seems no reason for believing, as some state, that it was secured by the Jesuits and taken abroad.[5] Not only is it not to be found in any Irish work printed abroad, but the Irish Seminary at Louvain possessed a fount of its own which, between 1616 and 1663, was in constant use.

After 1602 no serious attempt had been made to complete the translation of the Scriptures into Irish until Dr. Bedell, Bishop of Kilmore, undertook the task about 1630. For this purpose, being then at the age of 57, he devoted himself to the study of the language, and having secured the assistance of Murtagh King and the Rev. Denis Sheridan, both eminent Irish scholars, completed the translation of the *Old Testament* in 1640. Bedell, we are informed 'determined to publish the version immediately at his own expense and in his own house, and made an agreement with a person who undertook to print it: the types were even sent for to Holland'.[6] But the troubles and persecutions of the ensuing year, followed closely by the death of the Bishop, hindered the design, and the manuscript lay neglected for forty years.[7]

---

[1] *Tiomna Nuadh, &c.* (*The New Testament of our Lord and Saviour Jesus Christ, faithfully translated from the Greek into the Irish by William O'Donnell.*) *Séon Francke: a mbaile athá Cliath* (*Dublin*), 1602. fol. This work was printed in the house of Sir William Ussher, Clerk of the Council.

[2] *Leabhar na nurnaightheadh gcomhchoidchiond agus mheinisdraldachda na Sacrameinteadh, &c.* (Translated from the English by W. Daniel, Archbishop of Tuam), *a dtigh Shéon Francke, alias Franckton, a mbaile athá Cliath* (*Dublin*), 1608. fol. Not published till 1609. In his dedication, Daniel says that, 'having translated the book, I followed it to the presse with jealousy and daiely attendance, to see it perfected; payned as a woman in travell desirous to be delivered'.

[3] *A B C, or the Institution of a Christian. Printed by the Company of Stationers.* Dublin, 1631. 8vo.

[4] *The Catechism, with the Six points of W. Perkins, translated into Irish by Godfrey Daniel.* Dublin, 1652. 8vo. For other books in which this Irish type is found see Bruce Dickins, 'The Irish Broadside of 1571' in the Cambridge Bibl. Soc. *Transactions*, vol. i, pt. I, 1949.

[5] 'The publication of everything valuable in this language by the fathers of Donegal was unfortu-nately prevented by the troubles of the time of Charles I, by Cromwell's usurpation. These fathers had procured a fount for this purpose, which, when forced to fly, they carried with them to Louvain, where some fragments of this fount are yet to be found' (Theoph. O'Flanagan on the Ancient Language of Ireland, *Transac. of the Gaelic Soc.*, 8vo, Dublin, 1808, p. 212). Others stated that the fount had been removed to Douai, and there used to print several Catholic tracts. No Irish work whatever is known to have been printed at Douai. Respecting the various foreign Irish founts, the reader is referred to the account given in Chap. 2.

[6] *Life of William Bedell*, D.D., by H. J. Monck Mason, London, 1843, p. 287.

[7] In addition to the *A B C and Catechism*, already referred to as published by Bedell in 1631, some of his biographers record that he had printed a later edition about 1641, and at the same time the following tracts in Irish, viz.: Some forms of prayer, a selection of passages from Scripture, the first three of Chrysostom's Homilies on the rich man and Lazarus, and some sermons by Leo. There is no record of these works in the bibliographies cited above on p. 69.

In the year 1680, the *New Testament* of 1602 being then entirely out of print,[1] and no Irish types being available, the illustrious Robert Boyle determined on republishing it at his own expense. To this end he caused a fount of Irish type to be cut and cast in London, and had an able printer instructed in the language for the purpose of printing it. Moxon was the founder selected to produce the types, and the result was the curious Irish fount of which the matrices formed part of his foundry.[2] With this type Boyle had the *Church Catechism*, with the *Elements of the*

2lR ττúγ δο ċρυτaιδ Óιa nₑṁ aₑuγ τalaṁ. 2lₑuγ
δο bͼ an τalaṁ ₑan ċumaδ, aₑuγ ρolaṁ; aₑuγ δο
δορċaδuγ ₑ aₑaιδ a naιₑéιn. Óé ₑ aₑaιδ na nₓιγ

FIG. 38. Moxon's Irish. From the original matrices.

Irish Language, printed in 1680,[3] and in the following year was issued in London, with a preface in Irish and English, the new edition of Daniel's Irish *New Testament*.[4]

God hath raised up [says this preface] the generous Spirit of Robert Boyle, Esq., son to the Right Honourable Richard, Earl of Cork, Lord High Treasurer of Ireland, renowned for his Piety and Learning, who hath caused the same Book of the New Testament to be Reprinted at his proper Cost; And as well for that purpose, as for Printing the *Old Testament*, and what other Pious Books shall be thought convenient to be published in the Irish Tongue, has caused a New Set of fair Irish Characters to be Cast in London, and an able Printer to be instructed in the way of Printing this Language.

The printer was Robert Everingham,[5] at the Seven Stars, in Ave Maria Lane, who in 1685 was further employed by Boyle to print, in the same Irish types,[6] Bishop Bedell's translation of the *Old Testament*,[7] the manuscript of which had fortunately been preserved. The whole *Bible* being thus complete, it was issued in two 4to volumes, and in 1690 was reprinted in roman characters at Everingham's press for the use of the Highlanders.[8]

Our space forbids us to give here anything like a list of the different works in which Moxon's Irish type appeared after 1690. An interesting note as to the early use of the fount in Ireland occurs in a petition presented in 1709 to the Lord-Lieu-

[1] Most of the copies were stated to have been bought up, like the type, by Roman ecclesiastics.

[2] Dr. Lynam considers that Moxon's fount was modelled on the first type of the Irish Franciscans at Louvain and that the designs were perhaps supplied by Andrew Sall, an Irish scholar and ex-Jesuit from Douai.

[3] *Teagasg Criosduighe*, R. Everingham, London, 1680. 8vo.

[4] *Tiomna Nuadh.* (*The New Testament of our Lord and Saviour Jesus Christ, faithfully translated from the Greek into the Irish by William O'Donnell*.) R. Everingham. 1681. 4to.

[5] 'Mr. Everingham and Mr. Whiteledge', says Dunton (*Life*, p. 331), 'were two partners in the trade; I employ'd 'em very much, and look'd upon 'em to be honest and thriving men. Had they confin'd 'emselves a little sooner to Household Love, they might possibly have kept upon their own Bottom; however, so it happen'd, that they lov'd themselves into Two Journey-men Printers again.' Everingham was the printer, in 1680, of a *Weekly*

Advertisement of Books for some London publishers.

[6] Writing to Dr. Marsh of Dublin, 17 Jan. 1681–2, Boyle refers to a projected Irish Grammar and offers the use of his type. 'I am glad that so useful a designe as that of frameing a compendious Irish Grammar has been conceived by one that is so able to execute it well; but I presume you will want letters for many of the Irish words; in which case you may please to consider what use may be made of those I have already, that may be consistent with the printing of the Old Testament in the language they relate to; for all the designe I had in having them cut off was, that they might be in a readiness to print useful bookes in Irish, whether there or here' (Monck Mason's *Life of Bedell*, p. 301).

[7] *Leabhuir na Seintiomna, &c.* (*The Books of the Old Testament translated into Irish by Dr. William Bedell, late Bishop of Kilmore. London.*) 1685. 4to.

[8] *An Biobla Naomhtha.* (*W. Bedell's and W. O'Donnell's Irish Bible, revised, and printed at London by R. Everingham.*) 1690. 8vo.

tenant by several of the clergy and gentry of Ireland for the printing of a new edition of the *New Testament* 'in the Irish character and tongue, in order to which the only set of characters now in Britain is bought already'.[1]

This petition does not appear to have been successful; but in 1712 a *Book of Common Prayer*,[2] translated by Dr. John Richardson, Rector of Annah (Chaplain to the Lord-Lieutenant), with the assistance of the Christian Knowledge Society, was printed by Elinor Everingham, at the Seven Stars in Ave Maria Lane. Dr. Richardson also published some *Irish Sermons*[3] at the same press, and a *History of the Attempts . . . to Convert the Popish Natives of Ireland*, London, 1712.

In 1700, in the London *Oratio Dominica*, Moxon's Irish type was used, as also in the reprint in 1713, after which the fount frequently reappeared until 1820, when it was used in the *Transactions of the Iberno Celtic Society* for printing the titles of E. O'Reilly's 'Chronological Account of Irish Writers' there given. The 'punches and matrices', said Mores, writing in 1778, 'have ever since continued in England. The Irish themselves have no letter of this face, but are supplied with it by us from England; though it has been said, but falsely, that the University of Louvain have lately procured a fount to be cut for the use of the Irish Seminary there.'[4] We are glad to add to this statement that the punches of this interesting fount are still in existence in the possession of Messrs. Stephenson, Blake & Co.

Among the other peculiar characters cut by Moxon may be mentioned the symbols used in George Adams's scientific works, and the Philosophic or 'Real Character' designed by Bishop John Wilkins for his learned *Essay towards a Universal Language*, printed in 1668.[5] The correcting marks used in the *Mechanick Exercises*, as well as other mathematical and astronomical symbols, were also the work of this versatile artist, whose scientific genius appears to have had a special bent towards the more curious by-paths of typography.

Moxon's foundry descended to Robert Andrews, with whom it is possible he was, during the close of his career, associated either as a master or a partner. Rowe Mores is unable to distinguish, beyond the peculiar founts above noted, and the Canon roman and italic (which subsequently came into Caslon's hands), what were the precise contents of his foundry. He therefore omits his usual list and includes the whole in Andrews's.

The date of Moxon's death is uncertain, but he was certainly dead by 1692, as we learn from the dedication to the second edition of his *Mathematicks made easy*, issued by his son James from Warwick Lane in that year. In the dedication to Christopher Seaton, signed by James, occurs the following passage: 'It was above twelve years since this book was first compos'd by my Father and then dedicated to a Noble Patron of this Nation [Sir George Wharton, d. 1681]; who are both Deceased.' Mores states that he founded in London from 1659 to 1683, from which it would seem that he retired from the type business some time before his death.

---

[1] Mason's *Life of Bedell*, p. 305.

[2] *The Book of Common Prayer, Irish and English, with the Elements of the Irish Language*, by John Richardson. London, 1712. 8vo.

[3] *Practical Sermons*. London, 1711.

[4] *Dissertation*, p. 33. It is worthy of note that at the date when Mores wrote an almost universal cessation in Irish printing was taking place at home and abroad.

[5] *An Essay towards a Real Character and a Philosophical Language, by John Wilkins, D.D., Dean of Ripon. London, printed . . . for the Royal Society*. 1668. Fol.

He was a voluminous writer on scientific and mathematical subjects, and many of his works ran through several editions. Mores describes him cordially as an admirable mechanic and an excellent artist, and states that he was made a Fellow of the Royal Society, 30 November 1678. His name appears on the List of Fellows for 1679, 1680, and 1681. He was succeeded in his office of Hydrographer to the King by Captain Greenvile Collins, who so styles himself on the title-page of his *Coasting Pilot*, 1693. Our portrait of Moxon is taken from the frontispiece to the fourth edition of his *Tutor of Astronomy and Geography*, 1686, printed by Samuel Roycroft for the author.

It is doubtful whether his investigations and theories had any sensible effect on the practice of English letter-founding. They may have tended to encourage the favour with which Dutch letter was regarded at the beginning of the eighteenth century; but it is not clear that his attempt to confine to rule and compass the art of letter-cutting either secured general adoption or was productive of any appreciable reform in our national typography.

SPECIMENS OF SEVENTEENTH-CENTURY ENGLISH TYPES

In the Bagford collection in the British Museum there are a number of specimen-sheets, Dutch and English, signed and unsigned, many of them unknown from other sources. John Bagford was born in 1650 and was originally a shoemaker; he wrote a tract on fashions in shoes. For most of his life he was a book-buyer and was commissioned to purchase books by the Earl of Oxford; John Moore, Bishop of Norwich; Sir Hans Sloane; and others. He became an enthusiastic collector of ballads, documents relating to the antiquities of England, and all manner of papers relating to the production of books. He planned a history of printing based on his collections and issued proposals for the works. If one may judge from the manuscripts left by Bagford, the plan seems to have made little progress, and it may be doubted whether he was competent to write such a history. Thomas Hearne was well acquainted with him, and in his *Remarks and Collections* published by the Oxford Historical Society, 1885–1921, 11 vols., there are many letters exchanged between the two. From Bagford's letters it appears that he had little education, and even his friend Hearne had to agree that he wanted judgement as well as learning. Another contemporary, the Rev. John Lewis, who published a Life of Caxton in 1737, says of him, and of Hearne also, that they lacked judgement and even common sense. Bagford may not have mutilated books in amassing his collection of title-pages to the extent generally supposed. Booksellers used additional title-pages for advertising, and further Bagford is said to have made use of refuse from the Great Fire of London. A note in the collections (5910, pt. 3, fol. 120 b) states that he was allowed to take what he wanted from the waste books of Christopher Bateman. In the *Philosophical Transactions* of the Royal Society, April–June 1707, pp. 2397 seq., there is a paper by Bagford entitled 'An Essay on the Invention of Printing', which is chiefly concerned with Coster and the author's visits to Holland in search of early books. The paper is followed by a brief description of Bagford's collection by Humphrey Wanley, in the form of letters to Sir Hans Sloane. Wanley was librarian to the Earl of Oxford, who finally bought the collections after Bagford's death in 1716. They came to the British Museum with the Harleian MSS. by purchase in 1753. The only evidence that Bagford was a printer consists of a card which he printed on the frozen Thames in January 1716. This is reproduced in Dibdin's *Bibliographical Decameron*, iii. 282. He died in May of the same year.[1]

---

[1] There is a portrait of Bagford from an engraving by George Virtue in Dibdin's *Bibliographical Decameron*, iii. 281, and a further account of him in the same author's *Bibliomania*, pp. 430–7. There are also a number of references to him in Nichols's *Literary Anecdotes* and *Literary Illustrations*.

An examination of the English specimen-sheets contained in Bagford (5915) will help us to discover some of the English-cut types used in this country in the seventeenth century. Three of the sheets are unsigned and undated, not in fact published specimens, but miscellaneous collections of letters struck off, perhaps for Bagford himself or for some contemporary printer. They may be dated as about 1700. We will number them 1–3. Sheet No. 1 (5915, No. 37), measuring for the type area 294 × 390 mm., shows two alphabets of capitals, three romans, one black-letter, and one italic, all of large size. The first alphabet of capitals is the five-line Pica already found in the Oxford specimen of 1693, said to be cut by George Edwards. Four letters appear on the title-page of an edition of *Paradise Lost*, printed by Thomas Hodgkin for Jacob Tonson in 1688. (There was another edition in 1695.) Of the second alphabet of roman capitals I know only that they appear in the headings of proclamations, issued by the official printers, from 1659. Of the third alphabet the upper-case is common on the title-pages of English books and on specimen-sheets. The earliest appearance on a title-page noted is of 1639—*Relation of a Conference between William Laud and Mr. Fisher the Jesuite*, R. Badger. We have already found it in the Oxford specimen-books. It appears also on the specimen-sheet of the Heirs of Andrew Anderson, Edinburgh, 1698, and in James Watson's book of 1713. On our anonymous sheet No. 2 it is called 'Fatt Cannon'. The lower-case is less common; on the title-page of the Milton of 1688, already mentioned, the words *Paradise Lost* are set in this type. The words *in twelve books*, on the same title-page, are in Moxon's Canon, which is the fourth type on our sheet. An account of this design is given under Moxon (p. 171). Next follows the two-line Great Primer black which was one of the commonest heading types in England from 1530 to 1730. We have said something of its origin and history in the chapter on sixteenth-century types. The last roman on the sheet, a Double Pica, is found in English books at least as early as 1638, e.g. in *The Letters of J. L. Guez, Sieur de Balzac*. This roman is followed by a very poor italic of Great Primer size, of about the same date. On this curious sheet all the types shown are most probably English cut.

Sheet No. 2 (5915, No. 453), measuring 265 × 150 mm. type area, is surrounded by printers' flowers. At the top are acorns. The earliest appearance of this flower noted in England is in Giovanni della Casa's *Galateo*, G. Webb, Oxford, 1628. The flower appears to be of Dutch origin and is found at Arnhem as early as 1619 and on several Dutch specimen-sheets. On the Bagford sheet, at the sides, are harps, and at the foot, vases, and a third decorative unit. The harp and vase appear in R. Montacutius's *Apparatus ad origines ecclesiasticas*, L. Lichfield, Oxford, 1635. The harp, at any rate, is English. Under a crown it represents Ireland. Similarly one finds the rose, leek, and thistle, each under a crown.

The type used for the descriptions is the Elzevir Double Pica italic of which an account is given in Johnson's *Type Designs*, p. 160. It was used by James Flesher at London from 1657 and is the earliest certainly Dutch type found in England. It is found at Oxford, for instance, in the running titles of the folio Bible of 1680, and in London as late as 1723. Type 1, the 'Fatt Cannon', is the third alphabet on anonymous sheet No. 1 just described; type 2, the 'French Cannon', is Moxon's; type 3, the 'Lean Cannon', is unknown to me. Types 4 and 5, the two-line English and Double Pica romans, are heavy faces of Dutch origin. They were used by the Elzevirs and appear to be identical with the Cicerones Duplices and Ascendonica shown in the specimen of Johannes Elzevir, Leyden, 1658, and the Dubbelde Augustyn and Dubbelde Mediaan in Abraham Elzevir's *Proeve der Drukkerye*, 1713. The Double Pica was used in Hugo Grotius's *The Rights of War and Peace*, London, 1682. Type 6, the 'Great Primmer', was a sixteenth-century type, probably of Antwerp origin (see p. 93). For its appearance in a seventeenth-century book, see *The Works of King Charles I*, J. Flesher for R. Royston, 1662, where it is used for the main text of the book. Type 7, English, again dates from the sixteenth century; it is John Day's 95 roman, of which some account was given on p. 94. It should be noted that these two sizes have been given a capital U of the same design as the lower-case u, a form peculiar to the seventeenth century. Of the three smaller sizes, 'Pica', 'Long Primmer', and 'Brevier', it is difficult to say anything definite, but they also may possibly be of the sixteenth century. Sheet No. 2, then, shows some English heading types, three Dutch types, and a number of sixteenth-century designs still in use after 150 years.

Sheet No. 3 (5915, No. 457), measuring 272 × 151 mm. type area, shows two romans, two blacks, and two italics (Fig. 39). First come the capitals of Moxon's Canon. Next is a two-line Great Primer black, which is the same as that shown in the Oxford book of 1706, 'purchased 1701', different from the one in the Grover Foundry. Then follows a two-line English italic, a Dutch type, or probably a Dutch type. It belongs to the series of so-called 'Janson' romans and italics, which have survived and been much used in the last generation, especially in Germany. The series is of some historical interest because of its large x height and other tendencies towards the modern face. In No. 11 of *Signature*, 1939, in an article entitled 'Leipzig as a centre of Typefounding', Mr. Morison contributed a study of the series and its connexion with Anton Janson, typefounder of Leipzig. In *Signature*, No. 15, 1940, Mr. Morison added an appendix, in which it was shown that Janson was in fact a Dutchman, who was trained as a typefounder at Amsterdam, and that he worked also at Frankfort before proceeding to Leipzig. In an article in *The Library*, September 1939, I traced some of the early appearances of the pseudo-Janson series, which was certainly not cut by Anton Janson. One size only of the italic and none of the romans reached England. The italic is the two-line English on sheet No. 3. It is found also in the Oxford specimen-book of 1695, on the sheet of the Heirs of Andrew Anderson, Edinburgh, 1698, and on that of James Orme, 1698. In English books the earliest appearance noted is on the title-page of John Shower's *Mourner's Companion*, London, 1692. Thomas Rymer's *Foedera*, the first volume of which was published in 1704, has a fine display of this italic in the preliminaries.

The next sizes on sheet No. 3 are the 'Fell' Double Pica roman and italic, often found in London printed books. Finally is a black-letter. Except for this black, all the types shown on the sheet were at Oxford.

In the Bagford collection is also 'A Specimen of Mr. J. Orme's Printing-House; which is now to be disposed of' (5915, No. 38). This sale took place in 1698. The sheet shows several types already found on the anonymous sheets. (Fig. 40.) There is the second set of capitals of sheet No. 1, the capitals of the third type on that sheet, which were also at Oxford, and the 'Fell' Double Pica roman and italic. There is also a copy of Moxon's Canon roman, and the two-line Great Primer black of the Grover Foundry; it is difficult to be certain of these two, when only a few over-inked words are given. But I mention this sheet especially on account of a Great Primer roman, which introduces another series of English types. The design has a distinctive lower-case g with a steeply descending loop, a capital R with a curled tail, a form peculiar at this date to English types and already found in Nicholas Nicholls's roman, and the capital U with the lower-case design, also a peculiarity of the seventeenth century. There were at least three sizes, Double Pica, Great Primer, and English. The last size may be seen on the sheet of the Heirs of Andrew Anderson, Edinburgh, 1698. The English size was used for the Latin text of the *Catena in Job*, 1637 (p. 132). They appear also in books of 1636 and 1637, printed by Nathaniel Okes and Richard Hodgkinson. Nos. 3583 A, 15717, 18806, and 24660 in the *Short Title Catalogue of Books printed in England to 1640*, show one or more of the sizes. Presumably the italics used with these romans are from the same hand. The series is of very inferior design and execution, but is certainly from an English founder. In this case the Dutch took the trouble to copy the design, and improve it. On an undated specimen-sheet of an Amsterdam printer, Johannes Kannewet, also in the Bagford collection (5915, No. 544), a Text roman is shown, which is clearly based on the Great Primer of the English series. This Dutch copy was used by the Amsterdam printer Jan Jannson in 1647, e.g. in H. Alting's *Exegesis logica Augustanæ Confessionis*. It is found also in the *Hollantsche Mercurius*, 1650. It is also worth mentioning that Hodgkinson, one of the first printers to use the English type, was in trouble in March 1637 for failure to pay for types received from the London founder, Arthur Nicholls, father of Nicholas Nicholls. (See *Domestic State Papers*, Charles I, vol. 324 f. 307b.)

ABCDEFGHIJK
LMNOPQRSTV
UWXYZÆ

(Blackletter alphabet specimen)
A a B b C c D d E e F f G g
H h I i j K k L l M m N n
O o P p Q q R r z S l s T t
U u v W w x r Y y Z z

(Italic alphabet)
*A a B b C c D d E e F f G g H h I J i j K k
L l M m N n O o P p Q q R r S f s T t U V
u v W w X x Y y Z z Æ æ œ &*

(Roman alphabet)
A a B b C c D d E e F f G g H h I J i j K k L l M m
N n O o P p Q q R r S f s T t U u V v W w X x Y y
Z z Æ æ œ &

(Italic swash alphabet)
*A A a B b C c D D d E e F f G g H h I J i j K k L l
M M m N n O o P P p Q q R r S f s T t U u V v X x
Y y Z z Æ æ œ &*

(Blackletter small)
A a B b C c D d E e F f G g H h J i j K k L l M m N n O o P p
Q q R r z S l s T t U u v W w x r Y z z

Acquaint thy Mind with the Quinteſſence of Wiſdom,
& let the ſparkling Excellency thereof blazon thy
Conversation.

(Blackletter:) Acquaint thy Mind with the Quintessence of Wisdom, & let the spark-
ling Excellency thereof blazon thy Conversation.

FIG. 39. Anonymous Specimen. From the Bagford collection. Reduced.

A
SPECIMEN
OF
Mr. *J. ORME's* PRINTING-HOUSE;

Which is now to be Disposed of; and Part of the House to be Lett.

ABCD
EFGH

ABCDE
FGHIK

ABCDEF
GHIKLM

ABCDEFG
HIKLMNO

ABCDEFGHI
KLMNOPQRS

ABCDEFGHIKLM
NOPQRSTUWXYZ

Our Father
which art in

𝕺𝖀𝕽 𝕱𝖆𝖙𝖍𝖊𝖗
𝖜𝖍𝖎𝖈𝖍 𝖆𝖗𝖙 𝖎𝖓 𝕳𝖊𝖆-
𝖛𝖊𝖓, &c.

Our Father, which
art in Heaven, Hallow-
ed be thy Name, *&c.*
Our Father, which art
in Heaven, Hallowed

Thy Kingdom come, thy Will be done in Earth as it is in Heaven.

Thy Kingdom come, thy Will be done in Earth as it in Heaven.

Give us this Day our daily Bread, and forgive us our Trespasses, as we forgive them that trespass against us.

Give us this Day our daily Bread, and forgive us our Trespasses, as we forgive them that trespass against us.

O God whose Nature and Property is ever to have Mercy and to forgive, receive our humble Petitions: and though we be tied and bound with the Chain of our Sins, yet let the pitifulness of thy Mercy loose us, for the honour of Jesus Christ our Mediator and Advocate.

O God whose Nature and Property is ever to have Mercy and to forgive, receive our humble Petitions: and though we be tied and bound with the Chains of our Sins, yet let the pitifulness of thy Mercy loose us, for the honour of Jesus Christ our Mediator and Advocate.

O God whose Nature and Property is ever to have Mercy and to forgive, receive our humble Petitions: and though we be tied and bound with the Chain of our Sins, yet let the pitifulness of thy Mercy loose us, for the honour of Jesus Christ our Mediator and Advocate.

O God whose Nature and Property is ever to have Mercy and to forgive, receive our humble Petitions: and though we be tied and bound with the Chain of our Sins, yet let the pitifulness of thy Mercy loose us, for the honour of Jesus Christ our Mediator and Advocate.

𝕺 𝕲𝖔𝖉 𝖜𝖍𝖔𝖘𝖊 𝕹𝖆𝖙𝖚𝖗𝖊 𝖆𝖓𝖉 𝕻𝖗𝖔𝖕𝖊𝖗𝖙𝖞 𝖎𝖘 𝖊𝖛𝖊𝖗 𝖙𝖔 𝖍𝖆𝖛𝖊 𝕸𝖊𝖗𝖈𝖞 𝖆𝖓𝖉 𝖙𝖔 𝖋𝖔𝖗𝖌𝖎𝖛𝖊, 𝖗𝖊𝖈𝖊𝖎𝖛𝖊 𝖔𝖚𝖗 𝖍𝖚𝖒-𝖇𝖑𝖊 𝕻𝖊𝖙𝖎𝖙𝖎𝖔𝖓𝖘: 𝖆𝖓𝖉 𝖙𝖍𝖔𝖚𝖌𝖍 𝖜𝖊 𝖇𝖊 𝖙𝖎𝖊𝖉 𝖆𝖓𝖉 𝖇𝖔𝖚𝖓𝖉 𝖜𝖎𝖙𝖍 𝖙𝖍𝖊 𝕮𝖍𝖆𝖎𝖓 𝖔𝖋 𝖔𝖚𝖗 𝕾𝖎𝖓𝖘.

O God whose Nature and Property is ever to have Mercy and to forgive, receive our humble Petition: and though we be tied and bound with the Chain of our Sins, yet let the pitifulness of thy Mercy loose us, for the honour of Jesus Christ our Mediator and Advocate.

O God whose Nature and Property is ever to have Mercy and to forgive, receive our humble Petitions: and though we be tied and bound with the Chain of our Sins, yet let the pitifulness of thy Mercy loose us, for the honour of Jesus Christ our Mediator and Advocate.

𝕺 𝕲𝖔𝖉 𝖜𝖍𝖔𝖘𝖊 𝕹𝖆𝖙𝖚𝖗𝖊 𝖆𝖓𝖉 𝕻𝖗𝖔𝖕𝖊𝖗𝖙𝖞 𝖎𝖘 𝖊𝖛𝖊𝖗 𝖙𝖔 𝖍𝖆𝖛𝖊 𝕸𝖊𝖗𝖈𝖞 𝖆𝖓𝖉 𝖙𝖔 𝖋𝖔𝖗𝖌𝖎𝖛𝖊, 𝖗𝖊𝖈𝖊𝖎𝖛𝖊 𝖔𝖚𝖗 𝖍𝖚𝖒𝖇𝖑𝖊 𝕻𝖊𝖙𝖎𝖙𝖎𝖔𝖓𝖘: 𝖆𝖓𝖉 𝖙𝖍𝖔𝖚𝖌𝖍 𝖜𝖊 𝖇𝖊 𝖙𝖎𝖊𝖉 𝖆𝖓𝖉 𝖇𝖔𝖚𝖓𝖉 𝖜𝖎𝖙𝖍 𝖙𝖍𝖊 𝕮𝖍𝖆𝖎𝖓 𝖔𝖋 𝖔𝖚𝖗 𝕾𝖎𝖓𝖘, 𝖞𝖊𝖙 𝖑𝖊𝖙 𝖙𝖍𝖊 𝖕𝖎𝖙𝖎𝖋𝖚𝖑𝖓𝖊𝖘𝖘 𝖔𝖋 𝖙𝖍𝖞 𝕸𝖊𝖗𝖈𝖞.

O God we have heard with our Ears, and our Fathers have declared unto us the noble Works that thou didst in their Days, and in the Old Time, yea, even in the times before them. Almighty God, who hath given us Grace at this time with one accord to make our common Supplication unto thee, and dost promise that when when two or three are gathered together in thy Name, thou wilt grant their Requests. Fulfil now, O Lord the desires and petitions of thy Servants, as may be most convenient for them, granting us in this World knowledge of thy Truth, and in the World to come Life everlasting.

O God we have heard with our Ears, and our Fathers have declared unto us the noble Works that thou didst in their Days, and in the Old Time, yea, even in the Times before them. Almighty God, who hath given us Grace at this time with one accord to make our common Supplications unto thee, and dost promise that when two or three are gathered together in my Name, thou wilt grant their requests. Fulfil now, O Lord, the desires and petitions of thy Servants, as may be most expedient for them, granting us in this World knowledge of thy Truth, and in the World to come Life everlasting.

Almighty God who hath given us Grace at this time with one accord to make our common Supplications unto thee, and dost promise that when two or three are met together in thy Name, thou wilt grant their Requests. Fulfil now, O Lord, the desires and Petitions of thy Servants, as may be most expedient for them, granting us in this World a Knowledge of thy Truth, and in the World to come Life everlasting.

Almighty God, who hath given us Grace at this time with one accord to make our common Supplications unto thee, and dost promise that when two or three are gathered together in thy Name, thou wilt grant their Requests. Fulfil now, O Lord the desires and petitions of thy Servants, as may be most expedient for them, granting us in this World knowledge of thy Truth, and in the World to come Life everlasting.

𝕬𝖑𝖒𝖎𝖌𝖍𝖙𝖞 𝕲𝖔𝖉, 𝖜𝖍𝖔 𝖍𝖆𝖙𝖍 𝖌𝖎𝖛𝖊𝖓 𝖚𝖘 𝕲𝖗𝖆𝖈𝖊 𝖆𝖙 𝖙𝖍𝖎𝖘 𝖙𝖎𝖒𝖊 𝖜𝖎𝖙𝖍 𝖔𝖓𝖊 𝖆𝖈𝖈𝖔𝖗𝖉 𝖙𝖔 𝖒𝖆𝖐𝖊 𝖔𝖚𝖗 𝖈𝖔𝖒𝖒𝖔𝖓 𝕾𝖚𝖕𝖕𝖑𝖎𝖈𝖆𝖙𝖎𝖔𝖓𝖘 𝖚𝖓𝖙𝖔 𝖙𝖍𝖊𝖊, 𝖆𝖓𝖉 𝖍𝖆𝖙𝖍 𝖕𝖗𝖔𝖒𝖎𝖘𝖊𝖉 𝖙𝖍𝖆𝖙 𝖜𝖍𝖊𝖓 𝖙𝖜𝖔 𝖔𝖗 𝖙𝖍𝖗𝖊𝖊 𝖆𝖗𝖊 𝖌𝖆𝖙𝖍𝖊𝖗𝖊𝖉 𝖙𝖔𝖌𝖊𝖙𝖍𝖊𝖗 𝖎𝖓 𝖙𝖍𝖞 𝕹𝖆𝖒𝖊, 𝖙𝖍𝖔𝖚 𝖜𝖎𝖑𝖙 𝖌𝖗𝖆𝖓𝖙 𝖙𝖍𝖊𝖎𝖗 𝕽𝖊𝖖𝖚𝖊𝖘𝖙𝖘. 𝕱𝖚𝖑-𝖋𝖎𝖑 𝖓𝖔𝖜, 𝕺 𝕷𝖔𝖗𝖉 𝖙𝖍𝖊 𝖉𝖊𝖘𝖎𝖗𝖊𝖘 𝖆𝖓𝖉 𝖕𝖊𝖙𝖎𝖙𝖎𝖔𝖓𝖘 𝖔𝖋 𝖙𝖍𝖞 𝕾𝖊𝖗𝖛𝖆𝖓𝖙𝖘, 𝖆𝖘 𝖒𝖆𝖞 𝖇𝖊 𝖒𝖔𝖘𝖙 𝖊𝖝𝖕𝖊𝖉𝖎𝖊𝖓𝖙 𝖋𝖔𝖗 𝖙𝖍𝖊𝖒, 𝖌𝖗𝖆𝖓𝖙𝖎𝖓𝖌 𝖚𝖘 𝖎𝖓 𝖙𝖍𝖎𝖘 𝖂𝖔𝖗𝖑𝖉 𝖐𝖓𝖔𝖜𝖑𝖊𝖉𝖌𝖊 𝖔𝖋 𝖙𝖍𝖞 𝕿𝖗𝖚𝖙𝖍, 𝖆𝖓𝖉 𝖎𝖓 𝖙𝖍𝖊 𝖂𝖔𝖗𝖑𝖉 𝖙𝖔 𝖈𝖔𝖒𝖊 𝕷𝖎𝖋𝖊 𝖊𝖛𝖊𝖗𝖑𝖆𝖘𝖙𝖎𝖓𝖌, 𝕬𝖒𝖊𝖓.

Μὲν Ὁ ὅτι τιμὴν ἡ προηγμένου ἰσίον ἱαυϊὸν παραγίγνε, ἡ ἀριλμα δίου τελείων ἱ ἱαυϊὸ ψυχὴν, ὁ τοὺς εἰς εὐποδίγκε Τὸ δέον πωτὸς τὸν ἱαυτῷ Θαρεύωμεν νιν· ψυχὴς καθαρᾶς τὸν σκείτηση γὴς δέδε τὶς ἔχε εἰς, ἡ ὁ ΠὶΰεΘ συμπάιησ, λέγων, Εὐσεβίστω ἡ βμῆτις μόνομεν πόσον ἱλὸμμτο.

Almighty God, who hath given us Grace at this time with one accord to make our common Supplications unto thee, and doth promise that when two or three are gathered together in thy Name, thou wilt grant their Requests. Fulfil now, O Lord the desires and petitions of thy Servants, as may be most expedient for them, granting us in this World knowledge of thy Truth, and in the World to come Life everlasting, Amen.

Almighty God, who hath given us Grace at this time with one accord to make our common Supplications unto thee, and doth promise that when two or three are gathered together in thy Name, thou wilt grant their Requests. Fulfil now, O Lord the Desires and Petitions of thy Servants, as may be most expedient for them, granting us in this World knowledge of thy Truth, and in the World to come Life everlasting, Amen.

רָשָׁע יְדַבְּרֶנִי עַל־טֵּם פֻּשְׁעוֹ־לְרֶוֶד יְהֹוָה רַע לֹא־אֹתֶה׃

ה. לְמַעַן שְׁמֶ ; גַּם סְטוֹתָי וְעֲוֹלֵנִי ; נַפְשִׁי שׁוֹבֵב בְּנְאֹת אַלֶּךְ מַיֵּא צֶלְמֹתֵי׃

𝕬𝖑𝖒𝖎𝖌𝖍𝖙𝖞 𝕲𝖔𝖉, 𝖜𝖍𝖔 𝖍𝖆𝖙𝖍 𝖌𝖎𝖛𝖊𝖓 𝖚𝖘 𝕲𝖗𝖆𝖈𝖊 𝖆𝖙 𝖙𝖍𝖎𝖘 𝖙𝖎𝖒𝖊 𝖜𝖎𝖙𝖍 𝖔𝖓𝖊 𝖆𝖈𝖈𝖔𝖗𝖉 𝖙𝖔 𝖒𝖆𝖐𝖊 𝖔𝖚𝖗 𝖈𝖔𝖒𝖒𝖔𝖓 𝕾𝖚𝖕𝖕𝖑𝖎𝖈𝖆𝖙𝖎𝖔𝖓𝖘 𝖚𝖓𝖙𝖔 𝖙𝖍𝖊𝖊, 𝖆𝖓𝖉 𝖉𝖔𝖙𝖍 𝖕𝖗𝖔𝖒𝖎𝖘𝖊 𝖙𝖍𝖆𝖙 𝖜𝖍𝖊𝖓 𝖙𝖜𝖔 𝖔𝖗 𝖙𝖍𝖗𝖊𝖊 𝖆𝖗𝖊 𝖌𝖆𝖙𝖍𝖊𝖗𝖊𝖉 𝖙𝖔𝖌𝖊𝖙𝖍𝖊𝖗 𝖎𝖓 𝖙𝖍𝖞 𝕹𝖆𝖒𝖊, 𝖙𝖍𝖔𝖚 𝖜𝖎𝖑𝖙 𝖌𝖗𝖆𝖓𝖙 𝖙𝖍𝖊𝖎𝖗 𝕽𝖊𝖖𝖚𝖊𝖘𝖙𝖘. 𝕱𝖚𝖑𝖋𝖎𝖑 𝖓𝖔𝖜, 𝕺 𝕷𝖔𝖗𝖉 𝖙𝖍𝖊 𝖉𝖊𝖘𝖎𝖗𝖊𝖘 𝖆𝖓𝖉 𝖕𝖊𝖙𝖎𝖙𝖎𝖔𝖓𝖘 𝖔𝖋 𝖙𝖍𝖞 𝕾𝖊𝖗𝖛𝖆𝖓𝖙𝖘, 𝖆𝖘 𝖒𝖆𝖞 𝖇𝖊 𝖒𝖔𝖘𝖙 𝖊𝖝𝖕𝖊𝖉𝖎𝖊𝖓𝖙 𝖋𝖔𝖗 𝖙𝖍𝖊𝖒, 𝖌𝖗𝖆𝖓𝖙𝖎𝖓𝖌 𝖚𝖘 𝖎𝖓 𝖙𝖍𝖎𝖘 𝖂𝖔𝖗𝖑𝖉 𝖐𝖓𝖔𝖜𝖑𝖊𝖉𝖌𝖊 𝖔𝖋 𝖙𝖍𝖊 𝕿𝖗𝖚𝖙𝖍, 𝖆𝖓𝖉 𝖎𝖓 𝖙𝖍𝖊 𝖂𝖔𝖗𝖑𝖉 𝖙𝖔 𝖈𝖔𝖒𝖊 𝕷𝖎𝖋𝖊 𝖊𝖛𝖊𝖗𝖑𝖆𝖘𝖙𝖎𝖓𝖌, 𝕬𝖒𝖊𝖓.

Likewise Three Presses, Two Imposing-Stones, a Lye-Trough, and Sink; with Racks, Frames, Composing-Sticks, Gallies, Chases, *&c.*

Fig. 40. Printer's Specimen. From the Bagford collection. Reduced.

It is, no doubt, true that between 1700 and 1720 there was probably more Dutch type in England than English. These dates have been extended, until it is supposed that from the time of the Restoration much Dutch type was being imported. The only Dutch type we have found earlier than the 'Fell' purchases is the Elzevir italic mentioned above, used in England from 1657. James Watson, or John Spotswood, who is said to have written the preface to Watson's specimen-book of 1713, states that the Edinburgh printers Robert Sanders and John Cairns had both brought workmen and material from Holland. Cairns's successor, David Lindsay, among whose partners were two Dutchmen, issued a single-sheet advertisement in 1681. This sheet is set in a Dutch roman, the Augustin (English) roman of Bartholmaeus Voskens of Amsterdam, shown on his specimen-sheet issued about 1670 when he was working at Hamburg (reproduced by G. Mori in *Die Schriftgiesser B. und R. Voskens*, 1923). Lindsay and his partners printed several books in the type, e.g. *The Laws and Acts of Parliament*, 1681, and Robert Sibbald's *Scotia illustrata*, 1683. The italic used by Lindsay to accompany this roman was not that of Voskens, but that of the best of the Amsterdam founders, Christoffel van Dijk, an italic later to be copied by William Caslon. These were probably the first Dutch types used in Scotland. The Voskens roman has not been found in any English printed book, and the Van Dijk italic not until about 1697 when it was purchased by the Cambridge University Press. As we shall see, it was at Cambridge that the best display of Van Dijk was to be found in England.

THE LATER FOUNDERS OF THE SEVENTEENTH CENTURY

JOSEPH LEIGH, 1649?

THE Joseph Leigh[1] whose name appears in imprints from 1662 to 1665, according to Plomer's *Dictionary*, is probably identical with the founder. His address was in Basinghall Street, near the Nag's Head Tavern, in 1665. Presumably this is the Nag's Head Tavern which was on London Wall. From the records of the Stationers' Company we learn that in 1669 Leigh, along with Thomas Goring, is 'to give at the next Court an account in writing, what sorts of letter they have made, and for whom, since the Act of Parliament in that case was provided'. The record of his dealings with Oxford begins in 1668.[2] At the meeting of the Delegates on 17 October 1668 it was agreed that £40 or £50 be paid to Leigh 'in order to a fount of Greek and Latin Letters'. On 8 April 1669 he was paid £136. 7s. 6d. for Greek, Latin, and 'Italica' founts, ordered 17 October 1668 and delivered January 1669. In 1670 £175 was paid to Leigh and Nicholls, £40 to Leigh in 1671, and finally £55 late in 1672. From a letter of Leigh's to Samuel Clarke, the Architypographus of the Press, of 4 February 1669 (reproduced in Hart, op. cit.), it appears that the types delivered in January 1669 were for use in William Beveridge's Συνόδικον, 1672 (Madan, No. 2916). Leigh writes about a difference in body: 'acquaint Mr. Hall how you and Mr. Scott appointed the difference of body's to save underruning in the Latin Collu[mn] in this edition, viz. that the Greek and the Italica is a two line Brevier body and the Roman is an English body.' Two different bodies were used in order to get the same amount of Latin and Greek, in parallel columns, on the page. The Beveridge is an interesting volume of Oxford pre-Fell printing, with some sixteenth-century types, such as Day's Double Pica roman and italic and Day's English roman for the main text. Nicholls's roman is used for the Prolegomena and the capitals dating from 1639 (cf. p. 180) are found. As far as the evidence of this volume goes, Leigh appears to have been only a caster of letters.

In 1675 Leigh served as Steward at the Brotherly Meeting of Printers, and in the same year he signed a petition to the Lord Mayor's Court, along with Thomas

[1] One Joseph Lee was made free of the Stationers by patrimony on 17 Sept. 1649. In one of the Registers (Calendar I) he is called a Primer Binder. Possibly all the same man.
[2] See Madan, iii, p. xxxv.

Goring and Godfrey Head, begging that they may be allowed to keep their Journeymen Foreigners (see below, p. 200). The latest mention of Leigh is in the Domestic State Papers for 26 March 1678, where he is recorded as making an affidavit about a secret press on information received from William Paxton. The authorities were searching for the printers of an attack on the government entitled *An Account of the Growth of Popery*, written by Andrew Marvel according to the *D.N.B.* A reward of £100 was offered for the discovery of the anonymous author.

THOMAS GORING, 1657

Thomas Goring's father was John, apprenticed to the founder Thomas Wright, 1 June 1635 and free 4 Aug. 1645. Thomas was apprenticed to his father, 31 May 1650 and free 2 Nov. 1657. One of his apprentices was Robert Littleboy.

Little more of him is known beyond what is recorded in two short entries in the books of the Stationers' Company, viz.:

1668. The Master and Wardens requested to certify to the Archbishop of Canterbury that Thomas Goring, a member of this Company, is an honest and sufficient man, and fit to be one of the *four* present founders; there being one now wanting, according to the Act of Parliament.

1669. Mr. Joseph Lee and Mr. Goring to give at the next Court an account in writing, what sorts of letter they have made, and for whom, since the Act of Parliament in that case was provided.

In 1675, along with Joseph Leigh and Godfrey Head, Goring signed the petition to the Lord Mayor's Court asking for permission to keep their Journeymen Foreigners (see below, p. 200). In 1678 he served as Steward at the Brotherly Meeting of Printers.

ROBERT ANDREWS, 1683

This founder, who was born in 1650, was made free of the Stationers 4 September 1676. He succeeded Joseph Moxon, probably about the year 1683,[1] and transferred his foundry to Charterhouse Street, where he continued in business till 1733. His foundry, of which, Mores informs us, Moxon's matrices formed the most considerable part, was next to that of the Grovers the most extensive of its day; and it would appear that, for some time at any rate, these two shared between them the whole of the English trade. Andrews's foundry consisted of a large variety of roman letter and Titlings; and in 'learned' founts was specially rich in Hebrew, of which there were no less than eleven founts, and five rabbinical. Of peculiar sorts, he possessed the matrices of Bishop Wilkins's 'Real Character', also the correcting-marks used by Moxon in his *Mechanick Exercises*, and other symbols, besides three or four founts of square-headed music.

He also possessed the Hebrews and the Ethiopic[2] used in Walton's *Polyglot*, the Irish cut by Moxon for Boyle's *New Testament*, and an alphabet of Great Primer Anglo-Norman. Such capitals are usually called Lombardic and were in very

---

[1] His name occurs in the list of Masters and Workmen Printers as having served as Steward at the sixty-ninth Feast (1680). Charterhouse St. is not the present street of that name. It ran north from Long Lane to Charterhouse Sq. and is now called Hayne St.

[2] Mores's *Dissertation*, p. 13.

general use towards the end of the fifteenth century. The Enschedés have an alphabet which they trace to Hendrik De Lettersnijder, 1498 (cf. C. Enschedé, op. cit., p. 18). In this country similar capitals were used by Pynson before 1500, and in the sixteenth century by William Faques, Robert Copland, and others. Among Andrews's old blacks, several of which have survived to this day, are some

בראשית ברא אלהים את השמים ואת האן : והאין היתה תהו ובהו וחשך על פני תהום ורוח אלהים
מרחפת על פני המים : ויאמר אלהים יהי אור ויהי אור : וירא אלהים את האור כי טוב ויבדל אלהים בין
האור בבין החשך : ויקרא אלהים לאור יום ולחשך קרא לילה ויהי ערב ויהי בקר יום אחד : ויאמר

Fig. 41. Nonpareil Rabbinic Hebrew. From Andrews's foundry.

Of the grete sorowe that Achylles demened for the deth of hys frende Patroclus, and of the armes that Thetys his moder dyde doo forge by Ulcan. Capitulo decimoquinto.

'De la description des Armes que forga Ulcan a Achiles.
'En lescu fut, par tres grāde ȝ subtille maistrise, figuree
'ȝ pourtraite la deuise des elemens, leurs substances ȝ leurs
'natures et toutes leurs differēces, si y fut pourtrait le fir=
'mamēt et les estoilles, chascune en sa propriete. Et les
'douze signes du Zodiacke en leurs propres natures ȝ leur

m̄ ā c̄ ī n̄ ō ȫ p̄ q̄ q̄ r̄ i ū ū ᵹ ꝗ ꝙ ᵹ ᴣ ℄ ꞇ ꞇ ꝓ ꝑ m̄ ꝛ

Fig. 42. Old Blacks. From Andrews's foundry.

of Dutch cut.[1] His son, Silvester Andrews, as we shall notice later on, founded at Oxford, whither he appears to have taken matrices of some of the romans and one fount of Hebrew from his father's foundry.

The following is the list of matrices in the foundry in 1706, as given by Mores. Founts of which the punches or matrices were still in existence *c.* 1890 are distinguished by an asterisk, and those still in existence by two asterisks; those descended from the *Polyglot* foundry are marked [P.], and those from Moxon's [M.]. The table on pp. 220 and 222 shows which of them are displayed in the James Sale Catalogue.

MR. ROBERT ANDREWS' FOUNDERY, 1706.

ORIENTALS.

Hebrew.—2-line English, 32. [P.?]
Double Pica, 68. [P.?]
Great Primer, 35.
English (the common German face), 47.
English, 73. [P.?]
Pica, 65.
Long Primer, 35.
Brevier, 35.
Small Pica, old, 42.
 ,, another, 77.
 ,, another, 73.
Nonpareil, 35.

Rabbinical Hebrew.—English (German), 30.
Rashi, Pica, 29.
 ,, Long Primer,* 30.
 ,, Brevier,* 29.
 ,, Nonpareil,* 29.
Large face points, 42.
Accents, 27.
Small face points, 28.
Samaritan.—(Leusdenian), 21.
Syriac.—Great Primer, 47; Points, 13.
Arabic.—Great Primer, 104.
English, 62.

---

[1] For the use of these blacks in the nineteenth century, see below, pp. 296, 297.

MERIDIONALS.

Æthiopic.—Great Primer,** 212.　[P.]

OCCIDENTALS.

Greek.—English.　⎱　'These three were purchased
Long Primer.　　⎰　by Thos. James, 20th April
Brevier.　　　　　1724, ten years before the
　　　　　　　　　sale of the foundery.'
Long Primer, 457.
Brevier, 331.
Nonpareil, 329.
Roman and Italic.—2-line English full face
　　caps, 31.
2-line English Roman, 147.
　　,,　　　　Italic, 108.
Double Pica large face Roman, 122.
　　,,　　　small face　,,　　115.
　　,,　　　Italic, 107.
　　,,　　　2, Roman, 118.
　　,,　　　,, Italic, 66.
Another, 126.
Great Primer 1, Roman, 114.
　　,,　　　　,,　Italic, 102.
　　,,　　　　2, Roman, 110.
　　,,　　　　,,　Italic, 66.
English Roman and Italic, . . .
　　,,　　2, Roman, 92.
　　,,　　3,　,,　96.
　　,,　　Roman lower-case, 32.
Pica Roman, 117.
　　,,　　,,　lower-case, 27.
　　,,　　,,　and Italic, long face, . . .
Roman and Italic.
Long Primer Roman, 84.
　　,,　　　Italic, 80.
　　,,　　　Roman lower-case, 42.
　　,,　　　　,,　　　,, another, 38.
　　,,　　　Italic capitals and double-
　　letters, 45.
Brevier Roman lower-case, 57.
　　,,　　　,,　　　,, another, 57.
　　,,　　Italic, . . .
Title Letters and Irregulars.—4-line Pica full
　　face caps, 30.
Canon Roman, 27.　[M.]

Canon Roman, Italic, 74.　[M.]
2-line Double Pica Roman, 127.
　　,,　　Great Primer full face caps, 31.
　　,,　　Pica full face caps, 31.
　　,,　　Pica Roman lean face, 58.
Paragon Roman, 122.
　　,,　　Italic, 100.
Small Pica Roman, 76.
　　,,　　Italic, 82.
　　,,　　　,,　another, 98.
　　,,　　　,,　another, 80.
Small Pica Roman and Italic, . . .
Bourgeois Italic, 72.
Nonpareil Roman, 80.
Pearl Roman, 2 sets.

SEPTENTRIONALS.

Anglo-Saxon.—Pica, 16.
　Pica, another, 21.
Anglo-Norman (Lombardic).—Great
　　Primer capitals, 24.
English.—Great Primer with law, 116.
　English*　　　　　,,　　106.
　Pica　　　　　　,,　　125.
　Pica small face, 71.
　Long Primer,* 78.
　Brevier with law, 118.
　Small Pica*　,,　120.
　Small Pica,* 58.
　Nonpareil,* 43.
Secretary.—Great Primer capitals, 15.
Hibernian.—Pica,** 60.　[M.]
Bishop Wilkins' Real Character, English,
　　160.　[M.]
Mr. Adam's symbols, 20.　[M.]
Mr. Moxon's correcting marks, English, 16.
　　[M.]
Mathematical Characters, English and
　　Small Pica, 42.　[M.]
Astronomical and Astrological, 31.　[M.]
Music.—2-line Great Primer, 54.
　Paragon, square-headed, 44.
　Large old　　,,　　61.
　Sundry ,,　　　,,　　155.

Although he accumulated a large quantity of matrices, Robert Andrews does not appear to have been a good workman. The very indifferent manner in which he cut the punches for Miss Elstob's Saxon *Grammar* has been elsewhere recorded,[1] and the fact that his apprentice, Thomas James, after quitting his service and setting up for himself, furnished his new foundry entirely with foreign matrices, speaks somewhat unfavourably for the merits of the English letter then in common use.

[1] See p. 148.

Three of the Greek founts, however, James did subsequently purchase, in 1724, for his own use; and nine years later, on Andrews's retirement from business, he purchased the whole of his foundry, and that of his son, with the exception of the Canon roman and italic, which were acquired by Caslon.

Andrews appears to have been also a printer. The Oxford Press have a document, dated 20 September 1703, being the articles of agreement between the

Elstob Saxon

Eornuʒtlice ʒebiooað eop þuʒ:- Fæoen upe þu þe eapt on heoʒenum. Si þin nama ʒehalʒoo:- To-becume þin pice:- Lepupðe þin pilla on eopþan. ppa ppa on heoʒenum:- Upne oæʒhpamlican hlaʒ ʒyle uʒ to oæʒ:- Ano ʒopʒyʒ uʒ upe ʒyltaʒ. ppa ppa pe ʒopʒiʒað upum ʒyltenoum:- Ano ne ʒelæooe þu uʒ on coʒtnunʒe. ac alyʒ uʒ oʒ yʒele:- Soðlice:-

FIG. 43. Saxon cut by R. Andrews. From the original matrices.

University of Oxford and W. Phillips, H. Mortlock, and R. Andrews, London Stationers, to exercise the privilege of printing within the precincts of the University for five years. They were to pay £200 a year for the privilege.[1] Presumably these three acted on behalf of the Stationers' Company. This agreement lasted until 1712.

Robert Andrews was one of the Assistants of the Stationers' Company. He only survived his retirement two years, and died 27 November 1735, at the age of 80.

His name appears as a contributor of £5. 5s. towards the subscription raised by Bowyer's friends in 1712, after the destruction by fire of that eminent printer's office.

THE GROVER FOUNDRY, 1674

This foundry, situated in Angel Alley (now Edmund Place), Aldersgate Street, is said to have been established about 1674 by James and Thomas Grover. James Grover was apprenticed to James Young 6 October 1651 and became free 4 October 1658. When Thomas Grover on 3 April 1671 apprenticed his son Thomas to Andrew Crook, he was described in the Stationers' Register as 'of St. Gyles Cripplegate, Founder'. James Grover is in the list of stewards of the Brotherly Meeting of Printers for 1672; Thomas appears as steward for the year 1674. In 1676 the name J. Grover appears in the imprint of Thomas Hobbes's *A Letter on Liberty and Necessity*, and in an edition of *Herodotus* in Greek and Latin edited by Thomas Gale in 1679 the imprint reads 'Typis E. Horton et J. Grover'. The edition is set in double columns, with the Latin text in a Pica roman which is of some interest. This roman is a condensed design, with narrow H, K, M, and R, and lower-case h.

[1] See *The First Minute Book of the Delegates*, Oxford Bibl. Soc., 1943.

It would seem to have been cut for setting in a narrow column but is larger in size than that commonly used in contemporary newspapers. It cannot have been cut by the Grovers, as it is found in 1647 in George Hughes's *Vae-Euge-Tuba, or the Wo-Joy Trumpet*, printed by E. G. for John Rothwell, although only for half of the book, and again in some parts of Alexander Ross's *History of the World*, John Clark, London, 1652. The footnotes and index of the *Herodotus* are set in a Long Primer roman of similar design, which does seem to have been used for newspaper work. It appears to be the type of Ichabod Dawks's *The Protestant Mercury* (see a reproduction in Mr. Morison's *Ichabod Dawks*), though it must be admitted that the miserable press-work and worn types of this journal and other early newspapers make it impossible to speak with any certainty.

We may assume that these types were in the Grover Foundry, but whether they are included in the list of matrices given by Rowe Mores in his account of the foundry it is impossible to say. When Mores came to the account of the matrices in the James Foundry, including those acquired from the Grover Foundry, he was not sufficiently interested in the romans and italics to list them and describe their origin. We are left with the reproductions in the James's Sale Catalogue, which are only a small selection as far as the romans and italics are concerned. The number of matrices is given against each type, and that is almost the only clue. But even when, as in a few cases, we can recognize a type as having been in the Grover Foundry, the number of matrices seldom agrees. There was only one roman reproduced which we can be confident was from the Grovers, and that is Day's Double Pica roman, shown on p. 34 of the Catalogue (the italic is not shown) and one italic, the Diamond on p. 39 (in this case the roman is not shown), which probably came from the Voskens of Amsterdam.

The following is the full list of the matrices in the foundry, *c.* 1700, as given by Mores. Founts of which punches or matrices were still in existence *c.* 1890 are marked with an asterisk, and those in existence to-day with two asterisks.

THE FOUNDERY OF THE TWO Mr. GROVERS, *circ.* 1700

ORIENTALS.

Hebrew.—Great Primer, 30.
  Pica, 80.
  Long Primer, 60.
  Brevier, 130.
Samaritan (with English face).—English,** 32. [P.]
Syriac.—Double Pica, 60. [P.]
  Pica, 80.
Arabic.—Double Pica, 30. *Great Primer*, [P.?]

MERIDIONALS.

Coptic (the new hand),* 81.

'This seems to be a mistake of the cataloguers, who had fallen upon something which they did not understand; we suppose the Alexandrian fount, which from the semblance they took to be Coptic; the number 81 was made up with something else they were strangers to; and so are we. But whatever it was (if it is in the foundery) it is now in its proper place.'[1]

OCCIDENTALS.

Greek.—
  Double Pica large face, 183. [Royal.]
    „   small face, . . .   „
  Great Primer, 144.
  English, 350.
  Pica, 380.
    „   another, 120.
  Long Primer, 120.
  Brevier, 426. Very fine.
    „   another, imperfect.
  2-line full face capitals, 23.

[1] Mores's *Dissertation*, p. 46.

Roman and Italic.—2-line English full face
  capitals, 31.
2-line English Roman, 100.
  ,,   Italic, 77.
Double Pica Roman large face, 120.
  [Day?] [P.?]
  ,,   Italic, 98.   [Day?] [P.?]
  ,,   Roman small face, 126.
  ,,   Italic, 98.
Great Primer Roman large face, 102.
  ,,   Italic, 105.
  ,,   Roman small face, 153.
  ,,   Italic, 105.
  ,,   small capitals, 27.
English Roman, 159.
  ,,   Italic, 114.
Two other English Roman and Italic.
  (One called the *Old English*.)
English small capitals, 27.
Pica Roman broad face, 85.
  ,,   Roman, 146. (Called *King's House*.)
  ,,   Roman and Italic, 292.
  ,,   Italic, 42.
  ,,   small capitals, 27.
Long Primer Roman and Italic, 177.
  ,,   another,   226.   (Called
            King's House.)
  ,,   another, 219.
  ,,   two others.
Small capitals, 27.
Brevier Roman large face, 96.
  ,,   Roman and Italic, 241.
  ,,   ,,   ,,   small face.
  ,,   Italic.
Title Letters and Irregulars.—5-line Pica full
  face capitals, 31.
Canon Roman, 87.
  ,,   Italic, 70.
  ,,   Roman lean face capitals, 57.
2-line Double Pica full face capitals, 26.
  ,,   Great Primer ,,   ,,   31.
  ,,   ,,   Roman, 86.
  ,,   ,,   Italic, 68.
  ,,   Pica full face capitals, 31.
  ,,   ,, Roman, 83.
  ,,   ,, Italic, 77.
  ,,   Small Pica full face capitals, 27.
  ,,   Long Primer ,,   ,,   31.
  ,,   Brevier   ,,   ,,   21.
Paragon Roman, 106.
  ,,   Italic, 38.
Small Pica Roman and Italic, 175.
  ,,   ,,   ,,   another, 233.

Small Pica small capitals, 27.
Minion Roman and Italic, 175.
Nonpareil ,,   ,,   174.
  ,,   ,,   ,,   another, 175.
Pearl Roman and Italic, 167.
Diamond ,,   ,,   94.

SEPTENTRIONALS.

Anglo-Saxon.—Great Primer, . . .
Pica, 30.
English.—Double Pica, 69.
Great Primer, 66.   [De Worde?]
  ,,   another, with law, 73.
English, 82.
  ,,   another, with law, 128.
Long Primer, 1, 74.
  ,,   2, 89.
  ,,   3, 74.
Brevier, 73.
2-line Great Primer, 69.   [De Worde?]
Small Pica, 70.
Nonpareil, 88.
Scriptorial.—Double Pica Court, 80.
English Court,* 100.
Great Primer Secretary, 105.
Double Pica Union Pearl,** 61.
Cursive.—Double Pica, . . .
Great Primer, 69.
English, 1, 68.
  ,,   2, 57.
Pica,**
Long Primer, 68.   [missing]
Geometrical and Algebraical Symbols.
Astronomical, Astrological, and Pharma-
  ceutical Characters.—English, 55.
Figures struck in circles and squares.—
  English, 22.
Pica Astronomical Characters belonging to
  Pica *King's House*, 22.
Pica Algebraical and Pharmaceutical Marks,
  and cancelled figures, 3 sets.
Long Primer Dominical Letters, Astro-
  nomical and Pharmaceutical Marks and
  Characters.
Long Primer Fractions, 20.
Music.—Great Primer, 176.
Flowers, 200.
Space Rules, Metal Rules, Braces, 150.
Punches.—Some for Pica, Long Primer, and
  Nonpareil Greek.
Long Primer and other Punches.

Respecting one of the founts in this foundry a special interest exists which calls for particular reference here. Among the 'Meridionals' in the list is included a 'Coptic (the new hand) 81 matrices', an entry which Mores considers to be 'a mistake of the cataloguers.' Later on, in noting the various founts missing in the collection of John James, he again refers to this 'New Coptic', adding, 'it certainly was the Alexandrian which they called New Coptic';[1] and a specimen of this Alexandrian Greek duly appears in the catalogue of James's foundry, prepared by Mores in 1778. This fount, which we are thus enabled to trace back with tolerable certainty to an earlier date than 1700, is interesting as being the first attempt at facsimile

ΠΑΤΕΡΗΜΩΝΟΕΝΤΟΙϹΟΥΡΑΝΟΙϹ
ΑΓΙΑϹΘΗΤΩΤΟ ΟΝΟΜΑϹΟΥΕΛΘΕΤΩ
ΗΒΑϹΙΛΕΙΑϹΟΥΓΕΝΗΘΗΤΩΤΟ
ΘΕΛΗΜΑϹΟΥΩϹΕΝΟΥΡΑΝΩΚΑΙΕΠΙ

ΑΒΓΔΕΖΗΘΙΚΛΜΝΞΟΠΡϹΤΥΦΧΨΩ

FIG. 44. The Alexandrian Greek. From the original matrices.

reproduction by means of type. The history of its origin is vague, but there seems reason to believe that it may have been in existence at least half a century before coming into the hands of the Grovers.

In the year 1628 Cyrillus Lucaris, a native of Crete and Patriarch of Constantinople, sent to King Charles I, by the hand of Sir Thomas Rowe (or Roe),[2] English ambassador to the Grand Seignor, a manuscript of the Bible in four volumes, written in Greek uncial or capital letters, without accents or marks of aspiration, held to be of the fifth century. An Arabic note of the thirteenth or fourteenth century led to the supposition that it was written by the martyr Thecla, said to be a noble Egyptian lady who lived in the sixth century. This precious work was received by Charles I and deposited in the Royal Library of St. James, of which at that time Patrick Young was the Keeper.

Young applied himself with enthusiasm to the work of collating and examining the manuscript, with a view to putting forward a literal transcript of its contents in print. Having published at Oxford, in 1633, an edition of Clemens Romanus, *Ad Corinthios Epistola prior*, in Greek and Latin, the text of which is included in the Alexandrian MS., he was encouraged to put forward, in 1637, his *Catena in Job*, which contained the entire text of that book transcribed from the same codex. This book was printed in the Greek types of the Royal Printing Office, purchased under the peculiar circumstances already detailed.[3] After this, says Gough, Young 'formed the design of printing the entire text of the Codex in facsimile type, of which, in 1643, he printed a *Specimen*, consisting of the first chapter of *Genesis*, with notes, and left behind him scholia as far as to the fifteenth chapter of *Numbers*'.[4]

[1] Mores's *Dissertation*, p. 67.
[2] This distinguished ambassador belonged to an honourable family, of whom by no means the least worthy member was Miss Elizabeth Rowe, who in 1785 married Henry Caslon, and subsequently—first with her mother-in-law, and afterwards by her own exertions—ably conducted the affairs of the Chiswell St. Foundry. See p. 245.
[3] See pp. 130–2.
[4] *Gent. Magaz.* lvi. 497. Nichols's *Lit. Anec.* ix. 9.

Of this specimen, unfortunately, no copy can be discovered; although as to the existence of such a document there is no lack of contemporary evidence. In his Prolegomena to the *London Polyglot* of 1657 Bishop Walton, who had made a careful study of the codex, and availed himself freely of Young's notes, distinctly states that he had seen the specimen, and that the proposal to carry through the work had been discouraged by the advice of Young's friends.[1] Walton shows a few words of the Alexandrian Greek, poorly cut in wood, among the specimens in his Prolegomena: a circumstance which would suggest that in 1657 the matrices used for Junius's facsimile, if in existence, were not then available.

Walton's statement was confirmed by J. E. Grabe, John Mill,[2] and others, who made a study of the codex and its history; and in 1707 Young's biographer and successor in the task of preparing the codex for print, Dr. Thomas Smith, repeated it with the authority of one who had also personally inspected the specimen.[3] It has been assumed by later writers that both Walton and Thomas Smith made reference to a proposed *facsimile* reprint of the manuscript; and Gough's circumstantial statement, already quoted (which is adopted by Nichols and copied by others, such as Horne, Edwards, &c.), leaves little doubt that the chapter of *Genesis* was actually put forward in 1643, in facsimile type, as a specimen of the forthcoming work. The evidence as to the existence of the types receives further countenance from the presence of these matrices in Grover's foundry, certainly before the year 1700.

Anthony à Wood states that Young's project excited much curiosity and expectation, and that in 1645 an ordinance was read for printing and publishing the *Septuagint*, under the direction of Whitelock and Selden.[4] The troublous times which ensued, however, as well as certain doubts as to the fidelity with which the original text was being treated by the transcriber, led to the abandonment of the scheme during Young's tenure of office, which ceased in 1649. In that year Bulstrode Whitelock became Library Keeper, and consequently custodian of the manuscript. It would appear, however, from a sentence in one of Usher's letters,[5] that as late as 1651 Young retained his purpose of publishing the Bible from the text of the codex, but his death in the following year finally stopped the enterprise.

What became of the specimen chapter of *Genesis* it is impossible to say. Bishop Walton, as he himself states, acquired possession of the scholia to the end of *Numbers*, and the remainder of Young's Greek and Latin manuscripts, Wood informs

---

[1] 'Proposuit quidem D. Junius multis antehac annis MS. hoc typis evulgare, cujus etiam specimen impressum vidi; sed consilium illius, multis viris doctis merito improbatum, ejus progressum retardavit; dum multa pro arbitrio ex MS. detruncaret et mutaret, idque cùm nulla premebat necessitas, prout ex Catalogo satis magno vocabulorum per pauca *Geneseos* capita, quae ipse mutaverat et expunxerat (quem mihi ostendit Typographus) constat' (*Proleg.* sec. ix, § 34).

[2] J. E. Grabe published an account of the codex in 1705, and John Mill in 1707 in his edition of the Greek *New Testament*.

[3] *Vitae quorundam eruditissimorum et illustrium Virorum.—Patricii Junii*, London, 1707. 4to. 'Utcunque futuri operis specimen, quod jam prae oculis meis habeo, primum nimirum caput libri

Geneseos, una cum doctissimis Scholiis, edere placuit. Omnes illud certamen arripiunt, avidisque oculis legunt perleguntque, ac optimâ spe de promissâ editione, quam cum maximo et vix continendo affectu exspectant efflagitantque, conceptâ, quasi moram pertaesi, Orbem Christianum hoc eximio thesauro, quod dudum fuisset locupletandus, nimium diu hactenus caruisse amicè queruntur' (p. 32).

[4] See also *Journal of the House of Commons*, vols. iv and v, where there are several references to this project.

[5] Usher's *Works*, vol. xvi, Letter 288. Usher to Boate, June 1651: '. . . the Alexandrian copy (in the Library of St. James) which he intendeth shortly to make publick, Mr. Selden and myself every day pressing him to the work.'

o

us, came to the hands of Dr. John Owen, Dean of Christ Church, Oxford. Subsequently the manuscripts were acquired by Isaac Vossius and finally by the University of Leyden. Assuming the matrices to have existed, their natural location would be either the Royal Printing Office or the foundry in which already had been deposited the Greek types and matrices used in the *Catena in Job*. If, however, they remained in the St. James's Library, it is possible to conceive of their disappearance for a considerable period, as Whitelock's principal duties during his term of office appear to have been to check the depredations which in Young's own time had already deprived the library of many of its treasures.[1]

At the Restoration the Keepership of the Library was bestowed on Thomas Rosse, by whom was once more revived the suggestion of reproducing the Alexandria Codex in facsimile, not this time by means of type, but by copperplate. This circumstance is thus related by Aubrey in his *Remains of Gentilism and Judaism*, preserved among the Lansdowne MSS. in the British Museum.[2]

. . . ye Tecla MS. in St James Library . . . was sent as a Present to King Charles the First, from Cyrillus, Patriark of Constantinople: as a jewell of that antiquity not fit to be kept among Infidels. Mr. . . . Rosse (translator of Statius) was Tutor to ye Duke of Monmouth who gott him the place (of) Library-Keeper at St James's: he desired K. Cha. I (*sic*) to be at ye chardge to have it engraven in copper-plates, and told him it would cost but £200; but his Maty would not yeild to it. Mr. Ross sayd 'that it would appeare glorious in History, after his Maty's death'. 'Pish,' sayd he, 'I care not what they say of me in History when I am dead.' H. Grotius, J. G. Vossius, Heinsius, etc., have made Journeys into England purposely to correct their Greeke Testaments by this Copy in St James's. Sr Chr. Wren sayd that he would rather have it engraved by an Engraver that could not understand or read Greek, than by one that did.

The manuscript was subsequently handed, in 1678, to Dr. Thomas Smith to collate and edit, with a view to its reproduction; but once again the scheme fell through, and (with the exception of Walton's *Polyglot*) it was not till J. E. Grabe, in 1707, published his *Octateuch* (accompanying his preface by a small copperplate specimen of the manuscript), that any considerable portion of the Bible appeared from this ancient text.

Of the subsequent successful attempt to produce the entire manuscript in facsimile type we have spoken elsewhere.[3] Meanwhile, we find from the facts here given, that in 1643 a specimen of a portion of the text of the codex is said to have been issued in facsimile type; that constant efforts had been made during the latter half of the seventeenth century to carry out Patrick Young's purpose of reproducing the entire Bible in this form; that in 1657 Bishop Walton was presumably unaware of the existence of any matrices from which to exhibit a specimen of the uncial Greek of the codex; that Grabe, similarly ignorant, made use of copperplate in 1707 for a similar purpose; but that prior to the year 1700, concealed under the erroneous name of 'Coptic—the new hand', there existed in the foundry of the Grovers (where already were deposited several of the 'King's House' matrices, as well as those of the Greek fount used in Junius's *Catena in Job* in 1637) a set of

---

[1] Wood, *Fasti Oxon.* i. 308; also Edwards, *Libraries and Founders of Libraries*, London, 1865, 8vo, p. 168.

[2] Lansd. MSS., No. 231, fol. 169. An edition was published by James Britten in 1881.
[3] See p. 316.

ΟΙΗϹΑϹ ΑΥΤΟΥϹ ΤΩ ΘΩ ΗΜΩΝ
.ΛΕΙϹ ΚΑΙ ΙΕΡΕΙϹ ΚΑΙ ΒΑϹΙΛΕΥϹΟΥ
ϹΙΝ ΕΠΙ ΤΗϹ ΓΗϹ ΚΑΙ ΕΙΔΟΝ ΚΑΙ ΗΚΟΥ
ϹΑ ΩϹ ΦΩΝΗΝ ΑΓΓΕΛΩΝ ΠΟΛΛΩΝ
ΚΥΚΛΩ ΤΟΥ ΘΡΟΝΟΥ ΚΑΙ ΤΩΝ ΖΩΩΝ
ΚΑΙ ΤΩΝ ΠΡΕϹΒΥΤΕΡΩΝ ΚΑΙ ΗΝ Ο Α
ΡΙΘΜΟϹ ΑΥΤΩΝ ΜΥΡΙΑΔΕϹ ΜΥΡΙΑ
ΔΩΝ ΚΑΙ ΧΙΛΙΑΔΕϹ ΧΙΛΙΑΔΩΝ ΛΕΓΟΝ
ΤΕϹ ΦΩΝΗ ΜΕΓΑΛΗ ΑΞΙΟΝ ΕϹΤΙ ΤΟ
ΑΡΝΙΟΝ ΛΑΒΕΙΝ ΤΗΝ ΔΥΝΑΜΙΝ ΚΑΙ
ΠΛΟΥΤΟΝ ΚΑΙ ϹΟΦΙΑΝ ΚΑΙ ΙϹΧΥΝ ΚΑΙ
ΤΙΜΗΝ ΚΑΙ ΔΟΞΑΝ ΚΑΙ ΕΥΧΟΓΙΑΝ ΚΑΙ
ΠΑΝ ΚΤΙϹΜΑ Ο ΕϹΤΙΝ ΕΝ ΤΩ ΟΥΡΑΝΩ
ΚΑΙ ΕΠΙ ΤΗϹ ΓΗϹ ΚΑΙ ΥΠΟΚΑΤΟ ΤΗϹ
ΓΗϹ ΚΑΙ ΕΠΙ ΤΗϹ ΘΑΛΑϹϹΗϹ Α ΕϹΤΙ
ΚΑΙ ΤΑ ΠΑΝΤΑ ΕΝ ΑΥΤΟΙϹ ΗΚΟΥϹΑ ΛΕ
ΓΟΝΤΑ ΤΩ ΚΑΘΗΜΕΝΩ ΕΠΙ ΤΟΥ ΘΡΟ
ΝΟΥ ΚΑΙ ΤΩ ΑΡΝΙΩ Η ΕΥΑΛΟΓΙΑ ΚΑΙ Η
ΤΙΜΗ ΚΑΙ Η ΔΟΞΑ ΚΑΙ ΤΟ ΚΡΑΤΟϹ ΕΙϹ
ΤΟΥϹ ΑΙΟΝΑϹ ΤΩΝ ΑΙΩΝΩΝ ΑΜΗΝ
ΚΑΙ ΤΑ ΤΕϹϹΑΡΑ ΖΟΑ ΛΕΓΟΝΤΑ ΑΜΗΝ
ΚΑΙ ΟΙ ΠΡΕϹΒΥΤΕΡΟΙ ΕΠΕϹΟΝ ΚΑΙ ΠΡΟ
ϹΕΚΥΝΗϹΑΝ ΖΟΝΤΙ ΕΙϹ ΤΟΥϹ ΑΙΟΝΑϹ
ΤΩΝ ΑΙΩΝΩΝ ΚΑΙ ΕΙΔΟΝ ΟΤΕ ΑΝΟΙΞΕ
ΤΟ ΑΡΝΙΟΝ ΜΙΑΝ ΕΚ ΤΩΝ ϹΦΡΑΓΙΔΩΝ
ΚΑΙ ΗΚΟΥϹΑ ΕΝΟϹ ΕΚ ΤΩΝ ΤΕϹϹΑΡΩΝ
ΖΩΩΝ ΛΕΓΟΝΤΟϹ ΩϹ ΦΩΝΗϹ ΒΡΟΝ
ΤΗϹ ΕΡΧΟΥ ΚΑΙ ΒΛΕΠΕ ΚΑΙ ΕΙΔΟΝ ΚΑΙ
ΚΑΙ ΕΙΔΟΝ ΚΑΙ ΕΙΔΟΥ ΙΠΠΟϹ ΛΕΥΚΟϹ
ΚΑΙ Ο ΚΑΘΗΜΕΝΟϹ ΕΠΙ ΑΥΤΩ ΕΧΩΝ
ΤΟ ΞΟΝ ΚΑΙ ΕΛΟΘΗ ΑΥΤΩ ϹΤΕΦΑΝΟϹ
ΚΑΙ ΕΞΗΛΘΕ ΝΙΚΩΝ ΚΑΙ ΙΝΑ ΝΙΚΗϹΗ ΚΑΙ
ΟΤΕ ΑΝΟΙΞΕ ΤΗΝ ΔΕΥΤΕΡΑΝ ϹΦΡΑΓΙ
ΔΑ ΗΚΟΥϹΑ ΤΟΥ ΔΕΥΤΕΡΟΥ ΖΩΟΥ
ΛΕΓΟΝΤΟϹ ΕΡΧΟΥ ΚΑΙ ΒΛΕΠΕ ΚΑΙ ΕΞΗΛ
ΘΕΝ ΑΛΛΟϹ ΙΠΠΟϹ ΠΥΡΡΟϹ ΚΑΙ ΤΩ ΚΑ
ΘΗΜΕΝΩ ΕΠΙ ΑΥΤΩ ΕΔΟΘΗ ΑΥΤΩ
ΛΑΒΕΙΝ ΤΗΝ ΕΙΡΗΝΗΝ ΑΠΟ ΤΗϹ ΓΗϹ ΚΑΙ
ΙΝΑ ΑΛΛΗΛΟΥϹ ϹΦΑΓΩϹΙ ΚΑΙ ΕΔΟΘΗ ΑΥ
ΤΩ ΜΑΧΑΙΡΑ ΜΕΓΑΛΗ ΚΑΙ ΟΤΕ ΕΝΟΙΞΕ
ΤΗΝ ΤΡΙΤΗΝ ϹΦΡΑΓΙΔΑ ΗΚΟΥϹΑ ΤΟΥ

FIG. 45. The Alexandrian Greek. From a specimen in Bagford. (Harl. 5966 (36).)

matrices consisting of a single alphabet of the Alexandrian Greek, which apparently lay undetected until 1758, when that foundry came into the hands of John James, or more probably until 1778, when Rowe Mores applied himself to the task of arranging and cataloguing the various matrices of interest in that miscellaneous collection.

It may be added that the letters of this fount (like those of the old Greek, Court Hand, Scriptorial, and Union Pearl in the same foundry) are struck inverted in the copper,[1] a peculiarity which may be due either to their foreign execution or to the ignorance of the English striker, and which, in either case, goes far to account for the confusion which existed respecting their identity. Unfortunately, the link which might definitely connect the Alexandrian matrices with the facsimile types of Patrick Young is, in the absence of any copy of the specimen chapter of *Genesis* of 1643, wanting. But, apart even from this, the fount undoubtedly claims the distinction of being the first attempt at facsimile by means of type.[2]

Among other interesting matrices there are several which go back to the sixteenth century. Day's Double Pica roman and italic has already been mentioned; some account of this type was given above (pp. 91–93). There was also a Double Pica and a Great Primer black; of the Double Pica Mores said he held some punches. 'They are truly vetustate formâque et squalore venerab. and we would not give a *lower-case* letter in exchange for all the leaden cups of Haerlem.' In the account of some of the types of Wynkyn De Worde (p. 85) we have said something of the origin of the designs and found reasons for rejecting Mores's supposition that his punches descended from that printer, although they may very well date from the sixteenth century. We have already met the Double Pica on several seventeenth-century specimens and as a heading it may be seen on many contemporary newspapers. The other sixteenth-century fount is the Great Primer Secretary, called Running Secretary by Mores, a type based on Elizabethan handwriting and resembling the French *Civilité*. It was used from 1576 to 1614 at least, among others by Sir Walter Raleigh on wine licences issued under his monopoly. This English script was described in Johnson's *Type Designs*, pp. 186 seq., together with two other gothic scripts, which are not known to have survived in any foundry. (See Fig. 46.)

Of seventeenth-century types the earliest appear to be the Double Pica large face and small face (i.e. Great Primer cast on the same body) Greeks, which were used in Patrick Young's *Catena Græcorum patrum in beatum Job*, 1637, as related above (pp. 130–1). They were copies of the French Royal Greeks of Claude Garamond, and the Great Primer might be the same as the Savile Greek, which went to

---

[1] The matrices of all these curious founts were examined by Reed *c.* 1885. They bore strong evidence of having been justified and finished by the same hand.

[2] From this assertion we except, of course, the letter of the first printers, which, if not imitating the actual handwriting of one particular scribe, was a copy of the conventional book-writing hand of the period. Some of the earliest scripts, italics, and cursives are also reputed to have been modelled on the handwriting of some famous calligrapher or artist, e.g. the italics of Ludovico degli Arrighi

(Vicentino), Rome, 1523. One of the first instances of printing with facsimile types was the copy of the famous Medicean *Virgil*, produced at Florence in 1741. The types are for the most part ordinary roman capital letters with a certain number of 'discrepants' or peculiar characters. The title of this fine work is: *P. Vergilii Maronis Codex Antiquissimus . . . qui nunc Florentiæ in Bibliotheca Mediceo-Laurentiana adservatur. Bono publico Typis descriptus Anno MDCCXLI. Florentiæ. Typis Mannianis.* 8vo.

James, by the grace of God, King of England, Scotland, France and Ireland, defender of the faith &c. To all our welbeloued subiects, greeting.

Whereas our louing Subiect, John Stowe (a meere aged, & most bee member of our city of London) his fiue & forty yeers hath to his greate charge, & with neglect of his ordinary meanes of maintenance ((for the generall good of posteritie, as of the present age) compiled and publ. diuerse necessary bookes & chronicles, & therefore wee, in recompense of these his painfull labours, & for encouragement to the like, haue (in our royall inclination) bene pleased to graunt our Letters Patents vnder our great seale of England, dated the eighth of March, 1603, therby authorizing him, the said John Stowe, and his deputies, to collect, amongst our louing subiects, their voluntary contribution & liberall gratuities, as by the said Letters Patents more at large may appeare: Now seeing that our said Patents (being but one in them selues) cannot be shewed forth in diuers places or passes at once (as the occasions of his speedy putting them in execution, may require) Wee haue therefore thought expedient, in this manner manner, to recommend his cause vnto you, hauing already, in our owne person, and of our speciall grace, begun the largesse, for the example of others,

Giuen at our palace of Westminster,

Fig. 46. Grover's Great Primer Secretary. Letters patent granted to John Stowe, 1604. (Harl. MSS. 367(8).)

Oxford. The Double Pica large face is shown in the James's Sale Catalogue on p. 10. The Great Primer there shown, also from the Grover Foundry, is a different face. A Pica and a Long Primer roman are described as *King's House* and were presumably used in the office which printed the *Catena in Job*, namely, the King's printers in Blackfriars, but there seems to be no way of identifying them.

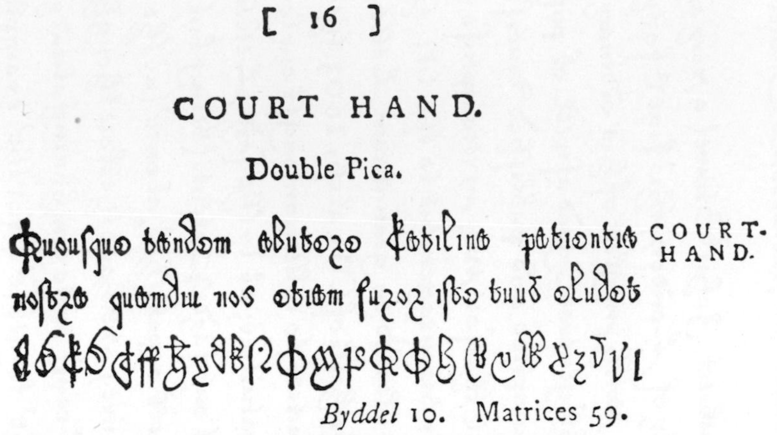

[16]

COURT HAND.

Double Pica.

Byddel 10.   Matrices 59.

Fig. 47. Grover's Court Hand. From the James's Sale Catalogue, 1782.

Fig. 48. Union Pearl. From the original matrices.

Next we come to the very unusual Scriptorials and Cursives. The Scriptorials include two sizes of the old legal Court Hand, Mores's Base Secretary, one of which survived in 1887, but of neither of which is there any record outside the foundries (cf. Johnson's *Type Designs*, p. 191), the Great Primer Secretary already dealt with, and a Double Pica Union Pearl. Union Pearl is described by Mores (pp. 32, 33) as 'a letter of fancy, it is English and of recent date, for nothing exactly correspondent is given us amongst the whims of Yciar. . . . It receives the name from the pearls which grow in couples, to which the nodules of the letters were conceived to bear some resemblance.' He goes on to reject on the score of date the notion that the Union had reference to the union of the kingdoms of England and Scotland in 1704. Mr. Morison, who showed a specimen of the type cast from the original matrices in *The Fleuron*, No. VI, 1928, p. 110, calls it the first-known English decorated letter. The only use of the type recorded in contemporary printing is the one word 'Scriptographia' in the notice of the printer H. Meere referred to below. But it is found on the specimen-sheet of Benjamin Franklin Bache of Philadelphia, now in the Library of Columbia University, of which a reproduction was published in 1925 by Douglas McMurtrie.

The Cursorial, says Mores, 'is a flimsy type imitating a pseudo Italian handwriting, and fitted for ladies and beaux'. There were seven founts, Double Pica to Long Primer, with two sets of English, in the Grover Foundry, the matrices of some of which still exist. In 1696 Ichabod Dawks began to print his *News Letter* in the English No. 2, with the Double Pica as a subsidiary. It seems likely that it was Dawks who had these sizes cut for the purpose of reproducing more or less in facsimile the manuscript news-letter which was handed about in the coffee-houses. Mr. Morison in his *Ichabod Dawks*, 1931, showed the English, Pica, and Small Pica in type cast from the original matrices, and a reproduction of the Double Pica as used by Dawks and also in *Jones's Evening News Letter* of 1716. H. Meere, the dates of whose activity given by Plomer are 1708–24, inserted in *The Observator* of 7 February 1708 a notice of 'Scriptographia', described as suitable for blank law-

Quousque tandem abutere Catilina patientia nostra. Quamdiu nos etiam furor iste tuus eludet. acbefilmuqrstv
ABCDEFGHIJKLMNOPQRSTUVWXYZ

Fig. 49. Scriptorial in Grover's Foundry, 1700. From the original matrices.

forms; the type is the Grover Pica Cursorial, with the word 'Scriptographia' in Union Pearl. This same printer issued an undated specimen-sheet of his types, preserved in the Bagford collection, in which are shown six sizes of romans and italics, Canon to Long Primer, and the Small Pica Cursorial. Meere was a printer of newspapers and was married to Cassandra, daughter of Thomas Grover. The Double Pica Cursorial was used in 1710 for the printing of a single sheet poem, entitled *Fair Warning*, and also in *An Old Maid's Fortune or the Bride at her Wit's End*, John Applebee, 1727. The English No. 1 appears in the *British Legacy or Fountain of Knowledge*, printed for Thomas Chandler, 1732. This size and the Pica are shown on the specimen of B. F. Bache of Philadelphia.

These Cursorials, an English version of the Italian hand, had been preceded by another script of the same school and a much finer one, which was described and illustrated by Mr. Morison in his article 'On Script Types' in *The Fleuron*, No. IV, 1925, and also in his *Ichabod Dawks*. Nothing is known of the designer of this script and it has been found on a few sheets only, mostly of an official nature, the earliest being of 1672. Besides the publications mentioned by Mr. Morison the type was used for *Instructions for the better ordering of His Majesty's Fleet*, issued by James, Duke of York, as Lord High Admiral, *c.* 1680, fourteen folio pages without imprint, and again in the address 'To the Reader' to some manuscript music,

Sonatas of Henry Purcell, 1683. Mr. Morison calls attention to its resemblance in some particulars to the scripts of the Paris founder, Pierre Moreau, and considers that it may be the work of a foreign hand.

In his *Ichabod Dawks* Mr. Morison quotes a petition from the three London founders, Joseph Leigh, Thomas Goring, and Godfrey Head, addressed to the Lord Mayor of London, in 1675, in which they pray that in view of the shortage of labour due to the 'late visitation' they may be allowed still to employ their Journeymen Foreigners.[1] In the same petition there is reference to the limitation of the number of foundries to four, a regulation renewed in the Act of the fourteenth year of Charles II. This limitation was imposed in the Star Chamber Decree of 1637, was renewed in 1662, and again frequently down to 1693. This seems to indicate that the terms were strictly enforced. Who then were the four founders in 1675? Moxon was still in the business and the Grovers are said to have started about 1674. If Nicholls was still active, then the three petitioners must have been in partnership and regarded as one foundry. But there are records of these men acting separately, and possibly these three and Moxon made up the four, and the Grover Foundry was established after 1675, perhaps some years after. Moxon, however, writing in 1683, says that the number of founders had grown very many.

Thomas Grover had several daughters, one of whom, Cassandra, was the wife of Hugh Meere;[2] and Meere's daughter Elizabeth was the wife of Richard Nutt.[3] On Thomas Grover's death[4] his foundry became the joint property of all his daughters, who attempted to dispose of it by private contract in 1728, when it was appraised by Thomas James and William Caslon. Caslon actually made an offer for its purchase, but at so low a figure that it was not accepted. The foundry therefore remained locked up in the house of R. Nutt, a printer, who appears to have provided himself with type for his own use during his tenure of the matrices. Finally, on the death of all Grover's daughters, the foundry became Nutt's absolutely, and was by him sold on 14 September 1758 to John James.

GODFREY HEAD, 1675

Godfrey Head was apprenticed 5 August 1650 to Alexander Fifield and was free 2 November 1657. We have noted already that he was a petitioner, along with Leigh and Goring, to the Lord Mayor's Court in 1675. In *The Library* for September 1944, pp. 28–29, Mr. S. Hodgson gave some extracts from the Court Minutes of the Stationers' Company relating to Head. He was summoned before the Court on 22 December 1685 for not giving due account of letters cast, as the Act of Parliament prescribed. Head admitted that about a year and a half ago he had delivered on board ship 'a presse & Lett^r of abt 200 & ½ weight that it was sent to Pensilvania & that Mr. Warren the Joyner made the Presse'. On 1 February 1686 Head apologized to the Court and it was ordered that his dividend be paid him on

---

[1] Foreigners meant journeymen who had not served a regular apprenticeship in the City of London. See *The Case and Proposals of the Free Journeymen Printers in London*, 23 Oct. 1666.

[2] We have already referred to Meere's specimen of types.

[3] Richard Nutt, printer in the Savoy from 1724, died 11 March 1780, aged 80 years.

[4] Grover contributed £2. 2s. in 1712 towards defraying the loss incurred by the elder Bowyer on the occasion of the fire at his printing-house. The date of Grover's death is not known. If this is still the same Thomas who apprenticed his son in 1671 he must by 1712 have been about eighty years of age. He cannot have been the son, as stated by Rowe Mores, of James Grover.

his giving 20 shillings to the Poor Box. It is not stated who was the New England printer who ordered the type.

In 1677 Head's name appears as a steward at the Brotherly Meeting of Printers. His foundry, Mores informs us, was in St. Bartholomew's Close. Whether Head succeeded to it or established it we are unable to ascertain. Of his productions, two founts only can be traced with any certainty, the Pica Greek and the English black, both of which subsequently passed into Caslon's foundry.[1] He was succeeded by

ROBERT MITCHELL

who had formerly been servant to Grover. Mitchell removed the foundry first to Jewin Street, and afterwards, says Mores, 'lived over Cripplegate, and afterwards in Paul's Alley, between Aldersgate Street and Red Cross Street. His foundry, containing nothing very curious, unless it were the Blacks, was on the 26th July 1739 purchased by William Caslon and John James jointly, and divided between them'.

The following is Mores's summary of the contents of this foundry, at its partition:

Mr. ROBERT MITCHELL'S FOUNDERY

Mr. Caslon's Choice.	Mr. James's Share.
Greek.—Pica.	*Roman and Italic.*—Canon, 2-line Great Primer, 2-line English, Double Pica (small faced), Great Primer (3 founts), English (large face), Pica, Brevier (3 founts), Small Pica, Minion, Pearl (2 founts).
Roman and Italic.—	
4-line Pica	
2-line Great Primer ⎱ full-face capitals.	
„ English ⎰	
„ Pica	
and Great Primer, English, Long Primer, Brevier, and Nonpareil.	*Algebra.*—English.
English (Black).—Great Primer, English, Pica, Long Primer, Brevier, Small Pica.	*Cancelled Figures.*—Pica.
The *Music* matrices. The *Flower* matrices.	*Almanac* matrices.—Long Primer.

The Canon italic is shown on a single sheet in the collection of 'Various Alphabets' made by Joseph Ames, now in the British Museum. Cf. Berry and Johnson, p. 3.

THE 'ANONYMOUS' FOUNDRY

Over and above the foundries described by Mores as having been absorbed by that of Thomas and John James, there remained in his possession a certain number of matrices—some of them of some importance—of whose former owners he was unable to give an account. 'These may be considered as a distinct foundery,' he says, 'and distinguished by the title of "anonymous," for we know not whence they came. Our account of Mr. James's purchases is accurate, and these are not included amongst them, but at the end of our scrutiny remained unclaimed. Let them then be called "The Anonymous Foundery".' We do not presume to step in where Rowe

---

[1] In 1692 the Stationers' Company came to an agreement with the University of Oxford and became lessees of the Bible Press. A new stock was formed to raise capital for this undertaking. In a document among the Stationers' Records relating to this stock there is mention of Letter for Printing sent to Oxford 'by Mr. Robert Andrews and Mrs. Maryx Head Letter founders'. The Mrs. Head is presumably the widow of Godfrey Head. The document is reproduced in *Print and Privilege at Oxford*, p. 186.

Mores fears to tread, and therefore leave the matrices, of which the following is his list, still unappropriated:

THE ANONYMOUS FOUNDERY, *absq. dat.*

ORIENTALS.
Arabic.—Double Pica.
Æthiopic.—English.

OCCIDENTALS.
Greek.—Great Primer.
Roman and Italic.—Great Primer.
  English.
  Long Primer.
  Brevier.
  2-line Double Pica full face capitals.
    ,,   Great Primer ,,   ,,
    ,,   English   ,,   ,,
    ,,   Pica   ,,   ,,

Small Pica.
Bourgeois.
Nonpareil.
Pearl.

SEPTENTRIONALS.
Gothic.—Pica.
Anglo-Norman.—Pica.
English.—English.
  Pica.
  Long Primer.
  Small Pica.
("of all of which a more full account will be given in the ensuing catalogue.")

OXFORD FOUNDERS

PETER WALPERGEN, or Walberger, as we have stated in our account of the Oxford foundry, was successor to Hermansen and doubtless the individual alluded to by Bagford when, in recounting Fell's services to Oxford, he says: 'The good Bishop provided from Holland . . . a Letter Founder, a Dutchman by birth, who had served the States in the same quality at Batavia in the East Indies.'[1] Bagford, it is true, does not name this founder, but as there exists in the Bodleian Library (also in the British Museum) a copy of a Portuguese version of *Æsop's Fables*, edited by Jo. Ferreira d'Almeida, and printed at Batavia by Pedro Walberger in 1672,[2] we have no hesitation in identifying our founder with this Dutch typographer, and in fixing his settlement at Oxford soon after the above date, which, it will be remembered, was the year in which Fell and others took upon them the charge of the University Press, and furnished from abroad all the necessaries for its use and advancement. There is a record of payment to Walpergen for his journey to Oxford on 28 February 1676.[3]

That he was well known at Oxford in 1683 is also apparent from a casual reference to 'Mr. Walberger of Oxford' in Moxon's *Mechanick Exercises*,[4] where the writer dwells with some minuteness on a peculiar and elaborate tool, called the 'Joynt-Flat-Gauge', contrived by this founder for polishing the faces of his punches after hardening them, and before striking them into the copper. It was doubtless from this casual notice that Rowe Mores derived his scant reference to Walpergen, of whom he knows nothing, save that he founded at Oxford in 1683, was sometimes called Walperger, and by name appears to have been a foreigner, therefore probably a 'transient', by means of his countryman Michael Burghers, the University engraver.

Of Walpergen's work little is known beyond the fact that he appears to have devoted his attention chiefly to the production of music type, impressions of

[1] See *ante*, p. 137.
[2] Cotton's *Typographical Gazetteer*, Second Series, 1866, p. 17.
[3] See Madan's 'Oxford Oddments' in *The Library*, vol. ix, 1929, p. 347.
[4] Vol. ii, p. 120.

which appear in the University *Specimen* of 1695. The punches and matrices of this interesting fount are still preserved at Oxford, and are singular relics of the old letter-founders' art.[1] Although the music was the only fount cut by Walpergen of which we have any certain knowledge, it is probable that the experienced Dutch artist, whom Bagford describes as an excellent workman, did not confine his labours to that class of work. What his exact relations were with the University Press is also a matter of conjecture. But it seems probable, from the manner in which he

FIG. 50. Walpergen's music. From the original matrices.

is spoken of by Moxon, and in the Oxford *Specimen*, that he practised as a letter-founder on his own account, and not wholly as an official of the University. From the papers of the Vice-Chancellor's Court it is known that he did work for others, including Godfrey Head and Robert Andrews. Fell declared that 'he would not allow him to worke for any one else, saying that he was his servant and they (meaneing Head and Andrews) were Knaves for employing of him'.[2]

He died in 1714.[3] Among the University archives is preserved an inventory of his chattels, which, if a full account of his earthly possessions, speaks poorly for the profits of the profession of letter-founding in those days. This highly interesting document runs as follows:

An inventory of the Chattels of Peter De Walpergen, deceased, taken the tenth day of January 1714–5.

Being the Moiety of a Fount of Musick.

	£	s.	d.
Two hunderd and two pounds weight of Mettal (? cast type) at four pence per pound his part is	1	13	8
One hunderd fourty seven Matrices at one Shilling per piece his part is .	3	13	6
Nine quadrats at two pence per piece his part is . . .	0	0	9
Four moulds at two shillings six pence per piece his part . . .	0	5	0
Sixty three puncheons at five shillings (*i.e.*, for the lot) his part . .	0	2	6
Four cases at four shillings his part	0	2	0
Two galleys at two shillings his part	0	1	0
A box at sixpence his part	0	0	3

Appraised by us, LEONARD LICHFIELD.
RICHARD GREEN.

[1] Some of the matrices are without sides, which were probably supplied by a peculiar adaptation of the mould.
[2] See *Print and Privilege at Oxford*, p. 51.
[3] Bagford (writing in 1714) states that Walpergen 'was succeeded by his son, who has long since been succeeded by Mr. Andrews'. If this be the case, the Peter Walpergen whose death occurred in 1714 was probably the son, of whom nothing is known as distinguished from his father.

The extraordinarily low value of the punches is quite consistent with the esteem in which these now precious steel originals were held at the time, after once being struck.

Walpergen's music matrices were secured by the University Press, in whose *Specimens* the type had already figured for some years; it was used in the *Yattendon Hymnal* of 1895–9, edited by Robert Bridges. Some account of the fount is given in the preface to that edition.

SYLVESTER ANDREWS, who succeeded to Walpergen's foundry before the year 1714, was the son of Robert Andrews, the London founder. His foundry, which, with the exception of one alphabet of Hebrew, consisted entirely of roman and italic, was, Rowe Mores informs us, nothing compared with that of his father, and was indeed a part of his father's. The following is the list of his matrices:

MR. SILVESTER ANDREWS' FOUNDERY; *furtim:*

Hebrew.		Long Primer Italic . . .	102
Brevier (at first 33) . . .	30	Brevier Roman, large face .	130
		,, ,, small ,, .	135
Roman and Italic		,, Italic (2 sets of Capitals) .	105
2-line English Capitals . .	. . .	2-line Pica Italic . . .	. . .
Great Primer Roman, large face .	125	Small Pica Roman . . .	146
,, Italic . . .	82	,, Italic . . .	28
English Roman . . .	148	Minion Roman and Italic .	. . .
,, Italic . . .	98	Nonpareil Roman, large face . .	140
Pica Roman, large face . . .	153	Nonpareil Italic . . .	105
,, ,, small ,, .	148	,, Roman, small face .	94
,, Italic . . .	110	Pearl Roman . . .	98
,, Roman, lower case .	27	,, Italic . . .	38
Long Primer Roman . .	119		

Although his stock of matrices was limited, he appears to have done a considerable business, not only with the University, in whose service he was probably retained, but also with other printers practising in Oxford, notably with John Baskett, the King's printer, to whom, with John Williams and Samuel Ashurst, the 'Chancellor, Masters and Scholars of the University', leased their 'privilege and interest in printing' for twenty-one years from March 1713.[1]

In the year 1719 Baskett, who had two years previously produced the magnificent 'Vinegar' *Bible*[2] at Oxford, mortgaged his stock and privilege at the University to James Brooks, stationer, of London, as security for a loan of £3,000. And in a schedule attached to an indenture, dated 23 May 1720, having reference to this transaction, occurs an inventory of the type at that time in the printer's possession, which is highly interesting, not only as throwing light on Andrews's business, but as indicating the contents of a large office of the period, and the extent to which

---

[1] See *The First Minute Book of the Delegates,* Oxford, 1943.

[2] *The Holy Bible, containing the Old Testament and the New, etc. Oxford, Printed by John Baskett,* *Printer to the King's Most Excellent Majesty, for Great Britain; and to the University,* 1716, 1717. 2 vols., folio. The running title of Luke xx reads, *The parable of the vinegar.*

Dutch type at that time competed in this country with English. The schedule is as follows:

An Account of the Letter Presses and other Stock and Implements of and in the Printing house at Oxford belonging to John Baskett, Citizen and Staconer of London:—

A Large ffount of Perle Letter Cast by Mr. Andrews.

A Large ffount of Nonp[l] Letter, New-Cast by ditto.

Another ffount of Nonp[l] Letter, Old, the whole standing and Sett up in a Com'on Prayer in 24mo Compleat.

A large ffount of Min[n] Letter, New-Cast by Mr. Andrews.

Another Large ffount of Min[n] Letter, New-Cast in Holland.

The whole Testament standing in Brev[r] and Min[n] Letter, Old.

A Large ffount of Brev[r] Letter, New-Cast in Holland.

A very Large ffount of Lo. Prim[r] Letter, New-Cast by Mr. Andrews.

A large ffount of Pica Letter, very good, cast by ditto.

Another Large ffount of ditto, never used, Cast in Holland.

A small Quantity of English, New-Cast by Mr. Andrews.

A small Quantity of Great Prim[r], New-Cast by ditto.

A very Large ffount of Double Pica, New, the largest in England.[1]

A Quantity of Two Line English Letters.

A Quantity of ffrench Cannon.

Two line Letters of all Sorts and a Sett of Silver Initiall Letters.

Cases, Stands, etc.

ffive Printing Presses, very good, with other Appurtenances, etc.

The schedule is signed 'Jno. Baskett'.[2]

In 1733 Sylvester Andrews's foundry was purchased, at the same time with that of his father, by Thomas James, and removed to London. His epitaph remains, and gives an amusing glimpse of his character and the reputation he bore at Oxford.

On a Letter-Founder at Oxford

Underneath this stone lies honoured Syl
Who died, though much against his will;
Yet, in his fame he will survive—
Learning shall keep his name alive;
For he the parent was of letters,—
He founded, to confound his betters;
Though what those letters should contain
Did never once disturb his brain.
Since, therefore, reader, he is gone,
Pray let him not be trod upon.[3]

---

[1] This, in all probability, was the fount used for printing the 'Vinegar' *Bible*. It was, however, the Fell Double Pica.

[2] The contents of this very interesting document were communicated to the *Athenaeum* of 5 Sept.

1885, by J. H. Round, in whose possession the original then was.

[3] Timperley's *Songs of the Press*, London, 1833, 8vo, p. 85.

THOMAS AND JOHN JAMES, 1710

THOMAS JAMES was the son of the Rev. John James, vicar of Basingstoke.[1] He was apprenticed to Robert Andrews on 3 June 1700 and free 3 February 1708. Impressed, doubtless, with the present low condition of the art in England, and lacking the skill to regenerate it by his own labour, he determined to visit Holland and procure for himself, from that famous typographical market, the matrices and moulds necessary for establishing a successful foundry in London. The characteristic letters in which he describes this expedition to his brother are given by Rowe Mores,[2] and present so instructive and entertaining a picture of the Dutch typefounders of the day that we are tempted to copy them *in extenso*.

Rotterdam, 22 *June* 1710.—I have been with all the Letter Founders in Amsterdam, and if I would have given —— for matrices, could not persuade any of 'em but the last I went to, to part with any. So far from it that it was with much ado I could get them to let me see their business. The Dutch letter founders are the most sly and jealous people that ever I saw in my life. However this last man (being as I perceived by the strong perfume of Geneva waters a most profound sot) offers to sell me all his house for about —— I mean the matrices: for the punchions with them he will not sell for any money. But there being about as much as he would have —— for, Hebrew and other Oriental languages such as Syrian, Samaritan and Russian characters, I would not consent to buy 'em. But the rest consisting of about 17 sets of Roman and Italic capitals and small letters, and about 5 sets of capital letters only, and 3 sets of Greek, besides a set or two of Black with other appurtenances, these I design to buy. He is not very fond of selling them because it will be a great

---

[1] Nichols's note on the James family (*Anecdotes of Mr. Bowyer*, pp. 585, 609) is at variance with the account given by Rowe Mores. According to the former, Thomas, John, and George James were all brothers, and sons of the notorious half-crazy Elianor James, whose husband, Thomas James, the printer, was a large benefactor to Sion College, and died in 1711. On this point, however, Mores, whose relations with the family gave him special opportunities for information, may be considered as more correct in representing Thomas and John as sons of the Rev. John James. Mores's account is supported by Baigent and Millard's *History of Basingstoke*, 1889. The article on John James, the architect, in the *D.N.B.* follows Nichols. George James, the son of Thomas and Elianor, was City Printer in 1724. His office was in Little Britain, where he wrote and printed the *Post Boy*. He was Common Councilman for the Ward of Aldersgate Without,

and died in 1735. His great-grandfather, Dr. Thomas James, Dean of Wells, was the first Keeper of Bodley's Library at Oxford in 1605. Portraits of this Dr. Thomas James, and of Thomas and Elianor, the parents of George James, are preserved in Sion College, as is also a portrait of Elizabeth, their daughter, who married Jacob Ilive, the printer, and who was herself a benefactor to the College. Nichols mentions another member of the family, one Harris James, who, he says, was originally a letter-founder, and 'formerly of Covent Garden Theatre, where he represented fops and footmen'.

[2] *Dissertation*, pp. 51 seq. The brother is presumably John the architect of Greenwich. From *William Ged's Narrative* (see below, p. 212) it is clear that the architect was the brother of James the founder. There is no information as to what became of the James's letters.

while before he can furnish himself again. However I believe I shall have 'em for less than
—— a matrice, which as he says is cheaper than ever they were his; but having most of
the punches he can sink 'em again and so set himself to rights with little trouble and less
charge.

The next letter, dated Rotterdam, 14 July 1710, describes graphically the difficulties which James encountered in driving his bargain to a conclusion.

I took a place in the waggon for Tergoes and from thence in a scayte for Amsterdam,
where I arrived at 5 o'clock on Monday morning 10 July. As soon as I thought the person
I have dealt with was stirring I went to confer with him farther about his matrices; but
instead of finding all things set in order for sale, I found him less provided than when I was
with him before; for indeed he had lent about eight sets of matrices to another Letter
Founder. I let him know my mind by an interpreter. He told me what a disposition his
things were in, and said he had rather part with some particular sets than with all. In short,
I found he had not a mind to part with any but those which he esteemed least, and those of
which he had the puncheons by him to sink again when he pleased. I told him that I came
expecting to make an end of the bargain, if he would part with all the sets I had seen in his
proof for the price I had offered. The man hesitated a good while and at last told me he
would advise about it. I told him I'd have him resolve presently, and showed him the bill. . . .
The sight of the bill made the man begin to be a little more serious than before; so after a
few more words he told me he would send for his other sets in the afternoon. I told him
that he might do, but in the meantime I would survey those he had by him; so he had a
table set and he fetched his matrices to me. The reason why I would not stir out of his house
till I had taken a survey of his matrices was, because I was fearful that he might pick and
cull (as we call it) a great many things which are useful in printing besides just the alphabets; and indeed lest he might change some whole sets; though indeed the man declares he
would not do a thing so ill for his life. However I having all the matrices brought into one
room locked 'em up and took the key away with me, and went to dinner. In the afternoon
I went again with my interpreter (being an Exchange Broker) where we sat all the afternoon viewing the matrices. At night I locked 'em up again and took the key with me, and
on Tuesday morning presented my bill, which was accepted and paid immediately. But I
should have told you that the afternoon before he sent his wife to speak to the people to
send home the other sets; but she brought a note from the house and said the master who
had the key and keeping of 'em was gone a great way out of town to the burial of his mother,
and they did not expect him back till Wednesday. This news was very disagreeable to me;
but not knowing how to help myself, on Tuesday, after having viewed all day those he had,
I paid him ——, and took 'em along with me to my lodging when it was too late to send
to you by the post from Amsterdam. On Wednesday I went again but could not find the
man at home. He was gone for the other sets. So I tarried till yesterday and went again
and received 3 of the 8 sets. The rest are not to be had yet, the man being not returned,
only his wife who gave him those three sets. So there are wanting but five sets more which
are all Greeks but one. I took 'em, molds and all, and packed them up in a box and sent
'em by an Amsterdam scayte appointed to carry goods for Rotterdam. This I did, fearing
the *Catherine* yacht might sail if I tarried for the rest. At 8 o'clock last night I took scayte
for Tergoes, and arrived there this morning. From thence I came hither by waggon and
arrived here before 9.

The next letter, dated Rotterdam, 27 July 1710, describes his purchase more in
detail, and gives particulars as to the Dutch foundries visited.

You are desirous to know whether the matrices I have bought excel those which are in
the hands of the Letter Founders in England. The beauty of letter like that of faces is as
people opine; but notwithstanding I had no choice, all the Romans excel what we have in

England in my opinion, and I hope being well wrought, I mean cast, will gain the approbation of very handsome letters. The Italic I do not look upon to be unhandsome, though the Dutch are never very extraordinary in those. An account of the names that I think I shall give the sets I have bought is as follows: The largest size I shall distinguish by the name of *Four-line Pica*, the next by that of *French Canon*, the next by that of *Two-line Pica*; these three consist of Capitals only. The fourth size is a small *Canon Italic*, the fifth a *Two-line English* Roman and Italic, the sixth *Great Primer* Roman, of which I have two sets, a great face and a small one, with one Italic to them both. The seventh size is an *English* Roman and Italic; the eighth a *Pica*, of which I have three sets Roman, and one Italic; the ninth a *Small Pica* Roman and Italic, the tenth *Long Primer*, three sets Roman and one Italic, the eleventh, *Brevier* Roman and Italic. Besides these I have one set of *Great Primer Greek*, one of *English Greek*, one of *Pica Greek*, one of *Brevier Greek*, as also one set of *Pica Black* and one of *Brevier Black* together with matrices of divers sorts of flowers useful as ornaments in printing. To which I have 15 molds. All the sizes except the three first have Capitals, small letters, double letters, figures and points, as also all the accents, amounting in the whole to the number of about 3500 matrices. As for sets of Nonpareil and Pearl, I am informed nobody in this country has any but the Jew whose name is Athias. Him I was with first of all, who assured me he would part with none of any size whatever, as did likewise another man whose name is Foskins.[1] The next I went to was Cupi by name. He said he must consult a friend of his before he could give me my answer, which friend being gone out of town it would be two or three days before he could certify me. The next and last I went to the same day: his name was Rolij, a German by birth. Him I soon perceived I should agree with, as afterwards I did. But before I went to him I called upon Cupi. He told me he would sell no matrices, but he would cast me as much letter as I would have as cheap as anybody. I went to him before I agreed with Rolij because I would see which would sell cheapest. But finding them all so inflexible I was obliged to agree with Rolij upon his own terms, who, however, did not know but I had come to him first, since himself and Cupi are the only letter-cutters in this country, and he did not imagine but that if he would not have sold me matrices Cupi would, as I found by him afterwards. When Cupi perceived that Rolij would sell me some matrices (as, indeed, then Rolij and I had agreed and he received 1700 gilders in part), he comes to the Exchange-Broker and told him he would sink his puncheons again and in half a year's time deliver me all the matrices he has, perfect, after the rate of —— per matrice, but that except I would take all one with another, he would sell none at all.

His Roman letters are very handsome and his Italics ugly, but all printed upon a proof of the best paper; with all the care taken in composing and printing imaginable, which adds much to the lustre of his letter. In a book it is quite another thing; not so handsome as Rolij's, whose letter in the proofs I could see in matter looks much better than it does in his printed Specimen, which is done with all disadvantage, being wretchedly composed and worse printed off, upon very sorry paper. However I can see when letters are well proportioned. I have two specimens of his letter in matter which look very beautiful. Rolij says whatever matrices I want, whether great or small, he'll cut 'em for me as soon as I give him orders, provided it happens before a peace. He told me likewise he would see if he could procure any Nonpareil and Pearl of the Jew, I allowing him a reasonable profit for his pains. Rolij says he was the man who made Foskins[1] father by the letter he cut for him. Foskins[1] is a man of great business, having five or six men constantly at the furnace, besides boys to rub, and himself and a brother to do the other work. How many men the Jew keeps at work I do not know, for he would not permit me to go up into his work-house. Foskins thought I wanted letter to be cast, but when he knew that I was a letter founder he looked very sly, and watched me as if I had been a thief, being I suppose very fearful that I should steal some of their art from them. Cupi was not very forward to let me see his work-house, and the first time avoided it by saying he could not stay for he was just going out, but the

[1] Voskens.

second time I did see it though he was as loth then as before, saying he believed there was nobody at work. But I told him the person who was with me wanted to see the trade, and he would oblige me by showing it. He had places for four to work, although there was but one casting. I did not ask Rolij to show me his work-house the first time I went to him, but the second time I went up and saw places for four men and nobody at work. I asked him where his men were; he told me they were gone to a fair at Harlem, but I believe he had lent them out as well as his matrices to some other letter founder. As I was going along the street with him, he told me there was an English gentleman that had lodged at such a house (pointing to it), for whom he had cast three hundred pounds worth of work not long ago, which if true must have been for Tonson.

I have bought of Rolij in all thirty sets of matrices, besides the box of flowers and 15 molds made of brass as almost all the Dutch molds I saw were. Mr. Cupi has in all but eighteen sets of matrices, but is continually, as I hear, cutting more, designing in time to set up printing and bookselling too. He is a very close and very civil fellow. I do not know but one time or other I may take another trip into this country for matrices, for there's no trusting to anybody here to manage business for one. There's hardly such a thing as an honest man to be found. They all live by buying and selling, and whatever they can bite anyone of, they count it fairly got in the way of trade. I hear but a very indifferent character of the young man, the broker, who interprets for me. He is very expert indeed at that, and I do not know what I should have done without him: but I am informed that if it lay in his power to come at any of my money, he would contrive some way or other to cozen me of it, or part of it at least; for which reason I took particular care. He stood very hard with me for a gilder per cent. for every hundred I laid out. The moulds and matrices together stand me in ———. I have enquired very diligently of abundance of Printers, Booksellers, and of Mr. Rolij whether there are any letter founders at Harlem, Leyden, The Hague, Delft or Utrecht. I was told by some they knew of none, and by others that there were none, and Rolij assured me there were none at any of those places; and I myself saw at Foskins[1] a box with letter in it, directed for Utrecht; and it seems very probable there may be none at any of these places, because letter may be sent from Amsterdam to any of these places as cheap by water as a porter in London will carry a burthen half a mile. The box of molds and matrices which I bought was brought hither from Amsterdam for twelve stivers into the house, the distance about forty English miles. I am told there is one letter founder at Tergoes, but I can't hear of one Englishman or English house in the whole town. However I'll endeavour to find the founder before I leave the country. I have been through Tergoes three times, and as often through Harlem, Leyden and Delft, but never made any stay in any one of them. I have been twice to the Hague, but at such times that I could not see the States House. The town is very fine. One's charges thither and back again are not above a gilder. 'Tis very easy, and travelling would be very pleasant if one were not destitute of company.

From these letters it will be seen that James made all his purchases from Johannes Rolu of Amsterdam, formerly of Frankfort, in all about 3,500 matrices of Greeks, romans, italics, and blacks. The Athias mentioned in the letter of 27 July was Emanuel, son of Joseph Athias, a Lisbon Jew, who had won distinction as a printer of Hebrew books. In 1681 Joseph Athias bought from the widow of Daniel Elzevier the foundry of Christoffel van Dijk and shortly afterwards issued a specimen which was a repetition of that issued by the former owner. Owing to the jealousy of the other Amsterdam founders he seems to have had difficulty in carrying on, and issued another specimen, showing the same types, with a somewhat disguised heading, reading: *Proeven van letteren die gesneden zijn door wylen*

---

[1] Voskens.

P

Christoffel van Dijck, welke gegoten werden by Jan Bus, ten huyse van Dr. Joseph Athias woonst in die Swanenburg Street, tot Amsterdam. Finally, he sold the foundry to the widow of J. J. Schipper, but he still retained the matrices of his Hebrew types, one of which, the Text size, had been cut by Van Dijk. Athias died in 1692. The Cupi mentioned was Willem Cupi, also a Jew according to Enschedé, who had a number of Hebrew matrices. All this material ultimately reached the Enschedé Foundry. In the Bagford collection (5930) there are fragments of a specimen by M. Cupi.

The Voskens referred to in the letters is Bartholomeus, son of Dirk Voskens, who had died in 1688. There is also a reference in the last letter to Jacob Tonson, who visited Holland in 1703 to buy material for his great edition of Caesar, edited by Samuel Clarke, which was published in 1712. During his visit Tonson met Joseph Addison, and in Addison's letters from Amsterdam there is an account of their intercourse, but no mention of typefounders.

Thomas James returned with the matrices bought from Rolu and started his foundry in Aldermanbury. Afterwards he moved to Town Ditch, and in 1719 to Bartholomew Close, where the founding-house adjoined a dwelling-house, which in the previous century had been occupied by Thomas Roycroft, then by one Houndeslow, and afterwards by Samuel Palmer, with whom Benjamin Franklin worked as a journeyman in 1725. Later James occupied this dwelling-house also. The list of matrices with which James began is as follows, as worked out by Mores from the letter of 27 July:

Greek. Great Primer, 191; Pica, 161; Brevier, 141; Small Pica, 130.

Roman and Italic. Two-line English Roman, 148; Italic, 90.
Great Primer Roman, 111; another Roman, 101; Italic, 123.
English Roman, 86; Italic, 78.
Pica Roman, 109; another, 180; another, 82; Italic, 95.
Long Primer Roman, 140; another, 141; Italic, 94.
Brevier Roman, 112; Italic, 97.

Titles and Irregulars.
Four-line Pica Roman, 35.
Canon Roman (Two-line Great Primer it is), 33.
Small Canon (Two-line English) *missing.*
Two-line Pica Roman, 31.
Small Pica Roman, 136; Italic, 73.

English (Blacks). Pica, 60; Brevier, 65.
Mathematical Marks, Flowers, etc.

We have set this list out in full because we have three documents which throw some light on the origin of the types. First there is the specimen-sheet of Johannes Rolu in the Bagford collection (5930, Nos. 531, 532, and 539), presumably the same as the one referred to by James in his letters. The title reads: *Proeven van Letteren dewelcke gegooten worden by Mr. Johannes Rolu, Letter-Snyder woonende tot Amsterdam in de laetste Lely dwars-streat.* Rolu came from Frankfort and, as there is extant a specimen of Hebrews issued by his widow in 1711, he must have died soon after James's visit. There was a Cornelius Anton Rolloux who published a specimen of Frakturs and Schwabachers at Frankfort in 1714. The second document, given by Kleerkooper in *De Boekhandel de Amsterdam*, s' Gravenhage, 1914, pp. 737 seq., is an account of the sale of the whole of the stock of the foundry of Johan Adolph Smit of Frankfort by his widow to Johan Roluw, dated 25 June 1697. The third document consists of fragments of a specimen of J. A. Smit, which is also in the Bagford collection (5915).

J. A. Schmid (his name is variously spelt) was trained in the Luther Foundry at Frankfort, and about 1670 acquired the foundry of Reinhard Voskens, formerly of Amsterdam, and brother of the first Bartholomeus Voskens. Schmid, whilst still at Frankfort, issued two specimens of Frakturs and Schwabachers and one of exotics (Nos. 55, 56, and 58, in *Schriftproben deutscher Schriftgiessereien*, 1926, edited by G. Mori). By 1695 he was in Amsterdam, where his foundry was 'op Rapenburg in de Foely dwaers-straat'. The document in Kleerkooper gives a list of the matrices and punches sold. Two of the fragments in Bagford, the Mediaen roman and italic, bear Schmid's name. From a comparison of these fragments with the specimens on Rolu's sheet and with the list of matrices sold by the widow Schmid to Rolu it appears that the great majority of the types shown by Rolu came from Schmid's foundry. Among these types are most of the romans and italics, including the two bearing Schmid's name, four of the five Greeks, four Hebrews, a Mediaen Samaritan, a Text Syriac, and a Garmont Duyts or Black. Schmid shows a Text Russian, probably the fount bought for the Oxford Foundry (cf. p. 143), whereas Rolu has a Mediaen Russian. As to the types bought by James in 1710, of the romans and italics we know practically nothing. If they were among those shown on Rolu's sheet, then they were not displayed in the sale catalogue of 1782, with the one exception of the four-line Pica capitals, which are on Rolu's sheet but did not come from Schmid. One might have supposed that the Long Primer black, Dutch-cut, was Rolu's Garmont Duyts, but according to Mores James bought a Pica and a Brevier black from Rolu. Perhaps the Long Primer came from Andrews, who had several Dutch-cut founts of this family. The most interesting types purchased of Rolu are the four sizes of non-ligatured Greeks, all of which are on his sheet, together with a fifth size, Augustin or English.[1] The Brevier is not among the Schmid fragments but is mentioned in the list of matrices as sold by the widow Schmid.

James's later years were embittered by transactions which tended neither to his credit nor his fortunes, and which one would be tempted to pass by unnoticed, but that the history of English typefounding is closely involved in the narration. In the year 1725 a Scotch printer complained to William Ged, a respectable goldsmith of Edinburgh, of the inconvenience of being compelled to send to London or Holland for type, there being no foundry in Scotland at the time, and urged him to undertake the business of typefounder. Ged, in considering the matter, was struck with the idea of producing plates from whole pages of composed type, and after several experiments, satisfied himself that the idea was practicable.[2] In 1727

---

[1] See below, pp. 224, 225.

[2] 'The matter was first composed in the usual way, then the form was affused with some sort of *gypsum*, which after it was indurated, became a complication of matrices for casting the whole page in a single piece' (*Mores*, p. 59). As early as the year 1705 a Dutchman, named J. Van der Mey, had, with the assistance of Johann Muller, a German clergyman, devised a method of soldering together the bottoms of common types imposed in a forme,

he entered into a contract with an Edinburgh printer to prosecute the invention, but the latter being intimidated by the rumoured costliness of the process, withdrew from the bargain at the end of two years. In 1729 Ged entered into a new partnership with William Fenner, a London stationer, who offered, for one-half of the profits, to find the requisite capital and work the undertaking. Fenner introduced him to Thomas James, the founder, and a company was shortly afterwards formed, consisting of Ged, Fenner, Thomas James, John James, his brother, an architect at Greenwich, and James Ged, son of the inventor. Ged's narrative, which is simple, and to all appearances straightforward, represents Thomas James as having played from the first a highly dishonourable part in the proceedings of the new company. Being naturally selected to provide the necessary type, he supplied worn and battered letter, which Ged was compelled to reject as useless. Ged next applied to the King's printers, who had recently discarded James's type in favour of the highly superior letter of William Caslon, for permission to take plates from some formes of their new letter. The printers consulted Caslon, who not only denied the utility of the invention, but asserted that he could, if he chose, make as good plates as Ged.[1] A wager of £50 ensued. Each of the disputants was furnished with a page of type, and allowed eight days for producing the plate. At the end of a single day Ged produced three plates to the umpire, who was bound to admit his success. This feat becoming known, the partners applied for, and obtained a privilege from the University of Cambridge in 1731, to print Bibles and Prayer Books by the new method.

Ged was, however, again thwarted in every direction by the treachery of his colleagues, especially of Thomas James, who continued to supply imperfect type, and actively intrigued with the King's printers for the purpose of upsetting the University contract and discrediting the invention. With wonderful courage and perseverance Ged struggled against the opposition, and, it is said, completed two Prayer Books. The printers engaged on the work, however, were influenced by James, the compositors making malicious errors in the text, and the pressmen damaging the formes with their ink-balls. The complaint thus raised against the type was the motive for sending James in 1732 to Holland, to procure fresh letter. This second expedition lacked all the interesting features of the first, and he returned after being absent for two months and spending £160, with only one fount of type, far too large for the requirements of the undertaking. Meanwhile, however, in consequence of the persistent animosity of the printers, the books were suppressed by authority, and the plates sent to the King's printing-house, and thence

so as to form solid blocks of each page. By this method, two Bibles, a Greek Testament, and a Syriac Testament with Lexicon were produced, the plates of all of which, except the last-named, were preserved in 1801. See T. Hodgson, *Essay on the Origin and Progress of Stereotype Printing*, Newcastle, 1820, 8vo. The French claimed priority for the invention over Ged. Camus in his *Histoire et procédés polytypages*, 1802, gives an impression from a plate to be used in calendars in Books of Hours by a Paris printer Valleyre, but the date of the plate is a matter of doubt. In America Cadwallader Colden wrote a paper making suggestions as to a method of producing stereotype plates in 1743, but nothing further was done. The paper, together with correspondence on the subject with Benjamin Franklin, was printed in the *American Medical and Philosophical Register*, New York, 1811, vol. i, pp. 439–50.

[1] 'Being called into our company', says Ged, in his *Narrative*, 'he bragged much of his great skill and knowledge in all the parts of mechanism, and particularly vaunted, that he, and hundreds besides himself, could make plates to as great perfection as I could: which occasioned some heat in our conversation.'

to Caslon's foundry to be broken up.[1] Ged, shattered in health and fortune, returned to Edinburgh in 1733, where, by the assistance of his friends, he was enabled, after some delay, to finish his edition of Sallust.[2] He died in 1749.[3]

The dishonourable part taken by James in this business reacted on himself, for we find that he suffered considerably both in purse and business in consequence of his connexion with the undertaking. 'The printers', says Mores, 'would not employ him, because the block printing, had it succeeded, would have been prejudicial to theirs.'[4] The rising fame of Caslon at this particular period contributed also, and with equal force, to the ill success of his later years.

Before his death, however, he added considerably to his foundry, chiefly by the purchase of the foundries of his old master, Robert Andrews, and of his son Sylvester at Oxford. By the former he acquired not only a large number of roman and italics, but also several oriental and curious founts (some of which had formed the foundry of Moxon), which constituted the nucleus of that large collection for which his foundry subsequently became notorious. He died in 1736,[5] after a long illness, during which his son John James managed the business. The following circular, addressed to the printing trade at the time of his death, is interesting, not only as notifying the fact, but as being put forward as a specimen of the type of the foundry:

ADVERTISEMENT.

The death of Mr. Thomas James of Bartholomew Close, Letter Founder, having been industriously published in the Newspapers, without the least mention of any person to succeed in his business, it is become necessary for the widow James to give as public notice that she carries on the business of letter founding, to as great exactness as formerly, by her son John James, who had managed it during his father's long illness; the letter this adver-

---

[1] Hansard (*Typog.*, p. 823) shows an impression of two pages of a *Prayer Book*, from plates which had escaped 'Caslon's cormorant crucible'. A cast of pages of a *Common Prayer* were shown at the Caxton Celebration, 1877. See p. 465 of the catalogue.

[2] *C. Crispi Sallustii Belli Catilinarii et Jugurthini Historiæ. Edinburgi; Guilielmus Ged, Aurifaber Edinensis, non typis mobilibus, ut vulgo fieri solet, sed tabellis seu laminis fusis, excudebat.* 1739, 8vo (reprinted 1744). According to the account given by Ged's daughter in the narrative above referred to, the *Sallust* was completed in 1736. No copy of that date is, however, known. Some of the plates of the work were still in existence in 1887. His second book was H. Scougall, *The Life of God in the Soul of Man*, 1742.

[3] The story may be read in detail in *Biographical Memoirs of William Ged, including a particular account of his progress in the art of Block printing.* London, 1781, 8vo. Fenner died insolvent about the year 1735. James Ged, after working for some time with his father, engaged in the rebellion of 1745, and narrowly escaped execution. He ultimately went to Jamaica, a year before his father's death.

[4] Despite Mores's prophecy that Ged's invention, even if at first successful, would soon have sunk under its own burden, the method was successfully revived, or rather re-invented, about the year 1781 by Dr. Tilloch of Edinburgh, in conjunction with Foulis, printer to the University of Glasgow, at whose press were printed a stereotype edition of

Xenophon's *Anabasis* in 1783, and several chapbooks. Messrs. Tilloch and Foulis did not persevere with their venture, which was about the year 1800 successfully revived and perfected by Earl Stanhope, who employed a London printer, Andrew Wilson, to carry on the work. For a description of the Stanhope process and the sale of the secret to the Oxford University Press in 1805, see Hart's 'Charles Earl Stanhope and the Oxford University Press' in *Collectanea*, 3rd series, Oxford Historical Society, 1896. A similar contract had already been made in 1804 with Cambridge University Press; cf. S. C. Roberts. The Stanhope process was based on making a mould in plaster of Paris. The paper mould or flong was introduced into England by an Italian, Vanoni, in 1846, and patents were taken out in 1855 and 1861 by a Swiss, James Dellagana. See J. Southward's *Progress in Printing during the Victorian Era*, 1897. See also Ellic Howe's *The London Compositor*, p. 259. In France Firmin Didot, in 1795, attempted a method similar to that of Van der Mey in 1705; but abandoning this, succeeded in 1798 in producing good stereo plates by a system of *polytypage*. The reader is referred to Hodgson's *Essay* for specimens and particulars of the successive efforts to perfect the stereotype process at home and abroad.

[5] Mores contradicts himself as to this date, giving it as 1738 in one place, and 1736 in another. As, however, he is particular to mention that John James, in 1736, *after his father's death*, commenced his specimen of the foundry, the earlier date may be assumed to be correct.

tisement is printed on being his performance.[1] And he casts all other sorts from the largest to the smallest size. Also the Saxon, Greek, Hebrew, and all the Oriental types, of various sizes.

Although the above seems to indicate that John James was a practical letter-cutter, he does not appear to have contributed much to the increase of his foundry by his own handiwork. In 1739 he purchased, jointly with William Caslon, the foundry of Robert Mitchell, and took a half of the matrices.[2] A year later he bought Ilive's foundry. Of this purchase Rowe Mores mentions that the two founts of Nonpareil Greek, though duly paid for, never came to James's hands. The remaining matrices, consisting of roman and italics and a few sundries, were transferred to Bartholomew Close, where they lay, apparently unused, in the boxes distinguished by the name of Jugge.

A far more important purchase was made some eighteen years later, when Grover's foundry, after having lain idle for thirty years in the possession of his family, was finally sold to James by Richard Nutt in 1758. By this purchase James became possessed of a stock of matrices, the number of which nearly doubled his own foundry, and which included many of the most interesting relics of the art.[3] At the same time, he combined in one no fewer than nine of the old English foundries, and remained, with Caslon and Baskerville, as one of only three representatives of the trade in the country.[4] The following table will present in a clear form the gradual absorption of all the old foundries into that of James:

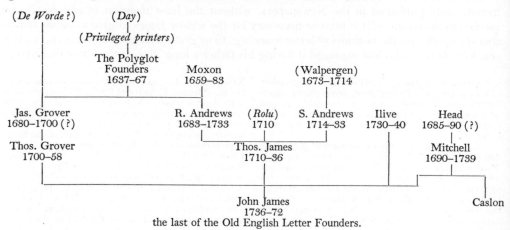

the last of the Old English Letter Founders.

With the exception of the circular already mentioned, nothing of the nature of a specimen of this large foundry appeared during the lifetime of its owner. As early as 1736, Rowe Mores informs us, a specimen was begun, designed to show the variety of matrices with which the foundry then abounded, and from which types could be supplied to the trade. But although so early begun, and progressed with

---

[1] Timperley, who quotes this document (*Encycl.*, p. 655), gives no particulars as to the letter in which it is printed.

[2] See p. 201.

[3] See p. 200.

[4] The Oxford University foundry must, of course, be included as a fourth foundry existing at this time, but does not rank as a trading establishment. Cottrell's foundry was also started in 1757, but it is doubtful whether he had yet finished cutting his punches. John Smith, in *The Printer's Grammar*, 1755, in comparing the standard bodies in use at that time in England, names Caslon and James as the only English founders.

for several years, the work was left incomplete at the time of James's death in 1772.[1]
Two causes may be assigned for this fact, one being the frequent and numerous
additions to the foundry from time to time, which would render any specimen
undertaken at an early stage of its existence incomplete; and the second and more
cogent reason is to be found in the fact that the excellence and growing popularity
of Caslon's founts at this particular period tended rapidly to depreciate the productions of the old founders, and, as Rowe Mores himself states, to render many
of their founts altogether useless in typography; so that a letter which in 1736
might have commanded a tolerable sale would in 1756 be despised, and in 1770
scoffed at.

At John James's death his foundry passed by purchase[2] into the hands of Rowe
Mores,[3] a learned and eccentric antiquary and scholar, who had devoted himself,

R. Van Bleeck pinxo   *J. Mynde fc.*

EDWARD ROWE MORES, M.A. & F.A.S.

FIG. 51. Portrait of Rowe Mores.

among other matters, to the study of typographical antiquities, a pursuit in which he
received no little stimulus from the possession of a collection of punches and matrices,
some of which were supposed to be as old as the days of Wynkyn de Worde.
Whether any motive besides a pure antiquarian zeal prompted the purchase, or
whether he held the collection in the capacity of trustee, is not known, but it seems
probable he had been intimately acquainted with the foundry and its contents for

---

[1] John Smith's *Printer's Grammar*, 1755, in referring to the use of flowers in typography, makes
mention of 'the considerable augmentation which
Mr. Caslon has made here in flowers, and in which
Mr. James likewise has so far proceeded that we
may soon expect a specimen of them' (p. 137).

[2] Nichols, *Illust. Lit.* viii. 450.

[3] Edward Rowe Mores was born 13 Jan. 1730,
at Tunstall in Kent, of which place his father was
rector. He was educated at Merchant Taylors'
School and Queen's College, Oxford, and being
originally intended for holy orders, took his M.A.
degree. He did not, however, enter the Church, but
devoted himself to literary and antiquarian pursuits.
Besides his *Dissertation upon English Typographical
Founders*, he spent some time in correcting Ames,
and in other investigations into the early history of
printing. On one occasion, as he himself narrates,
he assisted Ilive in correcting the Hebrew proofs of
M. Calasius, *Concordantiae Bibliorum Hebraicorum*,
ed. G. Romaine, 4 vols., London, 1747, fol., for the
press. His latter life was marred by habits of negli-
gence and intemperance, which hastened his death
in 1778 at Low Leyton. His valuable library of
books and manuscripts was sold by auction by
Paterson in Aug. 1779, on which occasion the
eighty copies of the *Dissertation*, being the entire
impression, were bought up by John Nichols and
given to the public with a short appendix. See
D.N.B.

some time before James's death. He speaks emphatically of it as 'our' foundry, and his disposition of its contents for sale is made with the authority of an absolute proprietor. It does not appear, however, that during the six years of his possession any steps were taken to extend or even continue the old business, which we may assume to have died with its late owner.

Mores found himself the owner of a vast confused mass of matrices, many of them unjustified, and others imperfect, which to an ordinary observer might have been summarily condemned as rubbish, but which he, with an enthusiasm quite remarkable, set himself to catalogue and arrange in order, considering himself amply repaid for his pains by the discovery of a few veritable relics of Wynkyn de Worde and other old English printers. The result of his labours he minutely relates in his *Dissertation*,[1] a work written, as he himself says, 'to preserve the memory of this Foundry, the most ancient in the kingdom, and which may now be dispersed', and intended as an introduction to the completed specimen of its contents. Despite its eccentric style and crabbed diction, the work, by virtue of its learning and acuteness, will always remain one of the most interesting contributions to the history of English typography.

The condition of the foundry will be best described in its author's own words. After giving a list of matrices lost,[2] and quoting a catalogue of the matrices of the learned languages in the foundry in 1767, written by James himself (which varies considerably from the catalogue presented at the sale, to be given later on), he observes:

The specimen will show that several of the matrices are unjustified. This being but an accidental circumstance, does not in the least affect the goodness of the type, though it affects its appearance in *the casting*. The matrices were amassed at all events to augment the collection, and the operation of the file was suspended till a call for the type should make it necessary. So this defect is no more than a proof that the matrices have not been impaired by use.

Another circumstance it may be necessary to mention relating to the difference in the number of matrices of the same face and body, which may lead to a suspicion that those of a lesser number are imperfect. But this is not the fact. The difference arises from a difference in the quantity of ligations, which have been always cut in a greater or smaller number according to the humour or fancy of the artist. We own ourselves admirers of ligatures, for they are certainly ornamental and elegant, and it is to be wished that they could be used in typography with the same ease as they are displayed in calligraphy. But this is impossible; fusile types are not so tractable as the pen of a ready writer, and we scruple not to call a fount complete though it be destitute of every jugation. . . .

A word or two must be added in relation to the Specimen. It was begun by Mr. James in the year 1736, in which year, after the decease of his father, he entered into business for himself, and was designed to show the variety of matrices with which his foundery abounded. Therefore it is a specimen only of the types which he could cast for those who wanted; no reference being made to the situation of the matrices from which he would have cast them. But notwithstanding the number of years intermediate, the Specimen was left unfinished by Mr. James at the time of his death, and that which was left has been mangled since his

---

[1] *A Dissertation upon English Typographical Founders and Founderies, by Edward Rowe Mores, A.M., A.S.S.* London, 1778. 8vo (only 80 copies printed). It was reprinted by the Grolier Club in 1924, with an introduction by D. B. Updike.

[2] Consisting of eight founts of Hebrew, four of Samaritan, three of Arabic, four of Greek, five of roman or italic, three of Saxon, one of Anglo-Norman, and four of black.

A

CATALOGUE AND SPECIMEN

Of the Large and Extensive

PRINTING-TYPE-FOUNDERY

Of the late ingenious

Mr. JOHN JAMES, Letter-founder,

Formerly of Bartholomew-Close, London, deceased:

Including several other FOUNDERIES,
English and Foreign.

Improved by the late Reverend and Learned
EDWARD ROWE MORES, deceased:

COMPREHENDING

A great Variety of Punches and Matrices of the Hebrew,
Samaritan, Syriac, Arabic, Æthiopic, Alexandrian, Greek,
Roman, Italic, Saxon, Old English, Hibernian, Script,
Secretary, Court-Hand, Mathematical, Musical.
and other Characters, Flowers, and Ornaments;

Which will be Sold by Auction,

By Mr. PATERSON,

At his Great Room (No. 6), King's-Street, Covent-Garden,
London,

On Wednesday, 5th June, 1782; and the **Three** following Days.

To begin exactly at 12 o'Clock.

To be viewed on Wednesday, May 29, and to the Time of Sale.

Catalogues, with Specimen of the Types, may be had at the Place
of Sale.
[Price One Shilling.]

FIG. 52. Title-page of James's Sale Catalogue, 1782.

decease. Not that there was any occasion for such references, for Mr. James was possessed of the matrices, and consequently of the secret of adapting them to his purpose. To supply this deficiency in a specimen of the matrices (for as such the specimen is now to be considered) has been attended with trouble incredible to anyone but one who upon a like occasion shall attempt the same. And such an occasion we believe there will never be.

For the Specimen some apology is to be made; neither the form nor the matter is so judicious as we could wish, but the greatest part of it was composed long ago, and it was almost impossible now to alter it. Incorrectness must be overlooked, because Letter Founders generally compose their own specimens, and this might be sufficient to apologise for deficiencies in the Composing part. But we must use another plea in extenuation of enormities in this part unavoidable; the confinement of large-bodied letters to a narrow measure; though for blemishes of this sort the just allowance will be made by those of judgement. It shows the letter, the common purpose of this kind of specimens.

We have inserted specimens of several matrices which the great improvements made in the art of letter-cutting have rendered altogether useless in typography; but these specimens will be found of critical use to an antiquary, for whose sake we have inserted them, regardless of the charge that we deform our Specimen, or of another more material accusation, that by multiplying particulars we endeavour to enhance the value of our foundery. The latter we can easily refute; for the sets we speak of, besides the rudeness of the workmanship, are imperfect, and consequently unsaleable, and will probably be taken from the foundery before it is disposed of to prevent the trouble of a future garbling,[1] and this consideration must extend to those objections which may be made against things cast in haste without justification, for the purpose only of shewing the faces.

Hitherto we have spoken only of Matrices. The punches though in order they are first must come last; and of them we have but little to say; for these having performed their office by formation of the matrice are generally like other useful instruments which have discharged their duty, neglected discarded and thrown away.

The *entire loss*, the *waste* and the *rubbish* in our foundery in this article are great. The *waste* and *rubbish* are in weight about 120 lb., and were we to put down *tale* instead of *weight* (the pusils which seem to make the greater part of this quantity not much exceeding in largeness the little end of a poinctrel) the number would be very great. But covetous of preserving the remembrance of everything which in Mr. James' Foundery was curious or uncommon, we have re-scrutinized these, and have left behind us nothing but the *Rom.* and *Ital.* in which is nothing either curious or uncommon.

The same likewise have we done to the matrices, the *waste* of which now remaining and disposed of in order, is in number about 2,600,[2] the rubbish in weight about ½ cwt.

A work of some trouble, but *virtù* hath been gratified amongst the rubbish of punches by some originals of Wynkyn de Worde, some punches of the Two-line Great Primer English.[3] They are truly *vetustate formáque et squalore venerabiles*, and we would not give a lower-case letter in exchange for all the leaden cups of Haerlem.[4]

Mores, unfortunately, did not live to see the publication of his *Dissertation*, or to complete the specimen which was to accompany it. He died in 1778, and four years elapsed before the foundry was put up to auction, and the catalogue with its

---

[1] 'Such as those which being uniques cannot be perfected without new punches, and if they were made complete, it would be no more than *oleum et operam, etc.*, because they are either out of use or the times afford better, as the Antique Hebrew (spec. 7); Leusden's Samaritan (spec. 27); 2-line Great Primer Hebrew (spec. 38); the Runic, Gothic, and some other recondites, the matrices for which are incomplete or useless. But of the founts which are in daily use the imperfects will continue, as they mutually aid and help out one another. For the same reason also will continue those which have been cast aside (not by their owner) under the name of *waste.*'

[2] In another place Mores states that the 'waste and pye' of the foundry contained upwards of 6,000 matrices.

[3] This is the old black from Grover's foundry; see above, p. 196.

[4] This sly allusion leaves little doubt as to the light in which Mores viewed the Coster legend so industriously defended by such writers of his own day as Meerman, Bowyer, and Nichols.

OCCIDENTALS.

GREEK.

English. *Alexandrian.*

ΜΑΚΑΡΙΟCΛΝΗΡΟCΟΥΚΕΠΟ GREEK.
ΡΕΥΘΕΝΒΟΥΔΗΛCΕΒΩΝΚΛΙΕΝ
ΟΔΩΛΜΑΡΤΩΔΩΝΟΥΚΕCΤΗΚΛ

De Worde 8. Matrices 31.

Double Pica.

Α Β Γ Δ Θ Λ Ξ Π Ρ Σ Τ Ψ Ω
α β ϛ γ Γ δ ε ζ η ϑ θ ι κ λ μ ν
ξ ο π ϖ ρ σ ς ϛ τ] υ φ χ ψ ω

Ἐνῆκεν ὁ Θεὸς τῇ τῦ ἀνθρώπυ φύ-
σει τὰ σπέρματα τῆς ἀρετῆς.

De Worde 1 & 2. Matrices 284.

. Great Primer.

Α Δ Ζ Λ Μ Ξ Γ Σ Τ Φ Χ Ψ Ω
α β ϛ γ δ ε η θ κ μ ν ξ π ϖ ρ σ ς ϛ τ φ χ ω

De Worde 9. Matrices 131.

FIG. 53. Page from the James's Sale Catalogue, 1782.

specimen attached finally appeared. Of this interesting document we need only observe that in point of execution and printing it calls for all the apology which Mores offers on its behalf;[1] for one could hardly imagine a specimen doing less justice to the collection it represents. Yet, in spite of its imperfections, it is a work of the highest importance to anyone interested in the history of the old English letter-founders, and we regret that space forbids quoting the catalogue in full.[2] We shall, however, present our readers with an abstract of the specimen as far as it relates to the matrices of the 'learned' languages in the foundry; adding, as far as possible, the initials of the foundries through which each fount had come into James's hands.[3]

The specimens shown are as follows:

Hebrew (Biblical).[4]—2-line English Mod. [A.][5]		Rashi Nonpareil.*	[A.]
2-line English No. 2.		*Samaritan.*[6]—Double Pica (Leusden's).	[A.]
„ Ancient.	[P.]	English** (with English face).	[P.] [G.]
Double Pica.	[P.] [A.]	*Syriac.*—Double Pica.	[P.] [G.]
Great Primer.	[A.]	Great Primer.	[A.]
English Antique.		Pica.	[G.]
„ Ancient, No. 2.	[P.] [A.]	*Arabic.*[7]—Double Pica (Gt. Primer?)* [P.?] [G.]	
„ „ No. 3.		Great Primer.	[A.]
„ Modern.		*Æthiopic.*—Gr. Primer or English.** [P.] [A.]	
Pica Ancient.	[G.?]		
„ Modern.	[A.]	English.	[Anon.]
Small Pica Antique.	[A.]	*Greek.*[8]—Double Pica.[9]	[Royal] [G.]
„ „ No. 2.	[A.]	Great Primer.*	[G.]
„ Modern.		„ No. 2.	
Long Primer.	[G.?]	„ No. 3.	[R.]
Brevier.	[A.]	English.	
„ No. 2.	[S.A.]	„ No. 2.	
Nonpareil.	[A.]	Pica.	[R.]
Hebrew (Rabbinical).—English German (a spurious Rashi).	[A.]	„ No. 2.	
Rashi Pica.	[A.]	Small Pica.	[P.]
„ Long Primer.*	[A.]	„ No. 2.	[R.?]
„ Brevier.*	[A.]	„ No. 3.	[P.]

[1] 'Excusatos nos habeant eruditi quibus obvenerit typorum *Jamesianorum* specimen accuratis perlustrare oculis, quod minus quam expetendum esset, in linguis praesertim reconditoribus, elimatum prodeat; in animo erat dedisse emendatissimum et si sat se fecisse existiment opifices, si, posthabitis preli ceterisque maculis, ostendatur literarum facies—limae non defuit labor,—at cessante Fusore cessavit fornax et defuerunt fusi ad emaculandum typi.'—*Preface to the Specimen.*

[2] No copy of the catalogue is known in this country. The British Museum has a photographic reproduction of the copy in the possession of the late D. B. Updike, presented by Mr. Morison.

[3] i.e. [P.] Polyglot, [A.] Andrews, [G.] Grover, [R.] Rolu, [N.] Nicholls, [S.A.] Sylvester Andrews, [Anon.] 'Anonymous'. Of founts marked *, punches or matrices still existed *c.* 1890. Those marked with two asterisks are in existence to-day.

[4] Two sets of Small Pica and two sets of Pearl not shown in specimen, were also sold. A Canon, 2-line Great Primer, three Great Primers, an English, Pica, and Bourgeois, had been lost.

[5] It is to be borne in mind that Andrews's foundry included that of Moxon, from whom many of his oldest founts doubtless came.

[6] A Great Primer, Pica, Small Pica, and Long Primer had been lost, but the Long Primer punches remained.

[7] A 2-line English, Double Pica, and Pica had been lost.

[8] There were also, not in specimen, a 2-line Great Primer, Double Pica, Pica, two Small Picas, and a set of 2-line Nonpareil Capitals. A Paragon, Bourgeois, and two sets of Nonpareil had been lost.

[9] This was the fount used in the *Catena in Job*, 1637.

Pica.

That about this time (1450) the Art of Printing SCRIPTO-
and Casting Single Types was found out in the City of RIAL.
ABCDEEFGHIKLMNOPQRSTUW

Byddel 11. Matrices 78.

Small Pica.

That about this time (1450) iae Art of Printing
and Casting Single Tipes mae found out in tde Cirl

Byddel 12. Matrices 69.

SECRETARY.

Great Primer.

And may it be enacted by The Authority SECRE-
Aforesaid that from and after the said TARY.
A BCDFGHIK LMNO

Byddel 10. Matrices 114.

HIEROGLYPHICS, &c.

Pica.

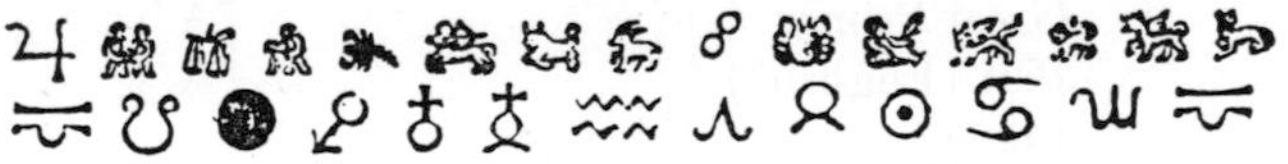

Berthelet 7. Matrices 33.

FIG. 54. Page from the James's Sale Catalogue, 1782.

Greek.—Brevier.	[A.]		*Secretary.*—Great Primer.		[G.]
Brevier No. 2.	[R.]		*Hieroglyphics.*—A Set.		
„ No. 3.[1]	[G.]		*English.*[5]—2-line Great Primer.		
Nonpareil.	[A.]			[De Worde?]	[G.]
Pearl.	[N.?]		Great Primer.	[De Worde?]	[G.]
English Alexandrian.*	[G.]		„ No. 2.		[A.]
Gothic.—Pica.	[Anon.]		English.		[Anon.]
Anglo-Saxon.[2]—Great Primer.	[G.]		„ No. 2.**		[A.]
Great Primer, No. 2.	[G.]		„ No. 4.		[G.]
English (Pica).	[A.]		Pica.		[A.]
Long Primer.	[A.?]		„ No. 2.		[Anon.]
Anglo-Norman.[3]—Great Primer.	[A.]		„ No. 3.		[R.?]
English.	[Anon.]		Small Pica No. 2.		[A.]
Runic.—Pica.			„ No. 3.		[Anon.?]
Court Hand.—Double Pica.	[G.]		„ No. 6.		[A.]
English.*	[G.]		„ No. 7.		[A.?]
Union.—Double Pica.**	[G.]		Long Primer (Dutch cut).		[G.?]
Scriptorial (Cursive).[4]—Double Pica.	[G.]		„ No. 2.		[G.]
English.	[G.]		„ No. 3.		[G.]
„ No. 2.	[G.]		Brevier.		[G.?]
Pica.**	[G.]		„ No. 4.		[R.?]
Small Pica.	[G.]		Nonpareil.*		[G.]

Of roman capitals, eight founts were shown,[6] and of roman and italic from Canon to Diamond, there were thirty-seven founts in the specimen and 108 not shown. In addition to the above, the specimen included ninety-seven varieties of flowers, chiefly from the Grovers's foundry; while other odd flowers, with signs, rules, braces, and various imperfect founts (contained in sixteen drawers) were also sold, though not shown. At the end of the list of matrices came what was perhaps the most interesting feature of the sale, viz. a set of punches contained in a press named 'Caxton', consisting of twenty drawers. Of these the majority were roman and italics, which we will not specify, as it is impossible to determine whose handiwork they were in the first instance. We give, however, the contents of drawers A, E, F, and G, which contained the following punches of the learned languages:[7]

A.—Æthiopic	English*	[P.]	[A.]
Samaritan	Pica* (English?)	[P.]	[G.]
„	Long Primer		
Syriac	English (Pica?)		[G.]
Arabic	Great Primer		[A.]
„	Pica (English?)		[A.]
Greek	Brevier		
Saxon	Pica		[A.]

[1] 'Remarkably beautifully cut and justified.'
[2] A Double Pica, Pica, and Long Primer had been lost.
[3] A 2-line English had been lost.
[4] Also a Double Pica not in specimen. Matrices of the English and Small Pica are also in existence though not starred by Reed.
[5] i.e. black—of which the following sets, not in specimen, were also sold: Double Pica, two Great Primers, two English, four Small Picas, Long Primer, three Breviers, and Nonpareil. A 2-line Great Primer, Double Pica, Long Primer, and Bourgeois had been lost.
[6] Of these, one was a 4-line Pica, to which belonged a set of 'leaden' lower-case matrices.
[7] There is more difficulty in tracing these to their original sources than in the case of the matrices, as not only are the numbers not given, but the bodies named may very likely vary from the actual bodies to which the matrices were justified.

A.—Hibernian[1]	Pica*			[M.] [A.]
E.—Greek	Great Primer,* points and ligatures			[G.]
F. „	Pica,	„	„	
G. „	Nonpareil,	„	„	[A.]

It is at least remarkable that so few punches should have existed in so large a foundry; but it is to be remembered that the wear and tear of the matrices in those days was not so great as now, and the necessity for a new set of strikes from the punches was consequently less frequent. We may even suppose, from Mores's own reference to the subject, already quoted, that it was a common practice to discard a set of punches as useless as soon as they had left their impression in the matrices.

The concluding items of the catalogue are 'about 60 or 70 moulds, from 5-line Pica down to Nonpareil, some 2, some 3 or more of a sort which will be lotted according to their bodies; also a parcel of iron ladles; a vice, 33 lb. weight, several gauges, dividers, blocks, setting-up sticks, dressing sticks, &c.'—a meagre list, which, if it represents the working plant of the foundry, points to a rough-and-ready practice of the art which, even in Moxon's time, would have been considered primitive.

A word must be added respecting the catalogue. Whether it was taken precisely as Mores left it, or whether Paterson, the auctioneer (whose 'talent at Cataloguing' Nichols, in his *Anecdotes*, approvingly mentions[2]), completed it, we cannot say. It is as precise, perhaps, as any catalogue of so confused a collection could be. An opening was, however, left for a good deal of misapprehension, by the fact that the nests of drawers in which the matrices were stored, instead of bearing distinguishing numbers, bore the names of famous old printers, which duly figured in the cata-logue.[3] Misled by this circumstance, it seems more than likely that Paterson may have enhanced the importance of his lots by dwelling on the fact that one fount was 'De Worde's', another 'Cawood's', another 'Pynson's', and so on. The absurdity of this delusion becomes very apparent when we see the Alexandrian Greek some years later puffed by its purchasers as the veritable production of De Worde (who lived a century before the Alexandrian MS. came to this country), and find Hansard, in 1825, ascribing seven founts of Hebrew and a Pearl Greek to Bynneman.

What was the result of the sale financially we cannot ascertain. Of the fate of its various lots we know very little either, except that Dr. Fry secured most of the curious and 'learned' matrices. How far the other foundries of the day, at home and abroad, enriched themselves, or how much of the collection fell into the hands of the coppersmiths, are problems not likely to find solution. With the sale, how-ever, disappeared the last of the old English foundries, and closed a chapter of English typography which, though not the most glorious, is certainly not the least instructive through which it has passed.

---

[1] Though the matrices of this fount do not appear in the catalogue, they were evidently in James's foundry, as they are mentioned in the list drawn up by James in 1767, and are not specified among the matrices lost. They were acquired at the sale by Dr. Fry, and may possibly have been included with the Saxons, or with the imperfect lots.

[2] *Lit. Anec.* iii. 438.

[3] See our facsimiles from the specimen at Figs. 53 and 54.

APPENDIX I
GREEK WITHOUT LIGATURES

The fact that our printers continued down to the beginning of the eighteenth century to wrestle with Greek founts of over 400 sorts is no doubt due to the success of the Aldine Greek classics and the beauty of Garamond's 'Grecs du Roi'. The story of the breaking down of this tradition and the manner in which the reform was achieved has not been fully worked out. P. S. Fournier in his *Manuel Typographique*, 1764 (tom. i, p. 235), states that the Dutch were the first to cut non-ligatured Greeks and that the innovation was due to the Hebrew scholar Jan Leusden of Amsterdam. In 1698 Heinrich Wetstein printed at Amsterdam ʽΗ Καινὴ Διαθήκη edited by Leusden. In the preface the editor writes: 'Do tibi hic Novum Testamentum Graecum nitidissime & correctissime impressum, sine ullis litterarum compendiis, quae vulgo abbreviaturae dicuntur. Hae saepius Tyronibus, & quandoque etiam doctoribus, molestias facessere & remoram injicere solent.' This passage is probably the source of Fournier's note. Wetstein printed several other editions of this Greek Testament, in which the preface was repeated, even after the death of the editor in 1699.

The type in which these editions are set is the smallest of a series of non-ligatured Greeks owned by the Wetstein Foundry, which was started at Haarlem in 1735 by Rudolph Wetstein, the son of Heinrich. Four sizes are shown in a specimen issued by the grandson H. F. Wetstein in 1743. After the death of Rudolph in 1742 the stock was bought by Isaac and Johan Enschedé in 1743. In the Enschedé specimen-book of 1744 a series of seven Greeks is shown, the sizes being Text, Augustyn, Mediaan, Dessendiaan, Garmond, Brevier, and Collonel (Great Primer down to Minion in English). They are shown again in the Enschedé specimen-book of 1768 and from the notes it appears that the Augustyn and Dessendiaan were cut by J. M. Fleischman in 1740 and 1742 respectively. Incidentally it may be noted that even as late as 1765 Fleischman thought it worth while to cut the ligatured sorts also, so that printers who wished could follow the earlier practice. The original five sizes are again displayed on p. 112 of Charles Enschedé's *Fonderies de caractères dans les Pays-Bas*. In the 'Advertissment' of the book of 1744 the Enschedés write: 'Les Lettres Grecques, qui se trouvent dans cette Epreuve se trouvoient plusieurs années auparavant seulement chez la Famille des Wetsteins, qui en avoit fait faire les Poinçons à ses depens, & imprimés quelques ouvrages en Grec avec ces Lettres.' In the preface to the specimen of 1768 Johan Enschedé says that Rudolph Wetstein had three or four Greeks which his father and grandfather had bought or had cut in Basle. Charles Enschedé, writing in 1908, said that H. Wetstein got his type from Basle, probably from Pistorius. Wetstein, who was himself a Greek scholar, certainly came of a Basle family, but the source of his new Greek is still to be traced. P. S. Fournier in another passage of his *Manuel* (tom. ii, p. xxxv) says that the father had had them engraved in Geneva. We know of no founders at Geneva at that period, and as to Pistorius, that firm showed their Greeks in a specimen issued about 1710, and I am informed by Herr Gustav Mori of Frankfort that these Greeks follow the old models. Herr Mori also states that he can find no evidence that any member of the Pistorius firm was a punch-cutter.

Wetstein was printing with non-ligatured Greek some years before the appearance of Leusden's *New Testament* and it seems that undue credit has been given to that scholar. In 1688 Wetstein printed an edition of Thomas Gale's *Opuscula mythologica*, in which the Greek is set in a non-ligatured type different from any shown in the later specimens. In the preface, dated 1687, Gale says, speaking of Marcus Meibomius, who helped in the preparation of the volume, 'optimo etiam consilio characterem adduxit in usum facilem, & expeditum, nexibus, & ligaturis, quas vocant, liberum'. Meibomius (1630–1711) was a well-known German philologian who, after many wanderings, spent the last part of his life in Amsterdam. The credit is again given to him in the edition of Diogenes Laertius, printed by Wetstein in 1692 in a similar but larger size of non-ligatured Greek. In the address to the reader Wetstein writes: 'De characteribus graecis quibus (suadente Cl. Meibomio) usi sumus solutis nullisque litterarum nexibus intricatis . . . te morari nolumus.' This passage was quoted in 1902 by Wilhelm Meyer in *Henricus Stephanus über die Regii Typi Graeci.* In a passage on p. 29 dealing with the end of the 'Grecs du Roi', Meyer noted that the scholar who began the movement was Meibomius. It is, of course, quite possible that the printer Wetstein in his first experiments, e.g. in the Gale and the Diogenes Laertius, made use of an old Greek, merely leaving out the tied letters. If this was so, I have not succeeded in identifying the type.

APPENDIX II
THE ROMAN AND ITALIC TYPES OF THE JAMES FOUNDRY

The romans and italics of the James Foundry were not acquired by Fry and therefore were irretrievably scattered. These types have never been discussed, so that a few notes on the origin of some of them may be useful. The Sale Catalogue shows, besides Hebrews, Greeks, black-letter, &c., two pages of titlings, thirty-seven roman types, and twenty-nine italics. They are badly printed from worn types, and inadequately displayed in that unfortunate text, *Quousque tandem . . .* , which all English founders had adopted from Caslon. But still, at any rate for the larger sizes, some results can be arrived at. In the facsimile of Rowe Mores's *Dissertation,* edited in 1924 by D. B. Updike for the Grolier Club of New York, pp. 1, 10, 14, 20, 24, 26, and 43 of the specimen are reproduced.

Of the titlings the only one of which I know anything is the four-line Pica (p. 24) which was bought from Johannes Rolu and is shown on his specimen-sheet of *c.* 1710. The French Canon No. 3 (on p. 26) I imagine to be a seventeenth-century English type, as it is common on English title-pages and will be found on Proclamations from the year 1659. It appears also on the title-page of the specimen-book of the Edinburgh printer James Moncur, 1709, of which a reproduction is given in Berry and Johnson's *Catalogue of Specimens of Printing Types,* 1935, pl. 20. The Canon italic on p. 27 seems to be that of Robert Mitchell, described by Berry and Johnson, op. cit., p. 3. The two-line Great Primer roman and italic (p. 28) are in James Watson's specimen-book, Edinburgh, 1713, where they are more fully displayed. These may be presumed to be Dutch types, since Watson declared that his stock came from Holland. However, not all Watson's types were Dutch; he shows, for instance, Moxon's Canon. Nor is this two-line Great Primer known on any Dutch founder's specimen. In English printed books the type may be seen in Pope's *Essay on Man,* 1733. The second two-line Great Primer (p. 29) can be seen on the title-page of Pope's *Sermon against Adultery,* 1734. Pope's works, both collected and single, were frequently lavishly printed in folio, and offer a fine display of the popular types of his day.

The two-line English, No. 2, roman and italic (p. 30), are shown also in the Oxford University Press specimen-book of 1695 (they are not in the first edition, 1693). The italic belongs to a series surviving to-day, known as 'Janson', although almost certainly *not* cut by Anton Janson, of Leipzig. This series has already been discussed (see above, p. 181). It is a curious fact that only this one size of the italic reached England, and that as early as 1692. The accompanying roman, both at Oxford and in the James Foundry, is not the so-called 'Janson', nor is it the roman shown with the 'Janson' italic on the specimen-sheet of the Widow of J. Adamzoon and A. Ente at Amsterdam. The two-line English, No. 3, roman and italic (pp. 30 and 31), are again in Watson, op. cit., and again much better displayed. There is a good show of this type in Mark Catesby's *Natural History of Carolina,* London, 1731, in the 'Address to the Queen'.

Of the Double Picas (there are five in all), that shown at the top of p. 32 was a favourite London type for the printing of poems in folio, a fashion in the time of Pope; cf., for example, *The Battle of the Books*, J. Roberts, 1725, an anonymously published poem by Thomas Cooke. That shown at the top of p. 33 may possibly be from a minor founder, Jacob Ilive; the reasons for this attribution are given below in describing that founder's Great Primer. The fourth Double Pica, roman and italic (p. 33), is a Fell type, perhaps the best known of the Fell collection. Oxford appears to have sold their types, and this Double Pica and also the Fell Great Primer are commonly found in London printed books. The Double Pica in particular was even more popular than the type already mentioned in connexion with the printing of verse in folio. The Double Pica No. 2, the fifth (p. 34), is probably the oldest surviving roman in the James Foundry. It was brought to England by John Day and was formerly thought to have been cut by him (cf. above, pp. 91–93). The italic shown after it is Dutch, and, as far as traced, was first used by the Elzevirs in 1631. It was in London by 1657 (see above, p. 180). The Paragon roman on p. 34 is, I think, Joseph Moxon's Double Pica, as shown on his specimen-sheet of 1669. A full display of this roman will be found in the preliminaries of John Evelyn's *Discourse of Medals*, 1697.

Of Great Primers eight examples are given. The first (p. 35) is the Fell type already mentioned. The one at the foot of p. 36 may be by Jacob Ilive. According to Rowe Mores, Ilive's types were in boxes marked 'Jugge' (the boxes were given names after early English printers), and this Great Primer bears the name Jugge. Also I find the type in the pre-liminaries of a small book written by Ilive, *The Oration spoke at Trinity Hall, etc.*, printed for J. Wilford, London, 1738; presumably the *Oration* was printed also by Ilive. Other types bearing the name Jugge are the Double Pica mentioned above, the first of the two Picas (p. 39) and the second Small Pica (p. 40). All four resemble one another in design; note in particular the capital M in both roman and italic. In design they are the worst of all the types shown and are not flattering to Jacob Ilive, if he was the cutter. The second Pica (p. 39), with which there is no italic, I have found in a number of London-printed books dating from the early days of the James Foundry. The earliest appearance noted of this roman, with its conspicuous large serified M, is in a *Sermon* by Matthew Clarke, 1714. I know nothing of its origin. Finally, the Diamond (italic only) may be presumed to be that from the Grover Foundry; the first roman of that size in this country was probably that cut by Voskens about 1680. This is, perhaps, a very meagre harvest. It is quite possible that among the types not discussed are concealed known designs, unrecognized because so poorly displayed. As to the Dutch types bought by James, he seems to have been saddled with a poor lot, and acquired nothing from the two foundries which in 1710 had the best stock, the Voskens and the successors of Van Dijk.

APPENDIX III
TYPOGRAPHY AT THE CAMBRIDGE UNIVERSITY PRESS, *c.* 1700

Much has been written about the Fell types and the reform in printing at the Oxford University Press towards the end of the seventeenth century, but little about the contemporary revival at Cambridge. No type-foundry was established at Cambridge, but with the help of new types purchased from Holland in 1697 and the few following years, a number of books were produced well worthy to be compared with Oxford books printed with the Fell types.

For details of the measures taken by the University from 1696 towards the improvement of their press, the reader may be referred to S. C. Roberts's *History of the Cambridge University Press*, chap. v. We learn that on 10 July 1696 the famous Dr. Richard Bentley, who to some extent played the part of Dr. John Fell at Oxford, was given authority to buy types. In January 1698 we hear that a large consignment of Dutch types (fifty-two alphabets) had reached Harwich on its way to Cambridge. Again, on 23 August of the same year, the inspector of the press, Cornelius Crownfield, has 'leave to send to Rotterdam for 300 l.

weight of the double Pica letter in order to the printing of Virgil, Horace, &c.'. On 3 May 1699 it was ordered that 400 lb. weight of Paragon Greek Letter be sent for to the Widow Voskens (i.e. the widow of the founder, Dirk Voskens) in Holland. We see that Cambridge bought types, not matrices, and bought them in Holland. From a comparison of books printed at Cambridge from 1697 onwards, with the specimen-sheets of contemporary Dutch founders, many of the new founts can be identified, and it appears that most of the dealings were with the Van Dijk firm. Nowhere in England was there such a fine display of Van Dijk's romans and italics as at Cambridge in the early years of the eighteenth century.

Christoffel Van Dijk was the most distinguished type-cutter in Holland in the seventeenth century. He was born in 1601, and worked in Amsterdam at first as a goldsmith. In 1648 he was established as typefounder, and between that year and his death in 1671 or 1672 he cut many types—romans and italics, Greeks, Hebrews, and 'Flamands'. His stock ultimately came into the hands of the firm of Enschedé of Haarlem, and to this day that house still possesses a few of his types: one Greek, one Hebrew, three 'Flamands', but no romans, and only one size of italic, Text, i.e. Great Primer. No specimen-sheet issued by Van Dijk himself is known, but we have several issued by his successors. Van Dijk's son Abraham died shortly after his father, and the foundry was purchased by Daniel Elzevir, whose widow printed a specimen-sheet of the stock in 1681. This sheet—the earliest we know—is reproduced in Willem's *Les Elzevir*, 1880, and there is also a reduced reproduction in Updike's *Printing Types*, Fig. 207. Charles Enschedé, in his *Fonderies de caractères dans les Pays-Bas*, gives specimens of the surviving types of Van Dijk, and also a table showing which of the types on the sheet of 1681 were cut by Van Dijk and which were from other foundries. From the records of his firm Enschedé knew that in some cases his ancestor had acquired the actual punches, and these types he judged to have been cut by Van Dijk. Of the rest we know, in any event, that some were older than Van Dijk; some, for instance, were sixteenth-century types acquired from the Luther Foundry at Frankfort.

I propose now to trace some of the Van Dijk types in Cambridge-printed books.

Although the first document relating to the arrival of Dutch types at Cambridge is of 1698, yet it appears from existing printed books that the press had some Van Dijk types already in 1697. A collection of poems entitled *Gratulatio Academiae Cantabrigiensis de reditu Gulielmi III* is set in Van Dijk's Text (Great Primer) roman and italic; this size of the italic is the one which has survived to this day. The verses at the end in Greek and Hebrew are grouped separately because, as we are told, the new types had not arrived 'quod typi novi Academici nondum ad nos pervenerint'. In 1698 the press was using the Augustijn (English) roman and italic of Van Dijk, e.g. in a sermon of Francis Hutchinson. In the edition of *Horace* published by Jacob Tonson for the press in 1699 we meet a whole series of Dutch types, most of them Van Dijk's. The main text is set in a Double Pica roman, Van Dijk's Ascendonica. The dedication is in his Kleene Kanon, with a little of the italic. The address 'Lectori' before the notes is in the Text size, which the press had by 1697. Finally, the notes are set in a Pica roman and italic, among the most interesting of the types acquired at this time, which we will describe more fully. We may add that the editions of *Virgil*, 1701, and of *Catullus*, *Propertius*, and *Tibullus*, 1702, are exactly similar volumes in typography.

The Pica roman used for the notes is also shown on the Van Dijk specimen-sheets. It is the Mediaen romeyn, No. 2. Charles Enschedé says that this type was not cut by Van Dijk, for he found that no punches were acquired by his firm. His conclusion in this case is borne out by the fact that the type was in existence long before Van Dijk's day. This roman has several spot letters which make it easily recognizable. In the upper-case the E has the lower arm distinctly longer than the upper and middle arms, the M has no serif on the right-hand upright, and the P is an oddly small letter. In the lower-case the 'g' has a long link, and is quite different in design from the Garamond 'g'. This type is a Paris design of the sixteenth century; the earliest book in which I have found it is the octavo edition of Geofroy Tory's *Champ fleury*, V. Gaultherot, 1549. About that time the well-known French type-designer, Robert Granjon, printed a few books in Paris in partnership with Michel Fezendat. Our Pica roman appears in those books, so that it is no surprise to find it under the title 'Cicero Antiqua de Granjon' on the specimen-sheets of J. P. Fievet, 1664 and of J. D. Fievet, 1682, of Frankfort. (On the 1664 sheet the wrong roman is so described, corrected on the 1682 sheet.) The type had a fairly wide sale in Europe; we have noted its use in Venice by Paolo Manuzio, and by Girolamo Scotto in 1557, at Antwerp in 1558, and in Frankfort in 1574. The italic which the Cambridge Press used with this Pica is not on the Van Dijk sheets. Except for the swash J, this italic agrees with the Cicero italic shown by Voskens, which is a sixteenth-century type cut by Robert Granjon, and shown on most of the specimens of the Luther Foundry at Frankfort.

There is in existence at the press, 'A Specimen of the Letters belonging to the University of Cambridge', a unique sheet which displays romans and italics from two-line English to Minion, and also a few exotics. Unfortunately, so little of each size is shown that identification is difficult. In the case of the Pica roman, however, we are helped by the fact that this size is used for the headings. We can confidently identify the 'Old Pica' as the roman used for the notes of the *Horace* of 1699 and in the edition of Tory of 1549, the 'Cicero Antiqua de Granjon'. We can also identify the 'Old Great Primer' and 'Oldest Great Primer' as Van Dijk's Text, roman and italic, and the 'New Great Primer' as Caslon's. The sheet is not dated, but on two of the specimens the dates 1730 and 1721 occur, apparently with no special significance. Since Caslon's Great Primer is shown, the sheet can hardly have been printed before 1732.

There are still two other Dutch types, or types purchased in Holland, found in Cambridge books of this period. The edition of Sir Thomas Browne's *Christian Morals*, 1716, is set in a roman, English in size, which was used for the main text of the edition of John Selden's works printed at London in three large volumes in 1726, and it is so like Caslon that it has been mistaken for his (see below, p. 232). The italic used with it is Van Dijk's Augustijn. Part of the second volume of the *Selden* is set in a different roman, still with the same Van Dijk italic, a type which also was at Cambridge and which is shown on the Van Dijk sheets. It is his Augustijn No. 2, which according to Enschedé was not cut by Van Dijk, but came from the Luther Foundry at Frankfort. It does not appear on the earliest Frankfort sheets, but on a sheet of 1664. This roman has a lower-case 'g', in which the loop is rather wider than the bowl, and if we may trust to this one letter, it appears to be the 'Old English No. 2' of the Cambridge specimen-sheet. As to its use in Cambridge-printed books, it will be found in several volumes of the octavo edition of the works of Cicero. This edition, known as the edition *cum notis variorum*, began to appear in 1725, and its publication extended over a number of years. The *Academica*, 1725, edited by John Davies, is set in the Augustijn No. 2 of the Van Dijk sheet, and with it is used the italic also shown by Van Dijk. This second Augustijn italic of the Dutch founder is a mixed affair, the upper-case only, according to Enschedé, being cut by Van Dijk, while the lower-case is Granjon, dating from about 1560. The succeeding volumes of the Cambridge *Cicero* remained the same in format and in typography, until we come to the *De Oratore*, 1732, in the edition of Zachary Pearce. This volume is in the same format, but the type used is Caslon's English roman and italic. This size of Caslon had been used already at Cambridge in Cicero's *De Divinatione*, 1730, but only in the address to the reader. Caslon's Great Primer, which, as already mentioned, appears on the Cambridge specimen-sheet, I have not found before 1733, in *Remarks on Christianity as Old as Creation* by M. Tindall.

We have enumerated seven romans and five italics used at Cambridge which were Dutch, or at least purchased in Holland, and this list could, no doubt, be extended. There were probably some Dutch titlings, and almost certainly some of the sizes below Pica were similarly acquired. As to these smaller sizes, it is more difficult to identify designs with confidence. All the main body types used at Cambridge in this period were of Dutch origin, and these new types were chiefly responsible for the decided improvement in the University printing.

⌈ 11 ⌋

WILLIAM CASLON, 1720

P RINTING had reached a low ebb in England in the early years of the eighteenth century. A glance through any of the common public prints of the day, such, for instance, as official broadsides, political pamphlets, works of literature, or even Bibles,[1] points to a depression and degeneration so marked that one is tempted to believe that the art of Caxton and Pynson and Day was rapidly becoming lost in a wilderness of what a contemporary satirist terms

Brown sheets and sorry letter.

Few printers of the day were contributing anything towards the revival of good printing, or even towards the maintenance of such a standard as did exist. Grover and Andrews, the heritors of the old founders, originated little or nothing; and where their efforts were put into requisition (as in the case of Andrews's attempt to cut the Anglo-Saxon for Miss Elstob's *Grammar*) they failed. Scarcely a work with any pretension to fine printing was the impression of honest English type. Watson, the Scottish historian of printing, openly rebuked his brethren of the craft for not stocking their cases with Dutch type. Tonson, a king among English printers, on one occasion lodged in Amsterdam while a founder there was casting him £300 worth of type; and James, the only English founder whose business showed any vitality, owed his success chiefly, if not entirely, to the fact that all his letter was the product of Dutch matrices; and even these, in his hands, were so indifferently cast as to be often as bad as English type.

What was the reason for this lamentable decline—how far it was chargeable on the printer, how far on the founder, or how far both were the victims of that system of Star Chamber decrees, monopolies, patents, restraints, and privileges which had characterized the illiberal days of the Stuarts—this is not the place to inquire. Nor, happily, are we called upon to speculate as to what would have been the consequence to English typography of an uninterrupted prolongation of the malady under which it laboured. But it is necessary to remind ourselves of the critical nature of that malady in order to appreciate properly the providential circumstance which turned

---

[1] In 1703, in the Convocation of Clergy in the Lower House, a complaint was exhibited against the printers of the Bible for the careless and defective way in which it was printed by the patentees. The editions specially complained of were those printed by Hayes, of Cambridge, in 1677 and 1678, and an edition in folio printed in London by the King's printers in 1701. The printers continued, however, to print the Bible carelessly, with a defective type, on bad paper; and when printed, to sell copies at an exorbitant price. See John Lewis's *A Complete History of the several translations of the Bible*, London, 1818, 3rd edition, p. 350.

the attention of William Caslon to typefounding, and thus served to avert from England the disgrace which threatened her.

William Caslon[1] was born at Cradley, Halesowen, in Shropshire in the year 1692. He served his apprenticeship to an engraver of gun-locks and barrels in London, and at the expiration of his term followed his trade in Vine Street, near the Minories.

FIG. 55. William Caslon.

The ability he displayed in his art was conspicuous, and by no means confined to the mere ornamentation of gun-barrels—the chasing of silver and the designing of tools for bookbinders frequently occupying his attention. While thus engaged, some of his bookbinding punches were noticed for their neatness and accuracy by John Watts,[2] the eminent printer, who, fully alive to the present degenerate state of the typographical art in this country, was quick to recognize the possibility of raising it once more to its proper position. He accordingly encouraged Caslon to persevere in letter-cutting, promising him his personal support, and favouring him meanwhile with introductions to some of the leading printers of the day.

About the same time, it is recorded that another great printer, the elder Bowyer,[3] 'accidentally saw in the shop of Mr. Daniel Browne, bookseller, near Temple Bar, the lettering of a book, uncommonly neat; and enquiring who the artist was by whom the letters were made, Mr. Caslon was introduced to his acquaintance, and was taken by him to Mr. James's foundery in Bartholomew Close. Caslon had

[1] The following sketch of William Caslon is mainly taken, and in parts quoted, from the interesting particulars of his career preserved in Nichols's *Anecdotes of Bowyer* and the larger work into which that was subsequently expanded. The elder Bowyer's intimate connexion with Caslon's first ventures in letter-founding give Nichols's work a special authority in the matter. At the same time there exists a certain confusion in the earlier part of the narrative which it is difficult completely to harmonize.

[2] John Watts, for some time partner with Jacob Tonson II in Covent Garden. It was in Watts's printing-office in Wild Court, off Great Wild Street

(now Wild St.), that Benjamin Franklin worked as journeyman in 1725. Watts died in 1763, aged 85.

[3] William Bowyer, the elder, regarded as one of the foremost printers of his time, was born in 1663. In 1699 he had his office in Dogwell Court, Whitefriars. His premises were burnt in 1713, and in the conflagration he lost all his types and presses. For all particulars respecting Bowyer and his learned son, see Nichols's *Anecdotes of William Bowyer*, London, 1782, 4to, and *Literary Anecdotes of the 18th Century*, London, 1812–15, 9 vols., 8vo, a work the foundation of which is a bibliography of the productions of this celebrated press.

never before that time seen any part of the business; and being asked by his friend if he thought he could undertake to cut types, he requested a single day to consider the matter, and then replied he had no doubt but he could. From this answer, Mr. Bowyer lent him £200, Mr. Bettenham[1] (to whom also he had been introduced) lent the same sum, and Mr. Watts £100.'[2]

With this assistance Caslon established himself in a garret in Helmet Row, Old Street, and devoted himself with ardour to his new profession.[3] An opportunity for distinguishing himself presented itself shortly afterwards. In the year 1720 the Society for Promoting Christian Knowledge,[4] acting on a suggestion made by Salomon Negri, a native of Damascus, and a distinguished Oriental scholar, 'deemed it expedient to print for the Eastern Churches the *New Testament* and *Psalter* in the Arabic language for the benefit of the poor Christians in Palestine, Syria, Mesapotamia, Arabia and Egypt, the constitution of which countries allowed of no printing'. A new Arabic fount being required for the purpose, Caslon, whose reputation as a letter-cutter appears already to have been known, was selected to cut it. This he did to the full satisfaction of his patrons, producing the elegant English Arabic which figures in his early specimens. The Society was, according to Rowe Mores, already possessed of a fount of Arabic cast from the Polyglot matrices in Grover's foundry. But Caslon's fount was preferred for the text, and in it appeared, in due time, first the *Psalter* in 1725,[5] and afterwards the *New Testament* in 1727.[6]

الحبيب القاري اللبيب * ان الاب الفاضل
كافة العلوم نامه * كبركبر اعلم ايها الاخ
الرومية ـفي الامصار الكلبي احترامه والذابع ـفي

FIG. 56. Caslon's Arabic.

Mr. Caslon, after he had finished his Arabic fount, cut the letters of his own name in Pica Roman, and placed the name at the bottom of a specimen of the Arabic[7]; and Mr. Palmer

[1] James Bettenham, husband of the elder Bowyer's step-daughter, was born 1683. He printed in St. John's Lane, and attained to considerable eminence as a printer, although after sixty years' labour he left behind him only £400. 'He died', says Rowe Mores, 'in 1774, *ferè centenarius sanaeque mentis et memoriae.*' [2] *Anecdotes of Bowyer*, p. 585.

[3] A tradition in the Caslon family that William Caslon began his career as a letter-founder in 1716 induced H. W. Caslon to adopt this as the date of the establishment of the foundry. In the absence, however, of any testimony in support of the statement, and in the face of the clear announcement by Caslon himself that his foundry was begun in the year 1720, there seems to be no ground for attaching any importance to the use of this earlier date.

[4] This Society, which was established in 1698, had already displayed considerable activity in the introduction of printing into the distant fields of its missionary effort. In 1711 it sent out to the Danish missionaries of Tranquebar, on the Coromandel Coast, a printing press furnished with Portuguese types, paper, &c., which, after an adventurous voyage, in which the vessel was plundered by the French of all her other cargo, reached its destination and enabled the missionaries to commence the printing of a Tamulic *New Testament*, of which the

Gospels appeared in 1714, with the imprint *Tranquebariae in littore Coromandelino, typis Malabaricis impressit G. Adler*, 1714. It is related that the publication of the remainder of the work was delayed from a scarcity of paper, their types being very large; till at length the expedient was adopted of casting a new fount of letter from the leaden covers of some Cheshire cheeses, which had been sent out to the missionaries by the Society. The attempt succeeded, and with these new and smaller types the remainder of the Testament was printed, the whole being published together in 1719. (Cotton, *Typographical Gazetteer*, 2nd edit., p. 289.) The Tamil type, the one which proved too large, was procured from Halle. See above, p. 69.

[5] *Liber Psalmorum . . . una cum decem Praeceptis . . . et Oratione Dominicâ . . . Arabicè; sumptibus Societatis de Propagandâ Cognitione Christi apud Exteros*, London, 1725. 8vo.

[6] *Novum Testamentum, Arabicè. Londini. Sumptibus Societatis de Propagandâ Cognitione Christi apud Exteros*, 1727. 4to.

[7] 'This circumstance', says Nichols (*Anec. Bowyer*, p. 317) 'has lately been verified by the American, Dr. Franklin, who was at that time a journeyman under Mr. Watts, the first printer that employed Mr. Caslon.'

(the reputed author of Psalmanazar's *History of Printing*), seeing this name, advised Mr. Caslon to complete the fount of Pica. Mr. Caslon did so; and as the performance exceeded the letter of the other founders of the time, Mr. Palmer—whose circumstances required credit with those who, by his advice, were now obstructed (*i.e.*, whose business was likely to suffer from this new rival)—repented having given the advice, and discouraged Mr. Caslon from any further progress.

PICA ROMAN.

Melium, novis rebus ftudentem, manu fua occîdit.
Fuit, fuit ifta quondam in hac repub. virtus, ut viri
fortes acrioribus fuppliciis civem perniciofum, quam

Pica Italick.

Melium, novis rebus ftudentem, manu fua occîdit.
Fuit, fuit ifta quondam in hac repub. virtus, ut viri
fortes acrioribus fuppliciis civem perniciofum, quam a-

FIG. 57. Caslon's Pica Roman and Italic.

Mr. Caslon, disgusted,[1] applied to Mr. Bowyer, under whose inspection he cut, in 1722, the beautiful fount of English [Roman] which was used in printing *Selden's Works*,[2] 1726.

John Nichols, then, was responsible for these irreconcilable accounts of Caslon's introduction to typefounding and for the statement that Caslon's English roman was used in Selden's *Works*. Rowe Mores in his story of the origin of the Caslon Foundry makes no mention of Selden, but subsequent writers have generally repeated Nichols's inaccurate account.[3] The roman, of English size, used for most of the text, is in fact Dutch, and also the italic, which is that of Christoffel van Dijk. In an appendix we add a fuller account of the typography of this work.

Caslon's next performance was a fount of Pica Coptic for Dr. Wilkins's[4] edition of the *Pentateuch*,[5] a letter which Rowe Mores commends as superior to the Oxford Coptic in which Dr. Wilkins's *New Testament* had been printed in 1716.[6] This

---

[1] Dibdin, in repeating this anecdote, uses rather stronger language. 'Caslon,' he says, 'after giving (I would hope) that wretched pilferer and driveller Samuel Palmer (whose *History of Printing* is only fit for chincampane paper) half a dozen good canings for his dishonesty, betook himself to Mr. Bowyer.' (*Bibl. Decam.* ii. 379.)

[2] *Joannis Seldeni Jurisconsulti Opera Omnia, tam edita quam inedita. In tribus voluminibus. Collegit ac recensuit . . . David Wilkins, S.T.P. . . . Londini, Typis Guil. Bowyer.* 1726. Fol. (Begun in 1722.)

[3] In the notes, dated 16 Nov. 1779, to Mores's *Dissertation*, on p. 98, after mentioning the Hebrew used in Selden, Nichols continues: 'The first font which he [Caslon] cast was an English roman and italic for the elder Mr. Bowyer, which was also used in Selden.' In the *Biographical and Literary Anecdotes of William Bowyer*, 1782 (p. 317), and later in his *Literary Anecdotes of the Eighteenth Century*, 1812 (vol. ii, p. 356), he says that in 1722 Caslon cut the beautiful fount of English which was used in printing Selden's *Works*, 1726.

[4] Dr. David Wilkins, F.S.A., was Keeper of the Lambeth Library under Archbishop Wake, and drew up a Catalogue of all the manuscripts and books there in his time. Besides editing the *Selden* and the *Coptic Testament* and *Pentateuch*, he published some important works in Anglo-Saxon literature, and edited the learned Prolegomena to Chamberlayne's *Oratio Dominica* in 1715 and the *Concilia*, 1737. He died in 1740. Rowe Mores considers that in his Coptic studies Dr. Wilkins was indebted to Kircher, the Jesuit, whose *Prodromus Coptus*, published in Rome in 1636, the doctor had severely handled. His name was originally Wilke; he was of Prussian parentage. See *D.N.B.* and D. C. Douglas, *English Scholars*, 1939.

[5] *Quinque Libri Moysis Prophetae in Linguâ Aegyptiâ. Ex M.S.S. . . . descripsit ac Latine vertit Dav. Wilkins. Londini* 1731. 4to. Only 200 copies were printed.

[6] See above, pp. 141, 142. Nichols, writing about 1813, mentioned that the Coptic fount, having escaped the conflagration of his printing-office in 1808, was still in his possession.

fount Caslon also cut under the direction of Bowyer, his generous patron, whom he always acknowledged as his master from whom he had learned his art.

Πενιωτ ετ ⳁεнни φнοϯ ⸭- ⲙⲙ-
ρεϥ τοⲩⲃοⲛⳉε ⲡⲉⲕⲣⲁⲛ ⸭- ⲙⲙⲣⲉⲥ
ⲓⲛⳉⲉⲧⲉⲕⲙⲙⲉ τοⲩⲣⲟ ⸭- ⲛⲉⲧⲉⲅⲛⲁⲕ

Fɪɢ. 58. Caslon's Coptic.

Caslon's business, thus established, rapidly advanced in fame and excellence. Although at the outset it depended mainly on the support of his three chief patrons, it was soon able to stand alone and compete with the best houses in the trade.

It is difficult [observes Hansard] to appreciate the obstacles which Mr. Caslon encountered at the commencement of his career. At present the theory and practice of letter-founding are not, as in his time, an 'art and mystery', and efficient workmen in every branch are easily procured. He had not only to excel his competitors in his own particular branch of engraving the punches, which to him was probably the easiest part of his task, but to raise an establishment and cause his plans to be executed by ignorant and unpractised workmen. He had also to acquire for himself a knowledge of the practical and mechanical branches of the art, which require, indeed, little genius, but the most minute and painful attention to conduct successfully. The wishes and expectations of his patrons were fulfilled and exceeded by his decided superiority over his domestic rivals and Batavian competitors. The importation of foreign types ceased; his founts were, in fact, in such estimation as to be frequently, in their turn, exported to the Continent.[1]

In 1728 Caslon narrowly escaped committing an error which might seriously have affected his after career. The foundry of the Grovers being then in the market, he contracted for the purchase of it.[2] Fortunately for English typography, the business fell through, and Caslon was still left a free man to pursue his own method, unburdened by the incubus of a large and useless stock of matrices, which, had they been suffered to mingle with his own beautiful productions, would have degraded his foundry to a patchwork establishment little better than that of his competitors at home and abroad. As it was, he had the advantage of completing his specimens after his own plan, and impressing with the mark of his own genius every fount which bore his name.

His fame in 1730 was such that (as Ged, in his narrative of the invention of block-printing, states) he had already eclipsed most of his competitors, had introduced his founts into some of the chief printing-houses of the metropolis, and even secured the custom of the King's printers to the exclusion of all others. Although Ged's narrative goes to show that Caslon shared the scepticism of his contemporaries with regard to the utility of stereotyping, and was even ready to back his opinion with his money, it is satisfactory to observe that he was no party to the discreditable persecution to which that unfortunate inventor was subjected by other members of the craft. Indeed, the only successful experiment made by Ged appears to have been a cast from Caslon's type.

That the success of the new foundry was not achieved wholly without opposition

---

[1] *Typographia*, p. 349.   [2] See p. 200.

is apparent from the following anecdote preserved by Nichols, and told in connexion with the account of Bishop Hare's *Hebrew Psalter*, published by Bowyer in 1736.[1] This work, it appears, had been originally intended to be printed at the press of Palmer, with whom Caslon, as we have seen, had already had dealings of a not altogether satisfactory character.

His Lordship, however, [says Nichols] (quoting Psalmanazar's account of the transaction), had excepted against Mr. Palmer's Hebrew types which were of Athias' font, and a little battered, and insisted upon his having a new set from Mr. Caslon, which greatly exceeded them in beauty. But Mr. Palmer was so deeply in debt to him (Caslon) that he knew not how to procure it from him without ready money, which he was not able to spare. The Bishop likewise insisted upon having some Roman and Italic types cast with some distinguishing mark, to direct his readers to the Hebrew letters they were designed to answer, and these required a new set of punches and matrices before they could be cast; and that would have delayed the work, which Mr. Palmer was in haste to go about that he might the sooner finger some of his Lordship's money. This put him upon such an unfair stratagem as, when discovered, quite disgusted his lordship against him; namely, representing Mr. Caslon as an idle, dilatory workman, who would in all probability make them wait several years for those few types, if ever he finished them. That he was indeed the only Artist that could supply him with those types, but that he hated work and was not to be depended upon; and therefore advised his Lordship to make shift with some sort which he could substitute and would answer the same purpose, rather than run the risk of staying so long and being perhaps disappointed.

The Bishop, however, being resolved, if possible, to have the desired types, sent for Mr. Bowyer, and asked him whether he knew a letter-founder that could cast him such a set out of hand, who immediately recommended Mr. Caslon; and being told what sad and disadvantageous character he had heard of him, Mr. Bowyer not only assured his Lordship that it was a very false and unjust one, but engaged to get the above-mentioned types cast by him, and a new font of his Hebrew ones, in as short a time as the thing could possibly be done. Mr. Caslon was accordingly sent for by his Lordship, and having made him sensible of the time the new ones would require to be made ready for use, did produce them according to his promise, and the book was soon after put to the press.[2]

Among the other interesting founts cut by Caslon about this time may be mentioned the Pica black, of which we show a specimen, and which received special commendation for its faithful following of the traditional Old English character first used by Wynkyn de Worde.

FIG. 59. Caslon's Pica black.

He also cut an Armenian for the Whistons' edition of *Moses Chorenensis*,[3] and an Etruscan for John Swinton of Oxford,[4] the learned antiquary and philologist (a few

---

[1] *Anec. Bowyer*, p. 537.
[2] *Psalmorum Liber in Versiculos metrice divisus, etc.* (*Heb. et Lat.*). *Londini*, 1736. 2 vols., 8vo.
[3] *Moses Chorenensis Historiae Armeniacae Libri iii. Armeniacè ediderunt, Latinè verterunt notisq: illustr.*

Guil. et Geo. Whistoni, London, 1736. 4to.
[4] See Mores's *Dissertation*, p. 35. The type was shown on the Caslon specimen-sheet of 1748. The Coptic, Gothic, Armenian, Syriac, Samaritan, and Arabic appeared on the first sheet of 1734.

letters appear in Swinton's *De primogenio Etruscorum alphabeto*, 1746); as well as a Gothic and several other of the foreign and learned characters.

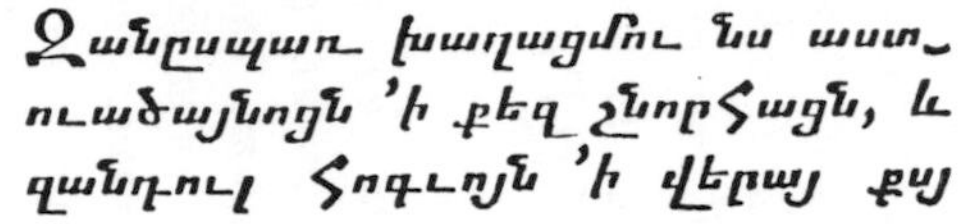

Fig. 60. Caslon's Armenian.

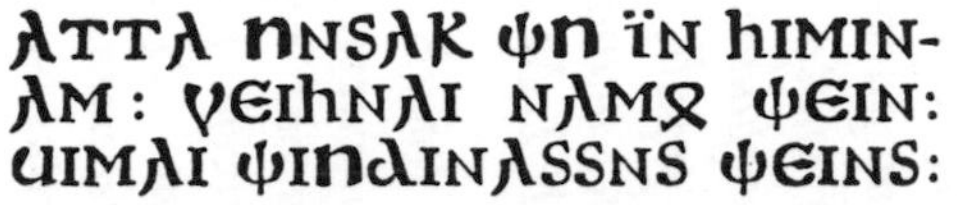

Fig. 61. Caslon's Gothic.

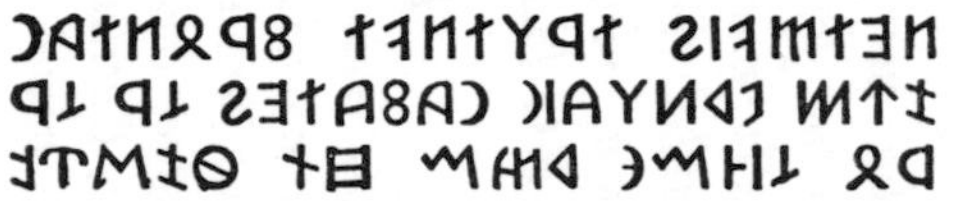

Fig. 62. Caslon's Etruscan.

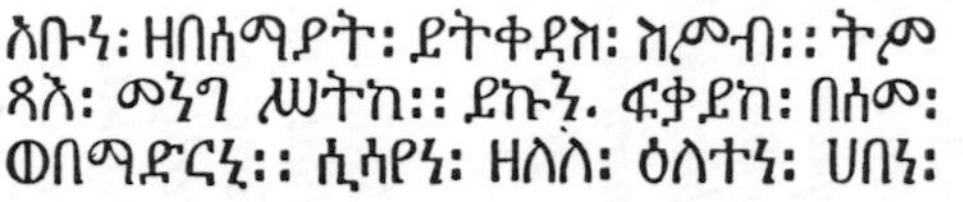

Fig. 63. Caslon's Ethiopic.

All of these, with the exception of the Etruscan and an Ethiopic cut by Caslon junior, were completed before 1734, in which year the first *Specimen* of his foundry appeared. This famous broadside, of which very few copies are now extant, dates from Ironmonger Row,[1] to which address Caslon had transferred the Helmet Row Foundry.

The sheet is arranged in four columns and displays altogether thirty-eight founts, namely:

Titlings.—Five-line Pica, four-line Pica, two-line Great Primer, two-line English, two-line Pica, two-line Long Primer, two-line Brevier.

Roman and Italic.—French Canon, two-line Great Primer, two-line English, Double Pica, Great Primer, English, Pica, Small Pica (2), Long Primer (2), Brevier, Nonpareil, and Pearl.

Saxon.—Pica and Long Primer.

Black.—Pica and Brevier.

Gothic, Coptic, Armenian, Samaritan.—Pica of each.

Syriac and *Arabic.*—English of each.

Hebrew.—English, English with points, Brevier.

Greek.—English, Pica, Long Primer, Brevier.

Flowers.—Seven designs.

Of these, all, with three exceptions, are Caslon's own handiwork, and represent the untiring industry of fourteen years. Of the excellence of the performance it is sufficient to say that the specimen placed Caslon absolutely without rival at the head of his profession; 'and,' as Nichols says, 'for clearness and uniformity, for the use of the reader and student, it is doubtful whether it has been exceeded by any subsequent production'.

From the entries in the Rate Book we find that Caslon was in Ironmonger Row from 1727 to 1737.

Great Primer Roman.

Quousque tandem abutére, Catilina, patientia noſtra ? quamdiu nos etiam furor iſte tuus eludet? quem ad finem ſeſe effrenata jactabit audacia ? nihilne te
nocturnum præſidium palatii, nihil urbis vigiliæ, nihil timor populi, nihil con-
ABCDEFGHIJKLMNOPQRS

English Roman.

Quouſque tandem abutére, Catilina, patientia
noſtra? quamdiu nos etiam furor iſte tuus eludet?
quem ad finem ſeſe effrenata jactabit audacia ?
nihilne te nocturnum præſidium palatii, nihil ur-
urbis vigiliæ, nihil timor populi, nihil conſen-
fus bonorum omnium, nihil hic munitiſſimus ſe-
ABCDEFGHIJKLMNOPQRSTVU

Pica Roman.

Melium, novis rebus ſtudentem, manu ſua occidit.
Fuit, fuit iſta quondam in hac repub. virtus, ut viri
fortes acrioribus ſuppliciis civem pernicioſum, quam
acerbiſſimum hoſtem coërcerent. Habemus enim ſenatuſconſultum in te, Catilina, vehemens, & grave:
non deeſt reip. conſilium, neque autoritas hujus ordinis: nos, nos, dico aperte, conſules defumus. De-
ABCDEFGHIJKLMNOPQRSTVUWX

Small Pica Roman. No 1.

At nos vigeſimum jam diem patimur hebeſcere aciem horum
autoritatis. habemus enim hujuſmodi ſenatuſconſultum, ve-
rumtamen incluſum in tabulis, tanquam gladium in vagina
reconditum: quo ex ſenatuſconſulto confeſtim interfectum te
eſſe, Catilina, convenit. Vivis: & vivis non ad deponendam, ſed ad confirmandam audaciam. Cupio, P. C., me
effe clementem ; cupio in tantis reipub. periculis non diſ

Great Primer Italick.

Quouſque tandem abutére, Catilina, patientia noſtra ? quamdiu nos etiam furor iſte tuus eludet ? quem ad finem ſeſe
effrenata jactabit audacia ? nihilne te
nocturnum præſidium palatii, nihil urbis vigiliæ, nihil timor populi, nihil con-
ABCDEFGHIJKLMNOPQR

English Italick.

Quouſque tandem abutére, Catilina, patientia noſtra? quamdiu nos etiam furor iſte tuus eludet?
quem ad finem ſeſe effrenata jactabit audacia ?
nihilne te nocturnum præſidium palatii, nihil urbis vigiliæ, nihil timor populi, nihil conſenſus bonorum omnium, nihil hic munitiſſimus habendi ſe-
ABCDEFGHIJKLMNOPQRSTVU

Pica Italick.

Melium, novis rebus ſtudentem, manu ſua occidit.
Fuit, fuit iſta quondam in hac repub. virtus, ut viri
fortes acrioribus ſuppliciis civem pernicioſum, quam a-
cerbiſſimum hoſtem coërcerent. Habemus enim ſenatuſconſultum in te, Catilina, vehemens, & grave: non deeſt
reip. conſilium, neque autoritas hujus ordinis: nos, nos,
dico aperte, conſules defumus. Decrevit quondam ſenatus
ABCDEFGHIJKLMNOPQRSTVUWXYZ

Small Pica Italick. No 1.

At nos vigeſimum jam diem patimur hebeſcere aciem borum
autoritatis. habemus enim bujuſmodi ſenatuſconſultum, verum-
tamen incluſum in tabulis, tanquam gladium in vagina reconditum: quo ex ſenatuſconſulto confeſtim interfectum te eſſe, Catilina, convenit. Vivis: & vivis non ad deponendam, ſed ad
confirmandam audaciam. Cupio, P. C., me eſſe clementem :
cupio in tantis reipub. periculis non diſſolutum videri, ſed jam

The three founts referred to as not the product of Caslon's hand were the Canon roman, from Andrews's foundry, formerly Moxon's, and exhibited in the *Mechanick Exercises*;[1] the English Syriac, which is from the matrices of the *Polyglot*;[2] and the Pica Samaritan, which was cut by a Dutchman named Dummers.

Fame appears to have followed rapidly on the appearance of this specimen. The sheet, dated 1734, but with the address altered to Chiswell Street,[3] was included as an inset plate in the second edition of Ephraim Chambers's *Cyclopaedia* in 1738,[4] with the following flattering notice: 'The above were all cast in the foundery of Mr. W. Caslon, a person who, though not bred to the art of letter-founding, has, by dint of genius, arrived at an excellency in it unknown hitherto in England, and which even surpasses anything of the kind done in Holland or elsewhere.'

Caslon made a further addition to his stock of matrices in 1739 by the purchase of half of Mitchell's foundry,[5] of which the most interesting items were a Pica Greek, sets of music and flower matrices, and six sizes of black. The remainder, consisting of romans and italics, do not appear to have added much to the resources of the Chiswell Street Foundry.[6] Some of these possibly appear on the sheet issued in 1742. There are some additional titlings and flowers, harps, and crowns, which may be of the seventeenth century. In particular the Long Primer black differs in design from Caslon's other blacks. On this 1742 sheet twelve of the specimens are signed 'W. Caslon junior sculp.'.

Nichols says, 'the abilities of the second Caslon appeared to great advantage in the specimen of the types of the learned languages in 1748.'[7] A copy of this sheet was described by D. B. Updike in No. 1 of *The Fleuron*, p. 117. It contains thirty-three founts of learned types, fourteen being signed: 'W. Caslon Junior Sculp.' The style of the firm has now become 'William Caslon and Son'. A further specimen was issued in the following year, in broadside form, which displayed a large variety of letters, from Canon to Pearl, many of them being the handiwork of Caslon the younger. It is possible that this last sheet may have been sent, for the most part, abroad; for while no copy of it is to be found in this country, we find one

[1] This fount may be seen also in Nichols's Appendix to Rowe Mores's *Dissertation*, p. 96, and in Ames's *Typographical Antiquities*, 1st edit., p. 571.

[2] If these were the matrices which Mores, in his summary of the Polyglot Foundry (p. 160, above), described as Great Primer, it is difficult—unless they were duplicates—to determine through whose foundry they passed into Caslon's hands. Andrews had a Great Primer, and Grover a Double Pica and Pica; but all these came to James, in whose foundry they remained when Mores wrote in 1778.

[3] When Caslon first moved to Chiswell Street in 1737, the houses were not numbered. It was only after Acts passed in 1765 and 1766 that the numbering of houses was carried out in general. Caslon's house was on the north side of the street and in the *Directory* for 1774 appears as No. 62. It remained 62 down to 1824, but in 1825 appears as No. 22. The whole street must have been renumbered at this time. The firm ultimately moved to the opposite side of the street, to Nos. 82 and 83. There is nothing left of either site after the bombing raids of 1940 and 1941.

[4] *Cyclopaedia, or an Universal Dictionary of the Arts and Sciences, etc.*, by E. Chambers, F.R.S.,

London, 1738. 2 vols., fol. (Caslon's specimen faces the article 'Letter'.) For the various issues of the sheet see Berry and Johnson, pp. 13–15. The first edition of this valuable work—the first repertory of general knowledge published in Britain—appeared in 1728. It subsequently formed the basis of Rees's *Encyclopaedia*.

[5] See p. 201.

[6] Rowe Mores's account of the Caslon Foundry in 1778, wherein he attributes several of the founts which originally appeared in the 1734 specimen to Mitchell, might suggest at first sight that Caslon had acquired Mitchell's foundry prior to 1739. Mores is, however, particular to give the exact date of the purchase, 26 July 1739. It seems more probable that, finding the bodies in Caslon's specimen corresponding generally with the description of the matrices he was known to have bought from Mitchell, he concluded hastily that the founts shown were Mitchell's, whereas a reference to the specimen would have proved that Caslon preferred his own original faces, in most cases, to those he had bought. See also our notes, pp. 243–4.

[7] *Anec. Bowyer*, p. 586.

mentioned with commendation by Fournier in 1766,[1] and another preserved to this day in the Sohmian Collection at Stockholm, where, along with several other rare English and foreign specimens, it was discovered by William Blades.

In Ames's *Typographical Antiquities*,[2] published in 1749, appears a specimen of 'Mr. Caslon's Roman letter and the names of the sizes now in use', the introductory note to which affords the first literary notice of the younger Caslon in connexion with the foundry. 'The art', says Ames, 'seems to be carried to its greatest perfection by Mr. William Caslon, and his son, who, besides the type of all manner of living languages now by him, has offered to perform the same for the dead, that can be recovered, to the satisfaction of any gentleman desirous of the same.'

Another contemporary record of equal interest, which seems, moreover, to allude to one or more of the three specimens above mentioned, is contained in a little essay on the *Original, Use, and Excellency of Printing*, published in 1752;[3] in which the anonymous writer, after dealing with the invention, remarks:

Altho' the chief honour is due to the Inventor, yet the perfection and beauty that Printing is now arrived at is very much owing to them that came after. Many in the present age have not a little contributed thereto. Among whom I cannot but particularly mention Mr. William Caslon and his Son, Letter Founders in Chiswell Street, who have very much by their indefatigable labours promoted the honour of this Art, and who have lately printed three broadsheet specimens of their curious types; one of them consisting of all the common sorts of letter used in printing; the second sheet is divers sorts of their Orientals, Old-English, and Saxon; and the third contains a great variety of curious Flowers and Fancies for Ornamenting of Title Pages, Tickets, &c., also several sorts of Titling letter of Roman, Old-English and Greek; and the whole, for their master strokes and curious flourishes, outdo all that have been cast in England, Holland or any other place before.

The above is one of many compliments paid to Caslon at this period by his contemporaries. John Smith, in his *Printer's Grammar* in 1755, goes out of his way more than once to commend the founder by whose genius 'letter is now in England of such a beautiful cut and shape as it never was before'. Baskerville, in a passage quoted elsewhere,[4] frankly acknowledges him as the greatest master of the art. Ames and Chambers, as has been noticed, vie with one another in proclaiming his pre-eminence; Mores himself styles him the Coryphaeus of modern letter-founders, and Lemoine awards him the title of the English Elzevir. In 1750 Caslon's reputation was such that His Majesty George II placed him on the Commission of the Peace for Middlesex, which office he sustained with honour to himself and advantage to the community till the time of his death.

In June of the same year the *Universal Magazine*[5] contained an article on Letter

---

[1] 'Les caractères de Caslon ont été gravés, pour la plus grande partie, par Caslon fils, avec beaucoup d'adresse et de propreté. Les épreuves qui en ont été publiées en 1749 contiennent beaucoup de sortes différentes de caractères' (*Man. Typog.* II. xxxviii). The Sohmian Typographical Collection was made by Peter Sohm, printer at Stockholm, 1750–1819. A catalogue of the collection was published in 1812 and another edition in 1815. It now forms part of the Royal Library at Stockholm.

[2] *Typographical Antiquities*, London, 1749, p. 571. The names of William Caslon, sen., and William Caslon, jun., letter-founders, figure among the sub-

scribers to the work; and the plate of facsimiles of Caxton's types is dedicated 'to Mr. Wm. Caslon, a good promoter of this work, and as suitable to the principal Letter Founder'.

[3] *An Essay on the Original, Use, and Excellency of the Noble Art and Mystery of Printing*, London, 1752. 8vo. The work is of little interest apart from the references to the Caslons, and a curious poem at the end.

[4] See below, p. 274.

[5] *The Universal Magazine of Knowledge and Pleasure*, London, vol. vi, June 1750, p. 274.

Founding, extracted chiefly from Moxon, and accompanied by a view of the interior of Caslon's foundry, containing portraits of six of his workmen (see our Frontispiece). The view represents four casters at work, one rubber (Joseph Jackson), one dresser (Thomas Cottrell), and three boys breaking off, &c. Considering the extent of the business at the time, it may be doubted whether this represents the entire working staff of the establishment, or whether the view is of a portion only, in which, for the convenience of the artist, the four processes of the manufacture are assembled. The processes of punch-cutting and justifying were conducted in private by the Caslons themselves; yet not, as history shows, in such secrecy as to prevent their two apprentices, Cottrell and Jackson, from observing and learning the manual operation of that part of the 'art and mystery'.[1]

A movement among the workmen of the foundry in 1757 for a higher scale of wages, although decided in favour of the men, resulted in the dismissal of the two ex-apprentices, who were supposed to have been ringleaders in the movement. With the experience acquired during their term of service at Chiswell Street, both these men were enabled to establish foundries of their own; and it is to the credit of Cottrell's good sense, if not of his good feeling, that he subsequently supported his own claim to the patronage of the trade by announcing on his specimens that he had 'served his apprenticeship to William Caslon, Esq.'.

The active part taken by the second Caslon in the operations of the foundry may be best judged of by a reference to the specimen-books of 1763 and 1764. In the 1764 book the number of founts which originally appeared on the broadside of 1734 is more than doubled,[2] most of the additions (with the exception of those which had formed part of Mitchell's foundry) being the handiwork of Caslon II. There are included flowers in the rococo style copied from the Paris founders, Louis Luce and P. S. Fournier. The following advertisement appears on the last page:

This new Foundery was begun in the year 1720, and finish'd 1763; and will (with God's leave) be carried on, improved, and inlarged, by William Caslon, Letter-Founder, in London.—Soli Deo Gloria.

Rowe Mores, whose prejudice against the second Caslon is undisguised, waxes facetious on the head of this innocent declaration,[3] although he can find but little to blame in the specimen itself, 'in which', he says, 'is nothing censurable but the silly notion and silly fondness of multiplying bodies'—the specimen showed a long-bodied English and a large-face Long Primer and Bourgeois—'as if the intrinsic of a foundery consisted in the numerosity of the heads!' Such animadversions, however, leave untouched the younger Caslon's reputation as an able and successful typefounder, which was, indeed, so well established that during the later years of his father's life he appears to have had the sole management of the business.

Caslon I, having lived to see the result of his genius and industry in the regeneration of the art of printing in England, retired, universally respected, from the active

---

[1] See below, p. 311.

[2] Forty-four new founts appear in all, viz.: 2 Titlings, 15 romans, 4 Greeks, 9 Hebrews, 1 Ethiopic, 1 Etruscan, 2 Saxons, 8 blacks, and 2 Music, while the Flowers now number 63 varieties.

[3] '"This New Foundery was begun in the year 1720 and finished 1763." So we are told by a note at the end of their Specimen published in 1764, although the same note tells us that though it was finished, yet it was not finished, "but would (with God's leave) be carried on, etc." Amen!' (*Dissert.*, p. 80.)

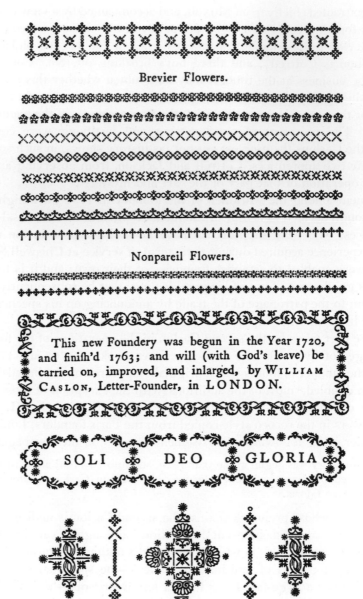

Brevier Flowers.

Nonpareil Flowers.

This new Foundery was begun in the Year 1720, and finiſh'd 1763; and will (with God's leave) be carried on, improved, and inlarged, by WILLIAM CASLON, Letter-Founder, in LONDON.

SOLI ✷ DEO ✷ GLORIA

FIG. 65. Page from the Caslon specimen-book, 1764.

management of the foundry, and took up his residence first in a house opposite the Nag's Head in the Hackney Road, removing afterwards to Water Gruel Row, and finally settling in what was then styled a country house at Bethnal Green, where he resided till the time of his death.

'Mr. Caslon', says Nichols, 'was universally esteemed as a first-rate artist, a tender master, and an honest, friendly, and benevolent man.'[1] The following anecdote, preserved by Sir John Hawkins in his *History of Music*, gives a pleasing glimpse into his private life, and shows that in his devotion to the severer arts the gentler were not neglected.

Mr. Caslon [says Sir John] settled in Ironmonger Row, in Old Street; and being a great lover of music, had frequent concerts at his house, which were resorted to by many eminent masters. To these he used to invite his friends and those of his old acquaintance, the companions of his youth. He afterwards removed to a large house in Chiswell Street, and had an organ in his concert room. After that, he had stated monthly concerts, which, for the convenience of his friends, and that they might walk home in safety when the performance was over, were on that Thursday in the month which was nearest the full moon; from which circumstance his guests were wont humourously to call themselves 'Luna-tics'. In the intervals of the performance the guests refreshed themselves at a sideboard, which was amply furnished; and when it was over, sitting down to a bottle of wine, and a decanter of excellent ale, of Mr. Caslon's own brewing, they concluded the evening's entertainment with a song or two of Purcell's sung to the harpsicord, or a few catches; and, about twelve, retired.[2]

Caslon's hospitalities were not confined to his musical friends merely. His house was a resort of literary men of all classes, of whom large parties frequently assembled to discuss interesting matters relating to books and studies.[3]

Caslon was thrice married. His first wife was Sarah Pearman, his second a Miss Longman, and the third Elizabeth Warter. By his first wife he had two sons and a daughter: William, who succeeded him at Chiswell Street; Thomas, who became an eminent bookseller in Stationers' Hall Court, where he died in 1783, after having in the previous year served the office of Master of the Stationers' Company; and Mary, who married first Godfrey Shewell, one of the original partners in Whitbread's brewery, Chiswell Street, and afterwards Thomas Hanbey, an ironmonger of large fortune. A brother of Caslon, named Samuel, is mentioned by Rowe Mores, and appears to have served at Chiswell Street for a short time as mould-maker, leaving there subsequently, on some dispute, to work in the same capacity for George Anderton of Birmingham.

Caslon died, much respected, at Bethnal Green, on 23 January 1766, aged 74, and was buried in the Churchyard of St. Luke's, the parish in which his three foundries were all situated. The monument to his memory, kept in repair by bequest of his daughter, Mrs. Hanbey, is thus briefly inscribed:

W. CASLON, Esq., ob. 23rd Jan., 1766, aetat 74.

---

[1] Among the relics of the Caslon Foundry is a copy of the 1764 specimen-book presented by Caslon to his friend Phil. Thicknesse the poet. At the end of the book appears Thicknesse's letter of thanks to the donor, execrably printed by the poet himself, in type given him by Caslon.

[2] *A General History of the Science and Practice of Music*, London, 1776, 4to, vol. v, p. 127.

[3] The Rev. Dr. Charles Lyttelton writes to Ames, 25 April 1744, 'Some unforeseen business prevents Dr. [Richard] Pococke and myself dining with Mr. Caslon to-morrow. I give you this notice that you may defer your visit till some day next week, when we will endeavour to meet there.'—Nichols's, *Illustrations of Literature*, iv. 231.

A life-size portrait of him by Francis Kyte was preserved at Chiswell Street, representing him holding in his hand the famous specimen-sheet of 1734.[1]

William Caslon II issued in the year of his father's death a specimen in small
quarto, bearing his own name and containing the same founts as those exhibited in

FIG. 66. The Chiswell Street Foundry.

the 1764 book.[2] This specimen, consisting of thirty-eight leaves, was again reprinted in 1770 by Luckombe in his *History of Printing*,[3] of which work it occupies
pages 134 to 173.

In 1767 the Chiswell Street Foundry was called upon to supply a Syriac fount for
the Oxford University Press, and Caslon produced the Long Primer Syriac which

ܠܝܘܢ ܩܘܡܢܝ ܒܠܝܗܠܒܡ ܂ ܡܚܠܐ ܡܛܚܝܗ
ܚܪܒ ܗܣܩ ܠܢ ܚܠܠܐ ܚܠܐ ܂ ܗܝܢ ܒܪܬܪܝ܃
ܐܗܢ ܐܠܘܝ ܠܐ ܡܚܡܕܟܒܡ ܚܠܐ ܐܠܥܡ ܟܗ ܂

FIG. 67. Caslon Syriac, 1767.

occurs in his subsequent specimens. He had previously supplied the University
with a Long Primer Hebrew, and the old ledgers of the foundry show that numerous
transactions of a similar kind took place during the latter half of the eighteenth
century.

---

[1] Reproduced as the frontispiece in McRae's *Two
Centuries of Typefounding*, 1920. It is now in possession of the Monotype Corporation.

[2] Copies of which he continued to circulate,
erasing with pen and ink the words 'and Son' from
the title-page and advertisement.

[3] *A Concise History of the Origin and Progress of
Printing*, etc., London, 1770. 8vo. Reissued in the
following year with the title: *The History of the Art
of Printing, in two Parts*, etc., *J. P. Luckombe,
M.T.A.*, London, 1771. 8vo.

In 1770, besides the specimen of Luckombe, another indirect specimen of the Caslon types was issued by J. D. Cornish, printer, in Blackfriars, in a very small form—32mo—exhibiting a series of romans, two founts of black, and three pages of flowers. The Society of Antiquaries has a copy.

It was probably on the specimen of 1766 that Rowe Mores founded his summary of the contents of the Caslon Foundry; and it will be interesting to reproduce this list, as it presents a view of the state of the foundry as it then existed, and, at the same time, distinguishes the authors of the several founts with which it was supplied. Rowe Mores seizes the opportunity afforded by this enumeration for another sneer at Caslon II. 'This is the best account', he says, 'we can give of this capital and beautiful foundery, the possessor of which refused to answer the natural questions, because, forsooth, "answering would be of no advantage to us; if we wanted letter to be cast, he would cast it". But this we can do ourselves.'[1]

The summary is as follows:

Mr. CASLON'S FOUNDERY.

ORIENTALS.		
Hebrew.—2-line English.	[Caslon I]	
Double Pica.	[Caslon II]	
Great Primer.	do.	
English.	[Caslon I]	
English open.[2]	do.	
Pica.	[Caslon II]	
Long Primer.[3]	do.	
Brevier.	do.	
2-line Great Primer.	do.	
Samaritan.—Pica.	[Dummers]	
Syriac.—English.	[Polyglot]	
Arabic.—English.	[Caslon I]	
Armenian.—Pica.	do.	

MERIDIONALS.	
Coptic.—Pica.	[Caslon I]
Ethiopic.—Pica.	[Caslon II]

OCCIDENTALS.	
Greek.—Double Pica.	[Caslon II]
Great Primer.	do.
English.[4]	do.
Pica.[5]	[Head]-[Mitchell]
Long Primer.	[Caslon I]

Brevier.	do.
Small Pica.	[Caslon II]
Nonpareil.	do.
Etruscan.—English.	[Caslon I]
Roman and Italic.—All the regulars.	
Irregulars and Titlings.—5-line.	[Caslon I]
4-line.[4]	do.
Canon.	[Moxon]-[Andrews]
2-line Double Pica.	[Caslon II]
2-line Great Primer.[4]	[Caslon I]
2-line English.[4]	do.
2-line Pica full face.	[Mitchell]
2-line Pica.	[Caslon II]
Paragon.	do.
Small Pica.	do.
Bourgeois.	do.
Minion.	do.
Nonpareil.	do.
Pearl.[6]	do.
Proscription.—20-line to 4-line.[7]	do.

SEPTENTRIONALS.	
Gothic.—Pica.	[Caslon I]
Anglo-Saxon.—English.	[Caslon II]

[1] *Dissertation*, p. 81.

[2] Mores calls this 'excavated' or 'Hutter's leading-string' Hebrew. A specimen may be seen in *The Scholar's Instructor. An Hebrew Grammar of Israel Lyons*, Cambridge, 1735, 8vo. The open Hebrew is here used to distinguish the servile from the radical letters. Lyons in his preface deprecates Hutter's method of printing the entire Bible in this character, thereby keeping the learners 'too long in leading-strings' (see also above, p. 56).

[3] Mores omits a Small Pica Hebrew, which is the same as the Brevier shown in the sheet of 1734.

[4] These founts are not Head's or Mitchell's, as Mores states, but were cut by Caslon I, and shown on the 1734 sheet.

[5] The Pica Greek shown on the 1734 sheet was discarded in favour of this fount.

[6] 'But', adds Mores, 'Mr. Caslon is cutting a *Patagonian* which will lick up all these diminutives as the ox licketh up the grass of the field.' But no such type is found in the specimens.

[7] 'Supported by arches.' Doubtless cast in sand.

Anglo-Saxon.—Pica.[1]	[Caslon I]	Pica.[2]	do.
Long Primer.[1]	[Caslon I]	Long Primer.	do.
Brevier.	[Caslon II]	Brevier.	[Caslon I]
English.—Double Pica.	do.	2-line Great Primer.	[Caslon II]
Great Primer.	do.	Small Pica.[3]	do.
English.	[Head]-[Mitchell]	Music.—Round Head.	do.
English Modern.[2]	[Caslon II]	Flowers and the rest of the Apparatus.	

Caslon II died in 1778, aged 58, and was buried in the family vault at St. Luke's, the following line being added to his father's inscription:

Also W. Caslon, Esq. (son of the above) ob. 17 Aug., 1778, aetat. 58 years.

Of him, too, an excellent oil portrait was preserved at Chiswell Street. He had married Elizabeth Cartlitch,[4] a lady of beauty, understanding, and fortune, who during the latter years of her husband's life had taken an active share in the management of the foundry.

Caslon dying intestate, his property was divided equally between his widow and her two sons, William and Henry, the chief superintendence of the business devolving on William Caslon III, at that time quite a young man (b. 1754). The chief event of the new régime was the issue of the admirable specimen-book of 1785, a work which, for its completeness and excellent execution, has received high approbation. It consists of sixty-four sheets, twenty-two of which are devoted to romans and italics, ten to 'learned' letter[5] and blacks, two to music, two to script, and no fewer than twenty-eight to flowers arranged in artistic combinations and designs. The volume is dedicated to King George III, Caslon assuming the title allowed a century earlier to Nicholas Nicholls, of 'Letter Founder to His Majesty'.

The 'Address to the Public', which prefaces this specimen, naturally lays claim on behalf of the Caslon Foundry to the merit of having rescued the type trade in England from the hands of foreigners. But it also suggests, by the somewhat acrid tone in which it refers to its 'opponents', that the competition of the newly established foundries of Cottrell, Fry, Wilson, and Jackson was already beginning to tell on the temper of the third of the Caslons, who evidently did not regard as flattery the avowed imitation of the Caslon models by some of his rivals.[6]

[1] These were not cut, as Mores states, by Caslon II, but by Caslon I, and appeared on the sheet of 1734, when Caslon II was but 14 years of age.

[2] 'These', says Mores, 'are one and the same. The Acts of Parliament are printed in them, therefore we call them as Dr. Ducarel and the Act call them, "the common legible hand and character".'

[3] Mores omits here the Pica black, cut by Caslon I, and shown on the sheet of 1734.

[4] Not Cartledge, as erroneously given by Nichols. This lady was the only child of a Mr. Cartlitch, an eminent refiner in Foster Lane, Cheapside, and was born 31 May 1730.

[5] With the addition of the Long Primer Syriac cut for Oxford University, the 'learned' founts in the 1785 specimen are precisely the same as those which appeared in the book of 1764.

[6] The address is a literary curiosity: 'The acknowledged excellence of this Foundry, with its rapid success, as well as its unexampled Productions having gained universal Encomiums on its ingenious Improver and Perfecter (whose uncommon Genius transferred the Letter Foundry Business from HOLLAND to ENGLAND, which, for above Sixty years, has received, for its beauty and Symmetry, the unbounded praises of the Literati, and the liberal encouragement of all the Master Printers and Booksellers, not only in this Country but of all EUROPE and AMERICA) has excited the Jealousy of the Envious and the Desires of the enterprising, to become Partakers of the Reward due to the Descendants of the Improver of this most useful and important Art.

'They endeavour, by every method to withdraw, from this Foundry, that which they silently acknowledge is its indisputable Right: Which is conspicuous by their very Address to the Public, wherein they promise (in Order to induce Attention and Encouragement) that they will use their utmost Endeavours to IMITATE the Productions of this Foundry; which assertion, on inspection, will be found impracticable, as the Imperfections cannot correspond in size.

'The Proprietor of this Foundry, ever desirous of retaining the decisive Superiority in his Favour, and

The specimen contains one new feature—a Double Pica Script—which, however, is of no particular merit though faithfully enough rendering the contemporary clerkish hand.[1] Two other scripts in this style had preceded Caslon's, that of Thomas Cottrell (see p. 291) and the one cut for the Rev. John Trusler (see p. 342).

The year 1785 was prolific in specimens of the Chiswell Street Foundry. In addition to the book above referred to, an eight-page specimen in post-folio, appeared, intended for use as inset plates to encyclopaedias,[2] in which the principal founts of the foundry, roman and oriental, were displayed. In addition to this, there was issued a folio specimen of two sheets of large letter[3] showing the sand-cast types of the foundry in sizes from nineteen- to seven-line Pica.

In 1785 also Caslon III had issued his specimen of cast ornaments—the first of the kind exhibited by an English founder—displaying sixty-five designs of various size and merit at prices ranging from 3*d*. to 7*s*. each. In his introductory note to the second edition, dated 20 July 1786, he takes to himself the credit of an invention 'completed with infinite attention and at an inconceivable expence', whereby the trade is in future to be supplied with typographic designs equal to copperplate and less costly than the commonest woodcuts. The process thus originated was that of sharply impressing a wood block in cooling metal so as to form a lead matrix from which to 'dab' further impressions as required. The specimen of 1785 contained a few small ships of imposing appearance, but these were produced by the usual method of punch and matrix.

It does not appear that the third Caslon's connexion with the business resulted in any large addition to its founts. As, however, no specimen-book of the foundry is known between 1786 and 1800, it is difficult to judge of its progress during that period. In the year 1792 Caslon disposed of his interest in the Chiswell Street business to his mother and sister-in-law. Henry Caslon had died in 1788. He had married Miss Elizabeth Rowe, a lady of good family,[4] between whom and their only son, Henry (at that time an infant of two years), he left his share of the foundry.

It will not appear extraordinary [says Hansard] that a property so divided, and under the management of two ladies, though both superior and indeed extraordinary women, should be unable to maintain its ground triumphantly against the active competition which had for some time existed against it. In fact, the fame of the first William Caslon was peculiarly disadvantageous to Mrs. Caslon, as she never could be persuaded that any attempt to rival him could possibly be successful.

---

full of the sincerest Gratitude for the distinguished Honour, by every Work of Reputation being printed from the elegant Types of the Chiswell-street Manufactory, hopes, by every Improvement, to retain and merit a Continuance of their established Approbation, which, in all Quarters of the Globe, has given it so acknowledged an Ascendency over that of his Opponents.'

The address prefixed to the 1785 specimen-book of the Worship Street Foundry had evidently been the inspiration of this tirade, which in turn evoked a spirited reply from the Frys in the following year. See p. 303.

In this script was printed Mary Potter's *The*

Poetry of Nature . . . from the Works of the Caledonian Bards, London, 1789. 4to.

[2] The sheets appear (along with some of Fry & Son's and Wilson's) in *Chambers's Cyclopaedia—incorporated in one alphabet by Abraham Rees, London, 1784–6*. 4 vols., fol.

[3] These are sometimes (as in the case of the British Museum copy) bound up with the 1785 8vo specimen-book as folding plates.

[4] See p. 192. Hansard observes that besides Queen Elizabeth's Ambassador, the same family had produced Sir Henry Rowe, a Lord Mayor of London; and Owen Rowe, the Regicide.

Mrs. Caslon, sen., was an active member of the Association of Typefounders of her day, which first met in 1793. The original members were Elizabeth Caslon & Co., William Caslon, Edmund Fry & Co., Vincent Figgins, Simon Stephenson, and Myles Swinney.[1] In this capacity Mrs. Caslon gained the esteem of her fellow founders as well as of the printers, and on one occasion formed one of a deputation

Fig. 68. Founders' signatures.

of two to confer with the latter on certain questions affecting the price of type. She died from the effects of a paralytic stroke in October 1795. The esteem in which she was held by all who knew her was amply testified by numerous notices in the public prints of the day. 'Her merit and abilities', says one, 'in conducting a capital business during the life of her husband and afterwards, till her son was capable of managing it, can only be known to those who had dealings with the manufactory. In quickness of understanding and activity of execution she has left few equals among her sex.' And, in the same strain, the *Freemason's Magazine* of March 1796 thus speaks of her: 'The urbanity of her manners, and her diligence and activity in the conduct of so extensive a concern, attached to her interest all who had dealings with her, and the steadiness of her friendship rendered her death highly lamented by all who had the happiness of being in the extensive circle of her acquaintance.' The latter notice is accompanied by a portrait of this worthy lady.

Mrs. Caslon's will becoming the object of some litigation, her estate was thrown

[1] The Minute Book of this Association is now in the possession of Mr. R. G. Stevens, who has kindly allowed us to consult it. Reed was familiar with the book. See above, p. 110.

into Chancery, and in March 1799, the foundry was, by order of the Court, put up for auction and purchased by Mrs. Henry Caslon for £520. The smallness of this figure is the more remarkable since only seven years previously, on the retirement of Caslon III, a third share of the concern had sold for £3,000.

On the decease of Mrs. Caslon [writes Hansard, in 1825] the management of the Foundry devolved on Mrs. Henry Caslon, who, possessing an excellent understanding, and being seconded by servants of zeal and ability, was enabled, though suffering severely under ill-health, in a great measure to retrieve its credit. Finding the renown of William Caslon no longer efficacious in securing the sale of his types, she resolved to have new founts cut. She commenced the work of renovation with a new Canon, Double Pica and Pica, having the good fortune to secure the services of Mr. John Isaac Drury, a very able engraver, since deceased. The Pica, an improvement on the style of Bodoni,[1] was particularly admired, and had a most extensive sale. Finding herself, however, from the impaired state of her health, which suffered from pulmonary attacks, unable to sustain the exertions required in conducting so extensive a concern, she resolved, after the purchase of the Foundry, to take as an active partner Mr. Nathaniel Catherwood, (a distant relation), who by his energy and knowledge of business fully equalled her expectations. This connection gave a new impetus to the improvements of the Foundry, which did not cease during the lives of the partners, and their exertions were duly appreciated and encouraged by the printers. In 1808 the character of the Foundry may be considered as completely retrieved, but the proprietors did not long live to enjoy their well-merited success. In 1799, Mrs. Henry Caslon had married Mr. Strong, a medical gentleman, who died in 1802. In the spring of 1808 she was afflicted with a serious renewal of her pulmonary attack, in consequence of which she was advised to try the effect of the air of Bristol Hotwells, which probably protracted her life during a twelvemonth of extreme suffering, but could not eradicate the fatal disease. Her fortitude and resignation under this long continued, and helpless affliction could not be surpassed, and were truly admirable. Her sufferings were terminated in March 1809, when she was buried in the Cathedral of Bristol. The worthy and active Mr. Nathaniel Catherwood did not long survive his associate, being seized with a typhus fever which baffled the medical art. He died on the 6th of June, aetat. 45, very generally regretted.[2]

In 1805 was published the first specimen containing the new romans of Caslon and Catherwood, among which, however, the Canon and Double Pica referred to by Hansard are not included. The dates affixed to the various specimens[3] show that

---

[1] The celebrated typographer, born at Saluzzo, in the Sardinian States, in 1740. At an early age he visited Rome, and obtained a situation in the printing-office of the Propaganda, where he gained great credit for his printing. In 1768 he settled at Parma, where he published many famous works, and established a European reputation. He never visited England, although one or two works were printed by him in our language, viz. Lord Orford's *Castle of Otranto*, 1791, 8vo; Gray's *Poems*, 1793, 4to; Thomson's *Seasons*, 1794, fol. and 4to. He died in 1813, and his widow finished and published in 1818 the *Manuale Tipografico*, 2 vols., royal 4to, a most sumptuous work, containing upwards of 250 exquisite specimens of type and ornaments. A monument was erected to him in Saluzzo in 1872. Of Bodoni's office at Parma the following interesting particulars are preserved in Sir James E. Smith's *Tour on the Continent*, 2nd edit., vol. iii, 1807: 'A very great curiosity in its way, is the Parma printing-office, carried on under the direction of M. Bodoni, who has brought that art to a degree of perfection hardly known before him. Nothing could exceed his civility in showing us numbers of the beautiful productions of his press, of which he gave us some specimens, as well as the operations of casting and finishing the letters. The materials of his type are antimony and lead, as in other places, but he showed us some of steel. He has sets of all the known alphabets, with diphthongs, accents, and other peculiarities in the greatest perfection. His Greek types are peculiarly beautiful, though of a different kind of beauty from those of old Stephens, and perhaps less free and flowing in their forms.' The tour was made in 1786 and 1787. See also Updike, vol. ii, pp. 163–73, and the references there given. A translation of Bodoni's preface to his *Manuale*, 1818, by H. V. Marrot was published in London in 1925.

[2] *Typographia*, p. 352.

[3] Two-line Great Primer—1803
Great Primer—May 1802
English 1—Aug. 1802
English 2—Apr. 1805
Pica 2 and 3—Mar. 1805
Small Pica 1, 2, and 3—July 1804
Long Primer 1, 2, and 3—July 1804
Bourgeois 1 and 2—July 1802
Brevier 1 and 2—May 1805
Minion—May 1805
Nonpareil 1 and 2—Oct. 1803

most of them were completed between 1802 and 1805, the earliest being the Great Primer, dated May 1802. The specimen also contained the Caslon orientals. In 1808 a further specimen of the romans, including a few additional founts, appeared as a supplement to Stower's *Printers' Grammar*.[1]

These two specimens indicate clearly the important revolution through which the Chiswell Street Foundry, in common with all the other foundries of the day, had passed in respect of the model of its characters. All the once-admired founts of the originator of the foundry have been discarded, and between the specimen of 1785 and that of 1808 there is absolutely no feature in common.[2]

On the death of his mother and her partner, Henry Caslon II (b. 1786) assumed the management of the business, and fully maintained its reputation. The former name of the firm was retained. In 1814 Caslon took into partnership John James Catherwood,[3] brother to Nathaniel Catherwood, and in this association proceeded vigorously with the improvement of the foundry. The partnership continued until 1821, during which period, says Hansard, 'the additions and varieties made to the stock of the Foundry have been immense. Nothing that perseverance in labour and unsparing effort could effect, either to meet the fashion and evanescent whim of the day, or with the superior view of permanent improvement, has been wanted to keep the concern up to its long-established eminence, and to enable it to rank high among the many able competitors of the present age. The ancient stock can never be equalled—the modern never excelled.'[4]

Among the more important accessions to the stock of the foundry may be mentioned the acquisition in 1817 of the foundry of William Martin of Duke Street, St. James's, which, as elsewhere stated,[5] included several good roman and oriental letters.

The partnership between Caslon and Catherwood being dissolved in 1821 by the withdrawal of the latter,[6] Caslon admitted to a share of the business Martin William Livermore, 'who for many years', says Hansard, 'had evinced ample talent, indefatigable zeal, and obliging attention, as active foreman and manager of the mechanical department'.

The specimen-books of 1821, 1825, and 1829 show the first Caslon examples of the new advertising types, Fat Faces, including Fat Face blacks, ornamented letters, Antiques (the Caslon name for Egyptian), and Italian (a sort of reversed Egyptian and the only one of these designs originated by the Caslons). It may be interesting

---

[1] *The Printers' Grammar, etc.*, by C. Stower, *Printer*, London, 1808. 8vo. The following note is prefixed to the specimen: 'A 4-line Pica, Canon, and Double Pica of a bold and elegant shape were not quite ready to introduce with these specimens.'

[2] Savage, in his *Hints on Decorative Printing*, London, 1822, 4to, chapter ii, shows specimens of Mrs. Caslon's roman letter contrasted with the old models of the foundry on the one hand, and its more recent developments on the other.

[3] 'Chiswell Street, January 19, 1814. Henry Caslon respectfully informs his friends and the printers in general, that the term of his partnership with the executors of the late Mr. Nathaniel Catherwood having expired, he has entered into a new engagement with Mr. John James Catherwood,

brother to his late partner, and that the firm is now carried on under the firm of Henry Caslon and J. J. Catherwood. He embraces this opportunity of expressing his grateful sense of the distinguished patronage the Foundry has received, and the kind encouragement he has individually experienced from his friends in the printing business, since the death of his mother and late partner.'

[4] *Typographia*, p. 353.

[5] See below, pp. 324–27.

[6] See below, p. 351, s.v. 'Bessemer'. In Andrew Johnstone's *Commercial Directory*, 1817, and in the Directory at the end of Johnson's *Typographia*, 1824 (ii. 652), a Catherwood is mentioned among the Letter Founders, at 19 Charles' Sq., Hoxton.

to quote the list given by Hansard of matrices of the 'learned' languages in the foundry at the time when he wrote, i.e. 1825:

Arabic.—English.
Armenian.—Pica.
Coptic.—Pica.
Ethiopic.—Pica.
Etruscan.—Pica.
German.—Pica, Long Primer, Brevier.
Greek.—Double Pica,[1] Great Primer,[1] English, Pica, Small Pica, Long Primer, Bourgeois, Brevier, Nonpareil, Pearl, Diamond.[2]
Gothic.—Pica.
Persian.—English.
Hebrew.—Two-line Great Primer, Two-line English, Double Pica, Great Primer; ditto, with points; English; ditto, with points; Pica; ditto, with points; Small Pica, Long Primer, Bourgeois, Brevier.
Samaritan.—Pica.
Sanscrit.—English.[3]
Saxon.—English, Pica, Long Primer, Brevier.
Syriac.—English (*Polyglot*), Long Primer.
Music.—Large, Small.
Black.—Two-line Great Primer, Double Pica, Great Primer, English, Pica, Small Pica, Long Primer, Brevier, Nonpareil.

Caslon and Livermore issued specimens in 1830 and 1834, the latter appearing exactly 100 years after the first broadside published by William Caslon I. Numerous specimens followed the issue of 1834, that of 1839 bearing the title of Caslon, Son, and Livermore, Letter-founders to Her Majesty's Board of Excise—the new partner being Caslon's son, Henry William Caslon. Shortly afterwards, Livermore's connexion with the business ceased, and the next few specimens bear the name of Henry Caslon alone.

In 1843 a revival of the Caslon old-style letter took place under the following circumstances, which, as they initiated a new fashion in the trade generally, call for reference here. In the year 1843 Charles Whittingham of the Chiswick Press waited upon Caslon to ask his aid in carrying out the then new idea of printing in appropriate type *The Diary of Lady Willoughby*,[4] a work of fiction, the period and diction of which were supposed to be of the reign of Charles I. The original matrices of the first William Caslon having been fortunately preserved, Caslon undertook to supply a small fount of Great Primer. So well was Whittingham satisfied with the result of his experiment that he determined on printing other volumes in the same style, and eventually he was supplied with the complete series of all the old founts. Then followed a demand for old faces, which has continued up to the present time.

In Whittingham's report as a juror at the Great Exhibition of 1851 he writes: 'Mr. Whittingham at the suggestion of Mr. Pickering first reintroduced the old letters of Garamond and Jenson, and many of the London printers have since followed.' Presumably by the letters of Garamond he meant those of Caslon, but why he should not have given credit directly to Caslon one cannot understand. Equally mysterious is the reference to Jenson, unless the Chiswick Press Basle roman was already cut (see below, p. 365). The remark that many of the London printers

---

[1] Cut by William Martin.

[2] This beautiful little fount was cut for Pickering's *Greek Testament*, 1826, and for clearness and minuteness eclipses both the Sedan Greek and that of Blaeu of Amsterdam. It was also used in the *Homer* of 1831. Dibdin (*Introd. to the Classics*, 1827, i. 166) shows a specimen of the type.

[3] Cut for Dr. C. Wilkins, Oriental Librarian to the East India Company.

[4] *The Diary of Lady Willoughby, as relates to her Domestic History in the Reign of King Charles I*, London, 1844. 4to. However, Whittingham had already used Caslon Old-Face on the title-pages of several books printed for Pickering in 1840. See G. Keynes, *William Pickering*, 1924, pp. 25, 26.

had since followed is also surprising, since it is difficult to find books in the forties set in Caslon, except those of the Chiswick Press. Whittingham's chief follower was an Anglo-Catholic printer, Joseph Masters, and another printer, at a rather later date, was the Catholic John Philp. In the fifties there appeared a whole group of books in old face intended for Christmas presents, bound in embossed cloth covers. But many years were yet to pass before it could be said that the general typography of the nineteenth century had begun to change. It should also be noted that Whittingham revived not only the Caslon roman but also his blacks. Pickering had for years been using black-letter on title-pages, and published a number of editions of early English authors printed entirely in black-letter at the Chiswick Press. One of the finest examples was the reproduction of the *Common Prayer* of 1549, printed in 1844, the year in which *The Diary of Lady Willoughby* appeared.

The Caslons themselves had not forgotten their old faces. In the specimen-book of 1825 they refer with regret to the original Caslon types, which were no longer displayed. In the specimen of 1842 there is included a price list, dated 1838, which is actually set in old face. In the specimen of 1857 they again showed the old types including the old blacks and exotics. Some of the pages are evidently taken from the old books and inserted. But even in 1875, when the publication of *Caslon's Circular* began, it was not thought desirable to break with the modern face, and it was only with the issue for July 1880 that the *Circular* was set in Old Style.

In 1846 there was a crisis in the history of the firm owing to the increasing infirmities of Caslon, and there was an attempt to sell the foundry. The title of the catalogue then issued reads: *Particulars of a most valuable property for Investment called the Caslon Letter Foundry; also a most extensive Modern Foundry on which has been expended upwards of £50,000, which will be sold by auction by W. Lewis and Son . . . on Wednesday Dec. 16, 1846.* This is a most interesting and unusual document, since it consists of a list of the punches and matrices of the modern foundry with the names of the punch-cutters added. On the obscurity usually surrounding the actual punch-cutter we may compare the story told by Vincent Figgins II (see below, p. 331). Fifteen names of different cutters are given, and most of these are mere names to us. Highest on the list is HUGHES with 88 entries. It seems a likely assumption that this is Hugh Hughes who had a foundry from 1824 to his death in 1841. There is no record of the sale of his stock, but it seems that, apart from the music, most of the punches and matrices were bought by Caslon. The entries in the catalogue show a complete set of romans and italics down to Pearl, as well as a few Greeks. Next is SELKIRK with 60 entries; these include many blacks, Antiques (Egyptians), two Italians, and one Ionic. I can find no information about this cutter, and he was possibly a regular employee of the firm. DRURY has 47 entries, no doubt the John Isaac Drury who cut the first modern faces of the Caslons, as already mentioned. The entries show a series of romans and italics from Canon to Nonpareil. He, too, does not appear to have traded as an independent founder. Fourth is KING with 46 entries, probably Thomas King, a London founder from *c.* 1825 (see below, p. 368). His types are mostly Placard types, including Trafalgar, and also a Nonpareil Greek. Fifth is BESSEMER with 44 entries. This is Anthony Bessemer, who according to his son, Sir Henry, recut the Caslon types from Pica to Diamond. This series is entered, and in addition an English roman, italic, and Greek. PEEK has 42 entries, nearly all Placard types, called Sanspareil. This was the name given to a new method of cutting large types, invented by William Caslon IV, of the other branch of Caslons (see below, p. 321). As already recorded a John Peek took out a patent in 1809 for a type-casting machine. High on the list are the BOILEAUS, but as some entries are to E. Boileau, some to F. Boileau, and some to Boileau without initial, it is impossible to estimate the number due to any one of them, although the three together amount to over 100. There was an E. Boileau who took out a patent in 1854 in connexion with printing in colour. A Frederick Boileau appears in the *Post Office Directory* as a Die Sinker. Their types are mostly scripts and display types, including Albion (a fat-faced series of romans), Ionic, and six sizes of Doric (the Caslon name for Sans Serif). There are sixteen entries described as French, presumably not the name of a cutter but an indication of French importation. This is borne out by the fact that matrices only are entered for these founts. This is also the case with the four entries described as German, which include one Hebrew and three Germans, probably Frakturs. Eleven entries are assigned to DODD, including coronets and cheques. Perhaps this was the Daniel George Dodd, who appears in the *Directory* for 1841 as an engraver. Eleven entries also are given to EDMISTON, including Diamond roman, italic, and Greek; the Greek must be the type mentioned above as used by Pickering. Harvey is probably the engraver who was in partnership with Barton in 1824 (see below, p. 358). Was he the well-known William Harvey? I find no information about Edmiston, nor about PERRY or PHILLIPS. A six-line Pica roman and a two-line Pica Ornamented are assigned to POUCHÉE, i.e. Louis Jean Pouchée (see below, p. 355), a Long Primer Greek to MARTIN, i.e. William Martin, whose foundry had been acquired in 1817, and a two-line English Ornamented to AUSTIN, no doubt Richard Austin. Caslon had no punches, but the type is not in the Austin specimen of 1827. As a large number of these types can be checked in the Caslon specimen book of 1842, the Sale Catalogue is a most illuminating document.

No acceptable offer was made at this sale, and the business continued as Caslon & Son.[1] Henry Caslon died on 28 May 1850, and in the same year another important purchase was made, that of the London branch of the Wilson or Glasgow Letter Foundry, and Alexander and Patrick Wilson, grandsons of the original Glasgow founder, joined the Caslon firm (cf. below, p. 264). The style of the firm now became H. W. Caslon & Co., and it was also called the 'Caslon and Glasgow Letter Foundry'. The specimen-book of 1857 is very different from the book of 1842. Very few types are the same; the body types, roman and italic, although differing little in design, all bear higher numbers than those shown in 1842. Some of them are doubtless from the Wilson Foundry. There are also some new display types, such as 'Ecclesiastic' and the so-called 'Anglo-Saxon'. The total stock of the foundry was by this time of great extent. However, the years in which the last of the Caslons, Henry William Caslon, was head of the firm were not a prosperous period. H. W. Caslon is described by T. W. Smith as 'a man of generous impulse, but of little wisdom in business matters'. In 1865 there was a strike in the firm

[1] For the later history of the firm, see J. M. McRae, *Two Centuries of Typefounding*, London, 1920, 4to.

followed by a lock-out, which brought the business almost to a standstill for eight months. As a result the Wilsons finally retired and T. W. Smith sought employment elsewhere. It was during this period, in 1879, that the firm opened a branch in Paris, the manager being Henry J. Tucker, who was the editor of the periodical *La Typologie Tucker*. In 1872 Caslon, being in ill health, invited T. W. Smith to rejoin the firm as manager. In 1874 the last of the Caslons died at his country-house at Medmenham.

Under the management of T. W. Smith a new and more prosperous era in the history of the firm opened. Thomas White Smith was born at Tavistock in 1835, and was apprenticed to a printer in Newport, Isle of Wight, and finally in London. His first employment after completing his apprenticeship was with Messrs. Stephenson and Blake. From 1857 until the strike in 1865 Smith was employed by the Caslon firm and returned again as manager in 1872. From the account given by Smith in his privately circulated autobiography he found the business in a neglected state, but nevertheless he succeeded in restoring the position of the firm. In January 1875 there appeared the first number of *Caslon's Circular*. The *Circular* was at first set in a modern face, but from July 1880 it was set in Old Style. In spite of the vogue for Caslon Old Face the firm found it expedient to cut their own copy of Old Style, which was first shown in 1877 and the range of sizes completed in 1880. The new Caslon types, including American jobbing types with which the Caslons became more and more concerned, were, of course, displayed in the *Circular*, but the paper included much else of interest. In July 1880 they printed the letter of Sir Henry Bessemer to T. W. Smith about Anthony Bessemer's work as a punch-cutter; in the spring of 1887 they reprinted from the *Leeds Mercury* a long review of the first edition of this present work and in the summer of 1890 reprinted Reed's paper read to the Royal Society of Arts on roman type. In 1878–9 there were articles by T. L. De Vinne advocating the introduction of the point system of type measurement. T. W. Smith was interested in this reform and was one of the leaders of the campaign in this country. His proposal was put forward in 1886, but apparently was not acceptable to the other founders and the Caslons had to abandon the scheme. It was not until 1898 that agreement among the founders was reached and the American point system adopted. By this time there was much American type in the country and printers had become more accustomed to the new nomenclature. Even then the change-over was naturally a slow process and, according to J. Southward's *Modern Printing* (1924 edition, vol. i, p. 106), it was not until 1905 that the system can be said to have been in general use. In the *Circular* there was much controversial matter, e.g., repeated complaints against the unfairness of the copying of designs with matrices produced by the electrotype process. The Caslons had attacked this method of piracy continually since the London Exhibition of 1862. They also reproached certain of the trade papers for their unjustified accusations brought against the old foundries for obstructing the progress of mechanical invention. On the question of the introduction of the point system T. W. Smith was certainly no obstructionist. Smith had also invented and patented a method of combining matrices in a line, which foreshadowed the Linotype. The Linotype Company, in fact, recognized this and bought up his rights.

In 1896 T. W. Smith took into partnership his three sons, who assumed the name of Caslon-Smith and finally by deed-poll the name of Caslon. In 1900 their father, who had been called the second founder of the most famous of the old English letter foundries, retired. He died in 1907. The foundry came to an end in 1936 and the stock was bought by Messrs. Stephenson, Blake & Co. of Sheffield (now called also the Caslon Foundry).

APPENDIX

Caslon's First Types

Joannis Seldeni Opera omnia, edited by David Wilkins, was published in 1725 and 1726, but was begun in 1722. It was issued in three folio volumes, each in two parts, printed in double columns. With the preliminaries to each of Selden's books and the many extracts in Greek, oriental languages, and Anglo-Saxon, the work includes a very large number of types. The first volume has the imprint of William Bowyer. On the title-page are some of the capitals used at Oxford and found in London as early as 1639 (see p. 180) and some of Moxon's Canon roman. The Double Pica roman and the Great Pica roman and italic used in the preliminaries are probably Dutch, although I can say nothing of their origin. They occur frequently in books printed by William Bowyer. The English roman of the main text is Dutch; it is found on the specimen-sheet of an Amsterdam printer, Johannes Kannewet, where it is headed 'Klyne Augustyn Romyn'. Kannewet appears to have died in 1718 (see Kleerkooper's *De Boekhandel te Amsterdam*), and in any case, as the sheet is in the Bagford collection it cannot be later than 1716. In English books the roman appears in tom. xv of Rymer's *Foedera*, 1713, and subsequent volumes. We have already mentioned its use at Cambridge from 1716 (p. 228) and it will be found in many of Bowyer's books of earlier date than the *Selden*, for example, in *The Second Part of the Proceedings against Dr. Bentley*, printed for J. Bettenham, 1719, and the edition of Charles Leslie's *Theological Works*, 1721, a book described by Updike and one in many respects like the *Selden*. As to the confusion between this type and Caslon's English roman, the two are not very close. One has only to compare the upper- and lower-case G and the upper-case M to see marked differences.

The italic used with this Dutch roman—and there is a great deal of italic in the main text of the *Selden*—is the 'Augustijn Cursijf' of Christoffel van Dijk, shown on the various specimen-sheets of his heirs. This italic was already in use by 1656, as may be seen in an edition of the *Epistolae* of Claude Saumaise, printed at Leyden. We have referred to its appearance at Edinburgh in 1681 (p. 184) and its frequent use at Cambridge (p. 227). In London it was used for the address 'Lectori' in Jacob Tonson's well-known edition of *Caesar*, edited by Samuel Clarke, 1712, another book selected with approval by Updike. The italic is common in Bowyer's books beginning with Pope's translation of the *Iliad*, 1715, where it is used for the list of subscribers. In design Caslon's italic is clearly modelled on Van Dijk's. The English founder has not tried to make an exact copy; some letters he has deliberately altered, e.g. the J, in which the bar has been moved higher up the stem, and the N, where the foot serif on the right stem has been dropped.

To continue with the types found in vol. i of the *Selden*, a Long Primer roman is used for footnotes and the Index, and further we find an English Greek, Hebrew, Arabic, Syriac, and black-letter. The Hebrew is said by Nichols to have been cut by Caslon, and this appears to be correct. The black-letter is exactly of the design of Caslon's Pica black, but is probably a much older type which Caslon took as a model. The second volume of *Selden* has the imprint of Samuel Palmer. Clearly the work was too big a task for Bowyer alone. The italic of the main text is the same, but the English roman used by Palmer is different. It is the 'Augustijn Romeyn no. 2' on the Van Dijk sheets, which was not cut by Van Dijk,

impares) *& tempus Abib, seu frugum maturef-*
centium nondum ita prope sit, visum est mihi,
& collegis meis adjicere huic anno dies triginta.
Sic legitur in Gemara Hierosolymitana. Tam in hac
autem, quam in Babylonia tribuitur hoc edictum
Gamalieli synedrii magni principi, Rabban Si-
meonis filio, atque ut non immerito existimatum
est, Pauli Apostoli [d] praeceptori. Commemorat
quidem edictum hoc, vir summus Josephus Scaliger [e], paulo ante ad hunc modum praefatus.
Ab ultima, inquit, *antiquitate consistorium ju-*
dicum Hierosolymitanum ex libro τ ψηφοφορίας
(ελωναϊκῆς, de quo paulo ante egimus quotannis
mittebant, item in alias regiones finium Israel;
in Galilaeam formam anni proxime imminentis
quod & hodie a Samaritanis fieri in eorum com-
puto demonstravimus. Ejusmodi epistolae pon-
tificis maximi, & consistorii ad Galilaeos subje-
cimus. Dein subjicit formulam edicti a synedrio
etiam emissi [f], de indicando tempore τ מעבר
quod vertens ille *excussuram,* & triturae voce
explicans, non dubitat quin edictum ipsum sit
anni communis praemonitio, quam & sic fieri
ait eleganter. Et demum pro anni proxime imminentis intercalationis indictione edictum supra
allatum sumit; quasi tam annum communem fore, edicto synedrii praedici fuisset solitum (ex
eo quod fruges jam maturescentes etiam triturae
ferme idoneae essent) quam fore aliquem inter-

& dictasse, & emisisse edictum illud intercalare,
nec pontifici hic jus aliquod a Talmudicis quidem, ut mox dicetur, permissum, sed omnino,
ut judici hac de re nimis impari, negatum. Con-
troversia autem est aliqua utrum edictum illud de
paschate [k] celebrando mense [l] secundo sub Eze-
chia rege, ad intercalationem etiam anni attine-
ret. Et plerumque quidem attinere recipitur,
uti etiam ad synedrii hic potestatem. Dicitur e-
nim *יחל המלך* id est, *& iniit rex consilium*
cum principibus suis, atque universo coetu Hi-
erosolymis ut facerent pascha in mense secundo,
seu ut vulgata, *decreverunt ut facerent pascha*
in mense secundo. Id quod complures non ac-
cipiunt perinde ac si mense Jiar, contra institu-
tum numinis, qui in mensium ordine est secundus, pascha primum (nam non ut secundum [m] hic
agitur) fuisset celebrandum. Sed quoniam ante
dies Nisan decimus sextus [n], dum in templi fa-
crorumque instauratione occuparentur, adeoque
legitimum in anni communis ratione paschatis
tempus praeterierat, ideo ne non omnino eo in
anno celebraretur, aiunt annum sic adjecto tunc
mense intercalatum, ut mensis hic secundus dictus
fieret saltem alter Nisan, priori velut pro Adare
secundo habito. Qua tamen de re loquuntur
fere magistri ut de eo, quod שנה *pro tem-*
poris necessitate factum est nec moribus avitis
consonum. Nam neque rite intercalatione adhi-

but which came from Frankfort. It is the 'Mittel Antiqua' on the Luther specimen of 1664 and is shown on other Frankfort specimens contemporary with the *Selden*, e.g. J. H. Stubenvoll, 1718, and J. F. Halle, 1724. We have already found the type at Cambridge (p. 228), and in London it was used by Roger Daniel in 1656.

KLYNE AUGUSTYN ROMYN.

Vir qui fæpius correptus obdurat cervicem, re-
pentè confringetur ita ut non fit curatio. Quum
augentur jufti, lætatur populus: quum autem
dominatur improbus, fuspirat populus. Vir a-
mans fapientiam, lætificat patrem fuum, qui autem confociat fe meretricibus, perdit fubftantiam
ABCDEFGHIJKLMNOPQRSTVU.

(GROOTE) MEDIAAN ROMYN.

Tranquillitate confcientiæ nihil beatius excogitari
poteft. Nihil fapientia pulchrius, nihil virtute ama-
bilius. Nihil eft libertate prefiofius. Fidelis vir om-
ni auro melior. Radix eruditionis amara, fed fructus
melle dulcior eft. Et genus & virtus nifi cum re, vi-
lior alga eft. Ingrato homine, terra nihil pejus creat.

FIG. 70. From Johannes Kannewet's specimen-sheet, Amsterdam, not later than 1715.

cidiffet Aperte InimicumNollet; cui Virium
hijklmnopq fstvuw ABCDEFGHI
ABCDEFGHIKLMNOP Q STVUXYZÆ

Auguftijn Curfijf.

Æadem, is admonenti Gubernatrici ut abiret
Amftelodamo, non modo non a paruerit, fed etiam
Miffum a Guberna trice Turrium a fecretis pri
vatæ Concilii, qui Regis nomine Juberet illum
urbe Protinus abfcendere, non Exaudito Re-
AABCDE FGHJI KLM MNOP

Auguftijn Romeyn Nº. 2.

Alexander aute factus annorum duodecim, rebus bellicis admodum de lectari, & excelfæ indolis

FIG. 71. Van Dijk's Types from a specimen-sheet of 1681.

The subsidiary types are much as in vol. i, except that there are several Oxford types, the Fell Double Pica and Great Primer roman and italic, and the two-line English italic, while the black-letter is of Dutch origin very like the Small Pica of the Andrews Foundry, shown in the James' Sales Catalogue, p. 22, No. 6. In coll. 1612–21 there is an Anglo-Saxon of English size. Oddly enough, from col. 1439 the English roman changes back again to the fount used in vol. i. Perhaps this section was not printed by Palmer. The third volume was printed by Thomas Wood, who worked also at Oxford as well as in London. The main part of the text is set in the same types as vol. i, and the same Great Primer roman is used, but with a different and earlier italic. There is also the Fell Double Pica and Great Primer roman and italic. In all the numerous types of the three volumes of the *Selden*—and we have not exhausted all the subsidiary types—the only one cut by Caslon appears to be the Hebrew.

When did Caslon's romans and italics first appear in books? With the help of the list of the books printed and published by Bowyer given by Nichols we can answer this question, if we may assume that Bowyer was likely to use them as early as any printer. The first to appear was the Pica roman in the notes at the end of the *Anacreon*, issued in 1725. It was used also in William Baxter's *Reliquae Baxterianae*, 1726, and in the *Common Prayer*, J. Basket, 1727. (It is not found in Baxter's edition of 1726.) On the sheet of Johannes Kannewet, below the 'Klyne Augustyn Romyn', the type found in the *Selden*, is shown a 'Groote Mediaan Romyn', which is also on the specimens of the Voskens house. It is not on the sheets of the two elder Voskens and I have not found it earlier than 1684. If it dates from about that year, it is presumably the work of Dirck Voskens. It is the type used in Bowyer's books down to 1724, and is clearly Caslon's model for his Pica roman. In particular the resemblance of the lower-case 'g' is striking.

Caslon's English roman and italic I have not found before 1728. In *A Discourse of the Judicial Authority belonging to the Office of Master of the Rolls*, 1728, the long preface is set in the same roman and italic as the *Selden*, and the main text shows the same italic, but with Caslon's English roman. In T. Bisse's *Sermon*, 1728, there is the roman only, but both the roman and italic in B. Motte's *Miscellanies in Prose and Verse*, 1728, and John Ecton's *Liber valorum*, 1728. We have already mentioned the use of this size at Cambridge in 1730. David Wilkins's edition of the *Pentateuch* in Coptic appeared in 1731 in the type cut by Caslon, and along with this we find his Small Pica roman. Caslon's Great Primer and Double Pica I have not found until 1732, the first in M. Maittaire's *Marmorum Arundellianorum editio secunda*, and the second in the Dedication to Rapin's *History of England*.

[12]

ALEXANDER WILSON, 1742

IN the early years of the eighteenth century printing in Scotland was in a condition even more depressed and unsatisfactory than in England. Except in Glasgow and Edinburgh the art was almost wholly neglected; and in those two cities the disadvantages at which printers were placed, owing partly to restrictive patents and monopolies, partly to jealousies among themselves, but chiefly to the absence of any letter foundry in their own country, were sufficient bar to all prosperity, either as an industry or an art.

A graphic sketch of this lamentable state of affairs is given in James Watson's *History of Printing*, published in Edinburgh in 1713,[1] a work which, while professing to give a general history of the art, derives its chief interest from the brief account of printing in Scotland given in the preface. That the art was derived in that country from Holland the author entertains no doubt, and that it was indebted for its maintenance and any measure of excellence it might claim to the same foreign source, he boldly asserts. It was the intervention of Dutch workmen that mainly contributed to relieve the deadlock into which the monopolies and patents of the seventeenth century had brought the trade generally, and it was only by a continuous supply of Dutch workmen, Dutch presses, and Dutch type that printing in Scotland was to be raised from its present low condition. And, as a crowning argument, he exhibits with some pride a selection of indifferent Dutch types and 'Bloomers', with which his own office is provided, as a suggestion of the excellence to which Scottish typography might yet attain.[2] This avowal of entire dependence on foreign labour and workmanship is significant; and the absence of any suggestion for remedying the evil by the establishment of a foundry in Scotland itself only emphasizes the helpless condition into which the art had sunk.

[1] *The History of the Art of Printing, containing an Account of its Invention and Progress in Europe, with the names of the famous Printers, the places of their birth and the works printed by them, and a Preface by the Publisher to the Printers in Scotland. Edinburgh, printed by James Watson. Sold at his shop opposite the Lucken Booths, and at the shops of David Scot in the Parliament Close, and George Stewart a little above the Cross*, 1713, 12mo. Watson's preface is stated to have been written by John Spotswood, Advocate. The historical portion is a condensed translation of De la Caille's *Histoire de l'Imprimerie*, published at Paris in 1689. The preface was re-edited in 1913 by W. J. Couper. For a list of books printed by Watson see J. S. Gibb in the *Publications of the Edinburgh Bibliographical Society*, 1896.

[2] *Specimen of Types in the Printing House of James Watson*, 1713. 48 pp., of which 26 are devoted to Dutch 'Bloomers' or Initials, and the remainder to romans and italics from French Canon to Nonpareil, with a fount of Greek, one of black, and a few signs, &c. Some of these initials must be cast pieces, since the original blocks are still with the Enschedés of Haarlem. Not quite all the types are Dutch; we find the English-cut capitals described above on p. 180 and Moxon's Canon roman. The 2-line Great Primer English also is not Dutch.

s

But although such a notion was too wild a dream for James Watson, others of his countrymen were bold enough to entertain it, and we find that in 1725 a Scottish printer clearly represented to William Ged the disadvantage under which the country laboured from having no foundry nearer than London or Holland, and urged him to undertake the business. Of Ged's career we have spoken elsewhere.[1] He failed, and Scotch typography, despite the rising fame of Caslon, might have remained many years longer in its depressed condition but for the accident which directed the genius of Alexander Wilson to letter-founding.[2]

Fig. 72. Alexander Wilson.

Born at St. Andrews in 1714, young Wilson was originally intended for the medical profession, and it was with a view to push his fortunes in that direction that he came up to London in 1737 and took employment as assistant to a surgeon and apothecary in the great city. While thus engaged he obtained an introduction to Dr. Stewart, physician to Lord Isla, afterwards Duke of Argyle, and in this way came under the notice of his lordship. A common interest in scientific pursuits, particularly astronomy, served to interest Lord Isla in the young doctor's assistant, and during the term of his service in London Wilson devoted much of his leisure to scientific study under the encouragement and favour of his new patron.

Of his first introduction to typography, we quote the following account given by Hansard on the authority of Alexander Wilson's son and grandson:[3]

While he was thus passing his time in a manner which he considered comfortable for one at his first entrance upon the world, a circumstance accidentally occurred which gave a new direction to his genius, and which in the end led to an entire change of his profession. This was a chance visit made one day to a letter-foundry with a friend, who wanted to purchase some printing types. Having seen the implements and common operations of the workmen usually shown to strangers, he was much captivated by the curious contrivances made use of in prosecuting that art. Shortly afterwards, when reflecting upon what had been shown him in the letter-foundry, he was led to imagine that a certain great improvement in the

[1] See pp. 211–13.
[2] The first Scottish typefounder appears to have been James Duncan, described as 'letter founder in Glasgow' in 1718 in McUre's *History of Glasgow*. See John Ferguson, 'The Brothers Foulis', in *The Library*, March 1889.   [3] *Typographia*, p. 362.

process might be effected; and of a kind too, that, if successfully accomplished, promised to reward the inventor with considerable emolument. He presently imparted his idea on the subject to a friend named Baine, who had also come from St. Andrews, and who possessed a considerable share of ingenuity, constancy and enterprise. The consequence of this was, the resolution of both these young adventurers to relinquish, as soon as it could be done with propriety, all other pursuits, and to unite their exertions in prosecuting the business of Letter Founding, according to the plan which had been contemplated with a view to improvements. After some further deliberation, Mr. Wilson waited upon his patron, Lord Isla, to whom he communicated his views, and the design of embarking in this new scheme; and derived much satisfaction from his Lordship's entire approbation and best wishes for his success.

Mr. Wilson and Mr. Baine then became partners in the project, and having taken convenient apartments, applied with great assiduity to the different preparatory steps of the business. At an early stage they had proofs of difficulties to an extent which had not been anticipated, and which, had their magnitude been foreseen, would probably have altogether deterred them from their attempt. But although they found their task grow more and more arduous as their experience improved, it may yet be mentioned, as a fact which bespeaks singular probity of mind, that they never once attempted to gain any insight whatever through the means of workmen employed in any of the London foundries, some of whom they understood could have proved of considerable service to them.[1]

Of the precise nature of the improved system of founding by which the two young Scotsmen proposed to prosecute their undertaking, the narrative given by Hansard affords no information. It has been suggested by some that it was no other than that of stereotyping by a method similar to, or better than, that attempted a few years earlier by Ged. But whatever it may have been, further experiment failed to justify the scheme as one of practical utility, and the two partners, who had by this time quitted the metropolis and returned to St. Andrews, determined to abandon it and to fall back on the ordinary method of manufacturing type.

In their attempt to prosecute this speculation [continues Hansard, still quoting the narrative furnished him by Wilson's successors] they found themselves in a more sure, though still in a difficult track, and in which they had no guide whatever but their own talent of invention and mechanical ability; and it was by the aid of these that they carried things forward until, at length, they were enabled to cast a few founts of Roman and Italic characters: after which they hired some workmen, whom they instructed in the necessary operations, and at last opened their infant letter-foundry at St. Andrews in the year 1742.

The Scottish printers were not slow in showing their appreciation of the convenience afforded them by the establishment of a foundry in their midst, and from the first Wilson and Baine appear to have received liberal encouragement in their new venture. They added steadily to the variety of their founts, and finding the demand for their type on the increase, not only in Scotland, but in Ireland and North America, they decided in 1744 to remove from St. Andrews to a more convenient centre at Camlachie, a small village a mile eastward of Glasgow.

In 1747 the claims of their Irish business necessitated the residence of one of the partners in Dublin. Baine was selected by lot for the duty, and accordingly departed for Ireland, leaving Wilson at Camlachie. Two years later the partnership was

---

[1] According to Southey's *Life of the Rev. Andrew Bell* the partners were assisted in their experiments by Alexander Bell, a barber in St. Andrews.

dissolved by mutual consent, and Baine quitted the business to make an independent venture in typefounding.[1]

Left to himself, Wilson actively prosecuted his business, and although no specimen of the foundry is known to exist, either during the partnership between Wilson and Baine or, indeed, during the entire period of its location at Camlachie, its productions very shortly attained some considerable celebrity.

During his residence at Camlachie [says Hansard] Mr. Wilson had contracted habits of intimacy and friendship with some of the most respectable inhabitants and eminent characters in that quarter, among whom may be particularly reckoned the professors of the University of Glasgow and Messrs. Robert and Andrew Foulis, the University printers.[2] The growing reputation of the University Press, conducted by these latter gentlemen, afforded more and more scope to Mr. Wilson to exercise his abilities in supplying their types; and being now left entirely to his own judgment and taste, his talents as an artist in the line to which he had become devoted became every year more conspicuous.

When the design was formed by the gentlemen of the University, together with the Messrs. Foulis, to print splendid editions of the Greek classics, Mr. Wilson with great alacrity undertook to execute new types, after a model highly approved. This he accomplished, at an expense of time and labour which could not be recompensed by any profits arising from the sale of the types themselves. Such disinterested zeal for the honour of the University Press was, however, upon this occasion, so well understood as to induce the University, in the preface to their folio *Homer*,[3] to mention Mr. Wilson in terms as honourable to him as they had been justly merited.

Of this magnificent work—one of the finest monuments of Greek typography which our nation possesses—it is sufficient to say that if the reputation of Alexander Wilson depended on no other performance, it alone would give him a lasting title to the distinction accorded to him in the preface, of 'egregius ille typorum artifex'.[4]

In 1760 Wilson was honoured with the appointment of the Practical Astronomy Professorship in the University of Glasgow, about two years after which the foundry

---

[1] For an account of Baine's subsequent career as a typefounder, see pp. 340, 341.

[2] These eminent printers, the most elegant typographers of which Scotland can boast, produced some of the finest editions of their generation. Robert was originally a barber, but began as a printer in 1740. In 1743 he was appointed printer to Glasgow University, one of his first productions being an edition of *Demetrius Phalereus* in that year. In 1744 he brought out his famous 'immaculate' edition of *Horace* in 12mo at Glasgow. Shortly afterwards his brother Andrew, who had been a teacher of French at the University, joined him, and the two together, by great industry and excellent artistic taste, produced a large number of beautifully printed works. Their classics, both Greek and Latin, were as remarkable for their exactness as for their beauty, and it is recorded that the brothers, following the example of some of the old masters, were in the habit of publicly exhibiting their proof sheets and offering a reward for the detection of any error. Andrew Foulis died in 1775, and Robert in the following year. The business was carried on under the old name of R. & A. Foulis for some years by Andrew Foulis, son of Robert. This printer it was who was associated with Tilloch in his patent for stereotype in 1784. He died in 1829 in great poverty. See a catalogue of the Foulis books in W. J. Duncan's *Notices and Documents illustrative of*

the *Literary History of Glasgow*, Maitland Club, 1831. See also D. Murray's *Robert and Andrew Foulis*, 1913, and James MacLehose's *The Glasgow University Press*, 1931.

[3] *Homeri Opera, Graece (ex edit. Sam. Clarke). Glasguae; in Ædibus Academicis excudebant Robertus et Andreas Foulis, Academiæ Typographi*, 1756–8, 4 vols., fol. This work is one of the most splendid editions of Homer ever printed. Each sheet was corrected six times before being finally worked. Flaxman's illustrations were designed for the work.

[4] After stating that it was the ambition of the publishers of this work to rival the finest productions of the Stephani of Paris, the preface continues (p. viii): 'Omnes quidem tres regios Stephanorum characteres graecos expresserat jam apud nos, atque imitatione accuratissimâ repraesentaverat *Alexander Wilson*, A.M., egregius ille Typorum artifex, quem et hoc nomine adscripserat sibi Alma Mater. In his autem grandioris formae characteribus Stephanianis id unum desiderari quodammodo videbatur, scilicet, si res ita ferre posset, ut, salvâ tamen illa solidae magnitudinis specie quâ delectantur omnes, existeret una simul elegantiae quiddam, magis atque venustatis. Rogatus est igitur ille artifex, ut, in hoc assequendo solertiam suam, quâ quidem pollet maximâ, strenue exerceret. Quod et lubenter aggressus est, et ad votum usque videtur consecutus vir ad varias ingenuas artes augendas natus.'

was removed to the more immediate vicinity of the college. After this appointment the further enlargement and improvement of the foundry devolved upon his two eldest sons; and he lived to witness its rise under their management to the highest reputation.

Among the later performances of Wilson, the most important was the beautiful fount of Double Pica cut in 1768 for the 4to edition of Gray's *Poems*[1] published by the brothers Foulis, who in their preface made public acknowledgement of the excellence of the letter and the expedition with which it had been provided.[2]

ΜΗΝΙΝ ἄειδε, ΘΕΑ, Πηληϊάδεω ΑΧΙΛΗΟΣ

Οὐλομένην, ἡ μυρί Ἀχαιοῖς ἄλγε ἔθηκε·

Πολλὰς δ᾿ ἰφθίμυς ψυχὰς ἄϊδι προΐαψεν

Ἡρώων, αὐτὺς δ᾿ ἑλώρια τεῦχε κύνεσσιν,

Οἰωνοῖσί τε πᾶσι Διὸς δ᾿ ἐτελείετο βυλή·

Ἐξ ὗ δὴ τὰ πρῶτα διασήτην ἐρίσαντε

Ἀτρείδης τε, ἄναξ ἀνδρῶν, κ᾿ δῖος Ἀχιλλεύς.

Τίς τ᾿ ἄρ σφῶε θεῶν ἔριδι ξυνέηκε μάχεσθαι;

Λητὺς καὶ Διὸς υἱός· ὁ γὰρ βασιλῆϊ χολωθεὶς

Νῦσον ἀνὰ στρατὸν ὦρσε κακήν· ὀλέκοντο δὲ λαοί·

Οὕνεκα τὸν Χρύσην ἠτίμησ᾿ ἀρητῆρα

Ἀτρείδης· ὁ γὰρ ἦλθε θοὰς ἐπὶ νῆας Ἀχαιῶν,

FIG. 73. Wilson's Greek, from the *Homer*, 1768.

Another high compliment was paid to Wilson's talents in 1775, when Dr. Edward Harwood, in the preface to his *View of the Greek and Roman Classics*,[3] singled out, along with Baskerville's types, the 'Glasgow Greek types which have not been used since the superb edition of *Homer* in 1757, and which are the most beautiful that modern times have produced', as fit to form the nucleus of a Royal typography for

[1] *Poems of Mr. Gray. Glasgow, printed by Robert and Andrew Foulis, Printers to the University*. 1768. 4to. This edition was published simultaneously with Dodsley's first collected edition of Gray's *Poems*, in London; and far exceeded it in beauty of typography and execution. Writing to Beattie in 1768, Gray says, 'I rejoice to be in the hands of Mr. Foulis (the famous printer of Glasgow) who has the laudable ambition of excelling the Etiennes and the Elzevirs as well in literature as in the proper art of his profession.'

[2] 'This is the first work in the Roman character which they (A. and R. Foulis) have printed with so large a type, and they are obliged to DOCTOR WILSON for preparing so expeditiously, and with so much attention, characters of so beautiful a form.'

[3] *A View of the Various Editions of the Greek and Roman Classics*, London, 1775. 12mo. Improved editions in 1778, 1782, and 1790.

England, dedicated to the improvement of the 'noblest art which human genius ever invented'.[1]

The first known specimen of the Glasgow Letter-Foundry, as it was now called, was published in 1772. It is at least remarkable that no specimen of its types should have been issued during the first thirty years of its successful career. But although Rowe Mores mentions with approval a sheet by Baine, he had apparently seen none bearing the name of Wilson. The specimen of 1772, which dated from the College of Glasgow, consisted of twenty-four 8vo leaves, and showed roman and italic only, in sizes from five-line to Pearl, there being several faces to most of the bodies. Certain of these, it is stated, are 'conformable to the London types'; and the enterprising proprietors undertake 'to cast to any body and range, on receiving a few pattern types'. Wilson's later founts show the influence of Baskerville, and since he issued no specimen before 1772, notes on the earliest appearance of some of these types will not be out of place. The Great Primer No. 2 is found in F. Hutcheson's *System of Moral Philosophy* and the *Callimachus*, both of 1755. The English roman No. 1, the type chosen as a model by Messrs. Collins for their 'Fontana' type of 1936, is used for the 'Vita' contained in the edition of *Horace* of 1760, and in the *Cornelius Nepos* of 1761. The Small Pica No. 1 appears in Dalrymple, 1766. The Double Pica of 1768 has already been mentioned.

In 1783 another specimen was issued in a broadside form, in four columns, and is usually to be met with in copies of Ephraim Chambers's *Cyclopaedia*, enlarged by Rees, where it is inserted to illustrate the article 'Printing'. It shows roman and italic from six-line to Pearl, with five sizes of black, six of Hebrew, and five of Greek, including the famous 'Glasgow Homer' Double Pica.[2] The general appearance of the sheet is good, and the founts compare favourably in shape and finish with those of any other foundry of the day. A note to the specimen intimates that the founts shown form a portion only of the contents of the foundry. A full specimen appeared in 1786 (the year in which Alexander Wilson died), and again in 1789, the latter being a small 4to volume of 50 pages, showing very considerable advance on its predecessors.[3] A further specimen appeared in 1812, showing the modern letters of the foundry, cut according to Hansard by Richard Austin.

With almost a monopoly of the Scotch and Irish[4] trade, the Glasgow Foundry became in course of time a formidable rival to the London houses, whose productions it contrived to undersell even in the English market. Its success, however, raised up competitors with itself in Scotland, foremost among which was the foundry of William Miller, a former manager in the Glasgow Foundry.

In 1825 the proprietors of the foundry were Andrew and Alexander Wilson, son and grandson to the originator. Andrew Wilson had been apprenticed to the

---

[1] Renouard, speaking of the twenty-volume edition of *Cicero* printed by the Foulis in 1749, prefers its type to that of the Elzevirs. *Catalogue de la Bibliothèque d'un Amateur*, Paris, 1819. 4 vols., 8vo, ii. 75.

[2] Hansard states that the Long Primer Greek matrices of the foundry were 'from the type cast in which the Elzevirs printed some of their editions' (*Typographia*, 404). The Long Primer Greek of the Elzevirs has been identified by Charles Enschedé with Robert Granjon's Garmond Greek. Wilson's

Greek as shown on the specimen-sheet of 1783 certainly bears a close resemblance to Granjon's.

[3] In a later specimen is shown a 'New Small Pica Italic' cut for the King's printer in Edinburgh, 1807.

[4] Lemoine, *Typographical Antiquities*, 1797, says, 'Ireland, by its connection with London and Scotland, produces some very neat printing; Wilson's types are much approved of at Dublin. Alderman George Faulkner may be considered as the first printer in Ireland in his time; but it must be remembered his letter was all cast in London.' p. 99.

London printer William Strahan, who was of Scottish origin and bought much of his type from the Glasgow Foundry.[1] Hansard summarizes their foreign and learned founts at this date as follows:

Greek.—Double Pica (*Glasgow Homer*), Great Primer, English, Pica, Small Pica, Long Primer ('Elzevir'), Brevier, Nonpareil.

Hebrew.—2-line English, Double Pica, Great Primer, English,[2] Pica, Small Pica, Long Primer, Brevier, Minion, Nonpareil.

Saxon.—English, Pica, Small Pica, Long Primer, Brevier.

Black.—2-line Great Primer, Double Pica, Great Primer, English, Pica, Long Primer, Brevier, Nonpareil.

In 1823 another complete specimen appeared and a further one in 1828, showing the new series of romans from Double Pica to Diamond, Greek, and fifteen pages of flowers.

Andrew Wilson dying in 1830, the management of the business devolved on his sons Alexander and Patrick, by whom it was decided, in 1832, to establish a branch house in Edinburgh.

A handsome 4to specimen of the roman letter of the foundry was published in 1833. This volume, and also those issued in 1823 and 1828, are interesting as being among the first to show the letter not only in the venerable 'Quousque tandem' paragraph, but also in an English garb.[3] It includes also five pages of Greek, in which the Double Pica 'Homer' is still prominent, and two pages of Hebrew, but no other orientals.

In 1834 the important step was taken of transferring the Glasgow Foundry to London, where, in premises at New Street, Gough Square, the business was carried on. The following extract from the preface to the 1834 specimen announces the removal:

'We had the honour some time ago of announcing the removing of the Glasgow Letter Foundry to London, and we beg leave to inform you that we have now carried our intentions into execution, and are prepared to receive your commands in our establishment in Great New Street, Gough Square, London. The operative department will be conducted by Mr. John Sinclair, whose integrity of conduct and thorough knowledge of his profession we now reward by making him a partner in our business.' London, Aug. 1, 1834.

The London foundry was carried on under the old name of Alex. Wilson & Sons, the Edinburgh branch, and that subsequently started in Dublin, being styled A. & P. Wilson, or occasionally Wilsons and Sinclair.

Briefly to trace the later vicissitudes of the foundry we may add that, about 1834, a further development of the business was completed by the establishment of a foundry at Two-Waters in Hertfordshire, where it was expected the cost of

---

[1] See R. A. Austen Leigh, *William Strahan and his Ledgers*, 1923.

[2] This fount (according to Savage, *Dict. of Printing*, p. 320) was cut after the classical and elegant type of Athias, for Mr. Jno. Wertheimer, of Leman Street, and was used in printing the Rev. D. A. De Sola's edition of the *Prayers of the Sphardim*. John Wertheimer (1799–1883) printed many Hebrew books from 1820. See the *Jewish Encyclopaedia*. The firm later became Wertheimer, Lea & Co., and is now Williams Lea Ltd.

[3] 'In conformity', says the preface, 'with ancient immemorial usage we have in Part I displayed our Founts in the Roman Garb—the venerable *Quousque tandem*—but lest it should be supposed we had adopted the flowing drapery of Rome for the purpose of shading or concealing defects, we have in Part II shown off our founts in a dress entirely English.' This had already been done to some extent in the specimen of 1772.

production would be considerably reduced by the cheaper labour attainable in the country. A strike occurring in 1837 among the London workmen, the Gough Square House was closed. In 1840 another branch was established at Dublin. Despite the activity of Alex. Wilson and the continued excellence of his types, the business declined. The latter years of his management were spent in fruitless endeavours to supersede the old method of handcasting by machinery. The various experiments made, however (one of which was by Sir Henry Bessemer, whose father[1] had been a typefounder), failed, and tended further to diminish Wilson's resources, until in 1845 he became bankrupt. The last specimen-book was issued in 1843.

The London and Two-Waters foundries being offered for sale by auction, the principal part of the matrices was purchased by the proprietors of the Caslon Foundry in 1850,[2] Wilson remaining for some time with Caslon as joint manager. He retired finally in 1865 and died in November 1874. There is an affectionate recollection of him in T. W. Smith's privately printed *Autobiography*.

The Edinburgh branch of the business, started in 1832, had continued for some time with Duncan Sinclair as managing partner. In specimens of 1832 and 1833 the firm is styled Wilsons and Sinclair. On the latter withdrawing from the concern and establishing himself as an independent founder at Whiteford House, Edinburgh, about 1839, the management was entrusted to John Gallie.

On the breaking up of the business, the plant of the Edinburgh and Dublin branches was acquired by Dr. James Marr, who, in association with Gallie, carried on the business under the firm of Marr, Gallie, & Co. In 1853 it was James Marr & Co., with branches in London, Edinburgh, and Dublin. The Dublin branch appears to have been closed after 1864. In *Specimens of Ancient and Modern Printing Types*, c. 1865, some sheets are signed 'Marr, Thom & Co., Dublin', and others 'Alex. Wilson & Sons'. There are seven pages of 'Ancient' types, i.e. founts dating from the end of the eighteenth century. J. Marr & Co. in 1869 appeared in the Trade Directory included in *The Printers' Register*, after the chief foundries had ceased to advertise in that journal (cf. below, p. 354). Dr. James Marr died in 1866, from which time till 1874 the business was carried on by his widow, with John Blair as manager. In 1874 it was converted into a limited company under the title of the Marr Typefounding Company, Limited, calling themselves 'Irish Letter Founders'; they removed the business from the old premises in New Street, Edinburgh, to Whiteford House. This foundry was subsequently absorbed by Messrs. Miller and Richard.

In *The Shops and Companies of London*, edited by Henry Mayhew, 1865, Part 8, is a description of a visit to the Marr Typefoundry. There is a long historical introduction and a detailed description of all the processes of type production. All this leads up to an account of the development of type-casting machinery as exemplified in the Marr foundry. First the old hand mould, called the Ring Tail mould, is described, and then the hand-lever mould. This improved mould, it is stated, was devised in 1832 by the American Edwin Starr, and was first used in this country

---

[1] See p. 351.

[2] In the copy now in St. Bride Institute of the Sale Catalogue of the Glasgow Letter Foundry, London, 1850, against the Long Primer No. 5, appears the following note: 'This was the fount used for the 1st edition of the Waverley Novels. T. B. R.'

by the Glasgow Foundry, the Wilsons. Another invention, that of the application of a pump to the furnace, so that the molten metal could be forced into the mould under some pressure, had already been made in 1830 by Bower and Bacon of Sheffield. This device was known as the 'hand-pump furnace' or the 'Sheffield furnace-pump'. It was a combination of these two inventions which led to the introduction of type-casting machines, and it was the Wilson foundry which was the first to make the attempt to use these machines in England. After the Wilsons had opened a branch in London in 1834 and were in fierce competition with the London houses, and moreover involved in labour disputes with their own work-men, they attempted to solve their troubles by the introduction of labour-saving machinery, namely, the type-casting machine invented by Henry Bessemer. But, as we have seen, their struggle ended in bankruptcy. The Marr foundry imported an American machine, presumably that of David Bruce, but this was found unsatis-factory. James Henry, the foreman of their smithy, attempted to improve the American machine. After repeated trials and alterations, and the addition of amendments from a revised version of the American machine, success was achieved and by 1862 the invention was in continual operation at the Edinburgh foundry. A detailed description, with illustrations of the machine, is given. It is stated that between thirty and forty of these casters were in use, each of which could do the work of four hand casters. No patents appear to have been taken out.

Like the other founders, the Marrs too had their hard metal. They had in fact four grades of type metal. There was no secret about the process. Anyone could make hard type by increasing the proportion of antimony, with tin to provide toughness. The problem was to produce a hard metal at a reasonable price; how not to use an excessive amount of the more expensive materials.

Duncan Sinclair, between whose specimens and those of the Wilson foundry there was an obvious similarity, continued for some years at Whiteford House, where his son John, formerly manager at the Two-Waters branch of the Glasgow Foundry, subsequently joined him. They published specimens in 1840, 1842, and 1846 (which latter included a fount of 'Gem'). In 1861 the Whiteford House Foundry was in the hands of John Milne & Co., who published a quarto specimen. In 1870 the contents of this foundry were dispersed at public auction in London and a catalogue was issued by J. M. Powell; the premises, as already stated, were shortly afterwards taken by the Marr Typefounding Company.

MALONE AND PERRY, DUBLIN, 1749. STEPHEN PARKER, 1765[1]

We have seen that John Bain conducted a branch of the Wilson foundry in Dublin from 1747 to 1749. Before that date there appears to have been no foundry in Ireland, although there is a record of the administration of the goods of 'Ralph Sadler, late of Dublin, Letter Founder', dated 7 May 1703. In February 1749 an advertisement appeared in *Faulkner's Dublin Journal*:

Daniel Malone and Robert Perry, Letter Founders in Dublin, beg leave to inform the printers and booksellers of this kingdom that they are preparing with the utmost diligence the proper materials for casting all manner of printing types in use; in the prosecution of

---

[1] See W. G. Strickland's *Typefounding in Dublin*, Bibliographical Society of Ireland, 1922.

which all imaginable care shall be taken to have them finished to equal perfection with any imported from abroad. It is humbly presumed there remains little doubt of this from the progress already made in the compass of one year, they accordingly hope for suitable encouragement.

Malone was an engraver and Perry a printer, so that Malone may be presumed to have been the punch-cutter. *Faulkner's Journal* further reports, in November 1750, that 'they produced before the Dublin Society several specimens of their printing with letters of their own making; and their letters and types appearing to be more correct and neat than any imported, the Society ordered that £10 be given to them for their encouragement'. The firm appears to have had financial assistance from George Grierson, King's printer in Ireland. His son, Boulter Grierson, in 1764 petitioned for the renewal of his father's patent, and in support of his claim says 'that the art of making types for printing was unknown in Ireland until very lately, when your petitioner's father encouraged it by laying out One Thousand pounds in that article alone, in order to establish that art in the said kingdom, and there are now as good types made here as any imported, by which means there is great saving to the public, and great part of the money that would be otherwise sent to foreign country's is left in this kingdom'. No foundry is mentioned, but presumably it was that of Malone and Perry.

Robert Perry died in November 1765 (the date of Malone's death is not known) and was succeeded by his nephew, Stephen Parker, who had been his apprentice. In 1769 Parker issued a small specimen-book of the types of the foundry, the first specimen of types cut in Ireland. Roman and italic types from four-line Pica to Brevier are shown, with four pages of flowers, the last page showing flowers built up into a border in quite the latest style. Stephen Parker died about 1790 and the firm was continued by his widow Mary Anne and then by his son Stephen until 1810. James Christie appears as a typefounder in the Dublin directories from 1809 to 1855, but the only known type of his cutting is the Irish fount mentioned above (p. 69). In 1840 the Wilson foundry once more opened a branch in Dublin. As already related, after the failure of the Wilson firm, James Marr & Co. acquired the plant and continued the Dublin branch until 1864. In 1869 William Miller started a new foundry, which is still working under the style of William Miller & Son.

$\begin{bmatrix} 13 \end{bmatrix}$

JOHN BASKERVILLE, 1752

JOHN BASKERVILLE was born at Sion Hill in the parish of Wolverley, in the county of Worcestershire, in the year 1706.[1] The story that he began life as a footman to a clergyman at King's Norton rests only on the evidence of the Rev. Mark Noble, an untrustworthy authority.[2] At the age of 20 he became

FIG. 74. John Baskerville.

a writing-master in Birmingham. This occupation he appears to have supplemented by, or exchanged for, that of engraving inscriptions on tombstones and memorials, a profession in which he is said to have shown much talent.[3] His name

---

[1] He was baptized on 28 Jan. 1706.

[2] See William Bennett, *John Baskerville*, 1937–9, 2 vols. That work gives the latest research on Baskerville's ancestry.

[3] There still exists, formerly in Samuel Timmins's collection of Baskerville relics and now in the Birmingham Central Library, a slate tablet beauti-fully engraved with the words 'Grave Stones cut in any of the Hands by John Baskervill, Writing Master', in which the admirable models of roman and italic for which he afterwards became famous are clearly prefigured. There is a reproduction in Straus and Dent's *John Baskerville*, 1907, and in W. Bennett, op. cit.

first appears in the rate books in 1733, when he had a school in the Bull Ring. By 1739 he was living in New Meeting Street and from 1740 to 1748 in Moor Street. His artistic tastes led him afterwards to enter into the japanning business, in which he prospered and became possessed of considerable property. He purchased an estate on the outskirts of the town, to which he gave the name of Easy Hill; and here built a handsome house, in which he carried on his business, and lived in considerable style.[1]

About the year 1750 his inclination for letters induced him to turn his attention to typography, and to add to his business of a japanner that of a printer.[2]

The condition of printing in England at this period was still anything but satisfactory. Fine printing was an art unknown; and although under the influence of Caslon's genius the press was recovering from the reproach under which it lay at the beginning of the century, England was still very far behind her neighbours both in typographical enterprise and achievement. Once more it was left to an outsider to initiate the new departure; and as in 1720 the art of letter-founding had been roused from its lethargy by the genius of a gunsmith's apprentice, so in 1750 the art of printing was destined to find its deliverer in the person of an eccentric Birmingham japanner. Whatever may be the judgement of posterity as to the merits of Baskerville's performances, to him is undoubtedly due the honour of the first real stride towards a higher level of national typography; an example which became the incentive to that outburst of enthusiasm—that 'matrix and puncheon mania', as Dibdin terms it—which brought forth the series of splendid typographical productions with which the eighteenth century closed and the nineteenth opened.

Baskerville's first essay in his new enterprise was deliberate, and gave ample proof of the enthusiasm of the man. Six years elapsed before any work issued from his press. During that period he is said to have sunk upwards of £600[3] in the effort to produce a type sufficiently perfect to satisfy his fastidious taste. He engaged the best punch-cutters that could be had,[4] in addition to which he made his own moulds, chases, ink, presses, and, indeed, almost the entire apparatus of the art.

The following extracts from letters formerly in the possession of Samuel Timmins of Birmingham,[5] to whose industrious researches the student of typography is indebted for much new light on the history of Baskerville's career, will best describe the marvellous industry and enthusiasm which carried our printer to the

[1] 'His carriage,' says Nichols, 'each panel of which was a distinct picture, might be considered the pattern-card of his trade, and was drawn by a beautiful pair of cream-coloured horses' (*Lit. Anec.* iii. 451).

[2] He appears to have continued his original business to the end of his days. Writing in 1760, Samuel Derrick, in a letter to the Earl of Cork, dated July that year, after describing Baskerville's printing achievements, adds: 'This ingenious artist carries on a great trade in the Japan way, in which he showed me several useful articles, such as candlesticks, stands, salvers, waiters, bread-baskets, tea-boards, etc., elegantly designed and highly finished.' The name of Baskerville had previously been associated with typography, as we find in the lists of the Stationers' Company a Gabriel Baskerville, who took up his freedom in 1622, and a John Baskerville, who took up his freedom in 1639.

[3] Dibdin (*Intr. to Classics*, ii. 555) says £800.

[4] An obituary notice in the *Gentleman's Magazine* (1793, p. 91) reads: 'Mr. John Handy, the artist who executed the admired types of the late celebrated Mr. Baskerville; and who, for the last 12 years, very materially assisted in the establishment of the present esteemed letter-foundry of Mr. Swinney, of Birmingham.'

[5] Baskerville's letters are given more fully, with some additional letters, in Straus and Dent's *John Baskerville*, 1907, and in William Bennett's *John Baskerville*. The location of the letters is also given in Bennett. Straus and Dent include also a catalogue of books printed by Baskerville, and other printers who used his types.

successful issue of his great enterprise. The letters form part of a correspondence between Baskerville and his friend Robert Dodsley, the publisher, respecting the preparations for his earliest printing venture:

Baskerville to R. Dodsley. 2 October 1752.

To remove in some measure your impatience, I have sent you an impression of fourteen punches of the Two-lines Great Primer, which have been begun and finished in nine days only, and contain all the letters Roman necessary in the Titles and Half-titles. I cannot forbear saying they please me, as I can make nothing more correct, nor shall you see anything of mine much less so. You'll observe they strike the eye much more sensibly than the smaller characters, tho' equally perfect, till the press shows them to more advantage. The press is creeping slowly towards perfection. I flatter myself with being able to print nearly as good a colour and smooth a stroke as the enclosed. I should esteem it a favour if you'd send me the Initial Letters of all the Cantos lest they should not be included in the said fourteen, and three or four pages of any part of the Poem from whence to form a Bill for the casting a suitable number of each letter. The R wants a few slight touches, and the Y half an hour's correction. This day we have resolutely set about thirteen of the same siz'd Italic Capitals, which will not be at all inferior to the Roman, and I doubt not to complete them in a fortnight. You need, therefore, be in no pain about our being ready by the time appointed. Our best respects to Mrs. Dodsley and our friend, Mr. Beckett.

Baskerville to R. Dodsley. 19 October 1752.

As I proposed in my last, I have sent you impressions from a candle of twenty Two-lines Great Primer Italick, which were begun and finished in ten days only. We are now about the figures, which are in a good forwardness, and changing a few of those letters we concluded finished. My next care will be to strike the punches into copper and justify them with all the care and skill I am master of. You may depend on my being ready by your time (Christmas), but if more time could be allowed, I should make use of it all in correcting and justifying. So much depends on appearing perfect on first starting. . . .

Baskerville to R. Dodsley. 16 January 1754.

I have put the last hand to my Great Primer, and have corrected fourteen letters in the specimen you were so kind to approve, and have made a good progress in the English, and have formed a new alphabet of Two-line Double Pica and Two-line Small Pica capitals for Titles, not one of which I can mend with a wish, as they come up to the most perfect idea I have of letters.

He then details his scheme for obtaining absolutely correct texts of the works he is about to print, as follows:

'Tis this. Two people must be concerned; the one must name every letter, capital, point, reference, accent, etc., that is, in English, must spell every part of every word distinctly, and note down every difference in a book prepared on purpose. Pray oblige me in making the experiment with Mr. James Dodsley in four or five lines of any two editions of an author, and you'll be convinced that it's scarcely possible for the least difference, even of a point, to escape notice. I would recommend and practise the same method in an English author, where most people imagine themselves capable of correcting. Here's another great advantage to me in this humble scheme; at the same time that a proof sheet is correcting, I shall find out the least imperfection in any of the Types that has escaped the founder's notice. I have great encomiums on my Specimen from Scotland.

The concluding sentence of this letter probably refers to the public announcement of the forthcoming quarto *Virgil*,[1] put forward about this time, together with a specimen of the type. This most interesting document, a very few copies of which still exist, is in the form of a quarto sheet, headed, *A Specimen By John Baskerville of Birmingham, in the County of Warwick, Letter-Founder and Printer*. It displays the roman and italic of the Great Primer fount, and is remarkable not only as a piece of exquisite printing,[2] but as the first known specimen of the famous Birmingham foundry (Fig. 75).

The following letters refer principally to the progress and completion of the *Virgil*:

Baskerville to R. Dodsley. Birmingham, 20 December 1756.

I shall have *Virgil* out of the press by the latter end of January, and hope to produce the Volume as smooth as the best paper I have sent you. Pray, will it not be proper to advertize how near it is finishing, and beg the gentlemen who intend favouring me with their names, to send them by that time? When this is done, I can print nothing at home but another Classick (a specimen of which will be given with it) which I cannot forbear thinking a grievous hardship after the infinite pains and great expense I have been at. I have almost a mind to print a pocket Classick in one size larger than the old Elzevirs, as the difference will, on comparison, be obvious to every Scholar; nor should I be very sollicitous whether it paid me or not.

R. Dodsley to Baskerville. 10 February 1757.

The account you give me of the *Virgil* pleases me much, and I hope you will in that have all the success your heart can wish. I beg if you have any objection, addition or alteration to make in the following Advertisement you will let me know by return of post:—

'To the Public.

'John Baskerville of Birmingham thinks proper to give notice that having now finished his Edition of *Virgil* in one Volume, Quarto, it will be published the latter end of next month, price one guinea in sheets. He therefore desires that such gentlemen who intend to favour him with their names, will be pleased to send them either to himself at Birmingham, or to R. and J. Dodsley in Pall Mall, in order that they may be inserted in the list of his encouragers.'

R. Dodsley to Baskerville. 7 April 1757.

I am very sorry I advertised your *Virgil* to be published last month as you have not enabled me to keep my word with the public; but I hope it will not be delayed any longer, as every day you lose now the season is so far advanced, is certainly a great loss to you. I hope I shall have the pleasure of seeing you and it together. However, if the delay is occasioned by your making corrections, I think that a point of so much consequence, that no consideration should induce you to publish till it is quite correct. As to the ornamented

---

[1] 'John Baskerville proposes, by the advice and assistance of several learned men, to print, from the Cambridge edition corrected with all possible care, an elegant edition of Virgil. The work will be printed in quarto, on a very fine writing royal paper, and with the above letter. The price of the Volume in sheets will be one guinea, no part of which will be required till the book is delivered. It will be put to press as soon as the number of Subscribers shall amount to five hundred, whose names will be prefixt to the work. All persons who are inclined to encourage the undertaking, are desired to send their names to John Baskerville in Birmingham; who will give specimens of the work to all who are desirous of seeing them. Subscriptions are also taken in, and specimens delivered by Messieurs R. and J. Dodsley, Booksellers in Pall Mall, London.'

[2] Of the two copies formerly in the possession of Samuel Timmins (now in the Birmingham Central Library) one is printed on very fine bank-note paper, and the other, more heavily, on a coarse brown. One copy is dated MDCCLIV.

Fig. 75. The first Baskerville specimen-sheet.

SPECIMEN

By *JOHN BASKERVILLE* of BIRMINGHAM,
In the County of Warwick, *Letter-Founder and Printer.*

To CNEIUS PLANCIUS.

I Am indebted to you for two letters, dated from Corcyra. You congratulate me in one of them on the account you have received, that I ſtill preſerve my former authority in the commonwealth: and wiſh me joy in the other of my late marriage. With reſpect to the firſt, if to mean well to the intereſt of my country and to approve that meaning to eve-ry friend of its liberties, may be conſidered as maintaining my authority; the account you have heard is certainly true. But if it conſiſts in rendering thoſe ſentiments effectual to the public welfare, or at leaſt in daring freely to ſupport

To *CAIUS CASSIUS,* proquæſtor.

MY own inclinations have anticipated your recommendation: and I have long ſince received Marcus Fabius into the number of my friends. He has extremely endeared himſelf to me indeed, by his great politeneſs and elegance of manners: but particularly by the ſingu-lar affection I have obſerved he bears towards you. Accordingly, tho' your letter in his behalf was not without effect, yet my own knowledge of the regard he entertains for you had ſomewhat more: you may be aſſured therefore I ſhall very faithfully confer upon him the good offi-ces you requeſt.

TO THE PUBLIC.

JOHN BASKERVILLE propoſes, by the advice and aſſiſtance of ſeveral learned men, to print, from the Cambridge edition corrected with all poſſible care, an elegant edition of Virgil. The work will be printed in quarto, on a very fine writing royal paper, and with the above letter. The price of the Volume in ſheets will be one guinea, no part of which will be required till the book is de-livered. It will be put to preſs as ſoon as the number of Subſcribers ſhall amount to five hundred, whoſe names will be prefixt to the work. All perſons who are inclined to encourage the undertaking, are deſired to ſend their names to JOHN BASKERVILLE in Birmingham; who will give ſpecimens of the work to all who are deſirous of ſeeing them.

Subſcriptions are alſo taken in, and ſpecimens delivered by Meſſieurs R. and J. DODSLEY, Bookſellers in Pall Mall, London. MDCCLIV.

paper, I will lower the price since you think it proper, but am still of opinion that it will not sell at our end of the town, tho' for what reason I cannot imagine. . . . I like exceedingly your specimen of a *Common Prayer*, and hope you are endeavouring to get leave to print one. There is an error in the Exhortation, *shall* for *should*. Your small letter is extremely beautiful; I wish I could advise you what to print with it. What think you of some popular French book—*Gil Blas*, *Molière*, or *Telemaque?* In the specimen from *Melmoth* I think you have used too many Capitals, which is generally thought to spoil the beauty of printing; but they should never be used to adjectives, verbs, or adverbs. My best compliments attend your whole family.

At length, after repeated delays, caused mainly by the nervous fastidiousness of the printer, who even corrected his work *currente prelo* up to the last moment, the famous *Virgil* appeared in 1757,[1] and with its publication Baskerville's reputation was made. Being the earliest performance of this press, the volume possesses a peculiar interest among the productions of English typography. Opinions may differ as to some of the eulogies pronounced on it by bibliographers and bibliophiles,[2] but as a typographical curiosity,[3] and as a pioneer of fine printing in our midst, it is a work to be treasured and reverenced.

From a letter-founder's point of view its chief interest consists in its being the earliest book printed in the type of the new Birmingham foundry. The fount used is a Great Primer, slender and delicate in form, combining, as Dibdin says, in a singularly happy manner, the elegance of Plantin with the clearness of the Elzevirs. The italic letter was specially admired for its freedom and symmetry—qualities in which it excelled even the beautiful founts of Aldus and Colines.[4]

Baskerville's merit met with prompt recognition in many quarters, amongst others, by the Delegates of the Oxford Press, who, in 1758 (apparently on his own application), entrusted him with the cutting and casting of a new Greek fount for their own use. A record of this important transaction remains in the following Minutes of the Delegates:

June 6, 1758.—Present (among others) Dr. (Sir W.) Blackstone. *Order'd* that this Delegacy will at their next meeting take into consideration Mr. Baskerville's Proposals for casting a Set of new Greek Types.

July 5, 1758.—*Ordered* that Dr. Blackstone be empowered to agree with Mr. Baskerville of Birmingham to make a new set of Greek Puncheons, matrices and moulds, in Great Primer, for the Use of the University, and also to cast therein 300 Weight of Types, at the Price of 200 Guineas for the whole. And that he and Mr. Prince (Warehouse-keeper) do give proper Directions for that Purpose.

Jan. 31, 1759.—*Agreed* that Mr. Musgrave have leave to print his *Euripides* at the University Press on Mr. Baskerville's Types as soon as they arrive.[5]

March 11, 1761.—*Ordered,* That a Greek Testament in Quarto and Octavo be printed on Baskerville's Letter, and three or four Gentlemen of Learning and Accuracy be desired separately to correct the Proofs.

June 23, 1761.—500 copies in Quarto and 2,000 in Octavo ordered to be printed.

---

[1] *Publii Virgilii Maronis Bucolica, Georgica, et Æneis. Birminghamiae Typis Johannis Baskerville.* 1757. 4to. There were several issues of the *Virgil*, for details of which see Straus and Dent.

[2] 'I have always considered this beautiful production as one of the most finished specimens of typography' (Dibdin, *Introduction to the Classics*, 2nd ed. ii. 335).

[3] 'My neighbour Baskerville at the close of this month (March 1757) publishes his fine edition of *Virgil*; it will for *type* and *paper* be a perfect curiosity' (Shenstone's *Letters and Works*, 1791, letter 88).

[4] For a specimen of Baskerville's jobbing printing of the year 1757 see *The Fleuron*, No. 7, pp. 155–6.

[5] Other type was used for this work.

In the accounts for 1761 the following entry records the conclusion of the business:

To Mr. Baskerville for Greek Types . . . . £210 0 0.

Considerable expectation was aroused by this order, which was considered of sufficient importance to deserve mention in the public press, as the following extract from the *St. James's Chronicle* of 5 September 1758 testifies:

The University of Oxford have lately contracted with Mr. Baskerville of Birmingham for a complete Alphabet of Greek Types of the Great Primer size; and it is not doubted but that ingenious artist will excel in that Character, as he has already done in the Roman and Italic, in his elegant edition of *Virgil*, which has gained the applause and admiration of most of the literati of Europe, as well as procured him the esteem and patronage of such of his own countrymen as distinguish themselves by paying a due regard to merit.

The anticipations thus expressed were destined to be disappointed; for Baskerville's genius appears to have failed him in his efforts to reproduce a foreign character. Even before the appearance of the Oxford *Greek Testament*, which did not occur till 1763, rumours of the failure of this undertaking had begun to circulate. Writing in 1763, respecting a forthcoming *Greek Testament* of his own, Bowyer says, 'Two or three quarto Editions on foot, one at Oxford, far advanced on new types by Baskerville,—by the way, not good ones.'[1]

The appearance of the work in question[2] justified, to some extent, the criticism. Regular as the Greek character is, it is stiff and cramped, and, as Dibdin says, 'like no Greek characters I have ever seen'. Rowe Mores goes to the length of styling it 'execrable'; and Bowyer appears to have had it specially in mind when he said to Jackson that the Greek letters commonly in use were no more like Greek than English. Be this as it may, Baskerville made no further excursions into the foreign and learned languages, and, fortunately (as we consider) for his reputation, confined his talents to the execution of the characters of his native tongue, a branch of the art in which he had no rival.

The punches, matrices, and some of the types of this interesting fount are still preserved at Oxford,[3] and are the only relics in this country of Baskerville's letter foundry. We are particularly glad, therefore, to be able to present here a facsimile

[1] *Lit. Anec.* ii. 411.
[2] H. Καινη Διαθηκη. *Novum Testamentum juxta exemplar Millianum. Typis Joannis Baskerville. Oxonii e Typographeo Clarendoniano.* 1763. *Sumptibus Academiae*, 4to and 8vo.
[3] Some of the punches were exhibited by the University Press at the Caxton Celebration in 1877. Since then, thanks to the energy of the then Controller, Horace Hart, to whom Reed was indebted for the above extracts and specimens, the matrices of the fount have come to light as well as the punches and matrices of the two-line letters and figures belonging to it. These were exhibited at the British Association Meeting at Birmingham in Aug. 1886, being catalogued as follows:
'Punchions of the Great Primer Greek—a large proportion of the fount, but not the whole.
'Matrices of the same.

'Punchions of the Two-line Great Primer, with Initial Letters. Complete.
'Matrices of the same, also complete.
'Punchions of one set of Figures, supplied with the above.
'Matrices of the same.'
Still later, Horace Hart was fortunate enough to discover part of the actual type in its original cases. It is interesting to note that these types, which are of rather a soft metal, are cast to the Oxford Learned-Side 'height-to-paper'.
The Oxford Press claim to have had some Brevier roman of Baskerville, which was used inadvertently in some books of the Daniel Press. See *Memorials of C. H. O. Daniel*, Oxford, 1921, p. 159. But this Brevier may have been a copy. See J. Dreyfus, 'The Baskerville Punches', in *The Library*, June, 1950.

T

from the Oxford Specimen of 1768–70, printed from the actual type cast by Baskerville in 1761.

Among the other important works which, says Nichols, 'Baskerville printed with more satisfaction to the literary world than emolument to himself', his *Paradise Lost*, in 4to, printed in 1758,[1] is of signal merit and beauty. As a work of fine printing it equals, if it does not excel, the *Virgil*.

The type [observes Hansard, who speaks of it as a Pica instead of an English] is manifestly an improvement on the 'slender and delicate' mentioned by Mr. Dibdin; I should think it, on the contrary, approaching to the *embonpoint*, and admirably calculated by extending the size (if in exact proportion), for works of the largest dimensions. The Italic possesses much room for admiration. . . . This work will, in my opinion, bear a comparison, even to its advantage, with those subsequently executed by the first typographer of our age. There is a clearness, a soberness, a softness, and at the same time a spirit, altogether harmonizing, in Baskerville's book, that neither of the others with which I am comparing it, can, I think, fairly claim.[2]

In his preface to the *Paradise Lost*, Baskerville gives an interesting account of his own labours and ambitions as a letter-founder. He says:

Amongst the several mechanic Arts that have engaged my attention, there is no one which I have pursued with so much steadiness and pleasure as that of *Letter Founding*. Having been an early admirer of the beauty of Letters, I became insensibly desirous of contributing to the perfection of them. I formed to myself ideas of greater accuracy than had yet appeared, and have endeavoured to produce a *Sett* of *Types* according to what I conceived to be their true proportion.

Mr. Caslon is an artist to whom the Republic of Learning has great obligations; his ingenuity has left a fairer copy for my emulation, than any other master. In his great variety of *Characters* I intend not to follow him; the *Roman* and *Italic* are all I have hitherto attempted; if in these he has left room for improvement it is probably more owing to that variety which divided his attention, than to any other cause. I honor his merit and only wish to derive some small share of Reputation, from an Art which proves accidentally to have been the object of our mutual pursuit.

After having spent many years, and not a little of my fortune, in my endeavours to advance this art: I must own it gives me great satisfaction to find that my edition of *Virgil* has been so favourably received. . . .

It is not my desire to print many books; but such only as are *books* of *Consequence*, of *intrinsic merit*, or *established Reputation*, and which the public may be pleased to see in an elegant dress, and to purchase at such a price, as will repay the extraordinary care and expence that must necessarily be bestowed upon them. . . . If this performance shall appear to persons of judgment and penetration, in the *Paper*, *Letter*, *Ink*, and *Workmanship* to excel; I hope their approbation may contribute to procure for me what would indeed be the extent of my Ambition, a power to print an Octavo *Prayer Book*, and a FOLIO BIBLE.

Both these ambitions were in due time fulfilled. In 1758 Baskerville had applied for the post of Printer to the University of Cambridge, an office which he obtained, with permission to print the folio *Bible*, and two editions of the *Common Prayer* in three sizes. This learned body, however, appear to have been influenced in the

---

[1] *Paradise Lost, etc., Paradise Regain'd, etc.*, Birmingham, 1758. 2 vols., 4to. The work was also published in the same year in 8vo, and again in 4to in 1759. The 4to edition of 1758 appears to be overlooked by some bibliographers, Hansard, among others, who refers in the extract here given to the reprint of 1759.

[2] *Typographia*, p. 310. It is worthy of note that the very high gloss on the paper which characterized most of Baskerville's later works is not always observable either in the *Virgil* of 1757 or the *Milton* of 1758.

ΑΒΓΔΕΖΗΘΙΚ

ΑΒΓΔΕΖΗΘΙΚΛΜΝΞΟΠΡΣΤΥΦΧΨΩ

Καὶ μετὰ ταῦτα ἤκεσα φωνὴν ὄχλου πολλῦ μεγάλην ἐν τῷ ἐρανῷ, λέγοντος· Ἀλληλέϊα· ἡ σωτηρία καὶ ἡ δόξα καὶ ἡ τιμὴ καὶ ἡ δύναμις, Κυρίῳ τῷ Θεῷ ἡμῶν· Ὅτι ἀληθιναὶ καὶ δίκαιαι αἱ κρίσεις αὐτῦ· ὅτι ἔκρινε τὴν πόρνην τὴν μεγάλην, ἥτις ἔφθειρε τὴν γῆν ἐν τῇ πορνείᾳ αὐτῆς, καὶ ἐξεδίκησε τὸ αἷμα τῶν δέλων αὐτῦ ἐκ τῆς χειρὸς αὐτῆς. Καὶ δεύτερον εἴρηκαν. Ἀλληλέϊα. Καὶ ὁ καπνὸς αὐτῆς ἀναβαίνει εἰς τὰς αἰῶνας τῶν αἰώνων. Καὶ ἔπεσον οἱ πρεσβύτεροι οἱ εἴκοσι καὶ τέσσαρες, καὶ τὰ τέσσαρα ζῶα, καὶ προσεκύνησαν τῷ Θεῷ τῷ καθημένῳ ἐπὶ τῦ θρόνῦ, λέγον{ε}ς· Ἀμήν· Ἀλληλέϊα. Καὶ φωνὴ ἐκ τῦ θρόνῦ ἐξῆλθε, λέγεσα· Αἰνεῖτε τὸν Θεὸν ἡμῶν πάντες οἱ δῦλοι αὐτῦ, καὶ οἱ φοβύμενοι αὐτὸν καὶ οἱ μικροὶ καὶ οἱ μεγάλοι. Καὶ ἤκεσα ὡς φωνὴν ὄχλε πολλῦ, καὶ ὡς φωνὴν ὑδάτων πσλλῶν, καὶ ὡς φωνὴν βροντῶν ἰχυρῶν, λέγοντας.

Fɪɢ. 76. Baskerville's Greek, 1763.
From the original matrices.

PARADISE LOST.

BOOK X.

MEAN while the hainous and defpiteful act
    Of Satan done in Paradife, and how
He in the ferpent, had perverted Eve,
Her hufband fhe, to tafte the fatal fruit,
Was known in Heav'n; for what can 'fcape the eye 5
Of God all-feeing, or deceive his heart
Omnifcient? who in all things wife and juft,
Hinder'd not Satan to attempt the mind
Of Man, with ftrength entire, and free will arm'd,
Complete to have difcover'd and repuls'd   10
Whatever wiles of foe or feeming friend.
For ftill they knew, and ought to' have ftill remember'd
The high injunction not to tafte that fruit,
Whoever tempted; which they not obeying,
Incurr'd (what could they lefs?) the penalty,   15
And manifold in fin, deferv'd to fall.
Up into Heav'n from Paradife in hafte
Th' angelic guards afcended, mute and fad
For Man, for of his ftate by this they knew,
Much wond'ring how the fubtle Fiend had ftol'n   20
Entrance unfeen. Soon as th' unwelcome news
                        From

FIG. 77. Baskerville's *Milton*, 1758.

THE ARGUMENT.

Man's transgression known, the Guardian Angels forsake Paradise, and return up to Heaven to approve their vigilance, and are approv'd, God declaring that the entrance of Satan could not be by them prevented. He sends his Son to judge the transgressors, who descends and gives sentence accordingly; then in pity clothes them both, and reascends. Sin and Death sitting till then at the gates of Hell, by wondrous sympathy feeling the success of Satan in this new world, and the sin by Man there committed, resolve to sit no longer confin'd in Hell, but to follow Satan their sire up to the place of Man: To make the way easier from Hell to this world to and fro, they pave a broad high-way or bridge over Chaos, according to the track that Satan first made; then preparing for Earth, they meet him proud of his success returning to Hell; their mutual gratulation. Satan arrives at Pandemonium, in full assembly relates with boasting his success against Man; instead of applause is entertained with a general hiss by all his audience, transform'd with himself also suddenly into serpents, according to his doom given in Paradise; then deluded with a show of the forbidden tree springing up before them, they greedily reaching to take of the fruit, chew dust and bitter ashes. The proceedings of Sin and Death; God foretells the final victory of his Son over them, and the renewing of all things; but for the present commands his Angels to make several alterations in the Heavens and elements. Adam more and more perceiving his fall'n condition heavily bewails, rejects the condolement of Eve; she persists, and at length appeases him: then to evade the curse likely to fall on their offspring, proposes to Adam violent ways, which he approves not, but conceiving better hope, puts her in mind of the late promise made them, that her seed should be reveng'd on the Serpent, and exhorts her with him to seek peace of the offended Deity, by repentance and supplication.

FIG. 78. Baskerville's *Milton*, 1758.

transaction more by a wish to fill their own coffers than by a desire to promote the interests of the art; and the heavy premiums exacted from Baskerville for the privilege thus accorded effectually deprived him of any advantage whatever in the undertaking. He continued to hold this unsatisfactory office till 1766.

Meanwhile he had laboured assiduously to complete his promised series of the roman and italic faces. At the time of the publication of the *Virgil*, he put forward a quarto sheet containing specimens of the Great Primer, English, Pica, and Brevier roman, and Great Primer and Pica italic, beautifully printed. This sheet, which is noted by Renouard,[1] and which is occasionally found bound up with copies of the *Virgil*, was very shortly followed, about the end of the year 1758, by a larger and more general specimen, consisting entirely of roman and italic letter in eight sizes, viz.: Double Pica, Great Primer, English, Pica, Small Pica, Long Primer, Bourgeois, and Brevier. Of the two last, roman only is shown. The whole is arranged in two columns on a broadside sheet, with appropriate titlings, and forms a beautiful display. The specimen exceeds in elegance and uniformity most, if not all, the productions of contemporary founders.[2]

It may be worth noting here that in point of body Baskerville appears to have followed an independent course, most of his bodies, even the Pica, varying from the usual standards. The punches of the Greek fount, preserved at Oxford, show marks of high finish, although unnecessarily, as it seems to us, rounded in the stem. It is probable that these and the other punches of his foundry were not his own handiwork, but cut by skilled artists under his critical supervision.

Unfortunately, very little is known of the operations of the Birmingham foundry as a trade undertaking. It is even doubtful whether, at first, Baskerville supplied his types to any press but his own; indeed, the activity of that press during the period when it was in the height of its prosperity was such that it is unlikely its proprietor would encumber himself with the duties of a letter-founder to the trade in general.

The magnificent works[3] which between 1759 and 1772 continued to issue from his press not only confirmed him in his reputation, but raised his name to a unique position among the modern improvers of the art. The paper,[4] the type, and the

---

[1] *Catalogue de la Bibliothèque d'un Amateur*, i. 310. After noticing the folio specimen following, he says: 'Un autre essai de Baskerville, sur une plus petite feuille, contient seulement quatre caractères romains et deux en italique. . . . Outre cette épreuve de grand essai, j'ai l'un et l'autre réunis à la fin de son *Virgile* in 4.' One example we have met with is that bound up with Lord Spencer's beautiful copy of the *Virgil* in the Althorp Library (now in the John Rylands Library, Manchester). There is no copy at Birmingham, as stated in Berry and Johnson.

[2] Writing to R. Richardson of Durham on 29 Oct. 1758, Dr. John Bedford says: 'By Baskerville's specimen of his types, you will perceive how much the elegance of them is owing to his paper, which he makes himself, as well as the types and ink also; and I was informed whenever they came to be used by common pressmen and with common materials they will lose of their beauty considerably. Hence, perhaps, this specimen may become very curious (when he is no more, and the types cannot be set off in the same perfection), and a great piece of

vertû.' (Nichols, *Illust. Lit.* i. 813.) Straus and Dent, op. cit., date this specimen *c*. 1762, since it accompanied the letter to Walpole of 2 Nov. 1762 quoted below. But the Birmingham Central Library, when they acquired the Walpole letter in 1899, found two sheets with the letter, the one here discussed, and a second sheet containing one more roman and three more italics, surrounded by a border of flowers. Cf. Berry and Johnson. The dates of issue of these sheets, Baskerville's third and fourth, remain, then, doubtful.

[3] Amongst which should be particularly singled out the *Horace* in 12mo printed in 1762, which Dr. Harwood describes as 'the most beautiful little book, both in regard to type and paper, I ever beheld'.

[4] Baskerville has been credited with the invention of wove paper. But in an article in *Signature*, No. 9, 1938, Mr. James Wardrop has shown that Whatman had made wove paper by 1759 and that his watermark is found on the paper of Baskerville's *Aesop*, 1761. It seems probable, then, that it was from Maidstone that Baskerville bought the paper of the

general execution of his works were such as English readers had not hitherto been accustomed to, while the disinterested enthusiasm with which, regardless of profit, he pursued his ideal, fully merited the eulogy of the printer-poet who wrote:

> O BASKERVILLE! the anxious wish was thine
> Utility with beauty to combine;
> To bid the o'erweening thirst of gain subside;
> Improvement all thy care and all thy pride;
> When BIRMINGHAM—for riots and for crimes
> Shall meet the long reproach of future times,
> Then shall she find amongst our honor'd race,
> One name to save her from entire disgrace.[1]

Baskerville's fourth specimen-sheet, undated, but probably issued in 1762, is an exquisitely printed large folio on highly glazed white paper. It completes the series of roman and italic displayed in the former sheet with a Nonpareil, and the whole is surrounded by an elegant light border. It is incomparably the most beautiful type-specimen of its day, although it must be admitted that not a little of its beauty is due to the brilliancy of the ink and the gloss of the paper.

Despite the applause bestowed on him, and the acknowledged excellence of his work, Baskerville failed to make his new business a paying one. His letter to Horace Walpole in 1762 best details the history of his struggles and disappointments:

To the Hon'ble Horace Walpole, Esq., Member of Parliament, in Arlington Street, London, this:

EASY HILL, BIRMINGHAM, 2 Nov. 1762.

SIR,—As the Patron and Encourager of Arts, and particularly that of Printing,[2] I have taken the Liberty of sending you a Specimen of Mine, begun ten Years ago at the age of forty-seven, and prosecuted ever since with the utmost Care and Attention, on the strongest Presumption, that if I could fairly excel in this divine Art, it would make my Affairs easy or at least give me Bread. But alas! in both I was mistaken. The Booksellers do not chuse to encourage Me, though I have offered them as low terms as I could possibly live by; nor dare I attempt an Old Copy till a Law Suit relating to that affair is determined.

The University of Cambridge have given me a Grant to print their 8vo and 12mo *Common-Prayer Books*, but under such Shackles as greatly hurt me. I pay them for the former twenty and for the latter twelve pounds ten shillings the thousand; and to the Stationers' Company thirty-two pound for their permission to print one edition of the *Psalms in Metre* to the small *Prayer Book*; add to this the great expense of Double and treble carriage, and the inconvenience of a printing house an hundred Miles off. All this Summer I have had nothing to print at Home. My folio *Bible* is pretty far advanced at Cambridge, which will cost me near £2000 all hired at 5 per cent. If this does not sell, I shall be obliged to sacrifice a small patrimony which brings me in £74 a year to this business of Printing, which I am heartily tired of and repent I ever attempted. It is surely a particular hardship, that I should not get Bread in my own country (and it is too late to go abroad)

Virgil. He does, however, appear to have experimented with paper-making. He was a competitor for a prize for making paper from silk, according to William Bailey's *Description of the Machines and Models at the Society of Arts*, 1772, p. 218. He had also some Dutch paper. See Straus and Dent, Appendix V, p. 140. He also sold and probably made writing-paper, as appears from two letters from Dodsley of 1767.

[1] *The Press, a poem. Published as a specimen of typography by John McCreery, Liverpool,* 1803, 4to,

p. 19.

[2] An interesting notice of Horace Walpole's famous private press at Strawberry Hill, with a Catalogue of the—many of them—finely printed works that issued from it, is given in Lemoine's *Typographical Antiquities*, p. 91. See also Austin Dobson, *Horace Walpole*, London, 1927. That Walpole procured his types from Caslon is shown in *Strawberry Hill Accounts*, ed. Paget Toynbee, 1927, pp. 97–8.

after having acquired the Reputation of excelling in the most useful Art known to mankind; while everyone who excels as a Player, Fiddler, Dancer, &c., not only lives in Affluence, but has it in their power to save a Fortune.

I have sent a few Specimens (same as the enclosed) to the Courts of Russia and Denmark, and shall endeavour to do the same to most of the Courts in Europe; in hopes of finding in some of them a purchaser of the whole scheme, on the Condition of never attempting another Type. I was saying this to a particular Friend, who reproached me with not giving my own Country the Preference, as it would (he was pleased to say) be a national Reproach to lose it: I told him nothing but the greatest Necessity would put me upon it; and even then I should resign it with the utmost reluctance. He observed the Parliament had given a handsome Premium for a great Medicine; and he doubted not, if My Affair were properly brought before the House of Commons, but some Regard would be Paid to it. I replied I durst not presume to Petition the House, unless encouraged by some of the Members, who might do me the honour to promote it; of which I saw not the least hopes or probability. Thus, Sir, I have taken the Liberty of laying before you my Affairs without the least Aggravation; and humbly hope your patronage: To whom can I apply for Protection, but the Great who alone have it in their power to serve me? I rely on your candor as a Lover of the Arts; to excuse this Presumption in your most obedient and most humble servant

JOHN BASKERVILLE.

P.S.—The folding of the Specimens will be taken out by laying them for a short time between damped Papers. N.B.—The Ink, Presses, Chases, Moulds for Casting, and all the apparatus for Printing were made in my own shops.[1]

The folio *Bible*[2] referred to in this letter has always been regarded as Baskerville's *magnum opus*, and is his most magnificent as well as his most characteristic specimen. It duly appeared in Cambridge in 1763, in a beautiful Great Primer type, fully meriting the applause which it evoked. It had been preceded in 1760 by some very elegant editions of the *Book of Common Prayer*,[3] all published at Cambridge in his capacity of University printer.

After the publication of the *Bible*, Baskerville wearied of his profession of printing, disheartened alike by the poor pecuniary returns for his labours, and the unfriendly criticism pronounced in various quarters upon his performances. Despite the splendid appearance of his impressions, the ordinary English printers viewed with something like suspicion the meretricious combination of sharp type and hotpressed paper which lent to his sheets their extraordinary brilliancy.[4] They objected to the dazzling effect thus produced on the eye; they found fault with the unevenness of tone and colour in different parts of the same book, and even discovered an irregularity and lack of symmetry in some of his types, which his glossy paper and bright ink alike failed to disguise. That these strictures were not wholly

---

[1] The original of this important letter, with the specimens attached, was in Samuel Timmins's possession, and is now in the Birmingham Central Library.

[2] *The Holy Bible, containing the Old Testament and the New, translated out of the Original Tongues, and with the former translations diligently compared and revised. By His Majesty's special command. Appointed to be read in Churches. Cambridge: printed by John Baskerville, Printer to the University. 1763. Cum Privilegio.* Fol. The prospectus of this work, with a specimen of the type, appeared in 1760. The folio *Bible* printed at Birmingham in 1772 is a much inferior performance.

[3] *The Book of Common Prayer, Cambridge,* 1760,

roy. 8vo (with long lines); 1760, roy. 8vo (in double columns); 1761, roy. 8vo; 1762, roy. 8vo (with long lines); 1762, 12mo.

[4] He appears always to have kept a large number of hot plates of copper ready, between which, as soon as printed, just as they were discharged from the tympan, the sheets were inserted. The moisture was thus expelled, the ink set, and the smooth, glossy surface put on all simultaneously. However well the method may have answered at the time, the discoloration of his books still preserved in the British Museum and elsewhere shows that the brilliance thus imparted was most tawdry and ephemeral.

the result of prejudice and jealousy, a careful examination of Baskerville's printed works in the light of the modern canons of fine printing will prove. Even his warmest admirers, like Fournier,[1] tempered their praise with some reservation; while hostile critics, like Mores, summarily denied him a place among letter-cutters at all.[2]

Of the prejudice rife against Baskerville at this time, an amusing anecdote is preserved in a letter of Benjamin Franklin to our printer, dated 1760:

CRAVEN STREET, LONDON, 1760.

DEAR SIR,—Let me give you a pleasant instance of the prejudice some have entertained against your work. Soon after I returned, discoursing with a gentleman concerning the artists of Birmingham, he said you would be a means of blinding all the readers of the nation, for the strokes of your letters being too thin and narrow, hurt the eye, and he could never read a line of them without pain. 'I thought,' said I, 'you were going to complain of the gloss of the paper some object to.' 'No, no,' said he, 'I have heard that mentioned, but it is not that; it is in the form and cut of the letters themselves, they have not that height and thickness of the stroke which makes the common printing so much more comfortable to the eye.' You see this gentleman was a *connoisseur*. In vain I endeavoured to support your character against the charge; he knew what he felt, and could see the reason of it, and several other gentlemen among his friends had made the same observation, etc. Yesterday he called to visit me, when, mischievously bent to try his judgement, I stepped into my closet, tore off the top of Mr. Caslon's specimen, and produced it to him as yours, brought with me from Birmingham, saying, I had been examining it, since he spoke to me, and could not for my life perceive the disproportion he mentioned, desiring him to point it out to me. He readily undertook it, and went over the several founts, showing me everywhere what he thought instances of that disproportion; and declared, that he could not then read the specimen, without feeling very strongly the pain he had mentioned to me. I spared him that time the confusion of being told, that these were the types he had been reading all his life, with so much ease to his eyes; the types his adored Newton is printed with, on which he has pored not a little; nay, the very types his own book is printed with (for he is himself an author), and yet never discovered this painful disproportion in them, till he thought they were yours.

I am, etc.,
B. FRANKLIN.[3]

In 1762 Baskerville, either when himself in Paris, or through the French ambassador in London, the Duc de Nivernais, made an offer of his foundry to the French Court for £8,000. This and two other attempts failing, a few years later Dr. Franklin undertook a similar good office in Paris, and with a similar result. 'The French,' he wrote in 1767, 'reduced by the war of 1756 were so far from being able to pursue schemes of taste, that they were unable to repair their public buildings, and suffered the scaffolding to rot before them.' In 1767 Baskerville was ready to accept £6,000. In a letter addressed to the President of the Royal Academy of

---

[1] 'Les caractères sont gravés avec beaucoup de hardiesse, les italiques sont les meilleures qu'il y ait dans toutes les Fonderies d'Angleterre, mais les romains sont un peu trop larges.' . . . And of his editions he adds, 'Quoiqu'elles fatiguent un peu la vue, on ne peut disconvenir que ce ne soit la plus belle chose qu'on ait encore vue en ce genre.' (*Man. Typ.* ii, p. xxxix.)

[2] 'Mr. Baskerville . . . made some attempts at letter-cutting, but desisted, with good reason. The Greek cut by him or his for the University of Oxford is execrable. Indeed, he can hardly claim a place amongst letter-cutters. His typographical excellence lay more in trim, glossy paper to dim the sight.' (*Dissert.*, p. 86.)

[3] *The Life of Benjamin Franklin, written by himself, etc.* (Bigelow's edition), Philadelphia, 1875, i. 413. Nichols, in error, gives the date of this letter as 1764.

Sciences in Paris, written on 2 December 1773, he made a fifth, also unsuccessful, attempt to open negotiations for a sale.

Having lost all spirit for the printing business, Baskerville, about 1766, declined to pursue it except through the medium of a confidential agent, and the following notice, issued about this period, announced this decision to the public:

Robert Martin has agreed with Mr. Baskerville for the use of his whole printing apparatus, with whom he has wrought as a journeyman for ten years past. He therefore offers his services to print at Birmingham for Gentlemen or Booksellers, on the most moderate terms, who may depend on all possible care and elegance in the execution. Samples, if necessary, may be seen on sending a line to John Baskerville or Robert Martin.

In the Cambridge University Library there is a single-sheet specimen, undated, of Robert Martin's, showing Baskerville's types. It was reproduced also in *The Fleuron*, No. v, p. 70.

After Martin had printed five books[1] Baskerville resumed work in 1769. The chief reason seems to have been jealousy of a Birmingham printer, Nicholas Boden, who proposed to print a folio Bible. The two printers carried on a war in the pages of the *Birmingham Gazette* respecting their rival editions.[2] Between 1770 and the time of his death Baskerville's fine series of the 4to classics bear the marks of unabated genius even in declining days, and suffice, had he printed nothing else, to distinguish him as the first typographer of his time.

It would appear from a passage in a letter of Franklin's in reference to the fine edition of Shaftesbury's *Characteristics*, published in 1773 (4to), that, in that year, Baskerville contemplated some further development of his typefounding business.[3] His press, at any rate, seems to have continued active till that date, and even later; although it is doubtful whether the latest works bearing his imprint received his personal oversight.

He died on 8 January 1775. Notwithstanding the poor success of his printing enterprise, he left behind him a fortune of £12,000, which, as he had no heir, went, together with the stock and goodwill of his business, to his widow.[4]

Of Baskerville's personal character, a biographer observes:

In private life, he was a humourist, idle in the extreme; but his invention was the true Birmingham model, active. He could well design, but procured others to execute; wherever he found merit, he caressed it; he was remarkably polite to the stranger, fond of shew; a figure, rather of the smaller size, and delighted to adorn that figure with gold lace. Although constructed with the light timbers of a frigate, his movement was stately as a ship of the line. During the twenty-five last years of his life, though then in his decline, he retained the singular traces of a handsome man. If he exhibited a peevish temper, we may consider that good nature and intense thinking are not always found together. Taste accompanied him through the different walks of agriculture, architecture, and the fine arts. Whatever passed through his fingers bore the living marks of John Baskerville.[5]

---

[1] These include Somerville's *Chace*, 1767, 8vo, and *Shakespeare*, 9 vols., 1768, 12mo.

[2] See Straus and Dent, Appendix II.

[3] Letter dated 21 Sept. 1773. 'You speak of enlarging your Foundery' (*Works*, viii. 88).

[4] The remaining copies of Baskerville's impressions were, after his death, purchased for £1,100 by W. Smart, bookseller, of Worcester, and publisher of J. Price's *Worcester Guide*, 1799.

[5] William Hutton, *History of Birmingham*, 1835, p. 197.

ORLANDO

FURIOSO

DI

LODOVICO

ARIOSTO.

TOMO PRIMO.

BIRMINGHAM,

Da' Torchj di G. BASKERVILLE:

Per P. MOLINI Librajo dell' Accademia

Reale, e G. MOLINI.

M. DCC. LXXIII.

FIG. 79. A Baskerville title-page.

A less pleasing sketch of his character is given by Mark Noble in his *Biographical History of England*:

I have very often [he says] been with my father at his house, and found him ever a most profane wretch, and ignorant of literature to a wonderful degree. I have seen many of his letters, which like his will, were not written grammatically, nor could he even spell well. In person he was a shrivelled old coxcomb. His favourite dress was green, edged with narrow gold lace, a scarlet waistcoat, with a very broad gold lace, and a small round hat, likewise edged with gold lace. His wife was all that affectation can describe. . . . She was originally a servant. Such a pair are rarely met with. He had wit; but it was always at the expense of religion and decency, particularly if in company with the clergy. I have often thought there was much similarity in his person to Voltaire, whose sentiments he was ever retailing.[1]

Professing a total disbelief of the Christian religion, he ordered that his remains should be buried in a tomb in his own grounds, prepared by himself for the purpose, with an epitaph[2] expressing his contempt for the superstition which the bigoted called Religion. Here, accordingly, his body was buried upright, and here it remained, although the building that contained it was destroyed by the Birmingham riots of 1791. In 1826 his body was exhumed and exhibited for some time in a shop in Birmingham.[3] In 1829 it was placed in the catacombs of Christ Church, where it was rediscovered in 1893.

There is a half-length portrait of Baskerville by James Millar, of which a woodcut copy is given in Hansard's *Typographia* (cf. Fig. 74). Of this portrait there is a copy by the elder Samuel Raven in the National Portrait Gallery. Another copy attributed to Exteth is in the Victoria and Albert Museum.

Mrs. Baskerville,[4] on succeeding to her husband's property, declined to continue the printing business, although continuing that of letter-founding; and thus advertised her intention to the public:

Mrs. Baskerville, being about to decline business as a printer, purposes disposing of the whole of her apparatus in that branch, comprehending, among other articles, all of them perfect in their kind, a large and full assortment of the most beautiful types, with the completest printing presses, hitherto known in England. She begs leave to inform the publick, at the same time, that she continues the business of Letter-founding, in all its parts, with the same care and accuracy that was formerly observed by Mr. Baskerville. Those gentlemen who are inclined to encourage so pleasing an improvement may, by favouring her with their commands, be now supplied with Baskerville's elegant types at no higher expence than the prices already established in the trade.[5] 6 *April* 1775.

---

[1] *Biographical History of England*, ii. 362.

[2]   'Stranger,
  beneath this cone, in *unconsecrated* ground,
  a friend to the liberties of mankind directed his
        body to be inurn'd.
May the example contribute to emancipate thy mind
      from the idle fears of *Superstition*,
      and the wicked arts of Priesthood.'
Touching this epitaph Archdeacon Nares has the following note: 'I heard John Wilkes, after praising Baskerville, add, "But he was a terrible infidel; he used to shock me!"'

[3] See Straus and Dent, op. cit.

[4] 'On Friday last, Mr. Baskerville, of this town, was married to Mrs. Eaves, widow of the late Richard Eaves, Esq., deceased' (*Birmingham Register*, 7 June 1765). She was separated from her husband and had been living with Baskerville since *c.* 1750. She died 1788. Two works exist, printed at Birmingham, with the imprint, Sarah Baskerville.

[5] On this occasion the last Baskerville specimen, a double sheet, was issued. See Berry and Johnson, pp. 30–31. It may be supposed that at this sale types were acquired by Thomas Chapman, Christopher Earl, James Bridgwater, Pearson, and Rollason, all Birmingham printers, and by James Smith of Newcastle-under-Lyme. The books they printed in these types are given in Straus and Dent. For portraits of Baskerville see Straus and Dent, Appendix V.

The following further advertisement intimates that two years later the type-founding business was still carried on under the same management:

The late Mr. Baskerville, having taken some pains to establish and perfect a Letter-foundry for the more readily casting of Printing-types for sale, and as the undertaking was finished but a little before his death, it is now become necessary for his widow, Mrs. Baskerville, to inform all Printers that she continues the same business, and has now ready for sale, a large stock of types, of most sizes, cast with all possible care, and dressed with the utmost accuracy. She hopes the acknowledged partiality of the world, in regard to the peculiar beauty of Mr. Baskerville's types, in the works he has published, will render it quite unnecessary here to say anything to recommend them—only that she is determined to attend to the undertaking with all care and diligence; and to the end that so useful an improvement may become as extensive as possible, and notwithstanding the extraordinary hardness and durability of these types above all others, she will conform to sell them at the same prices with other Letter founders. *25 Feb.* 1777.

Notwithstanding Mrs. Baskerville's avowed intention of continuing the business, many attempts had been made, and were still made, to dispose of the foundry. It was offered to the Universities and declined; and the London booksellers preferred the types of Caslon and his apprentices.[1] The stock lay a dead weight till 1779, when the whole was purchased by Beaumarchais for the Société Littéraire-Typographique, for the sum of £3,700,[2] and transferred to France.

Much blame and even contempt was bestowed at the time on the bad taste and unpatriotic spirit of the English nation in thus allowing the materials of this famous press to go out of the country.[3] *De gustibus non est disputandum.* Deprived of the master-hand of their designer, the types which startled the world into admiration in the *Virgil* of 1757 had lost their magic by 1779; and it seems hardly reasonable to blame the printers of this country for preferring the sterling types of Caslon and Jackson, in which works as beautiful were being produced, and by far simpler methods than those employed by the Birmingham genius. Nor does it appear that after the purchase by the French there was any general feeling of regret in this country at the opportunity missed. It is, however, a fact that for some important works produced towards the close of the century—particularly those of Bulmer's press—it was considered an advantage to secure the services of artists of the Birmingham school, both in the formation of the types and the execution of the press-work. As the pioneer of fine printing in England, Baskerville deserves, and will receive, the grateful approbation of all lovers of the art. But it would be idle to say that he was not speedily matched and even surpassed by the performance of others, or that his types, had they remained in this country, would have been more valuable on account of their intrinsic excellence than of their historical interest.

That the French were well satisfied with their bargain may be gathered from the following letter quoted by Nichols, dated Paris, 8 August 1780:

The English language and learning are so cultivated in France, and so eagerly learned, that the best Authors of Great Britain are now reprinting in this Metropolis: Shakespeare,

---

[1] This preference was so marked that about this time the proprietors of Fry and Pine's foundry, who had begun with an avowed imitation of the Baskerville models, were constrained to admit their mistake, and discard that fashion for new founts cut on the model of Caslon.

[2] Loménie says 150,000 *livres* and Pierre Didot's

letter quoted below says £20,000.

[3] As early as 1775 Dr. Harwood, in the preface to his *View of the Editions of the Classics*, had pleaded urgently for the purchase of Baskerville's types, and Wilson's famous Greek, as the nucleus of a Royal Typography in England.

Addison, Pope, Johnson, Hume, and Robertson, are to be published here very soon. Baskerville's types, which were bought it seems for a trifle, to the eternal disgrace of Englishmen, are to be made use of for the purpose of propagating the English Language in this country.[1]

Nichols himself adds, after deploring the comparative failure of Baskerville to receive appreciation in his native land:

We must admire, if we do not imitate, the taste and economy of the French nation, who, brought by the British arms in 1762 to the verge of ruin, rising above distress, were able, in seventeen years, to purchase Baskerville's elegant types, refused by his own country, and to expend an hundred thousand pounds in poisoning the principles of mankind by printing the *Works of Voltaire.*

This great work, for the express purpose of printing which Baskerville's types were procured, was thus announced to the English public in 1782:[2]

A complete edition of the *Works of Voltaire,* printed by subscription, with the types of Baskerville.

This work, the most extensive and magnificent that ever was printed, is now in the press at Fort Kehl, near Strasburgh, a free place, subject to no restraint or imprimatur, and will be published towards the close of the present year. It will never be on sale. Subscribers only can have copies. Each set is to be numbered, and a particular number appropriated to each subscriber at the time of subscribing. As the sets to be worked off are limited to a fixed and small number, considering the demand of all Europe, those who wish to be possessed of so valuable a work, must be early in their application, lest they be shut out by the subscriptions being previously filled. Voltaire's Manuscripts, and Port-Folio, besides his Works already published, cost twelve thousand guineas. This and the other expenses attending the publication, will lay the Editors under an advance of £100,000 sterling. The publick may from thence form a judgment of the extraordinary care that will be taken to make this edition a lasting monument of typographical elegance and grandeur, etc.

At the same time there was issued a specimen *Épreuves des caractères de Baskerville* of thirty-five leaves.[3]

Of this famous edition of *Voltaire* an interesting account is given in Loménie's *Beaumarchais et ses temps.*[4] The Society in whose name Beaumarchais undertook the work consisted of himself alone. Besides the Voltaire MSS. and the Baskerville types, he bought and set to work three paper-mills in the Vosges, and after much difficulty secured the old fort at Kehl as a neutral ground on which to establish in security his vast typographical undertaking. The enterprise was one involving labour, time, and cost vastly beyond his expectations, and his correspondence with his manager at Kehl presents an almost pathetic picture of his efforts to grapple with the difficulties that beset his task. 'How can we promise', he wrote in 1780, 'in the early months of 1782 an edition which has neither hearth nor home in March 1780? The paper-mills have to be made, the type to be founded, the printing press to be put up, and the establishment to be formed.' And on another occasion he

---

[1] *Lit. Anec.* iii. 460.

[2] *St. James's Chronicle,* 4 June 1782. There appeared also *Proposals for Printing by Subscription a Complete Edition of the Works of Voltaire, printed with the Types of Baskerville for the Literary and Typographical Society,* 1782, 12 pp. 8vo, with 4 pp. specimens of the type. The French proposal appears to have been put forward in 1780.

[3] Cf. Berry and Johnson, p. 31.

[4] *Beaumarchais and His Times. Translated by* H. S. Edwards, London, 1856. 4 vols., 8vo (iii, chap. 24). See also R. Diehl, *Beaumarchais als Nachfolger Baskerville,* Frankfort, 1925.

writes: 'Here am I, obliged to learn my letters at paper-making, printing and book-selling.'

It was not until 1784 that volume 1 appeared; and the whole work in two editions was not completed till 1789,[1] by which time France was in the throes of the Revolution, and little likely to heed the literary exploits even of one of her most talented sons. Of the 15,000 copies printed, only 2,000 found subscribers; and after the dissolution of the establishment at Kehl[2] (where, besides, he printed an edition of *Rousseau* and a few other works) all the benefit Beaumarchais received from his enterprise was a mountain of waste paper. In 1790 he moved the stock to Paris and operated a type foundry there until 1794. Several works by Alfieri printed at Kehl bear later dates, one as late as 1809. However they were published they were printed before 1790.[3]

The mystery as to what became of the Baskerville punches and matrices has now been cleared up by Mr. John Dreyfus. From the beginning confusion was caused by the activities of one Claude Jacob, calling himself 'élève de Baskerville'. At the time when Beaumarchais made his purchase he appears to have sent this Jacob to Birmingham to take charge of affairs. It is uncertain whether Jacob had been in Birmingham previously; his name was not known to Straus and Dent. Subsequently he quarrelled with Beaumarchais's manager Le Tellier and set up a rival establishment at Strasburg, called the 'Société Typographique de Strasbourg'. He added a foundry equipped with what appear to be copies of the Baskerville letters, and together with Henri Rolland issued a specimen in 1784. A second specimen appeared under the name of Jacob alone in 1787, and a further undated broadside.[4] The *Épreuves des caractères de la fonderie de Levrault Frères, à Strasbourg,* 1800, is said to display the same types, which are now in the possession of Berger-Levrault of Nancy. Books have been issued set in these types in recent years. Meanwhile, the true Baskerville types as used at Kehl were offered for sale in Paris during the Revolution, on which occasion a specimen was issued (described in Berry and Johnson, pp. 31–32).[5] The main stock of matrices was not sold, although some founts of type found purchasers, for they were used for printing the *Gazette National ou le Moniteur Universel.* John Bell stated that Didot was using Baskerville types in 1787. About the year 1818 the whole stock was bought, as a curiosity rather than with any intention of using the types, by Pierre Didot. We reproduce a letter from the Egerton MSS. in the British Museum, in which Didot offers the collection for 6,000 francs to Francis Egerton, afterwards 8th Earl of Bridgewater, then residing in Paris.

Le 16 Janvier 1819.

My Lord,

J'ai fait depuis peu l'acquisition de tous les types de Baskerville, c'est à dire de tous ses poinçons en acier, et de toutes ses matrices de cuivre, en nombre d'environ vingt deux

---

[1] *Œuvres Complètes de Voltaire. De l'Imprimerie de la Société littéraire et typographique* (Kehl),1784–9. 70 vols. in 8vo; and 92 vols. in 12mo.

[2] Renouard mentions having seen at Paris a broadside specimen of all the Baskerville types transported to Beaumarchais's establishment: 'Ce sont les mêmes types,' he adds, 'mais quelle différence dans leur emploi!' (*Catalogue,* i. 310).

[3] See Alfieri's *Life,* 1810, vol. ii, chap. 18, and John Dreyfus, *The Survival of Baskerville's Punches,* Cambridge, 1949.

[4] See *Ars Typographica,* vol. ii, No. 3, p. 237, and M. Audin's *Livrets typographiques,* Nos. 225, 231, and 232.

[5] Cf. also fig. 272 in Updike's *Printing Types* and Audin's *Le Baskerville,* 1931.

caractères différents depuis le plus petit jusqu'au plus gros romain et italique. C'est l'ensemble d'une des plus belles fonderies qui existent; et je l'ai acheté par occasion, et simple-
ment comme objet de curiosité, n'ayant pas eu envie d'y mettre un grand prix, ma nouvelle
fonderie à laquelle je travaille depuis huit années consécutives étant bientôt terminée. Cette
fonderie de Baskerville se compose de plus de trois milles poinçons en acier, et d'autant de
matrices. Beaumarchais la lui a payée vingt mille livres sterling. C'est de Madame Delarue,
fille de Beaumarchais, que j'ai fait cette acquisition, partie en argent, partie en éditions
imprimées par moi. Si, comme objet de curiosité, ce bel ensemble de types anglais paraît
vous convenir, j'ai l'honneur de vous le proposer pour le prix de six mille francs. De plus,
dans quelque pays que ce fût, cette fonderie pouvroit encore faire un état à quelqu'un que
vous auriez intention de récompenser, ou d'encourager.

J'ai l'honneur d'être avec respect, my Lord, Votre très humble et obéissant serviteur.

P. DIDOT, l'ainé.[1]

The offer was not accepted and the collection was acquired by Henri Plon, then by
the Fonderie Bertrand in Paris, and finally by Deberny and Peignot. Types from
this source were purchased about 1921 by the Harvard University Press and with
this material Mr. Bruce Rogers has printed several handsome volumes. Among
these are *The Cemetery at Souain*, 1921, and *The Wedgwood Medallion of Samuel
Johnson*, by C. B. Tinker, 1926. Other books in Baskerville in which Mr. Rogers
has been concerned may be found in I. Haas, *Bruce Rogers: a bibliography*, New
York, 1936.

The estimation in which the Baskerville design is held is higher to-day than it was
among his contemporaries, as may be judged by the popularity of the recutting made
by the Monotype and the Linotype Corporations. The D. Stempel Typefoundry of
Frankfort also reproduced the design in 1926. A critical appreciation of Baskerville's
type was contributed by Mrs. Warde to the *Monotype Recorder*, September to October
1927, and in the introduction to Berry and Johnson we have Mr. Morison's estimate. Baskerville's types are said to mark the beginnings of the transition in this
country from the old face to the modern face. This is true in so far as the stress in
his letters, as contrasted with Caslon, was rather more vertical and abrupt and the
serifs rather nearer the horizontal. But he did not carry the matter nearly so far as
the eighteenth-century French designers and probably intended no deliberate reform. He had been a writing-master and engraver of letters, and to that fact was
due the change in his designs rather than to a study of the letters of Grandjean and
Fournier. In the main he belongs to what Mr. Morison would call the Aldine
tradition and to printers of our day his roman certainly appears to be an old face.
The chief characteristic which strikes us is the roundness of his letters and not any
modification of the traditional design. The prejudice against him in his own day
was due partly to the fact that he was an interloper and partly to his methods of
printing. The trick played by Benjamin Franklin related above bears this out. In
any case the prejudice did not prevent subsequent designers from copying his letters,
as we shall see.

---

[1] See Robin Flower in *The Library*, 1909, p. 251 seq.

[14]

THOMAS COTTRELL, 1757
ROBERT THORNE, 1794
THE FANN STREET FOUNDRY

THOMAS COTTRELL, described by Mores as *à primo proximus* of modern letter-founders, served his apprenticeship in the foundry of the first Caslon. He was employed there as a dresser, and the portrait of him which is to be seen in the *Universal Magazine* of 1750, among a group of Caslon's workmen, represents him as engaged in that branch of the business. The Cottrells seem to have been a Birmingham family.[1]

It is not improbable that he joined with his friend and fellow apprentice, Joseph Jackson, in clandestinely observing the operation of punch-cutting, secretly practised by his master and his master's son at Chiswell Street, and being assisted by natural ability, and what Moxon terms a 'genuine inclination', he contrived during his apprenticeship to qualify himself not only in this but in all the departments of the art.

In 1757 a question as to the price of work having arisen among Caslon's workmen, Cottrell and Jackson headed a deputation on the subject to their employer, then a Commissioner of the Peace, residing at Bethnal Green. The worthy justice taking this action in dudgeon, the two ringleaders were dismissed from Chiswell Street, and thus thrown unexpectedly on their own resources. Cottrell, in partnership for a short time with Jackson, and (according to Rowe Mores) assisted also by a Dutchman, one Baltus de Graff, a former apprentice of Voskens of Amsterdam, established his foundry at No. 9 Nevil's Court, Fetter Lane. His first fount was an English roman, which, though it will compare neither with the performance of his late master, nor with the then new faces of Baskerville, was yet a production of considerable merit for a self-trained hand.

In 1758 an incidental record of Cottrell's foundry exists in the history, elsewhere recorded, of Miss Elstob's Saxon types, the punches and matrices of which, after remaining untouched for several years at Caslon's, were brought to Cottrell by Bowyer, to be 'fitted up' ready for use. This task Cottrell performed punctually and apparently to the satisfaction of his employer, returning them with a small fount of the letter cast in his own mould, as a specimen of the improvement made in them.[2]

---

[1] See Joseph Hill's *The Book Makers of Old Birmingham*, p. 57.   [2] See, p. 149.

In 1759 Jackson quitted the business to go to sea, and Cottrell, left to himself, busily proceeded with the completion of his series of romans, which he carried as low as Brevier, a size 'which', says Rowe Mores, 'he thinks low enough to spoil the eyes'.[1] He also cut a two-line English Engrossing in imitation of the Law-Hand, and several designs of flowers.

The Engrossing, or as Mores styles it, the Base Secretary, was a character designed to take the place of the lately abolished Court Hand in legal documents, and

And be it further hereby enacted,
That the Mayors Bailiff, and
head Officers of every Town and
THOMAS COTTRELL

FIG. 80. Engrossing cut by Cottrell. From the original matrices.

appears to have been designed for Cottrell by a law printer named William Richardson, a nephew of Samuel Richardson. On the completion of the fount, an impression of which we here give, Richardson issued a specimen of it,[2] claiming the design, and representing its advantages as the proper character for leases, agreements, indentures, &c. The matrices, however, remained with Cottrell, and the inclusion of the fount in his general specimen shows that Richardson ceased to retain any exclusive use of it. It was the only fount of the kind in England when Mores wrote in 1778.

The surviving Cottrell specimens are all undated and difficult to arrange. They consist, apart from the sheet of Engrossing cut for William Richardson, of four single sheets, of which the only known copies are in the Sohmian Collection at Stockholm,[3] and two specimen-books. The single sheets may be placed before the books, as they do not contain the Engrossing, shown in the books. One of the books may be placed before 1770, since it does not contain the Domesday fount, shown in Luckombe's *History and Art of Printing* of that year. Two of the sheets show his poster letters, no doubt cast in sand. Mores says (*Dissertation*, p. 83) that he was the first to produce such letters, 'some uncommon founts of proscription, or posting letter of great bulk and dimensions as high as to the measure of twelve-line Pica'. The two other sheets and the books show a range of romans and italics down to Brevier, cut on the Caslon model, and flowers in the eighteenth-century style. The second book includes the Domesday fount, which is headed 'The Character used in the time of William the Conqueror'. In a copy of one of the books belonging to the American Antiquarian Society there is inserted a note dated 14 July 1774

[1] *Dissertation*, p. 82.

[2] *A Specimen of a New Printing Type, in Imitation of the Law-Hand. Designed by William Richardson, of Castle Yard, Holborn.* London, n.d. Broadside. Present location not known. In an auction-sale catalogue of Samuel Paterson's, 1781, the type is called two-line English Secretary. It is reproduced in Berry and Johnson, pl. 5.

[3] For the Sohmian Collection see the note above on p. 238.

printed in Cottrell's Double Pica Script. This is a Latin script and, if the date may be trusted, the first of its kind to be cut in England, unless possibly the script cut for the Rev. John Trusler preceded it (see below, p. 342). Mores in his *Dissertation*, which is dated 1778, says that at the time of his writing Cottrell's Script was not ready.

The following note at the foot of the Long Primer on Bourgeois specimen is, perhaps, the most interesting feature of the first book:

This Foundery was begun in the Year 1757, and will (with God's leave) be carried on, improved and enlarged, by Thomas Cottrell, Letter Founder, in London.

N.B. Served my apprenticeship to William Caslon, Esq.

Fournier, in the second part of his *Manuel Typographique*, 1766, mentions Cottrell's foundry, but in such a manner as to lead one to suppose he had never seen his specimen, or heard of it except by the vaguest hearsay. He mentions him as 'Cottrell à Oxfort', at the head of his list of English founders.[1]

A more satisfactory contemporary record is contained in Luckombe's *History and Art of Printing*, 1770, where pages 169 to 174 are occupied by specimens of the Engrossing and Flowers already exhibited in the specimen-book, and a fount of English Domesday.

This latter fount, which appears to have been completed subsequent to the issue of the first specimen-book, Cottrell cut under the inspection of Dr. Charles Morton for the forthcoming issue of Domesday Book, begun in 1773, and 'which', Rowe Mores sarcastically observes, 'if the undertakers go on as they have begun, will by domes-day hardly finished'. The work was, however, finished and printed, but not in Cottrell's type, his performance having been eclipsed by that of his old colleague and partner Jackson, who, after returning from sea in 1763, had worked for a short time at the Nevil's Court Foundry, and then left to start business for himself, taking with him two of Cottrell's workmen. Cottrell was at this period a private in the Life Guards, a position considered highly respectable in those days, and not at all incompatible with business pursuits. His military ardour evidently had its effect in the foundry, for we find that Robinson and Hickson, his two workmen who left with Jackson, were also enlisted in the same service.

No specimen is to be found of the Russian fount, which Mores, writing in 1778, hopes Cottrell is about to cut 'for a gentleman who compiles a Russian Dictionary; the same gentleman who translated into English, *The Grand Instructions of Her Imperial Majesty Catherine II, for a new Code of Laws for the Russian Empire. London*, 1768, 4*to.*, to whom we wish success'.[2]

Cottrell died in 1785. He is described as obliging, good-natured, and friendly,

---

[1] *Manuel Typographique*, ii, p. xxxviii. This whole notice is so exceedingly incorrect as to call for mention here. 'L'Angleterre a peu de Fonderies, mais elles sont bien fournies en toutes sortes de caractères: les principales sont celles de Thomas Cottrell à Oxfort; de Jacques Watson à Edimbourg, de Guillaume Caslon & Fils à Londres, et de Jean Baskerville à Birmingham'! It would almost appear as if, having before him the names of Cottrell, Oxford, James, Wilson of Glasgow, Caslon of London, and Baskerville of Birmingham, the then existing foundries in this kingdom, Fournier had taxed his ingenuity to make four foundries out of six and had succeeded, altering Wilson's name to that of his long-defunct fellow citizen, Queen Anne's printer, in the process. This feat has, however, been eclipsed in his notice of the Voskens's foundry at Amsterdam, which, after the death of Dirk Voskens, passed to his widow and sons. 'Cette Fonderie', Fournier informs us, 'a passé à sa veuve et au Sieur Zonen'!

[2] The gentleman was M. Tatischev.

rejecting nothing because it was out of the common way, and expeditious in his performances. Nichols, in recording his death, says 'Mr. Cottrell died, I am sorry to
add, not in affluent circumstances, though to his profession of a letter-founder were
superadded that of a doctor for the toothache, which he cured by burning the ear;
and had also the honour of serving in the Troop of His Majesty's Life Guards'.[1]

The following is the summary of his foundry as gathered from his specimen-
book, together with the additional founts cut subsequently:

COTTRELL'S FOUNDRY

Roman.—Five-line, four-line, two-line
Double Pica, two-line Great Primer,
two-line English, two-line Small Pica,
two-line Long Primer.

Roman and Italic.—Canon, two-line Great
Primer, two-line English, Double Pica,
Great Primer, English, Pica 1, Pica 2,
Small Pica, Long Primer 1, Long Primer
2, Bourgeois, Brevier.

Flowers.—Small Pica, 29 varieties.

Engrossing.—two-line English.

Script.—Double Pica.

Domesday.—English.

Large letter.—From four-line up to twelve-
line.

Of the history of the foundry during the nine years following Cottrell's death,
no record remains. In 1794 it became the property of Robert Thorne, a former
apprentice of Cottrell's, who removed the business from Nevil's Court to No. 11,
Barbican, whence he issued in that year his first specimen and a price-list announcing
his new undertaking.[2] In Pendred's *Printer's Vade Mecum*, undated but issued in
1785, we find Thorne's name already as an independent founder at No. 6, Barbican.

The specimen-book of 1794 consists entirely of elegantly shaped large letters
cast in sand, from five-line up to nineteen-line, a then unprecedented size. The bulk
of these, comprising the sizes from five- to twelve-line, advancing by one pica em in
body, it may be surmised, are from Cottrell's models; the thirteen-, sixteen-, and
nineteen-line being added by Thorne. For his specimen of ordinary-sized letter
Thorne probably made use at first of Cottrell's book as it stood.[3]

But it is evident by the specimen published four years later, in 1798, that if he
ever was possessed of the matrices of these founts he entirely discarded them, in
conformity with the passing fashion, in favour of others more closely resembling
the beautiful faces of Jackson and Figgins. His specimen of 1798 is indeed one of
the most elegant of which that famous decade can boast. For lightness, grace, and
uniformity, the series of romans and italics which are exhibited excels that of
almost all his competitors. The book, which, except for the large letters of the
1794 book, contains not a single fount which had previously appeared in Cottrell's
book, consists of forty-five leaves, of which twenty are devoted to roman and italic,
and the remainder to titlings, shaded letters, and flowers, with one fount of Double-

---

[1] *Lit. Anec.* ii. 358.

[2] 'R. Thorne, Letter-Founder, takes the Liberty
of informing the Trade in general that he has begun
business upon his own account, and intends serving
them at the following old-established prices: [here
follows price-list]. He respectfully informs those
gentlemen that choose to favour him with their
orders, that they may depend upon the best workmanship and materials. Barbican, July 1, 1794.'

[3] It appears to have been no uncommon practice
in the trade to make use of a predecessor's book,
corrected on the title-page in pen and ink. The St.
Bride copy of Cottrell's specimen is thus altered to
the name of a broker; and the specimens of the Type
Street Foundry are many of them similarly corrected
to adapt them for the frequently changing style of
that firm.

Pica Script. A postscript to the specimen states that four more founts were nearly ready, completing the series, the preparation of which had evidently been the labour of many years.[1] It is therefore the more to be regretted that Thorne, in common with all his contemporaries, was compelled almost immediately, by the sudden change of public taste in favour of the new style of roman, to abandon the further prosecution of this excellent series, and devote himself to the production of founts according to 'modern' fashion.

In 1801 a revised price-list was issued announcing a rise in the price of type owing to the advanced cost of raw material and journeymen's wages;[2] and in 1803 appeared the specimen of the new roman series, representing the product of five years' incessant toil and sacrifice. It cannot be said that this specimen of 'Improved Types'[3]—one of the first completed in the trade—bears any comparison with the artistic elegance of its predecessor. It exhibits the new roman and italic in ten-, seven-, and five-line Pica, Canon, two-line Great Primer (two faces), two-line English (two faces), Double Pica (two faces), Great Primer (two faces), English, Pica, Long Primer (two faces), Bourgeois, Brevier, and Minion. Ornamenteds— two-line Pica (two faces), two-line Small Pica (two faces). Shadeds—two-line Small Pica (two faces), two-line Nonpareil (three faces). Script—Double Pica.

Thorne, indeed, having once abandoned the old style for the new, appears in the van of the innovating fashion. Not sharing in the regret expressed by his brethren in the art at the new departure, he still further advanced upon it by the production of some exceedingly thick and fat (and we may add unsightly) jobbing letters, which, though subsequently followed and even exceeded by others, were at the time unique for boldness and deformity.

In oriental and 'learned' letters he appears to have achieved nothing, as not a single fount, not even Cottrell's Domesday, appears in this specimen, or in the subsequent inventory of the foundry.

A curious document entitled *Rules and Regulations of the Letter-Foundry of Robert Thorne, London, Jan. 1806*, exists, and gives an interesting glimpse into the order and customs of the Barbican Foundry. To the general scope of these rules we have referred in another place;[4] but as being personal to Thorne in his relations with his men, we may mention here that he constituted himself treasurer of the fines for 'Footale', imposed by the men on all new workmen, with an obligation to account for and distribute the sum every Christmas Eve, and also made himself liable, equally with his men, to a fine of a shilling if he left his light burning when quitting the foundry for the night.

For some time (though the exact dates cannot be fixed) Thorne had a partner in Hugh Hughes, an able engraver and designer of music and other characters, who

---

[1] In a note he says, 'R. T. informs those gentlemen to whom he is at present unknown, that the Types of the Barbican Foundry are cast to the usual Height and Body; and that great care has been taken to have the Counterpart deeply cut, by which means they will wear much longer than any hitherto in use.'

[2] Pica, which in 1798 had been 1*s.* per lb., is raised to 1*s.* 2½*d.*, and Nonpareil is advanced from 5*s.* to 5*s.* 6*d.* The other sizes are in similar proportion.

[3] 'Sir,—Having published a Specimen of Improved Printing Types, I have taken the liberty of sending you a Copy, which I hope you will approve of; and be assured that every possible exertion shall be used in completing those orders you may favor me with.

'Barbican, 1803.

'I remain, your obedient Servant,
ROBERT THORNE.'

[4] See p. 109.

afterwards commenced a foundry in Dean Street, Fetter Lane.[1] This association does not appear to have lasted long or to have involved any alteration in the style of the firm. In 1808 Thorne removed from Barbican to No. 2 Fann Street, Aldersgate, where, in premises formerly occupied by a brewery, he continued his business under the name of the Fann Street Foundry.[2]

Considerable additions were made to the faces of the foundry during the next ten years. Two new Scripts were cut, the 'Sanspareil' matrices were adopted for the large letters, and a few new book founts appeared with light faces, which contrasted agreeably with the fat style generally predominating in Thorne's specimens. His fat faces were respected abroad. Not only were they copied, as we may see from an examination of contemporary Paris specimen-books, but Thorne was commissioned to cut such types for the Imprimerie Royale—the sole instance of that glorious printing-house and foundry seeking the services of a foreigner.

In 1817 declining health induced Thorne to attempt to dispose of his business to his fellow founders; but his offer being declined, he resumed his labours and continued actively at work until the time of his death, which occurred in 1820, at the age of 66. He was buried in Holloway churchyard, where a tablet is erected to his memory. No complete specimen of his type remains later than that of 1803; although the numerous loose sheets which appeared after that date, and the fact that as many as 132 pages of composed specimens were left in type at the time of his death, show that one if not several books had been issued during the interval.

On 21 June 1820 the foundry was put up to auction,[3] and purchased entire by William Thorowgood. This gentleman was previously unconnected with the typographical profession,[4] having been engaged as London manager and agent to a Patent Roller Pump business at Stone, in Staffordshire, of which concern he was one of the principal proprietors. With the proceeds, it is said, of a fortunate draw in one of the State Lotteries,[5] he became possessor of the Fann Street Foundry, and proceeded at once to throw himself into the new business with great energy and no small success. His first specimen-book was issued a few months after the purchase, and a second followed in January 1821, which may be taken as representing the contents of the foundry pretty much as Thorne left it; although even in this

---

[1] See p. 358.

[2] In Stower's *Printers' Price Book*, 1814, Thorne's roman are shown.

[3] *Particulars of the Lease and Valuable Plant of the Type Foundry of Mr. Robert Thorne, deceased, situate in Fann's Street, Aldersgate Street, . . . which will be Sold by Auction by Mr. W. Davies, at Garraway's Coffee House, on Wednesday, the 21st of June, 1820, at Twelve o'clock, in One Lot.* Besides the lease, plant, and fixtures, the catalogue comprised 316 lots of matrices and about 340 moulds. The matrices were as follows:

Roman and Italic.—5-line (3), 4-line (3), Canon (4), 2-line Double Pica (3), 2-line Great Primer (4), 2-line English (4), 2-line Pica (1), Double Pica (4), Great Primer (4), English (5), Pica (6), Small Pica (3), Long Primer (6), Bourgeois (3), Brevier (5), Minion (1), Nonpareil Roman (2), Pearl (1).

Black (plain or open).—5-line (5), 4-line (2), Canon (2), 2-line Great Primer (5), 2-line English (2), Double Pica (2), Great Primer (2), English (1), Pica (1), Small Pica (1), Long Primer (2), Bourgeois (1).

Shaded.—5-line to Brevier (21).

Flowers.—All bodies (15).

Ornamented.—Canon to 2-line Bourgeois (6).

Egyptian.—2-line Great Primer to Brevier (6).

Script.—2-line Pica, Double Pica, Great Primer.

Engrossing.—2-line English.

German.—English.

Two-line Letters, Signs, &c., &c.

Sanspareil Founts.—14-line to 4-line (24).

[4] He had a brother, Frederick Thorowgood, a printer, in Wood Street, Cheapside.

[5] It is curious to note that the matter of not a few of Thorowgood's early specimens has reference to the lucky numbers 'always found in great variety in the Grand State Lotteries'. Such gratuitous advertisements are no doubt so many grateful acknowledgements of his own obligations to a time-honoured institution.

short space of time some additions are apparent, which formed no part of his predecessor's stock.[1]

In the following year Thorowgood was sworn Letter-Founder to His Majesty, and put forth a specimen of a Greek fount of good cut, which, at the time, was the sole representative of the 'learned' languages in his foundry.[2] Further progress was, however, made in this direction during the next few years, specimen-books appearing in 1822, 1824, 1825, 1827, 1828, and 1829. Hansard, writing in 1825, mentions three sizes of German (Fraktur), two of Greek, one of Hebrew, and four

INDUSTRIAL CITIES OF ENGLAND
and convincing manner, has a direct and

AABCDEFGHIJKLMMNOPQRS
TUVVWWXYYZ

abcdefghijklmnopqrstuvwxyzfifffifflffifl
1234567890

Quousque

Fig. 81. Thorowgood Fat Face. From the original matrices.

of Russian, as forming part of his stock. The Germans, and the Pica and Bourgeois Russian, were procured from the foundry of Breitkopf and Härtel of Leipzig.[3]

In 1828 the retirement of Dr. Fry presented Thorowgood with the opportunity of making a most important addition to his business by the acquisition of the Type Street Foundry. This purchase transferred to the Fann Street Foundry not only the whole of Dr. Fry's interesting collection of oriental and 'learned' founts, which included many relics of the old foundries, but augmented his stock of book founts, blacks, titlings, and flowers, to almost double their former extent. The transfer was completed in 1829, and early in the following year a specimen of additions to the foundry contained an announcement that 'a new edition of the Greeks, Hebrews, and foreign characters of the Polyglot Foundry, late the property of Dr. Fry, is in preparation'. This promised specimen duly appeared in 1830, the sheets still bearing Dr. Fry's imprint; and after this date frequent supplementary specimens

---

[1] The address to the printers, prefixed to this specimen, is as follows: 'I cannot omit the opportunity offered in presenting my first specimen to your notice, to return my most sincere thanks to the profession for that portion of their patronage which I have received since my succession to Mr. Thorne. Although some difficulties presented themselves in redeeming the pledge I made of renovating my small founts and casting them of metal more durable than those in common use, yet I flatter myself that those friends who relied on my professions will bear ample testimony that they have not been disappointed, and that the superior facilities of manufacturing types possessed by myself in common with the other founders of the metropolis has been used

to their advantage', &c.

[2] Present location not known.

[3] This famous foundry, which still exists, was established by Bernard Christoph Breitkopf in 1719. His son, Johann Gottlieb Immanuel Breitkopf, was the inventor (simultaneously with Haas of Basle) of the art of map-printing with movable types, and is claimed also as the inventor of movable music types about 1748. Many eminent punch-cutters were employed on the founts of this foundry, which was in 1800 one of the largest in Germany. The first specimen appeared in 1739. See O. von Hase, *Breitkopf & Härtel, Gedenkschrift*, Leipzig, 1917, vol. i.

marked the development of the business of this now extensive foundry, although, except for a Great Primer black, none of the old types acquired from Dr. Fry were shown for many years. About 1838 Robert Besley (born at Exeter in 1794), who since 1826 had been in the service of the foundry as a traveller, became a partner, and the firm was styled Thorowgood & Co., or more commonly Thorowgood and Besley. In 1849 Thorowgood retired and the firm became Robert Besley & Co., Besley's partner being Benjamin Fox, a practical and skilful punch-cutter. Fox was responsible for the firm's *Court Hand* and *Clarendon* series. The Clarendon was registered in 1845 for three years, and on the expiry of the period of protection was immediately and widely copied, as the original founders complained. The type was an Egyptian with bracketed serifs and fulfilled a demand for a bold face suitable for dictionary work. It was so successful that the word Clarendon for a heavy type has become part of the common language. There had been types of similar design before Besley's, which went under the name of Ionic. Alderman Besley, who retired in 1861, took an active part in City affairs and was Lord Mayor of London in 1869–70. He died in 1876. In 1855 he had taken out a patent for an alloy for the production of hard metal and subsequent specimens of the foundry advertised their newspaper types in hard metal. In 1861 the firm was joined by Charles Reed (b. 1819), who had been at first engaged in the woollen trade at Leeds and then became editor of the *Leeds Repository*. By 1842 he had moved to London and became a printer with Tyler and Reed from 1842 to 1849, and with Reed and Pardon from 1849 to 1861. Reed and Pardon issued a specimen of their types in 1851. Reed and Fox, as the foundry was now styled, took part in the revival of the taste for eighteenth-century letters, not by resuscitating the original romans of Isaac Moore or Fry, but by copying Miller and Richard's *Old Style* of 1860 in a series to which they gave the name of *Mediaeval*. Mrs. Gray, in *XIXth Century Ornamented Types*, has pointed out that the distinction between the art of the Middle Ages and Renaissance art was not familiar to designers of the 1860's, and thus a letter in the Aldine tradition might excusably be called *Mediaeval* by a founder. The series was shown in *The Printer's Register* in 1868 and in most of the subsequent specimen-books of the Fann Street Foundry. Fox, who perhaps cut the *Mediaeval* series, died in 1877, and the firm became Sir Charles Reed & Sons. Charles Reed, who was knighted for his public services in 1874, was chairman of the London School Board, M.P. for Hackney from 1868 to 1874, and for St. Ives from 1880 until his death in 1881.[1] The two sons in the firm were Andrew Holmes and Talbot Baines. The elder shortly retired because of ill health, and T. B. was the sole manager until his own early death in 1893. He was born in 1852 and had entered the business at the age of seventeen. The interest taken by the Reeds in the early types acquired from the Fry Foundry is shown by the issue of an unusual book in 1884—*Specimens of Greek, Hebrew, Saxon, Irish, and Oriental Types*, which includes the Alexandrian Greek, the Samaritan and Ethiopic from the *Polyglot* of 1657, and Moxon's Irish. Another of the firm's old types, the Pica black No. 4, which came from the Andrews Foundry and was of Dutch origin, was

[1] See *D.N.B.* and a memoir by his eldest son Charles E. Baines Reed, who was Secretary of the British and Foreign Bible Society. The memoir deals with his public life; there is nothing about the foundry, and T. B. Reed is not mentioned.

used by the Grolier Club of New York for their edition of the *Philobiblion* of Richard Aungerville, printed by Theodore De Vinne in 1889. De Vinne has a note on the type, but supposes it was a French Textura of the sixteenth century and assigns it to Rouen. Reed also cast the types of the Kelmscott Press from punches cut by Edward Prince.

After the death of T. B. Reed the firm was made a limited company and was under the management of A. W. Tillie until 1905, when the stock was bought by Messrs. Stephenson, Blake & Co. of Sheffield.

15

JOSEPH AND EDMUND FRY, 1764

HIS foundry, first known as Fry and Pine's, had its origin in Bristol in the year 1764.

Joseph Fry, a prominent and enterprising Bristolian, was the son of John Fry, and was born in the year 1728. He entered the medical pro-

FIG. 82. Silhouettes of Joseph and Edmund Fry.

fession, where, says a biographer,[1] 'his affable, courteous manners and sound Christian principles soon secured to him a large practice amongst the highest class of his fellow citizens. Possessing uncommon energy and activity of mind, he was led to take a part in many new scientific undertakings, actuated more by the desire to be useful to society and advance the arts than by any hope of individual profit.'

This spirit of enterprise induced him, in the year 1764, to turn his attention to letter-founding, which, though hardly to be called a new scientific undertaking, was at least a novel industry for a provincial city. The success of Baskerville's foundry at Birmingham, at that time in the height of its celebrity, was undoubtedly an

[1] Hugh Owen, *Two Centuries of Ceramic Art in Bristol*, 1873, 8vo.

incentive to the adventurers of Bristol, whose first founts were avowedly cut in close imitation of those famous models.

William Pine, Fry's partner, was a practical printer from 1753, of some note in his native city. He was the first printer of the *Bristol Gazette*, and carried on a considerable business at his premises in Wine Street. The new foundry was attached to his office, and its productions may be traced in several works which issued from his press between the years 1764 and 1770.[1] Messrs. Fry and Pine's manager was one Isaac Moore, who (Rowe Mores informs us) was originally an ingenious whitesmith of Birmingham before he removed to Bristol. The practical superintendence of the foundry, if not the actual cutting of its punches, devolved on him; and his services appear to have been acknowledged by his admission into the partnership at an early stage of the undertaking, the business being carried on in his name.

Moore issued his first specimen in 1766.[2] Renouard mentions a *Specimen by Isaac Moore, Bristol*, in 1768, of which he possessed a copy mounted on linen,[3] and which he describes as displaying 'caractères assez bien gravés, et imitant ceux de Baskerville'. If this is not a mistake for 1766 and was, as it would appear from the title, issued at Bristol, we must conclude that the removal of the foundry to the metropolis took place in the same year, as there exists in the Sohmian Collection at Stockholm, where it was discovered by W. Blades, a broadside *Specimen by Isaac Moore and Co. in Queen Street, near Upper Moorfields, London*, showing the roman series from five-line to Brevier, bearing the same date. Whether the two specimens are the same or not, it is hardly likely that their contents could have varied much during the brief interval. Two years later, however, the progress of the undertaking was announced by the issue of a fresh broadside sheet containing the complete series of romans, cut after the Baskerville models, from eight-line to Pearl, with italics to most of the founts, besides a fair display of flowers. The general appearance of the letters is elegant, especially in the larger sizes.

Appended to the specimen, in the form of a postscript, is the following address to the public (the first of a series of florid effusions which characterized the specimens of this foundry), in which the proprietors announce the principles on which their venture is to be conducted, and refer with satisfaction to the success already achieved by their productions:

The Proprietors of the above Foundery having nearly compleated all the Roman and Italic Founts, desire with great Deference, to lay this Specimen before the Trade; and intreat the Curious and critical, before any decisive Judgement be passed, on the Merits or Demerits of the Performance, to make a minute Examination and Comparison of the respective letters and founts of each Size, with the same Letters and Founts of the most respectable Founders in the Kingdom; For as all Letters, whether Roman or Italic, bear a great Similitude to each other, to apprehend the peculiar Beauty or Deformity of them are only to be discovered by such a Comparison. In making which they hope the Candid and Judicious will set aside the Influence of Custom and Prejudice (those Great Barriers against

---

[1] See John Wesley's *Explanatory Notes on the Old Testament*, 1765, showing Great Primer for the text and Pica for the notes. Pine had been printing extracts from Wesley's *Journal* from 1761. The portion issued in 1767 is printed in a new type, the Long Primer of Moore. See also Wesley's *Hymns*, editions of 1767, 1768, and 1769.

[2] See a reproduction in Updike, *Printing Types*, fig. 276.

[3] *Catalogue*, i. 310. 'Grande feuille collée sur une toile ou batiste fine.'

Improvement) and attend to Propriety, Elegance and Mathematical Proportion. And as these have been objects particularly attended to in the Course of the Work, they apprehend it will appear on such a Disquisition, that all the above sizes bear a greater Likeness to each other, than those of any other Founder. They have been already favoured with the Encouragement and Approbation of several very respectable printers, who have wrought off many large Editions on their Founts, which have been Experienced to wear extremely well; owing to the Letter being clearly and deeply cut and to the Goodness of the Metal, which they make of an Extraordinary Composition; the Singular Advantage of which cannot but be obvious. Therefore hope that others will likewise make Trial of them, as they doubt not but they also will find it greatly to their Satisfaction.[1]

It is doubtful whether the encouragement accorded to the new foundry on its first establishment in the metropolis came up to the expectations of the proprietors; and a circular issued shortly afterwards by two of the partners suggests that some fillip was deemed necessary to awaken a more extended patronage of the concern. This curious document is entitled *Proposals for discovering a very great Improvement which William Pine, printer of Bristol, and Isaac Moore, Letter Founder, in Queen Street, Upper Moorfields, London, have made in the Art of Printing, both in the Construction of the Press and in the Manner of Beating and Pulling*, and publicly offers the secret of the invention (the precise nature of which is not apparent) to any customer of the new foundry ordering type to the value of ten pounds and upwards.[2]

How far this ingenuous offer had the effect of stimulating the type business is not recorded, but the proprietors were forced before long to recognize the desirability of adopting other and surer methods for gaining the popular favour.

Although Luckombe, writing in 1770,[3] mentions Moore along with Caslon and Jackson as one of the three London founders, the same authority makes a decidedly disparaging reference to his types;[4] a circumstance which may be accounted for by the then-growing prejudice amongst metropolitan printers against the Baskerville

[1] Rowe Mores, after quoting the above, adds drily: 'Their letter is neat. We *do* "set aside the influence of custom", and call it the law of fools, but we must recommend to the consideration of the proprietors the difference between scalping and counter-punching.' (*Dissertation*, p. 84.) The present location of the specimen of 1770, lent by A. W. Tuer for the Caxton Celebration, 1877 (No. 4371), is not known. Another, undated, sheet was issued by J. Moore from the address, No. 43 Drury-Lane, presumably not before 1776. Cf. Berry and Johnson, p. 39.

[2] 'The Inventors, sensible of the great utility of their Discovery, have mentioned it to several of the Trade, who have made very considerable offers to encourage the laying open the Secret: But as their desire is, that every Printer in the Kingdom might be benefited by it they propose to make the Discovery as universal as possible, by making an honourable and generous present of it to the whole trade: To many of whom they are under some Obligations for the kind encouragement of their new Foundery. And as that is an object they desire here to recommend, they would further propose, (as they have nearly compleated all their founts, and can serve the Trade on as good Terms as any in the Kingdom, and with Types they will warrant to wear as long) that every Printer who shall give them an order for Ten Pounds worth of Type or more (Five Pounds of which to be paid on ordering and the Re-

mainder on the Delivery) shall be made acquainted with the above improvements. So that the whole Advantage proposed is the selling some Founts of Letter which every Printer does or will want. And as they expect that the Trade in general will approve of their Plan, they beg that the Encouragers of it would send their orders with all convenient Speed to the above Foundery; (as they intend as soon as they have got a sufficient Number to lay open the whole) which they hope will not be less universal than the desire of being made Partakers of so interesting a Discovery: for it merits nothing less than the most cordial Encouragement of every Printer in Europe, though here so freely offered. And it will appear when laid open to be of such Service as nothing like it has been discovered in Printing for some Centuries. . . . The whole expence of altering the present presses to the above Improvement will be but about forty shillings.' A notice of this invention, as well as of a patent type-case designed by the same partners, is found in the *Abridgments of Specifications for Printing, 1617–1857*, London, 1859, 8vo, p. 88.

[3] *History and Art of Printing*, p. 244.

[4] After commending Caslon and Jackson, he says: 'As to the productions of other Founderies we shall be silent, and leave them to sound forth their own good qualifications, which by an examiner are not found to exist' (p. 230).

form of letter adopted by the new foundry. Representations of a similar nature having been made from several influential quarters, it became evident to the proprietors that if they were to retain public favour at all, it must be by adapting themselves to public taste and abandoning the formal, delicate models of Baskerville for the more serviceable, dashing characters of Caslon. This laborious task occupied several years in completion. Meanwhile the original founts were not discarded.

The printing-office connected with the foundry distinguished itself in the interval by the production of two highly interesting Bibles, the one a folio, published in 1774, and the other an 8vo, in five volumes, published 1774–6.[1] Both are elegantly printed in the clear Great Primer letter shown in the 1770 specimen, the latter being in long lines specially for the use of the aged. The general appearance of the folio edition compares not unfavourably with the Baskerville Bible of 1772.

In 1774 Pine printed at Bristol a very neat Bible in the Pearl type of the foundry, 'being', says the preface, 'the smallest a Bible was ever printed with, and made on purpose for this work'.[2]

Moore's connexion with the business appears to have terminated in 1776, after which the style of the firm became J. Fry & Co., who in the following year issued, in their own name, reprints of the folio and octavo Bibles above referred to.[3] Broadside specimens of their types appeared in 1778 and 1780. In 1782 Pine had also withdrawn from the business.[4] He continued to print the *Bristol Gazette* in Wine Street, Bristol, till the time of his death, which occurred in 1803 at the age of 64 years.

Left to himself, Fry, in the year 1782, admitted his sons Edmund and Henry into partnership, under whose supervision the work of recutting the romans of the foundry made active progress. Edmund Fry, probably the most learned letter-founder of his day, had, like his father, been educated for the medical profession, and had taken his doctor's degree. But the infirmity of deafness prevented him from following that walk in life, and he abandoned it for typefounding, applying himself to that pursuit not only with the enthusiasm of an ardent philologist, but also with considerable natural ability for conducting the practical operations of the art. The year of his entry into the business (1782) was signalized by an important event in the typefounding world—the sale of James's foundry. This event has been

---

[1] *The Holy Bible, containing the Old and New Testament, with Notes Explanatory, Critical and Practical, selected from the Works of several Eminent Divines.* London, I. Moore and Co., Letter Founders and Printers in Queen Street, near Upper Moorfields. 1774, fol. The same, in 5 vols., 8vo: Vols. i, ii, iii, 1774; vol. iv, 1776; vol. v (*Apocrypha*), 1775.

[2] *A Commentary on the Holy Bible, containing the Whole Sacred Text of the Old and New Testaments, with Notes, &c.* Bristol, Printed and Sold by William Pine. 1774, 12mo.

[3] *The Holy Bible, containing the Old and New Testament, with Notes Explanatory, Critical and Practical, selected from the Works of several Eminent Authors.* London. Printed and Sold by J. Fry and Co., Letter Founders and Printers in Queen Street, near Upper Moorfields. 1777, fol. The same, 4 vols., 1777, 8vo. In 1777 appeared James Kenton, *An*

Essay on Death. Printed and sold by I. Moore, letter founder and printer, No. 43 Drury Lane. From 1783 to 1787 John Paramore was printing Wesley Tracts at the Queen Street address. Moore is still, in 1785, entered as a letter-founder, in Drury Lane, in Pendred's *Printers' Vade Mecum*. There was a Joseph Moore, later J. Moore & Son, at No. 134 Drury Lane, styled letter-founder, in Holden's *Directory*, from 1799 until after 1820.

[4] Amongst other works printed by him there is preserved a tract, entitled *An Answer to a Narrative of Facts . . . lately published by Mr. Henry Burgum as far as relates to the Character of Wm. Pine.* Bristol. Printed in the year 1775. 8vo. This is a letter of rejoinder addressed by Pine to Burgum, repelling charges relating to the publication of an offensive pamphlet. Pine also printed several works for the Wesleys.

fully alluded to elsewhere,[1] but it is interesting to note that the Frys were considerable purchasers on the occasion, securing amongst other items the chief part of the 'learned' and foreign matrices, for which that collection was noted.

The following list of their purchases forms an interesting connecting-link between the old and the new letter foundries; particularly as either punches or matrices of all the founts (and in some cases both) still exist, many of the latter being to this day in occasional use:

Blacks.[2]—English.	[A.]	*Greek.*—Great Primer.		[G.]
Pica.	[A.]	Another.		[R.?]
Small Pica.	[A.]	Pica.		[R.?]
Long Primer.	[A.]	*Arabic.*—Great Primer.		[A.?]
Brevier.	[G.]	*Irish.*—Small Pica.	[M.]	[A.]
Nonpareil.	[G.]	*Ethiopic.*—English.	[P.]	[A.]
Hebrew.—English.	[A.?]	Pica.		
Small Pica.		*Samaritan.*—English.	[P.]	[G.]
Long Primer (or Bourgeois).		Long Primer.		
Brevier.		*Scriptorial.*—Pica.		[G.]
Rabbinical Hebrew.—Small Pica.	[A.]	English.		[G.]
Brevier.	[A.]	*Union Pearl.*—Double Pica.		[G.]
Nonpareil.	[A.]	*Court Hand.*—English.		[G.]
Greek.—Alexandrian.	[G.]	*Flowers.*—Nearly all.		

The business was shortly afterwards removed to No. 8 Worship Street,[3] hard by the old premises; and here, in 1785, the first specimen-book of the foundry was issued. This volume exhibits the greater part of the new Caslon series of romans, which the proprietors in their 'Advertisement' frankly admit to have been cut in the closest possible imitation of that ingenious artist's models.[4] It includes also two pages of Hebrew type. Later in the same year appeared a large broadside sheet printed both sides, containing an epitome of the specimen-book, and displaying, besides the Arabic, Hebrews, Greeks, and Samaritan recently acquired at James's sale, one or two fresh Hebrew founts lately finished. Considerable variety is thrown into this and later specimens by showing each size not only on its own body, but upon the bodies next larger and next smaller—short descending sorts being specially

[1] See p. 217.

[2] The pedigree of the matrices is indicated, as far as can be ascertained, by the initials; but in several cases, particularly in the case of the blacks, the origin is considerably more remote than the foundry named. The error of inferring anything as to their origin from the names of famous old printers appearing on the drawers in which they were stored at James's foundry has already been pointed out. Several of these founts Dr. Fry appears to have received in a defective state, necessitating in some cases a complete rejustifying of the matrices, and in others the cutting of a considerable number of punches, and casting on bodies which did not always agree with those named in the sale catalogue. This circumstance will account for many of the apparent discrepancies between the original founts and the renovated founts as they appear in the Type Street specimens.

[3] In Kent's *London Directory*, 1781 and 1783, the address is given as No. 8 Queen Street. This street ran south from Worship Street. See R. Horwood's *Map of London*, 1794–9.

[4] 'It affords them'—the proprietors—'great Satisfaction to observe that the original Shape of their Roman and Italic Letters continues to meet the Approbation of the Curious, both in and out of the Printing Trade: nevertheless, to remove an Objection which the difference in Shape, from the letters commonly used here, raised in some, whereby their Introduction into several Capital Offices have been prevented; they have cut entire new sets of Punches, both Roman and Italic; and they flatter themselves they have executed the Founts, as far as they are done, in an elegant and masterly Manner, which in this Specimen are distinguished by the title NEW, and which will mix with and be totally unknown from the most approved Founts made by the late ingenious Artist, William Caslon.' For Caslon's acknowledgement of this compliment, see above, p. 244.

cut for the latter. The broadside also includes a Diamond roman, the first in England, for which the founders claim that it is 'the smallest letter in the world', adding subsequently that it 'gets in considerably more than the famous Dutch Diamond'. This sheet appeared also in Chambers's *Cyclopaedia*, edited by A. Rees, 1786, vol. i.

Another specimen followed in 1786, showing several more of the new founts, and including seven pages of orientals. This volume is dedicated to the Prince

בראשית ברא אלהי
ם את השמים ואת
בְּרֵאשִׁית בָּרָא אֱלֹהִים

FIG. 83. Hebrew cut by Edmund Fry.

of Wales, and is prefaced by an address to the public of the usual self-laudatory character, with a somewhat aggressive reference to the rival foundry at Chiswell Street.[1]

In the following year Joseph Fry retired from the business. Besides founding a chocolate business in his native city, and becoming a considerable partner in the new Bristol Porcelain Works, he had added to his other enterprises that of a Chemical Works at Battersea, and later still had established some important Soap Works in partnership with Alderman Fripp of Bristol. He did not long survive his retirement, and died, after a few days' illness, on 29 March 1787, aged 59, greatly respected. He was buried in the Friends' burial-ground at the Friars, Bristol. A silhouette portrait of him is to be seen in Hugh Owen's *Two Centuries of Ceramic Art in Bristol*, where also many interesting details of his life are to be found.[2]

In 1787 was issued a *Specimen of Printing Types by Edmund Fry and Co.*—the first mention of the firm under its new title. This was followed in the next year by a full specimen of the foundry, with a preface and dedication similar to those of the 1786 edition, but showing several fresh additions, particularly among the orientals, which occupy twelve pages. Of the latter, several founts had been cut by Dr. Fry himself.

The specimen of 1787 was included in John Smith's *Printer's Grammar*[3] published in that year—a work which makes considerable reference to the Frys'

---

[1] 'However desirous the proprietor of another Foundery may be to persuade the public into an idea of a superiority in his own favour, owing to *Rapid* improvements for upwards of *Sixty* years, a little time may, perhaps, suffice to convince impartial and unbiassed Judges that the very elegant Types of the WORSHIP STREET MANUFACTORY, though they cannot indeed boast of their existence longer than about *Twenty* years! will yet rank as high in Beauty, Symmetry, and intrinsic Merit as any other whatever, and ensure equal approbation from the Literati not only in this Country but in every quarter of the Globe.'

[2] For a short time following Fry's death his widow is said to have been associated with her sons in the conduct of the letter foundry. Mrs. Fry lived at Great Marlow, and afterwards in Charterhouse Square, London, where she died, 22 Oct. 1803, aged 83.

[3] *The Printer's Grammar, London, printed by L. Wayland.* 1787, 8vo.

foundry, whose specimens and standards are used in illustration of the various subjects dealt with. The introductory note to the specimen gives the following account of the then condition of the foundry. It

was begun in 1764 and has been continued with great perseverance and assiduity, at a very considerable expence. The plan on which they first sat out, was an improvement of the Types of the late Mr. Baskerville of Birmingham, eminent for his ingenuity in his line, as also for his curious Printing, many proofs of which are extant and much admired: But the shape of Mr. Caslon's Type has since been copied by them with such accuracy as not to be distinguished from those of that celebrated Founder. They have at present Twenty-seven complete Founts in punches and matrices of Roman and Italic, besides many sizes of larger Letter cast in Sand; also an elegant assortment of Blacks, with Hebrews and Greeks, and many other Orientals: They have also a greater variety of Flowers than are to be met with in any other Foundery in this Kingdom.

The premises at Worship Street becoming inadequate for the type and printing business combined, Dr. Fry took a plot of ground opposite Bunhill Fields in Chiswell Street—then open fields—and there built the foundry which gave its name to Type Street (now Moor Lane). To these premises the business was removed in 1788; and the specimen of that year dates from the Type Street Foundry.

Among many elegant works printed at this time in the types of this foundry was the Rev. Henry Homer's fine edition of the classics,[1] printed by Millar Ritchie,[2] in which the somewhat rare compliment was paid the founder of adding his name to the list of typographers engaged on the work. The printing business was about the same time dissociated from the typefounding, and remained at Worship Street under the management of Henry Fry, who styled his office the 'Cicero Press'.[3]

In the year 1794 Dr. Fry took Isaac Steele into partnership, and the specimen of this year, under the title of 'Edmund Fry and Isaac Steele, Letter-Founders to the Prince of Wales', shows a marked advance on its predecessors. Besides the additional romans, it includes the Irish fount originally cut by Moxon in 1680, and is further supplemented by a considerable display of 'Metal Cast Ornaments, curiously adjusted to paper', of which a specimen had already appeared in the preceding year. Rude as many of these cuts now appear, they were much affected at the time, while a few of their number bear evident testimony to the wholesome revolution then being effected in the art of engraving by Thomas Bewick. A distinct improvement in the same direction may be traced in the series of 'Head and Fable Cuts' for Dilworth's *Spelling Book*, a specimen of which was issued shortly afterwards.[4]

The Frys had considerable custom in the American colonies. William Cobbett's

[1] Cf. *C. Plinii Cæcilii Secundi Epistolarum libri x. sumptibus editoris excudebant M. Ritchie et J. Sammells. Londini,* 1790. 8vo. At end: *Typis Edmundi Fry.*

[2] This excellent artist was a Scotsman (1752–1828), and printed in Bartholomew Close in 1785. He was one of the first who started in emulation of Baskerville as a fine printer; his series of Homer's Classics (*Sallust,* 1789; *Pliny,* 1790; *Tacitus,* 1790; *Q. Curtius* and *Cæsar,* 1790; *Livy,* 1794) established his reputation. His quarto *Bible* and the *Memoirs of the Count de Grammont* are also celebrated. He printed on Whatman's paper with admirable ink and most careful press-work, and is stated to have produced most of his books by his own personal and manual labour.

[3] From this press the following elegantly printed volume was issued in 1788: *The Beauties of the Poets, being a Collection of Moral and Sacred Poetry, etc.,* compiled by the late Rev. *Thomas Janes of Bristol. London, printed at the Cicero Press by and for Henry Fry, No. 5 Worship Street, Upper Moorfields.* 1788, 8vo. At one time Henry Fry had as a partner Stephen Couchman. They printed John Bell's *Shakespeare,* 1785–8.

[4] *A New Guide to the English Tongue in five parts by Thomas Dilworth . . . Schoolmaster in Wapping. Stereotype Edition. London. Andrew Wilson, Camden Town.* 1812, 8vo. Contains portraits, tail-piece, and twelve fable cuts.

Porcupine's Gazette printed its title in Fry's handsome four-line Pica upper- and lower-case, and other newspapers of the day show Fry founts (see B. Fry's *Notes on the American Press at the end of the XVIII Century*, New York, Grolier Club, 1927). Isaiah Thomas of Worcester was a constant customer, and in 1790 procured a Bible in Nonpareil set at Type Street and shipped to him in the set-up pages. It was published in 1797 at Worcester, Massachusetts, United States of Columbia (see McMurtrie, *The Isaiah Thomas Standing Bible*, Chicago, 1928).

THE ORIGINAL MATRICES

ABCDEFGHIJKLMNOPQRSTUVWXYZ&

FIG. 84. Fry's Titling Old Face Open. From the original matrices.

BRIGHTER prospects opened when George Third came to the throne to those men of literary merit who had been honoured with no *mark of royal favour* during the reign

ABCDEFGHIJKLMNOPRSTUVQU
abcdefghijklmnopqrstuvwxyz

FIG. 85. Georgian Old Face, perhaps from the Fry Foundry. From the original matrices.

In 1798 Dr. Fry put forth proposals for publishing the important philological work on which he had for sixteen years been engaged, and which, in the following year, was issued under the title of *Pantographia*, with a dedication to Sir Joseph Banks, President of the Royal Society. This important work,[1] which displays great learning and research, was favourably received. It exhibits upwards of 200 alphabets, amongst which are 18 varieties of the Chaldee and no less than 39 of the Greek. Many of the letters were cut by the author expressly for the work, under the direction or with the advice of some of the most eminent scholars of the day, and not a few subsequently found a place among the specimens of the foundry.

In 1799 George Knowles was admitted into partnership, and the firm became Fry, Steele & Co.

A new revolution in the public taste necessitated at this stage the abandonment of the Caslon Old Style faces, and the adoption of the modern cut roman letter then coming into vogue; and the specimens between 1800 and 1808 are interesting as

[1] *Pantographia; containing accurate copies of all the known Alphabets in the World, together with an English explanation of the peculiar Force or Power of each Letter; to which are added specimens of all well authenticated Oral Languages; forming a comprehensive Digest of Phonology. By Edmund Fry, Letter Founder, Type Street, London, 1799. Roy. 8vo. A few copies were printed on vellum, one of which is in the Cambridge University Library.*

x

marking the gradual accomplishment of this task. The specimen of 1803 showed the first of the new romans, and in 1808 Stower's *Printer's Grammar* contained the series almost complete.[1]

The new style may have been considered an improvement at the time, but a later judgement has endorsed the regret with which Dr. Fry and others witnessed the then entire abandonment of the time-honoured and graceful characters of the first Caslon.

Naturally conservative in most matters pertaining to his art, Dr. Fry viewed with the utmost displeasure another innovation of the same period, in the introduction of ornamental type; and to the end of his career he strenuously resisted the 'pernicious fashion', as he styled it; yielding only to the extent of one small series of flowered titling-letters, which crept into his later specimens. But, although opposed to ornaments in this form, the Type Street specimens show no lack of flowers, and Stower's book includes a profuse specimen of these ornaments, arranged in fantastic designs by Samuel Hazard, the printer, of Bath.[2] Fry, however, did cut fat faces and antiques (Egyptians).

A *Specimen of Modern Cut Printing Types* was issued by Fry and Steele in 1814. Both Steele and Knowles appear to have retired by 1816, when Dr. Fry assumed the sole management of the business. In the specimen of 1816 he styles himself 'Letter-Founder to the King and Prince Regent'. Soon afterwards, his own health failing, he admitted his son, Windover Fry, into partnership, and the firm became Edmund Fry & Son.

The subsequent specimens of the foundry are not marked by any special feature of interest, if we except the introduction of Firmin Didot's Great Primer Script in 1820, containing upwards of sixty lower-case sorts, in a system of ligatures and connectors so elaborate as to necessitate the printing of a scheme to facilitate their composition, and the manufacture of special cases to hold them.

Dr. Fry's philological studies had not ceased with the publication of *Pantographia*, and he was constantly adding to the stock of punches and matrices of the 'learned' languages, in which his foundry was already rich. His excellence as a cutter of oriental punches led to his selection by the University of Cambridge[3] to execute several founts for that learned body; in addition to which he was employed to produce types for the works of the British and Foreign Bible Society, and similar biblical publications.

His most important effort in this direction was an English Syriac for Bagster's *Polyglot*, with the points cast on the body, the entire fount consisting of nearly 400 matrices.

The specimen of 1824, which was issued both in octavo and (more sumptuously) in quarto, for presentation, signalized the completion of his efforts in this depart-

---

[1] *The Printer's Grammar or Introduction to the Art of Printing: containing a concise History of the Art, etc.*, by C. Stower, Printer. London. *Printed by the Editor*. 1808, 8vo. The same work also shows extracts and specimens from *Pantographia*. The present location of the specimen of 1803 is not known.

[2] Hazard was also the designer of a pair of cases,

a plan of which is shown by Stower, p. 463. A single sheet of flowers, printed by Hazard, is reproduced in Berry and Johnson, pl. 8.

[3] The Rev. Samuel Lee, B.D., Regius Professor of Hebrew at Cambridge, was a constant visitor at Type Street, and personally directed the cutting of many of the founts.

ment, and at the same time notified that the name of the foundry had been changed —not inappropriately—to the Polyglot Foundry.

It is to be regretted that Dr. Fry's energy in one particular branch of his art, congenial as it was to his own tastes, did not turn out lucrative from a business point of view, and the last few years of his career as a typefounder were not prosperous. His latest specimen was a broadside sheet of Newspaper founts in 1827.

In the same year he produced a raised type for the blind, under the following circumstances: The Scottish Society of Arts, anxious to promote the welfare of the blind, and desirous to determine, among the many systems at that time proposed, which was the most suitable method of printing for their instruction, offered a gold medal of the value of £20 for the best communication on the subject. Twenty designs were sent in in 1833, of which Dr. Fry's was the only one retaining the ordinary alphabetical characters. His specimen consisted of large and small square 'sanserif' capitals working in combination, with no deviation from the regular form. The committee occupied four years in arriving at a decision; employing the time in corresponding with and eliciting the opinion of all the chief persons interested and experienced in the education of the blind, in reference to the various designs. Amongst others they received a long communication from the Rev. W. Taylor of York, who commended Dr. Fry's system, approving specially of the absence of a 'lower-case' letter.[1] The report was published 31 May 1837, awarding the medal to Dr. Fry, who, however, was at that time no more, his death having occurred two years previously.

The following summary of the contents of the Polyglot Foundry, as far as its foreign and rare founts were concerned, is taken from the specimen-book of 1824, and corresponds closely to the list given in Hansard's *Typographia* in the following year. With the exception of the founts purchased at James's sale in 1782 (which are distinguished by the initials), most of the characters were cut by, or under the direction of, Dr. Fry himself.

DR. FRY'S FOUNDRY

Arabic.—Great Primer.	[J.?]	*Greek.*—Small Pica.	
Ditto, No. 2.		Long Primer.	
English.		Ditto, No. 2.	
Amharic.—English.		Brevier.	
Ethiopic.—English.	[P.] [A.] [J.]	Nonpareil.	
Ditto, No. 2.		*Greek Alexandrian.*—Pica.	[G.] [J.]
Pica.	[J.]	*Guzerattee.*—Great Primer.	
German.—Long Primer.		Long Primer.	
Greek.—Double Pica.		*Hebrew.*—two-line Great Primer.	
Great Primer.		two-line English.	
English.		Double Pica with points.	
Pica.		English with points.	
Pica, No. 2.		Pica.	

[1] Dr. Fry's system was virtually that first introduced by John Alston, of Glasgow, to which reference is made on p. 74, where details are also given as to the other principal systems of type for the blind. A 'lower-case' was subsequently added to Dr. Fry's fount by his successors, and in this form the type was largely used by the various Type Schools following Alston's method. Full particulars of this award, with specimens, may be seen in vol. i of the *Transactions of the Royal Scottish Society of Arts.*

Hebrew.—Small Pica.
  Long Primer.
  Bourgeois.
  Brevier.
  Nonpareil.
Hebrew Rabbinical.—Small Pica. [A.] [J.]
  Brevier. [A.] [J.]
  Nonpareil. [A.] [J.]
Irish.—Pica.
  Small Pica. [M.] [A.] [J.]
    Ditto, No. 2.
Malabaric.—English.
  Pica.
Russian.—Double Pica.
Samaritan.—Pica. [P.] [G.] [J.]
  Long Primer. [J.]
Saxon.—Double Pica.
  Great Primer.
  English.
  Pica.

Saxon.—Small Pica.
  Long Primer.
  Brevier.
Syriac.—English.
  Long Primer.
Music.—Large Plein Chant.
  Small   ,,
  Psalm.
Blacks.—four-line.
  two-line Great Primer.
  two-line English.
  Double Pica.
  Great Primer.
  English, No. 1. [A.] [J.]
    Ditto, No. 2.
  Pica, No. 1.
    Ditto, No. 2. [A.] [J.]
  Small Pica.
  Long Primer. [A.] [J.]
  Brevier.[1]

In 1828, being now of an advanced age, and after forty-six years' incessant labour, Dr. Fry decided to dispose of his foundry; and a circular was issued announcing the fact to the public. This document, throwing as it does considerable light on the history of the Type Street Foundry, is interesting enough to quote at length. After enumerating generally the contents of the foundry and stating the conditions of sale, Dr. Fry remarks:

The Substructure of this Establishment was laid about the year 1764; commencing with improved imitations of Baskerville's founts, of which every size was completed, from the largest down to the Diamond: but they did not meet the encouraging approbation of the Printers, whose offices generally, throughout the kingdom, were stored from the London and Glasgow Founderies with Types of the form introduced by the celebrated William Caslon, early in the last century; chiefly from the admired Dutch models, which gained so much credit to the Elzevirs of Amsterdam, Leyden, &c.

By the recommendation, therefore, of several of the most respectable Printers of the Metropolis, Doctor Fry, the proprietor, commenced his imitation of the Chiswell Street Foundery, which he successfully finished throughout all it's various sizes, at a vast expense, and with very satisfactory encouragement, during the completion of it. At which period a rude, pernicious, and most unclassical innovating System was commenced, which, in a short time was followed by the most injurious and desolating ravages on the property of every Letter Founder and Printer in the kingdom, by the introduction of fancy letters of various anomalous forms, with names as appropriate—disgraceful in a Profession, once held so *Sacred*, as to have it's operations confined to consecrated Buildings, and those of the highest class.

The Baskerville and Caslon imitations, all completed with Accents, Fractions, &c., were, in consequence of this revolution, laid by for ever; and many thousand pounds weight of new letter in Founts, estimated on the average at selling prices, at 2*s.* 6*d.* per pound, were taken from the shelves, and carried to the melting-pot to be recast into Types, no doubt, in many instances, more beautiful; but no instance has occurred to the attentive observation of the Proprietor of this Foundery, where any Founts of book letter on the present

---

[1] Hansard mentions a two-line English Engrossing, two sizes of Music, and the matrices of Dr. Wilkins's *Philosophical Character*; none of which, however, formed part of this foundry.

system, have been found equal in service, or really so agreeable to the reader, as the true *Caslon*-shaped Elzevir Types; and this is the undisguised sentiment of many judicious Printers.

When that eminent Printer, the late William Bowyer, gave instructions to Joseph Jackson to cut his beautiful Pica Greek, he used to say 'Those in common use were no more Greek than they were English.' Were he now living, it is likely he would not have any reason to alter that opinion.

The Greeks of this Foundery were many of them made in Type Street, copied from those of the celebrated Foulis of Glasgow; and there are two, a Pica, and a Long Primer, on the Porsonian plan. The Codex Alexandrinus was purchased at James' Sale in 1782.[1]

The Hebrews were also chiefly cut by Dr. Fry, subject to the direction and approbation of the most learned Hebraists.

The two Arabics,[2] Great Primer and English, were cut from the original drawings of, and under the personal direction of Dr. Wilkins, Oriental Librarian to the East India Company; and have no rival either in beauty or correctness.

The Syriac[3] has been made within the last two years, with all it's vowel points, reduced to an English body, from the Double Pica of the eminent Assemann's edition of Ludolph's Testament.

The English, No. 1, and Pica Ethiopics—the Pica and Long Primer Samaritans, were purchased at James's sale. The other Orientals, viz. two Malabarics—the Amharic—Ethiopic, No. 3, and Guzerattee, were all cut at this Foundery. As was the fine collection of Blacks, or pointed Gothics, except the English, No. 1,—Pica, No. 2,—Long Primer, No. 1,—and Brevier, which were collected by the late John James. There is good authority for believing that this Pica Black, No. 2, was once the property of William Caxton;[4] Doctor

---

[1] Of the antiquity of this interesting fount an account has already been given at pp. 192–5. By a curious confusion of names and dates, Dr. Fry, in his specimens, stated that 'this character was cut by *Wynkyn de Worde*, in exact imitation of the *Codex Alexandrinus* in the British Museum'! This absurd anachronism—the more extraordinary as emanating from an antiquary of Dr. Fry's standing—appears to have arisen from the fact that at the sale of James's foundry the matrices lay in a drawer which bore the name, 'De Worde'. This circumstance misled Paterson, the auctioneer, into advertising the fount as the genuine handiwork of De Worde, a printer who lived a century before the codex was brought into this country. The further coincidence that Dr. Woide of the British Museum was, at the time of the sale, engaged in producing an edition of the codex, with facsimile types prepared by Jackson the founder, doubtless added—by the similarity of the names De Worde and Dr. Woide—to the confusion. After its purchase, the fount first appeared in Joseph Fry & Sons' specimen of 1786, without note. But, in the subsequent specimens of the foundry, bearing his own name, Dr. Fry introduced the fiction, which remained unchallenged for a quarter of a century.

[2] In addition to which Dr. Fry possessed, in an imperfect condition (many of the characters having been recut), the Great Primer Arabic of Walton's *Polyglot*. According to Hansard he also had a set of matrices, English body, from the first punches cut by William Caslon; but this seems to be an error.

[3] Used in Bagster's *Polyglot*. The same fount was cast on Long Primer with movable points. Hansard is in error in stating that Dr. Fry cut a Nonpareil Syriac. The remark about Assemann is not understood. There were three Assemanns, members of a Maronite family, who in the 18th century described Oriental MSS. in the Vatican Library and other Italian libraries. Ludolph is perhaps a mistake for Leusden.

[4] An error still less explicable than that of the Alexandrian Greek, but which not only Dr. Fry's successors, but Hansard himself has copied. The following seems to be the 'good authority' on which the assertion is based. In 1819 Bulmer, the eminent printer, printed for the Roxburghe Club Hibbert's transcript of the manuscript fragment of the translation of Ovid's *Metamorphoses*, made by Caxton about 1480, and preserved in the library of Pepys at Magdalene College, Cambridge. The body of the work was set in the English black bought by Dr. Fry at James's sale—but in two places a smaller size of type was required to print passages omitted in Caxton's translation, but supplied by the editor in the original French of Colard Mansion's edition. For these passages the Pica black was selected, and as the French text contained several accents and contractions, these had to be specially cut. This task Dr. Fry performed, and understanding that the letter was to be used for printing a work of Caxton's, he appears, without further inquiry, to have assumed that the work in question was a facsimile reprint, and that his old matrices had been discovered to bear the impress of the veritable character used by that famous man. Had he seen the book in question he would have discovered that not only was it a transcript from a manuscript of which no printed copy had ever been known to exist, but that the very passages in which the boasted type was used were passages which did not even appear in a work of Caxton at all. The matrices are very old. They were in Andrews's foundry about 1700, and in all probability came there from Holland, as they closely resemble the other old Dutch blacks in James's foundry. In 1924 the Shakespeare Head Press printed an edition of this translation of Ovid in a roman type.

Fry having recut for a reprint of a work published by the celebrated man, all the contractions and accented letters exhibited in the Specimen Book.

The Occidentals, as termed by Moxon, Mores, and others, viz. the Saxons, Hibernians,[1] German, and Russian, were also produced at this Foundery. As were the two Plein Chants, and the Psalm Music.

The Great Primer Script, which, it must be acknowledged, is the *Ne plus ultra* of every effort of the Letter Founder in imitation of writing, was made for the Proprietor by the celebrated Firmin Didot, at Paris; the Matrices are of Steel, and the impressions from the Punches sunk in *inlaid Silver!* [2]

In taking leave of a Profession, which has for many years engaged his whole attention, the Proprietor begs to convey, through this channel, the high sense of obligation he hopes to retain during his life, for the great encouragement with which he has been favoured for so long a period; as well as for the generous assistance and advice of many of his learned Friends, in the *getting up*, and accurate completion of various undertakings. It is also with much gratification, that he can look back and recall to recollection, that he has carefully followed their advices, in not admitting into his Foundery any article degrading or disgraceful, or unbecoming the dignity of that Art, which deserves to be looked up to and revered as the 'Head of the republic of letters':—claiming Permission to recommend to his Successor and Contemporaries, the steady pursuit of that plan which will secure the reputation of the *once Sacred* Profession, and restore to it the honourable Character it obtained several Centuries ago, of

'ARS ARTIUM OMNIUM CONSERVATRIX'.

Polyglot Letter Foundery, 2nd month 14th, 1828.

The foundry met with a purchaser in William Thorowgood, of Fann Street, to whose premises the entire stock was removed in 1829, and now forms part of the foundry of Messrs. Stephenson, Blake & Co.[3]

Dr. Fry retired to his residence at Stratford Green, and subsequently removed to Dalby Terrace, City Road, where he died 22 December 1835.[4] He was an old member of the Stationers' Company. In private life he was a man of genial disposition. A portrait of him, painted by Frederique Boileau, was exhibited in the Caxton Celebration of 1877 by his son, Arthur Fry, and an excellent silhouette was also in possession of the family of Francis Fry, F.S.A., of Bristol.

---

[1] In the Small Pica, No. 2, was printed *The Two First Books of the Pentateuch, or Books of Moses, as a preparation for learners to read the Holy Scriptures. The types cut by Mr. Edmund Fry, Letter Founder to His Majesty, from Original Irish Manuscripts, under the care and direction of T. Connellan (2nd Edit.) Printed at the Apollo Press, London, J. Johnson, Brook Street, Holborn, 1819. 12mo.*

[2] Whatever singularity Didot may have indulged in in the first strikes from his famous punches for his own use, the matrices now in the possession of Dr. Fry's successors are of most unmistakable copper throughout. And it does not appear that more than one set of the strikes was needed to meet all the demands made upon this complicated letter by the printers of the day.

[3] Cf. p. 295.

[4] *Gentleman's Magazine*, May 1836.

16

JOSEPH JACKSON, 1763
WILLIAM CASLON III, 1792
WILLIAM CASLON IV, 1807
STEPHENSON, BLAKE & CO.

JOSEPH JACKSON, apprentice to Caslon I, was born in Old Street, London, on 4 September 1733. He was the first child baptized in St. Luke's, and received his education at a school in that neighbourhood, the gift of a Mr. Fuller. During the term of his service at Chiswell Street he was, says Nichols,[1] exceedingly tractable in the common branches of the business. Rowe Mores states that he was an 'apprentice to the whole art',[2] but this term evidently does not comprehend the most important branch of that art, namely, the cutting of punches. This was kept a profound secret at Chiswell Street, Caslon and his son constantly locking themselves into the apartment in which they practised it. Jackson, who had a great desire to learn the mystery, bored a hole through the wainscot and was thus, at different times, able to watch his employers through the process, and to form some idea how the whole was performed; and he afterwards applied himself at every opportunity to the finishing of a punch.

When he had completed one to his own mind, he presented it to his master, expecting to be rewarded for his ingenuity: but the premium he received was a hard blow, with a threat that he should be sent to Bridewell if he again made a similar attempt. This circumstance being taken in dudgeon, his mother bought him what tools were necessary, and he improved himself at her house whenever he had an opportunity.

He continued [adds Nichols] to work for Mr. Caslon after he came out of his time,[3] till a quarrel arose in the foundery about the price of work; and a memorial, which terminated in favour of the workmen, being sent to the elder Caslon (who was then in the Commission of the Peace, and had retired to Bethnal Green), young Jackson and Mr. Cottrell were discharged, as supposed ringleaders.

Compelled thus to seek employment, they united their slender stock in a partnership, and went on prosperously till, Jackson's mother dying, he entered in 1759, on board the 'Minerva' frigate, as armourer; and in May 1761 was removed, with Capt. Alexander Hood, into the same situation in the 'Aurora'; and proved somewhat successful, having about £40 prize money to receive at the Peace of 1763. During the time he was at sea,

---

[1] Nichols's *Lit. Anec.* ii. 358–9, and *Gentleman's Magazine*, 1792, p. 93.　　[2] *Dissertation*, p. 83.　[3] Probably as a rubber, in which occupation he is represented as engaged in the 'View of the Caslon Foundry' given in the *Universal Magazine* for June 1750. (Cf. our Frontispiece.)

he was visited by a severe fit of sickness, in which he vowed, if he recovered, to lead in future a very penitent life; which promise he punctually fulfilled.

Quitting the navy, he returned to London and rejoined once more his old comrade and partner, now a fully established typefounder in Nevil's Court, Fetter Lane. He worked for some time under Cottrell, but at length, at the instigation, it would appear, of two of his fellow workmen, Robinson and Hickson (who shared with Cottrell the distinction of serving as privates in the Life Guards), he determined to set up in business for himself. The necessary capital for the new concern was found by Robinson and Hickson, who agreed to allow Jackson, as his salary for conducting the business under the partnership, the sum of £62. 8s. per annum, and to supply money for carrying on the trade for two years. A small house in Cock Lane was taken for the purpose, and such was the modest beginning of this famous foundry. The hazardous adventure succeeded, thanks to the genius of Jackson, who was able soon to satisfy his partners that the business would be productive before the time promised.

When he had pursued his labours about six months, Mr. Bowyer accidentally calling to inspect some of his punches (for he had no specimen), approved them so much, that he promised to employ him; adding, 'My father was the means of old Mr. Caslon riding in his coach, how do you know but I may be the means of your doing the same?'

A short time after this, he put out a small specimen of one fount; which his former young master carried to Bethnal Green with an air of contempt. The good old justice treated it otherwise; and desired his son 'to take it home and preserve it; and whenever he went to cutting again to look at it'. It is but justice to the third William Caslon to add that he always acknowledged the abilities of Mr. Jackson; and though rivals in an art which requires the greatest exertions of ingenuity, they lived in habits of reciprocal friendship.

It is much to be regretted that no copy of Jackson's first specimen-sheet (which we may assume to have been issued about 1765) is now to be discovered.

Business increasing, he removed from Cock Lane to more commodious premises in Dorset Street, Salisbury Square, Fleet Street, and here his foundry and reputation made rapid advances.

About the year 1771 [Nichols relates] he was applied to by the Duke of Norfolk to make a mould to cast a hollow square. Telling the Duke that he thought this was practicable, his Grace observed that he had applied to all the skilful mechanicks in London, Mr. Caslon not excepted, who declared it impossible. He soon convinced the Duke of his abilities, and in the course of three months, producing what his Grace had been years in search of, was ever after held in great estimation by the Duke, who considered him as the first mechanick in the kingdom.

In 1773 it would appear that Jackson issued a further specimen of his now-increasing foundry. Of this performance Rowe Mores makes flattering mention in presenting his summary of the contents of the foundry as it stood in that year:

Mr. Jackson [he says] lives in Salisbury Court in Fleet Street. He is obliging and communicative, and his Specimen will, *adjuvante numine,* have place amongst the literate specimens of English letter cutters. The prognostics are these:—

Mr. JACKSON'S FOUNDERY.

ORIENTALS:	OCCIDENTALS:

ORIENTALS:

Hebrew.—Double Pica.

Persic.—English.

Bengal.—(or Modern Sanskrit), a corruption of the older characters of the Hindoos, the ancient inhabitants of Bengal.

OCCIDENTALS:

Greek.—English, Long Primer, Brevier.

Roman and Italic.—*sicut et reliqui.*

SEPTENTRIONALS:

English.—2-line Great Primer.

Scriptorial.[1]—Double Pica, nearly finished.

He has likewise Proscription letters beginning at 12-line Pica, the same with those of Mr. Cottrell, the first who cut letters of this dimension.

With regard to the Bengalee letter, Rowe Mores states that this was cut by Jackson 'for Mr. William Bolts, Judge of the Mayor's Court of Calcutta, for a work in which he had been engaged at the time of his sudden departure from England about 1774'.[2]

The work here referred to was the *Grammar of the Bengal Language*, projected by the East India Company as part of a scheme for the dissemination of a knowledge of the Indian languages in Europe. It appears, however, that although Bolts was supposed to be in every way competent for the fabrication of this intricate character, his models, as copied by Jackson, failed to give satisfaction, and the work was for the time abandoned;[3] to be revived and executed some few years later in a more masterly and accurate manner by Charles Wilkins,[4] then in the service of the East

---

[1] Nothing more is known of Jackson's Script.

[2] *Dissertation*, p. 83.

[3] N.B. Halhed thus refers to this circumstance in the introduction to his *Bengal Grammar* (see *below*): 'That the Bengal letter is very difficult to be imitated in steel will readily be allowed by every person who shall examine the intricacies of the strokes, the unequal length and size of the characters, and the variety of their positions and combinations. It was no easy task to procure a writer accurate enough to prepare an alphabet of a similar and proportionate body throughout, with that symmetrical exactness which is necessary to the regularity and neatness of a fount. Mr. Bolts (who is supposed to be well versed in this language) attempted to fabricate a set of types for it with the assistance of the ablest artists in London. But, as he has egregiously failed in executing even the easiest part, or primary alphabet, of which he has published a specimen, there is no reason to suppose that his project when completed would have advanced beyond the usual state of imperfection to which new inventions are constantly exposed.'

[4] This distinguished scholar and self-made typographer was born in the year 1751. He entered the East India Company's Civil Service, where he devoted himself not only to the study of the oriental languages, but to the actual production of the types necessary to extend the study of those languages among his fellow countrymen, with extraordinary skill and perseverance. He succeeded in cutting the punches and casting the types for Halhed's *Grammar of the Bengal Language*, published at Hoogly in Bengal in 1778, 4to. In his preface to that work, Halhed, after referring to Bolts's failure, in the passage quoted in the preceding note, thus describes the undertaking: 'The advice and even solicitation of the Governor-General prevailed upon Mr. Wilkins, a gentleman who has been some years in the India

Company's Civil Service, to undertake a set of Bengal Types. He did, and his success has exceeded every expectation. In a country so remote from all connection with European artists, he has been obliged to charge himself with all the various occupations of the Metallurgist, the Engraver, the Founder, and the Printer. To the merit of invention he was compelled to add the application of personal labour. With a rapidity unknown in Europe, he surmounted all the obstacles which necessarily clog the first rudiments of a difficult art, as well as the disadvantages of solitary experiment; and has thus singly, on the first effort, exhibited his work in a state of perfection which in every part of the world has appeared to require the united improvements of different projectors and the gradual polish of successive ages.' Wilkins persevered in his noble undertaking of rendering the oriental languages available to the English scholar through the medium of typography. With this view he compiled from the most celebrated native grammars and commentaries a work entirely new to England on the Structure of the Sanskrita tongue. Of the difficulties and discouragements attendant on the execution of this self-imposed task he thus speaks in his Preface: 'At the commencement of the year in 1795, residing in the country and having much leisure, I began to arrange my materials and prepare them for publication. I cut letters in steel, made matrices and moulds, and cast from them a fount of types of the Deva Nagari character, all with my own hands; and, with the assistance of such mechanics as a country village could afford, I very speedily prepared all the other implements of printing in my own dwelling-house; for by the second of May of the same year I had taken proofs of 16 pages, differing but little from those now exhibited in the first two sheets. Till two o'clock on that day everything had succeeded to my expectations; when alas! the premises

India Company in Bengal, who with an extraordinary combination of talents succeeded, by the work of his own hand, in designing, engraving, casting, and printing the *Grammar* published at Hoogly in 1778.

Bolts's failure in this particular reflects no discredit on Jackson, who faithfully reproduced the models given him, and who displayed his talent in the same direction shortly after by the production of a fount of Deva Nagari, cut under the direction of Captain William Kirkpatrick, of the East India Service, and Persian Secretary to the Commander-in-Chief for India, for the purpose of printing a *Grammar and Dictionary* in that language.

Of this fount a specimen remains—the only specimen extant, we believe, bearing Jackson's name. It is a broadside, displaying in table form the alphabet and combinations of the Sanskrit, and exhibits no small delicacy of workmanship, not only in the oriental character itself, but in the few lines of roman letter composing the title. There is no date to the specimen.[1]

Captain Kirkpatrick's *Dictionary* was never completed. One part only appeared in 1785,[2] containing the Glossary of the Arabic and Persian words incorporated with the Hindu, and in this no Nagari is used. All the remaining parts of the work, as first projected, depended on the new type; but as they never appeared, the object for which the fount was cut was lost.

The next important undertaking which engaged Jackson's talents was one of national interest. The House of Lords had, in the year 1767, determined upon printing the Journals and Parliamentary records, 'a work, which', says Nichols, 'will ever reflect honour on the good taste and munificence of the present reign' (George III). Jackson had been employed to cut several varieties of letter for this work; and he was now called upon to assist in a further outcome of the same good taste and munificence, in the production of type for the splendid facsimile of the *Domesday Book*, begun in 1773. This important work was projected and carried through by Nichols himself, and a brief account of the circumstances under which it saw the light may be interesting and not out of place here.

The Lords, it appears, being petitioned to sanction the printing of the *Domesday Book*, the most important of the Anglo-Saxon records, as a matter of national importance, referred, through the Treasury Board, to the Society of Antiquaries as to the mode in which it should be published, whether by printing-types or by having a copy of the manuscript engraved in facsimile. By the examination of several eminent printers it was learned that according to the first plan very many

were discovered to be in flames, which, spreading too rapidly to be extinguished, the whole building was presently burned to the ground. In the midst of this misfortune, I happily saved all my books and manuscripts, and the greatest part of the punches and matrices; but the types themselves having been thrown out and scattered on the lawn, were either lost or rendered useless.' About ten years afterwards the Directors of the East India Company encouraged Dr. Wilkins, then Librarian to the Company, to resume his labours and cast new types, as the study of the Sanskrita had become an important object in their new College at Hertford. Dr. Wilkins complied, and the *Grammar of the Sanskrita Language*, London, 1808, 4to, duly appeared from Bulmer's Press, and was allowed to be a monument at once of beautiful typography and erudite industry. Dr., subsequently Sir Charles, Wilkins died 13 May 1836, at the advanced age of 85. Specimens of his Bengali and Sanskrit may be seen in Johnson's *Typographia*, ii. 389–94.

[1] A specimen of Jackson's Pica roman and italic appears in W. Hay's undated specimen. See Berry and Johnson, p. 91.

[2] *A Vocabulary, Persian, Arabic, and English, containing such words as have been adopted from the two former of these languages, and incorporated into the Hindvi; together with some hundreds of compound verbs formed from Persian or Arabic nouns and in universal use. Being the seventh part of the new Hindvi Grammar and Dictionary.* London, 1785. 4to.

unavoidable errors would occur; a tracing of the record was then proposed, to be transferred to copper plates. An estimate of the expense of this was next ordered by the Treasury Board, which amounted to £20,000 for the printing and engraving of 1,250 copies, each containing 1,664 plates; but this sum, however proportionate, was considered too large, and the first plan was again reverted to.

It was then proposed by the learned Dr. Charles Morton that a fount of facsimile types should be cut under his superintendence. This undertaking, however, failed, and Dr. Morton received £500 for doing little or nothing, and nearly £200 more for types that were of no use. The founder to whom Dr. Morton applied was Thomas Cottrell, a specimen of whose unsuccessful fount appeared shortly afterwards in Luckombe's *History of Printing*, 1770.

Dr. Morton's plan being abandoned, on account of the difficulty of producing in type letters which, in the manuscript, were constantly differing in their forms, the work was entrusted to Abraham Farley, F.R.S., a gentleman of great Record learning, and who had had access to the ancient manuscripts for upwards of forty years. His knowledge, however, did not induce him to differ from his original in a single instance, even when he found an apparent error; he preserved in his transcript every interlineation and contraction, and his copy was ultimately placed in Nichols's hands. Jackson was then employed to cut the types, and successfully accomplished the difficult undertaking.[1] The work occupied ten years in printing, and appeared in 1783, in two folio volumes.[2] The type was destroyed in the fire which consumed the printing-office of Nichols in Red Lion Court, Fleet Street, in 1808, previous to which, however, it was used in Kelham's Introduction and Glossary to the *Domesday Book* in 1788.[3]

It was Jackson's success, no doubt, in his facsimile letter for the *Domesday Book* which led to his selection shortly afterwards by Nichols to cut the type for Dr. Woide's[4] facsimile of the New Testament of the *Alexandrian Codex* in the British Museum. To the history of this priceless relic reference has been made once or twice in the course of this work.[5] Only one attempt had previously been made to reproduce its character in type—that of Patrick Young, in 1643, within a few years of the arrival of the manuscript in this country. In this letter was printed a specimen containing the first chapter of Genesis. But the project was abandoned, and the matrices, there is reason to believe, subsequently passed into Grover's foundry, and afterwards, through James, into the possession of Dr. Fry in 1782.[6] That Nichols was acquainted with their existence in 1778 is almost certain, since they are mentioned in Rowe Mores's *Dissertation*, which he himself edited and annotated. But not being sufficiently exact for the purpose, and, at the same time, it being decided that the facsimile should be produced through the medium of type in preference to other process,[7] Jackson was fixed on to cut a new set of punches

---

[1] The Domesday letter of Cottrell and Jackson may be seen in juxtaposition in Fry's *Pantographia*, 1799, pp. 50 and 314; also in Stower's *Printer's Grammar*, 1808, p. 253. Jackson's also appears in Johnson's *Typographia* (ii, p. 248), from which work our account is chiefly taken.

[2] *Domesday Book seu Liber Censualis Willelmi primi Regis Angliae inter Archivos Regni in Domo capitulari Westmonasterii asservatus. Jubente Rege*

Augustissimo Georgio Tertio prelo mandatus. Londini. Typis J. Nichols. 2 vols. Fol. 1783.

[3] *Domesday Book Illustrated.* London, 1788. 8vo.

[4] Dr. Woide was appointed Assistant Librarian at the British Museum in 1782.   [5] See pp. 192–5.

[6] A specimen of this letter may be seen in Dr. Fry's specimens, also in his *Pantographia*, p. 126.

[7] Gough, writing in the *Gentleman's Magazine*, vol. lvi, p. 497, says: 'It was reserved, therefore, for

from the transcript made by Dr. Woide's own hand. To this task he proved fully equal, and the work issued from Nichols's press in 1786[1]—a splendid folio edition, worthy alike of its subject and the artists who produced it. The unusual compliment was, in this instance, paid to the letter-founder of mentioning his name on the title-page as the author of the types employed in the work.

The matrices were afterwards deposited in the British Museum, and were again brought into requisition when, in 1812, H. H. Baber produced his facsimile of the *Psalms*[2] from the Alexandrian MS., and afterwards, in 1816–21, at the press of R. and A. Taylor, completed the entire *Old Testament*.[3] Thus concluded this great enterprise, which has been justly characterized by the Abbé J. N. Jager as *opus plane aureum*, in his edition of the *Greek Old Testament*, 1840.

Jackson having now become famous for his skill in this particular branch of his art, was called upon shortly before his death to execute a work of scarcely less importance than the facsimile of the Alexandrian Greek. This was to cut the punches for Dr. Kipling's facsimile of the celebrated *Codex Bezae*, a sixth-century manuscript presented in 1581 by Théodore Beza of Geneva to the University of Cambridge. The character of this manuscript differs considerably from that of the Alexandrine; and, being less regular in its execution, the difficulty of reproducing it in type is proportionately greater. Jackson, however, accomplished his task faithfully and with marked success. Unhappily his death in 1792 prevented him from seeing in print the fruit of his labours, as the work did not appear till the following year, when it was published at Cambridge in two beautiful folio volumes[4] —a work which, says its reviewer, 'reflects honour on the University of Cambridge, and its editor, and, we may add, on the late excellent letter-founder, Mr. Jackson, who cut the types for this handsome book, as well as for the Alexandrine MS. and for *Domesday*'.[5]

Jackson's reputation was not by any means wholly dependent on his skill in expressing in type the character of ancient and difficult manuscripts. During the

the industry and application of Dr. Woide . . . to rescue this valuable MS. from the fate which befel a MS. of the Septuagint in the Cottonian Library of equal antiquity, type, and value, of which a very few fragments escaped the fire in 1733, by adopting the facsimile mode of reproduction, which, from the great expense attending it, has unfortunately been adopted in so few instances.' The transcript with facsimiles of the Laudian Codex, a 6th-century manuscript presented by Archbishop Laud to the Bodleian Library, comprising the *Acts of the Apostles*, published by Hearne at Oxford in 1715, had been the only previous partial attempt of this kind in England. Hearne's facsimile, however, was engraved, and not from type. A list of the most important subsequent facsimile reproductions from codices of the Holy Text is given in T. H. Horne's *Introduction* (1856), iv, pp. 682–3.

[1] *Novum Testamentum Graecum è Codice MS. Alexandrino qui Londini in Bibliothecâ Musei Britannici asservatur, descriptum a Carolo Godofredo Woide . . . Musei Britannici Bibliothecario Londini. Ex prelo Joannis Nichols. Typis Jacksonianis*, 1786. Fol.

[2] *Psalterium Graecum è Codice MS. Alexandrino qui Londini in Bibliothecâ Musei Britannici asservatur Typis ad similitudinem ipsius Codicis Scripturae fideliter descriptum. Curâ et labore H. H. Baber. Londini*, 1812. Fol.

[3] *Vetus Testamentum Graecum è Codice MS. Alexandrino qui Londini in Bibliothecâ Musei Britannici asservatur, Typis ad similitudinem ipsius Codicis Scripturae fideliter descriptum. Curâ et labore H. H. Baber, Londini*, 1816–21. 4 vols. Fol. Baber, the better to preserve the identity of the original in his facsimiles, introduced a considerable number of fresh types as well as numerous woodcuts. Finally a photographic facsimile of the *Codex Alexandrinus* was published in four volumes in 1879–83, with a preface by Sir Edward Maunde Thompson. Jackson's type was used again in 1851 for *A Fragment of the Iliad*, edited by William Cureton from a manuscript in the British Museum.

[4] *Codex Theodori Bezae Cantabrigiensis, Evangelia et Acta Apostolorum complectens, quadratis literis, Graeco-Latinus. Academia auspicante summâ qua fide potuit, adumbravit, expressit, edidit, codicis historiam praefixit, notasque adjecit T. Kipling. Cantabrigiae è prelo Academico, impensis Academiae*, 1793. 2 vols. Fol. A photographic facsimile of this codex was published in 1899.

[5] *Gentleman's Magazine*, 1793, p. 733.

time he was occupied in the works above described he made several useful additions to his foundry. Amongst others, he cut a beautiful fount of Pica Greek for Bowyer, 'who', says Nichols,[1] 'used to say that the types in common use were no more Greek than they were English'.

'He had also, under the direction of Joseph Steele, the ingenious author of *Prosodia Rationalis*,[2] augmented the number of musical notes by such as represent the emphasis and cadence of prose.' This curious work, designed to show how the recitation of Garrick and other eminent speakers might be transmitted to posterity in score, was printed by Nichols in 1779, being an amplified edition of a treatise published four years previously,[3] in which Jackson's 'expression symbols' were made use of.

The most important work of his later years was undoubtedly the splendid fount of two-line English roman, cut for Bensley, about the year 1789, for Macklin's *Bible*.[4] As in the case of the Beza *Gospels*, he did not live to see the completion of his labours in the publication of this grand edition, which did not appear till some years after his death, and then in a type not wholly his own, but supplemented, in close facsimile, by a fount cut by his former apprentice and manager, Vincent Figgins.[5] Jackson's grand letter is justly counted among his greatest achievements, exhibiting, as Nichols observes, 'a pattern of the most perfect symmetry to which the art had at that time arrived'.[6]

A crowning monument to the skill of this excellent artist is Robert Bowyer's sumptuous edition of Hume's *History of England*, printed by Bensley[7] in 1806, in a Double Pica type, on which Jackson was engaged at the time of his death. On the execution of this fount he appears to have staked his reputation; 'Mr. Jackson', says his biographer in the *Gentleman's Magazine*,[8] 'had been engaged to cut the letter for the projected edition of Hume's *History of England*, which he declared should "be the most exquisite performance of the kind in this or any other country". And accordingly he had, in a great degree, accomplished his purpose, but his anxiety and application were so intense that his health suffered and he fell a victim to the great undertaking.'

This circumstance was made the occasion of a curious and affecting elegy, of which we will venture to inflict a specimen on the reader, not on account of its merit, but as being a rare instance of a letter-founder becoming the object of a poetical tribute:

> Patrons of merit, heave the sadden'd sigh!
> Ye brilliant dewdrops, hang on Beauty's eye!
> Let heavy hearts beat with the tolling bell,
> And mourn the fatal hour when *Jackson* fell!
> His were the gifts the Gods alone impart—
> A *tow'ring genius* and a *tender heart!*

---

[1] Mores's *Dissertation*, Appendix, p. 98.

[2] *Prosodia Rationalis, an Essay towards establishing the Melody and Measure of Speech by Symbols*, London, 1779. 4to.

[3] *An Essay towards Establishing the Melody and Measure of Speech, to be expressed and perpetuated by peculiar Symbols*, London, 1775. 4to.

[4] *The Holy Bible, embellished with Engravings from Pictures and Designs by the most eminent Artists.*

London: printed for *Thomas Macklin by Thomas Bensley*, 1800. 7 vols. Fol.

[5] See p. 330. Jackson's fount is used to the end of *Numbers*.

[6] *Lit. Anec.* ii. 360.

[7] *The History of England from the Invasion of Julius Caesar to the Revolution in 1688. By David Hume*, London: printed by *T. Bensley, for Robert Bowyer*, 1806. 10 vols. Fol.

[8] *Gentleman's Magazine* 1792, p. 166.

A greatness equalled only by his skill—
A goodness greater than his greatness still;
An ardent zeal each purpose to *obtain*,
Which Virtue and the Arts might entertain.
But Fate in jealous fury snatched him hence
The moment he accomplished excellence!
Tenax propositi—his art he tried,
Achieved perfection—and achieving died!   &c.

Although anxiety and overwork may have contributed to Jackson's death, the immediate cause was a severe attack of scarlet-fever, which carried him off on

Fig. 86. Joseph Jackson.

14 January 1792, in the 59th year of his age. The last few years of his life had been considerably troubled. In 1790 his foundry was destroyed by a fire in which his moulds and matrices were seriously damaged. The shock of this calamity affected both his health and his energy, and the management of his business was, during his later years, left almost entirely in the hands of his trusted servant, Vincent Figgins. The foundry was rebuilt, and the damaged materials were, as far as possible (though not wholly), replaced at the time of his death.

Jackson was twice married—first to Elizabeth Tassell, originally a whinster[1] in Spitalfields, 'a very worthy woman', says Nichols, 'and an excellent wife, who greatly contributed by her care and industry to his getting forward in his first entering into business'. She died in 1783, and, in the following year, Jackson married Mary Pasham, widow of a well-known printer in Blackfriars,[2] a union

[1] This is Nichols's spelling of the word which appears as 'windster' in the *Oxford English Dictionary*.

[2] John William Pasham, originally of Bury St. Edmunds, where he published the *Bury Flying Weekly Journal*. He removed to Blackfriars in London, where, in 1776, he published a beautiful pocket edition of the Bible in 24mo, which obtained the title of the *Immaculate Bible*, on account of the rarity of its errors. It had footnotes, which could be cut off in the binding if required. Of this Bible, Lemoine says 'it is spoiled by being dried in a kiln, which has

which materially assisted him in the means of carrying on his business. This lady died in 1791, her husband surviving his bereavement only a few months. He was buried in the same grave with his two wives in the ground of Spa Fields Chapel, Clerkenwell.

Of Jackson's private character his contemporaries concur in speaking very highly. 'By the death of this ingenious artist and truly worthy man', says Nichols, 'the poor lost a most excellent benefactor, his own immediate connexions a steady friend, and the literary world a valuable coadjutor in their labours.' He was a deacon at the Meeting-House in Barbican,[1] where a funeral sermon was preached by the Rev. John Towers, who also delivered a 'neat funeral oration' at the grave. He died possessed of some considerable property. There is an oil portrait of him formerly in the possession of William Blades, and an engraved portrait in Nichols's *Literary Anecdotes*.

It is unfortunately impossible to ascertain in what condition his foundry was left at the time of his death—how far it had recovered from the consequences of the fire, or how far that calamity had destroyed, beyond replacing, any of its contents. It was offered for sale in 1792, and Figgins, the presumptive successor to the business, not finding himself in a position to become its purchaser, it was acquired by William Caslon III, who had recently disposed of his share in the Chiswell Street Foundry, over whose affairs he had for some years been presiding.[2] He removed the foundry from Dorset Street to Finsbury Square, where for about two years it remained located. In 1794 Caslon became bankrupt[3] and the house in Finsbury Square was bought and converted by James Lackington, the celebrated bookseller, into the 'Temple of the Muses', one of the largest and most popular bookshops of the day.[4] Caslon started again in the old quarters in Dorset Street.

In the hands of Caslon, Jackson's foundry was greatly enlarged and improved. A specimen was issued in 1796, and a larger specimen of 1798, dedicated to the King, exhibits 19 pages of titlings and open letters, 1 of ornamental, 35 of roman and italic, 8 of foreign letter and blacks, 1 of script, 5 of sundry specimens, and 12 of flowers.[5] The book has many features in common with the Chiswell Street specimen of 1785, many of the founts in which reappear here. Indeed, it would seem that on relinquishing his share in the parental business William Caslon III had provided himself with duplicate matrices of several of the Chiswell Street founts, particularly of the foreign and oriental letters, which figure prominently in this and subsequent specimens of the Salisbury Square Foundry. Bound with the book is a specimen of cast ornaments, a species of typographical embellishment which Caslon III had had the merit of introducing into this country in 1784, while

entirely changed the colour of the paper; besides, the colour of the print is uneven, one side being darker than the other'. This Bible is said to have been printed in a house on Finchley Common. Pasham died Dec. 1783.

[1] This chapel was built in 1784 for John Towers. See W. Wilson's *History and Antiquities of the Dissenting Churches in London*, 1808–14. 4 vols.

[2] See p. 244.

[3] See a notice in the *Gazette* for 13–17 May 1794.

[4] Cf. C. Knight, *Shadows of the Old Booksellers*, 1865. The building was at the south-west corner of Finsbury Square. It was destroyed by fire in 1841. Lackington's shop had previously been in Chiswell Street.

[5] The prefatory note to this specimen runs as follows: 'Sir, Having completed my new Specimen, I take the opportunity of sending you a copy, and flatter myself it will meet with your approbation. I shall be happy to receive your future orders, and you may be assured of every possible attention being paid to the execution of those you may favour me with. I remain, your obedient humble servant, William Caslon. Salisbury Square, Jan. 1, 1798.'

still at Chiswell Street. In this particular, too, the Salisbury Square specimen is a reproduction of that of the Chiswell Street house.

About the year 1803 Caslon took his son, the fourth William Caslon, into partnership, and the firm became W. Caslon & Son. The specimen of this year exhibits a slight increase on that of 1798, the chief additions being in the modern-faced romans, then becoming fashionable. The learned and oriental founts remain

Fig. 87. William Caslon III.

unaltered from the 1798 specimen, and as this is the last specimen of the foundry in which these occupy a prominent place, it will be convenient to give the list here:

Greek.—Double Pica, Great Primer, English, English new, Pica, Small Pica, Long Primer, Brevier, Nonpareil.

Hebrew.—Two-line Great Primer, two-line English, Double Pica, Great Primer, ditto with points, English, ditto with points, Pica, ditto with points, Small Pica, Long Primer, Brevier.

Syriac.—English, Long Primer.

Arabic.—English.

Armenian.—Pica.

Samaritan.—Pica.

Saxon.—English, Pica, Brevier.

Blacks.—Two-line Great Primer, Double Pica, Great Primer, English 1, English 2, Pica 1, Pica 2, Small Pica, Long Primer, Brevier.

The whole of these founts, with the exception of the new English Greek, are identical with those shown in the Chiswell Street specimen of 1785.

The specimen-book of 1803 appears to have served the foundry for several years, as copies exist in which the date is altered by hand to 1807, and the name of the firm changed from 'W. Caslon & Son' to 'W. Caslon, Junior'. This last alteration was consequent on the retirement of William Caslon III from the business in 1807. Although this gentleman's connexion with typefounding ceases here,[1] we cannot refrain from quoting the few sentences in which Hansard, in 1825, describes his personal character, while the subject of his notice was yet living:

If his friends had not yet the pleasure of occasionally receiving his lively salutations—of enjoying the gay and gentlemanlike converse, the whim, the anecdote, and the agreeable

---

[1] He made an offer in 1817 to travel on commission for the founders generally, but his services in this direction were not made use of.

bagatelle of William Caslon aforesaid, I might be induced to amplify on these points. . . . The mention, however, of one thing must not be omitted. Some years ago he was deprived of sight by the formation of a cataract in each eye; still his musical ear furnished the faculty of distinguishing persons whom he knew by their voices; and his cheerful spirits enabled him to sustain the calamity with a becoming temper of mind. At length, his courage, in undergoing the operation of couching three several times, was rewarded with the perfect restoration of his sight; and his friends again experience the delight of hearing him truly say, 'Ah! I'm happy to see you, by ———'. But although ever ready with anecdote and whim to enliven, still more to his honour as a man, may it be added, that he can at once turn the cheerful smile into serious solicitations, for the assistance of a decayed old friend, his orphan, or his widow.

Caslon died in 1833.

William Caslon IV, being left in sole possession of the foundry, made consider-able progress in extending the business, especially by the addition of the new-fashioned fat-faced types, at that period so largely affected. His chief improvement, however, was the introduction in 1810 of the Sanspareil matrices for large letters.[1] This invention, which Hansard somewhat extravagantly describes as the greatest improvement in the art of letter-founding that 'has taken place in modern times', consisted in the substitution of pierced, or rather built-up matrices, in place of the old sand moulds hitherto in use, and it rapidly secured favour in the trade, and was as early as possible adopted by the other founders. There is a short description of the process in *Caslon's Circular*, July 1877. The matrix is said to be 'a stencil plate of sufficient thickness backed by another plate rivetted closely to it to form the face of the type'.

In 1812 Caslon also took out a patent for a new form of type for imposing on a cylinder, of a size from one-third to one-seventh that of ordinary type, and cast wedge-shaped, or larger at the end containing the face than at the foot; an attempt which reflected more credit on the ingenuity of its author than upon his practical judgement, and which was not proceeded with.[2]

Caslon IV's last specimen appeared in 1816. It includes the Sanspareil large letters, and an 'Egyptian', a Sans-serif type, a design which elsewhere is not known before 1832. See Berry and Johnson, pl. 18.

In 1819 Caslon, jun., disposed of his foundry to Blake, Garnett & Co., of Sheffield (now Stephenson, Blake & Co.), to which town the entire stock was removed. After his retirement from typefounding he devoted himself actively to the scheme for lighting London with coal-gas. For some of his appliances in connexion with this business—the sliding water-joints for pendants and chandeliers amongst others —he received the medal of the Society of Arts (his only reward, for he did not patent his invention). In 1832 he went to reside at Henley, and ten years later was afflicted with total blindness, an operation for cataract having proved unsuccessful. In this state he continued for twenty-seven years, 'tired', as he said, 'of having been so long in the dark', but serene in temper, and his mind illuminated with Christian hope. He taught himself to read the embossed printing for the blind, and was able

[1] The circular announcing this improvement is dated Salisbury Square, 1 Jan. 1810. The new types are offered at 1s. 10d. per lb., and, as an encourage-ment to buyers, 1s. per lb. is offered for old metal.

[2] See above, p. 111. This appears to have been intended as an improvement on the invention of Nicholson, who was the first (in 1790) to suggest the casting of types wedge-shaped, for fixing on cylinders (p. 110).

to write by the aid of a simple apparatus constructed for that purpose. He lived, in spite of his affliction, to a cheerful old age, and died in 1869, aged 88. He left no son.

To estimate the complete revolution which had taken place in the productions of this foundry during the interval between 1807 and 1819 it is only necessary to glance through the first specimen-book of the new proprietors, issued in the latter year, which may be taken to represent the state of the foundry pretty nearly as it was at the time of its transfer to Sheffield. There is not a single fount in the one book which reappears in the other. The modern fat-face romans take the place of Jackson's elegant old style letters. The orientals have completely disappeared, and the general appearance of the book reflects as much as any specimen of the period the prevalent taste of a so-called improved art. It was, apparently, highly esteemed in its day. 'Mr. Caslon', says Hansard, writing only six years after the event, 'transferred to the Sheffield founders such a specimen of type and flowers as will ever cause us printers to regret the loss of such a competitor for fame in this difficult business.'

Blake, Garnett & Co., a firm formed for the special purpose of acquiring the type business, issued their first specimen, above referred to, very shortly after the transfer of the business to its new quarters. Their prefatory note is interesting, not only as recording the transaction, but as intimating that the oriental and foreign founts, which had formed so conspicuous a feature of the previous specimens of the foundry, had also found their way to Sheffield:

> Blake, Garnett and Co. beg leave respectfully to inform the trade that they have purchased the whole of Mr. Caslon's Foundery, which, in addition to the Specimens here offered to their inspection, contains founts of Greek, Hebrew, Syriac, Arabic, Saxon, German, etc. from Brevier to Double Pica, chiefly modern, also every kind of Accented letters, . . . and a variety of other Sorts, of which Specimens are not yet printed.

The activity of the new proprietors resulted in a rapid increase in the extent and business of the foundry. Supplementary specimens were frequently issued between 1820 and 1830, when the style of the firm became Blake and Stephenson. John Stephenson was a man of great energy, practical skill, and artistic taste, and it is to his exertions that the rapidly achieved eminence of the house was chiefly due. In 1841 the firm took the style of Stephenson, Blake & Co. Stephenson directed the operations of the Sheffield Foundry until 1860, when the management devolved on his son, Henry (afterwards Sir Henry) Stephenson and W. G. Blake, who both died in 1904.

The firm was now on an equal footing with the chief London founders and was in fact classed with them by the innovators. An examination of one of their specimen-books may be taken as an example of the contents of the average specimen book of the Victorian age. They were all very much alike, showing more or less the same types under varying names. Their *Specimen of Printing Types*, 8vo edition, is as usual undated, but has a preface dated 1878. There is mention of their 'well-known hard metal' and they announce that they are prepared to cast type for their continental customers to the 'Didot' body and height, a reminder of the fact that in England there was still no such uniform system. Incidentally, it may be added that in 1904 Sir Henry K. Stephenson delivered a lecture entitled *Typefounding of To-day and the Point System*, which was partly a reply to attacks on the old founders for their dilatoriness in establishing a point system. The preface in the 1878 specimen is followed by price lists, not only of types but also of composing-room furniture, presses, and other machinery. The founders in general were now supplying much more than type. Then follows the series of old style types from two-line English to Nonpareil, with some old style ornaments. Next come Newspaper founts and the main series of modern-face body types, from Pearl to Canon. Many of the founders had a Diamond also. After some two-line capitals, some of them condensed, we come to the display of jobbing types, forming the largest part of the book. There are many examples of the three early designs of advertising types, Fat Faces, Egyptians, and Sans-serifs, some of them 'condensed', some 'elongated', and others 'expanded'. Some of the Fat Faces áre given the name 'Elephant', while the Stephenson Blake name for Egyptian is 'Antique'. For Sans-serifs they have two names, 'Sans Surryphs' and 'Grotesque', of which there are many varieties including 'Open', 'Shaded', and letters in three dimensions. By this time italic Sans-serifs are shown. There are many specimens of corrupt blacks, called 'Saxon', 'Old English', 'Augustan', and 'Columbian Text', but none of the genuine old blacks are shown. There are many scripts, for the most part the usual commercial copperplate, but some 'Rondes' copied or acquired from the French, and a few more fanciful scripts. Of the more ornamented letters the display is not so lavish as in the books of some of the London founders, but there are examples of most of the styles. Their usual name for decorated capitals is 'Tuscan'. They show also the popular 'Rustic', a type in imitation of woodwork which started with the Figgins in the forties. A thin series of capitals with elongated strokes called 'Ancient' appears with other founders under the name 'Venetian' or 'Monastic'. There is also a series of the 'Latin' face, a type with stubby but pointed serifs, which retained its name with most founders and is even now not extinct. For the usual Clarendon the firm had a series called 'Antique Old Style'.[1] Finally, the book ends with a display of flowers or 'Combination Borders' and cast ornaments.

In a large quarto specimen issued by the firm in 1924, when the chief directors were Sir Henry K. Stephenson and Mr. R. G. Blake, there is an introduction giving a brief account of the history of the firm, and also a genealogical tree, showing how the surviving types of the old English letter-founders are now concentrated in the Sheffield firm. By the purchase of the Fann Street Foundry in 1905 they acquired the old matrices which Dr. Fry had bought at the sale of the stock of the James Foundry in 1782. They had already acquired the John Bell types and since 1938 have added to their stock the original matrices of the Caslon firm. Thus Messrs. Stephenson, Blake & Co. have become the sole repository of such of the early English types as have survived.

---

[1] On the fanciful letters of the Victorian age see Mrs. N. Gray's *XIXth Century Ornamented Types*.

17

WILLIAM MARTIN, 1790

WILLIAM MARTIN was brother to Robert Martin,[1] Baskerville's apprentice and successor. He appears to have acquired his first knowledge of the art at the Birmingham foundry, and about the year 1786 to have come to London and entered into the service of George Nicol,[2] as a punch-cutter. Nicol was at that time engaged in maturing his plans for the production of a magnificent edition of *Shakespeare*, and kept Martin at his own house 'to cut sets of types after approved models in imitation of the sharp and fine letter used by the French and Italian printers'.

On the establishment of the famous 'Shakespeare Press',[3] by Boydell & Nicol, in 1790, at Cleveland Row, St. James's, with William Bulmer as presiding genius, Martin was established in premises hard by, in Duke Street; his foundry being a sort of private foundry in connexion with the press. Here it was that he produced the founts in which the magnificent works, issued during the next twenty years from Bulmer's Press, were printed.

The appearance of the first part of the *Shakespeare*[4] in 1791 at once established the fame of the printer and his types; and the completion of the work, in nine volumes, in 1810, may be regarded as marking an epoch in British typography. 'No work of equal magnitude', says the enthusiastic Dibdin, 'ever presented such complete accuracy and uniform excellence of execution. There is scarcely one perceptible shade of variation from the first page of the first volume, to the last page of the work, either in the colour of the ink, the hue of the paper, or the clearness and sharpness of the types.'[5]

The *Milton*,[6] which followed, is considered a still finer specimen of typography.

---

[1] See above, p. 282.

[2] George Nicol was born in 1741, and was for many years bookseller to King George III. He married a niece of Alderman John Boydell in 1787. The idea of the Boydell *Shakespeare* originated with him. He was a prominent member of the literary clubs of his day, and a personal friend of the Duke of Roxburgh. He died in 1829, aged 88.

[3] A history of this celebrated press would almost involve a history of fine printing in the first quarter of the last century. Dibdin, in the second volume of his *Bibliographical Decameron*, has given a list of its most famous impressions. Bulmer was a personal friend of Thomas Bewick, the engraver, many of whose blocks were cut for his books. He

spared no pains to render the typography of his press the most correct and beautiful England had hitherto known. He retired in 1819, leaving Wm. Nicol, only son of his friend George Nicol, to carry on the business. Bulmer died 9 Sept. 1830, in his 74th year, greatly honoured and respected. See also H. V. Marrot, 'William Bulmer', in *The Fleuron*, No. 3, pp. 62–91.

[4] *The Dramatic Works of William Shakespeare. Revised by G. Steevens*, London, 1791–1802. Eighteen parts in 9 vols. Atlas folio. With 100 engravings. [5] *Bibl. Decam.* ii. 384.

[6] *The Poetical Works of John Milton, with a Life of the Author by William Hayley*, London, 1794–7. 3 vols. Fol.

The enthusiasm animating all concerned in the new undertaking was remarkable, and attracted universal attention. 'The nation', says Dibdin, 'appeared to be not less struck than astonished; and our venerable monarch, George III, felt anxious not only to give such a magnificent establishment every degree of royal support, but, infected with the matrix and puncheon mania, he had even contemplated the creation of a royal printing office within the walls of his own palace.' One of the King's great ambitions was for England to rival Parma in the productions of Bodoni, and Dibdin alludes to a story current at the time of 'his majesty being completely and joyfully taken in, by bestowing upon the efforts of Mr. Bulmer's press that eulogy which he had supposed was due exclusively to Bodoni's'.

In the advertisement of his edition of the *Poems by Goldsmith and Parnell*,[1] printed in 1795 and dedicated to Boydell and Nicol, the founders of the Shakespeare Press, Bulmer thus bears testimony to the talents of those who had contributed to the performance:

The present volume, in addition to the *Shakespeare*, the *Milton*, and many other valuable works of elegance which have already been given to the world through the medium of the Shakespeare Press, are [*sic*] particularly meant to combine the various beauties of printing, type founding, engraving, and paper making; as well as with a view to ascertain the near approach to perfection which those arts have attained to [in] this country, as to invite a fair competition with the typographical productions of other nations. How far the different artists who have contributed their exertions to this great object have succeeded in the attempt, the public will now be fully able to judge.

In all these encomiums Martin claims a share; and, regarded simply as type specimens, the productions of the Shakespeare Press justify his reputation as a worthy disciple of his great master Baskerville. His roman and italic types were cut in decided imitation of the famous Birmingham models, although Hansard points out with disapproval that in certain particulars he attempted unwisely to vary the design. 'As to the type,' he says, 'the modern artist, Mr. Martin, has made an effort to cut the ceriphs and hair strokes excessively sharp and fine; the long ſ is discarded, and some trifling changes are introduced; but the letter does not stand so true or well in line as Baskerville's, and, as to the italic, the Birmingham artist will be found to far excel.'[2]

The Shakespeare Press, along with all the other presses of the land, had to bow before the revolution which in the closing years of the eighteenth century swept aside the beautiful old-face roman, and set up in its stead the modern character; and Hansard's strictures above quoted doubtless refer to Martin's endeavour, while adhering to the Baskerville form as his model, to modify it so as to conform to the new fashion. We are among those who deplore the change thus inaugurated; but at the same time it must be admitted that Martin succeeded as well in the new departure as any of his contemporaries.

Nor did he confine himself to roman and italic. He produced several founts of Greeks and orientals, which eventually came to form the most valuable part of his collection.[3] His Greek character, however, like the Greeks attempted by Baskerville

---

[1] *Poems by Goldsmith and Parnell*, London, 1795. 4to. This work was illustrated with woodcuts by Bewick. It is said that George III ordered his bookseller to procure the blocks of the engravings for his inspection, that he might convince himself they were wood and not copper.

[2] *Typographia*, p. 311.

[3] Nichols, *Illust. Lit.* viii. 485.

and Bodoni, was not a success; and the otherwise beautiful edition of *Musaeus*, printed in 1797,[1] and bearing on the title-page his name as the cutter of the type, is marred by the cramped and inelegant effect of that character. In John Richardson's *Dictionary, Persian, Arabic, and English*, edited by Charles Wilkins, W. Bulmer, 1806, the editor in the Advertisement says of the new Arabic types that he himself had designed the punches which had been executed by 'that ingenious mechanic, Mr. William Martin'.

Although Martin's foundry was entirely supported by, and, indeed, belonged to the Shakespeare Press, he appears occasionally to have supplied his types to outsiders—amongst others to McCreery, the author of the well-known poem on the *Press*, and himself a very elegant printer. *The Press*[2] was printed in 1803 from Martin's type, as a specimen of typography, and in his preface the author pays the following tribute to that artist's abilities:

The extraordinary efforts which have of late years been made to produce the finest models of Printing Types, must be highly gratifying to those who have in any measure interested themselves in raising the credit of the British Press. The spirit for this species of beauty has long been gaining an ascendancy, having received a strong impulse from the talents of Baskerville, who endeavoured to combine sharpness and perfection of impression with graceful types, giving to his works a finish which was before unknown in this kingdom. Mr. Martin, whose abilities are so conspicuously displayed in the productions of the Shakespeare Press, is a pupil of that celebrated school. By the liberality of George Nicol, Esq., I am enabled to boast of being the first who has participated with Mr. Bulmer in the use of these types, a mark of kindness for which my warmest acknowledgements are the least recompense he has a right to expect.

Several of the other productions of McCreery's press were also printed from Martin's type.

Among the finest specimens of the Shakespeare Press printed in Bulmer's time, the three great bibliographical works of Dibdin, viz. the *Typographical Antiquities*,[3] the *Bibliotheca Spenceriana*,[4] and the *Bibliographical Decameron*,[5] will always take a foremost place. Martin, whose roman type rarely appeared to greater advantage, unfortunately did not live to see the completion of the whole of these typographical masterpieces, as he died in the summer of 1815. He was buried in St. James's Church, Westminster. After his death, the foundry (of which unfortunately no specimen-book exists[6]) appears to have been continued for a short time by Bulmer, who, between 1815 and 1819, when he himself retired, produced several fine works.[7]

---

[1] Musaeus, *The Loves of Hero and Leander.* (*Greek and English.*) London: printed by *W. Bulmer & Co. Typis Gulielmi Martin*. 1797. 4to. This work was privately printed by Bulmer for Grosvenor Bedford, the translator.

[2] *The Press: a poem. Published as a specimen of typography by John McCreery. Liverpool: printed by J. McCreery*. Houghton Street, 1803. 4to.

[3] *Typographical Antiquities, &c., greatly enlarged, with copious notes*, by *T. F. Dibdin*, London, 1810–19. 4 vols. 4to. The work was not completed. The first volume was not printed at the Shakespeare Press.

[4] *Bibliotheca Spenceriana; or, a descriptive catalogue of books printed in the XVth century, and of many valuable first editions in the Library of George John, Earl Spencer*, London, 1814–15. 4 vols. 8vo.

[5] *The Bibliographical Decameron; or, ten days'* pleasant discourse upon Illuminated Manuscripts, and subjects connected with early engraving, typography and bibliography, London, 1817. 3 vols. 8vo. The types used in the Dibdin volumes are not Martin's transitional types, but his later, full modern faces.

[6] His types are shown in *A Specimen of the Improved Types of G. F. Harris*, Liverpool, 1807. See Berry and Johnson, p. 92.

[7] Amongst which were the early publications of the Roxburghe Club, instituted by Earl Spencer, in 1812, for the republication of rare books or unpublished manuscripts. Renouard censures Bulmer for the use of worn type in the edition of Ben Jonson's *Works*, 1816. 9 vols. 8vo. 'L'habile M. Bulmer aurait dû jeter à la fonte les caractères usés dont il a fait usage pour cette volumineuse édition, et les libraires entrepreneurs n'auroient pas dû lui en permettre l'emploi.'

Prior to that event—in 1817—Nichols states that the foundry was united with that of the Caslons.[1] There is, however, reason for supposing that some of the matrices were retained for the use of the Shakespeare Press, and that others went into the market and were secured by other founders.[2]

The Shakespeare Press, under the supervision of W. Nicol, continued in active operation till 1855, when he retired, and his printing materials were sold; thus closing one of the most memorable chapters in the history of British typographical enterprise.

No. 18.

It is now sixteen or seventeen years since I saw the Queen of France, then the Dauphiness, at Versailles; and surely never lighted on this orb, which she hardly seemed to touch, a more delightful vision. I saw her just above the horizon,

ABCDEFGHIJKLMNOPQRSTVUWXYZÆŒ

It is now sixteen or seventeen years since I saw the Queen of France, then the Dauphiness, at Versailles; and surely never lighted on this orb, which she hardly seemed to touch, a more delightful vision. I saw her just above the horizon, decorating and cheering the

ABCDEFGHIJKLMNOPQRSTVUWXYZÆŒ

FIG. 88. Martin's types, from the specimen of G. F. Harris, 1807.[3]

[1] *Illust. Lit.* viii. 485.
[2] An early specimen of Thorowgood's shows a black, the matrices of which, it is stated, 'were purchased by Messrs. Fry & Steele at the breaking up of the Cleveland Row Foundry'. As, however, Fry & Steele's partnership had terminated by 1816, we consider the whole statement doubtful.
[3] Reproduced from Mr. B. Wolpe's copy.

18

VINCENT FIGGINS, 1792

THIS excellent letter-founder was bound apprentice to Joseph Jackson in the year 1782, at the age of sixteen, and remained in his service till Jackson's death in 1792. During the last three years of his master's life, as has been already said, the entire management of the foundry devolved on him; and the experience and connexion so acquired fully qualified him to succeed to and increase the business to whose success he had materially contributed. Contrary to expectation, however, Vincent Figgins found himself, on Jackson's death, left in the position of an ordinary outsider; and not being able or willing to pay the sum demanded, which was in excess of what he conscientiously considered the concern to be worth, he failed in succeeding to the foundry, which was purchased by William Caslon III.

Left thus to his own resources, Figgins was constrained to enter on an independent undertaking. Encouraged by the advice of John Nichols (who, as the intimate friend of Jackson, had had many opportunities of observing the character and talent of his apprentice), he determined to rear a foundry in his own name. 'A large order', says Hansard, 'for two founts, Great Primer and Pica, of each 2,000 lbs— even before he had printed a single specimen—gave the young adventurer the best heart to proceed; neither did his liberal patron suffer him to want the sinews of trade as long as such assistance was required.' Writing to Nichols fifteen years afterwards, in reference to a passage in the *Literary Anecdotes*, Figgins thus gracefully acknowledged the generosity which befriended him at the beginning of his career:

I am greatly obliged to you for the very flattering mention of my name, but you have not done yourself the justice to record your own kindness to me: that, on Mr. Jackson's death, finding I had not the means to purchase the foundry, you encouraged me to make a beginning. You gave me large orders and assisted me with the means of executing them; and during a long and difficult struggle in pecuniary matters for fifteen years, you, my dear Sir, never refused me your assistance, without which I must have given it up. Do mention this—that, as the first Mr. Bowyer was the means of establishing Mr. Caslon—his son, Mr. Jackson—it may be known that Vincent Figgins owes his prosperity to Mr. Bowyer's successor.[1]

Figgins established himself in Swan Yard, Holborn Bridge, and at the outset of his undertaking an opportunity occurred which served as largely as any other to establish his reputation as an excellent artist. This was the completion of Macklin's

---

[1] *Lit. Anec.* ii. 361.

Bible, for which, as has already been narrated, Jackson had, in 1789, cut the beautiful two-line English roman fount, in which the first part of the work is printed. 'When Mr. Bensley had proceeded some way in the work he wished to renew the fount; but not choosing to purchase it of Mr. Caslon, the then possessor of Jackson's

TWO-LINE ENGLISH.

Quouſque tandem abu-
tere, Catilina, patientia
noſtra? quamdiu nos e-
tiam furor iſte tuus elu-
det? quem ad finem ſeſe
effrenata jactabit auda-
cia? nihilne te noctur-
num præſidium palatii,
nihil urbis vigiliæ, ni-
hil timor populi, ni-
hil conſenſus bonorum
omnium, nihil hic mu-
A B C D E F G H I J K
L M N O P Q R S T
U V W X Y Z

FIG. 89. V. Figgins's roman.

matrices, he applied to Mr. Figgins to cut a fount to correspond with that he had begun upon. Mr. Figgins undertook the task; and the fount, which was a perfect imitation of the other, was put into use to begin *Deuteronomy* about the year 1793.'[1] Of the excellence of this performance both as a facsimile and as a work of art, a reference to the splendid *Bible*[2] itself and the no less splendid edition of

[1] Hansard, *Typographia*, p. 359.   [2] See p. 317.

Thomson's *Seasons*,[1] in which the same type was used in 1797, is the most eloquent testimony. Figgins received the honour of being named on the title-page of the latter work, which still remains one of the finest achievements of English typography. His services were also employed in a similar manner to complete the Double Pica fount for R. Bowyer's edition of *Hume*, which, it will be remembered, was in course of execution by Jackson at the time of his death. The splendid types in which these masterpieces of the typographic art were executed established Figgins at once in all the reputation he could desire.

In 1792 he put forward a single-leaf specimen of the two-line English fount on its completion. In the following year, having added a 'long-bodied' English and a Pica, he issued his first specimen-book. This interesting document of five leaves (title, address, and three specimens) was printed by Bensley, and contained the following prefatory note, which will be read with interest as the first public announcement of this foundry:

At a period when the Art of Printing has, perhaps, arrived to a degree of excellence hitherto unknown in the annals of literature, the improvement of Types will no doubt be generally considered an object worthy of attention. Vincent Figgins having had the advantage of ten years' instruction and servitude under the late ingenious Mr. Joseph Jackson (great part of which time he had *the management of* his Foundery), flatters himself he shall not be thought arrogant in soliciting the patronage of the Master Printers, and other Literary Gentlemen, when he has commenced an entire new Letter Foundery, every branch of which, with their support and encouragement, he hopes he shall be enabled to execute in the most accurate and satisfactory manner; assuring them that his best endeavours shall be exerted to complete so arduous an undertaking. Although as yet he has but few founts finished, he is anxious to submit a specimen for approbation. All orders he may be favoured with shall be duly attended to and punctually executed. . . . The Italics of the following founts, with a Long Primer, Brevier and English, are in great forwardness—specimens of which shall be printed as soon as possible. *May* 1793.[2]

One of the first public appearances of the English fount was in the 8vo edition of Milton's *Paradise Lost*, begun in 1794 in monthly parts, and published by Parsons in 1796.[3] The announcement accompanying Part I makes special reference to 'a new and beautiful Type cast on purpose for this work by Vincent Figgins'. The italic of this fount is specially elegant.

Figgins's indefatigable industry enabled him to issue in the next year an enlarged specimen-book with the same title and address as before, but containing twelve sheets of specimens, four of which were dated 1794.[4]

He met with further encouragement in his new undertaking by the patronage of the Delegates of the Oxford Press. An Oxford edition of the *Gospels* printed in 1798 in a Pica Greek has the imprint 'Typis Vincentii Figgins'. Under the direction of the Oxford Press he completed a fount of Double Pica Greek, the progress of which had been interrupted by the death of Jackson. In connexion with this circumstance, Vincent Figgins the younger, in the remarks appended to his facsimile reprint of Caxton's *Game of the Chesse*, has preserved an anecdote which it will be interesting to repeat here, not only as having reference to Figgins's early productions, but as illustrating a curious phase of the mystery of typefounding at that day:

The mystery thrown over the operations of a Type foundry [says Vincent Figgins II in 1855] within my own recollection (thirty-four years), and the still greater secrecy which had existed in my father's experience, testifies that the art had been perpetuated by a kind of Druidical or Masonic induction from the first. An anecdote of my father's early struggles may illustrate this. At the death of Mr. Joseph Jackson, whom my father had served ten years as apprentice and foreman, there was in progress for the University Press of Oxford a new fount of Double Pica Greek, which had progressed under my father's entire management. The then delegates of that Press—the Rev. Dr. Randolph and the Rev. W. Jackson—suggested that Mr. Figgins should finish the fount himself. This, with other offers of support from those who had previously known him, was the germ of his prosperity (which was always gratefully acknowledged). But when he had undertaken this work, the difficulty presented itself that he did not know where to find the punch-cutter. No one knew his address; but he was supposed to be a tall man, who came in a mysterious way occasionally, whose name no one knew, but he went by the *sobriquet* of '*The Black Man*'. This old gentleman, a very clever mechanic, lived to be a pensioner on my father's bounty—gratitude is, perhaps, the better word. I knew him, and could never understand the origin of his *sobriquet*, unless Black was meant for dark, mysterious, from the manner of his coming and going from Mr. Jackson's foundry.

The actual cutter of the punches had now become an anonymous mechanic. Richard Austin in the preface to his specimen of 1819 asserted that the fact that the founders themselves no longer cut punches was one explanation of the faults in the new modern faces.

Shortly after the completion of the Greek fount, Figgins was called upon to execute a fount of Persian under the direction of the eminent Orientalist, Sir William Ouseley.[1] This type was used in Francis Gladwin's *Persian Moonshee*[2] in 1801, and other works; and was commended by Dr. Adam Clarke as a beautiful letter in the finest form of the Nustaleek character. About the same time he cut a fount of English Telegu from a manuscript, for the East India Company, in whose library, says Hansard, the 'matrices or moulds' were afterwards deposited. Of this fount he issued two specimens about 1802, one a folio, the other a quarto; and about the same time put forward a specimen of 'Two-line letters' in the same form.[3]

In the year 1800 Figgins was engaged by Messrs. Eyre & Strahan, His Majesty's Printers, to cut and cast an improved fount of Small Pica Domesday; and, in 1805, a new Pica of the same character, expressly for the purpose of printing the splendid

---

[1] Sir William Ouseley was born in 1771, and accompanied his brother Sir Gore Ouseley, the ambassador to Persia, to that country as secretary. He published *Persian Miscellanies* in 1795, and *Oriental Collections* in 1797–1800. In the advertisement at the close of the first volume of the latter work, he states, 'I have employed a few leisure hours in superintending the execution of a new Persian Type, which will, I trust, exhibit as faithful a representation of the true Taleek character as can be effected by any imitative powers of the Typographick Art'. Of this new fount he shows a single line as specimen, which, however, if cut by Figgins, is not the Paragon Persian which subsequently appeared in his specimen-books. Nor did it appear, as promised, in the *Oriental Collections* of 1798, the quotations in which continued to be printed in Arabic characters.

[2] *The Persian Moonshee, by Francis Gladwin, Esquire. Calcutta. London, reprinted* 1801. 4to.

[3] The present location of the Telegu specimens and the 'Two-line letters', all formerly in the possession of James Figgins, is not known.

and valuable publications of the Commission of Enquiry into the State of the Records of the Kingdom.[1] In the years 1807 and 1808 he was also employed by His Majesty's Printers in Scotland on three further founts (Pica, Long Primer, and Brevier) for the purpose of printing the records of that portion of the Empire.[2] This improved Domesday (a specimen of which may be seen in Johnson's *Typographia*) differs considerably from that of Jackson, in which the *Domesday Book* had been printed in 1783,[3] and became, subsequently, the uniform character adopted for extracts from Domesday and other ancient charters and records quoted in modern typographical works.

Figgins's good fortune in the first results of his new business was somewhat tempered by the fact that, within a few years of the establishment of his foundry, the public taste with regard to the ordinary roman letter experienced a complete revolution, setting aside the elegant models on which the punches of Jackson and his contemporaries had been cut, in favour of the new fashion which came in with the nineteenth century. To accommodate himself to this fashion must have involved Figgins in a considerable sacrifice of his early labour and industry, and the circumstance may possibly account for the somewhat remarkable absence of any specimen bearing his name for a lengthened period. In the appendix to Stower's *Printers' Grammar*, 1808, which exhibits the 'modern faces' of Caslon and Fry, the compiler regrets not being able to show specimens of the new cut types from Figgins's foundry, 'but understands that in a few months Mr. F. will have fully completed his specimens'. These new founts appear in a specimen of 1815, a book which contains 24 pages of large letter from sixteen-line to four-line; 35 pages of roman and italic from French Canon to Pearl; together with titlings, black-letter, and flowers, a few Greeks, and a Syriac. There are also shown 'Antiques', i.e. Egyptians, being the earliest appearance in any known specimen of this letter. Two years later, Figgins put forward a specimen of Newspaper founts, showing a series of eight sizes, on a broadside sheet—the first specimen of the kind, we believe, specially addressed to the proprietors of the public press. The title of this sheet is printed in the five-line German Text, which Hansard describes as a typographical curiosity.[4]

Speaking of Figgins about 1812, Nichols remarks (in the passage which called for the acknowledgement already quoted): 'With an ample portion of his kind

---

[1] This important inquiry was the result of an address of the House of Commons to the King, in 1800, setting forth the necessity of a better provision for the arrangement, preservation, and use of the various Public Records scattered among the numerous offices of the kingdom. The Commission thereupon appointed were empowered to take all necessary measures to 'methodize, regulate and digest the records, etc.', preserved in all Public Offices and repositories, and 'to superintend the printing of such calendars and indexes and original records and papers' as it should be deemed desirable to print. With this large task before them, the Commissioners went actively to work, and in 1800 and 1806 published their first reports. The following important publication, issued under the Direction of the Commission, was commenced in 1800: *Reports from the Commissioners appointed to execute the measures recommended by a Select Committee of the House of Commons respecting the Public Records of the Kingdom, etc.*, London, 1800–19, 2 vols., fol. The appendix forming the second volume contains facsimiles of all the Charters (including Magna Charta) and Inrollments from Stephen to William and Mary, with the Seals inserted in the several works printed under the Commission. The list of the subsequent publications of the Commission is very extensive, and includes verbatim copies, with all abbreviations and contractions, of the most important documents in the kingdom.

[2] The first important work in connexion with the Scottish Record Commission was *Inquisitionum ad Capellam Domini Regis retornatarum quae in publicis Archivis Scotiae adhuc servantur Abbrevatio cum Indicibus*, Edinburgh, 1811–16, 3 vols., fol., and a Supplement.

[3] These types perished in the fire at Nichols's printing office in 1808.

[4] This sheet is bound into the copy of the 1815 specimen at the Oxford University Press.

instructor's reputation, he inherits a considerable share of his talents and industry, and has distinguished himself by the many beautiful specimens he has produced, and particularly of Oriental Types.'[1]

The foundry had, in the year 1801, been removed from Swan Yard, Holborn, to 17 West Street, West Smithfield,[2] where, besides the work of completing the founts most commonly in use, several important and interesting tasks of a special character had engaged Figgins's attention. Among these may be mentioned the Small Pica Hebrew for Bagster's *Polyglot*,[3] in 1817, which had the distinction in its day of being the smallest Hebrew with points in England. Dibdin, in his *Biblio-graphical Decameron* (ii. 408), while specially commending the *Polyglot*, quotes a letter from Bagster in reference to the Figgins Hebrew fount, which it will be interesting to repeat here. Writing to Dibdin, Bagster remarks:

The difficulty to the compositor of the Hebrew with points far exceeds every other language. You are doubtless aware that every line is composed of three distinct lines; i.e. points and accents both above and below the line of letters. I wrote to the printer and letter founder to display these, and one of the letters (*that of Mr. Figgins which follows*) is enclosed as their accounts nearly agree. The difference between the fount with points, and that which is without them is very striking. The former requires 25 points and accents and 136 mixed letters; whereas the latter has only 32 altogether and one stop—a difference between the founts of 132 characters—the first with points exceeding by so considerable a number, and some are so minute that one ounce is found to contain no less than 236.

When I embraced the design of this work, no suitable fount of Hebrew existed. It became therefore necessary to cut the steel punches and the brass [*sic*] matrices before the fount of letter could be cast; and thus our country is enriched by the *creation* of this new fount.

The Greek and Roman type I think will also be admired for the delicate neatness of their execution. The Hebrew and Greek types are of the neatest form, and the latter is that of Porson. . . .

Figgins's letter enclosed is as follows:

The number of Hebrew matrices are 82; these are all first cast on a minion body, and 54 of them are again cast on a diamond body, to admit of marks and accents being put over them. The accents and points are 25 in number, of which there are, of the thinnest sort, about 240 to the ounce. The number of boxes required to contain the fount are:—

Minion Hebrew	82
Spaces (4), em and en quads (2), large quad (1) . .	7
Diamond Hebrew	54
Spaces same as Minion	7
Minikin accents and marks	25
Spaces, etc., same as Minion	7
	182

I am, Sir, your obedient servant,

West Street, London, 16th Oct., 1816.　　　　　　　　　　　　　V. Figgins.

[1] *Lit. Anec.* ii. 361.

[2] Both Swan Yard and West Street disappeared at the time of the construction of the Holborn Viaduct. Both are shown on Horwood's *Map of London*, 1799.

[3] *Biblia Sacra Polyglotta, Textus Archetypos, Versionesque praecipuas ab Ecclesiâ Antiquitùs receptas complectentia*, London, 1817–28. Five parts, 4to, 4 vols. 8vo. This Bible comprises the original Hebrew text of the Old Testament, the Samaritan Pentateuch, the Septuagint Greek version of the Old Testament, the Vulgate Latin, and the Authorized English version of the entire Bible, the original Greek of the New Testament, and the venerable Peschito or Syriac version of it. This *Polyglot* was republished with the addition of Spanish, French, Italian, and German versions in 1831, with learned prolegomena by Dr. Samuel Lee. Most of the first edition was destroyed in 1822 in a fire at Baxter's shop in Paternoster Row. See the·*Historical Catalogue* of the British and Foreign Bible Society.

The Syriac used in Bagster's *Polyglot*[1] was cut by Edmund Fry; but Figgins had previously produced three sizes of this character, viz.: a Double Pica, English, and Long Primer (two founts), under the direction and partly at the expense of Dr. Claudius Buchanan, the eminent Indian missionary and Orientalist, whose work on *Christian Researches in Asia, with notices of translations of the Scriptures into the Oriental Languages*, had been published at Cambridge in 1811. At the time of his death, in 1815, Dr. Buchanan was engaged in editing for the British and Foreign Bible Society a Syriac *New Testament*, which appeared in the following year, printed in Figgins's type.[2]

The founts already specified—to which may be added a Small Pica Irish, copied from the copperplate engravings in Charles Vallancey's *Irish Grammar*, and some additional Greeks, cut after the Porson model—constituted the chief features of Figgins's foundry in respect of the learned and foreign founts. With regard to its progress in the characters of more general use, it will be sufficient to quote Hansard's note, written in 1825, and based doubtless on an examination of the excellent specimen of 1821, with its additions in 1822 and 1823:

No foundry existing is better stocked with matrices for those extraneous sorts which are cut more with a view to accommodation than profit; such as astronomical, geometrical, algebraical, physical, genealogical, and arithmetical sorts; and I feel it particularly incumbent on me to add that, as his specimen bears equal rank with any for the number and beauty of its founts, so he has strayed less into the folly of fat-faced preposterous disproportions, than either Thorne, Fry or Caslon. I consider his Five-line Pica German text a typographical curiosity.[3]

The following is Hansard's summary of the foreign and learned founts contained in this foundry in 1825:

FIGGINS'S FOUNDRY

Domesday.[4]—Pica, Small Pica.

German Text (Ornamental).—Five-line Pica.

Greek.[5]—Great Primer, English, Pica, Small Pica, Long Primer, Brevier.

Hebrew.—English with points, Pica, Small Pica, Ditto with points.[6]—Long Primer, Nonpareil.

Irish.—Small Pica.

Persian.—Paragon.

Saxon.—Pica, Small Pica, Long Primer, Brevier.

Syriac.—Double Pica, English, Long Primer, Brevier.

Télegú.[7]—English.

Black.—Double Pica, Great Primer, English, Pica, Long Primer.

Further specimens were issued in 1824 and 1826, each indicating the rapid growth of the rising foundry between those dates. They were followed in 1827 by a compact little 16mo volume; and from that date specimens are frequent. In the

---

[1] See p. 306.

[2] *Novum Testamentum Syriace denuo recognitum atque ad fidem Codicum MSS. emendatum. Impressit R. Watts*, London, 1816, 4to. Dr. Buchanan was born in 1766 and went to India in 1796, where his researches led to the discovery, among other things, of some interesting Hebrew Manuscripts of portions of the Bible, on goat skins and tablets of brass. He died in 1815. The Syriac *Testament* was corrected by him as far as the Acts, and completed by Dr. Samuel Lee, Arabic Professor at Cambridge.

[3] *Typographia*, p. 360.

[4] The matrices of the Long Primer and Brevier cut for the Scottish Record Commission were given up to the Government.

[5] Hansard omits the Double Pica Greek cut for Oxford University, the matrices of which were retained by Figgins.

[6] The fount for Bagster's *Polyglot*.

[7] The punches, matrices, and moulds of this fount were deposited in the East India Company's Library.

specimen of 1832 the Sans-serif design first appeared under that name, though William Caslon IV had shown the type in 1816, calling it Egyptian.

Figgins died at Peckham, 29 February 1844. He was for several years Common Councillor for the Ward of Farringdon Without; 'an amiable and worthy character,' says Nichols, 'and generally respected.' He had relinquished business in 1836, leaving it to his two sons, Vincent Figgins II and James Figgins, who issued their first specimen-book, a handsome quarto, under the style of V. & J. Figgins, in 1838. Vincent Figgins II, as already noted, had cut some Chinese letters in 1826, shown on a sheet dated 1843. In 1855, for the facsimile reprint of the second edition of Caxton's *Game of the Chesse*, he cut a fount of type after the original, 'which', he remarks, 'is a mixture of black-letter and the character called secretary', the black predominating. The 'Caxton Black', a copy of Caxton's type 2, was the first attempt to produce such a facsimile. In his remarks Figgins gives his reason for concluding, from the variety in the form of the letters, that they were not cast from a matrix but cut separately by hand. This theory Blades, in his *Life of Caxton*, disproves, pointing out that type 2^x used in the second edition of Caxton's work is really an old fount originally cast from matrices and, when worn, trimmed up by hand to form the punches for a new fount—a circumstance amply sufficient to account for the irregularities observed.[1] Blades, in his copy of the reproduction, has added a comment that Figgins's remarks showed great ignorance of early typography. For the whole fount 133 punches were cut. Two other facsimiles of Caxton's books were printed in this type, *The Governal of Helthe* in 1858, and *The Moral Proverbs of Chrystine of Pise* in 1869.

In Hansard's summary quoted above there is no mention of Sanskrit. The Figgins specimen-book in quarto issued about 1850 shows their exotic types and contains also a note to the effect that 'V. & J. Figgins have also the matrices of an English Sanskrit, which was cut in Calcutta under the superintendence of Professor Wilson and is known there as Wilson's Sanskrita'. H. H. Wilson was the librarian of the East India Company and the type was presumably that used in his *Dictionary Sanscrit and English*, Calcutta, 1819, and various editions of Sanskrit texts.

At the Great Exhibition of 1851 the Figgins were awarded a medal for their display of types. At the same time the reporters made some adverse comment on the firm's attitude to type-casting machinery. We give some account below (p. 368) of the opposition of the old-established founders to new inventions and of James Figgins the Younger's reply to the attack made by J. R. Johnson in 1872. The

[1] John Whittaker's famous restorations of Caxtonian and other early printed works were to a certain extent accomplished by means of typography. Dibdin, in his *Bibliographical Decameron* (ii. 415), describes the operation as follows: 'He has caused to be engraved or cut four founts of Caxton's letter. These are cut in the manner of binders' tools for lettering, and each letter is separately charged with ink, and separately impressed on the paper. Some of Caxton's types are so riotous and unruly that Mr. Whittaker found it impossible to carry on his design without having at least twenty of such irregular letters engraved. The process of executing the text with such tools shall be related in Mr. Whittaker's own words:—"A tracing being taken with the greatest precision from the original leaf, on white tracing paper, it is then laid on the leaf (first prepared to match the book it is intended for) with a piece of blacked paper between the two. Then by a point passing round the sides of each letter, a true impression is given from the black paper on the leaf beneath. The types are next stamped on singly, being charged with old printing ink prepared in colour exactly to match each distinct book. The type being then set on the marks made by tracing, in all the rude manner and at the same unequal distances observable in the original, they will bear the strictest scrutiny and comparison with their prototype; it being impossible to make a facsimile of Caxton's printing in any other way, as his letters are generally set up irregularly and at unequal distances, leaning various ways," ' &c.

Figgins's part in the revival of old faces took the form of a display of the original romans of Vincent Figgins I on a sheet dated 1795 in their specimen-book issued *c.* 1857. After the death of Vincent II in December 1860 the business was continued by his brother James and by the latter's son James II. At the Exhibition in London in 1862 the Figgins, as well as Caslon, made vigorous and public protest against the practice of producing matrices by the electrotype process, but in vain. In 1865 the foundry was moved to Ray Street, Farringdon Road, and was further enlarged by the purchase in 1872 of the stock of J. & R. M. Wood. In that year the firm began a new series of specimen-books in octavo and the fact that 5,000 copies of the book of 1874 were issued gives an idea of the importance of the business at that time.

Alderman James Figgins I—like several of his fellow founders of the Victorian age he devoted much of his time to public affairs—retired from the firm on being elected to Parliament for Shrewsbury in 1868 (he lost his seat in 1874), and for the last years of the firm's history the sole manager was James Figgins the Younger. The last of the Figgins died in 1907, when a new firm was established by his nephew, Mr. R. H. Stevens. The business is still carried on under the style of Stevens, Shanks & Sons.

ENGLISH ANTIQUE.

Quousque tandem abutere, Catilina, patientia nostra? quamdiu nos etiam furor iste tuus eludet? quem ad finem sese effrenata jactabit audacia? nihilne te nocturnum præsidium palatii, nihil urbis vigiliæ, nihil timor populi, nihil consensus bonorum omnium, nihil hic munitis-ABCDEFGHIJKLMNOPQRSTU £1234567890.

Fig. 90. Figgins's Antique.

MINOR FOUNDERS OF
THE EIGHTEENTH CENTURY

SKINNER, *circa* 1710

THIS founder is mentioned by Mores as a contemporary of Robert Andrews and Head. Nothing, however, is known of his types.

SAMUEL JALLESON, *circa* 1727

According to John Smith's *Printers' Grammar*, p. 31, Jalleson came from Germany. Plomer's *Dictionary* spells the name Jallasson, while Enschedé writes Jalisson. He was in London by 1727 and in that year printed Voltaire's *Essay on the Civil Wars of France*. There is a copy in the British Museum presented by the author to Sir Hans Sloane. He lived in Prujean Court, Old Bailey, where he attempted an economical way of multiplying founts by casting six different bodies of letter from three sets of punches, viz. Brevier and Long Primer from one set, Pica and English from another, Great Primer and Double Pica from a third. 'Accordingly,' says Smith, 'he charged his Brevier, Pica, and Great Primer with as full a face as their respective bodies would admit of, and, in order to make some alteration in the advancing founts, he designed to cut the ascending and descending letters to such a length as should show the extent of their different bodies. But though he had cast founts of the three minor sorts of letters, he did not bring the rest here to perfection.'

While in England, 'he printed the greatest part of a Hebrew *Bible* with letter of his own casting; but was, by adverse fortune, obliged to finish the said work in Holland'. This Bible is unknown to the *Historical Catalogue* of the Bible Society. In 1730 he was in Amsterdam and cut some punches for the Wetsteins. C. Enschedé, op. cit., p. 200, shows part of a Malay fount cut by him. Jalleson's system, though apparently unsuccessful at the time, was eventually adopted, to a certain extent, by English founders.

DUMMERS, *circa* 1734

Mores says he was a Dutchman who founded in this country, where he cut the fount of Pica Samaritan which appears in Caslon's specimen of 1734.[1] He subsequently returned to his native country. Smith, in his *Printers' Grammar*, after

---

[1] See p. 237.

referring to the genius of Van Dijk, mentions Voskin and Dommer [*sic*] as having 'been considered as two Worthies, for their abilities in their profession'.

JACOB ILIVE, *circa* 1734

This eccentric individual was a connexion of James's the printers, his mother, Elizabeth, being the daughter of Thomas James, grandson of Thomas James of the Bodleian.[1] His father, Thomas, was a printer resident in Aldersgate Street,[2] and his two brothers, Abraham and Isaac, also followed the same calling. About the year 1734 he applied himself to letter-founding, and carried on a foundry and printing-house together in Aldersgate Street over against Aldersgate Coffee-house, where he was resident in 1734.

But, afterwards [says Mores] when *Calasio*[3] was to be reprinted under the inspection of Mr. Romaine, or of Mr. Lutzena, a Portuguese Jew who corrected the Hebrew—as we ourselves did sometimes another part of the work—he removed to London House (the habitation of the late Dr. Rawlinson) on the opposite side of the way, where he was employed by the publishers of that work. This was in the year 1746.[4]

From 1736 to 1738 he was the publisher of the rival *Gentleman's Magazine*, after having worked for Edmund Cave on the staff of the original *Gentleman's Magazine*. In 1737 he was the printer of *The Maidstone Journal*, of which only one number is known, No. 3, 6 October, preserved at the Maidstone Museum.

His foundry was only a small one, and does not appear to have received much patronage or to have issued a specimen. The following is Mores's summary of its contents:

MR. ILIVE'S FOUNDERY, 1734

OCCIDENTALS

Greek.—Nonpareil, 200; another, 80 lb.
Roman.—2-line English, the small letters only, 27; Pica, similiter, 27; Brevier broadface, 54; Small Pica, 70; another, the small letters and double only, 39; Nonpareil cap. 27.

Roman and Italic.—Double Pica, 154; Great Primer, 212; English, 236; Pica, 214; Long Primer, 230; Brevier, 255; Sm. Pica, 248.
Figures.—Pica fractions, 20; Mercantile marks, Pica, 17.
Braces, Rules and Flowers, 30.

In 1740 (3 July) the foundry was purchased by John James, in whose premises, says Mores, it lay in the boxes named *Jugge*, and underwent very little alteration. With regard to the sets of Greek matrices, Mores also states that though James paid for these they never came to his hands. Some suggestions about Ilive's romans were made above, p. 226.

Although abandoning typefounding early, Ilive continued to print until the time of his death in 1763. Mores says he was an expeditious compositor and knew the

---

[1] See p. 206.
[2] Thomas Ilive is named in Samuel Negus's list of Printers, published by Bowyer in 1724, as one of those 'said to be high flyers'. He was a benefactor to Zion College, and printed the classical catalogue of their library from the letter P.
[3] Marius de Calasio, *Concordantiae Bibliorum*

Hebr. et Lat. edente Guil. Romaine, 4 vols., London, 1747, fol.
[4] London House, on the west side of Aldersgate, originally Petre House, was acquired by the Bishop of London after the Restoration. It was destroyed by fire in 1768, and when rebuilt became No. 150 Aldersgate.

letters by touch. He was, however, less noted for his typography than for his opinions. Nichols tells us he was somewhat disordered in his mind. In 1733 he published an *Oration* proving the plurality of worlds, that this earth is hell, that the souls of men are apostate angels, and that the fire to punish those confined to this world at the day of judgement will be immaterial. This discourse was composed in 1729, and spoken at Joiners' Hall pursuant to the will of his mother, who died in 1733 and held the same singular opinions in divinity as her son.[1] A second pamphlet, entitled *A Dialogue between a Doctor of the Church of England and Mr. Jacob Ilive upon the Subject of the Oration*, also appeared in 1733.[2]

In 1751 Ilive perpetrated a famous literary forgery in a pretended translation of the *Book of Jasher*,[3] said to have been made by one Alcuin of Britain.

The account given of the translation [says Mores] is full of glaring absurdities, but of the publication, this we can say, from the information of the Only-One who is capable of informing us, because the business was a secret between the Two: Mr. Ilive in the night-time had constantly an Hebrew *Bible* before him (*sed qu. de hoc*) and cases in his closet. He produced the copy for *Jasher*, and it was composed in private, and the forms worked off in the night-time in a private press-room by these Two, after the men of the Printing-house had left their work. Mr. Ilive was an expeditious compositor, though he worked in a nightgown and swept the cases to *pye* with the sleeves.[4]

In 1756, for publishing *Modest Remarks on the late Bishop Sherlock's Sermons*, Ilive was imprisoned in Clerkenwell Bridewell, where he remained for two years, improving the occasion by writing and publishing *Reasons offered for the Reformation of the House of Correction in Clerkenwell*, in 1757. He also projected several other reforming works.[5]

In the last year of his life, 1762, he once more became notorious as the ringleader of a schism among the members of the Stationers' Company, of which the following narrative (communicated by Bowyer) is given by Gough:

He called a meeting of the Company for Monday the 31st of May, being Whit-Monday, at the Dog Tavern, on Garlick Hill, 'to rescue their liberties,' and choose Master and Wardens. Ilive was chosen chairman for the day; and, standing on the upper table in the hall, he thanked the freemen for the honour they had done him—laid before them several clauses of their two charters—and proposed Mr. Christopher Norris and some one else to them for Master; the choice falling upon Mr. Norris. He then proposed, in like manner, John Lenthall, Esq., and John Wilcox, Gent., with two others for Wardens; when the two first nominated were elected. A Committee was then appointed by the votes of the Common Hall to meet the first Tuesday in each month at the Horn Tavern, in Doctors' Commons, to inquire into the state of the Company, which Committee consisted of twenty-one persons, five of whom (provided the Master and Wardens were of the number), were empowered to act as fully as if the whole of the Committee were present. July the 6th being the first Tuesday in the month, the newly-elected Master, about twelve o'clock, came into the Hall,

---

[1] *Anecdotes of Bowyer*, p. 130.

[2] 'Emboldened by his first adventure, he determined to become the public teacher of infidelity. For this purpose he hired the use of Carpenters' Hall, where for some time he delivered his Orations, which consisted chiefly of scraps from Tindal and other similar writers' (Chalmers's *Biog. Dict.* xix. 228).

[3] *The Book of Jasher. With testimonies and notes explanatory of the text. To which is prefixed various readings. Translated into English from the Hebrew,* by *Alcuin of Britain, who went a Pilgrimage into the Holy Land, &c. Printed in the year 1751*. 4to. The fraud was immediately detected and exposed. The work was reprinted, without acknowledgement and with some variations, at Bristol in 1829, by a Rev. C. R. Bond. Both editions are now rare. There are copies in the British Museum.

[4] *Dissert.*, p. 65.

[5] These are enumerated in Gough's *British Topography*, i. 637.

and being seated at the upper end of it, the Clerk of the Hall was sent for and desired to swear Mr. Norris into his office; but he declined, and Mr. Ilive officiated as the Clerk in administering the oath. A boy then offered himself to be bound; but no Warden being present, he was desired to defer until next month, when several were bound; some freemen made; and others admitted on the livery; one of whom, at least, has frequently polled at Guildhall in contested elections.[1]

No particular notice appears to have been taken of the proceedings, and the rebellion was short-lived. Previous to its outbreak, Ilive had published a pamphlet on *The Charter and Grants of the Company of Stationers; with Observations and Remarks thereon*, in which he recited various grievances and stated the opinion of counsel upon several points. 'I have a copy of this pamphlet,' says Hansard, 'now lying before me, the twentieth page of which concludes with the line, "Excudebat, edebat, donabat, Jacob Ilive, Anno 1762".' Ilive died in the following year.

THE WESTONS

Some founders of this name are mentioned by Ames; but Mores supposes that Ames, 'who', he adds, 'was an arrant blunderer', has made Englishmen of the Wetsteins of Amsterdam, who founded in that city about 1733–43. The Wetsteins, though they doubtless had considerable type dealings with this country, are not known at any time to have practised typefounding in England.

JOHN BAINE, 1749

After the dissolution of partnership between Wilson and Baine in 1749,[2] the latter appears to have come to London, where, Rowe Mores informs us, 'he published a specimen (very pretty) without a date. It exhibits Great Primer and Pica Greek and (we take no notice of title letters) the roman and italic regulars beginning at Great Primer; and the bastard Small Pica. Mr. Baine left England and is now (1778), we think, alive in Scotland.' He appears to have carried his foundry with him, for we find in a specimen of types belonging to a printer, John Reid, in Edinburgh, in 1768,[3] two founts, a Small Pica and a Minion, marked as having been supplied by him. In 1787 was published a *Specimen by John Baine and Grandson in Co.* at Edinburgh, a copy of which is in the Library of the American Antiquarian Society, Worcester, Mass.

About the same date they established a foundry in Philadelphia, the grandson having probably taken charge of the new venture before being joined by his relative. Isaiah Thomas[4] speaks in high praise of the mechanical ability of the elder Baine, and adds that his knowledge of typefounding was the effect of his own industry; for he was self-taught. It may be confessed that quite apart from design the Small Pica and Minion shown in John Reid's specimen do not bear comparison with the Caslon and Wilson's founts in point of workmanship. Both, says Thomas, were good workmen and had full employment. They appear to have been moderately

[1] *British Topography*, i. 597.
[2] See above, p. 260.
[3] *A Specimen of the Printing Types and Flowers belonging to John Reid, Printer, Bailie Fyfe's Close, Edinburgh, &c.*, Edinburgh, 1768. 8vo. All the other founts shown are either Wilson's or Caslon's. Copy at St. Bride's.
[4] *History of Printing in America*. 2nd edition, Albany, 1874, i. 31.

successful in America.[1] The elder Baine died in 1790, aged 77. His grandson relinquished the business soon after, and, says Thomas, died at Augusta in Georgia about the year 1799.

GEORGE ANDERTON, 1753

George Anderton, an engraver, of Birmingham, appears to have been one of the earliest of English provincial letter-founders. He lived in Temple Street between 1740 and 1753. In 1752 he published *A New Plan of the University of Oxford*.[2] Mores says he 'attempted' letter-founding, and in the year 1753 printed a little specimen of Great Primer roman and italic. No copy of this specimen appears to have survived. Samuel Caslon, brother to Caslon I, worked as a mould maker in this foundry after having left the latter on account of some dispute.

HENRY FOUGT, *circa* 1766

This man, a German, lived in St. Martin's Lane about the year 1766, and in the following year took out a patent for 'Certain new and curious types by me invented for the printing of music notes as neatly and as well, in every respect, as hath usually been done by engraving'. The invention consisted in the use of sectional types 'in many respects similar to what in former ages was used in printing-offices and known by the name of choral type'. An explanatory note, setting forth the details of his scheme, accompanies the specification.[3] He appears to have copied the system of Breitkopf of Leipzig. Fougt issued a specimen of his new type in 1768,[4] and is said to have been the only printer of music from type of his day who produced any good work. Mores says that he returned to Germany, after selling his patent to one Falconer, a disappointed harpsichord maker. This is R. Falkener, whose shop was at 3 Peterborough Court, Fleet Street, and later at 45 Salisbury Court.

JOSEPH FENWICK, *circa* 1770

Mores's quaint account of this unlucky person is as follows:

Mr. Joseph Fenwick was a locksmith, and worked as a journeyman in David Street in Oxford Road. Invited by an advertisement from Mr. Caslon for a smith who could file smooth and make a good screw, he applied, and is now mould-mender in ordinary to Mr. Caslon. But his ingenuity hath prompted him to greater things than a good screw. He hath cut a fount of Two-line Pica Scriptorial for a divine, the planner of the Statute at Plaisterers' Hall for demising and to farm letting servants of both sexes and all services. Of him Mr. Caslon required an enormous sum when he thought that nobody could do the work but himself. Mr. Fenwick succeeded at a very moderate expence; for he has not been

---

[1] The first attempt to introduce typefounding in America had been made by David Mitchelson, a Scotsman, about 1768, but appears to have failed. In 1769 Abel Buel, of Connecticut, succeeded in casting a Pica and a Long Primer. Christopher Sower, in 1772, brought over a foundry from Germany to Germantown in Pennsylvania. Jacob Bay and Justus Fox also founded in the same town about 1774. Benj. Franklin and his grandson Bache brought over a foundry from France in 1785 to Philadelphia, which, however, had ceased its operations when Baine and his grandson established their foundry in the same city. See L. C. Wroth's *The Colonial Printer*, 1938, pp. 98–114.

[2] See Joseph Hill's *Bookmakers of Old Birmingham*.

[3] See *Abridgments of Specifications relating to Printing*, p. 87. See also p. 73.

[4] Copy in the British Museum.

paid for his labour. The plausible design of the fount was the relief and ease of our rural vineyarders, and the service of those churches in which the galleries overlook the pulpit.

The divine mentioned in Mores's account is surely the Rev. Dr. John Trusler,[1] although the allusion to the Statute at Plaisterers' Hall cannot be explained. Mr. Morison contributed an article, with reproductions, on 'The Trusler Script Types' to *The Fleuron*, No. 7, pp. 157–66. Trusler's idea was to provide clergymen with printed sermons which would look like manuscript. Such copies as survive are undated, but the project is referred to in a list of Trusler's publications at the Literary Press dated 1790. Two hundred and fourteen sermons had been printed by that year. Timperley says that the project was started in 1771. Trusler's script bears a close resemblance to that of Thomas Cottrell, which was certainly in existence by July 1774, and may have been cut several years earlier. It seems more likely that Cottrell cut the first of the Latin scripts rather than the obscure Fenwick. In the synopsis of founts given at the end of Mores's book, Fenwick's Scriptorial, or Cursive, is mentioned as being at that time (1778) obtainable. A Fenwick is entered as a Printers' Broker at 63 Snow Hill in 1785 in Pendred's *Printer's Vade Mecum*.

JOHN MATTHEWSON, *after* 1771

William Chambers, in his *Memoir of Robert Chambers, etc.*, chapter VI—1819 to 1821, has the following account of Matthewson:

My means being somewhat improved, it did not appear unreasonable that I should enlarge my stock of letter, by ordering a moderate fount of longprimer adapted for pamphlet-work, from an aged type-founder, named Matthewson, who carried on business at St. Leonard's, and with whom I had become acquainted. In his walks, he occasionally called to rest in passing, and hence our business dealings. His cut of letter was not particularly handsome, but in the decline of life and in easy circumstances, he did not care for new fashions.

Disposed to be familiar, Matthewson gave me an outline of his history. He had, he said, been originally a shepherd boy, but from his earliest years had possessed a taste for carving letters and figures. One day, while attending his master's sheep, he was accidentally observed by the minister of the parish to be carving some words on a block of wood with a pocket-knife. The clergyman was so pleased with his ingenuity, that he interested himself in his fate, and sent him to Edinburgh to pursue the profession of a printer. Shortly afterwards, he began to make himself useful by cutting dies for letters of a particular description required by his employer; there being then no typefounder in the city. While so occupied, he attracted the notice of Benjamin Franklin on his second visit to Scotland. This was about 1771. Franklin was pleased with the skill of the young printer, and offered to take him to Philadelphia, and there assist him in establishing a letter-foundry. Matthewson was grateful for the disinterested offer, of which, unfortunately, for family reasons he could not take advantage. He set up the business of letter-founding in Edinburgh, which he had all to himself until the commencement of establishments with higher claims to taste in execution.'

This man was founding in Edinburgh in 1810, at which date he had some correspondence with the Associated Founders respecting prices. Hansard mentions him

---

[1] On Trusler see W. J. Pinks's *History of Clerkenwell*, 1881, pp. 291–3. He lived at one time in Red Lion Street, Clerkenwell.

as an incipient founder even in 1825, and a competitor of Miller's. Nothing is known of the fate of his foundry; the American Typefounders have an undated specimen. (The library is now at Columbia University.)

T. RICHARDS, 1778

Mores says he lived near Hungerford Bridge, and called himself letter-founder and toyman, but appears to have been an instrument maker for marking the shirts of soldiers 'to prevent plunder in times of peace'. 'But we have seen no specimen,' he adds, 'either on paper or on rags.'

McPHAIL, 1778

Mores describes him as a Scotsman without address.

It is said that he hath cut two full-faced founts, one of Two-line English, the other of Two-line Small Pica; hath made the moulds, and casts the letter his self. If this be true (and we have reason to believe it is not altogether false) he must travel like the circumforanean printers of names from door to door soon after the invention of the art, with all the apparatus in a pack upon his shoulders; for he is a *nullibiquarian,* and we cannot find his founding house.

To this account Hansard adds in 1825:

I have reason to believe that, some years ago, the foundry of McPhail, which Mores has commemorated by a most humorous paragraph, was carried on either by the same individual or a descendant; but it continues to be screened from observation by the same cloud which obscured it from the curiosity of that illustrious typographical historian.

JOHN WALTER AND THE LOGOGRAPHIC PRESS, 1784

In 1783 Henry Johnson, a former employee of Caslon, published *An Introduction to Logography,* an account of an invention for which he had taken out patents in 1778 and 1780.[1] The process consisted in cementing together separately cast type. Johnson's intention was to produce a series of figures in one piece and to use them for filling in the blanks on lottery tickets. The extension to general letterpress printing, making slugs of commonly occurring words or syllables, was planned by John Walter, who in 1784 established a foundry for exploiting the 'logographic' process. He bought the King's Printing House in Blackfriars, which had been rebuilt after the fire in 1738. In 1785 Walter issued *Miscellanies in prose and verse intended as a specimen of the types, at the Logographic Printing Office.* This specimen shows eight sizes of type, from English to Pearl, the type being Caslon. In the same year was published a four-page folio in which Walter defended the system and added a list of titles of forty works set up. Later, in 1789, there was a fuller account: *An Address to the Public, by J. Walter, shewing the great improvement he has made in the art of printing by logographic arrangements,* a volume of 96 pages,

[1] François Barletti de Saint-Paul had preceded Johnson. In 1776 he published at Paris his *Nouveau système typographique . . . découvert en 1774, par Mme. de ***.* He gives tables of all the syllables proposed to be cast as logotypes and claims that the system would reduce the time of composition, correction, and distribution by one-third. The tract was mentioned by Benjamin Franklin in his letter to John Walter of 17 April 1784. Franklin himself seems to have experimented with logographs after reading Barletti de Saint-Paul's tract.

containing many letters of prominent men interested in the process. Among these men was Benjamin Franklin, at that time the representative of his government in France. The letters exchanged between Walter and Franklin were published in 1929 by the American Antiquarian Society, Worcester, Mass. On 1 January 1785 appeared the first number of Walter's newspaper *The Daily Universal Register* 'printed logographically' (the title was changed to *The Times* from 1 Jan. 1788), and it was not until the beginning of 1792 that these words were dropped. The author of *The History of The Times*, vol. i, 1935, says that up to 1790 the newspaper was 'scarcely more than a piece of daily publicity, designed to promote the publications of the Logographic Press'. The last book of any size published was John Meares's *Voyages to the North West Coast of America*, 1790, 2 vols.[1]

By the year 1792 John Walter had abandoned logotypes and in 1854 we find that *The Times* was firmly resolved not to reintroduce them. In 1854 Major Bartholomew Beniowski, a Polish refugee, published a pamphlet about his various inventions. His first patent was taken out in 1846, at which time his address was in Bow Street, Covent Garden. He had already found financial support and in 1853 'The Patent Printing Machinery and Printing Company' had been formed with a capital of £130,000. On 18 July 1854 John Greene, M.P. for Kilkenny, one of Beniowski's financial supporters, moved in the House of Commons for the appointment of a Select Committee to consider the cheapest mode of providing printing for the public service. He got his Select Committee, if little more. Great hopes were based on Beniowski's invention of a system of composing by logotypes. He designed a series of drawers which he called an 'Authoriton' and hoped by this device to cope with the very large number of sorts needed for any system based on logotypes. He claimed that a compositor could set from 4,500 to 6,000 letters in an hour as against the usual 1,000. In a leader of 20 July *The Times* said as to logotypes the idea was a favourite one with those who knew nothing about the business. Beniowski's printing machine was one of *The Times* rotatory machines turned inside out. They had examined Beniowski's inventions and rejected them.

This was the last determined attempt to introduce logotypes, although their history was not ended. In 1879 Noizette took out a patent for a system by which he claimed to be able to set 3,000 letters in the hour. Some of the composing machines have made a partial use of logotypes, as, for instance, the Frederic Wicks machine of 1880. In the same year the Marr Typefounding Company showed logotypes at the London Printing Exhibition.

IMISSON, 1785

Lemoine mentions an ingenious person of this name, 'who, among other pursuits, made some progress in the art of Letter Founding, and actually printed several small popular novels at Manchester with woodcuts cut by himself. But other mechanical pursuits took him off, and death removed him in 1791.'[2]

---

[1] John Bell's dealings with the Logographic Press are recorded in Mr. Morison's *John Bell*, pp. 97–102. For a printer's criticism of logography see Timperley, pp. 749–50.

[2] *Typog. Antiq.*, p. 81. This appears to be the person whom Gough, in his list of departed worthies of the eighteenth century, includes among the letterfounders, as 'Jurisson, d. 1791'. (*Gent. Magaz.* lxxiii, part. i, p. 161.)

MYLES SWINNEY, 1785

This provincial typographer was printer and proprietor of the *Birmingham Chronicle* from 1771 till his death in 1812, and appears to have commenced a letter foundry shortly after the breaking up of Baskerville's establishment. His shops were in the High Street, Birmingham; and in James Bisset's *Magnificent Directory* (1800) a view of his premises is given, including the type foundry called the Phoenix Foundry. He is styled Letter-Founder, Bookseller and Printer in the Directories of 1785, and subsequently added to his other pursuits that of Medicine Vendor. In 1793 he was a member of the Association of Founders at that time in existence (see p. 246,) but, according to the Minute Book, he was present at one meeting only. In 1796 he had some dispute with the Association about the price of his types. Possibly he ceased to be a member from that time, but there is a gap in the minutes between June 1796 and Dec. 1799. About the year 1802 he issued a neat specimen-book of twenty pages, comprising a series of roman and italic and a few ornamented and shaded letters. There is a copy in the Birmingham Central Library. The letters show the influence of Baskerville and there are no modern faces. There was issued also an undated broadside, of which D. B. Updike had a copy. The notice accorded to him in the *Magnificent Directory* is very complimentary: 'This useful Branch of the Typographic Art, immediately on the demise of the late celebrated Baskerville, was resumed and is now continued, with persevering industry and success, by Mr. Swinney, whose elegant specimens of printing add celebrity to the other manufactures of this Emporium of the Arts.'

The *Poetic Survey round Birmingham* accompanying the Directory immortalizes our founder in the following couplet:

> The Gods at Swinney's Foundry stood amaz'd,
> And at each curious Type and Letter gaz'd.

Among his workmen was John Handy, a former punch-cutter for Baskerville.[1] Swinney died in 1812, aged 74, having been printer and proprietor of the *Birmingham Chronicle* for nearly fifty years. Details of books printed by him are given in Joseph Hill's *Bookmakers of Old Birmingham*.

JOHN BELL AND THE BRITISH LETTER FOUNDRY, 1788

John Bell had already made a reputation as a publisher and editor of newspapers, when in 1787 he turned his attention to typefounding. In the number of *The World* for 9 June 1787 he announced that he was establishing his new foundry at his premises in the Strand, near Exeter Exchange, and was casting a new type on improved principles. His first specimen, showing an English roman and italic, was dated May 1788, and stated that the types had been 'completed under his directions by William Coleman, Regulator, and Richard Austin, punch-cutter'. What a regulator was is not recorded and nothing is known of William Coleman, though he may perhaps be the — Coleman described by Timperley as 'a very ingenious engraver in wood', died December 1807. Richard Austin was at the beginning of

---

[1] See above, p. 268.

a distinguished career and we shall meet him again. In an 'Address to the World', dated 1 July 1788, Bell announced an edition of *The Book of Common Prayer* to be printed in the Paragon size of his new types, of which a specimen is appended to the address. The *Common Prayer* never reached publication, but a further size of the type, Pica, was cut, and shown in another specimen, undated but also of 1788. These specimens were discovered by Mr. Stanley Morison in the Anisson collection in the Bibliothèque Nationale and are reproduced in full in his book *John Bell*, Cambridge, 1930.[1]

What exactly Bell meant by the new and improved principles is not clear, but probably, in view of what Austin says in the preface to his own specimen of 1819, quoted below (p. 352), the reference is to the method of cutting the serifs, flat but bracketed and cut to a fine point. In order to show effectively the sharpness of the cutting Bell had new and improved presses and inks made and printed on silky wove paper. The design of the Austin letters is modern face, with flat serifs, vertical stress, sharp contrast of thick and thin strokes, and ranging figures. In the roman Bell and Austin were no doubt influenced by Firmin Didot's design of 1784, but the italic has more resemblance to Baskerville, although the harmony between roman and italic was more completely attained. Bell's first English modern face was a letter of great historical importance, since it introduced a fashion in type design which was to prevail for more than a century. Unfortunately it was not the Bell type itself which was to be the model of the nineteenth century, but the exaggerated and inferior type introduced by Robert Thorne.

In 1789 Bell took into partnership Simon Stephenson, but even with a partner he found, as he said, that his other extensive concerns engrossed so much of his time that he was forced to relinquish the foundry business. An advertisement appeared in *The Oracle* for 4 December 1789, announcing the close of the partnership and stating that the business would be carried on by S. Stephenson.

The style was altered to Simon Stephenson & Co., and subsequently to Simon and Charles Stephenson, who removed the foundry to Bream's Buildings, Chancery Lane. Both the partners were members of the Association of Founders existing at that time.

Of the Stephenson Foundry little is known beyond what may be gathered from their elegant specimen-books of types and ornaments issued between 1791 and 1797. The punches were still cut by Richard Austin, and the address to the trade[2] in the specimen dated 1797 refers to the flattering encouragement hitherto received by the proprietors from the public. The specimen exhibits ten pages of large titling letters, fourteen pages of roman and italic, from Double Pica to Minion,[3] and the remainder chiefly ornaments.

---

[1] This edition of Reed is set in Monotype Bell.

[2] 'British Foundry. S. & C. Stephenson respectfully submit the present edition of their Specimen to the public with the hope that they shall continue to experience the flattering encouragement hitherto received, and for which they beg to return their most sincere thanks.

'To those of the Trade who have not hitherto used the Types of the British Foundry, it may be necessary to observe, that they are composed of the very best Metal, and that they are justified to paper and body agreeable to the usual standard.

'As the Establishment of this Foundry comprises eminent engravers on wood and brass, orders in either of these branches will be executed in the best stile of the Art. *February*, 1797.'

A first part of the specimen appears to have been issued in 1796, and the whole book in 1797.

[3] The English and Pica are the 'Bell' design.

Despite the merit of its productions the British Foundry was not successful, and in 1797 was put up for auction. Whether it was purchased as a whole by some other founder, or whether it was dispersed, we cannot say. It seems, however, that Austin recovered some of the punches cut by him, and used them when starting his own foundry in Worship Street.

The Bell types were little used after the sale of the British Letter Foundry in 1797. In 1864 H. O. Houghton of the Riverside Press, Cambridge, Mass., visited England, and took back some Bell founts, which he called English Copperface. Mr. Bruce Rogers, who joined the Riverside Press in 1895, called the type 'Brimmer'. An account of how he used 'Brimmer' will be found in *John Bell*, pp. 134, 135. D. B. Updike also, of the Merrymount Press, discovered the type independently (cf. *Printing Types*, ii. 243) and made use of it. The original punches and matrices are in the possession of Messrs. Stephenson, Blake & Co. of Sheffield. The type was cast afresh for Mr. Morison's book.

English Roman

ABCCDEFGHIJJKKLMNOPQQRRSTUVWXYZ

ÆŒ   £ 1 2 3 4 5 6 7 8 9 0

ABCDEFGHIJJKKLMNOPQRRSTUVWXYZ   ÆŒ

abcdefghijkklmnopqrstuvwxyz   æœ   fi ff fl ffi ffl

ct st f fb fh fi fk fl ff ft ffi   [ ] ( ) . , : ; ' - ? ! &

* † ‡ § ‖ ¶ ☞

English Italic

A A BCDEFGHIJJKKLMNNOPQQRRSTTUVVW

XYZ ÆŒ abcdefghijkklmnopqrstuvwxyz æœ fi ff fl ffi

ffl ct st ſ ſb ſh ſi ſk ſl ſſ ſt ſſi ( ) . , : ; ' - ? ! &

FIG. 91. Bell's English roman and italics.

20

WILLIAM MILLER, 1807

WILLIAM MILLER, the originator of this now great foundry, was for some time a foreman in the Glasgow Letter Foundry. In 1807 he left that service to begin a foundry of his own in Edinburgh under the style of William Miller & Co. The first specimen is stated to have been published in 1809,[1] but no copy unfortunately has been found still to exist.

A further specimen was issued in 1813, followed in the ensuing year by another of twenty-eight pages, consisting entirely of roman and italic letter, of which there was a complete series from Double Pica to Pearl, with two-line letters and one page of borders. As Hansard observes respecting early founts of this foundry, the letters so much resemble those of Messrs. Wilson as to require minute inspection to distinguish the one from the other.[2]

The business, once started, made rapid progress, and in due time became a formidable rival not only to the Glasgow foundry but to the London founders. The specimen of 1815 showed further additions to the founts, some of which, we have it on Hansard's authority, were cut by Richard Austin of London.[3] In 1822 the firm is described as William Miller only, Letter-Founder to His Majesty for Scotland. The energy and care displayed by Miller in the prosecution of his business rapidly brought his foundry to the front rank, and secured for him the support not only of English printers but of some of the most important newspapers of the day, including *The Times*.

In 1832 Walter Richard was admitted a partner; and the style of the firm became once more William Miller & Co., and so continued until 1838, when it became Miller and Richard. They were the first house successfully to introduce machinery for the casting of type in this country, using the American Bruce machine from 1849. For the Exhibition of 1851 the proprietors produced a 'Brilliant' type, the smallest then in England,[4] and subsequently cut a 'Gem', a size between Brilliant and Diamond, expressly for John Bellows's *French Dictionary*[5]—a book which for clearness and minuteness combined ranks as a typographical curiosity.

---

[1] Bigmore and Wyman, ii. 42.
[2] *Typog.*, p. 366.
[3] Ibid., p. 361. Miller's title-page to the specimen of 1831 bears a fine device of the royal arms signed by Austin.
[4] A specimen of this type, 'the smallest ever manufactured in this country', was exhibited, and contains the whole of Gray's *Elegy* in 32 verses, in 2 columns, measuring $3\frac{3}{4}$ inches each in depth. The type is called *Ruby* in the *Reports by the Juries*.
[5] *Dictionary for the Pocket; French and English; English and French, &c.*, by *John Bellows, Gloucester, from type cast specially for the work by Miller and Richard, Type founders to the Queen, Edinburgh.* 1873. 24mo.

In 1860 Miller and Richard issued *Specimens of Old Style*, an octavo booklet showing eight sizes, Great Primer to Pearl, of their modernized old face, cut by their employee in Edinburgh, Alexander C. Phemister. The founders state that it was intended to meet the growing demand for old faces and explain that 'they have endeavoured to avoid the objectionable peculiarities, whilst retaining the distinctive characteristics of the mediaeval letters'. The design has the bracketed and inclined serifs and gradual stress of earlier letters, but the stress is vertical and there is a sharpness of cut and uniformity of width in the capitals which are characteristics of the modern face. The small eye to the 'e' and the short 't' of the real old faces, no doubt thought to be objectionable peculiarities, are avoided. By 1866 the copies began to appear. In September of that year Messrs. Stephenson, Blake & Co. showed in *The Printers' Register* their 'New Series of Old Style Types', and in October in the same paper Reed and Fox displayed their 'New Series of Mediaeval Founts', both close copies. In 1868 the Patent Typefounding Company produced an Old Style, and even the Caslons found it expedient to follow the fashion in 1877. The success of the new design was so great that before long every foundry had to stock an Old Style, a fact which holds good even to-day. Old Style is the single example of an accepted original design cut by an English foundry and intended for bookwork throughout the Victorian age.[1]

This firm also had its hard metal and was accused by the Patent Typefounding Company of infringing their patent. However, in an action brought in 1862 against the Edinburgh firm, who had supplied *The Times* with their hard-metal newspaper founts, the Court found that there was nothing secret about the alloy. After Miller and Richard in 1863 had acquired the jobbing types of Wood and Sharwood they could compete with the London firms in this class of work and their subsequent specimen-books usually showed 'Jobbing and Ornamental Types'. Their *Tudor Black* was a revival of the early Rotundas, whilst their *English Union* of about the same date was as fanciful as anything of that generation.

After the death of Miller in 1843, the business was carried on by Richard and his son until 1868, when, on the retirement of Richard, senior, the active management of the foundry (which since 1850 has had a branch house in London) devolved upon his sons, J. M. and W. M. Richard. The firm is still active.

---

[1] For the use of Old Style in contemporary books, see Updike, ii. 201 and Johnson's *Type Designs*, pp. 112–20.

21

THE MINOR FOUNDERS, 1800-30

BOWER, BACON, & BOWER, *circa* 1810

THIS foundry was begun in Sheffield about the beginning of the nineteenth century. The first specimen-book was issued in 1810 under the style of Bower, Bacon & Bower, the types being all modern face. In the same year Bower issued a price-list below those of the London founders, whose founts he succeeded occasionally in underselling. In 1830 they issued an *Improved Specimen of Printing Types*, and further specimens in 1832 and 1837, when the firm was G. W. Bower, late Bower & Bacon. The Bacon was H. A. Bacon, presumably the Henry Andrew Bacon who printed the *Sheffield Independent* from 1819 to 1830.

A later specimen bears the name of G. W. Bower alone, and in 1841 the firm was Bower Brothers, who published *Proposals for establishing a graduated scale of sizes for the bodies of Printing Types, and fixing their height-to-paper, based upon Pica as the common standard*.[1]

After the death of G. W. Bower the foundry was continued by Henry Bower till his death, about 1851, in September of which year the plant and stock were sold by auction and dispersed among the other founders. The catalogue of this sale contained about 50,000 punches and matrices; many of them, however, being obsolete or of small value.

BROWN, 1810; LYNCH, 1810

These two individuals are included among the letter-founders whose names are given in William Mason's *Printer's Assistant*[2]—the former having had his place of business in Green Street, Blackfriars, and the latter in Featherstone Buildings. They do not appear to have continued long in business, and their names are not included in the list of letter-founders given in Johnson's *Typographia* in 1824. In 1816 one W. Brown made an offer to the Association of Letter Founders respecting some process, the details of which were not revealed. He proposed a partnership with one of the leading founders, or, for a premium of £200, he offered to surrender the process and himself retire from the trade. His address was No. 9 Great Warner

---

[1] Sheffield, 3rd edit., 1841, 12mo. A similar proposal, only with Nonpareil as the standard, was made about 1824 by James Fergusson, a printer in Newman Street, Oxford Street, whose scheme is quoted *in extenso* by Hansard in his *Typographia*,

p. 388. In 1807 Fergusson was in the employment of Earl Stanhope, who was engaged with several inventions relating to printing.

[2] *The Printer's Assistant, containing a sketch of the history of printing*, etc., London, 1810. 12mo.

Street, Cold Barthfields [*sic*]. He was evidently a minor founder and perhaps this same Brown. The Associated Founders declined to deal. In Pigot's *Directory* for 1822, 1823, and later, there are three founders of the name of Lench, one of whom may be this Lynch.

ANTHONY BESSEMER, 1813

Anthony Bessemer was born in London and at the age of 11 was taken by his parents to Holland. He was a man of remarkable inventive genius. In his twentieth year he distinguished himself by the erection at Haarlem in Holland of pumping-engines to drain the turf pits. In 1787 he proceeded to Paris, and before he had attained the age of twenty-five he was elected a member of the Académie at Paris for improvements in the microscope. He subsequently turned his attention to letter-founding and was an assistant in the foundry of P. F. Gando at Paris. While still in Paris he cut a Cicero roman and italic, modern face, for the Enschedés, which is shown in Charles Enschedé's book on p. 386. Soon after the Revolution he moved to London and later established a foundry at Charlton, near Hitchin. Of the exact date of this undertaking we are uncertain; but as his son, Sir Henry Bessemer, was born at Charlton in 1813, it is evident that the father was already settled there at that date. Hansard states[1] that 'Mr. Bessimer' cut the Caslon Diamond letter. If the person referred to is Anthony Bessemer, as is probable, it would appear that during the early years of his business as a founder he placed his energies occasionally at the disposal of his brethren in the art. According to a letter of Sir Henry Bessemer, written in 1880, he recut all the Caslon types from Pica to Diamond.

In 1821 he issued a specimen of Modern-cut Printing Types, and shortly afterwards took into partnership J. J. Catherwood, formerly a partner of Henry Caslon II, who, since his retirement from that business, appears for a short time to have had a foundry of his own at Charles Street, Hoxton.[2] Messrs. Bessemer & Catherwood issued a specimen in 1825, on the title-page of which the new partner styles himself 'late of the Chiswell Street Foundry, London'.

Bessemer's romans were, in conformity with the fashion of the day, somewhat heavy, but finely cut. His chief performance was a Diamond, which was, as Hansard informs us, cut to eclipse the famous Diamond of Henri Didot, of Paris, at that time the smallest known. The execution of this feat, particularly in the italic, was highly successful. The partnership between Bessemer and Catherwood was not of long duration, and terminated either by the death or the retirement of the latter prior to 1830. Bessemer then removed his foundry to London, and established it at 54 Red Lion Street, Clerkenwell, whence, in 1830, he issued his final specimen-book, consisting almost entirely of roman founts.

In 1832 he retired from the business, and his foundry was put up to auction and dispersed. The catalogue of the sale mentions that the 2,500 punches included in the plant had been collected at an expense of £4,000, and that not a single strike had been taken from them but for the proprietor's own use. From a marked copy of the catalogue it appears that several of the lots of punches and matrices fetched

---

[1] *Typographia*, p. 382.   [2] See above, p. 248; also Johnson's *Typographia*, ii. 652.

high prices. The list of implements and utensils shows that the foundry employed about seven casters and an equal number of rubbers and dresssers.

Bessemer's son, Henry, appears to have been for some time in his father's foundry, where he mastered the mechanics of the trade. In 1838, being then 25 years old, he took out a patent for improvements in type-casting machinery, embodying several ingenious contrivances, some of which have since been adopted.[1] In his *Autobiography*, London, 1905, he states that he sold his invention to the Wilson Foundry in Edinburgh, who allowed it to fall into oblivion. He also invented a type-composing machine at the suggestion of James Young, in whose name the patent was taken out. There is an illustration of the machine in the *Autobiography* at p. 45.

RICHARD AUSTIN, *circa* 1815

Richard Austin began business as a punch-cutter in the employ of John Bell about 1786, and was later with S. and C. Stephenson of the British Letter Foundry.[2] On the title-page of the specimens issued by that foundry in 1789 and 1796, his name is mentioned as the cutter of the punches, and the excellent specimen itself is no mean testimony to his abilities. Austin was also a wood-engraver. His trade card, issued from 7 Chiswell Street and 11 Paul's Alley, Red Cross Street,[3] has survived. Some account of the blocks he cut was given by Mr. Stanley Morison in a privately printed pamphlet, Cambridge, 1937. They range in date from 1789 to 1827. The British Museum Print Room has an album containing 213 prints from signed and unsigned blocks. In 1817 he was living at 57 Great Sutton Street, Clerkenwell, according to Andrew Johnstone's *Commercial Directory*.

The activity prevailing throughout the trade generally at that period, consequent on the transition of the roman character from the old style to the modern, brought the punch-cutter's services into much request, and Hansard informs us that Austin executed most of the modern founts both for Messrs. Wilson of Glasgow and Miller of Edinburgh. He also cut, about 1808, the 'Great Porson Greek', English in size, after the designs of Richard Porson and with the assistance of Richard Watts, at that time printer to the University of Cambridge. The type was first used in 1811 for an edition of the *Hippolytus* of Euripides.[4]

Prior to the year 1819 he began a foundry of his own at Worship Street, Finsbury, in which subsequently his son, George Austin, joined him and in the year 1824 succeeded to the business. This foundry was styled the Imperial Letter Foundry, and carried on under the style of Austin & Sons. The earliest-known specimen was issued in 1819. This 8vo volume is prefaced by a somewhat lengthy address to the Trade (quoted at length in Berry and Johnson, p. 76), in which, after criticizing the letter-founding of the day and the faults of the modern-face romans, the proprietors boldly claim to be the only letter-founders in London who

[1] See also a letter of April 1880 addressed to T. W. Smith of the Caslon Foundry, quoted in Berry and Johnson, p. 82. Cf. below, p. 360.

[2] The title 'British Type Foundry' was adopted by Messrs. Fred. W. Tarrant and W. Howard Revell who conducted a foundry first at 116 Camberwell Road, S.E., and afterwards at 87 Newington Butts, S.E. (see their specimen, dated 1896). The firm appears in the *Post Office Directory* from 1895 to 1899. This foundry, of course, had no connexion with Bell, Austin, or the Stephensons.

[3] Reproduced in S. Morison's *John Bell*.

[4] See Christopher Wordsworth's *Scholae Academicae*, Cambridge, 1877, p. 392.

cut their own punches, which they do in a peculiar manner so as to ensure perfect sharpness in outline. They also announce that they cast their type in an extra-hard metal. Another edition appeared in 1827.

Austin appears to have been a man of considerable force and independence of character. It is related of him that once, on receiving—what to any founder at that day must have been a momentous mandate—an intimation that *The Times* wanted to see him, he replied, with an audacity which sends a shudder even through a later generation, 'that if *The Times* wanted to see him, he supposed it knew where to find him!'

On the death of George Austin, his foundry was acquired by Richard Mason Wood, who subsequently, in 1833, in partnership with Samuel and Thomas Sharwood, transferred it to 120 Aldersgate Street, under the title of the Austin Letter-Foundry. Wood and Sharwood's first specimen was issued in 1839. In their preface, reference is again made to Austin's hard metal, the superiority of which, it is stated, 'was owing to one peculiar article being used in the mixture which is unknown to our brethren in the Art'. They state that they have expended a very large sum in the purchase of the secret, doubtless the secret of Richard Austin.

Wood died in 1845, and the firm became S. and T. Sharwood, who, in 1853–4, published two specimens, one of Types, the other of Polytyped Metal Ornaments. This latter collection had been begun more than twenty years previously by Vizitelly, Branston & Co.,[1] who in 1832 had issued a specimen of Cast Metal Ornaments, 'produced by a new improved method'. This method appears to have consisted of the soldering of the casts on metal mounts—at that time a novelty. The Sharwoods subsequently acquired this collection of blocks and considerably increased it.

In addition to these cast ornaments the firm had some of the most elaborate of the fancy letters which were a speciality of the Victorian age. Some of these are illustrated in Mrs. Gray's *XIXth Century Ornamented Types*, London, 1938, a book which gives a conspectus of neo-gothicism in display types. Some of the fancy letters shown in the Austin Foundry's specimen of *c.* 1853 were imported or copied from Germany. In the Blades's copy of this book there are some manuscript notes in Blades's hand as to the designers of a few of the body types. The English No. 2, Pica No. 2, Small Pica No. 1, Bourgeois No. 3, Brevier No. 2, Minion No. 2, and Nonpareil roman are said to be cut by 'Mr. Austin'. It is not clear whether this is Richard Austin or his son George. The smaller sizes are not in the only specimen issued by Richard Austin in 1819, but no doubt more sizes were cut before his death. The Minion No. 5 was cut by Stuart, possibly the Andrew Stuart (1805–91) who was brought to London in 1834 by Alexander Wilson. There is a short obituary notice of this punch-cutter in *The British and Colonial Printer* for 16 July 1891. Lastly, the Nonpareil No. 2 in the Sharwood specimen was cut by one Skyring, that is John Skyring who appears in the *Directory* in the fifties as a Type Punch-cutter, at the address 6 Artillery Place West (off Chiswell St.).

---

[1] Robert Branston was an engraver, and resided at Beaufort Buildings, Strand, in 1824. He attempted a new system of printing music, by striking the punches deeper than usual in the plate, so that when a stereo cast was taken from it, the notes appeared sufficiently in relief to be printed at a type press.

The two Sharwoods died in 1856; the foundry was thrown into Chancery and put up for auction. According to a notice in *Caslon's Circular*, Winter Number 1892, where the date is given as 1857, the stock was bought by Caslons, R. Besley of the Fann Street Foundry, and Figgins, except for some odd items. According to Bigmore and Wyman the contents of the foundry passed into the hands of two sons of R. M. Wood, James and Richard Mason Wood. In the *Printers' Register* for 1863 Miller and Richard of Edinburgh announce that they have acquired 'the principal modern jobbing founts of Wood and Sharwood'. It is at least doubtful whether the foundry of J. and R. M. Wood established in 1856 at 89 West Smithfield, later, in 1867, at Farringdon Road, and called the Austin Letter Foundry, should be regarded as a continuation of the firm of S. and T. Sharwood. In a specimen-book issued about 1865 they displayed their new types and say that they have excluded the Austin series, but that specimens of these types could be obtained on application. In the same book they showed a Great Primer Old Face, which is a copy of Miller and Richard's Old Style. From 1862 to 1866 the firm issued a monthly periodical, *Wood's Typographic Advertiser*. Besides displaying their jobbing types, 'Woodonian', 'Fleur de Lys', 'Peruvian', 'Pretty Face', and such-like, and advertising their newspaper founts in 'Adamantine' metal, the paper included also more general articles, accounts of exhibitions, and descriptions of composing-machines. In May 1863 they give some dates in the history of the Austin Foundry. For Richard Austin they give the year 1812. It seems hardly likely that Austin had started his foundry seven years before the appearance of his first specimen-book in 1819, considering the small number of types there shown. For R. M. Wood, they say 1820, which probably should be 1824. According to the *Gentleman's Magazine* Wood was only thirty-eight when he died in 1845. In 1872 the foundry was closed and the stock bought by James Figgins.

Still another firm took the style of the Austin Letter-Foundry, a firm established in 1864 by two other sons of R. M. Wood, Austin and Rowland Wood. They bought the foundry of George Williamson, who appears in the *Post Office Directory* from 1858 to 1864. According to *Caslon's Circular* Williamson bought three founts at the Sharwood sale in 1857. A. and R. Wood's address was Parkfield Street, Islington. The *Printers' Register* included a Trade Directory, in which were the names of the leading typefounders, until June 1868. The editor of this periodical, J. M. Powell, was a supporter of J. R. Johnson in his feud against the old founders, and no doubt that fact explains the transformation of the Trade Directory after that date. In 1869 the list of founders includes one American firm, Farmer, Little & Co., New York (for whom Powell was the English agent); G. Bullen, Judd Street; C. Hammond & Co., Exeter Street (this firm later moved to Sheffield and became Dover, Hammond & Co.); Marr & Co., Edinburgh; The Patent Typefounding Co., Red Lion Square, and Wood, Austin & Co.

The firm appears to have dealt largely in American display types. They advertised them in August 1883 in *The British and Colonial Printer* and again in March 1887. In their last specimen-books they call themselves 'Type Founders to Her Majesty's Government'. Austin Wood himself died in February 1883, and an obituary notice appeared in *The British and Colonial Printer*. According to that article Wood was himself a punch-cutter. Possibly it was he who cut the Caxton black, a facsimile of Caxton's type 4, for William Blades in 1877. I have not found any use of the type in a reproduction. The firm appeared in the *Post Office Directory* for 1889 under the old style, but then became Austin, Wood, Browne & Co., and later still the Austin Letter-Foundry until 1917.

LOUIS JOHN POUCHÉE, *circa* 1815

This Frenchman started a foundry in Great Wild Street (now Wild Street), Lincoln's Inn. He had probably been established a few years when his first specimen was issued in 1819, the most interesting portion of which was a somewhat lengthy address to the public, setting forth the principles on which his 'New Foundry' was to be conducted. He mentions that 'only four Type Foundries (exclusive of mine) are worked in London at this time', and declares his intention of breaking down the monopoly they assumed. The specimen itself is not remarkable.

In 1823 he took out the patent for this country for Henri Didot's system of polymatype[1] which consisted of a machine capable of casting from 150 to 200 types at each operation, each operation being repeated twice a minute. This result was to be obtained by means of a matrix bar which formed one side of a long trough mould into which the metal was poured; and, when opened, 'the types are found adhering to the break bar like the teeth of a comb, when they are broken off and dressed in the usual way'. Pouchée became agent in England for this novel system of casting which, says the editor of the partial reprint of Hansard's *Typographia*, writing in 1869, was still used successfully in France at that date.

The attempt to introduce this system into England went far to ruin Pouchée; and, according to the above authority, 'on his failure to sustain the competition of the associated founders,[2] Didot's machine and valuable tools were purchased by them through their agent, Mr. Reed, Printer, King Street, Covent Garden, and destroyed on the premises of Messrs. Caslon and Livermore'. A William Read appears in the *Post Office Directory* as an engraver and printer from 1821 to 1845.

Despite this unfortunate speculation, Pouchée (who appears for some time to have had a partner named Jennings)[3] issued a *Specimen of Printing Type* in 1823, said to include also types by Caslon and by Thorowgood. He published another specimen-book in 1827, dated from Little Queen Street, London, in the advertisement of which he again referred to the fact that there were still only four letter foundries in London (exclusive of his own), and took credit to himself for bringing about a reduction of 12 per cent. in the prices of his opponents. The specimen, which shows titlings, roman and italic, Egyptians, blacks, and flowers, is of little merit and is marked by a great preponderance of heavy faces.

---

[1] See p. 112, and the *London Journal of Arts and Sciences*, 1823, pl. XII. In the *Journal* his address is given as King Street, Covent Garden. Didot's invention had been previously tried by Henry Caslon, but unsuccessfully. In 1815 the Associated Founders were invited by Leger Didot, younger brother of Henri, to inspect his type-casting machine. He sent also a printed letter from T. Bensley dated 17 November 1809, who had experimented with the machine. The Founders were not impressed. Whether this machine was different from that of H. Didot does not appear.

[2] This appears to be a misnomer. There was no Association of Typefounders between 1820 and 1830.

[3] Hansard, *Typographia*, p. 361.

Fig. 92. The Pouchée type-casting machine.

About the same time[1] he issued a price-list of all kinds of printers' materials, styling himself 'Type Founder and Stereotype Caster'. In the beginning of 1830 he abandoned the business, which was sold by auction. The catalogue included a large quantity of stereotype ornaments, as well as 20,000 matrices and punches. moulds, presses, and 35 tons of type. The lots were variously disposed of at low prices among the other founders.

RICHARD WATTS, *circa* 1815

Richard Watts was Printer to the University of Cambridge from 1802 to 1809, and was associated with Andrew Wilson in the exploitation of the Stanhope method of printing from stereos (see p. 213). He may be the R. Watts, a bookseller at Oxford, who in 1795 issued with others a prospectus of the *Oxford Mercury*.[2] He resigned his post at Cambridge in 1809 and is next found printing at Broxbourne in 1812 for the British and Foreign Bible Society, whence in 1816 he removed to Crown Court, Temple Bar, and here, chiefly under the patronage of the Bible Society[3] and the Mission Presses in India and elsewhere, he produced the punches of a large number of languages hitherto unknown to English typography. He received the assistance and advice of many eminent scholars in his work, some of whom personally superintended the execution of certain of the founts. His collection increased at a rapid rate, and at the time of his death included almost every oriental language in which, at that time, the Scriptures had been printed. His death occurred in 1844 at Edmonton, in which place his foundry appears to have been for some time located.

John Watts, a brother of Richard, went to America before 1806. He began as a printer in Philadelphia and by 1809 had moved to New York. In 1813 he printed the first stereotype book produced in America, an edition of *The Larger Catechism*. In 1816 he returned to Europe, and in that year we find him making a contract with the Enschedé firm at Haarlem to teach them the process of making stereos. In 1819 he was in Vienna on a similar mission together with his nephew William.[4] The nephew was presumably the William Mavor Watts who succeeded to his father's business and in 1852 printed a broadside specimen of the collection of exotics, numbering sixty-seven languages. Besides the more usual exotics the collection included ten Indian languages, Calmuc, Manchu, Japanese, Hieroglyphics, and Wedge Inscription (Ninevah). This last type, intended for the reproduction of cuneiform inscriptions, was rivalled by the Babylonian of the Queen's printers, Harrison & Son, shown at the Great Exhibition of 1851.[5] W. M. Watts printed another broadside in 1859 showing ninety-seven languages, and prepared a sheet for the Exhibition of 1862 on which nearly 150 versions were displayed. To this specimen was prefixed a note on the origin of some of the founts. The collection

---

[1] Johnson, in 1824, gives a list of nine founders (including Pouchée), at that time trading in London. (*Typog.* ii. 652.)

[2] See S. C. Roberts's *The Cambridge University Press*, pp. 122 seq.

[3] See the *Historical Catalogue* of the British and Foreign Bible Society.

[4] See the *Catalogue of Books in the Library of the Typothetae of New York*, 1896, and *De Lettergietterij van Joh. Enschedé en zonen*, 1893, pp. 82–5.

[5] See C. R. Harrison's *The House of Harrison*, 1914, pp. 31–5, where many of the firm's exotics are shown, including, besides Indian languages, Egyptian (Hieroglyphic and Demotic), Assyrian, and Phoenician. The Phoenician was used in J. M. Macdonald's *Massilia-Carthago*, 1897.

was later acquired by Gilbert and Rivington, who in 1875 printed a specimen for the Bible Society, and showed them again at the Caxton Celebration in 1877. In 1908 the collection was finally acquired by Messrs. William Clowes & Son. The exotics shown in Legros and Grant, 1916, were set up by Messrs. Clowes.

THOMAS BARTON, 1817

In Andrew Johnstone's *Commercial Directory*, 1817, the firm of Barton & Harvey appears in the list of letter-founders. Hansard states that Barton was early initiated in mechanical science by Henry Maudslay, the engineer; he was formerly in partnership with Harvey, an engraver, by whom his founts were principally cut. His foundry was at 61 Stanhope Street, Clare Market, and is mentioned by Johnson as one of the nine foundries carried on in London in the year 1824. No specimen has come under observation. His name appears in Pigot's *Directory* from 1822–3 to 1828.

PAVYERS & BULLENS, 1822

In 1922 this firm published a short history of their activities for the preceding century. The founder of the firm of Pavyers, Benjamin Pavyer, 1794–1871, was originally apprenticed to Thorowgood. In 1822 he set up on his own account in Ball Alley, Old Street, and shortly afterwards purchased the small foundry of Stephen Black, retaining Black's services as a punch-cutter. But according to Pigot's *Directory*, from 1823 to 1825 he was in partnership with Thomas King at 31 Featherstone Street, City Road, and from 1826 he was in Bartholomew Close, alone. One son, James Pavyer, emigrated to the United States, and among other things invented a type-casting machine. Another son, Benjamin II, 1827–97, joined his father. It is stated that he cut a Gaelic type and a Persian. In 1901 the firm was amalgamated with the Bullens. George and Alfred Bullen were originally with the Figgins, and in 1840 established a foundry in Watford Street, Old Street (in Judd Street from 1868). Under the management of H. H. Sendars the foundry was moved to 119 Cromer Street, Gray's Inn Road, at which address the combined firms are still in business. George Bullen issued two specimen-books about 1870, largely devoted to advertising types.

HUGH HUGHES, 1824

This artist, described as a very able engraver, was for some time in partnership with Robert Thorne at the Fann Street Foundry. In 1824 he commenced a foundry of his own at 23 Dean Street, Fetter Lane, whence he published a specimen of Book and Newspaper type, without date, which, besides romans, scripts, and Egyptians, included also Saxon, Greek, flowers, and music.

He appears specially to have applied himself to the production of this last-named character, and attained the reputation of being the best music-type cutter in the trade. Savage, in his *Dictionary of Printing*, shows a specimen of Hughes's music, observing that 'the English musical types have never to my knowledge undergone any improvement till within a few years, when Mr. Hughes cut two new founts [Nonpareil and Pearl], which are looked upon as the best we have and the largest of which I have used for this article ("Music")'. Hughes's system appears to have been that originally introduced by Breitkopf in 1754, and the scheme of a pair of cases by which his specimen is accompanied shows that a complete fount comprised as many as 238 distinct characters. Besides music of the modern notation, Hughes had matrices for the Gregorian Plain Chant Music, of which a specimen is also shown by Savage.

After the death of Hughes, which took place before 1841, the punches and matrices of his different music founts, Gregorian and modern, were purchased by C. Hancock, of Middle Row, Holborn, by whom they were considerably improved, and who subsequently, after his removal to Gloucester Street, Queen Square, issued a specimen. The other contents of Hughes's foundry appear to have been bought by Caslon (see above, p. 250).

S. HEAPHY, 1825; JAMES SIMMONS, 1825; STEPHEN BLACK, 1825

To complete the list of minor founders prior to 1830, should be added the names of these three individuals, who are mentioned by Hansard in his *Typographia* as distinct London letter-founders in 1825. The Heaphy is presumably the S. Heafy of Pigot's *Directory* at the address 6 Granby Place, Lambeth. James Simmons was in Salisbury Square. The foundry of Stephen Black was purchased by Pavyer, and he himself was kept on as a punch-cutter. See Pavyers & Bullens.

22

THE TYPEFOUNDERS AND THE MECHANICAL INVENTIONS OF THE NINETEENTH CENTURY

W E have given a list above (pp. 110–13) of the patents concerning founding taken out up to 1831, but none of these inventions had brought about any considerable change in the method of producing types as practised since the fifteenth century. The only invention which disturbed the trade was that introduced by Pouchée in 1823, a machine for accelerating the casting of type, and we have seen what became of that attempt. Between the time of Pouchée and the end of the century there were to be great changes, resulting in a complete transformation of the methods of type-manufacture and in the driving out of business of the old letter-founders.

A full list of British and American patents relating to printing is given in Legros and Grant's *Typographic Printing-Surfaces*. Those relating to typefounding alone are far too numerous to be repeated here. We shall mention only those which were of some importance in the history of British typefounding. For descriptions of the machines the reader may be referred to Legros and Grant. There are three inventions which are of particular significance for founders: (1) the application of a pump to the old hand-casting mould, (2) type-casting machines, and (3) composing machines. Composing machines were designed, of course, for the printers, but ultimately, in combination with casting machines, they were to transform the methods of type-production. First came the pump, by means of which molten metal was forced into the matrix, so that the strange evolutions of the hand-caster became unnecessary. The first patents in this country for such a pump were taken out, as already noted, by A. F. Berte in 1806 and 1807. The same idea was embodied in the casting machine of the famous engineer, M. I. Brunel, in 1820. The first pump with a spring-propelled piston was the American patent of Mann and Sturdevant, 1831, forestalling the inventions of Sir Henry Bessemer and of the American David Bruce, both of 1838. Bessemer's machine is described in his *Autobiography*, published in 1905, where the author states that he sold his invention to Alexander Wilson of Edinburgh, who allowed it to fall into oblivion. In the *Reports by the Juries*, Class XVII, of the Great Exhibition of 1851 (the reporters for this section were A. F. Didot, Charles Whittingham, of the Chiswick Press, and Thomas De La Rue) complaint is made that England was behind America and the continental countries in the use of casting machinery. None but hand moulds were shown at the Exhibition. The jurors gave an account of the destruction of the Pouchée machine at the instigation of the founders, and in a footnote on p. 409 it is stated of some unnamed American invention that 'Messrs. Figgins, who purchased it, have abstained from putting it into practice, probably in deference to the journeymen type-founders'. J. R. Johnson, of the Patent Typefounding Company, who also invented a casting machine, at a later date repeated these accusations against the regular founders (see below), and it certainly appears that there was some reluctance among the old founders to encourage the spread of new inventions.

However, from about the middle of the century most type casting, at any rate in the larger houses and in newspaper offices, seems to have been done by machinery. The firm of Clowes, who printed the Exhibition catalogues in 1851, were at that time casting by machinery. Even in 1843 we find from G. Dodd's *Days at the Factory* (p. 329) that Clowes were casting their own types, though with hand moulds. It would be interesting to know from which founder they obtained their matrices. The model generally adopted at first was the machine, or some modification of it, of David Bruce, patented in America in 1838. Miller and Richard were using this machine from 1849. Bigmore and Wyman state that in 1862 the Marr Typefounding Company had an unrivalled plant for casting by machinery, partly the invention of their employee James Henry.

The record for speed was attained by the Rotary Casting Machine of Frederick Wicks, of *The Times* (1840–1910), first patented in 1881; after improvements had been made this machine could cast 60,000 types an hour. This meant that a newspaper could go to press every day with new type and dispense with the labour of distribution. On the other side it should be noted that in February 1863 J. and R. M. Wood inserted a curious notice in *Wood's Typographic Advertiser* to the effect that for the last fifteen years they had given up casting by machinery, because the types so produced were porous and liable to break under pressure.

The earliest composing machine patented in this country, but probably never tried out, was that of an American, William Church, patented in 1822. A similar machine, at least in the composing part, was designed by Henry Bessemer in 1840, though apparently Bessemer had not heard of his predecessor; both used the key-board or so-called guide plate system, by which on the striking of keys, types were released and poured down into the composing bed. The patent for Bessemer's design was taken out by J. H. Young and A. Delcambre,[1] both of Lille, and was known under their name. A description of the machine and an illustration will be found in Bessemer's *Autobiography*. No English composing machines were shown at the Great Exhibition of 1851, but three were shown at the Exhibition of 1862, Young's, Delcambre's (now separated), and the machine of the American, William H. Mitchell, patented 1853 and 1854. The Hattersley machine, invented by Robert Hattersley in 1853 and patented in 1857 and 1859, marked an advance, because the types were composed in a short line accessible to the compositor for justifying. The machine was described in the *Printers' Register* for September 1870, with a further article in October 1874, and again in 1877, at the time when it was exhibited at the

[1] See *London Journal of Arts and Sciences*, 1842, p. 174.

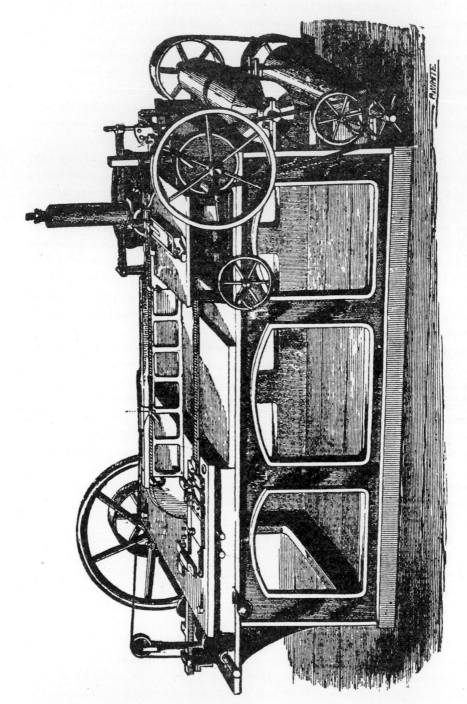

Fig. 93. J. R. Johnson's type-casting machine.

Caxton Celebration of that year. It was then accompanied by the Hattersley justifying machine. The *Printers' Register*, edited by the energetic J. M. Powell, was most encouraging to inventors, unlike some of the trade journals, and devoted many pages to descriptions of new machines. The use of a continuous paper strip for automatic setting was first suggested by D. Mackenzie in 1848, and the idea was utilized by Alexander Mackie in 1867 (described in the *Printers' Register* for Sept. 1870, and again in Dec. 1874, and by Ellic Howe in *The Monotype Recorder*, Spring 1937). The machine invented by Karl Kastenbein in 1869 was taken up by *The Times* and used in their office for many years. It is described in the *Printers' Register* for March 1876, and again in 1877 in connexion with the Caxton Celebration. Other machines described in the *Register* are the Hooker, in December 1873 (shown by Messrs. Clowes at the Caxton Celebration), the machine of Alexander Fraser, of the firm of Neill & Co., Edinburgh (patented 1872) in January 1878 (Fraser read a paper to the Royal Scottish Society of Arts in May 1875, printed in the Society's *Transactions*, 1878, describing his composing and his distributing machine), and the Wicks Logotype Composing Machine (cf. pl. xxix in Legros and Grant) in March 1880. Nevertheless, in the numbers for November and December 1878, we find that the question whether composing machines pay is still being debated. The Thorne type-setting and distributing machine, worked on the rotary system, was patented by J. Thorne in the United States in 1887 and in Great Britain in 1888. It is described in Legros and Grant, chap. xxvi. J. Southward, in *Type-Composing Machines*, 1891, was interested in this machine, although he holds that composing machines on the whole had proved a failure. The increased speed of composing was not sufficiently great as compared with hand-setting, when the initial cost, the wear on types, and the frequent breakdowns of the intricate mechanisms were taken into consideration. It was the overcoming of these difficulties which explains why composing machines were so slow in attaining final victory. Any composing machine could beat the hand compositors in speed, but the advantage might easily be lost from a variety of causes. With the Thorne 10,000 types an hour could be set, the keyboard was less fatiguing to work, and the wear on types slight. Southward prophesied that machines on the rotary principle would supersede all others, including the Linotype. In fact, before many years the Thorne patents were bought up by the Linotype organization.

If the founders were at first nervous about casting machines, the trade in general was naturally more outspokenly opposed to the introduction of composing machines. The *Compositors' Chronicle* from 1841 to 1843 contains several satirical articles about the Young–Delcambre machine and its use in printing the *Family Herald*.[1] The *Journal of the Typographic Arts* for 2 January 1860 has an unfavourable criticism of the Hattersley machine, and *The Printers' Journal* for 5 June 1865 has a leader declaring such machines to be a failure. However, in the number for 22 June 1865 this paper admits that the Alden machine (patented in 1857 by Timothy Alden in America) was an improvement. This machine had already in 1863 received favourable notices in *Wood's Typographic Advertiser*. No English machine had been shown in 1851 at the Great Exhibition, although there were shown three

---

[1] See Ellic Howe, *The Trade*, 1943, chap. ii.

German and one Danish machines. The Danish machine was that of Sörenson, of which there is a description in G. Dodd's *Curiosities of Industry*, 1852, where it is called a bird-cage-looking apparatus. The total number of inventions subsequently patented concerning composing, justifying, and distribution of types was very large. When finally in the Linotype the operations of casting and composing were successfully combined in one machine, the death-knell of the old English letter foundries had sounded.

FIG. 94. Hand casting machine.

23

FURTHER MINOR FOUNDERS, 1831-90

WILLIAM HOWARD, 1838

WILLIAM HOWARD (d. 1864) had a small foundry in Queen's Head Yard, Great Queen Street, from 1838 to 1859. He was employed by Charles Whittingham of the Chiswick Press and beyond his work for that press little is known of him. He served his apprenticeship to a typefounder and afterwards became a sailor. The first definite evidence of his work as a type-cutter is in the so-called 'Basle' roman of the Chiswick Press, used in 1854 for the Rev. William Calvert's book of verses entitled *The Wife's Manual*. The type was modelled on the usual German design of the first half of the sixteenth century, a design especially familiar in Basle-printed books. In 1889 William Morris had his prose romance *A Tale of the House of the Wolfings* set in Basle roman, but discarded the long 's' of the original design. It was used also for another romance by Morris, *The Roots of the Mountains*, 1890 (1889), with further modifications.

Howard also was the cutter of the Chiswick Press replica of Caxton's type 2, with some help from an anonymous French craftsman. It appears to have been used by the Whittinghams to make up imperfect Caxtons, and the only recorded use of it for the text of a whole book was another experiment made by William Morris. In 1890 *The Story of Gunnlaug Wormtongue*, translated by Morris from the Icelandic, was printed in this Caxton facsimile, but was never published, and only a few copies were circulated. The type was shown in the specimen-book issued by the Chiswick Press in 1867, and in Arthur Warren's *The Charles Whittinghams*, Grolier Club, 1890.

NEILL & CO., EDINBURGH, 1838

This firm were printers in Edinburgh from 1766, under Patrick and Adam Neill. In a specimen-book published in 1843 it is stated that they began typefounding upwards of fifty years ago and continued founding for thirty years. They resumed the business in 1838. In the specimen of 1843 modern-face types only are displayed. Alexander Fraser, the inventor of a composing machine patented in 1875 and 1877, was a member of the firm. A history of the house was issued in 1900.

MACBRAYNE & STIRLING, GLASGOW, *circa* 1840

This foundry, called the Glasgow Letter-Foundry, appeared in the *Directory* from 1840–1 to 1850–1. In 1847 a specimen-book was issued, described as a new edition. A series of modern-face romans and italics from Double Small Pica to Pearl is displayed.

BAUER, FERGUSON & HILL (FERGUSON BROS.), EDINBURGH, 1846

Johann Christian Bauer, the founder of the well-known Frankfort firm, the Bauersche Giesserei, was in Edinburgh from 1839 to 1847, at first working with the Edinburgh branch of the Wilson Foundry. According to Konrad Bauer's history

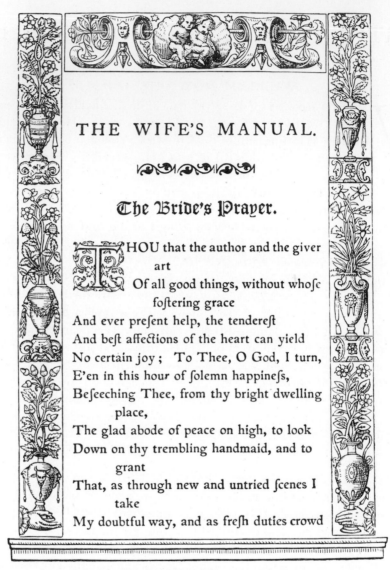

FIG. 95. The 'Basle' roman cut by W. Howard.

of the Bauersche Giesserei, 1937, he started his own foundry under the style of Bauer, Fergusson & Huie, but according to the *Edinburgh Directory* for 1846–7, the firm was Bauer, Ferguson & Hill, and after Bauer's return to Frankfort, Ferguson Bros., at the address of Callander House. At the Great Exhibition, 1851, Ferguson Bros. showed a series of roman types from Nonpareil to Pica. Their last appearance in the *Edinburgh Directory* was in 1857–8.

GEORGE CHAMBERS & CO., 1851

The firm, established in 1851, appears in the *Post Office Directory* from 1852 to 1904, in East Harding Street, Gough Square. In a specimen of 1857 Chambers states that he had 'had practical management of Caslons for nearly twenty years'. The specimen shows a series of modern-face romans from two-line Pica to Nonpareil, with Clarendon, flowers, and ornaments.

J. H. KING & CO., 1855: THE PATENT TYPEFOUNDING COMPANY, 1857

The severest critic of the old founders was John Robert Johnson, a chemist who became interested in typefounding at the time of the Great Exhibition of 1851. Johnson read a very interesting paper to the Royal Society of Arts in March 1873 (printed in the Society's *Journal* for 21 March 1873), in which he gave an account of the origin of his foundry, described his inventions, and entered on some outspoken criticisms of the state of typefounding in England. His paper starts with a short history of the application of machinery to English typefounding, and he quotes the official reports of the jurors for the Great Exhibition as to the backwardness of our founders compared with those of other countries. No English moulds other than the old hand-casting moulds had been exhibited, and no composing machines, although there had been shown three such machines from Germany and one from Denmark. Johnson describes the fate of Pouchée's machine and again quotes the jurors of the Great Exhibition as the authority for the story of its being bought by other founders and destroyed in the Caslon Foundry. In general he accuses the founders of pursuing a narrow policy injurious to human progress.

The first invention described by Johnson, for which he took out patents in 1852 and 1854, was an alloy for producing hard metal. His claim to have effected a revolution in this respect seems extravagant. The passage in which he appears to accuse the founders of pirating his invention is somewhat obscure. The founders in general were being forced to harden their types so that they might stand up to the pressure of power-driven machinery. Richard Austin claimed to have discovered an alloy which produced harder metal and Antony Bessemer, according to his son, had his own secret method. In January the Patent Typefounding Company against John Walter of *The Times* asked for an order to inspect the type used by *The Times*. This demand was at first refused, but in March of the same year permission was granted. As a result, in February 1861 an action was brought against Richard (Miller and Richard of Edinburgh), who had supplied the type which Johnson claimed infringed his patent. The defence was that there was no novelty in the alloy, and Johnson was non-suited. In his paper of 1873 Johnson refers to a patent taken out in 1855 by R. Besley, of the Fann Street Foundry, and jeers at its complicated process. Next came his casting machine, produced with the help of a founder, Josiah King. It was generally stated that the early casting machines were a failure because they produced 'big bodies'. This defect Johnson remedied by making his mould with a fixed opening. Subsequently he found that Sir Henry Bessemer had had the same idea, although in other respects the machines were different. Johnson's machine was bought by the Oxford University Press, adopted by the Imprimerie Impériale in Paris in 1855, and shown at the International Exhibition of 1862. An illustration of the machine was included in the *Journal of the Royal Society of Arts* for 1872, vol. xx, p. 909, and also in A. C. J. Powell's *A Short History of the Art of Printing in England*, 1877. (See Fig. 93.)

In 1855 Johnson formed a partnership with John Huffam King at 33*a* Liquorpond Street, Gray's Inn Lane. J. H. King was apparently a son of the Josiah King mentioned above, and presumably related to Thomas King, who appears as a founder first in Pigot's *Directory* for 1826–7. The firm of T. and J. H. King received an honourable mention for their music type at the Great Exhibition, 1851, and in the *London Directory* for 1854 the firm is entered as Thomas and John H. King, their address being 4 Bartlett's Buildings, Holborn.[1] Johnson found King's stock of types inconsiderable and proceeded to supply the deficiency by the electrotype process. He found that under the Registry of Designs Act, 1839, full property in any new character could be secured for four years, but that no copyright was recognized for merely modified forms of letters. He blandly admits that he had made use of this loophole and asserts that the other founders had been ready enough to copy each other's punches, but considered it immoral to make use of the electrotype process. The electrotype process of reproducing metal objects by means of a galvanic battery was invented in 1839 by M. H. von Jacobi of St. Petersburg, Thomas Spencer of Liverpool, and C. J. Jordan of London, independently (see the *Athenaeum*, 1839, p. 334[2]). As to who was the first to apply the process to the production of matrices from cast type we find that T. W. Starr took out a patent in the United States in 1845 for preparing matrices for type by the electrotyping process. According to De Vinne[3] Edwin Starr of Philadelphia first made such matrices for the James Connor Foundry, New York.

By the time of the Great Exhibition of 1851 the process was in use in the United States, and there is already mention of its misuse. In the display of the Austrian Imperial Printing Office at the Exhibition their electrotype matrices were commended. From 1862 onwards to the end of the century the older foundries were continually complaining of the unfairness of this practice. The firm of J. H. King & Co. further attempted to introduce a system of point measurements for types following P. S. Fournier and the Didots. In 1857 J. S. Atkinson formed a company to purchase J. H. King & Co.'s business and patents, and the new company was removed to 31 Red Lion Square under the name of the Patent Typefounding Company. Johnson, together with Atkinson, perfected one more invention, a machine for dressing the types after casting, patented in 1859, with improvements patented in 1862.

Johnson's paper was followed by an animated discussion. James Figgins defended the founders against the accusations brought by Johnson. He declared that Pouchée himself had found that his machine was unsatisfactory and had had the machine destroyed on his own premises. He denied that the founders had united to oppose the introduction of machinery; they had in fact bought the patents of Stewart and Duncan and of Kronheim and Newton, shared the expenses of the

---

[1] A grandson of J. H. King, Mr. Gaydon King, informs me that the family came originally from Bristol, where they practised type-founding.

[2] See also W. Savage, *A Dictionary of the Art of Printing*. London, 1841, art. 'Galvanism'.

[3] *Plain Printing Types*, p. 18.

machines, and offered them to all founders and printers, and there were at least 300 of these machines in use in England and Scotland. R. H. Gill, of Miller and Richard, stated that machinery for casting had been used by his firm from 1849. (According to A. C. J. Powell this was the machine of the American, David Bruce.)

The Patent Typefounding Company issued their first specimen in 1859, at which time the two managers were Joseph M. Powell and Peter Martin Shanks. J. M. Powell (1822–74) was an energetic type-broker, and among his many interests was the well-known monthly journal, *The Printers' Register*, of which he was the editor and proprietor. An obituary notice of Powell appeared in the October issue for 1874. In a supplement to the August issue for 1868 there appeared an article 'Progress of Typography', which is concerned with hard metal and the casting machine of the Patent Typefounding Company; the article is in fact a forerunner of Johnson's paper read to the Royal Society of Arts. Powell appears to have shared Johnson's opinions about the Associated Typefounders, and it is perhaps significant that about this time the old founders, who had been lavishly advertising their various Old Style types, ceased to use the pages of the *Printers' Register*. In October 1872 there is more about Johnson's hard metal, and in April 1873 a long summary of Johnson's paper.

For further criticism of the old founders reference may be made to an article in *The British and Colonial Printer* for 28 April 1892, entitled 'The "Associated Founders". An unsatisfactory retrospect'. Three main charges are made: first, that they opposed the introduction of typefounding machinery; next, that they obstructed the assimilation of type-bodies; and thirdly, the introduction of an improved alloy for type metal. After commending the fertility of invention of the Americans the writer follows much the same line as Johnson's paper, telling the story of Pouchée's machine. He accuses the Caslons of attempting to introduce a point system favourable to their own foundry, a charge firmly contradicted in *Caslon's Circular*. Another remarkable accusation is made to the effect that owing to the competition of the Wilson Foundry the Associated Founders in London combined to lower the height-to-paper of the types they cast. It is stated that this device was practised until early in the nineteenth century, and that the old height became known as Scotch height. I have found no other reference to this state of war among the founders. If there is any truth in it, one would have expected to hear of many complaints from the printers.

As to the assimilation of type-bodies, that is, the introduction of a point system of measurement, probably the conservatism of the printers was chiefly to blame for the long deferment of this reform in Great Britain. Before the final adoption of such a system there had been four attempts in this direction, one of them put forward by one of the old foundries. The first and second proposals, of James Fergusson, about 1824, and of Bower Brothers of Sheffield in 1841, have already been mentioned. Next came the system of J. H. King & Co., which the firm introduced about 1855, but which apparently had no influence on the other founders. P. M. Shanks wrote an article on this scheme in Ruse and Straker's *Printing and its Accessories*, 1860. It was based on Pica, which was divided into twenty points. The fourth system was the proposal of T. W. Smith, the director of Caslons, put forward in 1886. *Caslon's*

B b

Circular had already printed articles by T. L. De Vinne on the point system and that journal continued to press for the introduction of the system. It was not until 1898 that the English founders came to an agreement to adopt the American system, and even then some years elapsed before the new measurements can be said to have been in general use. J. Southward, in his *Modern Printing*, gives the year 1905 as the date of the completion of the reform. In 1904 Sir Henry K. Stephenson, of Stephenson, Blake & Co., gave a lecture on 'Typefounders and the Point System', which was largely a defence of the old founders against the accusation that they were to blame in this matter.

In 1873 H. A. Revell entered the firm and the style became Shanks, Revell & Co. After the death of Revell in 1881 it was P. M. Shanks & Co., and later P. M. Shanks & Sons. Finally, the firm was amalgamated with R. H. Stevens, successor of Figgins.

CHARLES MORTON, THE CITY TYPEFOUNDRY, 1869

The firm appears in the *Post Office Directory* from 1869 to 1912, at 167 City Road. A specimen-book was issued in 1875, and another in 1881, showing the 'latest collection of German and American novelties'.

CHARLES HAMMOND & CO., 1869

In the Trade Directory included in the *Printers' Register* for 1869, among the typefounders is Charles Hammond & Co. of 8 Exeter Street. In an advertisement in the same journal for November 1870 Hammond states that he was 'many years with Mr. Figgins'. On 6 May 1870 the firm appears as Dover, Hammond & Co. of Sheffield, and in the *Sheffield Directory* for 1871 as Charles Hammond & Co. Between 1874 and 1878 the firm is again in London in Bear Yard, Lincoln's Inn Fields.

LIST OF THE PRINCIPAL AUTHORITIES CONSULTED

THIS LIST DOES NOT INCLUDE TYPE SPECIMEN-BOOKS OR BOOKS REFERRED TO AS SPECIMENS OF TYPE

Adams (Eleanor N.). Old English Scholarship, 1566–1800. Yale Studies in English, No. 55. New Haven, 1917. 8°.

Allen (D. C.). Some Contemporary Accounts of Renaissance Printing Methods, *The Library*, ser. 4, vol. 17, 1937.

Ames (Joseph). Typographical Antiquities; being an historical account of printing in England. London, 1749. 4to.

——Typographical Antiquities; augmented by William Herbert. London, 1785–90, 3 vols. 4to.

—— Typographical Antiquities; now greatly enlarged by T. F. Dibdin. London, 1810–19, 4 vols. 4to.

Amman (Jost). Eygentliche Beschreibung aller Stände und . . . Handwerker. Frankfurt, 1568. 4to.

Arber (Edward). Transcripts of the Registers of the Stationers' Company. London, 1875–7, 4 vols. 4to.

Ars Typographica. New York, 1925–6, vol. 2, 3. fol.

Astle (Thomas). The Origin and Progress of Writing. London, 1784. 4to.

Athenaeum, vol. for 1839.

Aubrey (John). Remains of Gentilisme and Judaisme. London, 1881. 8°.

Audin (Marius). Le Baskerville. Paris, 1931. 8°.

—— Les Livrets typographiques des fonderies françaises. Paris, 1933. 8°.

Backer (A. de). Bibliothèque de la Compagnie de Jésus. Bruxelles, Paris, 1890–1909. 10 tomes. 4to.

Baigent (F. J.) and Millard (J. E.). A History of the Ancient Town . . . of Basingstoke. Basingstoke, 1889. 8°.

Bailey (William). The Advancement of Arts . . . or Descriptions of the Useful Machines and Models . . . of the Society for the Encouragement of Arts. London, 1772. 4to.

Baptist Mission, Serampore. Specimens of editions of the Sacred Scriptures in the Eastern Languages, 1818.

Baudrier (H. T.). Bibliographie lyonnaise. Recherches sur les imprimeurs . . . de Lyon au XVIe siècle. Lyon, 1895–1921, 12 vols. 8°.

Bauer (Konrad F.). Hiob Ludolf. Der Begründer der äthiopischen Sprachwissenschaft. Frankfurt, 1937. 8°.

Beaujon (Paul). *See* Warde (Beatrice).

Beaumarchais (P. A. C. de). Proposals for printing by subscription a complete edition of the Works of Voltaire, in the types of Baskerville. Kehl, 1782. 8°.

Beloe (William). Anecdotes of Literature and Scarce Books. London, 1807–12, 6 vols. 8°.

Bennett (William). John Baskerville. Birmingham, 1937–9, 2 vols. 8°.

Berjeau (J. P.). Speculum humanae salvationis . . . reproduit en facsimilé. Londres, 1861. 4to.

Bernard (A. J.). Antoine Vitré et les caractères orientaux de la Bible polyglotte de Paris. Paris, 1857. 8°.

—— De l'origine et des débuts de l'imprimerie en Europe. Paris, 1853, 2 vols. 8°.

—— Les Estienne et les types grecs de François Ier. Paris, 1856. 8°.

Berry (W. T.) and Johnson (A. F.). Catalogue of Specimens of Printing Types by English and Scottish Printers and Founders. Oxford, 1935. fol.

Bessemer (Sir Henry). An Autobiography. London, 1905. 4to.

Best (R. I.). Bibliography of Irish Philology. Dublin, 1913. 8°.

Bibliander (T.). De ratione communi omnium linguarum & literarum commentarius. Tiguri, 1548. 4to.

Bigmore (E. C.) and Wyman (C.). A Bibliography of Printing. London, 1880–6, 3 vols. 4to.

Binet (E.). Essay des merveilles de nature. Rouen, 1622. 8°.

Birch (J. G.). William Caxton's Stay at Cologne, *The Library*, ser. 4, vol. 4, 1923.

Birmingham Gazette, 1769.

Birmingham Register, 1765.

Bisset (James). Magnificent Directory. Birmingham, 1800. 8°.

Blades (William). The Life and Typography of William Caxton. London, 1861–3, 2 vols. 4to.
—— Some Early Type Specimen Books of England, Holland, France, Italy and Germany. London, 1875. 8o.
Blount (Thomas). Glossographia. London, 1656. 8o.
Bodoni (G.). Preface to the Manuale tipografico. *Tr.* H. V. Marrot. London, 1925. 8o.
Bower Bros. Proposals for establishing a graduated scale of sizes for printing types. Sheffield, 1841. 12mo.
British and Colonial Printer, April, 1892.
British and Foreign Bible Society. Historical Catalogue of the Printed Editions of Holy Scripture. . . . By T. H. Darlow and H. F. Moule. London, 1903–11, 4 vols. 8o.
British Museum. Catalogue of Books . . . printed in England, Scotland and Ireland . . . to 1640. London, 1884, 3 vols. 8o.
—— Catalogue of Books printed in the XVth Century, London, 1908, &c. fol.
—— Harleian MSS. (Bagford Collection.)
—— Lansdowne MSS.
—— Stowe MSS.
Bulgakov (Th. I.). Иллюстрированная исторія книгопечатанія. С.-Петербургъ, 1890. 8o.
Butler (Charles). Oratoriae libri duo. Oxoniae, 1629. 8o.
Butler (Pierce). The Origin of Printing in Europe. Chicago, 1940. 8o.
Byrom (H. J.). John Wayland, *The Library*, ser. 4, vol. 11, 1931.

Camus (A. G.). Histoire et procédés du polytypage. Paris, 1801. 8o.
Case (the) and Proposals of the Free Journeymen Printers in London. London, 1666.
Caslon's Circular. London, 1875, &c. 4to.
Caxton (William). Caxton's Prologues and Epilogues. *Ed.* W. J. F. Crotch. Early English Text Society, 1928. 8o.
Caxton Celebration. Catalogue of the Loan Collection . . . connected with the art of printing. London, 1877. 8o.
Chalmers (Alexander). The General Biographical Dictionary. London, 1812–17, 32 vols. 8o.
Chambers (Ephraim). Cyclopaedia. London, 1728, 2 vols. 8o. (Also editions of 1738 and 1784–6.)
Chevillier (A.). L'Origine de l'imprimerie de Paris. Paris, 1694. 4to.
Claudin (A.). Histoire de l'imprimerie en France. Paris, 1900–14, 4 vols., fol.
Colden (C.). New Method of Printing, *American Medical and Philosophical Register*. New York, vol. 1, 1814. 8o.
Compositors' Chronicle. London, 1840–3, fol.
Cotton (Henry). A Typographical Gazetteer. Oxford, 1831, 66, 2 ser. 8o.
Coyecque (E.). Recueil des actes notariés relatifs à l'histoire de Paris au XVIe siècle. Paris, 1905–21, 2 vols. fol.
Crotch (W. J. B.). Caxton Documents, *The Library*, ser. 4, vol. 8, 1928.
—— Caxtoniana, *The Library*, ser. 4, vol. 11, 1931.
Crous (E.). Die Schriftgiessereien in Berlin. Berlin, 1928. 4to.

Dahl (S.). Bibliotekshandbok. Uppsala, 1924. 8o.
Daniel (C. H. O.). Memorials of Oxford, 1921–2. 4to.
Degering (H.). Zedler: Von Coster zu Gutenberg. [A review.] *Zentralblatt für Bibliothekswesen*, 1922.
De Ricci (Seymour). A Census of Caxtons. Bibliographical Society, London, 1909. fol.
De Vinne (T. L.). The Invention of Printing. New York, 1877. 8o.
—— Plain Printing Types. (The Practice of Typography.) New York, 1925. 8o.
Dialogues françois pour les ieunes enfans. Anvers, 1567. 8o.
Dibdin (T. F.). The Bibliographical Decameron. London, 1817, 3 vols. 4to.
—— Bibliomania, or Book Madness. London, 1811, 6 pt. 8o.
—— Introduction to the knowledge of the rare and valuable editions of the Classics. 4th edition. London, 1827, 2 vols. 8o.
Dickson (Robert). The Introduction of the Art of Printing into Scotland. Aberdeen, 1885. 8o.
Dictionary of National Biography.
Diderot (D.). Encyclopédie. Genève, 1765–72, 17 vols. fol.

Didot (Pierre). Épître sur les progrès de l'imprimerie. Paris, 1784. 8º.

Diehl (R.). Beaumarchais als Nachfolger Baskervilles. Frankfurt, 1925. 8º.

Dix (E. R. M.) and Casaide (S. U.). List of Books printed in Irish. Dublin, 1905, 8º.

Dodd (George). Curiosities of Industry. London, 1858. 8º.

—— Days at the Factory. London, 1843. 8º.

Douglas (D. C.). English Scholars. London, 1939. 8º.

Dreyfus (John). The Survival of Baskerville's Punches. Cambridge, 1950. 8°.

Duerer (A.). Underweyssung der Messung. Nuremberg, 1525. fol.

Duff (E. Gordon). Fifteenth Century English Books. Bibliographical Society, London, 1917, fol.

—— The Printers, Stationers and Bookbinders of Westminster and London. Cambridge, 1906. 8º.

Duncan (W. J.). Notices and Documents illustrative of the literary history of Glasgow. Maitland Club. Glasgow, 1831. 8º.

Dunton (John). Life and Errors of. London, 1705. 12mo.

Dupont (Paul). Histoire de l'imprimerie. Paris, 1854, 2 vols. 8º.

Duverger (E.). Histoire de l'invention de l'imprimerie par les monuments. Paris, 1840. fol.

Dziatzko (K.). Der Drucker mit dem bizarren R. Berlin, 1904. 8º. Hft. 17 of the Sammlung bibliothekswissenschaftlicher Arbeiten.

Edinburgh Directory (Post Office), 1846–7—1857–8. 8º.

Edwards (Edward). Libraries and Founders of Libraries. London, 1865. 8º.

Encyclopaedia Britannica.

Encyclopaedia Judaica. Berlin, 1928, &c. 4to.

Enschedé (Charles). Die Druckerei der Elsevier und ihre Beziehung zu der Lutherschen Schriftgiesserei. (Die hochdeutschen Schriften von J. Enschedé en zonen.) Haarlem, 1919. 8º.

—— Fonderies de caractères . . . dans les Pays-Bas. Haarlem, 1908, fol.

Enschedé (J.) & Zonen. De lettergietterij van J. Enschedé en zonen. Haarlem, 1893. 4to.

Essay on the Original, use and excellency of the noble art . . . of printing. London, 1752. 8º.

Evelyn (John). Diary and Correspondence. London, 1850–2, 4 vols. 8º.

Faulmann (C.). Illustrierte Geschichte der Buchdruckerkunst. Wien, 1882. 8º.

Ferguson (John). The Brothers Foulis, *The Library*, March, 1889.

Figgins (V.). The Game of the Chesse by William Caxton. [A facsimile, with remarks by Figgins.] London, 1855. 4to.

Fineschi (V.). Notizie storiche sopra la stamperia di Ripoli. Firenze, 1781. 8º.

Fischer (G.). Essai sur les monumens typographiques de Jean Gutenberg. Mayence, 1802. 4to

Fournier (P.). Manuel typographique. Paris, 1764–6, 2 vols. 12mo.

Franklin (Benjamin). Works. London, 1793, 2 vols. 8º, and Philadelphia, 1875, 3 vols. 8º.

Freemason's Magazine. London, 1796. 8º.

Fry (B.). Notes on the American Press at the end of the XVIIIth century. Grolier Club, New York, 1927. 8º.

Fry (Edmund). Pantographia. London, 1799. 8º.

Fumagalli (G.). Lexicon typographicum Italiae. Florence, 1905. 8º.

Gamble (W.). Music Engraving and Printing. London, 1923. 8º.

Gand (M. J.). Recherches historiques et critiques sur la vie . . . de Thierry Martens. Alost, 1845. 8º.

Garamond (C.). Preface to D. Chambellan's Pia et religiosa meditatio. Paris, 1545. 8º.

Garrett (C. L.). Marian Exiles. Cambridge, 1938. 8º.

Ged (William). Biographical Memoirs of. London, 1781. 8º.

Gentleman's Magazine. Vols. for 1786, 1792, 1793, 1803, 1836.

Gesamtkatalog der Wiegendrucke. Leipzig, 1925, &c. 4to.

Gesellschaft für Typenkunde . . . des XV. Jahrhunderts. [Facsimiles.] Uppsala, 1907, &c. fol.

Gessner (Carl F.). Die so nöthig als nützliche Buchdruckerkunst. Leipzig, 1740–5, 4 vols. 8º.

Glasgow Post Office Directory, 1840–1—1850–1. 8º.

Gough (R.). British Topography. London, 1780, 2 vols. 4to.

Gray (G. J.). The Earlier Cambridge Stationers. Bibliographical Society Monographs XIII. London, 1904. 4to.

Gray (G. J.) and Palmer (W. M.). Abstracts from the Wills . . . of Printers of Cambridge, 1504–1699. Bibliographical Society, London, 1915. 4to.

Gray (Nicolette). XIXth Century Ornamented Types. London, 1938. 8º.

Great Exhibition, 1851. Reports by the Juries. London, 1852. 8º.

Greswell (W. P.). A View of the Early Parisian Greek Press. Oxford, 1838, 2 vols. 8º.

Guignes (J. de). Essai historique sur la typographie orientale et grecque de l'Imprimerie Royale. Paris, 1787. 4to.

Gutch (John). Collectanea Curiosa. Oxford, 1781, 2 vols. 8º.

Haas (I.). Bruce Rogers: a bibliography. New York, 1936. 8º.

Haebler (K.). Handbuch der Inkunabelkunde. Leipzig, 1925. 8º.

—— Italienische Fragmente vom Leiden Christi das älteste Druckwerk Italiens. Munich, 1927. 4to.

—— Schriftguss und Schriftenhandel in der Frühdruckzeit, *Zentralblatt für Bibliothekswesen*, Bd. xli, 1924.

—— Typenrepertorium der Wiegendrucke. Halle, 1905–10, 4 vols. 8º.

Halhed (N. B.). A Grammar of the Bengal Language. Hoogly, 1778. 4to.

Hansard (T. C.). Typographia. London, 1825. 8º.

—— the Younger. Treatises on Printing and Typefounding. Edinburgh, 1841. 8º.

Harleian Miscellany. London, 1744–6, 8 vols. 4to.

Harrison (Sir C. R.). The House of Harrison. London, 1914. 4to.

Hart (Horace). Charles Earl Stanhope and the Oxford University Press, *Collectanea*, ser. 3, Oxford Historical Society, 1896. 8º.

—— Notes on a Century of Typography at the University Press, Oxford, 1693–1794. Oxford, 1900. fol.

Harwood (Edward). A View of the Various Editions of the Greek and Roman Classics. London, 1775. 12mo.

Hase (O. von). Breitkopf & Härtel. Gedenkschrift. Leipzig, 1917–19, 2 vols. 4to.

Hawkins (Sir John). A General History of the Science and Practice of Music. London, 1776, 5 vols. 4to.

Hearne (Thomas). Remarks and Collections. Oxford Historical Society, 1885–1921, 11 vols. 8º.

Hill (Joseph). The Book Makers of Old Birmingham. Birmingham, 1907. 4to.

Historical Manuscripts Commission. Reports on the Manuscripts of the Duke of Buccleuch, London, 1899–1926, 3 vols. 8º.

Hodgkin (J. E.). Rariora. London, 1902, 3 vols. 4to.

Hodgson (Thomas). An Essay on the Origin and Progress of Stereotype Printing. Newcastle, 1820. 8º.

Holden (William). Triennial Directory. London, 1789–1811. 8º.

Horne (T. H.). An Introduction to the Critical Study . . . of the Holy Scriptures. London, 1818–21, 3 vols. 8º.

Horwood (R.). Plan of the Cities of London and Westminster. London, 1794–9.

Howe (Ellic). The Trade. London, 1943. 8º.

Howe (Olga) and (E.). Vignettes in Typefounders' Specimen Books, *Signature*, No. 11, 1939.

Howell (James). Lexicon Tetraglotton. London, 1659. fol.

Huntington (Robert). Epistolae. London, 1704. 8º.

Hupp (O.). Gutenberg und die Nacherfinder, *Gutenberg Jahrbuch*, 1929.

Hutton (William). An History of Birmingham, 6th edition, London, 1835. 8º.

Isaac (Frank). English and Scottish Printing Types, 1503–58. Bibliographical Society Facsimiles Nos. II and III, London, 1930–2, 2 vols. 4to.

—— English Printers' Types of the Sixteenth Century. Oxford, 1936. fol.

James (John). Catalogue and Specimen of the large and extensive Printing Type Foundry. London, 1782. 8º.

Jenkinson (Hilary). English Current Writing, *Transactions of the Bibliographical Society*, vol. 13, 1916.

Jewish Encyclopaedia. New York, 1925, 12 vols. 8º.

Johnson (A. F.). The 'Goût Hollandois', *The Library*, ser. 4, vol. 20, 1939.

Johnson (A. F.). Type Designs. London, 1934. 8°.

Johnson (John). Typographia. London, 1824, 2 vols. 12mo.

Johnson (John) and Gibson (S.). Print and Privilege at Oxford to the year 1700. Oxford, 1946. fol.

Johnson (John R.). On Certain Improvements in the Manufacture of Printing Types, *Journal of the Society of Arts*, March, 1873.

Johnstone (Andrew). London Commercial Guide. London, 1817. 8°.

Journal of the House of Commons, vols. IV and V.

Journal of the Typographic Arts. London, 1860.

Kent (Henry). Kent's Directory. London, 1738–1827. 8°.

Keynes (G. L.). William Pickering, publisher. London, 1924. fol.

Kidson (F.). British Music Publishers, Printers and Engravers. London, 1900. 8°.

Kinkeldey (O.). Music and Music Printing in Incunabula, *Papers of the Bibliographical Society of America*, 1932. 8°.

Kleerkooper (M. M.). De Boekhandel te Amsterdam. 's-Gravenhage, 1914–16, 3 vols. 8°.

Klemming (G. E.) and Nordin (I. G.). Svensk boktryckeri-historia. Stockholm, 1883. 8°.

Knight (Charles). Shadows of the Old Booksellers. London, 1865. 8°.

Laborde (L.). Débuts de l'imprimerie à Strasbourg. Paris, 1840. 8°.

La Caille (J. de). Histoire de l'imprimerie et de la librairie. Paris, 1689. 4to.

La Croix (P.). Histoire de l'imprimerie. [By La Croix, Fournier, and Seré.] Paris, 1851. 8°.

Lambinet (P.). Origine de l'imprimerie. Paris, 1810, 2 vols. 8°.

Latham (H.). Oxford Bibles and Printing in Oxford. Oxford, 1870. 8°.

Laud (William) Archbishop. Works. Oxford, 1847–60, 7 vols. 8°.

Legros (L. A.) and Grant (J. C.). Typographical Printing Surfaces. London, 1916. 8°.

Leigh (R. A. Austen). William Strahan and his Ledgers. London, 1923. 4to.

Le Long (J.). Discours historique sur les principales éditions des Bibles polyglottes. Paris, 1713. 12mo.

Lemoine (Henry). Typographical Antiquities. London, 1797. 12mo.

Linde (M. A. van der). The Haarlem Legend of the Invention of Printing by L. J. Coster. London, 1871. 8°.

Loménie (L. de). Beaumarchais and his Times. *Tr.* H. S. Edwards. London, 1856, 4 vols. 8°.

London Journal of Arts and Sciences. London, 1820, &c. 8°.

London Post Office Directory.

London Printer's Lamentation. London, 1660. 4to.

Luce (L.). Essai d'une nouvelle typographie. Paris, 1771. 4to.

Luckombe (P.). A Concise History of the Origin and Progress of Printing. London, 1770. 8°.

Lynam (E. W.). The Irish Character in Print, *The Library*, ser. 4, vol. 4, 1924.

McCreery (John). The Press, a poem. Liverpool, 1803–27, 2 pt. 4to.

McKerrow (R. B.). A Dictionary of Printers, 1557–1640. Bibliographical Society, London, 1910. 8°.

—— An Introduction to Bibliography. Oxford, 1927. 8°.

—— Printers' and Publishers' Devices in England and Scotland. Bibliographical Society Monographs, No. 16, 1913. fol.

MacLehose (James). The Glasgow University Press. Glasgow, 1931. 8°.

MacMurtrie (D. C.). The Isaiah Thomas Standing Bible. Chicago, 1928. 8°.

McRae (J. F.). Two Centuries of Typefounding. Annals of the Letter Foundry established by William Caslon. London, 1920. 4to.

Macray (W. I.). Annals of the Bodleian Library, Oxford. London, 1868. 8°.

McUre (John). The History of Glasgow. Glasgow, 1830. 8°.

Madan (Falconer). A Chart of Oxford Printing. Bibliographical Society Monographs, No. 12, 1904. fol.

—— Oxford Books: a bibliography, 1468–1600. Oxford, 1895–1919, 3 vols. 8°.

—— Oxford Oddments, *The Library*, ser. 4, vol. 9, 1929.

Madden (J. P. F.). Lettres d'un bibliographe. Paris, 1868–78, 5 vols. 8°.

Manzoni (G.). Annali tipografici dei Soncino. Bologna, 1883–6. 8°.

—— Studii di bibliografia analitica. Bologna, 1881–2, 3 pt. 8°.

Marrot (H. V.). William Bulmer—Thomas Bensley. London, 1930. 4ᵗᵒ.

Mason (Monck). Life of William Bedell. London, 1843. 8º.

Mason (William). The Printer's Assistant. London, 1810. 8º.

Mayhew (H.). The Shops and Companies of London and the Trades . . . of Great Britain. London, c. 1865. 4ᵗᵒ.

Meerman (G.). Origines typographicae. Hagae Com., 1765, 2 vols. 4ᵗᵒ.

Meyer (Kathi). The Liturgical Music Incunabula in the British Museum, *The Library*, ser. 4, vol. 20, 1939.

—— The Printing of Music 1473–1934, *The Dolphin*, 1935.

Meyer (Wilhelm). Henricus Stephanus über die Regii Typi Graeci, *Abhandlungen der K. Gesellschaft der Wissenschaften*, Göttingen, Bd. 6, No. 2, 1902.

Meynell (Sir F.) and Morison (S.). Printers' Flowers and Arabesques, *The Fleuron*, No. 1, 1923.

Mores (E. Rowe). A Dissertation upon English Typographical Founders and Founderies, London, 1778. 8º.

Mori (Gustav). Eine Frankfurter Schriftprobe von 1592. Frankfurt, 1920. fol.

—— Die Schriftgiesser B. und R. Voskens. Frankfurt, 1923. 4ᵗᵒ.

—— Schriftproben deutscher Schriftgiessereien. Frankfurt, 1926. 8º.

—— Was hat Gutenberg erfunden? Gutenberg-Gesellschaft, Mainz, 1921. 8º.

Morison (Stanley). Early Humanistic Script and the First Roman Type, *The Library*, ser. 4, vol. 24, 1943.

—— The Fell Types. (A poster.) Oxford, 1930.

—— Ichabod Dawks and his Newsletter. Cambridge, 1931. fol.

—— John Bell, 1745–1831. Cambridge, 1930. 8º.

—— Leipzig as a Centre of Typefounding, *Signature*, No. 11, 1939.

—— On Script Types, *The Fleuron*, No. 4, 1925.

—— Richard Austin, Engraver to the Printing Trade. Cambridge, 1937. 8º.

—— Towards an Ideal Type, *The Fleuron*, No. 2, 1924.

—— The Trusler Script Types, *The Fleuron*, No. 7, 1930.

—— The Type of the Hypnerotomachia Poliphili, *Gutenberg Festschrift*, 1925. fol.

Moxon (Joseph). Mechanick Exercises, or the Doctrine of Handy-Works. London, 1677–83, 2 vols. 4ᵗᵒ.

—— Regulae trium ordinum literarum typographicarum. London, 1676. 4ᵗᵒ.

—— Tutor to Astronomy and Geography. 4th edition. London, 1686. 4ᵗᵒ.

Murray (David). Robert & Andrew Foulis and the Glasgow Press. Glasgow, 1933. 4ᵗᵒ.

Neill & Co. History of the Firm. Edinburgh, 1900. 8º.

Neumann (C. F.). Versuch einer Geschichte der armenischen Literatur. Leipzig, 1836. 8º.

Nichols (John). Biographical and Literary Anecdotes of William Bowyer. London, 1782. 4ᵗᵒ.

—— Literary Anecdotes of the Eighteenth Century. London, 1812–15, 9 vols. 8º.

—— Illustrations of the Literary History of the Eighteenth Century. London, 1817–58, 8 vols. 8º.

Nijhoff (W.). L'Art typographique dans les Pays-Bas, 1500–48. La Haye, 1902–35. fol.

Noble (Mark). Bibliographical History of England. London, 1806, 3 vols. 8º.

Nouveau traité de la diplomatique. Paris, 1750–65, 6 tomes. 8º.

O'Lochlainn (Colm). Irish Script and Type in the Modern World, *Gutenberg Jahrbuch*, 1932.

Omont (Henri). Spécimens de caractères hébreux, grecs, latins et de musique gravés . . . par Guillaume Le Bé. Paris, 1889. 8º.

Ottley (W. Y.). An Inquiry concerning the invention of printing. London, 1863. 4ᵗᵒ.

Owen (Hugh). Two Centuries of Ceramic Art in Bristol. London, 1873. 8º.

Oxford University Press. The First Minute Book of the Delegates. Oxford Bibliographical Society, 1943, 4ᵗᵒ.

Palmer (Samuel). A General History of Printing. London, 1732. 4ᵗᵒ.

Panizzi (Sir A.). Chi era Francesco da Bologna? London, 1858. 16ᵐᵒ.

Panzer (G. W.). Annales Typographici. Nuremberg, 1793–1803, 11 vols. 4ᵗᵒ.

Parker (M.), Archbishop. Correspondence. Parker Society, 1853. 8º.

Patents for Inventions. Abridgments of Specifications relating to Printing. London, 1859. 8º.

Pater (Paulus). De Germaniae miraculo . . . dissertatio. Lipsiae, 1710. 4ᵗᵒ.

Pattison (B.). Notes on early Music Printing, *The Library*, ser. 4, vol. 20, 1939.

Pavyers and Bullens. One Hundred Years. London, 1922. 4to.

Peddie (R. A.). Printing. A Short History. London, 1927. 8°.

Pekarsky (P.). Введеніе въ исторію просвѣщенія въ Россіи. Санктпетербургъ, 1862. 8°.

Pendred (J.). London and County Printers, Booksellers and Stationers Vademecum. [1785] 8°.

Pepys (S.). Diary. *Ed.* H. B. Wheatley. London, 1903–4, 10 vols. 8°.

Philippe (J.). L'Origine de l'imprimerie. Paris, 1885. 4to.

Pierce (William). An Historical Introduction to the Marprelate Tracts. London, 1908. 8°.

Pigot and Co.'s Commercial Directory of London. 1825, &c. 8°.

Pine (William). Proposals for discovering a very great improvement which W. Pine and Isaac Moore have made in the art of printing. London, *c.* 1770.

Plomer (H. R.). A Dictionary of the Booksellers and Printers in England, Scotland and Ireland, 1641–67, 1668–1725, 1726–85. Bibliographical Society, 1907–32, 3 vols. 8°.

—— The Eliot's Court Printing House, *The Library*, ser. 4, vol. 2, 1921.

—— An Inventory of Wynkyn de Worde's House, ibid., vol. 6, 1915.

—— The King's Printing House under the Stuarts, ibid., vol. 2, 1901.

—— Some Petitions for Appointments as Master Printers, ibid., ser. 4, vol. 1, 1919.

Pocock (Edward). The Theological Works. London, 1740, 2 vols. fol.

Pollard (Graham). The Company of Stationers before 1557, *The Library*, ser. 4, vol. 18, 1938.

—— The Early Constitution of the Stationers' Company, ibid.

Printers' Journal and Typographic Magazine, 1865–9.

Printers' Register. 1868, &c. 4to.

Proctor (Robert). The French Royal Greek Types, *Bibliographical Essays*, 1905. 8°.

—— An Index of the Early Printed Books in the British Museum. Pt. 2. Germany, 1501–20. London, 1903. 4to.

—— The Printing of Greek in the Fifteenth Century. Bibliographical Society Monographs, No. 18, 1900. fol.

Reed (T. B.). Old and New Fashions in Typography, *Royal Society of Arts*, 1890.

Renouard (A.). Annales de l'imprimerie des Aldes. Paris, 1825, 3 vols. 8°.

—— Catalogue de la Bibliothèque d'un Amateur. Paris, 1819, 4 vols. 8°.

Repository of Arts. London, 1809–29. 8°.

Richardson (John). A Short History of the Attempts to convert the Popish Natives of Ireland. London, 1712. 8°.

Riemann (H.). Musik-Lexikon. Berlin, 1922. 8°.

—— Notenschrift und Notendruck. Leipzig, 1896. 8°.

Rivington (C. R.). Records of the Company of Stationers. London, 1883. 8°.

Roberts (S. C.). A History of the Cambridge University Press. Cambridge, 1921. 8°.

Roccha (A.). Bibliotheca Apostolica Vaticana. Roma, 1591. 4to.

Rooses (Max). Le Musée Plantin-Moretus. Anvers, 1913. fol.

Roper (H. R. Trevor). Archbishop Laud. London, 1940. 8°.

Rossi (Adamo). L'Ultima Parola sulla questione del cognome di M. Francesco da Bologna, *Atti della r. Deput. di storia patria per le Provincie di Romagna*, 1883.

Rossi (G. B. de). De Corano Arabico. Parma, 1805. 8°.

Round (J. H.). John Baskett, King's Printer, *Athenaeum*, Sept. 1885.

Royal Scottish Society of Arts. Transactions, vol. 1, 18.

Ruppel (A.). Johannes Gutenberg. Berlin, 1939. 8°.

Rushworth (John). Historical Collections. London, 1659–1701, 7 vols. fol.

Sabbe (M.) and Audin (M.). Die Civilité-Schriften des Robert Granjon in Lyon, &c. Wien, 1929. 8°.

Saltini (G. E.). Della Stamperia Orientale Medicea, *Giornale Storico degli Archivi Toscani*, vol. 4, 1860.

Sardini (G.). Storia critica di Nicolao Jenson. Lucca, 1796–98, 3 vols. fol.

Savage (William). A Dictionary of the Art of Printing. London, 1841. 8°.

—— Practical Hints on Decorative Printing. London, 1822. 4to.

Schoepflin (J. D.). Vindiciae typographicae. Argentorati, 1760. 4to.

Scholderer (V.). Adolf Rusch and the Earliest Roman Types, *The Library*, ser. 4, vol. 20, 1939.

—— Greek Printing Types, 1465–1927. British Museum, 1927. fol.

—— Printing at Venice to the end of 1481, *The Library*, ser. 4, vol. 5, 1924.

Scholderer (V.). The Shape of Early Type, *Gutenburg Jahrbuch*, 1927.

Schwab (M.). Les Incunables orientaux. Paris, 1883. 8°.

Schwenke (P.). Johann Gutenbergs zweiundvierzigzeilige Bibel, Leipzig, 1923. fol.

Shenstone (William). Works in Verse and Prose. London, 1791, 3 vols. 12mo.

Short Title Catalogue of Books printed in England, Scotland and Ireland, 1475–1640. Bibliographical Society, 1926. fol.

Simmons (J. S. G.). H. W. Ludolf and the printing of his *Grammatica Russica* at Oxford in 1696, *Oxford Slavonic Papers*, vol. 1, 1950.

Skeen (W.). Early Typography. Colombo, 1872. 8°.

Smith (John). The Printer's Grammar. London, 1755 and 1787. 8°.

Smith (Thomas). Vitae quorundam eruditissimorum . . . virorum. London, 1707. 4to.

Southward (John). Modern Printing. London, 1898–1900, 4 vols. 8°.

—— Progress in Printing and the graphic arts. London, 1897. 4to.

Specklin (D.). Les Collectanées. *Ed.* R. Reuss, *Fragments des anciennes chroniques d'Alsace*, 1890. 8°.

Star Chamber. A Decree . . . concerning Printing. London, 1637. 4to.

—— Reports of Cases in the Courts of Star Chamber and High Commission. *Ed.* S. R. Gardiner, London, 1886.

State Papers, Domestic, Calendars of.

Stationers' Company, Records of the Court. *Ed.* W. W. Greg and E. Boswell. Bibliographical Society, 1930. fol.

Steele (R.). The Earliest English Music Printing. Bibliographical Society, 1908. fol.

Stephenson (Sir H. K.). Type-founders of today and the Point System. Sheffield, 1904. 4to.

Stockum (W. P. van). La Librairie, l'imprimerie et la presse en Hollande. La Haye, 1910. 4to.

Stower (C.). The Printer's Grammar. London, 1808. 8°.

—— The Printer's Price Book. London, 1818. 8°.

Straus (R.) and Dent (R. K.). John Baskerville: a memoir. London, 1904. 4to.

Strawberry Hill Accounts. *Ed.* Paget Toynbee. Oxford, 1927. 4to.

Strickland (W. G.). Typefounding in Dublin. Bibliographical Society of Ireland, 1922. 8°.

Strype (John). The Life and Acts of Matthew Parker. London, 1711. fol.

Thiboust (C. L.). De typographiae excellentia: carmen. Paris, 1718. 8°.

Thomas (Sir Henry). Wilh. Caxton uyss Engelannt. London, 1938. 4to.

Thomas (Isaiah). The History of Printing in America, 2nd edition. Albany, 1874, 2 vols. 8°.

Thorne (R.). Rules and Regulations of the Letter-Foundry of. London, 1806.

Times, the History of the. London, 1935, &c. 8°.

Timperley (C.). Encyclopaedia of Literary and Typographical Anecdote. London, 1842. 8°.

—— Songs of the Press. London, 1833. 8°.

Todd (H. J.). Memoirs of the Life and Writings of Brian Walton. London, 1821, 2 vols. 8°.

Tory (Geofroy). Champ fleury. Paris, 1529. fol.

Trithemius (J.). Annales Hirsaugienses. St. Gall, 1690, 2 vols. 4to.

Twyn (Thomas). An Exact Narrative of the Trial and Condemnation of. London, 1664. 4to.

Type Facsimile Society. Publications. Oxford, 1900–9. 4to.

Universal Magazine. London, 1750. 8°.

Updike (D. B.). Printing Types. Cambridge, Mass., 1922, 2 vols. 8°.

Usher (James). Works. Dublin, 1847–64, 16 vols. 8°.

Volkmann (L.). J. G. I. Breitkopf und P. S. Fournier, *Gutenberg Jahrbuch*, 1928.

Warde (Beatrice). The Baskerville Types. A critique. *Monotype Recorder*, 1927. 4to.

—— The 'Garamond' Types, *The Fleuron*, No. 5, 1926.

Wardrop (James). Mr. Whatman, Papermaker, *Signature*, No. 9, 1938.

Warmholtz (C. G.). Biblioteca historica Sueo-Gothica. Stockholm, 1782–1815. 15 dl. 8°.

Warren (Arthur). The Charles Whittinghams. Grolier Club, New York, 1896. 4to.

Watson (James). The History of the Art of Printing. Edinburgh, 1713, 8°.

Wetter (J.). Kritische Geschichte der Erfindung der Buchdruckerkunst. Mainz, 1836. 8°.

Wharton (L.). Miscellaneous Notes on Slavonic Bibliography, *The Library World*, 1915.

Wilkins (David). Concilia Magnae Britanniae et Hiberniae. London, 1737, 4 vols. fol.

Willems (A.). Les Elzevier. Bruxelles, 1880–97, 2 pt. 8°.

Wood (Anthony a). Athenae Oxonienses. *Ed.* P. Bliss. London, 1813–20, 4 vols. 4to.

Wood's Typographic Advertiser. London, 1862–8. fol.

Wordsworth (Christopher). Scholae Academicae. Cambridge, 1877. 8o.

Worman (E. J.). Alien Members of the Book Trade during the Tudor Period. Bibliographical Society, 1906. 4to.

Wroth (L. C.). The Colonial Printer. 2nd edition. Portland, 1938. 8o.

Yattendon Hymnal. Oxford, 1895–9. 4to.

Yciar (J. de). Orthographia Pratica. Caragoça, 1548. 4to.

Young (Patrick). Patricius Junior. Mitteilungen aus seinem Briefwechsel. *Ed.* J. Kemke. Leipzig, 1898. 8o.

Zedler (G.). Von Coster zu Gutenberg. Leipzig, 1921. 4to.

INDEX

Books mentioned in the text as specimens of type are entered, but not books referred to as authorities, of which there is a separate list. The names of the British founders are set in small capitals.